ADVANCED TRADING RULES

Butterworth-Heinemann Finance

aims and objectives

- books based on the work of financial market practitioners, and academics
- presenting cutting edge research to the professional/practitioner market
- combining intellectual rigour and practical application
- covering the interaction between mathematical theory and financial practice
- to improve portfolio performance, risk management and trading book performance
- covering quantitative techniques

market

Brokers/Traders; Actuaries; Consultants; Asset Managers; Fund Managers; Regulators; Central Bankers; Treasury Officials; Technical Analysts; and Academics for Masters in Finance and MBA market.

series titles

Return Distributions in Finance
Derivative Instruments: theory, valuation, analysis
Managing Downside Risk in Financial Markets: theory, practice and implementation
Economics for Financial Markets
Global Tactical Asset Allocation: theory and practice
Performance Measurement in Finance: firms, funds and managers
Real R&D Options
Forecasting Volatility in the Financial Markets
Advanced Trading Rules

Series editor

Dr Stephen Satchell

Dr Satchell is Reader in Financial Econometrics at Trinity College, Cambridge; Visiting Professor at Birkbeck College, City University Business School and University of Technology, Sydney. He also works in a consultative capacity to many firms, and edits the journal *Derivatives: use, trading and regulations*.

ADVANCED TRADING RULES

Second edition

Edited by

E. Acar
Bank of America

S. Satchell
Trinity College, Cambridge, and Faculty of Economics,
University of Cambridge, Cambridge

BUTTERWORTH
HEINEMANN

OXFORD AMSTERDAM BOSTON LONDON NEW YORK PARIS SAN DIEGO
SAN FRANCISCO SINGAPORE SYDNEY TOKYO

Butterworth-Heinemann
An imprint of Elsevier Science
Linacre House, Jordan Hill, Oxford OX2 8DP
225 Wildwood Avenue, Woburn, MA 01801-2041

First published 1998
Reprinted 1998
Second edition 2002

British Library Cataloguing in Publication Data
Advanced trading rules. – 2nd ed. – (Quantitative finance series)
  1. International finance   2. Securities   3. Exchange   4. Futures
  I. Acar, E. (Emmanuel)   II. Satchell, Stephen E.
  332'.042

Library of Congress Cataloguing in Publication Data
A catalogue record for this book is available from the Library of Congress

ISBN 0 7506 5516X

For information on all Butterworth-Heinemann publications visit
our website at www.bh.com

Data manipulation by David Gregson Associates, Beccles, Suffolk
Printed and bound in Great Britain by Biddles Ltd., Guildford and King's Lynn

Contents

Foreword

It has been over 4500 years since the Egyptians coined the first metal money and foreign exchange dealing can be traced down to ancient middle eastern towns. It is not difficult to imagine ancient traders spending their day exchanging coins from one caravan to another, and after a long day of work, traders sitting down on the dusty streets of their middle eastern town wondering about the mysterious forces that move markets.

As exchanges grew over the centuries, so did the power of these forces, sometimes to the detriment of established ruling structures. Inevitably, over the centuries, many governments felt threatened by the freedom of markets. Their efforts to control or even suppress them, from the extreme case of communism to more subtle attempts such as price/salary or foreign exchange controls, all ended in costly failures and sometimes catastrophic changes of political systems.

Some businessmen have tried to harness market forces and become immensely rich in the process. They tried to corner markets by pooling large resources and using them to manipulate prices. They all failed and their attempts always ended in pain and sorrow. As markets continued to prosper they attracted the attention of academics who made the first serious efforts to understand their working. They first recognized that the flow of information was vital to any form of exchange. Indeed it is not by chance that the information age has brought an explosion of trading volumes. In their early attempts they – very logically – theorized that if and when information flows freely and is equally shared, markets develop into a 'random walk'; a most discouraging prospect to any trader.

Although the random walk explanation dominated the theoretical field, seasoned practitioners never believed this conclusion. They always felt that what the theory had failed to comprehend was that information did not move markets on its own. They knew by experience that it was rather the human interpretation of facts that did. As a result, they believed in mass and human psychology. As they were too busy trying, and succeeding to make money, despite the random walk threat, they never really tried to build their experience into a workable theory of markets.

In recent years however, more open minded academics and practitioners have joined forces and created the nascent field of Computer Aided System Trading (I propose to call it CAST). Supported by advanced risk management techniques, new mathematical theories, and the power of modern computers, CAST is developing fast. This is a time of invention and progress; in other words, a remarkable time to get involved in a field that could represent the biggest advance in market studies since the Egyptians.

Stochastic properties of trading rules such as neural networks, genetic algorithms, Markowitz curves will become indispensable tools. Very soon any serious investor will have to be familiar with these concepts or be left out of the rapidly progressing field of investment management.

This remarkable book has been written by the new breed of traders, well seasoned in some of the most active dealing rooms and with the best financial degrees. It certainly fills a gap in the financial literature by giving the reader a complete overview of this burgeoning field as well as acquainting him with the results of the most recent cutting edge research. In publishing this book, the contributors have taken a worthwhile initiative that will accelerate the progress of CAST.

The unanswered questions remain of course: Where will CAST lead? Will humans lose interest in trading? Will computers take over completely and, in the end, control markets in a way that humans never managed to do?

I personally believe that although, in the future, markets will become huge, move considerably faster and be more vibrant, they will firmly remain the expression of human freedom that they always have been.

They will not, therefore, be taken over by artificial intelligence and will be, as they have always been, controlled by humans. The fact remains, however, that there is a limit to human intellect and speed of thought and one might wonder how future traders will cope successfully with the explosion of information and action surrounding them.

It is clear that in order to survive, the descendants of ancient middle east caravan peddlers will have to harness the power of huge computers and use CAST with great expertise. And after a long day of work, they might sit down in a cyber café and talk about the early works on CAST and books such as this one that paved the way to a better understanding of market forces.

Robert Amzallag
Banque Nationale de Paris

Contributors

Emmanuel Acar is a Principal and Manager of Risk Management Advisory-London, at Bank of America. He previously worked at Citibank as a Vice-President in the FX Engineering Group. He was a proprietary trader for almost ten years at Dresdner Kleinwort Benson, BZW and Banque Nationale de Paris' London Branch. He has experience in quantitative strategies, as an actuary and having done his PhD on the stochastic properties of trading rules.

Olivier De Bandt is a senior economist in the Research Department of the Bank of France. He graduated from the University of Paris and the Institut d'Etudes Politiques (Paris). He holds a PhD in Economics from the University of Chicago.

Professor Bernard Bensaid is a consultant of the Research Department of the Bank of France. He graduated from the Ecole Polytechnique and earned a PhD in Economics from the University of Paris. He teaches at the University of Paris and Lille.

P. H. Kevin Chang is currently Vice-President at Credit Suisse First Boston, London. Since March 2001, he has been an Equity Derivatives Strategist, specializing in volatility strategies for indices and single stocks. He was previously Vice-President and Senior Strategist in Global Foreign Exchange, focusing on portfolio and derivative strategies as well as technical trading rules. Before joining CSFB in 1998, he was on the finance faculty at the Stern School of Business (New York University), Wharton School (University of Pennsylvania), and Marshall School of Business (University of Southern California), teaching international finance. His published academic research focused on the information content in foreign exchange options, macro-economic implications of FX option pricing, and technical trading rules in foreign exchange. He holds a PhD in Economics from MIT, and a Bachelor's in Economics from Harvard.

Christian L. Dunis is Girobank Professor of Banking & Finance at Liverpool Business School where he also heads the Centre for International Banking, Economics and Finance (CIBEF). He is also a consultant to asset management firms and a Senior Managing Consultant with Infacts. Before this, Christian Dunis was Global Head of Markets Research at Banque Nationale de Paris which he joined from Chase Manhattan Bank in 1996. At BNP, he managed the Markets Research Group, a 23-strong team covering Foreign Exchange and Fixed Income strategies, developing its technical capabilities and determining the overall architecture of BNP's quantitative models. At Chase Manhattan, where he stayed for 11 years, he headed the Quantitative Research & Trading group, a quantitative proprietary trading group using state of the art modelling techniques to trade a portfolio of spot currencies, stock indices and Government bond futures contracts.

Derek Edmonds graduated from Cornell University with a BA in Economics and joined RefcoFund Holdings Corporation in 1990, where he was involved in the development of the Refco Derivative Advisor Database. Since 1994, Edmonds has been responsible for the management of all the derivatives products at RefcoFund Holdings Corporation. His current functions include the evaluation of trading advisors, the development of innovative statistical analyses in the advisor selection and allocation process, and the structuring of unique products to meet the needs of clients.

Felix Gasser is currently Assistant Vice-President at Credit Suisse Private Banking in Zurich, Switzerland. Since October 1998, he co-writes the daily published newsletter on Forex and Commodities. As Quantitative Analyst he specializes in the development of systematic trading systems. This includes performance ratings of CTAs for the use of structured products. He was previously Marketing Manager for Analytical Software at Dow Jones, supporting the Swiss client base in the development of computer-driven trading strategies. Since the late 1980s he was involved in system-driven trading, having worked as a trader for some of the pioneers in the CTA business, like E.D.&F Man's Fund Division, AHL or as a trader for some of the original Turtles. He is a Chartered Market Analyst, has a Bachelor's in Economics and studied Economics for 2 years at the University of Zurich.

Risto Karjalainen is a fixed income portfolio manager at Merrill Lynch Investment Managers in London. He earned his PhD in Decision Sciences from the Wharton School in the University of Pennsylvania in 1994. Prior to that, he received an MSc in Systems and Operations Research in 1989 from the Helsinki University of Technology, Finland. Before joining Merrill Lynch, he worked for a hedge fund, developing and trading quantitative models, and for JP Morgan Investment Management as an analyst. In addition to evolutionary algorithms, his research interests include the valuation of bond and currency markets.

George W. Kuo studied and worked in Taiwan prior to coming to Cambridge University to enrol in a Master of Philosophy in Finance. He has completed a PhD in Finance, also at Cambridge. George is now working as an academic in Taiwan.

Blake LeBaron has a PhD in Economics from the University of Chicago. He is a Professor of Economics at the University of Wisconsin-Madison, a Faculty Research Fellow at the National Bureau of Economic Research, a member of the external faculty of the Santa Fe Institute, a Sloan fellow, and is currently visiting the Center for Biological and Computational Learning at MIT. LeBaron served as a director of the Economics Program at the Santa Fe Institute in 1993. His research has concentrated on the issue of nonlinear behaviour of financial and macroeconomic time series. He has been influential both in the statistical detection of nonlinearities and in describing their qualitative behaviour in many series. LeBaron's current interests are in understanding the quantitative dynamics of interacting systems of adaptive agents and how these systems replicate observed real-world phenomena. LeBaron is also interested in understanding some of the observed behavioural characteristics of traders in financial markets. This behaviour includes strategies such as technical analysis and portfolio optimization, along with policy questions such as foreign exchange intervention. In general, he seeks to find out empirical implications of learning and adaptation as applied to finance and macroeconomics.

Pierre Lequeux joined the Global Fixed Income division of ABN AMRO Asset Management London in June 1999. Being currently Head of Currency Management, he has the responsibility for both Quantitative and Fundamental Currency management processes. He previously was Head of the Quantitative Research and Trading desk at Banque Nationale de Paris, London branch, which he joined in 1987. Pierre is also an Associate Researcher at the Center for International Banking and Finance of Liverpool Business school and a member of the editorial board of *Derivative, Use Trading & Regulation.*

Andrew W. Lo is the Harris & Harris Group Professor of Finance at the MIT Sloan School of Management and the director of MIT's Laboratory for Financial Engineering. He received his PhD in Economics from Harvard

University in 1984, and taught at the University of Pennsylvania's Wharton School as the W. P. Carey Assistant Professor of Finance from 1984 to 1987, and as the W. P. Carey Associate Professor of Finance from 1987 to 1988. His research interests include the empirical validation and implementation of financial asset pricing models; the pricing of options and other derivative securities; financial engineering and risk management; trading technology and market microstructure; statistics, econometrics, and stochastic processes; computer algorithms and numerical methods; financial visualization; non-linear models of stock and bond returns; and, most recently, evolutionary and neurobiological models of individual risk preferences.

Harry Mamaysky received his doctorate in Financial Economics from MIT in 2000. Since then he has been an Assistant Professor of Finance at the Yale School of Management. His research ranges from trying to understand the factors affecting stock and bond prices to an analysis of why the mutual fund industry has such a broad range of products. His work on mutual funds sheds light on how the structure of the mutual fund industry reflects investor preferences. Another recent project investigates the fundamental determinants of movements in stock and bond prices – he has developed a statistical methodology to extract 'pure' factors from asset prices so that he can study their underlying economics.

Daan Matheussen is a Senior Consultant at ESR (CWA) where he specializes in risk, finance and insurance-related quantitative analysis. He has lived in Belgium and South Africa and studied Chemical Engineering at the University of Cape Town.

David Obert is a co-founder of Systeia Capital Management. He has been in the investment business for 15 years. As a Managing Director and Chief Investment Officer, he directs asset management activities and develops investment strategies including: Futures funds, Statistical Arbitrage, Event Driven and Fixed-income arbitrage. Previously, he was Managing Director of Barep Asset Management, a wholly owned subsidiary of SG Group specializing in alternative investment with Euro 6 Billion under management. David Obert created the Epsilon Futures Program (managed Futures Program) in 1994.

Professor John Okunev joined BT Funds Management as Head of Investment Process and Control in March 2001 from the University of New South Wales where he was Professor of Finance. Prior to joining the University of New South Wales, John was Manager of Investment Technology at Lend Lease where he was responsible for reviewing and developing new financial products. These products included equity trading strategies, in both domestic and international markets. He was also responsible for the implementation and maintenance of risk management systems. The major focus of John's research is the development of equity trading strategies in domestic and international markets.

Carol L. Osler is a Senior Economist at the Federal Reserve Bank of New York. She specializes in exchange rate dynamics and the role of financial markets in the real economy. After receiving a BA from Swarthmore College and a PhD from Princeton University she taught at the Amos Tuck School of Business Administration at Dartmouth College, the Kellogg School at Northwestern University, and at Columbia University. Her most recent work examines the effects of currency orders on high-frequency exchange rate dynamics.

Edouard Petitdidier is co-head of the Systematic and Statistical Hedge Fund Department of Systeia Capital Management and is co-responsible for the running of a Managed Futures Program (started in August 2001 with €75 million) and a Statistical European Pair Trading Fund (launched in November 2001 with €75 million). Systeia is a subsidiary of Credit Lyonnais based in Paris, created in early 2001 with an initial commitment of €250 million. He has 9 years' experience in the trading and investment business and was, from 1994 to March 2001, co-head of the systematic hedge fund department at Barep Asset Management, which included the running of the Epsilon Program (Managed Futures, up to $950 million under management) and a Relative Value Equity Hedge Fund.

Stephen Satchell has PhDs from the Universities of Cambridge and London. He is a fellow of Trinity College, Cambridge, and a Reader in Financial Econometrics at Cambridge University. His research interests include econometrics and finance and he has strong links with the City as an academic advisor and as a consultant. His current particular interests involve asset management, pension and risk.

Jiang Wang is the Nanyang Technological University Professor of Finance at the MIT Sloan School of Management. He received his PhD in Physics in 1985 and his PhD in Finance in 1990, from the University of Pennsylvania. His research is in the area of asset pricing, investments and risk management. Jiang Wang has served on the editorial board of several academic journals including the *Journal of Financial Markets*, *Operations Research*, *Quantitative Finance*, and the *Review of Financial Studies*. He was the recipient of the Trefftz Award in 1990, the Batterymarch Fellowship in 1995 and the LeoMelamed Prize in 1997. Jiang Wang is also a research associate of the National Bureau of Economic Research and a trustee of Nanjing University.

Derek White joined the University of New South Wales (UNSW) in August 1998 where he is currently the Director of the Masters of Commerce Studies Program in Finance. While at UNSW, Derek has served in various consulting positions within the funds management industry. Prior to joining the University, Derek completed his PhD at the University of Texas at Austin and worked in International Treasury for Electronic Data Systems developing programs to evaluate and hedge interest rate exposure. Derek's research interests include trading strategies for financial assets, simulation work, and compensation design for fund managers.

Introduction

In presenting the second edition of this book, we have added three new chapters, in particular focusing on the area of technical analysis (chartism). We feel that this material should be included in any broad contemporary study on trading rules and we hope this inclusion will encourage further research on this area.

The past few years have seen an extraordinary explosion in the use of quantitative systems designed to trade in the foreign exchange and futures markets. This is witnessed by exponential growth of alternative investments, namely futures funds and hedge funds. Curiously, research on this area has been fragmented and sporadic. The purpose of this book is to bring together leading academics and practitioners who are working on systematic trading rules. It is well known that futures fund managers, among others, tend to rely on some sort of systematic trading rules. Available statistics suggest that systematic traders outnumber their discretionary counterparts by a ratio of two to one. As we will see in Chapter 13, the gap is even bigger for sectorized markets such as foreign exchange, interest rates and stock index futures.

This book does not present an exhaustive review of dynamic strategies applied by traders and fund managers, as this would be a hazardous task given the speed at which forecasting techniques and markets evolve. The purpose of this book is rather to introduce the reader to the theory of trading rules and their application. Numerous forecasting strategies are covered in this book, including technical indicators, chartism, neural networks and genetic algorithms.

There are two common factors linking all the strategies investigated in this book. First, all forecasting techniques attempt to predict the direction of price movements. Second, the criterion used to assess forecasting accuracy is economic significance. Trading rules are built out of forecasting strategies and their profitability subsequently measured.

Our primary concern is to specify trading rule-based tools which allow proper testing of the efficient market hypothesis. A market is said to be informationally efficient if prices in that market reflect all relevant information as fully as possible. This demanding requirement for an efficient market is often relaxed to a statement that trading systems cannot use information to outperform passive investment strategies when transaction costs and risk are considered. This book shows that many financial markets, especially foreign exchange and futures, may not be efficient according to this definition.

This book hopes to combine intellectual challenge and practical application, as reflected by the distinction and variety of the contributors: academics, traders, central bankers, tracking agencies and fund managers. Some readers will be interested in this book for what it says about the practical use of technical analysis and others for what it says about the distributional properties of dynamic strategies. The interaction between mathematical theory and financial practice has intensified since the development of Modern Portfolio Theory in the 1950s and the Black–Scholes analysis of the early 1970s, and this has reached a point where no firm can ignore it.

Any virtue can become a vice if taken to extremes, and just so with the application of mathematical models in finance practice. At times the mathematics of the models become too interesting and we lose sight of the models' ultimate purpose: improving portfolio performance, risk management and trading book performance. Computer simulation of dynamic strategies using real data from foreign exchange, emerging and futures markets, will show that substantial risk-adjusted profits can be achieved. However, as with any computer simulation in financial markets, one cannot know how accurate the analysis is until one tries in real time with real money. Consequently, a complementary study of the usefulness of quantitative techniques must involve the review of fund managers' performance using systematic trading rules.

This book includes three sections: the stochastic properties of trading rules, applications to the foreign exchange market and trading the futures markets. We shall next discuss the contributions of each of the fifteen papers.

The first section deals with the stochastic properties of trading rules (six chapters).

1   Blake LeBaron uses moving-average based rules as specification tests on the process for foreign exchange rates. Several models for regime shifts and persistent trends are simulated and compared with results from the actual series. The results show that these simple models cannot capture some aspects of the series studied. Finally, the economic significance of the trading results is tested. Returns distributions from the trading rules are compared with returns on risk-free assets and returns from the US stock market.

2 Andrew Lo, Harry Mamaysky and Jiang Wang propose a systematic and automatic approach to technical pattern recognition using non-parametric kernel regression, and apply this method to a large number of US stocks from 1962 to 1996 to evaluate the effectiveness of technical analysis. By comparing the unconditional empirical distribution of daily stock returns to the conditional distribution – conditioned on specific technical indicators such as head-and-shoulders or double-bottoms – they find that over the 31-year sample period, several technical indicators do provide incremental information and may have some practical value.

3 Daan Matheussen and Stephen Satchell assess the performance of various trading rules for TAA (tactical asset allocation) modelling across equity indices in the emerging markets. The authors find that rules based on mean and variance information and using a rolling window of information outperform all others absolutely and in a risk-adjusted sense, even when they take into account transaction costs.

4 Emmanuel Acar establishes the expected return and variance of linear forecasting strategies assuming that the underlying logarithmic returns follow some Gaussian process. The necessary and sufficient conditions to maximize profits are specified. This chapter shows that many technical forecasts can be formulated as linear predictors. The effect of conditional heteroskedasticity is investigated using Monte Carlo simulations.

5 George Kuo derives some exact results about the probabilistic characteristics of realized returns from two simple moving-average trading rules. The first rule needs only the information contained in the asset return at the present time to issue trading signals while the second rule requires the whole past history of the asset price to do so.

6 Emmanuel Acar and Stephen Satchell establish the distribution of returns generated by a portfolio including two active strategies assuming that underlying markets follow an elliptical distribution. The timing is triggered by linear forecasts for the sake of tractability. The most important finding is that conventional portfolio theory might not apply to active directional strategies even when the underlying assets follow a multivariate normal distribution.

The second section of this book demonstrates that the foreign exchange markets may be seen as inefficient given the number of profitable strategies which can be built out of varied forecasts (four chapters).

7   John Okunev and Derek White evaluate the performance of multiple classes of foreign exchange trading rules across eight base currencies. Specifically, they compare trading rules that focus on individual currencies with those that follow a long–short strategy across multiple currencies. The trading rules include pure momentum, buying/selling based upon relative interest rates, and moving-average rules. They find that a long–short strategy across multiple currencies outperforms trading rules that focus on individual currencies. In addition, they find that significant benefits may accrue by combining long–short moving-average rules across multiple currencies with long–short positions based upon relative interest rates.

8   Christian Dunis considers Artificial Neural Networks (ANNs), and discusses their application to economic and financial forecasting and their increasing success. This chapter investigates the application of ANNs to intraday foreign exchange forecasting and stresses some of the problems encountered with this modelling technique. As forecasting accuracy does not necessarily imply economic significance, the results are also evaluated by means of a trading strategy.

9   Kevin Chang and Carol Osler assess the incremental value of the head-and-shoulders pattern (H&S), consistently cited by technical analysts as particularly frequent and reliable, relative to filter rules. On an incremental basis, they show that the H&S trading rules add noise but no value. Thus, a trader would do no better, and possibly worse, by following both H&S and filter rules instead of filter rules only.

10   Pierre Lequeux investigates the assumption that the interest rates market leads the currency markets as money flows from one country to another. For a systematic trader the hypothesis is quite attractive; indeed if such a cross-correlation exists it will enable him to devise profitable trading strategies.

Finally, the third section analyses the application of stop-loss rules and other technical strategies by futures traders (five chapters). The trading methodology and performance of futures funds managers is reviewed.

11   Bernard Bensaid and Olivier De Bandt explain the existence of stop-loss rules in financial institutions. They develop a principal/agent model, where an investment firm (the principal) has to rely on the expertise of a trader (the agent) to invest in a risky asset (a future contract, say). Using daily data on individual positions in the French Treasury bond future market, they find evidence that positions are more likely to be sold off when realized profits are very negative. More than 20 per cent of individual accounts seem to use stop-loss strategies in their database.

12   Risto Karjalainen uses genetic algorithm to find technical trading rules for S&P 500 futures. The rules are found to be profitable in an out-of-sample test period, with reduced volatility compared to the buy-and-hold strategy. It is also shown that there are characteristic patterns in option trading activity coinciding with the trading rule signals. The results are consistent with short-term overreaction that leads to a partial reversal of large returns on a few days' horizon.

13   Derek Edmonds examines the merits of using managed futures as a diversifying vehicle for traditional investments. The author carries out an in-depth examination of the performance characteristics of the two most popular schools of thought concerning trading: discretionary versus systematic. The relative performance for each style of trading is studied in each of the various market sectors, yielding some surprising results.

14   Edouard Petitdidier and David Obert explain precisely BAREP's management and techniques used to trade futures: choice of futures markets, creation and testing of strategies and money management. This structure has developed a Futures Funds' asset management based on two leading concepts: Technical non-discretionary asset management, with investment strategies based on models of historical behaviour in futures markets. The final section describes the funds' performance from 1994 to 1997.

15   Felix Gasser investigates the need for performance evaluation in technical analysis. He studies not only the indicators and trading systems that are commonly applied by technical traders, but also the analytical data used for evaluation.

The range of forecasting strategies investigated in this book is large but non-exhaustive. The pace of innovation is so fast that new trading concepts will appear which might be better suited to future market conditions. However, we hope that these contributions provide a host of ideas to help improve the risk–return profile of any trader or investor in the foreign exchange and futures markets. We also feel that our book will act as background for academics and other researchers who would like to find out more about this fascinating new area of financial research.

Chapter 1

Technical trading rules and regime shifts in foreign exchange

BLAKE LEBARON

1.1 INTRODUCTION

Techniques for using past prices to forecast future prices have a long and colourful history. Since the introduction of floating rates in 1973, the foreign exchange market has become another potential target for 'technical' analysts who attempt to predict potential trends in pricing using a vast repertoire of tools with colourful names such as channels, tumbles, steps and stumbles. These market technicians have generally been discredited in the academic literature since their methods are sometimes difficult to put to rigorous tests. This chapter attempts to settle some of these discrepancies through the use of bootstrapping techniques.

For stock returns, many early studies generally showed technical analysis to be useless, while for foreign exchange rates there is no early study showing the techniques to be of no use. Dooley and Shafer (1983) found interesting results using a simple filter rule on several daily foreign exchange rate series. In later work, Sweeney (1986) documents the profitability of a similar rule on the German mark. In an extensive study, Schulmeister (1987) repeats these results for several different types of rules. Also, Taylor (1992) finds that technical trading rules do about as well as some of his more sophisticated trend-detecting methods.

While these tests were proceeding, other researchers were trying to use more traditional economic models to forecast exchange rates with much less success. The most important of these was Meese and Rogoff (1983). These results showed the random walk to be the best out-of-sample exchange rate forecasting model. Recently, results using nonlinear techniques have been mixed. Hsieh (1989) finds most of the evidence for nonlinearities in daily exchange rates is coming from changing conditional variances. Diebold and Nason (1990) and Meese and Rose (1990) found no improvements using nonparametric techniques in out-of-sample forecasting. However, LeBaron (1992) and Kim (1989) show small out-of-sample forecast improvements. During some periods, LeBaron (1992) found forecast improvements of over 5 per cent in mean squared error for the German mark. Both of these papers relied on some results connecting volatility with conditional serial correlations of the series.

This chapter breaks off from the traditional time series approaches and uses a technical trading rule methodology. With the bootstrap techniques of Efron (1979), some of the technical rules can be put to a more thorough test. This is done for stock returns in Brock, Lakonishok and LeBaron (1992).[1] This chapter will use similar methods to study exchange rates. These allow not only the testing of simple random walk models, but the testing of any reasonable null model that can be simulated on the computer. In this sense, the trading rule moves from being a profit-making tool to a new kind of specification test. The trading rules will also be used as moment conditions in a simulated method of moments framework for estimating linear models.

Finally, the economic significance of these results will be explored. Returns from the trading rules applied to the actual series will be tested. Distributions of returns from the exchange rate series will be compared with those from risk-free assets and stock returns. These tests are important in determining the actual economic magnitude of the deviations from random walk behaviour that are observed.

Section 1.2 introduces the simple rules used. Section 1.3 describes the null models used. Section 1.4 presents results for the various specification tests. Section 1.5 implements the trading rules and compares return distributions and section 1.6 summarizes and concludes.

1.2   TECHNICAL TRADING RULES

This section outlines the technical rules used in this chapter. The rules are closely related to those used by actual traders. All the rules used here are of the moving average or oscillator type. Here, signals are generated based on the relative levels of the price series and a moving average of past prices:

$$ma_t = (1/L) \sum_{i=0}^{L-1} p_{t-i}$$

For actual traders, this rule generates a buy signal when the current price level is above the moving average and a sell signal when it is below the moving average.[2] This chapter will use these signals to study various conditional moments of the series during buy and sell periods. Estimates of these conditional moments are obtained from foreign exchange time series, and these estimates are then compared with those from simulated stochastic processes. Section 1.4 of this chapter differs from most trading rule studies which look at actual trading profits from a rule. Actual trading profits will be explored in section 1.5.

1.3   NULL MODELS FOR FOREIGN EXCHANGE MOVEMENTS

This section describes some of the null models which will be used for comparison with the actual exchange rate series. These models will be run through the same trading rule systems as the actual data and then compared with those series. Several of these models will be bootstrapped in the spirit of Efron (1979) using resampled residuals from the estimated null model. This closely follows some of the methods used in Brock, Lakonishok and LeBaron (1992) for the Dow Jones stock price series.

The first comparison model used is the random walk:

$$\log(p_t) = \log(p_{t-1}) + \varepsilon_t$$

Log differences of the actual series are used as the distribution for ε_t and resampled or scrambled with replacement to generate a new random walk series. The new returns series will have all the same unconditional properties as the original series, but any conditional dependence will be lost.

The second model used is the GARCH model (Engle, 1982; Bollerslev, 1986). This model attempts to capture some of the conditional heteroskedasticity in foreign exchange rates.[3] The model estimated here is of the form:

$$r_t = a + b_1 r_{t-1} + b_2 r_{t-2} + \varepsilon_t \qquad \varepsilon_t = h_t^{1/2} z_t$$

$$h_t = \alpha_0 + \alpha_1 \varepsilon_{t-1}^2 + \beta h_{t-1}$$

$$z_t \sim N(0,1)$$

This model allows for an AR(2) process in returns. The specification was identified using the Schwartz (1978) criterion. Only the Japanese yen series required the two lags, but for better comparisons across exchange rates the same model is used.[4] Estimation of this model is done using maximum likelihood.

Simulations of this model follow those for the random walk. Standardized residuals of the GARCH model are estimated as:

$$\frac{\varepsilon_t}{\sqrt{h_t}}$$

These residuals are scrambled and the scrambled residuals are then used to rebuild a GARCH representation for the data series. Using the actual residuals for the simulations allows the residual distribution to differ from normality. Bollerslev and Wooldridge (1990) have shown that the previous parameter estimates will be consistent under certain deviations from normality. Therefore, the estimated residuals will also be consistent.[5]

The third model has been proposed for foreign exchange markets in a paper by Engle and Hamilton (1990). It suggests that exchange rates follow long persistent swings following a two-state Markov chain. It is given by:

$$r_t = (\mu_0 + \mu_1 S_t) + (\alpha_0 + \alpha_1 S_t) z_t$$
$$P(S_t = 1 \mid S_{t-1} = 1) = p$$
$$P(S_t = 0 \mid S_{t-1} = 1) = 1 - p$$
$$P(S_t = 0 \mid S_{t-1} = 0) = q$$
$$P(S_t = 1 \mid S_{t-1} = 0) = 1 - q$$
$$z_t \sim N(0, 1)$$

This model allows both the mean and variance for exchange rate returns to move between two different states. Since this model is capable of generating persistent trends, it presents a strong possibility for generating the results seen using the trading rules. Estimation is done using maximum likelihood. For this model, the simulations will use normally distributed random numbers from a computer random number generator.

1.4 EMPIRICAL RESULTS

1.4.1 Data summary

The data used in this chapter are all from the EHRA macro data tape from the Federal Reserve Bank. Weekly exchange rates for the British pound (BP), the German mark (DM) and the Japanese yen (JY) are sampled every Wednesday from January 1974 to February 1991 at 12:00 pm EST.

Returns are created using log first differences of these weekly exchange rates quoted in dollars/fx. Table 1.1 presents some summary statistics for these return series. All three series show little evidence of skewness and are slightly leptokurtic. These properties are common for many high frequency asset returns series. The first ten autocorrelations are given in the rows labelled ρ_n. The Bartlett asymptotic standard error for these series is 0.033. The BP shows little evidence of any autocorrelation except for lags four and eight, while the DM shows some weak evidence of correlation, and the JY shows strong evidence for some autocorrelation. The Ljung–Box–Pierce statistics are shown on the last row. These are calculated for ten lags and are distributed $\chi^2(10)$ under the null of independently identically distributed. The p-values are included for each in parentheses. The BP and JY series reject independence, whereas the DM series does not.

Table 1.1   *Summary statistics*

Description	BP	DM	JY
Sample size	893	893	893
Mean * 100	−0.0162	0.0686	0.0875
Std. * 100	1.4398	1.4350	1.4012
Skewness	0.2107	0.3532	0.3785
Kurtosis	5.5931	4.3735	5.1425
ρ_1	0.0488	0.0636	0.1105
ρ_2	−0.0248	0.0609	0.0962
ρ_3	0.0367	0.0060	0.0592
ρ_4	0.0959	0.0414	0.0446
ρ_5	0.0164	−0.0200	0.0338
ρ_6	−0.0135	−0.0570	−0.0002
ρ_7	0.0070	−0.0028	−0.0359
ρ_8	0.0862	0.0625	0.0060
ρ_9	−0.0305	0.0146	−0.0036
ρ_{10}	−0.0047	0.0414	−0.0833
Bartlett	0.0335	0.0335	0.0335
LBP	20.16	15.53	26.41
p-values $(\chi^2(10))$	(0.027)	(0.115)	(0.003)

Summary statistics for BP (British pound), DM (German mark), JY (Japanese yen) weekly exchange rates from January 1974 to February 1991.

The interest rate series used are also from the EHRA macro data tape. For the dollar, the weekly eurodollar rate is used. For the pound, the international money market call money rate is used. For the mark, the Frankfurt interbank call money rate is used, and for the yen, the Tokyo unconditional lender rate. Weekly rates are constructed ex post from the compounded rates from Wednesday to Tuesday. These rates can only be viewed as proxies for the desirable situation of having a set of interest rates from the same offshore market at the same maturity. At this time that is not available.

1.4.2   Random walk comparisons

In this section, simulations are performed comparing conditional moments from the technical trading rules with a bootstrapped random walk generated from the actual returns time series scrambled with replacement. Three moving-average rules will be used, the twenty-week, thirty-week and fifty-week moving averages. These are fairly common lengths used by traders. We will see that the results are not very sensitive to the lengths used. The moving-average rules force us to start the study after a certain number of weeks have

Table 1.2 *BP random walk bootstrap*

Rule	Result	Buy	σ_b	Fraction Buy	Sell	σ_s	Buy–Sell
(1, 20)	Fraction > Xrate	0.080 00	0.560 00	0.460 00	0.980 00	0.420 00	0.000 00
	Simulation mean	−0.000 12	0.014 34	0.478 10	−0.000 14	0.014 29	0.000 02
	Xrate mean	0.000 91	0.014 26	0.486 24	−0.001 34	0.014 42	0.002 25
(1, 30)	Fraction > Xrate	0.010 00	0.630 00	0.340 00	1.000 00	0.370 00	0.000 00
	Simulation mean	−0.000 18	0.014 38	0.473 64	−0.000 10	0.014 27	−0.000 07
	Xrate mean	0.001 35	0.014 21	0.504 06	−0.001 84	0.014 52	0.003 19
(1, 50)	Fraction > Xrate	0.010 00	0.640 00	0.370 00	1.000 00	0.180 00	0.000 00
	Simulation mean	−0.000 19	0.014 36	0.468 09	−0.000 11	0.014 25	−0.000 09
	Xrate mean	0.001 45	0.014 10	0.494 66	−0.001 82	0.014 87	0.003 27
Average	Fraction > Xrate	0.010 00	0.660 00	0.390 00	0.990 00	0.320 00	0.000 00
	Simulation mean	−0.000 16	0.014 36	0.473 33	−0.000 12	0.014 27	−0.000 05
	Xrate mean	0.001 24	0.014 19	0.494 96	−0.001 66	0.014 60	0.002 90

Buy refers to the mean 1 week return during buy periods, σ_b, the standard deviation of these returns, and Fraction Buy is the fraction of buy weeks out of total weeks. Sell and σ_s are the same for the sell returns. Buy–Sell is the difference between the buy mean and sell mean. The row labelled Fraction > Xrate shows the fraction of the 500 simulations which generate a value for the statistic larger than that from the actual series. Simulation mean is the mean value for the statistic for the simulated random walks, and Xrate mean is the value from the original series.

passed. For this chapter, all tests for all the rules begin after week fifty. This gives the same number of weekly observations for all three rules.

Table 1.2 presents the results comparing the actual series for the BP with 500 simulated random walks. Six comparison statistics are computed in this table. First, the column labelled 'Buy' refers to the conditional mean during buy periods. This is:

$$m_b = (1/N_b) \sum_{t=0}^{N-1} r_{t+1} I_t^b$$

where N_b is the number of buy signals in the sample and I_t^b is an indicator variable for a buy signal at time t. The second column, labelled 'σ_b', looks at the standard deviation of this same set of returns. This is:

$$\left((1/N_b) \sum_{t=0}^{N-1} (r_{t+1} - m_b)^2 I_t^b \right)^{1/2}$$

This gives a simple idea of how risky the buy or sell periods might be and tells us something about what is happening to conditional variance. The third column, labelled 'Fraction buy', is just the fraction of buy weeks N_b/N. The next two columns, 'Sell' and 'σ_s' repeat the previous descriptions for the sell periods. Let m_s be the mean during the sell periods. The final column, 'Buy–Sell', refers to the difference between the buy and sell means, $m_b - m_s$.

This table presents several results for each test. The first is the fraction of simulated random walks that generate a given statistic greater than that for the original series. This can be thought of as a simulated p-value. For the twenty-week moving-average rules, this result is given in the first row of the table. For the BP series we see that 8 per cent of the simulations generated a mean return greater than that from the actual series. The next row, 'Simulation mean' shows the mean of m_b for the 500 simulated random walks. The third row, 'Xrate mean' shows m_b for the exchange rate series. For the BP series the table reports a mean one-week buy return of 0.091 per cent which is greater than the simulated mean of −0.012 per cent. The simulations show that this difference is weakly significant with 8 per cent of the simulations generating a m_b greater than 0.091 per cent.

The second column shows the results for the standard deviations of the buy returns σ_b. The column shows that 56 per cent of the simulations had standard deviations greater than that in the original series. This clearly shows no significant difference between the simulations and the original series. In other words, although the buys generate a larger mean, they do not have a larger variance. The next column reports that the fraction of buys to sells for the actual series, third row, is 0.486. This does not appear to be unusually large or small relative to the simulated random walks.

For the sells, m_s, for the BP series is −0.134 per cent which compares with −0.014 per cent for the simulation. Table 1.1 shows that 98 per cent of the simulated random walks generated m_s statistics larger than −0.134, indicating that the sell period returns for the original series are unusually small when compared with the random walk. The next column, σ_s, shows that these returns are not different from the entire sample in terms of volatility.

The final column reports the difference $m_b - m_s$. For this rule, the difference is about 0.2 per cent, but none of the simulated random walks generated such a large difference between buy and sell returns.

The next six rows of the table repeat the same results for the other two rules, the thirty- and fifty-week moving-average rules. The results for these rules are similar to the first two with the buy means unusually large and the sell means unusually small. There still appears to be no effect in volatility.[6]

The final set of tests performs a joint test based on all three rules. An average is taken for the statistics generated from each of the three rules. For the mean buys this would be:

$$m_b = 1/3(m_b(1, 20) + m_b(1, 30) + m_b(1, 50))$$

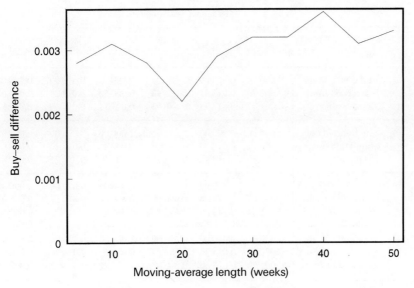

Figure 1.1 *British pound buy–sell differences*

Finding the distribution of this statistic would require knowledge of the joint distribution across all the rules. The results for each rule are clearly far from independent, so this would be a difficult job. With the simulated random walks the rules can now be compared with results for the same average statistics over the 500 simulated random walks. This section of the table shows that the pattern for each of the individual rules is repeated in the average rules.

A good question to ask at this point is how general these results are for different moving averages. This chapter has used only three different moving-average rules. These are chosen to be close to those used by actual traders. It is quite possible that there may be some data-snooping problems here in that these rules have already been chosen because of their past performance in the data. This problem is partially accounted for in Figure 1.1, which displays the buy–sell differences for several different lengths of moving averages. It is clear from this figure that the results are not overly sensitive to the length of the moving average chosen.

Tables 1.3 and 1.4, repeat the results for the DM and JY series. Turning to the average rows, we see very similar results to Table 1.2. The buy–sell differences are large for both with p-values of 0.

For the JY series, the standard deviations during the buy and sell periods are not unusually small or large. For the DM series, some weak differences appear between the standard deviations during the buy and sell periods. For

Table 1.3   *DM random walk bootstrap*

Rule	Result	Buy	σ_b	Fraction Buy	Sell	σ_s	Buy–Sell
(1, 20)	Fraction > Xrate	0.030 00	0.680 00	0.320 00	0.990 00	0.310 00	0.000 00
	Simulation mean	0.000 70	0.014 31	0.562 73	0.000 65	0.014 22	0.000 05
	Xrate mean	0.001 77	0.013 98	0.586 01	−0.001 12	0.014 54	0.002 88
(1, 30)	Fraction > Xrate	0.040 00	0.900 00	0.270 00	1.000 00	0.008 00	0.000 00
	Simulation mean	0.000 67	0.014 34	0.578 16	0.000 70	0.014 21	−0.000 03
	Xrate mean	0.001 69	0.013 52	0.618 77	−0.001 12	0.015 26	0.002 81
(1, 50)	Fraction > Xrate	0.050 00	0.960 00	0.550 00	0.960 00	0.010 00	0.000 00
	Simulation mean	0.000 69	0.014 34	0.600 50	0.000 66	0.014 17	0.000 03
	Xrate mean	0.001 64	0.013 30	0.597 86	−0.000 95	0.015 55	0.002 59
Average	Fraction > Xrate	0.030 00	0.870 00	0.430 00	1.000 00	0.120 00	0.000 00
	Simulation mean	0.000 68	0.014 33	0.580 24	0.000 67	0.014 20	0.000 02
	Xrate mean	0.001 70	0.013 60	0.600 85	−0.001 06	0.015 12	0.002 76

the average across the rules using the buy standard deviations, the simulated *p*-value is 0.87, indicating that 87 per cent of the simulations were more volatile than the actual exchange rate series. For the sells, this value is 0.12, indicating that 12 per cent of the simulations were more volatile than the original series. This shows some weak evidence that the buy periods were less

Table 1.4   *JY random walk bootstrap*

Rule	Result	Buy	σ_b	Fraction Buy	Sell	σ_s	Buy–Sell
(1, 20)	Fraction > Xrate	0.000 00	0.520 00	0.730 00	1.000 00	0.590 00	0.000 00
	Simulation mean	0.000 87	0.013 95	0.591 32	0.001 00	0.013 92	−0.000 13
	Xrate mean	0.002 50	0.013 88	0.548 17	−0.001 14	0.013 68	0.003 63
(1, 30)	Fraction > Xrate	0.000 00	0.490 00	0.790 00	1.000 00	0.530 00	0.000 00
	Simulation mean	0.000 89	0.013 97	0.614 37	0.001 00	0.013 88	−0.000 12
	Xrate mean	0.002 60	0.013 91	0.551 56	−0.001 16	0.013 72	0.003 76
(1, 50)	Fraction > Xrate	0.010 00	0.400 00	0.740 00	0.980 00	0.450 00	0.000 00
	Simulation mean	0.000 86	0.013 93	0.648 14	0.001 05	0.013 92	−0.000 18
	Xrate mean	0.002 13	0.014 02	0.594 31	−0.000 71	0.013 97	0.002 84
Average	Fraction > Xrate	0.000 00	0.470 00	0.720 00	1.000 00	0.520 00	0.000 00
	Simulation mean	0.000 87	0.013 95	0.617 61	0.001 02	0.013 90	−0.000 14
	Xrate mean	0.002 41	0.013 94	0.564 39	−0.001 00	0.013 79	0.003 41

Table 1.5 *Skewness kurtosis*

Rule	Result	Buy skew	Buy kurt.	Sell skew	Sell kurt.
BP					
(1, 20)	Fraction > Xrate	0.572 00	0.266 00	0.336 00	0.480 00
(1, 30)	Fraction > Xrate	0.504 00	0.306 00	0.422 00	0.488 00
(1, 50)	Fraction > Xrate	0.618 00	0.330 00	0.266 00	0.480 00
Average	Fraction > Xrate	0.564 00	0.296 00	0.326 00	0.480 00
	Simulation mean	0.198 99	5.416 80	0.217 49	5.459 27
	Xrate mean	0.134 46	5.941 69	0.335 41	5.511 24
DM					
(1, 20)	Fraction > Xrate	0.328 00	0.202 00	0.446 00	0.618 00
(1, 30)	Fraction > Xrate	0.300 00	0.168 00	0.354 00	0.666 00
(1, 50)	Fraction > Xrate	0.306 00	0.076 00	0.346 00	0.798 00
Average	Fraction > Xrate	0.312 00	0.136 00	0.350 00	0.724 00
	Simulation mean	0.341 52	4.282 22	0.353 44	4.279 91
	Xrate mean	0.443 44	5.553 64	0.394 10	3.437 40
JY					
(1, 20)	Fraction > Xrate	0.340 00	0.528 00	0.314 00	0.620 00
(1, 30)	Fraction > Xrate	0.364 00	0.524 00	0.334 00	0.628 00
(1, 50)	Fraction > Xrate	0.354 00	0.542 00	0.392 00	0.708 00
Average	Fraction > Xrate	0.330 00	0.530 00	0.346 00	0.668 00
	Simulation mean	0.383 54	5.089 46	0.407 57	5.052 35
	Xrate mean	0.490 69	4.964 34	0.541 88	4.631 71

volatile than average and the sells were more volatile than average. The results are fairly weak for the average rule, but checking the individual rules stronger rejections are found for the thirty- and fifty-week moving averages individually. This result moves counter to a simple mean variance connection for the exchange rate from a dollar perspective. The higher conditional returns from the buy period should be compensating for more risk, but these results show that for the DM the risk (in terms of own standard deviation) is lower. Although this is puzzling, measuring the riskiness of a foreign exchange series is more complicated than estimating the standard deviation, so strong conclusions about risk premia require more adequate modelling of the exact risk–return trade off.

Another check for changes in the conditional distributions of returns is performed in Table 1.5. In this table, skewness and kurtosis are estimated for the returns during the buy and sell periods. It is possible that these higher

Table 1.6   *Subsamples: random walk*

Rule	Result	Buy	σ_b	Fraction Buy	Sell	σ_s	Buy–Sell
BP first half							
(1, 20)	Fraction > Xrate	0.022 00	0.976 00	0.160 00	0.998 00	0.090 00	0.002 00
(1, 30)	Fraction > Xrate	0.012 00	0.946 00	0.106 00	0.998 00	0.058 00	0.000 00
(1, 50)	Fraction > Xrate	0.010 00	0.888 00	0.124 00	1.000 00	0.052 00	0.000 00
Average	Fraction > Xrate	0.006 00	0.952 00	0.118 00	1.000 00	0.064 00	0.000 00
	Simulation mean	−0.000 80	0.011 68	0.396 14	−0.000 59	0.011 72	−0.000 22
	Xrate mean	0.001 03	0.010 25	0.510 48	−0.002 67	0.012 88	0.003 70
BP second half							
(1, 20)	Fraction > Xrate	0.206 00	0.200 00	0.612 00	0.694 00	0.694 00	0.184 00
(1, 30)	Fraction > Xrate	0.070 00	0.244 00	0.462 00	0.834 00	0.648 00	0.050 00
(1, 50)	Fraction > Xrate	0.074 00	0.366 00	0.498 00	0.804 00	0.510 00	0.044 00
Average	Fraction > Xrate	0.094 00	0.246 00	0.518 00	0.788 00	0.630 00	0.052 00
	Simulation mean	0.000 11	0.016 47	0.524 70	0.000 50	0.016 52	−0.000 38
	Xrate mean	0.001 48	0.017 19	0.519 00	−0.000 47	0.016 09	0.001 95
DM first half							
(1, 20)	Fraction > Xrate	0.108 00	0.960 00	0.180 00	0.992 00	0.058 00	0.008 00
(1, 30)	Fraction > Xrate	0.196 00	0.996 00	0.122 00	0.966 00	0.008 00	0.020 00
(1, 50)	Fraction > Xrate	0.134 00	0.996 00	0.206 00	0.994 00	0.002 00	0.006 00
Average	Fraction > Xrate	0.134 00	0.994 00	0.174 00	0.992 00	0.010 00	0.004 00
	Simulation mean	0.000 08	0.012 59	0.521 43	0.000 26	0.012 65	−0.000 18
	Xrate mean	0.001 01	0.010 67	0.619 35	−0.001 64	0.014 76	0.002 64
DM second half							
(1, 20)	Fraction > Xrate	0.104 00	0.254 00	0.450 00	0.950 00	0.698 00	0.030 00
(1, 30)	Fraction > Xrate	0.046 00	0.392 00	0.454 00	0.996 00	0.600 00	0.002 00
(1, 50)	Fraction > Xrate	0.040 00	0.400 00	0.734 00	0.948 00	0.416 00	0.006 00
Average	Fraction > Xrate	0.048 00	0.330 00	0.562 00	0.986 00	0.566 00	0.000 00
	Simulation mean	0.001 03	0.015 69	0.626 56	0.001 41	0.015 77	−0.000 37
	Xrate mean	0.002 55	0.015 99	0.607 92	−0.000 84	0.015 49	0.003 39
JY first half							
(1, 20)	Fraction > Xrate	0.002 00	0.754 00	0.528 00	0.998 00	0.516 00	0.002 00
(1, 30)	Fraction > Xrate	0.000 00	0.782 00	0.536 00	0.998 00	0.414 00	0.000 00
(1, 50)	Fraction > Xrate	0.012 00	0.792 00	0.410 00	0.982 00	0.210 00	0.000 00
Average	Fraction > Xrate	0.000 00	0.792 00	0,488 00	0.998 00	0.330 00	0.000 00
	Simulation mean	0.000 07	0.012 46	0.528 96	0.000 39	0.012 43	−0.000 32
	Xrate mean	0.002 17	0.011 78	0.535 48	−0.001 85	0.012 74	0.004 02

Table 1.6 *(continued)*

Rule	Result	Buy	σ_b	Fraction Buy	Sell	σ_s	Buy–Sell
JY second half							
(1, 20)	Fraction > Xrate	0.100 00	0.432 00	0.690 00	0.958 00	0.908 00	0.016 00
(1, 30)	Fraction > Xrate	0.114 00	0.464 00	0.798 00	0.940 00	0.914 00	0.032 00
(1, 50)	Fraction > Xrate	0.082 00	0.260 00	0.802 00	0.964 00	0.942 00	0.014 00
Average	Fraction > Xrate	0.088 00	0.386 00	0.772 00	0.972 00	0.950 00	0.012 00
	Simulation mean	0.001 39	0.015 21	0.674 45	0.001 85	0.015 32	−0.000 46
	Xrate mean	0.002 62	0.015 50	0.604 69	−0.000 33	0.013 55	0.002 95

moments might give a better indication of the riskiness of returns during each of the periods. This table combines the results for the three series into one table. The individual tests are summarized with a single row entry giving their simulated p-value and the averages are presented in three rows for each exchange rate. This table shows little difference in the higher moments from the actual series buy and sell periods and their simulation counterparts.

Table 1.6 considers the stability of these results over various subsamples. It is quite possible that these rules may be picking up certain nonstationarities in the data series. The rules themselves are probably very good at checking for changes in regime. If these regime changes are relatively infrequent, then splitting the sample into two and repeating the tests makes it less likely that the rules will detect any differences between the buy and sell periods. Table 1.6 presents results from such an experiment, where each series is broken in half and the previous random walk simulations are repeated for each subsample.

For the BP, the results are basically unchanged across the subsamples. However, the trading rule results look slightly less significant in the second subsample. The simulated p-value for the average buy–sell difference moves from 0 to 0.052. Also, the average buy–sell difference falls from 0.37 per cent to 0.195 per cent. The DM series shows similar results for the buy and sell means in the two different subsamples. The p-value for the average buy–sell difference moves from 0.004 in the first subsample to 0 in the second subsample. The average buy–sell difference increases from 0.26 per cent to 0.34 per cent. For the standard deviations, the results look different. For the standard deviations, the small volatility during buy periods is coming entirely from the first subperiod. For the average standard deviations, the p-value for σ_b is 0.994 for the first subsample and 0.330 for the second subsample. The results on σ_s also are much stronger during the first subsample with a p-value of 0.01 during the first subsample and 0.566 during the second subsample.

Table 1.7   *GARCH(1, 1) parameter estimates*

$$x_t = a + b_1 x_{t-1} + b_2 x_{t-2} + \varepsilon_t \qquad \varepsilon_t = h_t^{1/2} z_t$$
$$h_t = \alpha_0 + \alpha_1 \varepsilon_{t-1}^2 + \beta h_{t-1}$$
$$z_t \sim N(0, 1)$$

Xrate	α_0	β	α_1	b_1	b_2	a
BP	2.2940	0.7287	0.1680	0.0832	0.0324	−3.4473
	(0.3504)	(0.0363)	(0.0303)	(0.0391)	(0.0393)	(4.5733)
DM	1.4131	0.7539	0.1889	0.0604	0.0935	6.8368
	(0.3480)	(0.0319)	(0.0289)	(0.0378)	(0.0349)	(4.2092)
JY	1.3460	0.7610	0.1875	0.1179	0.0832	6.3114
	(0.2403)	(0.0321)	(0.0308)	(0.0380)	(0.0389)	(4.1427)

Estimation is by maximum likelihood. Numbers in parentheses are asymptotic standard errors.

The results for the JY series change very little from the first to the second subsample. The mean buy–sell difference falls from 0.4 per cent to 0.3 per cent. The p-value for this number goes from 0 to 0.012.

1.4.3   GARCH comparisons

Table 1.7 shows the parameter estimates for GARCH(1,1)-AR(2) model for each of the three exchange rate series. The estimates show very similar estimates for the variance parameters, β and α_1, for the three exchange rate series. The AR(2) parameters show some significant persistence in exchange rate movements for all three series, but the yen and the mark both show a somewhat larger amount of persistence with both the AR(1) and AR(2) parameters significant.

Standardized residuals from this model are run back through the same model to generate simulated time series for the three exchange rate series. Results of these simulations are presented in Table 1.8. This table shows that the GARCH model combined with the AR(2) causes some increase in the mean buys and some decrease in the mean sells. Most of this is probably coming from the persistence in the AR(2). However, the magnitude of these differences is not as great as that for the actual series.

For the BP, the average buy–sell difference for the three tests is 0.07 per cent which compares with 0.29 per cent for the actual series. The simulated p-value here is 0.01. For the BP, the GARCH model leaves the previous

Table 1.8 *GARCH bootstrap*

Rule	Result	Buy	σ_b	Fraction Buy	Sell	σ_s	Buy–Sell
BP							
(1, 20)	Fraction > Xrate	0.176 00	0.552 00	0.394 00	0.818 00	0.530 00	0.094 00
(1, 30)	Fraction > Xrate	0.048 00	0.574 00	0.276 00	0.958 00	0.504 00	0.008 00
(1, 50)	Fraction > Xrate	0.020 00	0.588 00	0.304 00	0.970 00	0.424 00	0.008 00
Average	Fraction > Xrate	0.056 00	0.570 00	0.316 00	0.944 00	0.486 00	0.010 00
	Simulation mean	0.000 08	0.014 74	0.465 59	−0.000 58	0.014 92	0.000 66
	Xrate mean	0.001 24	0.014 19	0.494 96	−0.001 66	0.014 60	0.002 90
DM							
(1, 20)	Fraction > Xrate	0.284 00	0.782 00	0.404 00	0.928 00	0.646 00	0.076 00
(1, 30)	Fraction > Xrate	0.258 00	0.858 00	0.322 00	0.942 00	0.494 00	0.070 00
(1, 50)	Fraction > Xrate	0.232 00	0.878 00	0.556 00	0.934 00	0.422 00	0.050 00
Average	Fraction > Xrate	0.250 00	0.850 00	0.426 00	0.944 00	0.522 00	0.054 00
	Simulation mean	0.001 22	0.015 82	0.589 33	0.000 21	0.015 58	0.001 01
	Xrate mean	0.001 70	0.013 60	0.600 85	−0.001 06	0.015 12	0.002 76
JY							
(1, 20)	Fraction > Xrate	0.134 00	0.734 00	0.682 00	0.920 00	0.642 00	0.046 00
(1, 30)	Fraction > Xrate	0.086 00	0.718 00	0.738 00	0.944 00	0.606 00	0.026 00
(1, 50)	Fraction > Xrate	0.132 00	0.670 00	0.634 00	0.896 00	0.568 00	0.038 00
Average	Fraction > Xrate	0.114 00	0.710 00	0.692 00	0.932 00	0.602 00	0.028 00
	Simulation mean	0.001 46	0.016 11	0.596 72	0.000 16	0.015 19	0.001 30
	Xrate mean	0.002 41	0.013 94	0.564 39	−0.001 00	0.013 79	0.003 41

Results from simulations of 500 GARCH models. These models are generated from estimated parameters and standardized residuals from maximum likelihood.

results unchanged. Also, there are no effects on volatility as previously mentioned.

For the DM and JY series, the GARCH model has a slightly stronger effect. The simulations generate average buy–sell differences of 0.10 and 0.13 per cent respectively. The *p*-values for these differences are now 0.054 and 0.028 respectively. The added persistence of the AR(2) has caused a large buy–sell difference for these series. Although this does have a small impact on the results from the simulations, the differences remain small relative to the buy–sell difference for the actual series.

1.4.4   Regime shift bootstrap

Some of the results for the GARCH model suggest that although this model is moving in the right direction, the persistence generated is not strong enough to generate the trading rule results that are seen in the data. The rules used continue to generate buy or sell signals after the price has cut through the moving average, not just in the neighbourhood of the moving average.

Long-range persistence could be generated using the regime shifting model used by Engle and Hamilton (1990). In this model, conditional means and variances follow a two-state Markov process. The parameter estimates for this model are given in Table 1.9. For only one of the three series, the JY, are both the conditional mean parameters significantly different from zero. For the BP series, they are both insignificantly different from zero. There is also a sign pattern reversal on the JY series. For this series, high variance periods are high mean periods. For the other two series, this result is reversed.

It seems doubtful that the magnitudes of the regime shift parameters will be large enough to generate the conditional mean differences. For example, for the BP series, the conditional mean for $S_t = 0$ is 0.05 per cent and for the $S_t = 1$ period it is -0.02 per cent. It is difficult to see how this will generate a buy–sell spread of 0.29 per cent. This is confirmed in Table 1.10 which shows the results for simulations of this model using a normal random number generator to generate errors. There is little evidence of this model capturing

Table 1.9   *Regime shift parameter estimates*

$$x_t = (\mu_0 + \mu_1 S_t) + (\alpha_0 + \alpha_1 S_t)z_t$$
$$P(S_t = 1 \mid S_{t-1} = 1) = p$$
$$P(S_t = 0 \mid S_{t-1} = 1) = 1 - p$$
$$P(S_t = 0 \mid S_{t-1} = 0) = q$$
$$P(S_t = 1 \mid S_{t-1} = 0) = 1 - q$$
$$z_t \sim N(0, 1)$$

Xrate	$\alpha_0 * 1000$	$\alpha_1 * 1000$	$\mu_0 * 1000$	$\mu_1 * 1000$	p	q
BP	2.7811	12.2139	0.4923	−0.7119	0.9933	0.9260
	(0.2447)	(0.3578)	(0.3851)	(0.6374)	(0.0033)	(0.0342)
DM	6.7422	9.0407	1.1889	−0.6388	0.9940	0.9738
	(0.4188)	(0.5350)	(0.5313)	(0.7815)	(0.0034)	(0.0136)
JY	4.8973	11.8531	−0.7646	2.4587	0.9387	0.8773
	(0.2892)	(0.5093)	(0.3632)	(0.7655)	(0.0157)	(0.0266)

Estimation is by maximum likelihood. Numbers in parentheses are asymptotic standard errors.

Table 1.10 *Regime shift bootstrap*

Rule	Result	Buy	σ_b	Fraction Buy	Sell	σ_s	Buy–Sell
BP							
(1, 20)	Fraction > Xrate	0.048 00	0.482 00	0.538 00	0.972 00	0.566 00	0.020 00
(1, 30)	Fraction > Xrate	0.004 00	0.512 00	0.394 00	0.994 00	0.494 00	0.002 00
(1, 50)	Fraction > Xrate	0.004 00	0.620 00	0.424 00	0.998 00	0.270 00	0.000 00
Average	Fraction > Xrate	0.008 00	0.530 00	0.430 00	0.994 00	0.442 00	0.000 00
	Simulation mean	−0.000 25	0.014 20	0.484 42	−0.000 07	0.014 49	−0.000 18
	Xrate mean	0.001 24	0.014 19	0.494 96	−0.001 66	0.014 60	0.002 90
DM							
(1, 20)	Fraction > Xrate	0.036 00	0.532 00	0.538 00	0.996 00	0.600 00	0.000 00
(1, 30)	Fraction > Xrate	0.042 00	0.700 00	0.434 00	0.996 00	0.326 00	0.006 00
(1, 50)	Fraction > Xrate	0.056 00	0.780 00	0.644 00	0.982 00	0.230 00	0.008 00
Average	Fraction > Xrate	0.028 00	0.684 00	0.552 00	0.994 00	0.370 00	0.000 00
	Simulation mean	0.000 64	0.014 05	0.608 95	0.000 80	0.014 81	−0.000 16
	Xrate mean	0.001 70	0.013 60	0.600 85	−0.001 06	0.015 12	0.002 76
JY							
(1, 20)	Fraction > Xrate	0.008 00	0.734 00	0.642 00	1.000 00	0.428 00	0.000 00
(1, 30)	Fraction > Xrate	0.004 00	0.650 00	0.732 00	0.998 00	0.452 00	0.000 00
(1, 50)	Fraction > Xrate	0.024 00	0.572 00	0.666 00	0.978 00	0.412 00	0.004 00
Average	Fraction > Xrate	0.004 00	0.630 00	0.684 00	0.996 00	0.422 00	0.002 00
	Simulation mean	0.000 89	0.014 22	0.597 01	0.000 87	0.013 64	0.000 02
	Xrate mean	0.002 41	0.013 94	0.564 39	−0.001 00	0.013 79	0.003 41

Results from simulations of 500 regime-shift models. These models are generated from estimated parameters and computer generated normal random numbers.

what the trading rules are picking up for any of the series. For the DM and BP series, the buy–sell differences are actually negative. For all the series, the *p*-values for the buy–sell differences are all close to zero.

This should not rule out this model in general, but at these relatively high frequencies (weekly) it does not seem to capture what is going on. There may be some numerical problems in estimation as the probabilities, *p* and *q*, are close to one at this time horizon. In Engle and Hamilton (1990), the conditional mean estimates are significant and larger than those found here. This may be due to the use of quarterly data. It remains to be seen whether other estimation techniques can help repair these results for the regime shift model.

1.4.5   Interest rate differentials

The use of the previous simple processes for foreign exchange movements ignores much of the information available in world financial markets. This section incorporates some of this information into further simulations.

The relation that will be used here is uncovered interest parity. This relation can be written as:

$$E_t(s_{t+1}) - s_t = i_t - i_t^*$$

where i and i^* are the domestic and foreign interest rates and s_t is the log of the exchange rate. In a risk-neutral world, the interest rate differential over the appropriate horizon should be equal to the expected drift of the exchange rate.

Although uncovered parity, and theories closely related to it, have been rejected by several studies, it is important to see if this long-range persistent drift could be causing what the trading rules are picking up. For this test a model of the form:

$$s_{t+1} = s_t + i_t - i_t^* + \varepsilon_t$$

where ε_t is independently identically distributed noise will be used. One major problem is getting the interest rates and their timing correct. This is extremely difficult. For the weekly exchange rates used here, weekly eurorates would be the most useful series to have. This study is constrained by what is available on the EHRA tapes. For the dollar, weekly eurorates are available at daily frequency and will be used as the risk-free dollar rate for each week beginning at the close on Wednesday. Unfortunately, the other currencies do not have such rates available. The weekly rates are constructed from daily ex post overnight rates from Wednesday to the following Tuesday. Assuming the expectations hypothesis holds at the very short end of the term structure:

$$i_{t,7} = \sum_{i=0}^{6} E_t i_{t+1,1}$$

or

$$i_{t,7} = \sum_{i=0}^{6} i_{t+i,1} + e_t$$

where $E_t(e_t) = 0$. The expected drift term $i_t - i_t^*$ is therefore $i_t - i^* + e_t$ where i^* is the ex post rate constructed from the overnight rates. Therefore:

$$s_{t+1} - s_t = i_t - \tilde{i}_t^* + \eta_t$$

where $E_t(\eta_t) = 0$.

The time period studied is shortened due to data availability. For the BP and DM, the series now starts in January 1975. For the JY, the series begins in October 1977. The lengths of the BP, DM and JY series are 832, 832 and 690 weeks respectively.

Rather than immediately adjusting these series for the interest differential, a slightly different approach is taken at first. Representative series of the form:

$$s_{t+1} = s_t + \mu_t + \varepsilon_t$$

will be simulated. The drift, μ_t, is obtained from the appropriate interest differential. An estimate of the residual series $\hat{\varepsilon}_t$ is obtained by removing the drift from the actual exchange rate changes. This is then scrambled with replacement, and a new series is generated using the original drift series and the scrambled residuals. This gives us representative exchange rate series reflecting the appropriate information from the interest rates.

These simulations are then run through the same trading rule tests run in previous sections. Results of these tests are presented in Table 1.11. The results are comparable to those found for the random walk simulations in Tables 1.2, 1.3 and 1.4. For all three series, none of the rules generate buy–sell differences as large as those generated from the original series. The adjustment for the interest differential appears to have had little effect on the trading-rule results.

Table 1.12 repeats some of the earlier GARCH simulations accounting for interest differentials. In this case, the more traditional approach of subtracting the expected drift from the exchange rate returns is done. A GARCH model is then fitted to these 'zero drift' terms and simulated back using scrambled, standardized residuals as in section 1.4.3. Comparing Table 1.12 with Table 1.8 shows very few differences. Adjusting the exchange rate series using the expected drift has very little impact on the GARCH simulations. The large (small) returns during buy (sell) are still not replicated well by the simulated null model.

1.4.6   Simulated method of moments estimates

The previous tests have not incorporated the trading-rule diagnostic tests into the estimation procedure. This section presents a method where the two can be brought together in one combined procedure.

One problem with the trading-rule measures is that it is difficult to derive analytic results for these measures. One technique for estimating parameters using conditions which can only be simulated is simulated method of moments. This technique was developed for cross-section data by McFadden (1989) and Pakes and Pollard (1989). It is extended to time series cases in Duffie and Singleton (1993) and Ingram and Lee (1991).

Table 1.11   *Interest rate drift*

Rule	Result	Buy	σ_b	Fraction Buy	Sell	σ_s	Buy–Sell
BP							
(1, 20)	Fraction > Xrate	0.012 00	0.312 00	0.406 00	0.982 00	0.650 00	0.002 00
(1, 30)	Fraction > Xrate	0.010 00	0.616 00	0.284 00	0.992 00	0.296 00	0.000 00
(1, 50)	Fraction > Xrate	0.006 00	0.714 00	0.328 00	0.994 00	0.152 00	0.000 00
Average	Fraction > Xrate	0.006 00	0.552 00	0.320 00	0.994 00	0.330 00	0.000 00
	Simulation mean	−0.000 14	0.014 68	0.476 60	−0.000 11	0.014 61	−0.000 02
	Xrate mean	0.001 55	0.014 57	0.507 31	−0.001 65	0.014 91	0.003 20
DM							
(1, 20)	Fraction > Xrate	0.032 00	0.462 00	0.544 00	0.990 00	0.606 00	0.004 00
(1, 30)	Fraction > Xrate	0.110 00	0.756 00	0.540 00	0.960 00	0.212 00	0.024 00
(1, 50)	Fraction > Xrate	0.046 00	0.822 00	0.750 00	0.972 00	0.166 00	0.008 00
Average	Fraction > Xrate	0.040 00	0.704 00	0.630 00	0.982 00	0.294 00	0.004 00
	Simulation mean	0.000 28	0.015 41	0.538 98	0.000 48	0.015 44	−0.000 20
	Xrate mean	0.001 57	0.015 05	0.510 50	−0.001 35	0.015 82	0.002 92
JY							
(1, 20)	Fraction > Xrate	0.022 00	0.354 00	0.762 00	0.996 00	0.638 00	0.002 00
(1, 30)	Fraction > Xrate	0.002 00	0.350 00	0.866 00	0.996 00	0.664 00	0.000 00
(1, 50)	Fraction > Xrate	0.124 00	0.576 00	0.812 00	0.978 00	0.594 00	0.012 00
Average	Fraction > Xrate	0.024 00	0.424 00	0.814 00	0.992 00	0.642 00	0.000 00
	Simulation mean	0.000 77	0.015 21	0.596 42	0.000 98	0.015 33	−0.000 21
	Xrate mean	0.002 26	0.015 31	0.527 17	−0.001 21	0.015 02	0.003 48

Results from simulations of 500 replications of series generated with conditional drift equal to given interest rate differentials. $r_t = \mu_t + \varepsilon_t$ where μ_t corresponds to the interest rate differential at time t.

We will follow the procedure of fitting a linear process to the data using a set of moment conditions which include the trading rules. The trading rules must first be modified to fit into a moment condition framework. Define r_t as the returns series of interest. Also, let p_t be the price at time t, where:

$$r_t = \log(p_t) - \log(p_{t-1})$$

Again, use the moving average of length L at time t:

$$ma_t(L) = (1/L) \sum_{i=0}^{L-1} p_{t-i}$$

Table 1.12 *GARCH zero drift*

Rule	Result	Buy	σ_b	Fraction Buy	Sell	σ_s	Buy–Sell
BP							
(1, 20)	Fraction > Xrate	0.064 00	0.368 00	0.362 00	0.902 00	0.660 00	0.036 00
(1, 30)	Fraction > Xrate	0.030 00	0.514 00	0.278 00	0.934 00	0.420 00	0.006 00
(1, 50)	Fraction > Xrate	0.014 00	0.548 00	0.342 00	0.978 00	0.332 00	0.004 00
Average	Fraction > Xrate	0.024 00	0.480 00	0.318 00	0.944 00	0.444 00	0.006 00
	Simulation mean	0.000 51	0.014 80	0.512 14	−0.000 35	0.015 19	0.000 85
	Xrate mean	0.001 97	0.014 62	0.541 96	−0.001 49	0.015 02	0.003 46
DM							
(1, 20)	Fraction > Xrate	0.156 00	0.698 00	0.270 00	0.916 00	0.608 00	0.050 00
(1, 30)	Fraction > Xrate	0.138 00	0.792 00	0.182 00	0.894 00	0.486 00	0.054 00
(1, 50)	Fraction > Xrate	0.034 00	0.788 00	0.388 00	0.950 00	0.466 00	0.008 00
Average	Fraction > Xrate	0.092 00	0.762 00	0.298 00	0.924 00	0.536 00	0.026 00
	Simulation mean	0.000 52	0.015 76	0.477 58	−0.000 69	0.015 13	0.001 21
	Xrate mean	0.001 59	0.013 85	0.519 42	−0.001 76	0.014 62	0.003 35
JY							
(1, 20)	Fraction > Xrate	0.024 00	0.360 00	0.568 00	0.962 00	0.528 00	0.006 00
(1, 30)	Fraction > Xrate	0.016 00	0.436 00	0.556 00	0.970 00	0.478 00	0.002 00
(1, 50)	Fraction > Xrate	0.194 00	0.352 00	0.598 00	0.932 00	0.636 00	0.040 00
Average	Fraction > Xrate	0.050 00	0.372 00	0.576 00	0.970 00	0.546 00	0.000 00
	Simulation mean	0.000 60	0.015 22	0.492 50	−0.000 52	0.015 13	0.001 12
	Xrate mean	0.002 01	0.015 43	0.473 34	−0.001 93	0.014 99	0.003 94

Results from simulations of 500 GARCH models. These models are generated from estimated parameters and standardized residuals from maximum likelihood. Models are estimated and simulated using foreign exchange returns series with interest rate differentials removed.

One first guess for trading rule related moment might be:

$$E\left\{ S\left(\frac{p_{t-1}}{ma_{t-1}} \right) r_t \right\}$$

where $S(x) = 1$ if $x \geq 1$ and $S(x) = -1$ if $x < 1$. This will not do for simulated method of moments, since the first derivatives of this moment will not necessarily be continuous in the parameters of the process r_t. The condition must be replaced with a 'smooth substitute'. The hyperbolic tangent does a good job of being just such a function.[7] Replace the above condition with:

$$E\left\{\tanh\left((1/\mu)\left(\frac{p_{t-1}}{ma_{t-1}}-1\right)\right)r_t\right\}$$

This condition can now be added to a more standard set of moment conditions.[8]

The estimation procedure will attempt to fit an AR(2) to each of the exchange rate series. When using any method of moments estimator, choosing the moment conditions to use is not always a trivial procedure. Here, the choice of moments will follow the goal of trying to see whether a linear model does a good job of replicating some properties of the data (autocovariances) as well as the trading-rule results. This goal does not intend to get the tightest estimates of the parameters on the model. For this reason, the set of moment conditions will be rather small relative to other studies. The actual data will be aligned to simulated data using the mean variance, the first three lagged autocovariances and one trading-rule moment. This gives a total of six moment conditions. For the trading-rule moment condition, the thirty-week moving average is used. The results are generally similar across the other rules.[9]

There are two final details left for estimation. The variance–covariance matrix is estimated using the Newey–West (1987) weighting using ten lags. The lag length has been moved from five to fifty and the results have not changed greatly. This is important in this case, since the moving average may generate very long-range dependence in the estimated moments. Finally, the number of simulations is set to fifty times the sample size. For most of these series, this gives simulation samples in the range of 40 000 to 45 000.

Results of the estimation are given in Table 1.13. This table shows the estimated parameters and the chi-squared goodness-of-fit estimate for the AR(2). For the BP series, the results show a weak, but insignificant AR(1) parameter combined with a rejection of the moment conditions as indicated by the χ^2 test. The AR(2) is not able to match up with both the covariances and the trading-rule results. The next rows present results for similar estimation removing the trading-rule moment condition. Similar parameter estimates are obtained, but now the goodness-of-fit statistic is only significant at the 18 per cent level. The trading-rule condition has clearly added an important restriction for this time series.

The row labelled 'DM' repeats this procedure for the DM series. In this case, the model estimates two larger AR coefficients and the goodness-of-fit test is only significant at the 13 per cent level. The AR(2) is not strongly rejected here. Part of the reason for this can be seen in Table 1.1. There is some correlation in this series at the first two lags which allows the estimated AR coefficients to be larger. When the rule is removed the chi-square statistic still remains small with a significance level of 73 per cent.

Table 1.13   *SMM estimation*

$$r_t = \mu + \rho_1(r_{t-1} - \mu) + \rho_2(r_{t-2} - \mu) + \sigma\varepsilon_t$$
$$\varepsilon_t \sim N(0,1)$$

Series	Condition	μ	σ	ρ_1	ρ_2	χ^2
BP	Rule	−0.046	1.407	0.043	−0.017	8.261
		(0.054)	(0.074)	(0.035)	(0.041)	(0.016)
BP	No rule	−0.023	1.450	0.031	−0.029	1.793
		(0.057)	(0.073)	(0.034)	(0.039)	(0.181)
DM	Rule	0.099	1.410	0.051	0.042	3.989
		(0.052)	(0.061)	(0.031)	(0.043)	(0.136)
DM	No rule	0.071	1.427	0.052	0.045	0.120
		(0.054)	(0.062)	(0.031)	(0.043)	(0.729)
JY	Rule	0.152	1.364	0.104	0.103	6.819
		(0.055)	(0.062)	(0.039)	(0.042)	(0.033)
JY	No rule	0.125	1.405	0.100	0.088	2.066
		(0.059)	(0.062)	(0.039)	(0.040)	(0.150)
BPZD	Rule	0.075	1.463	0.063	−0.017	8.540
		(0.059)	(0.078)	(0.035)	(0.041)	(0.014)
BPZD	No rule	0.043	1.492	0.043	−0.022	1.773
		(0.063)	(0.078)	(0.035)	(0.040)	(0.183)
DMZD	Rule	0.021	1.404	0.063	0.047	3.035
		(0.055)	(0.063)	(0.031)	(0.045)	(0.219)
DMZD	No rule	0·011	1·428	0·063	0·048	0·009
		(0.058)	(0.063)	(0.031)	(0.045)	(0.924)
ZYZD	Rule	0·061	1·501	0·098	0·113	5·734
		(0.070)	(0.062)	(0.040)	(0.043)	(0.057)
JYZD	No rule	0.006	1.509	0.100	0.083	1.230
		(0.073)	(0.064)	(0.042)	(0.044)	(0.541)

Parameters estimated by simulated method of moments. Numbers in parentheses are asymptotic standard errors for the parameters and the *p*-value for the chi-squared goodness-of-fit test. Moments used are the mean, variance, 3 autocovariances and the 30-day moving-average trading rule. The chi-squared statistic has $6 - 4 = 2$ degrees of freedom when the trading rule is used and $5 - 4 = 1$ degrees of freedom when it is not used. The variance–covariance matrix is estimated using the Newey–West (1987) technique with 10 lags.

For the JY series, the AR(2) specification is rejected at the 3 per cent level. In this case, the model is estimating the largest AR parameters of the three series. However, these appear to not be enough to match the trading-rule condition. This is again demonstrated by removing this condition. After this is done, the chi-squared statistic drops to 2.1, which has a significance level of 0.5. The next rows in the table repeat these results for the zero drift series. These series generate results similar to those for the original series.

The simulated method of moments procedure has added to the earlier results. The procedure rejected the simple linear specification for two of the three foreign exchange series. This rejection followed from a procedure that combined standard autocovariance moments with conditions based on the trading rules.

1.5   ECONOMIC SIGNIFICANCE OF TRADING-RULE PROFITS

The tests run in the previous section have shown the moving-average trading rules to be able to detect periods of high and low returns. These returns are statistically large when compared with several different stochastic processes for the exchange rate series. These results are interesting in attempting to model the exact dynamics in the foreign exchange market, but they do not give us the economic significance of these rules. This section will attempt to measure the trading-rule results. Transaction costs and interest rates will be accounted for and some attempts will be made to measure the riskiness of the strategies relative to other assets.

The moving-average trading rules will be implemented as suggested by the previous tests. When the current price is above the long moving-average buy is indicated and when it is below a sell is indicated. The implementation tests performed here will concentrate on the thirty-day moving average alone. When a buy is indicated in a currency, the trader takes a long position in that currency and deposits this in foreign bonds. In the rules used here, the trader also will borrow dollars and invest these funds in the foreign currency. The trader will take a 50 per cent leveraged position.[10] This generally follows the procedure used in Dooley and Shafer (1983). Sweeney (1986) takes a slightly more cautious route of never borrowing and moving only from domestic bonds to foreign bonds conditional on the signal. This strategy leaves the trader exposed to foreign exchange risk only part of the time. There is obviously a continuous range of adjusting the leverage parameter which moves the outcome of the strategy both in terms of risk and return. In this study, the 50 per cent leverage strategy will be used for comparability with other studies and for the purpose of risk comparisons with the stock market.

Trading is done once a week. When the rule signals a change in position, a

Table 1.14   *Rule implementation summary*

Series	Trades	Return/ year	Return/ week	Std/week	β	BH	BH/week	BH(std)
BP	36	16.7	0.35	2.25	−0.07	9.9	0.20	1.57
DM	43	12.6	0.26	2.19	−0.08	6.2	0.13	1.54
JY	26	20.1	0.41	2.17	−0.03	8.4	0.17	1.52
CRSP VW		15.2	0.32	2.18				
$ RF		9.5	0.18	0.05				

This table summarizes the results of the trading rules over the full sample. β is the estimated CAPM beta for the trading strategy estimated using weekly data. t(return-CRSP) is a t-statistic for equality of the returns for the strategy and CRSP. BH stands for the buy and hold strategy in the foreign currency holding foreign bonds.

trade is made. Transactions costs are assumed to be 0.1 per cent of the size of the trade. This appears to be a reasonable estimate and is used in Dooley and Shafer (1983). Some studies are slightly above this number (Sweeney, 1986, uses 1/8 per cent), while others claim that this is a maximum for foreign exchange trading. The weekly eurodollar rate series and daily call money overnight rates are used again with compounding occurring at daily frequencies for the daily series. An interest rate differential of 3 per cent per year is used to estimate the borrowing rates from the lending rates from the tape. This is probably an upper bound on the borrowing and lending spread and is estimated from the current prime rate CD spread. Results will be compared with those from buying and holding stocks in the US market. The CRSP value weighted index, including dividends, will be used to represent this asset. All tests begin in October 1977 and end in December 1989.

Table 1.14 presents some summary statistics comparing the results for the various assets. The row labelled 'BP' gives the trading strategy for the pound. The table shows that the strategy executed thirty-six trades and yielded an average return of 16.7 per cent per year continuously compounded. It had a weekly standard deviation over the period of 2.25 per cent. The column labelled 'β' estimates the CAPM beta for the dynamic strategy using the CRSP portfolio as the market proxy. Although a static CAPM based only on domestic securities is probably not a good representation of risk, it is still interesting to observe how correlated the strategy is with the stock market and how much potential there is for diversification. For all currency strategies, the β is negative and very close to zero. The last three columns present results for a buy and hold strategy in the foreign currency and bonds. For the pound, this is 9.9 per cent with a weekly standard deviation of 1.57 per cent. This should be compared with the return to only holding dollar bonds (reported in the last row) of 9.5 per cent with a weekly standard deviation of 0.05 per cent.

The next three rows present results for the DM, JY and CRSP series respectively. All the series have similar standard deviation and beta risk characteristics. The DM underperforms CRSP by about 2.6 per cent and the JY exceeds the CRSP series by about 5 per cent. In each case, the strategies dramatically dominate the buy and hold portfolios.

Two currencies give returns in excess of the CRSP return. The important economic question is whether these dynamic strategies offer an important new security in terms of risk and return. This is a difficult question to answer without an appropriate model for risk or the exact stochastic process for either foreign exchange or stocks. A fairly straightforward technique will be used to try to get some initial answers to this question. Returns will be measured over fixed horizons chosen at random out of the entire sample. In other words fix the horizon at one year and estimate returns at randomly chosen one-year periods during the sample. This will generate a joint distribution of stock and exchange rate returns which can be compared.[11]

Results for 500 simulations at the 1-year horizon are presented in Table 1.15. For the BP series, the simulations gave an average annual return of 19.5 per cent with a standard deviation of 13.7 per cent. This compares with a return of 16.2 per cent with a standard deviation of 18 per cent for the CRSP series. The table also presents some other risk measures. The first, $\text{prob}(< RF - 5\%)$, reports the estimated probability of getting a return of less than 5 per cent below the risk-free rate. This number attempts to capture some aspect of 'drawdown' risk. For the BP series, this happens in 15 per cent of the simulations as compared with 29 per cent for the CRSP series. The next column reports the probability of the exchange rate return falling below CRSP. This is 46 per cent for the BP. The next column, $T < RF$, estimates the fraction of time that the compounded return on the strategy was below the compounded return on a risk-free bond. For the BP series this is 34 per cent. The final column reports the average beta and the standard deviation of the estimated beta across the simulations. Beta is estimated weekly for each simulation. This again shows that there is very little correlation between the strategy and the CRSP series. Results for the buy and hold strategy for the BP are shown in the next row. This gives a mean return of 11.0 with a standard deviation of 15.7. Buy and hold falls below the dynamic strategy in mean return and it shows little improvement in riskiness.

The distribution of these returns along with the CRSP distribution is shown in Figure 1.2. These are the one-year holding period simulated returns. This figure clearly shows strong evidence that the BP series may first-order stochastically dominate its equivalent buy and hold position. The comparison

Table 1.15 *One-year horizon*

Series	Return/year	Std	Prob(<RF − 5%)	Prob(<CRSP)	T < RF	β
BP	19.5	13.7	0.15	0.46	0.34 (0.31)	−0.04 (0.26)
BP BH	11.0	15.7	0.42	0.59	0.50 (0.39)	0.06 (0.16)
DM	14.3	18.7	0.32	0.50	0.46 (0.34)	−0.06 (0.18)
DM BH	5.6	14.7	0.55	0.65	0.62 (0.37)	0.07 (0.19)
JY	22.2	24.0	0.19	0.37	0.39 (0.35)	−0.04 (0.21)
JY BH	9.4	16.6	0.45	0.59	0.56 (0.37)	0.03 (0.17)
CRSP	16.2	18.0	0.29		0.41 (0.35)	
CRSP + BP	17.9	11.2	0.14	0.46	0.36 (0.32)	0.47 (0.13)
3FX + CRSP	17.4	12.8	0.18	0.38	0.37 (0.32)	0.47 (0.10)

Simulation results for one year trading business. Results of 1000 simulations of randomly selected 2 year intervals during the sample. Prob(<RF − 5%) is the probability of underperforming the domestic risk-free rate by more than 5%. Prob(<CRSP) is the probability that the strategy underperforms the CRSP index. T < RF is the fraction of time that the cumulative return on the strategy spends below the cumulative return on the risk free asset. β is again the beta estimated against the CRSP index. CRSP + BP is a portfolio which is started with portfolio weights of 1/2 and 1/2 on CRSP and the trading strategy respectively. 3FX + CRSP is a portfolio which is started with weights of 1/2 on a buy and hold stock position, and 1/2 on an equally weighted position in the three foreign exchange strategies.

with CRSP is more difficult, but the graph suggests that the pound strategy may second-order stochastic dominate CRSP. Both these comparisons await more detailed statistical testing.[12]

Results for the DM series are given in the next two rows of Table 1.15. This series gives a mean return less than CRSP with similar risk characteristics. Its returns are again much larger than the equivalent buy and hold strategy. Figure 1.3 plots the distribution for the DM strategies. There is a clear indication that the strategy first-order stochastically dominates the buy and hold strategy. No simple comparisons can be made between the DM strategy and CRSP.

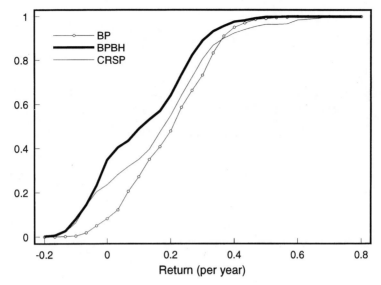

Figure 1.2   *Simulated return distribution – one-year period*

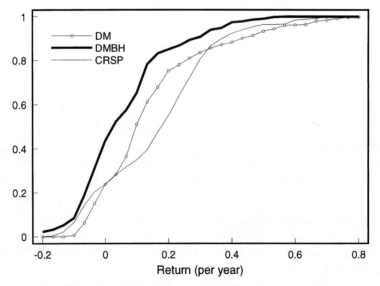

Figure 1.3   *Simulated return distribution – one-year period*

Results for the JY are given in the next two rows. The JY outperforms CRSP by 6 per cent and its buy and hold by 10 per cent. It has a larger standard deviation, but its other risk measures are equivalent to CRSP. Figure 1.4 shows the distributions. Once again, it appears that the strategy first-order stochastically dominates buy and hold. The strategy appears close to first-

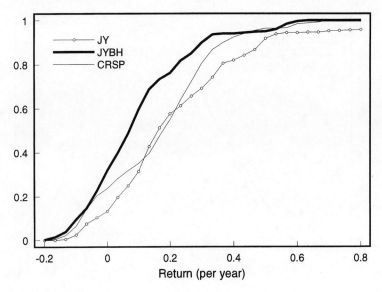

Figure 1.4   *Simulated return distribution – one-year period*

order stochastically dominating CRSP except for a small section. However, it shows strong evidence for second-order stochastic dominance.

For all three currencies the betas are very low. This suggests the possibility for diversification. The next row in Table 1.15, labelled 'CRSP + BE' presents results for a portfolio formed by starting out invested half in stocks and half in the BP dynamic strategy. The portfolio increases returns and reduces standard deviation over the original CRSP portfolio. It is easy to select an optimal portfolio using currencies determined by looking at the results ex post. The next row tests a strategy that might have been followed had the investor not known the relatively poor performance of the DM. In this strategy, wealth is split equally between a buy and hold CRSP portfolio and the dynamic portfolios. The half in the dynamic foreign exchange portfolios is split 1/3 to each currency. This strategy performs similarly to the BP + CRSP portfolio, showing that there is probably little diversification gain across foreign exchange strategies themselves.

Results for all these strategies and CRSP are plotted in Figure 1.5. The two dynamic strategies are close to each other and appear close to second-order dominating the CRSP returns alone. This is consistent with the properties of the dynamic foreign exchange strategies which suggested that they were zero beta securities exhibiting similar risk–return characteristics to the stock portfolio.

These results are further tested in Table 1.16. This table compares the previous distributions using a myopic one-year investor with constant relative

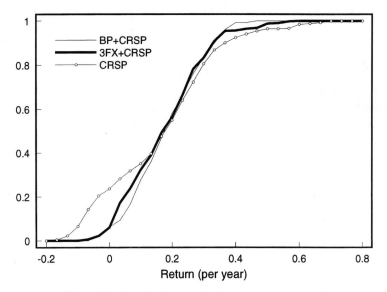

Figure 1.5   *Simulated return distribution – one-year period*

Table 1.16   *Utility distribution comparisons: one-year horizon*

Series	BH	CRSP	3FX + CRSP
BP	0.92	0.95	0.99
DM	0.93	1.01	1.05
JY	0.91	0.96	1.00
BP + CRSP		0.96	0.99
3FX + CRSP		0.96	

Utility comparisons of myopic 1 year crra investors. Fraction
of wealth α that would make an investor indifferent between
the row rule used on αW and the column rule on W. Degree
of relative risk aversion is fixed at 4.

risk aversion utility. The coefficient of relative risk aversion is set to four. The
table finds α that sets:

$$Eu(\alpha W \tilde{R}_1) = Eu(W \tilde{R}_2),$$

$$u(x) = \frac{1}{(1-\gamma)} x^{1-\gamma}$$

where R_1 is the return given by the labels on the left side of the rows, and R_2 is
the return given in the columns. For each currency, it is clear that this
consumer would be willing to give up close to 8 per cent of the invested wealth

to shift to the dynamic strategy from BH. Comparisons with CRSP, suggest the consumer would be willing to give up 4–5 per cent of wealth for each strategy except for the DM where CRSP is preferred. This improvement holds for the three exchange rate CRSP portfolio. The last column compares the diversified portfolio with each of the strategies. Interestingly, the portfolio shows little improvement over the BP and JY strategies separately.

Finding an optimal portfolio ex post is not a confirmation of an inefficient market. It should always be easy to find portfolios which dominate the market portfolio in an ex post data search. The evidence shows some performance improvements for currency and currency-stock portfolios when compared to the stock portfolio. This should be viewed with some caution as it awaits further statistical testing. All the trading rules do offer similar performance characteristics to the market portfolio with no beta risk. To the stock market investor wondering whether to speculate in the foreign exchange market, the evidence at this point appears somewhat uncertain. However, for any economic agent whose job requires some amount of liquidity in various foreign exchange markets, the recommendation is clear. These agents are comparing the risk-free rates of return in all markets and will have to maintain some exposure to foreign exchange risk. There are very dramatic improvements in moving from buy and hold strategies to the trading rules for these agents.[13]

There are several problems that could move these conclusions in either direction. First, the data used may not represent interest rates that traders could actually use. Also, there may be some timing problems in terms of settlements. For example, the rules as implemented, assume that traders can get the closing price on the day of the signal. This may not always be the case. Also, settlement procedures are not considered here.[14] Finally, measurement of risk with respect to a US stock portfolio probably misses much of the exposure to international portfolio risk to which the exchange rate portfolios are exposed. Estimating betas on a world portfolio or using a multifactor model might be more appropriate here.

There are some problems in the analysis which work in favour of the trading rules. First, the rules used are very simple compared to what most traders use. Also, most traders would operate at the daily frequency or higher.[15] Second, the comparison series, the CRSP index, may be difficult to obtain in practice. No attempt was made to adjust for transactions costs on this series even though using the CRSP index implies that dividends are being continuously reinvested. The ability of the average investor to track this index should be more carefully considered.

There has been some recent evidence that the usefulness of technical trading strategies has diminished over time (Sweeney and Surajaras, 1989).

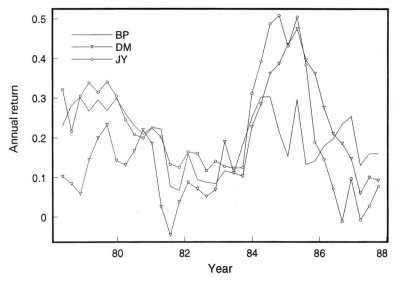

Figure 1.6   *Rolling strategy returns – two-year period*

To check the possibility of a trend in trading rule profits over time, a plot is made of the trading-rule returns measured over two-year horizons for the three currencies rolling the horizon forward one-quarter for each point plotted. This is plotted in Figure 1.6. There is some evidence for a drop off in profits in recent years. However, when analysing the entire series, it is unclear whether this period is at all unusual. There have been earlier periods when the rules did not perform very well. The time period around 1982–1983 appears to have also been relatively poor. It is interesting that these might be periods in which the two-year horizon is reaching into periods just after the Plaza Agreement when the dollar changed direction.

1.6   CONCLUSIONS

This chapter has presented evidence supporting the premise that exchange rates do not follow a random walk. Moreover, these deviations are detected by simple moving-average trading rules. These rules find that, in general, returns during buy periods are higher than returns during sell periods. Volatility appears to be indistinguishable during these two periods. Also, skewness and kurtosis show no discernible patterns over buy and sell periods.

These results are supportive of earlier work in Dooley and Shafer (1983), Schulmeister (1987), Sweeney (1986), Taylor (1980, 1986) and, more recently, Taylor (1992). These other authors perform extensive tests on the profitability of these tests and find that, in general, the rules make money even when adjusted for transactions costs, interest rate differentials and very simple measures of risk.

In this chapter, the rules are first used as specification tests for several different processes. The GARCH, regime shifting and interest rate adjusted models are unable to generate results consistent with the actual series. In each case, it is still possible that a modified version of the model could be capable of generating results consistent with the actual data, but this awaits further experimentation. The following two answers come from these results. First, it is possible that the series are non-stationary and are punctuated by strong changes in regime that cannot be captured by these simple models. Second, none of the models considered here allow for any connection between trend and volatility changes. This possibility is considered in Taylor (1986) and results in Bilson (1990), Kim (1989) and LeBaron (1992) suggest that there may be some connection.

The final section of this chapter runs some experiments to test the economic significance of these results. The trading rules are implemented on the data as they would be used in practice. Estimates for transaction costs and interest rate spreads are used to measure the realized returns from the strategies. For the three currencies tested, the trading-rule strategies generated return distributions similar to those from the CRSP stock index with very low correlation with the market. This suggests portfolios formed by combining the strategies with the CRSP index may dominate the stock index on its own.

While these results are interesting, they should still be viewed with some caution. There are still several interest rate and timing issues that are not worked out exactly. Also, the use of other risk factors than CAPM beta may be important. As in any trading-rules test, there are further questions about the parameters used and whether the prices used were actually tradeable. Given these issues and the lack of a statistical test on the distribution comparisons, the results cannot be taken as clear evidence that every economic agent is missing a big opportunity. However, for one group of agents, the results are fairly strong. For people who are involved in foreign exchange markets, either in trading goods or securities, and who maintain positions in foreign currencies, there appear to be major gains over buy and hold strategies. This is easily seen in Table 1.15 by comparing the buy and hold strategies with those for the rules. This may explain the large number of technical trading services available in the foreign exchange market.[16]

The results in this chapter may eventually lead to some better explanations for several effects in foreign exchange markets. Among these are the movements in forward and futures markets for foreign exchange.[17] Also, results from survey data found in Dominguez (1986) and Frankel and Froot (1990) may be relevant to some of the results found here.[18] Finally, foreign exchange markets differ from stock markets in that central banks play an important role. The behaviour of these large economic agents may differ greatly from that of ordinary traders. These agents may even be willing to lose money to satisfy other objectives.

This chapter has shown that technical trading rules may provide a useful specification test for examining foreign exchange markets. This chapter uses these rules to demonstrate some of the shortcomings of common parametric models for foreign exchange movements. Some evidence is given on the economic significance of these results and shows that the strategies generate returns similar to those from a domestic stock portfolio. Further tests will be necessary to completely answer the questions raised about the economic significance of these results.

REFERENCES

Bilson, J.F. (1990) 'Technical' Currency Trading, *The Currency-Hedging Debate* (ed. L.R. Thomas), IFR Publishing, London.

Bollerslev, T. (1986) Generalized autoregressive conditional heteroskedasticity, *Journal of Econometrics*, **21**, 3, 307–328.

Bollerslev, T. and Wooldridge, J.M. (1990) Quasi Maximum Likelihood Estimation and Inference in Dynamic Models with Time-varying Covariances, MIT, Department of Economics.

Bollerslev, T., Chou, R.Y., Jayaraman, N. and Kroner, K.F. (1990) ARCH Modelling in Finance: A Review of the Theory and Empirical Evidence, *Journal of Econometrics*, **52**, 1, 5–60.

Brock, W.A., Lakonishok, J. and LeBaron, B. (1992) Simple Technical Trading Rules and the Stochastic Properties of Stock Returns, *Journal of Finance*, **47**, 1731–64.

Diebold, F.X. and Nason, J.M (1990) Nonparametric exchange rate prediction?, *Journal of International Economics*, **28**, 315–32.

Dominguez, K.M. (1986) Are foreign exchange forecasts rational? New evidence from survey data, *Economics Letters*, **21**, 277–81.

Domowitz, I. and Hakkio, C.S. (1985) Conditional variance and the risk premium in the foreign exchange market, *Journal of International Economics*, **19**, 47–66.

Dooley, M.P. and Shafer, J. (1983) Analysis of short-run exchange rate behaviour: March 1973 to November 1981. In *Exchange Rate and Trade Instability: Causes, Consequences and Remedies* (eds D. Bigman and T. Taya) Cambridge, MA, Ballinger, pp. 43–72.

Duffie, D. and Singleton, K. (1993) Simulated Moments Estimation of Markov Models of Asset Prices, *Econometrica*, **61**, 4, 929–52.

Efron, B. (1979) Bootstrap methods: another look at the jackknife, *The Annals of Statistics*, **7**, 1, 1–26.

Engle, R.F. (1982) Autoregressive conditional heteroskedasticity with estimates of the variance of United Kingdom inflation, *Econometrica*, **50**, 987–1007.

Engle, R.F. and Bollerslev, T. (1986) Modelling the persistence of conditional variances, *Econometric Reviews*, **5**, 1, 1–50.

Engel, C. and Hamilton, J.D. (1990) Long swings in the dollar: are they in the data and do markets know it?, *American Economic Review*, **8**, 4, 689–713.

Frankel, J.A. and Froot, K.A. (1990) Chartists, fundamentalists and trading in the foreign exchange market, *American Economic Review*, **80**, 2, 181–5.

Goodhart, C. (1988) The foreign exchange market: a random walk with a dragging anchor, *Economica*, **55**, 437–60.

Hodrick, R.J. (1987) *The Empirical Evidence on the Efficiency of Forward and Futures Foreign Exchange Markets*, New York, Harwood Academic Publishers.

Hsieh, D. (1988) The statistical properties of daily foreign exchange rates: 1974–1983, *Journal of International Economics*, **24**, 129–45.

Hsieh, D. (1989) Testing for nonlinear dependence in daily foreign exchange rates, *Journal of Business*, **62**, 3, 339–68.

Kim, C.M. (1989) Volatility Effect on Time Series Behaviour of Exchange Rate Changes, Korea Institute for International Economic Policy.

Kunsch, H.R. (1989) The jacknife and the bootstrap for general stationary observations, *Annals of Statistics*, **17**, 3, 1217–41.

LeBaron, B. (1992) Forecast Improvements Using a Volatility Index, *Journal of Applied Econometrics*, **7**, S137–50.

Lee, B-S. and Ingram, B.F. (1991) Simulation estimation of time-series models, *Journal of Econometrics*, **47**, 197–205.

Levich, R.M. and Thomas, L.R. (1991) *The Significance of Technical Trading-Rule Profits in the Foreign Exchange Market: A Bootstrap Approach*, New York University, Graduate School of Business, New York.

McFadden, D. (1989) A method of simulated moments for estimation of discrete response models without numerical integration, *Econometrica*, **57**, 5, 995–1026.

Meese, R. and Rogoff, K. (1983) Empirical exchange rate models of the seventies: do they fit out of sample?, *Journal of International Economics*, **14**, 3–24.

Meese, R.A. and Rose, K.A. (1990) Nonlinear, nonparametric, nonessential exchange rate estimation, *American Economic Review*, **8**, 2, 192–6.

Newey, W. and West, K.D. (1987) A simple, positive definite, heteroskedasticity and autocorrelation consistent covariance matrix, *Econometrica*, **55**, 703–8.

Pakes, A. and Pollard, D. (1989) Simulation and the Asymptotics of Optimization Estimators, *Econometrica*, **57**, 5, 1027–58.

Rothschild, M. and Stiglitz, J. (1970) Increasing risk I: a definition, *Journal of Economic Theory*, **2**, 225–43.

Schulmeister, S. (1987) An Essay on Exchange Rate Dynamics. Wissenschafts-zentrum Berlin für Sozialforschung, Berlin, IIM/LMP, 87–8.

Schwarz, G. (1978) Estimating the dimension of a model, *Annals of Statistics*, **6**, 461–4.

Sweeney, R.J. (1986) Beating the foreign exchange market, *Journal of Finance*, **41**, 1, 163–82.

Sweeney, R.J. and Surajaras, P. (1989) The stability of speculative profits in the foreign exchanges. In *A Reappraisal of the Efficiency of Financial Markets* (eds R. Guimaraes, B. Kingsman and S.J. Taylor), Heidelberg: Springer-Verlag.

Taylor, S.J. (1980) Conjectured models for trends in financial prices, tests and forecasts, *Journal of the Royal Statistical Society*, **143**, 3, 338–362.

Taylor, S.J. (1986) *Modelling Financial Time Series*, Chichester: John Wiley & Sons.

Taylor, S.J. (1992) Rewards Available to Currency Futures Speculators: Compensation For Risk or Evidence of Inefficient Pricing, *Economic Record*, **68**, 105–16.

NOTES

1. Recently, Levich and Thomas (1991) have obtained some related results for several foreign exchange futures series.
2. There are many variations of this simple rule in use. One is to replace the price series with another moving average. A second modification is to only generate signals when the price differs from the moving average by a certain percentage. Many other modifications are discussed in Schulmeister (1987), Sweeney (1986) and Taylor (1992).
3. For more extensive descriptions of these results on exchange rates, see Hsieh (1988, 1989) and other references contained in Bollerslev et al. (1990).
4. Other specifications with changing conditional means related to volatility (GARCH-M) were also tried, but these turned out to be insignificant. This agrees with some of the results found in Domowitz and Hakkio (1985).
5. The convergence of the bootstrap distribution has not been shown for GARCH models. Brock, Lakonishok and LeBaron (1992) use a similar technique for stock returns. Their results are supported through large computer simulations.
6. This is generally the case for all the exchange rate tests used here. It differs from some of the results in Brock et al. (1992), where stock returns were found to be more volatile during sell periods than during buy periods.
7. $\tanh(x) = \dfrac{-e^{-x} + e^x}{e^{-x} + e^x}$
8. This condition brings in the problem of a free parameter, μ. This parameter is set to 1/10 the standard deviation of the price-moving-average ratio. Experiments with this parameter have shown the results to be insensitive to changes in the parameter ranging from 1 to 1/100 standard deviations.
9. This technique also allows the use of several trading-rule conditions simultaneously. Dependence across rules is captured in the variance–covariance matrix.
10. This means that an investor with one dollar who receives a buy signal will borrow one dollar domestically and invest two dollars in the foreign currency. The reverse is followed for a sell.
11. One drawback of this technique is that the first and last part of the series will be under-represented in simulations. One solution might be to think of the series as rolling around back onto itself on a circle. However, this imposes a severe pasting together of disjointed parts of the series. Another solution might be to use the m-dependent bootstrap of Kunsch (1989). Both of these

possibilities are left for the future. For the present, the reader should realize that the simulation does not adequately sample some parts of the series.

12. First-order stochastic dominance is obtained when

$$F(x) - G(x) \geq 0 \qquad \forall \quad x$$

for the distribution functions F and G, where the inequality is strict over a set of positive measure. Any consumer preferring more to less will prefer the distribution G. Second-order stochastic dominance is obtained when

$$\int_{-\infty}^{x} F(s) - G(s) \, ds \geq 0 \qquad \forall \quad x$$

In this case, only risk-averse consumers will prefer G (Rothschild and Stiglitz, 1970).

13. This may explain the extensive use of technical trading advice by many market participants.

14. An experiment was performed to test the robustness of the results to timing. The testing programs were modified so that investors could not get the interest rates at time t, but could get the rates given one day later. Results of this experiment are not presented since they are almost identical to those from the original series.

15. Most of the rules used here were repeated at daily frequency with little change in the results.

16. See Frankel and Froot (1990) for some evidence on the number of chartists.

17. See Hodrick (1987) for a survey of these results.

18. These papers, using survey data, find that short-range forecasts are more trend-following while longer-range forecasts are more mean reverting.

ACKNOWLEDGMENTS

The author is grateful to Robert Hodrick, Simon Potter, seminar participants at the Mid-West International Economics Meetings, The University of Iowa and Carnegie-Mellon University for comments on an earlier draft. This research was partially supported by the Economics Research Program at the Santa Fe Institute which is funded by grants from Citicorp/Citibank, the Russell Sage Foundation, the Alex C. Walker Educational and Charitable Foundation – Pittsburgh National Bank, and by grants to SFI from the John D. and Catherine T. MacArthur Foundation, the National Science Foundation (PHY-8714918) and the US Department of Energy (ER-FG05-88ER25054). The author also is grateful to the National Science Foundation (SES-9109671) for support.

Chapter 2

Foundations of technical analysis: computational algorithms, statistical inference and empirical implementation

ANDREW W. LO, HARRY MAMAYSKY AND JIANG WANG

2.1 INTRODUCTION

One of the greatest gulfs between academic finance and industry practice is the separation that exists between technical analysts and their academic critics. In contrast to fundamental analysis, which was quick to be adopted by the scholars of modern quantitative finance, technical analysis has been an orphan from the very start. It has been argued that the difference between fundamental analysis and technical analysis is not unlike the difference between astronomy and astrology. Among some circles, technical analysis is known as 'voodoo finance'. And in his influential book *A Random Walk Down Wall Street*, Burton Malkiel (1996) concludes that 'under scientific scrutiny, chart-reading must share a pedestal with alchemy'.

However, several academic studies suggest that despite its jargon and methods, technical analysis may well be an effective means for extracting useful information from market prices. For example, in rejecting the Random Walk Hypothesis for weekly US stock indexes, Lo and MacKinlay (1988, 1999) have shown that past prices may be used to forecast future returns to some degree, a fact that all technical analysts take for granted. Studies by Tabell and Tabell (1964), Treynor and Ferguson (1985), Brown and Jennings (1989), Jegadeesh and Titman (1993), Blume, Easley, and O'Hara (1994), Chan, Jegadeesh, and Lakonishok (1996), Lo and MacKinlay (1997), Grundy and Martin (1998), and Rouwenhorst (1998) have also provided indirect support for technical analysis, and more direct support has been given by Pruitt and White (1988), Neftci (1991), Brock, Lakonishok, and LeBaron (1992), Neely, Weller, and Dittmar (1997), Neely and Weller (1998), Chang and Osler (1994), Osler and Chang (1995), and Allen and Karjalainen (1999).

One explanation for this state of controversy and confusion is the unique and sometimes impenetrable jargon used by technical analysts, some of which has developed into a standard lexicon that can be translated. But there are many 'homegrown' variations, each with its own patois, which can often frustrate the uninitiated. Campbell, Lo, and MacKinlay (1997, pp. 43–44) provide a striking example of the linguistic barriers between technical analysts and academic finance by contrasting this statement:

> The presence of clearly identified support and resistance levels, coupled with a one-third retracement parameter when prices lie between them, suggests the presence of strong buying and selling opportunities in the near-term.

with this one:

> The magnitudes and decay pattern of the first twelve autocorrelations and the statistical significance of the Box-Pierce Q-statistic suggest the presence of a high-frequency predictable component in stock returns.

Despite the fact that both statements have the same meaning – that past prices contain information for predicting future returns – most readers find one statement plausible and the other puzzling, or worse, offensive.

These linguistic barriers underscore an important difference between technical analysis and quantitative finance: technical analysis is primarily *visual*, whereas quantitative finance is primarily algebraic and numerical. Therefore, technical analysis employs the tools of geometry and pattern recognition, and quantitative finance employs the tools of mathematical analysis and probability and statistics. In the wake of recent breakthroughs in financial engineering, computer technology, and numerical algorithms, it is no wonder that quantitative finance has overtaken technical analysis in popularity – the principles of portfolio optimization are far easier to program into a computer than the basic tenets of technical analysis. Nevertheless, technical analysis has survived through the years, perhaps because its visual mode of analysis is more conducive to human cognition, and because pattern recognition is one of the few repetitive activities for which computers do not have an absolute advantage (yet).

Indeed, it is difficult to dispute the potential value of price/volume charts when confronted with the visual evidence. For example, compare the two hypothetical price charts given in Figure 2.1. Despite the fact that the two price series are identical over the first half of the sample, the volume patterns differ, and this seems to be informative. In particular, the lower chart, which shows high volume accompanying a positive price trend, suggests that there may be more information content in the trend, e.g. broader participation among investors. The fact that the joint distribution of prices and volume contains important information is hardly controversial among academics.

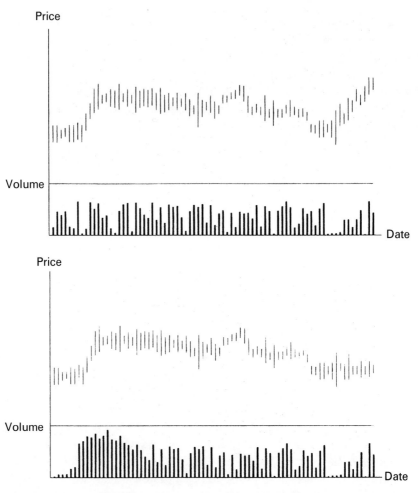

Figure 2.1   *Two hypothetical price/volume charts*

Why, then, is the value of a visual depiction of that joint distribution so hotly contested?

In this chapter we hope to bridge this gulf between technical analysis and quantitative finance by developing a systematic and scientific approach to the practice of technical analysis and by employing the now-standard methods of empirical analysis to gauge the efficacy of technical indicators over time and across securities. In doing so, our goal is not only to develop a lingua franca with which disciples of both disciplines can engage in productive dialogue, but also to extend the reach of technical analysis by augmenting its tool kit with some modern techniques in pattern recognition.

The general goal of technical analysis is to identify regularities in the time series of prices by extracting nonlinear patterns from noisy data. Implicit in this goal is the recognition that some price movements are significant – they contribute to the formation of a specific pattern – and others are merely random fluctuations to be ignored. In many cases, the human eye can perform this 'signal extraction' quickly and accurately, and until recently, computer algorithms could not. However, a class of statistical estimators, called *smoothing estimators*, is ideally suited to this task because they extract nonlinear relations $\hat{m}(\cdot)$ by 'averaging out' the noise. Therefore, we propose using these estimators to mimic, and in some cases, sharpen the skills of a trained technical analyst in identifying certain patterns in historical price series.

In the next section we provide a brief review of smoothing estimators and describe in detail the specific smoothing estimator we use in our analysis: kernel regression. Our algorithm for automating technical analysis is described in section 2.3. We apply this algorithm to the daily returns of several hundred US stocks from 1962 to 1996 and report the results in section 2.4. To check the accuracy of our statistical inferences, we perform several Monte Carlo simulation experiments and the results are given in section 2.5. We conclude in section 2.6.

2.2 SMOOTHING ESTIMATORS AND KERNEL REGRESSION

The starting point for any study of technical analysis is the recognition that prices evolve in a nonlinear fashion over time and that the nonlinearities contain certain regularities or patterns. To capture such regularities quantitatively, we begin by asserting that prices $\{P_t\}$ satisfy the following expression:

$$P_t = m(X_t) + \epsilon_t, \qquad t = 1, \ldots, T \tag{2.1}$$

where $m(X_t)$ is an arbitrary fixed but unknown nonlinear function of a state variable X_t and $\{\epsilon_t\}$ is white noise.

For the purposes of pattern recognition in which our goal is to construct a smooth function $\hat{m}(\cdot)$ to approximate the time series of prices $\{P_t\}$, we set the state variable equal to time, $X_t = t$. However, to keep our notation consistent with that of the kernel regression literature, we will continue to use X_t in our exposition.

When prices are expressed as Equation (2.1), it is apparent that geometric patterns can emerge from a visual inspection of historical price series – prices are the sum of the nonlinear pattern $m(X_t)$ and white noise – and that such patterns may provide useful information about the unknown function $m(\cdot)$ to be estimated. But just how useful is this information?

To answer this question empirically and systematically, we must first develop a method for automating the identification of technical indicators, i.e., we require a pattern-recognition algorithm. Once such an algorithm is developed, it can be applied to a large number of securities over many time periods to determine the efficacy of various technical indicators. Moreover, quantitative comparisons of the performance of several indicators can be conducted, and the statistical significance of such performance can be assessed through Monte Carlo simulation and bootstrap techniques.[1]

In section 2.2.1, we provide a brief review of a general class of pattern-recognition techniques known as *smoothing estimators*, and in section 2.2.2 we describe in some detail a particular method called *nonparametric kernel regression* on which our algorithm is based. Kernel regression estimators are calibrated by a *bandwidth* parameter and we discuss how the bandwidth is selected in section 2.2.3.

2.2.1   Smoothing estimators

One of the most common methods for estimating nonlinear relations such as Equation (2.1) is *smoothing*, in which observational errors are reduced by averaging the data in sophisticated ways. Kernel regression, orthogonal series expansion, projection pursuit, nearest-neighbour estimators, average derivative estimators, splines, and neural networks are all examples of smoothing estimators. In addition to possessing certain statistical optimality properties, smoothing estimators are motivated by their close correspondence to the way human cognition extracts regularities from noisy data.[2] Therefore, they are ideal for our purposes.

To provide some intuition for how averaging can recover nonlinear relations such as the function $m(\cdot)$ in Equation (2.1), suppose we wish to estimate $m(\cdot)$ at a particular date t_0 when $X_{t_0} = x_0$. Now suppose that for this one observation, X_{t_0}, we can obtain *repeated* independent observations of the price P_{t_0}, say $P_{t_0}^1 = p_1, \ldots, P_{t_0}^n = p_n$ (note that these are n independent realizations of the price at the *same* date t_0, clearly an impossibility in practice, but let us continue with this thought experiment for a few more steps). Then a natural estimator of the function $m(\cdot)$ at the point x_0 is:

$$\hat{m}(x_0) = \frac{1}{n}\sum_{i=1}^{n} p_i = \frac{1}{n}\sum_{i=1}^{n}[m(x_0) + \epsilon_t^i] \qquad (2.2)$$

$$= m(x_0) + \frac{1}{n}\sum_{i=1}^{n} \epsilon_t^i \qquad (2.3)$$

and by the Law of Large Numbers, the second term in Equation (2.3) becomes negligible for large n.

Of course, if $\{P_t\}$ is a time series, we do not have the luxury of repeated observations for a given X_t. However, if we assume that the function $m(\cdot)$ is sufficiently smooth, then for time-series observations X_t near the value x_0, the corresponding values of P_t should be close to $m(x_0)$. In other words, if $m(\cdot)$ is sufficiently smooth, then in a small neighbourhood around x_0, $m(x_0)$ will be nearly constant and may be estimated by taking an average of the P_ts that correspond to those X_ts near x_0. The closer the X_ts are to the value x_0, the closer an average of corresponding P_ts will be to $m(x_0)$. This argues for a *weighted* average of the P_ts, where the weights decline as the X_ts get farther away from x_0. This weighted-average or 'local-averaging' procedure of estimating $m(x)$ is the essence of smoothing.

More formally, for any arbitrary x, a smoothing estimator of $m(x)$ may be expressed as:

$$\hat{m}(x) \equiv \frac{1}{T} \sum_{t=1}^{T} w_t(x) P_t \tag{2.4}$$

where the weights $\{w_t(x)\}$ are large for those P_ts paired with X_ts near x, and small for those P_ts with X_ts far from x. To implement such a procedure, we must define what we mean by 'near' and 'far'. If we choose too large a neighbourhood around x to compute the average, the weighted average will be too smooth and will not exhibit the genuine nonlinearities of $m(\cdot)$. If we choose too small a neighbourhood around x, the weighted average will be too variable, reflecting noise as well as the variations in $m(\cdot)$. Therefore, the weights $\{w_t(x)\}$ must be chosen carefully to balance these two considerations.

2.2.2   Kernel regression

For the *kernel regression* estimator, the weight function $w_t(x)$ is constructed from a probability density function $K(x)$, also called a *kernel*:[3]

$$K(x) \geq 0, \qquad \int K(u)du = 1 \tag{2.5}$$

By rescaling the kernel with respect to a parameter $h > 0$, we can change its spread, i.e., let:

$$K_h(u) \equiv \frac{1}{h} K(u/h), \qquad \int K_h(u)du = 1 \tag{2.6}$$

and define the weight function to be used in the weighted average (Equation 2.4) as:

$$w_{t,h}(x) \equiv K_h(x - X_t)/g_h(x) \tag{2.7}$$

$$g_h(x) \equiv \frac{1}{T} \sum_{t=1}^{T} K_h(x - X_t) \tag{2.8}$$

If h is very small, the averaging will be done with respect to a rather small neighbourhood around each of the X_ts. If h is very large, the averaging will be over larger neighbourhoods of the X_ts. Therefore, controlling the degree of averaging amounts to adjusting the smoothing parameter h, also known as the *bandwidth*. Choosing the appropriate bandwidth is an important aspect of any local-averaging technique and is discussed more fully in section 2.2.3.

Substituting Equation (2.8) into Equation (2.4) yields the *Nadaraya–Watson* kernel estimator $\hat{m}_h(x)$ of $m(x)$:

$$\hat{m}_h(x) = \frac{1}{T}\sum_{t=1}^{T}\omega_{t,h}(x)\,Y_t = \frac{\sum_{t=1}^{T}\mathrm{K}_h(x - X_t)\,Y_t}{\sum_{t=1}^{T}\mathrm{K}_h(x - X_t)} \tag{2.9}$$

Under certain regularity conditions on the shape of the kernel K and the magnitudes and behaviour of the weights as the sample size grows, it may be shown that $\hat{m}_h(x)$ converges to $m(x)$ asymptotically in several ways (see Härdle, 1990 for further details). This convergence property holds for a wide class of kernels, but for the remainder of this chapter we shall use the most popular choice of kernel, the Gaussian kernel:

$$\mathrm{K}_h(x) = \frac{1}{h\sqrt{2\pi}}e^{-\frac{x^2}{2h^2}} \tag{2.10}$$

2.2.3   Selecting the bandwidth

Selecting the appropriate bandwidth h in Equation (2.9) is clearly central to the success of $\hat{m}_h(\cdot)$ in approximating $m(\cdot)$ – too little averaging yields a function that is too choppy, and too much averaging yields a function that is too smooth. To illustrate these two extremes, Figure 2.2 displays the Nadaraya–Watson kernel estimator applied to 500 datapoints generated from the relation:

$$Y_t = \sin(X_t) + 0.5\epsilon Z_t, \qquad \epsilon Z_t \sim N(0, 1) \tag{2.11}$$

where X_t is evenly spaced in the interval $[0, 2\pi]$. Figure 2.2(a) plots the raw data and the function to be approximated.

Kernel estimators for three different bandwidths are plotted as solid lines in Figure 2.2(b)–(c). The bandwidth in Figure 2.2(b) is clearly too small; the function is too variable, fitting the 'noise' $0.5\,\epsilon Z_t$ as well as the 'signal' $\sin(\cdot)$. Increasing the bandwidth slightly yields a much more accurate approximation to $\sin(\cdot)$ as Figure 2.2(c) illustrates. However, Figure 2.2(d) shows that if the bandwidth is increased beyond some point, there is too much averaging and information is lost.

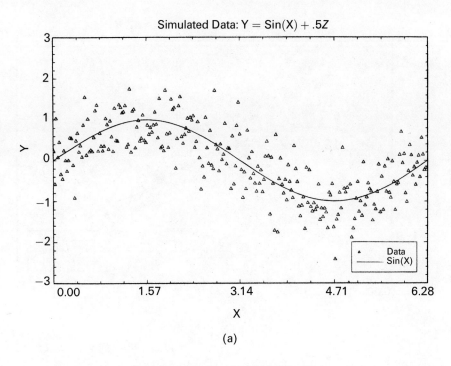

(a)

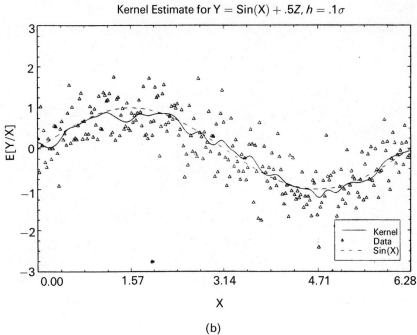

(b)

Figure 2.2 *Illustration of bandwidth selection for kernel regression*

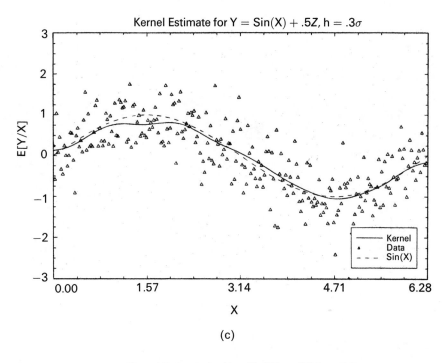

(c)

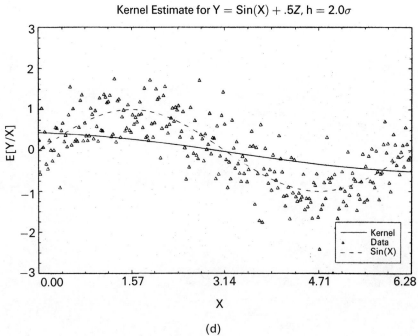

(d)

Figure 2.2   (*continued*)

There are several methods for automating the choice of bandwidth h in Equation (2.9), but the most popular is the *cross-validation* method in which h is chosen to minimize the cross-validation function:

$$\text{CV}(h) = \frac{1}{T}\sum_{t=1}^{T}(P_t - \hat{m}_{h,t})^2 \qquad (2.12)$$

where

$$\hat{m}_{h,t} \equiv \frac{1}{T}\sum_{\tau \neq t}^{T}\omega_{\tau,h}Y_\tau \qquad (2.13)$$

The estimator $\hat{m}_{h,t}$ is the kernel regression estimator applied to the price history $\{P_\tau\}$ with the tth observation omitted, and the summands in Equation (2.12) are the squared errors of the $\hat{m}_{h,t}$s, each evaluated at the omitted observation. For a given bandwidth parameter h, the cross-validation function is a measure of the ability of the kernel regression estimator to fit each observation P_t when that observation is not used to construct the kernel estimator. By selecting the bandwidth that minimizes this function, we obtain a kernel estimator that satisfies certain optimality properties, for example, minimum asymptotic mean-squared error.[4]

Interestingly, the bandwidths obtained from minimizing the cross-validation function are generally too large for our application to technical analysis – when we presented several professional technical analysts with plots of cross-validation-fitted functions $\hat{m}_h(\cdot)$, they all concluded that the fitted functions were too smooth. In other words, the cross-validation-determined bandwidth places too much weight on prices far away from any given time t, inducing too much averaging and discarding valuable information in local price movements. Through trial and error, and by polling professional technical analysts, we have found that an acceptable solution to this problem is to use a bandwidth of $0.3 \times h^*$, where h^* minimizes $\text{CV}(h)$.[5] Admittedly, this is an ad hoc approach, and it remains an important challenge for future research to develop a more rigorous procedure.

Another promising direction for future research is to consider alternatives to kernel regression. Although kernel regression is useful for its simplicity and intuitive appeal, kernel estimators suffer from a number of well-known deficiencies, e.g., boundary bias, lack of local variability in the degree of smoothing, etc. A popular alternative that overcomes these particular deficiencies is *local polynomial regression* in which local averaging of polynomials is performed to obtain an estimator of $m(x)$.[6] Such alternatives may yield important improvements in the pattern-recognition algorithm described in the next section.

2.3   AUTOMATING TECHNICAL ANALYSIS

Armed with a mathematical representation $\hat{m}(\cdot)$ of $\{P_t\}$ with which geometric properties can be characterized in an objective manner, we can now construct an algorithm for automating the detection of technical patterns. Specifically, our algorithm contains three steps:

1   Define each technical pattern in terms of its geometric properties, e.g., local extrema (maxima and minima).
2   Construct a kernel estimator $\hat{m}(\cdot)$ of a given time series of prices so that its extrema can be determined numerically.
3   Analyse $\hat{m}(\cdot)$ for occurrences of each technical pattern.

The last two steps are rather straightforward applications of kernel regression. The first step is likely to be the most controversial because it is here that the skills and judgement of a professional technical analyst come into play. Although we will argue in section 2.3.1 that most technical indicators can be characterized by specific *sequences* of local extrema, technical analysts may argue that these are poor approximations to the kinds of patterns that trained human analysts can identify.

While pattern-recognition techniques have been successful in automating a number of tasks previously considered to be uniquely human endeavours – fingerprint identification, handwriting analysis, face recognition, and so on – nevertheless it is possible that no algorithm can completely capture the skills of an experienced technical analyst. We acknowledge that any automated procedure for pattern recognition may miss some of the more subtle nuances that human cognition is capable of discerning, but whether an algorithm is a poor approximation to human judgement can only be determined by investigating the approximation errors empirically. As long as an algorithm can provide a reasonable approximation to *some* of the cognitive abilities of a human analyst, we can use such an algorithm to investigate the empirical performance of those aspects of technical analysis for which the algorithm is a good approximation. Moreover, if technical analysis is an art form that can be taught, then surely its basic precepts can be quantified and automated to some degree. And as increasingly sophisticated pattern-recognition techniques are developed, a larger fraction of the art will become a science.

More importantly, from a practical perspective, there may be significant benefits to developing an algorithmic approach to technical analysis because of the leverage that technology can provide. As with many other successful technologies, the automation of technical pattern recognition may not replace the skills of a technical analyst, but can amplify them considerably.

In section 2.3.1, we propose definitions of ten technical patterns based on their extrema. In section 2.3.2 we describe a specific algorithm to identify technical patterns based on the local extrema of price series using kernel regression estimators, and we provide specific examples of the algorithm at work in section 2.3.3.

2.3.1   Definitions of technical patterns

We focus on five pairs of technical patterns that are among the most popular patterns of traditional technical analysis (see, for example, Edwards and Magee, 1966, Chapters VII–X): head-and-shoulders (HS) and inverse head-and-shoulders (IHS), broadening tops (BTOP) and bottoms (BBOT), triangle tops (TTOP) and bottoms (TBOT), rectangle tops (RTOP) and bottoms (RBOT), and double tops (DTOP) and bottoms (DBOT). There are many other technical indicators that may be easier to detect algorithmically – moving averages, support and resistance levels, and oscillators, for example – but because we wish to illustrate the power of smoothing techniques in automating technical analysis, we focus on precisely those patterns that are most difficult to quantify analytically.

Consider the systematic component $m(\cdot)$ of a price history $\{P_t\}$ and suppose we have identified n local extrema, i.e., the local maxima and minima, of $\{P_t\}$. Denote by $E_1, E_2, \ldots, E_n$ the n extrema and $t_1^*, t_2^*, \ldots, t_n^*$ the dates on which these extrema occur. Then we have the following definitions:

Definition 1 (Head-and-Shoulders) Head-and-shoulders (HS) and inverted head-and-shoulders (IHS) patterns are characterized by a sequence of five consecutive local extrema $E_1, \ldots, E_5$ such that:

$$\text{HS} \equiv \begin{cases} E_1 \text{ is a maximum} \\ E_3 > E_1, E_3 > E_5 \\ E_1 \text{ and } E_5 \text{ are within 1.5 per cent of their average} \\ E_2 \text{ and } E_4 \text{ are within 1.5 per cent of their average} \end{cases}$$

$$\text{IHS} \equiv \begin{cases} E_1 \text{ is a minimum} \\ E_3 < E_1, E_3 < E_5 \\ E_1 \text{ and } E_5 \text{ are within 1.5 per cent of their average} \\ E_2 \text{ and } E_4 \text{ are within 1.5 per cent of their average} \end{cases}$$

Observe that only five consecutive extrema are required to identify a head-and-shoulders pattern. This follows from the formalization of the geometry of a head-and-shoulders pattern: three peaks, with the middle peak higher than the other two. Because consecutive extrema must alternate between maxima and minima for smooth functions,[7] the three-peaks pattern corresponds to a sequence of five local extrema: maximum, minimum, highest maximum, minimum, and maximum. The inverse head-and-shoulders is simply the mirror image of the head-and-shoulders, with the initial local extrema a minimum.

Because broadening, rectangle, and triangle patterns can begin on either a local maximum or minimum, we allow for both of these possibilities in our definitions by distinguishing between broadening tops and bottoms:

Definition 2 (Broadening) Broadening tops (BTOP) and bottoms (BBOT) are characterized by a sequence of five consecutive local extrema $E_1, \ldots, E_5$ such that:

$$\text{BTOP} \equiv \begin{cases} E_1 \text{ is a maximum} \\ E_1 < E_3 < E_5 \\ E_2 > E_4 \end{cases} \qquad \text{BBOT} \equiv \begin{cases} E_1 \text{ is a minimum} \\ E_1 > E_3 > E_5 \\ E_2 < E_4 \end{cases}$$

Definitions for triangle and rectangle patterns follow naturally.

Definition 3 (Triangle) Triangle tops (TTOP) and bottoms (TBOT) are characterized by a sequence of five consecutive local extrema $E_1, \ldots, E_5$ such that:

$$\text{TTOP} \equiv \begin{cases} E_1 \text{ is a maximum} \\ E_1 > E_3 > E_5 \\ E_2 < E_4 \end{cases} \qquad \text{TBOT} \equiv \begin{cases} E_1 \text{ is a minimum} \\ E_1 < E_3 < E_5 \\ E_2 > E_4 \end{cases}$$

Definition 4 (Rectangle) Rectangle tops (RTOP) and bottoms (RBOT) are characterized by a sequence of five consecutive local extrema $E_1, \ldots, E_5$ such that:

$$\text{RTOP} \equiv \begin{cases} E_1 \text{ is a maximum} \\ \text{tops are within 0.75 per cent of their average} \\ \text{bottoms are within 0.75 per cent of their average} \\ \text{lowest top} > \text{highest bottom} \end{cases}$$

$$\text{RBOT} \equiv \begin{cases} E_1 \text{ is a minimum} \\ \text{tops are within 0.75 per cent of their average} \\ \text{bottoms are within 0.75 per cent of their average} \\ \text{lowest top} > \text{highest bottom} \end{cases}$$

The definition for double tops and bottoms is slightly more involved. Consider first the double top. Starting at a local maximum E_1, we locate the highest local maximum E_a occurring after E_1 in the set of all local extrema in the sample. We require that the two tops, E_1 and E_a, be within 1.5 per cent of their average. Finally, following Edwards and Magee (1966), we require that the two tops occur at least a month, or 22 trading days, apart. Therefore, we have the following definition:

Definition 5 (Double Top and Bottom) Double tops (DTOP) and bottoms (DBOT) are characterized by an initial local extremum E_1 and subsequent local extrema E_a and E_b such that:

$$E_a \equiv \sup\{P^*_{t_k} : t^*_k > t^*_1, k = 2, \ldots, n\}$$

$$E_b \equiv \inf\{P^*_{t_k} : t^*_k > t^*_1, k = 2, \ldots, n\}$$

and

$$\text{DTOP} \equiv \begin{cases} E_1 \text{ is a maximum} \\ E_1 \text{ and } E_a \text{ are within 1.5 per cent of their average} \\ t^*_a - t^*_1 > 22 \end{cases}$$

$$\text{DBOT} \equiv \begin{cases} E_1 \text{ is a minimum} \\ E_1 \text{ and } E_b \text{ are within 1.5 per cent of their average} \\ t^*_a - t^*_1 > 22 \end{cases}$$

2.3.2   The identification algorithm

Our algorithm begins with a sample of prices $\{P_1, \ldots, P_T\}$ for which we fit kernel regressions, one for each subsample or *window* from t to $t+l+d-1$, where t varies from 1 to $T-l-d+1$, and l and d are fixed parameters whose purpose is explained below. In the empirical analysis of section 2.4, we set $l=35$ and $d=3$; hence each window consists of 38 trading days.

The motivation for fitting kernel regressions to rolling windows of data is to narrow our focus to patterns that are completed within the span of the window – $l+d$ trading days in our case. If we fit a single kernel regression to the entire dataset, many patterns of various durations may emerge, and without imposing some additional structure on the nature of the patterns, it is virtually impossible to distinguish signal from noise in this case. Therefore, our algorithm fixes the length of the window at $l + d$, but kernel regressions are estimated on a rolling basis and we search for patterns in each window.

Of course, for any fixed window, we can only find patterns that are completed within $l+d$ trading days. Without further structure on the systematic component of prices $m(\cdot)$, this is a restriction that any empirical analysis must contend with.[8] We choose a shorter window length of $l=35$ trading days to focus on short-horizon patterns that may be more relevant for active equity traders, and we leave the analysis of longer-horizon patterns to future research.

The parameter d controls for the fact that in practice we do not observe a realization of a given pattern as soon as it has completed. Instead, we assume that there may be a lag between the pattern completion and the time of pattern detection. To account for this lag, we require that the final extremum that completes a pattern occurs on day $t+l-1$; hence d is the number of days following the completion of a pattern that must pass before the pattern is detected. This will become more important in section 2.4 when we compute conditional returns, conditioned on the realization of each pattern. In particular, we compute post pattern returns starting from the end of trading day $t+l+d$, i.e., one day after the pattern has completed. For example, if we determine that a head-and-shoulders pattern has completed on day $t+l-1$ (having used prices from time t through time $t+l+d-1$), we compute the conditional one-day gross return as $Z_1 \equiv Y_{t+l+d+1}/Y_{t+l+d}$. Hence we do *not* use any forward information in computing returns conditional on pattern completion. In other words, the lag d ensures that we are computing our conditional returns completely out-of-sample and without any 'look-ahead' bias.

Within each window, we estimate a kernel regression using the prices in that window, hence:

$$\hat{m}_h(\tau) \;=\; \frac{\displaystyle\sum_{s=t}^{t+l+d-1} K_h(\tau - s)P_s}{\displaystyle\sum_{s=t}^{t+l+d-1} K_h(\tau - s)} \qquad t = 1,\ldots, T-l-d+1 \qquad (2.14)$$

where $K_h(z)$ is given in Equation (2.10) and h is the bandwidth parameter (see Section 2.3.3). It is clear that $\hat{m}_h(\tau)$ is a differentiable function of τ.

Once the function $\hat{m}_h(\tau)$ has been computed, its local extrema can be readily identified by finding times τ such that $\text{Sgn}(\hat{m}'_h(\tau)) = -\text{Sgn}(\hat{m}'_h(\tau+1))$, where $\hat{m}'_h$ denotes the derivative of $\hat{m}_h$ with respect to τ and $\text{Sgn}(\cdot)$ is the signum function. If the signs of $\hat{m}'_h(\tau)\,\hat{m}'_h(\tau+1)$ are $+1$ and -1, respectively, then we have found a local maximum, and if they are -1 and $+1$, respectively, then we have found a local minimum. Once such a time τ has been identified, we proceed to identify a maximum or minimum in the original price series $\{P_t\}$ in the range $[t-1, t+1]$, and the extrema in the original price series are used to determine whether or not a pattern has occurred according to the definitions of section 2.3.1.

If $\hat{m}'_h(\tau) = 0$ for a given τ, which occurs if closing prices stay the same for several consecutive days, we need to check whether the price we have found is a local minimum or maximum. We look for the date s such that

$s = \inf\{s > \tau : \hat{m}'_h(s) \neq 0\}$. We then apply the same method as discussed above, except here we compare $\text{Sgn}(\hat{m}'_h(\tau - 1))$ and $\text{Sgn}(\hat{m}'_h(s))$.

One useful consequence of this algorithm is that the series of extrema which it identifies contains alternating minima and maxima. That is, if the kth extremum is a maximum, then it is always the case that the $(k+1)^{\text{th}}$ extremum is a minimum and vice versa.

An important advantage of using this kernel regression approach to identify patterns is the fact that it ignores extrema that are 'too local'. For example, a simpler alternative is to identify local extrema from the raw price data directly, i.e., identify a price P_t as a local maximum if $P_{t-1} < P_t$ and $P_t > P_{t+1}$ and vice versa for a local minimum. The problem with this approach is that it identifies too many extrema, and also yields patterns that are not visually consistent with the kind of patterns that technical analysts find compelling.

Once we have identified all of the local extrema in the window $[t, t+l+d-1]$, we can proceed to check for the presence of the various technical patterns using the definitions of section 2.3.1. This procedure is then repeated for the next window $[t+1, t+l+d]$, and continues until the end of the sample is reached at the window $[T-l-d+1, T]$.

2.3.3 Empirical examples

To see how our algorithm performs in practice, we apply it to the daily returns of a single security, CTX, during the five-year period from 1992 to 1996. Figures 2.3–2.7 plot occurrences of the five pairs of patterns defined in section 2.3.1 that were identified by our algorithm. Note that there were no rectangle bottoms detected for CTX during this period, so for completeness we substituted a rectangle bottom for CDO stock that occurred during the same period.

In each of these graphs, the solid lines are the raw prices, the dashed lines are the kernel estimators $\hat{m}_h(\cdot)$, the circles indicate the local extrema, and the vertical line marks date $t+l-1$, the day that the final extremum occurs to complete the pattern.

Casual inspection by several professional technical analysts seems to confirm the ability of our automated procedure to match human judgement in identifying the five pairs of patterns in section 2.3.1. Of course, this is merely anecdotal evidence and not meant to be conclusive – we provide these figures simply to illustrate the output of a technical pattern-recognition algorithm based on kernel regression.

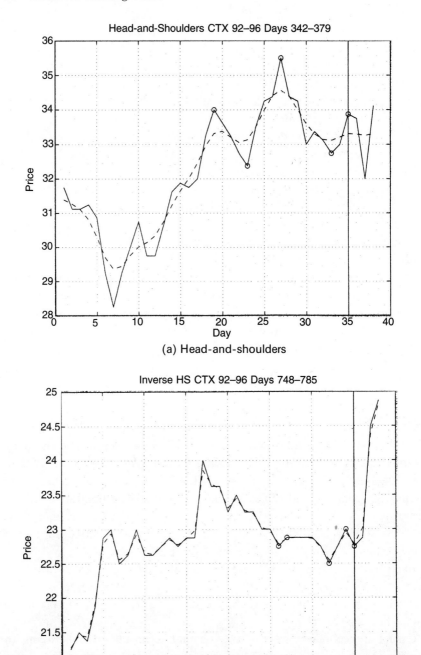

(a) Head-and-shoulders

(b) Inverse head-and-shoulders

Figure 2.3   *Head-and-shoulders and inverse head-and-shoulders*

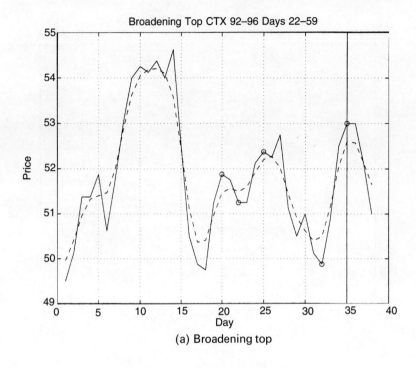

(a) Broadening top

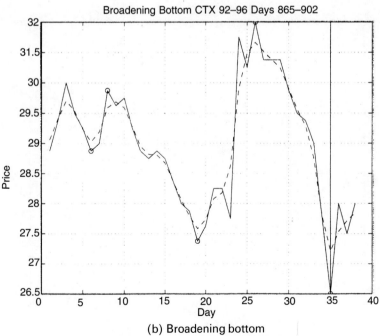

(b) Broadening bottom

Figure 2.4 *Broadening tops and bottoms*

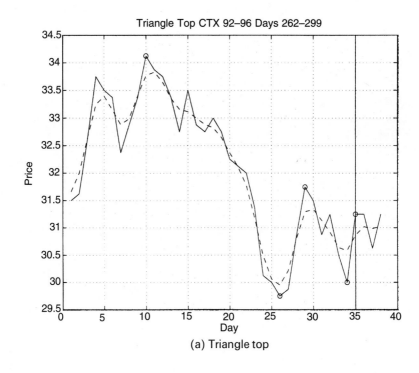

(a) Triangle top

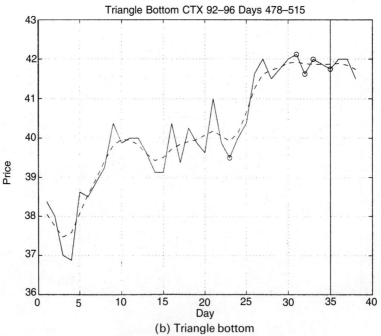

(b) Triangle bottom

Figure 2.5   *Triangle tops and bottoms*

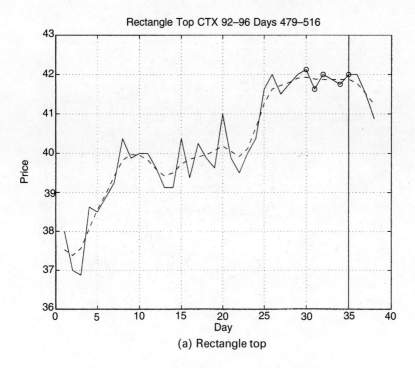

(a) Rectangle top

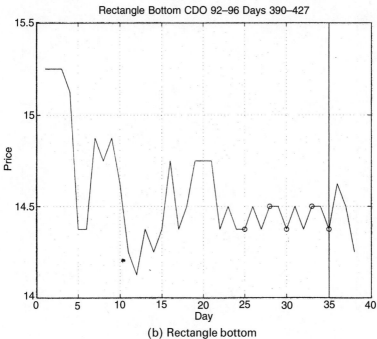

(b) Rectangle bottom

Figure 2.6 *Rectangle tops and bottoms*

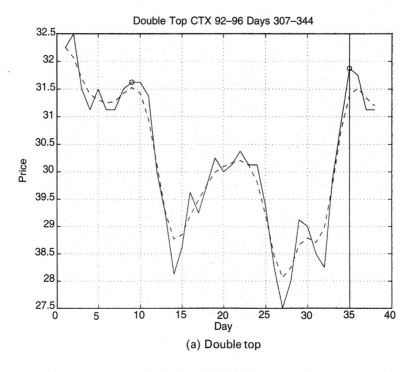

(a) Double top

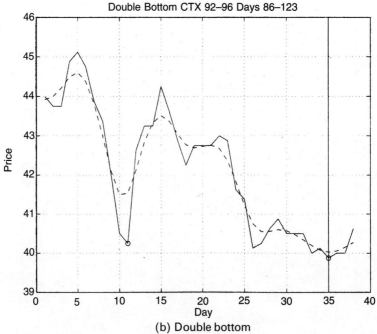

(b) Double bottom

Figure 2.7   *Double tops and bottoms*

2.4   IS TECHNICAL ANALYSIS INFORMATIVE?

Although there have been many tests of technical analysis over the years, most of these tests have focused on the profitability of technical trading rules.[9] Although some of these studies do find that technical indicators can generate statistically significant trading profits, they beg the question of whether or not such profits are merely the equilibrium rents that accrue to investors willing to bear the risks associated with such strategies. Without specifying a fully articulated dynamic general equilibrium asset-pricing model, it is impossible to determine the economic source of trading profits.

Instead, we propose a more fundamental test in this section, one that attempts to gauge the information content in the technical patterns of section 2.3.1 by comparing the unconditional empirical distribution of returns with the corresponding conditional empirical distribution, conditioned on the occurrence of a technical pattern. If technical patterns are informative, conditioning on them should alter the empirical distribution of returns; if the information contained in such patterns has already been incorporated into returns, the conditional and unconditional distribution of returns should be close. Although this is a weaker test of the effectiveness of technical analysis – informativeness does not guarantee a profitable trading strategy – it is, nevertheless, a natural first step in a quantitative assessment of technical analysis.

To measure the distance between the two distributions, we propose two goodness-of-fit measures in section 2.4.1. We apply these diagnostics to the daily returns of individual stocks from 1962 to 1996 using a procedure described in sections 2.4.2–2.4.4, and the results are reported in sections 2.4.5 and 2.4.6.

2.4.1   Goodness-of-fit tests

A simple diagnostic to test the informativeness of the ten technical patterns is to compare the quantiles of the conditional returns with their unconditional counterparts. If conditioning on these technical patterns provides no incremental information, the quantiles of the conditional returns should be similar to those of unconditional returns. In particular, we compute the deciles of unconditional returns and tabulate the relative frequency $\hat{\delta}_j$ of *conditional* returns falling into decile j of the unconditional returns, $j = 1, \ldots, 10$:

$$\hat{\delta}_j \equiv \frac{\text{Number of conditional returns in decile } j}{\text{Total number of conditional returns}} \tag{2.15}$$

Under the null hypothesis that the returns are independently and identically distributed (IID) and the conditional and unconditional distributions are identical, the asymptotic distributions of $\hat{\delta}_j$ and the corresponding goodness-of-fit test statistic Q are given by:

$$\sqrt{n}(\hat{\delta}_j - 0.10) \overset{a}{\sim} \mathcal{N}(0, 0.10(1-0.10)) \tag{2.16}$$

$$Q \equiv \sum_{j=1}^{10} \frac{(n_j - 0.10n)^2}{0.10n} \overset{a}{\sim} \chi_9^2 \tag{2.17}$$

where n_j is the number of observations that fall in decile j and n is the total number of observations (see, e.g. DeGroot, 1986).

Another comparison of the conditional and unconditional distributions of returns is provided by the Kolmogorov–Smirnov test. Denote by $\{Z_{1t}\}_{t=1}^{n_1}$ and $\{Z_{2t}\}_{t=1}^{n_2}$ two samples that are each IID with cumulative distribution functions $F_1(z)$ and $F_2(z)$, respectively. The Kolmogorov–Smirnov statistic is designed to test the null hypothesis that $F_1 = F_2$, and is based on the empirical cumulative distribution functions $\hat{F}_i$ of both samples:

$$\hat{F}_i(z) \equiv \frac{1}{n_i} \sum_{k=1}^{n_i} \mathbf{1}(Z_{ik} \le z) \qquad i = 1, 2 \tag{2.18}$$

where $\mathbf{1}(\cdot)$ is the indicator function. The statistic is given by the expression:

$$\gamma_{n_1,n_2} = \left(\frac{n_1 n_2}{n_1 + n_2}\right)^{1/2} \sup_{-\infty < z < \infty} |\hat{F}_1(z) - \hat{F}_2(z)| \tag{2.19}$$

Under the null hypothesis $F_1 = F_2$, the statistic γ_{n_1,n_2} should be small. Moreover, Smirnov (1939a,b) derives the limiting distribution of the statistic to be:

$$\lim_{\min(n_1,n_2)\to\infty} \mathrm{Prob}\left(\gamma_{n_1,n_2} \le x\right) = \sum_{k=-\infty}^{\infty} (-1)^k \exp(-2k^2 x^2) \qquad x > 0 \tag{2.20}$$

An approximate α-level test of the null hypothesis can be performed by computing the statistic and rejecting the null if it exceeds the upper 100αth percentile for the null distribution given by Equation (2.20) (see Hollander and Wolfe, 1973, Table A.23; Csáki, 1984; and Press et al., 1986, Chapter 13.5).

Note that the sampling distributions of both the goodness-of-fit and Kolmogorov–Smirnov statistics are derived under the assumption that returns are IID, which is not plausible for financial data. We attempt to address this problem by normalizing the returns of each security, i.e., by subtracting its mean and dividing by its standard deviation (see section 2.4.3), but this does not eliminate the dependence or heterogeneity. We hope to extend our analysis to the more general non-IID case in future research.

2.4.2 The data and sampling procedure

We apply the goodness-of-fit and Kolmogorov–Smirnov tests to the daily returns of individual NYSE/AMEX and Nasdaq stocks from 1962 to 1996 using data from the Center for Research in Securities Prices (CRSP). To ameliorate the effects of non-stationarities induced by changing market structure and institutions, we split the data into NYSE/AMEX stocks and Nasdaq stocks and into seven five-year periods: 1962 to 1966, 1967 to 1971, and so on. To obtain a broad cross-section of securities, in each five-year subperiod, we randomly select ten stocks from each of five market-capitalization quintiles (using mean market-capitalization over the subperiod), with the further restriction that at least 75 per cent of the price observations must be non-missing during the subperiod.[10] This procedure yields a sample of 50 stocks for each subperiod across seven subperiods (note that we sample with replacement; hence there may be names in common across subperiods).

As a check on the robustness of our inferences, we perform this sampling procedure twice to construct two samples, and apply our empirical analysis to both. Although we report results only from the first sample to conserve space, the results of the second sample are qualitatively consistent with the first and are available upon request.

2.4.3 Computing conditional returns

For each stock in each subperiod, we apply the procedure outlined in section 2.3 to identify all occurrences of the ten patterns defined in section 2.3.1. For each pattern detected, we compute the one-day continuously compounded return d days after the pattern has completed. Specifically, consider a window of prices $\{P_t\}$ from t to $t+l+d-1$, and suppose that the identified pattern p is completed at $t+l-1$. Then we take the conditional return R^p as $\log(1 + R_{t+l+d+1})$. Therefore, for each stock, we have ten sets of such conditional returns, each conditioned on one of the ten patterns of section 2.3.1.

For each stock, we construct a sample of *unconditional* continuously compounded returns using non-overlapping intervals of length τ, and we compare the empirical distribution function of these returns with those of the conditional returns. To facilitate such comparisons, we standardize all returns – both conditional and unconditional – by subtracting means and dividing by standard deviations, hence:

$$X_{it} = \frac{R_{it} - \text{Mean}[R_{it}]}{\text{SD}[R_{it}]} \tag{2.21}$$

where the means and standard deviations are computed for each individual stock within each subperiod. Therefore, by construction, each normalized return series has zero mean and unit variance.

Finally, to increase the power of our goodness-of-fit tests, we combine the normalized returns of all 50 stocks within each subperiod; hence for each subperiod we have two samples – unconditional and conditional returns – and from these we compute two empirical distribution functions that we compare using our diagnostic test statistics.

2.4.4   Conditioning on volume

Given the prominent role that volume plays in technical analysis, we also construct returns conditioned on increasing or decreasing volume. Specifically, for each stock in each subperiod, we compute its average share turnover during the first and second halves of each subperiod, τ_1 and τ_2, respectively. If $\tau_1 > 1.2 \times \tau_2$, we categorize this as a 'decreasing volume' event; if $\tau_2 > 1.2 \times \tau_1$, we categorize this as an 'increasing volume' event. If neither of these conditions holds, then neither event is considered to have occurred.

Using these events, we can construct conditional returns conditioned on two pieces of information: the occurrence of a technical pattern and the occurrence of increasing or decreasing volume. Therefore, we shall compare the empirical distribution of unconditional returns with three conditional-return distributions: the distribution of returns conditioned on technical patterns, the distribution conditioned on technical patterns and increasing volume, and the distribution conditioned on technical patterns and decreasing volume.

Of course, other conditioning variables can easily be incorporated into this procedure, though the 'curse of dimensionality' imposes certain practical limits on the ability to estimate multivariate conditional distributions nonparametrically.

2.4.5   Summary statistics

In Tables 2.1 and 2.2, we report frequency counts for the number of patterns detected over the entire 1962 to 1996 sample, and within each subperiod and each market-capitalization quintile, for the ten patterns defined in

Table 2.1 Frequency counts for ten technical indicators detected among NYSE/AMEX stocks from 1962 to 1996, in five-year subperiods, in size quintiles, and in a sample of simulated geometric Brownian motion. In each five-year subperiod, ten stocks per quintile are selected at random among stocks with at least 80 per cent non-missing prices, and each stock's price history is scanned for any occurrence of the following ten technical indicators within the subperiod: head-and-shoulders (HS), inverted head-and-shoulders (IHS), broadening top (BTOP), broadening bottom (BBOT), triangle top (TTOP), triangle bottom (TBOT), rectangle top (RTOP), rectangle bottom (RBOT), double top (DTOP), and double bottom (DBOT). The 'Sample' column indicates whether the frequency counts are conditioned on decreasing volume trend ('$\tau(\searrow)$'), increasing volume trend ('$\tau(\nearrow)$'), unconditional ('Entire'), or for a sample of simulated geometric Brownian motion with parameters calibrated to match the data ('Sim. GBM')

Sample	Raw	HS	IHS	BTOP	BBOT	TTOP	TBOT	RTOP	RBOT	DTOP	DBOT
All stocks, 1962 to 1996											
Entire	423 556	1611	1654	725	748	1294	1193	1482	1616	2076	2075
Sim. GBM	423 556	577	578	1227	1028	1049	1176	122	113	535	574
$\tau(\searrow)$	—	655	593	143	220	666	710	582	637	691	974
$\tau(\nearrow)$	—	553	614	409	337	300	222	523	552	776	533
Smallest quintile, 1962 to 1996											
Entire	84 363	182	181	78	97	203	159	265	320	261	271
Sim. GBM	84 363	82	99	279	256	269	295	18	16	129	127
$\tau(\searrow)$	—	90	81	13	42	122	119	113	131	78	161
$\tau(\nearrow)$	—	58	76	51	37	41	22	99	120	124	64
2nd quintile, 1962 to 1996											
Entire	83 986	309	321	146	150	255	228	299	322	372	420
Sim. GBM	83 986	108	105	291	251	261	278	20	17	106	126
$\tau(\searrow)$	—	133	126	25	48	135	147	130	149	113	211
$\tau(\nearrow)$	—	112	126	90	63	55	39	104	110	153	107
3rd quintile, 1962 to 1996											
Entire	84 420	361	388	145	161	291	247	334	399	458	443
Sim. GBM	84 420	122	120	268	222	212	249	24	31	115	125
$\tau(\searrow)$	—	152	131	20	49	151	149	130	160	154	215
$\tau(\nearrow)$	—	125	146	83	66	67	44	121	142	179	106

(continued)

Table 2.1 (continued)

Sample	Raw	HS	IHS	BTOP	BBOT	TTOP	TBOT	RTOP	RBOT	DTOP	DBOT
4th quintile, 1962 to 1996											
Entire	84780	332	317	176	173	262	255	259	264	424	420
Sim. GBM	84780	143	127	249	210	183	210	35	24	116	122
$\tau(\searrow)$	—	131	115	36	42	138	145	85	97	144	184
$\tau(\nearrow)$	—	110	126	103	89	56	55	102	96	147	118
Largest quintile, 1962 to 1996											
Entire	86007	427	447	180	167	283	304	325	311	561	521
Sim. GBM	86007	122	127	140	89	124	144	25	25	69	74
$\tau(\searrow)$	—	149	140	49	39	120	150	124	100	202	203
$\tau(\nearrow)$	—	148	140	82	82	81	62	97	84	173	138
All stocks, 1962 to 1966											
Entire	55254	276	278	85	103	179	165	316	354	356	352
Sim. GBM	55254	56	58	144	126	129	139	9	16	60	68
$\tau(\searrow)$	—	104	88	26	29	93	109	130	141	113	188
$\tau(\nearrow)$	—	96	112	44	39	37	25	130	122	137	88
All stocks, 1967 to 1971											
Entire	60299	179	175	112	134	227	172	115	117	239	258
Sim. GBM	60299	92	70	167	148	150	180	19	16	84	77
$\tau(\searrow)$	—	68	64	16	45	126	111	42	39	80	143
$\tau(\nearrow)$	—	71	69	68	57	47	29	41	41	87	53
All stocks, 1972 to 1976											
Entire	59915	152	162	82	93	165	136	171	182	218	223
Sim. GBM	59915	75	85	183	154	156	178	16	10	70	71
$\tau(\searrow)$	—	64	55	16	23	88	78	60	64	53	97
$\tau(\nearrow)$	—	54	62	42	50	32	21	61	67	80	59

All stocks, 1977 to 1981

Entire	62 133	223	206	134	110	188	167	146	182	274	290
Sim. GBM	62 133	83	88	245	200	188	210	18	12	90	115
τ(↘)	—	114	61	24	39	100	97	54	60	82	140
τ(↗)	—	56	93	78	44	35	36	53	71	113	76

All stocks, 1982 to 1986

Entire	61 984	242	256	106	108	182	190	182	207	313	299
Sim. GBM	61 984	115	120	188	144	152	169	31	23	99	87
τ(↘)	—	101	104	28	30	93	104	70	95	109	124
τ(↗)	—	89	94	51	62	46	40	73	68	116	85

All stocks, 1987 to 1991

Entire	61 780	240	241	104	98	180	169	260	259	287	285
Sim. GBM	61 780	68	79	168	132	131	150	11	10	76	68
τ(↘)	—	95	89	16	30	86	101	103	102	105	137
τ(↗)	—	81	79	68	43	53	36	73	87	100	68

All stocks, 1992 to 1996

Entire	62 191	299	336	102	102	173	194	292	315	389	368
Sim. GBM	62 191	88	78	132	124	143	150	18	26	56	88
τ(↘)	—	109	132	17	24	80	110	123	136	149	145
τ(↗)	—	106	105	58	42	50	35	92	96	143	104

Table 2.2 *Frequency counts for ten technical indicators detected among Nasdaq stocks from 1962 to 1996, in five-year subperiods, in size quintiles, and in a sample of simulated geometric Brownian motion. In each 5-year subperiod, ten stocks per quintile are selected at random among stocks with at least 80 per cent non-missing prices, and each stock's price history is scanned for any occurrence of the following ten technical indicators within the subperiod: head-and-shoulders (HS), inverted head-and-shoulders (IHS), broadening top (BTOP), broadening bottom (BBOT), triangle top (TTOP), triangle bottom (TBOT), rectangle top (RTOP), rectangle bottom (RBOT), double top (DTOP), and double bottom (DBOT). The 'Sample' column indicates whether the frequency counts are conditioned on decreasing volume trend ('τ(↘)'), increasing volume trend ('τ(↗)'), unconditional ('Entire'), or for a sample of simulated geometric Brownian motion with parameters calibrated to match the data ('Sim. GBM')*

Sample	Raw	HS	IHS	BTOP	BBOT	TTOP	TBOT	RTOP	RBOT	DTOP	DBOT
All stocks, 1962 to 1996											
Entire	411010	919	817	414	508	850	789	1134	1320	1208	1147
Sim. GBM	411010	434	447	1297	1139	1169	1309	96	91	567	579
τ(↘)	—	408	268	69	133	429	460	488	550	339	580
τ(↗)	—	284	325	234	209	185	125	391	461	474	229
Smallest quintile, 1962 to 1996											
Entire	81754	84	64	41	73	111	93	165	218	113	125
Sim. GBM	81754	85	84	341	289	334	367	11	12	140	125
τ(↘)	—	36	25	6	20	56	59	77	102	31	81
τ(↗)	—	31	23	31	30	24	15	59	85	46	17
2nd quintile, 1962 to 1996											
Entire	81336	191	138	68	88	161	148	242	305	219	176
Sim. GBM	81336	67	84	243	225	219	229	24	12	99	124
τ(↘)	—	94	51	11	28	86	109	111	131	69	101
τ(↗)	—	66	57	46	38	45	22	85	120	90	42
3rd quintile, 1962 to 1996											
Entire	81772	224	186	105	121	183	155	235	244	279	267
Sim. GBM	81772	69	86	227	210	214	239	15	14	105	100
τ(↘)	—	108	66	23	35	87	91	90	84	78	145
τ(↗)	—	71	79	56	49	39	29	84	86	122	58

4th quintile, 1962 to 1996

Entire	82 727	212	214	92	116	187	179	296	303	289	297
Sim. GBM	82 727	104	92	242	219	209	255	23	26	115	97
$\tau(\searrow)$	—	88	68	12	26	101	101	127	141	77	143
$\tau(\nearrow)$	—	62	83	57	56	34	22	104	93	118	66

Largest quintile, 1962 to 1996

Entire	83 421	208	215	108	110	208	214	196	250	308	282
Sim. GBM	83 421	109	101	244	196	193	219	23	27	108	133
$\tau(\searrow)$	—	82	58	17	24	99	100	83	92	84	110
$\tau(\nearrow)$	—	54	83	44	36	43	37	59	77	98	46

All stocks, 1962 to 1966

Entire	55 969	274	268	72	99	182	144	288	329	326	342
Sim. GBM	55 969	69	63	163	123	137	149	24	22	77	90
$\tau(\searrow)$	—	129	99	10	23	104	98	115	136	96	210
$\tau(\nearrow)$	—	83	103	48	51	37	23	101	116	144	64

All stocks, 1967 to 1971

Entire	60 563	115	120	104	123	227	171	65	83	196	200
Sim. GBM	60 563	58	61	194	184	181	188	9	8	90	83
$\tau(\searrow)$	—	61	29	15	40	127	123	26	39	49	137
$\tau(\nearrow)$	—	24	57	71	51	45	19	25	16	86	17

All stocks, 1972 to 1976

Entire	51 446	34	30	14	30	29	28	51	55	55	58
Sim. GBM	51 446	32	37	115	113	107	110	5	6	46	46
$\tau(\searrow)$	—	5	4	0	4	5	7	12	8	3	8
$\tau(\nearrow)$	—	8	7	1	2	2	0	5	12	8	3

All stocks, 1977 to 1981

Entire	61 972	56	53	41	36	52	73	57	65	89	96
Sim. GBM	61 972	90	84	236	165	176	212	19	19	110	98
$\tau(\searrow)$	—	7	7	1	2	4	8	12	12	7	9
$\tau(\nearrow)$	—	6	6	5	1	4	0	5	8	7	6

(continued)

Table 2.2 (continued)

Sample	Raw	HS	IHS	BTOP	BBOT	TTOP	TBOT	RTOP	RBOT	DTOP	DBOT
All stocks, 1982 to 1986											
Entire	61 110	71	64	46	44	97	107	109	115	120	97
Sim. GBM	61 110	86	90	162	168	147	174	23	21	97	98
$\tau(\searrow)$	—	37	19	8	14	46	58	45	52	40	48
$\tau(\nearrow)$	—	21	25	24	18	26	22	42	42	38	24
All stocks, 1987 to 1991											
Entire	60 862	158	120	50	61	120	109	265	312	177	155
Sim. GBM	60 862	59	57	229	187	205	244	7	7	79	88
$\tau(\searrow)$	—	79	46	11	19	73	69	130	140	50	69
$\tau(\nearrow)$	—	58	56	33	30	26	28	100	122	89	55
All stocks, 1992 to 1996											
Entire	59 088	211	162	87	115	143	157	299	361	245	199
Sim. GBM	59 088	40	55	198	199	216	232	9	8	68	76
$\tau(\searrow)$	—	90	64	24	31	70	97	148	163	94	99
$\tau(\nearrow)$	—	84	71	52	56	45	33	113	145	102	60

section 2.3.1. Table 2.1 contains results for the NYSE/AMEX stocks, and Table 2.2 contains corresponding results for Nasdaq stocks.

Table 2.1 shows that the most common patterns across all stocks and over the entire sample period are double tops and bottoms (see the row labelled 'Entire'), with over 2000 occurrences of each. The second most common patterns are the head-and-shoulders and inverted head-and-shoulders, with over 1600 occurrences of each. These total counts correspond roughly to four to six occurrences of each of these patterns for each stock during each five-year subperiod (divide the total number of occurrences by 7×50), not an unreasonable frequency from the point of view of professional technical analysts. Table 2.1 shows that most of the ten patterns are more frequent for larger stocks than for smaller ones, and that they are relatively evenly distributed over the five-year subperiods. When volume trend is considered jointly with the occurrences of the ten patterns, Table 2.1 shows that the frequency of patterns is not evenly distributed between increasing (the row labelled '$\tau(\nearrow)$') and decreasing (the row labelled '$\tau(\searrow)$') volume-trend cases. For example, for the entire sample of stocks over the 1962 to 1996 sample period, there are 143 occurrences of a broadening top with decreasing volume trend, but 409 occurrences of a broadening top with increasing volume trend.

For purposes of comparison, Table 2.1 also reports frequency counts for the number of patterns detected in a sample of simulated geometric Brownian motion, calibrated to match the mean and standard deviation of each stock in each five-year subperiod.[11] The entries in the row labelled 'Sim. GBM' show that the random walk model yields very different implications for the frequency counts of several technical patterns. For example, the simulated sample has only 577 head-and-shoulders and 578 inverted-head-and-shoulders patterns, whereas the actual data have considerably more, 1611 and 1654, respectively. On the other hand, for broadening tops and bottoms, the simulated sample contains many more occurrences than the actual data, 1227 and 1028 as compared to 725 and 748, respectively. The number of triangles is roughly comparable across the two samples, but for rectangles and double tops and bottoms, the differences are dramatic. Of course, the simulated sample is only one realization of geometric Brownian motion, so it is difficult to draw general conclusions about the relative frequencies. Nevertheless, these simulations point to important differences between the data and IID lognormal returns.

To develop further intuition for these patterns, Figures 2.8 and 2.9 display the cross-sectional and time-series distribution of each of the ten patterns for the NYSE/AMEX and Nasdaq samples, respectively. Each symbol represents a pattern detected by our algorithm, the vertical axis is divided into the five quintiles, the horizontal axis is calendar time, and alternating symbols

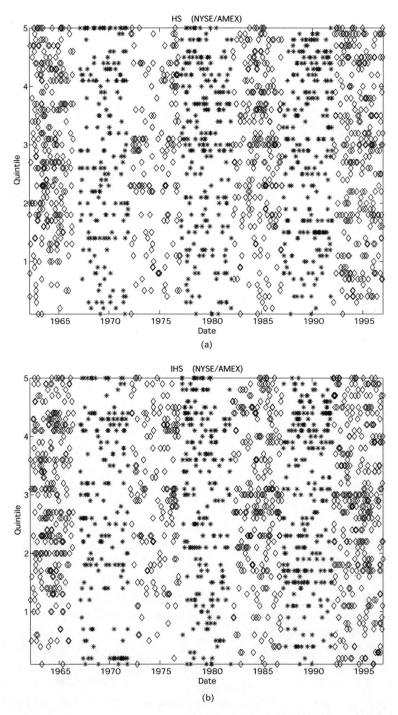

Figure 2.8   *Distribution of patterns in NYSE/AMEX sample*

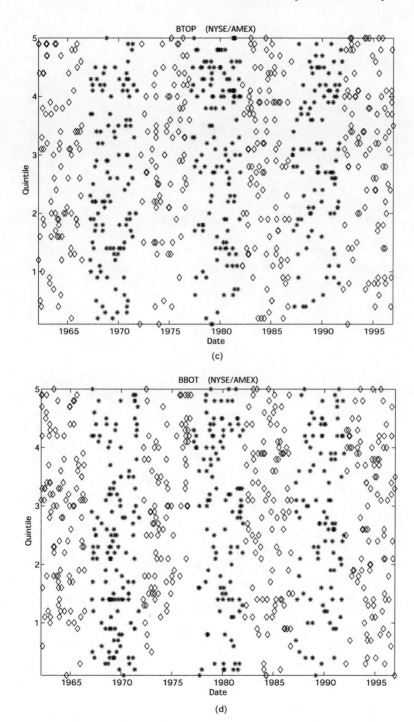

(c)

(d)

Figure 2.8 (*continued*)

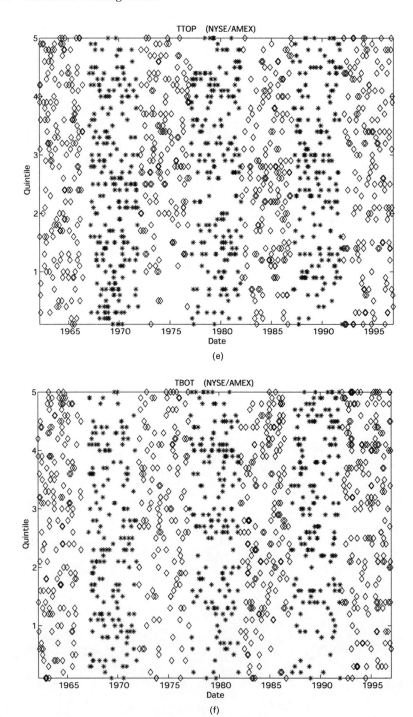

Figure 2.8   (*continued*)

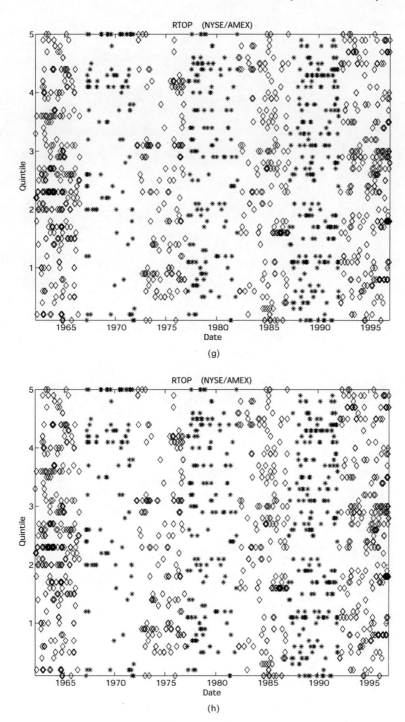

Figure 2.8 (*continued*)

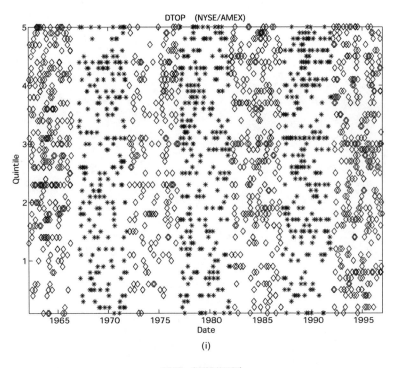

(i)

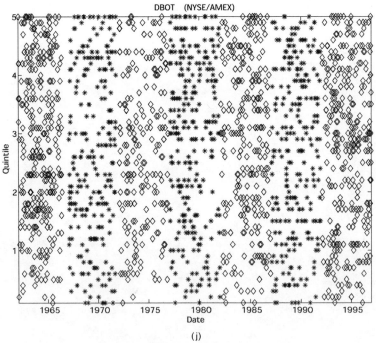

(j)

Figure 2.8   (*continued*)

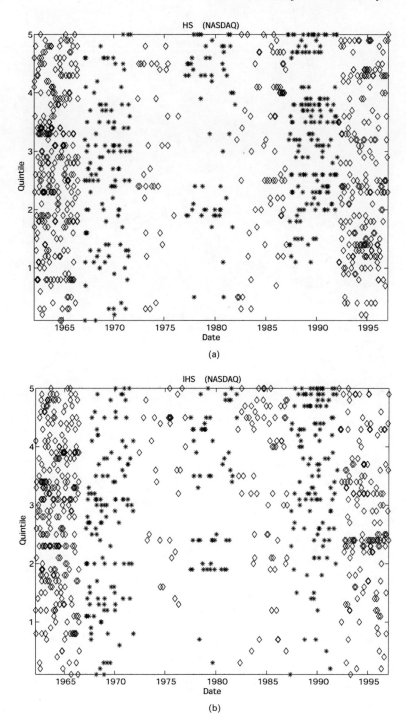

Figure 2.9 *Distribution of patterns in Nasdaq sample*

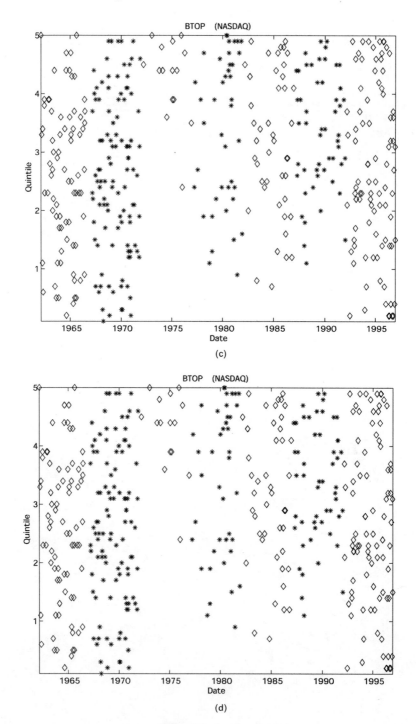

Figure 2.9   (*continued*)

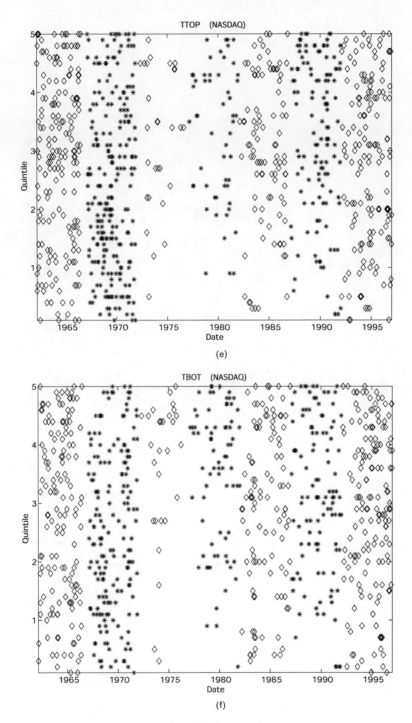

Figure 2.9 (*continued*)

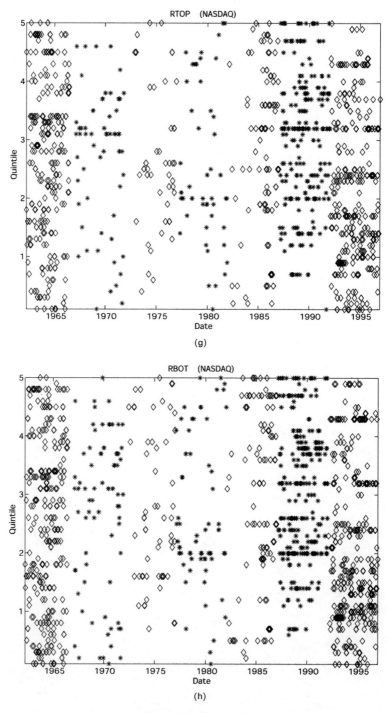

(g)

(h)

Figure 2.9   (*continued*)

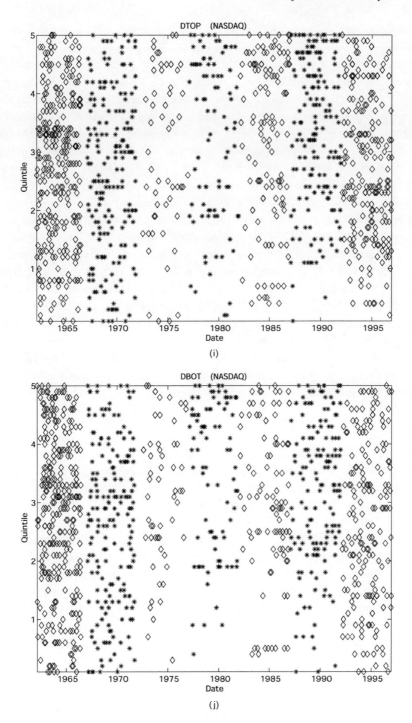

Figure 2.9 (*continued*)

(diamonds and asterisks) represent distinct subperiods. These graphs show that the distribution of patterns is not clustered in time or among a subset of securities.

Table 2.2 provides the same frequency counts for Nasdaq stocks, and despite the fact that we have the same number of stocks in this sample (50 per subperiod over seven subperiods), there are considerably fewer patterns detected than in the NYSE/AMEX case. For example, the Nasdaq sample yields only 919 head-and-shoulders patterns, whereas the NYSE/AMEX sample contains 1611. Not surprisingly, the frequency counts for the sample of simulated geometric Brownian motion are similar to those in Table 2.1.

Tables 2.3 and 2.4 report summary statistics – means, standard deviations, skewness, and excess kurtosis – of unconditional and conditional normalized returns of NYSE/AMEX and Nasdaq stocks, respectively. These statistics show considerable variation in the different return populations. For example, in Table 2.3 the first four moments of normalized raw returns are 0.000, 1.000, 0.345, and 8.122, respectively. The same four moments of post-BTOP returns are −0.005, 1.035, −1.151, and 16.701, respectively, and those of post-DTOP returns are 0.017, 0.910, 0.206, and 3.386, respectively. The differences in these statistics among the ten conditional return populations, and the differences between the conditional and unconditional return populations, suggest that conditioning on the ten technical indicators does have some effect on the distribution of returns.

2.4.6   Empirical results

Tables 2.5 and 2.6 report the results of the goodness-of-fit test (Equations (2.16) and (2.17)) for our sample of NYSE and AMEX (Table 2.5) and Nasdaq (Table 2.6) stocks, respectively, from 1962 to 1996 for each of the ten technical patterns. Table 2.5 shows that in the NYSE/AMEX sample, the relative frequencies of the conditional returns are significantly different from those of the unconditional returns for seven of the ten patterns considered. The three exceptions are the conditional returns from the BBOT, TTOP, and DBOT patterns, for which the p-values of the test statistics Q are 5.1 per cent, 21.2 per cent, and 16.6 per cent respectively. These results yield mixed support for the overall efficacy of technical indicators. However, the results of Table 2.6 tell a different story: there is overwhelming significance for all ten indicators in the Nasdaq sample, with p-values that are zero to three significant digits, and test statistics Q that range from 34.12 to 92.09. In contrast, the test statistics in Table 2.5 range from 12.03 to 50.97.

One possible explanation for the difference between the NYSE/AMEX and Nasdaq samples is a difference in the power of the test because of different sample sizes. If the NYSE/AMEX sample contained fewer conditional

Table 2.3 Summary statistics (mean, standard deviation, skewness, and excess kurtosis) of raw and conditional one-day normalized returns of NYSE/AMEX stocks from 1962 to 1996, in five-year subperiods, and in size quintiles. Conditional returns are defined as the daily return three days following the conclusion of an occurrence of one of ten technical indicators: head-and-shoulders (HS), inverted head-and-shoulders (IHS), broadening top (BTOP), broadening bottom (BBOT), triangle top (TTOP), triangle bottom (TBOT), rectangle top (RTOP), rectangle bottom (RBOT), double top (DTOP), and double bottom (DBOT). All returns have been normalized by subtraction of their means and division by their standard deviations

Moment	Raw	HS	IHS	BTOP	BBOT	TTOP	TBOT	RTOP	RBOT	DTOP	DBOT
All stocks, 1962 to 1996											
Mean	−0.000	−0.038	0.040	−0.005	−0.062	0.021	−0.009	0.009	0.014	0.017	−0.001
S.D.	1.000	0.867	0.937	1.035	0.979	0.955	0.959	0.865	0.883	0.910	0.999
Skew.	0.345	0.135	0.660	−1.151	0.090	0.137	0.643	−0.420	0.110	0.206	0.460
Kurt.	8.122	2.428	4.527	16.701	3.169	3.293	7.061	7.360	4.194	3.386	7.374
Smallest quintile, 1962 to 1996											
Mean	−0.000	−0.014	0.036	−0.093	−0.188	0.036	−0.020	0.037	−0.093	0.043	−0.055
S.D.	1.000	0.854	1.002	0.940	0.850	0.937	1.157	0.833	0.986	0.950	0.962
Skew.	0.697	0.802	1.337	−1.771	−0.367	0.861	2.592	−0.187	0.445	0.511	0.002
Kurt.	10.873	3.870	7.143	6.701	0.575	4.185	12.532	1.793	4.384	2.581	3.989
2nd quintile, 1962 to 1996											
Mean	−0.000	−0.069	0.144	0.061	−0.113	0.003	0.035	0.018	0.019	0.067	−0.011
S.D.	1.000	0.772	1.031	1.278	1.004	0.913	0.965	0.979	0.868	0.776	1.069
Skew.	0.392	0.223	1.128	−3.296	0.485	−0.529	0.166	−1.375	0.452	0.392	1.728
Kurt.	7.836	0.657	6.734	32.750	3.779	3.024	4.987	17.040	3.914	2.151	15.544
3rd quintile, 1962 to 1996											
Mean	−0.000	−0.048	−0.043	−0.076	−0.056	0.036	0.012	0.075	0.028	−0.039	−0.034
S.D.	1.000	0.888	0.856	0.894	0.925	0.973	0.796	0.798	0.892	0.956	1.026
Skew.	0.246	−0.465	0.107	−0.023	0.233	0.538	0.166	0.678	−0.618	0.013	−0.242
Kurt.	7.466	3.239	1.612	1.024	0.611	2.995	0.586	3.010	4.769	4.517	3.663

(continued)

Table 2.3 *(continued)*

Moment	Raw	HS	IHS	BTOP	BBOT	TTOP	TBOT	RTOP	RBOT	DTOP	DBOT
4th quintile, 1962 to 1996											
Mean	−0.000	−0.012	0.022	0.115	0.028	0.022	−0.014	−0.113	0.065	0.015	−0.006
S.D.	1.000	0.964	0.903	0.990	1.093	0.986	0.959	0.854	0.821	0.858	0.992
Skew.	0.222	0.055	0.592	0.458	0.537	−0.217	−0.456	−0.415	0.820	0.550	−0.062
Kurt.	6.452	1.444	1.745	1.251	2.168	4.237	8.324	4.311	3.632	1.719	4.691
Largest quintile, 1962 to 1996											
Mean	−0.000	−0.038	0.054	−0.081	−0.042	0.010	−0.049	0.009	0.060	0.018	0.067
S.D.	1.000	0.843	0.927	0.997	0.951	0.964	0.965	0.850	0.820	0.971	0.941
Skew.	0.174	0.438	0.182	0.470	−1.099	0.089	0.357	−0.167	−0.140	0.011	0.511
Kurt.	7.992	2.621	3.465	3.275	6.603	2.107	2.509	0.816	3.179	3.498	5.035
All stocks, 1962 to 1966											
Mean	−0.000	0.070	0.090	0.159	0.079	−0.033	−0.039	−0.041	0.019	−0.071	−0.100
S.D.	1.000	0.797	0.925	0.825	1.085	1.068	1.011	0.961	0.814	0.859	0.962
Skew.	0.563	0.159	0.462	0.363	1.151	−0.158	1.264	−1.337	−0.341	−0.427	−0.876
Kurt.	9.161	0.612	1.728	0.657	5.063	2.674	4.826	17.161	1.400	3.416	5.622
All stocks, 1967 to 1971											
Mean	−0.000	−0.044	0.079	−0.035	−0.056	0.025	0.057	−0.101	0.110	0.093	0.079
S.D.	1.000	0.809	0.944	0.793	0.850	0.885	0.886	0.831	0.863	1.083	0.835
Skew.	0.342	0.754	0.666	0.304	0.085	0.650	0.697	−1.393	0.395	1.360	0.701
Kurt.	5.810	3.684	2.725	0.706	0.141	3.099	1.659	8.596	3.254	4.487	1.853
All stocks, 1972 to 1976											
Mean	−0.000	−0.035	0.043	0.101	−0.138	−0.045	−0.010	−0.025	−0.003	−0.051	−0.108
S.D.	1.000	1.015	0.810	0.985	0.918	0.945	0.922	0.870	0.754	0.914	0.903
Skew.	0.316	−0.334	0.717	−0.699	0.272	−1.014	0.676	0.234	0.199	0.056	−0.366
Kurt.	6.520	2.286	1.565	6.562	1.453	5.261	4.912	3.627	2.337	3.520	5.047

All stocks, 1977 to 1981

Mean	−0.000	−0.138	−0.040	0.076	−0.114	0.135	−0.050	−0.004	0.026	0.042	0.178
S.D.	1.000	0.786	0.863	1.015	0.989	1.041	1.011	0.755	0.956	0.827	1.095
Skew.	0.466	−0.304	0.052	1.599	−0.033	0.776	0.110	−0.084	0.534	0.761	2.214
Kurt.	6.419	1.132	1.048	4.961	−0.125	2.964	0.989	1.870	2.184	2.369	15.290

All stocks, 1982 to 1986

Mean	−0.000	−0.099	−0.007	0.011	0.095	−0.114	−0.067	0.050	0.005	0.011	−0.013
S.D.	1.000	0.883	1.002	1.109	0.956	0.924	0.801	0.826	0.934	0.850	1.026
Skew.	0.460	0.464	0.441	0.372	−0.165	0.473	−1.249	0.231	0.467	0.528	0.867
Kurt.	6.799	2.280	6.128	2.566	2.735	3.208	5.278	1.108	4.234	1.515	7.400

All stocks, 1987 to 1991

Mean	−0.000	−0.037	0.033	−0.091	−0.040	0.053	0.003	0.040	−0.020	−0.022	−0.017
S.D.	1.000	0.848	0.895	0.955	0.818	0.857	0.981	0.894	0.833	0.873	1.052
Skew.	−0.018	−0.526	0.272	0.108	0.231	0.165	−1.216	0.293	0.124	−1.184	−0.368
Kurt.	13.478	3.835	4.395	2.247	1.469	4.422	9.586	1.646	3.973	4.808	4.297

All stocks, 1992 to 1996

Mean	−0.000	−0.014	0.069	−0.231	−0.272	0.122	0.041	0.082	0.011	0.102	−0.016
S.D.	1.000	0.935	1.021	1.406	1.187	0.953	1.078	0.814	0.996	0.960	1.035
Skew.	0.308	0.545	1.305	−3.988	−0.502	−0.190	2.460	−0.167	−0.129	−0.091	0.379
Kurt.	8.683	2.249	6.684	27.022	3.947	1.235	12.883	0.506	6.399	1.507	3.358

Table 2.4 Summary statistics (mean, standard deviation, skewness, and excess kurtosis) of raw and conditional one-day normalized returns of Nasdaq stocks from 1962 to 1996, in five-year subperiods, and in size quintiles. Conditional returns are defined as the daily return three days following the conclusion of an occurrence of one of 10 technical indicators: head-and-shoulders (HS), inverted head-and-shoulders (IHS), broadening top (BTOP), broadening bottom (BBOT), triangle top (TTOP), triangle bottom (TBOT), rectangle top (RTOP), rectangle bottom (RBOT), double top (DTOP), and double bottom (DBOT). All returns have been normalized by subtraction of their means and division by their standard deviations.

Moment	Raw	HS	IHS	BTOP	BBOT	TTOP	TBOT	RTOP	RBOT	DTOP	DBOT
All stocks, 1962 to 1996											
Mean	0.000	−0.016	0.042	−0.009	0.009	−0.020	0.017	0.052	0.043	0.003	−0.035
S.D.	1.000	0.907	0.994	0.960	0.995	0.984	0.932	0.948	0.929	0.933	0.880
Skew.	0.608	−0.017	1.290	0.397	0.586	0.895	0.716	0.710	0.755	0.405	−0.104
Kurt.	12.728	3.039	8.774	3.246	2.783	6.692	3.844	5.173	4.368	4.150	2.052
Smallest quintile, 1962 to 1996											
Mean	−0.000	0.018	−0.032	0.087	−0.153	0.059	0.108	0.136	0.013	0.040	0.043
S.D.	1.000	0.845	1.319	0.874	0.894	1.113	1.044	1.187	0.982	0.773	0.906
Skew.	0.754	0.325	1.756	−0.239	−0.109	2.727	2.300	1.741	0.199	0.126	−0.368
Kurt.	15.859	1.096	4.221	1.490	0.571	14.270	10.594	8.670	1.918	0.127	0.730
2nd quintile, 1962 to 1996											
Mean	−0.000	−0.064	0.076	−0.109	−0.093	−0.085	−0.038	−0.066	−0.015	0.039	−0.034
S.D.	1.000	0.848	0.991	1.106	1.026	0.805	0.997	0.898	0.897	1.119	0.821
Skew.	0.844	0.406	1.892	−0.122	0.635	0.036	0.455	−0.579	0.416	1.196	0.190
Kurt.	16.738	2.127	11.561	2.496	3.458	0.689	1.332	2.699	3.871	3.910	0.777
3rd quintile, 1962 to 1996											
Mean	−0.000	0.033	0.028	0.078	0.210	−0.030	0.068	0.117	0.210	−0.109	−0.075
S.D.	1.000	0.933	0.906	0.931	0.971	0.825	1.002	0.992	0.970	0.997	0.973
Skew.	0.698	0.223	0.529	0.656	0.326	0.539	0.442	0.885	0.820	−0.163	0.123
Kurt.	12.161	1.520	1.526	1.003	0.430	1.673	1.038	2.908	4.915	5.266	2.573

4th quintile, 1962 to 1996

Mean	0.000	-0.079	0.037	-0.006	-0.044	-0.080	0.007	0.084	0.044	0.038	-0.048
S.D.	1.000	0.911	0.957	0.992	0.975	1.076	0.824	0.890	0.851	0.857	0.819
Skew.	0.655	-0.456	2.671	-0.174	0.385	0.554	0.717	0.290	1.034	0.154	-0.149
Kurt.	11.043	2.525	19.593	2.163	1.601	7.723	3.930	1.555	2.982	2.807	2.139

Largest quintile, 1962 to 1996

Mean	0.000	0.026	0.058	-0.070	0.031	0.052	-0.013	0.001	-0.024	0.032	-0.018
S.D.	1.000	0.952	1.002	0.895	1.060	1.076	0.871	0.794	0.958	0.844	0.877
Skew.	0.100	-0.266	-0.144	1.699	1.225	0.409	0.025	0.105	1.300	0.315	-0.363
Kurt.	7.976	5.807	4.367	8.371	5.778	1.970	2.696	1.336	7.503	2.091	2.241

All stocks, 1962 to 1966

Mean	-0.000	0.116	0.041	0.099	0.090	0.028	-0.066	0.100	0.010	0.096	0.027
S.D.	1.000	0.912	0.949	0.989	1.039	1.015	0.839	0.925	0.873	1.039	0.840
Skew.	0.575	0.711	1.794	0.252	1.258	1.601	0.247	2.016	1.021	0.533	-0.351
Kurt.	6.555	1.538	9.115	2.560	6.445	7.974	1.324	13.653	5.603	6.277	2.243

All stocks, 1967 to 1971

Mean	-0.000	-0.127	0.114	0.121	0.016	0.045	0.077	0.154	0.136	-0.000	0.006
S.D.	1.000	0.864	0.805	0.995	1.013	0.976	0.955	1.016	1.118	0.882	0.930
Skew.	0.734	-0.097	1.080	0.574	0.843	1.607	0.545	0.810	1.925	0.465	0.431
Kurt.	5.194	1.060	2.509	0.380	2.928	10.129	1.908	1.712	5.815	1.585	2.476

All stocks, 1972 to 1976

Mean	0.000	0.014	0.089	-0.403	-0.034	-0.132	-0.422	-0.076	0.108	-0.004	-0.163
S.D.	1.000	0.575	0.908	0.569	0.803	0.618	0.830	0.886	0.910	0.924	0.564
Skew.	0.466	-0.281	0.973	-1.176	0.046	-0.064	-1.503	-2.728	2.047	-0.551	-0.791
Kurt.	17.228	2.194	1.828	0.077	0.587	-0.444	2.137	13.320	9.510	1.434	2.010

All stocks, 1977 to 1981

Mean	-0.000	0.025	-0.212	-0.112	-0.056	-0.110	0.086	0.055	0.177	0.081	0.040
S.D.	1.000	0.769	1.025	1.091	0.838	0.683	0.834	1.036	1.047	0.986	0.880
Skew.	1.092	0.230	-1.516	-0.731	0.368	0.430	0.249	2.391	2.571	1.520	-0.291
Kurt.	20.043	1.618	4.397	3.766	0.460	0.962	4.722	9.137	10.961	7.127	3.682

(continued)

Table 2.4 (continued)

Moment	Raw	HS	IHS	BTOP	BBOT	TTOP	TBOT	RTOP	RBOT	DTOP	DBOT
All stocks, 1982 to 1986											
Mean	0.000	-0.147	0.204	-0.137	-0.001	-0.053	-0.022	-0.028	0.116	-0.224	-0.052
S.D.	1.000	1.073	1.442	0.804	1.040	0.982	1.158	0.910	0.830	0.868	1.082
Skew.	1.267	-1.400	2.192	0.001	0.048	1.370	1.690	-0.120	0.048	0.001	-0.091
Kurt.	21.789	4.899	10.530	0.863	0.732	8.460	7.086	0.780	0.444	1.174	0.818
All stocks, 1987 to 1991											
Mean	0.000	0.012	0.120	-0.080	-0.031	-0.052	0.038	0.098	0.049	-0.048	-0.122
S.D.	1.000	0.907	1.136	0.925	0.826	1.007	0.878	0.936	1.000	0.772	0.860
Skew.	0.104	-0.326	0.976	-0.342	0.234	-0.248	1.002	0.233	0.023	-0.105	-0.375
Kurt.	12.688	3.922	5.183	1.839	0.734	2.796	2.768	1.038	2.350	0.313	2.598
All stocks, 1992 to 1996											
Mean	0.000	-0.119	-0.058	-0.033	-0.013	-0.078	0.086	-0.006	-0.011	0.003	-0.105
S.D.	1.000	0.926	0.854	0.964	1.106	1.093	0.901	0.973	0.879	0.932	0.875
Skew.	-0.036	0.079	-0.015	1.399	0.158	-0.127	0.150	0.283	0.236	0.039	-0.097
Kurt.	5.377	2.818	-0.059	7.584	0.626	2.019	1.040	1.266	1.445	1.583	0.205

Table 2.5 *Goodness-of-fit diagnostics for the conditional one-day normalized returns, conditional on ten technical indicators, for a sample of 350 NYSE/AMEX stocks from 1962 to 1996 (ten stocks per size-quintile with at least 80 per cent non-missing prices are randomly chosen in each five-year subperiod, yielding 50 stocks per subperiod over seven subperiods). For each pattern, the percentage of conditional returns that fall within each of the ten unconditional-returns deciles is tabulated. If conditioning on the pattern provides no information, the expected percentage falling in each decile is 10 per cent. Asymptotic z-statistics for this null hypothesis are reported in parentheses, and the χ^2 goodness-of-fitness test statistic Q is reported in the last column with the p-value in parentheses below the statistic. The ten technical indicators are as follows: head-and-shoulders (HS), inverted head-and-shoulders (IHS), broadening top (BTOP), broadening bottom (BBOT), triangle top (TTOP), triangle bottom (TBOT), rectangle top (RTOP), rectangle bottom (RBOT), double top (DTOP), and double bottom (DBOT)*

Pattern	\multicolumn{10}{c}{Decile}										Q (p-Value)
	1	2	3	4	5	6	7	8	9	10	
HS	8.9	10.4	11.2	11.7	12.2	7.9	9.2	10.4	10.8	7.1	39.31
	(−1.49)	(0.56)	(1.49)	(2.16)	(2.73)	(−3.05)	(−1.04)	(0.48)	(1.04)	(−4.46)	(0.000)
IHS	8.6	9.7	9.4	11.2	13.7	7.7	9.1	11.1	9.6	10.0	40.95
	(−2.05)	(−0.36)	(−0.88)	(1.60)	(4.34)	(−3.44)	(−1.32)	(1.38)	(−0.62)	(−0.03)	(0.000)
BTOP	9.4	10.6	10.6	11.9	8.7	6.6	9.2	13.7	9.2	10.1	23.40
	(−0.57)	(0.54)	(0.54)	(1.55)	(−1.25)	(−3.66)	(−0.71)	(2.87)	(−0.71)	(0.06)	(0.005)
BBOT	11.5	9.9	13.0	11.1	7.8	9.2	8.3	9.0	10.7	9.6	16.87
	(1.28)	(−0.10)	(2.42)	(0.95)	(−2.30)	(−0.73)	(−1.70)	(−1.00)	(0.62)	(−0.35)	(0.051)
TTOP	7.8	10.4	10.9	11.3	9.0	9.9	10.0	10.7	10.5	9.7	12.03
	(−2.94)	(0.42)	(1.03)	(1.46)	(−1.30)	(−0.13)	(−0.04)	(0.77)	(0.60)	(−0.41)	(0.212)
TBOT	8.9	10.6	10.9	12.2	9.2	8.7	9.3	11.6	8.7	9.8	17.12
	(−1.35)	(0.72)	(0.99)	(2.36)	(−0.93)	(−1.57)	(−0.83)	(1.69)	(−1.57)	(−0.22)	(0.047)
RTOP	8.4	9.9	9.2	10.5	12.5	10.1	10.0	10.0	11.4	8.1	22.72
	(−2.27)	(−0.10)	(−1.10)	(0.58)	(2.89)	(0.16)	(−0.02)	(−0.02)	(1.70)	(−2.69)	(0.007)
RBOT	8.6	9.6	7.8	10.5	12.9	10.8	11.6	9.3	10.3	8.7	33.94
	(−2.01)	(−0.56)	(−3.30)	(0.60)	(3.45)	(1.07)	(1.98)	(−0.99)	(0.44)	(−1.91)	(0.000)
DTOP	8.2	10.9	9.6	12.4	11.8	7.5	8.2	11.3	10.3	9.7	50.97
	(−2.92)	(1.36)	(−0.64)	(3.29)	(2.61)	(−4.39)	(−2.92)	(1.83)	(0.46)	(−0.41)	(0.000)
DBOT	9.7	9.9	10.0	10.9	11.4	8.5	9.2	10.0	10.7	9.8	12.92
	(−0.48)	(−0.18)	(−0.04)	(1.37)	(1.97)	(−2.40)	(−1.33)	(0.04)	(0.96)	(−0.33)	(0.166)

Table 2.6 Goodness-of-fit diagnostics for the conditional one-day normalized returns, conditional on ten technical indicators, for a sample of 350 Nasdaq stocks from 1962 to 1996 (ten stocks per size-quintile with at least 80 per cent non-missing prices are randomly chosen in each five-year subperiod, yielding 50 stocks per subperiod over seven subperiods). For each pattern, the percentage of conditional returns that fall within each of the ten unconditional-return deciles is tabulated. If conditioning on the pattern provides no information, the expected percentage falling in each decile is 10 per cent. Asymptotic z-statistics for this null hypothesis are reported in parentheses, and the χ^2 goodness-of-fitness test statistic Q is reported in the last column with the p-value in parentheses below the statistic. The ten technical indicators are as follows: head-and-shoulders (HS), inverted head-and-shoulders (IHS), broadening top (BTOP), broadening bottom (BBOT), triangle top (TTOP), triangle bottom (TBOT), rectangle top (RTOP), rectangle bottom (RBOT), double top (DTOP), and double bottom (DBOT)

Pattern					Decile						Q (p-Value)
	1	2	3	4	5	6	7	8	9	10	
HS	10.8	10.8	13.7	8.6	8.5	6.0	6.0	12.5	13.5	9.7	64.41
	(0.76)	(0.76)	(3.27)	(−1.52)	(−1.65)	(−5.13)	(−5.13)	(2.30)	(3.10)	(−0.32)	(0.000)
IHS	9.4	14.1	12.5	8.0	7.7	4.8	6.4	13.5	12.5	11.3	75.84
	(−0.56)	(3.35)	(2.15)	(−2.16)	(−2.45)	(−7.01)	(−4.26)	(2.90)	(2.15)	(1.14)	(0.000)
BTOP	11.6	12.3	12.8	7.7	8.2	6.8	4.3	13.3	12.1	10.9	34.12
	(1.01)	(1.44)	(1.71)	(−1.73)	(−1.32)	(−2.62)	(−5.64)	(1.97)	(1.30)	(0.57)	(0.000)
BBOT	11.4	11.4	14.8	5.9	6.7	9.6	5.7	11.4	9.8	13.2	43.26
	(1.00)	(1.00)	(3.03)	(−3.91)	(−2.98)	(−0.27)	(−4.17)	(1.00)	(−0.12)	(2.12)	(0.000)
TTOP	10.7	12.1	16.2	6.2	7.9	8.7	4.0	12.5	11.4	10.2	92.09
	(0.67)	(1.89)	(4.93)	(−4.54)	(−2.29)	(−1.34)	(−8.93)	(2.18)	(1.29)	(0.23)	(0.000)
TBOT	9.9	11.3	15.6	7.9	7.7	5.7	5.3	14.6	12.0	10.0	85.26
	(−0.11)	(1.14)	(4.33)	(−2.24)	(−2.39)	(−5.20)	(−5.85)	(3.64)	(1.76)	(0.01)	(0.000)
RTOP	11.2	10.8	8.8	8.3	10.2	7.1	7.7	9.3	15.3	11.3	57.08
	(1.28)	(0.92)	(−1.40)	(−2.09)	(0.25)	(−3.87)	(−2.95)	(−0.75)	(4.92)	(1.37)	(0.000)
RBOT	8.9	12.3	8.9	8.9	11.6	8.9	7.0	9.5	13.6	10.3	45.79
	(−1.35)	(2.52)	(−1.35)	(−1.45)	(1.81)	(−1.35)	(−4.19)	(−0.66)	(3.85)	(0.36)	(0.000)
DTOP	11.0	12.6	11.7	9.0	9.2	5.5	5.8	11.6	12.3	11.3	71.29
	(1.12)	(2.71)	(1.81)	(−1.18)	(−0.98)	(−6.76)	(−6.26)	(1.73)	(2.39)	(1.47)	(0.000)
DBOT	10.9	11.5	13.1	8.0	8.1	7.1	7.6	11.5	12.8	9.3	51.23
	(0.98)	(1.60)	(3.09)	(−2.47)	(−2.35)	(−3.75)	(−3.09)	(1.60)	(2.85)	(−0.78)	(0.000)

returns, i.e., fewer patterns, the corresponding test statistics might be subject to greater sampling variation and lower power. However, this explanation can be ruled out from the frequency counts of Tables 2.1 and 2.2 – the number of patterns in the NYSE/AMEX sample is considerably larger than those of the Nasdaq sample for all ten patterns. Tables 2.5 and 2.6 seem to suggest important differences in the informativeness of technical indicators for NYSE/AMEX and Nasdaq stocks.

Tables 2.7 and 2.8 report the results of the Kolmogorov–Smirnov test (Equation (2.9)) of the equality of the conditional and unconditional return distributions for NYSE/AMEX (Table 2.7) and Nasdaq (Table 2.8) stocks, respectively, from 1962 to 1996, in five-year subperiods, and in market-capitalization quintiles. Recall that conditional returns are defined as the one-day return starting three days following the conclusion of an occurrence of a pattern. The *p*-values are with respect to the asymptotic distribution of the Kolmogorov–Smirnov test statistic given in Equation (2.20).

Table 2.7 shows that for NYSE/AMEX stocks, five of the ten patterns – HS, BBOT, RTOP, RBOT, and DTOP – yield statistically significant test statistics, with *p*-values ranging from 0.000 for RBOT to 0.021 for DTOP patterns. However, for the other five patterns, the *p*-values range from 0.104 for IHS to 0.393 for TTOP, which implies an inability to distinguish between the conditional and unconditional distributions of normalized returns.

When we also condition on declining volume trend, the statistical significance declines for most patterns, but the statistical significance of TBOT patterns increases. In contrast, conditioning on increasing volume trend yields an increase in the statistical significance of BTOP patterns. This difference may suggest an important role for volume trend in TBOT and BTOP patterns. The difference between the increasing and decreasing volume-trend conditional distributions is statistically insignificant for almost all the patterns (the sole exception is the TBOT pattern). This drop in statistical significance may be due to a lack of power of the Kolmogorov–Smirnov test given the relatively small sample sizes of these conditional returns (see Table 2.1 for frequency counts).

Table 2.8 reports corresponding results for the Nasdaq sample, and as in Table 2.6, in contrast to the NYSE/AMEX results, here all the patterns are statistically significant at the 5 per cent level. This is especially significant because the the Nasdaq sample exhibits far fewer patterns than the NYSE/AMEX sample (see Tables 2.1 and 2.2), hence the Kolmogorov–Smirnov test is likely to have lower power in this case.

As with the NYSE/AMEX sample, volume trend seems to provide little incremental information for the Nasdaq sample except in one case: increasing volume and BTOP. And except for the TTOP pattern, the

Table 2.7 Kolmogorov–Smirnov test of the equality of conditional and unconditional one-day return distributions for NYSE/AMEX stocks from 1962 to 1996, in five-year subperiods, and in size quintiles. Conditional returns are defined as the daily return three days following the conclusion of an occurrence of one of ten technical indicators: head-and-shoulders (HS), inverted head-and-shoulders (IHS), broadening top (BTOP), broadening bottom (BBOT), triangle top (TTOP), triangle bottom (TBOT), rectangle top (RTOP), rectangle bottom (RBOT), double top (DTOP), and double bottom (DBOT). All returns have been normalized by subtraction of their means and division by their standard deviations. p-values are with respect to the asymptotic distribution of the Kolmogorov–Smirnov test statistic. The symbols '$\tau(\searrow)$' and '$\tau(\nearrow)$' indicate that the conditional distribution is also conditioned on decreasing and increasing volume trend, respectively

Statistic	HS	IHS	BTOP	BBOT	TTOP	TBOT	RTOP	RBOT	DTOP	DBOT
All stocks, 1962 to 1996										
γ	1.89	1.22	1.15	1.76	0.90	1.09	1.84	2.45	1.51	1.06
p-value	0.002	0.104	0.139	0.004	0.393	0.185	0.002	0.000	0.021	0.215
$\gamma\tau(\searrow)$	1.49	0.95	0.44	0.62	0.73	1.33	1.37	1.77	0.96	0.78
p-value	0.024	0.327	0.989	0.839	0.657	0.059	0.047	0.004	0.319	0.579
$\gamma\tau(\nearrow)$	0.72	1.05	1.33	1.59	0.92	1.29	1.13	1.24	0.74	0.84
p-value	0.671	0.220	0.059	0.013	0.368	0.073	0.156	0.090	0.638	0.481
γ Diff.	0.88	0.54	0.59	0.94	0.75	1.37	0.79	1.20	0.82	0.71
p-value	0.418	0.935	0.879	0.342	0.628	0.046	0.557	0.111	0.512	0.698
Smallest quintile, 1962 to 1996										
γ	0.59	1.19	0.72	1.20	0.98	1.43	1.09	1.19	0.84	0.78
p-value	0.872	0.116	0.679	0.114	0.290	0.033	0.188	0.120	0.485	0.583
$\gamma\tau(\searrow)$	0.67	0.80	1.16	0.69	1.00	1.46	1.31	0.94	1.12	0.73
p-value	0.765	0.540	0.136	0.723	0.271	0.029	0.065	0.339	0.165	0.663
$\gamma\tau(\nearrow)$	0.43	0.95	0.67	1.03	0.47	0.88	0.51	0.93	0.94	0.58
p-value	0.994	0.325	0.756	0.236	0.981	0.423	0.959	0.356	0.342	0.892
γ Diff.	0.52	0.48	1.14	0.68	0.48	0.98	0.98	0.79	1.16	0.62
p-value	0.951	0.974	0.151	0.741	0.976	0.291	0.294	0.552	0.133	0.840
2nd quintile, 1962 to 1996										
γ	1.82	1.63	0.93	0.92	0.82	0.84	0.88	1.29	1.46	0.84
p-value	0.003	0.010	0.353	0.365	0.505	0.485	0.417	0.073	0.029	0.478
$\gamma\tau(\searrow)$	1.62	1.03	0.88	0.42	0.91	0.90	0.71	0.86	1.50	0.97
p-value	0.010	0.242	0.427	0.994	0.378	0.394	0.703	0.443	0.022	0.298

$\gamma\tau(\nearrow)$	1.06	1.63	0.96	0.83	0.89	0.98	1.19	1.15	0.96	0.99
p-value	0.213	0.010	0.317	0.497	0.407	0.289	0.119	0.141	0.317	0.286
γ Diff.	0.78	0.94	1.04	0.71	1.22	0.92	0.99	0.79	1.18	0.68
p-value	0.576	0.334	0.228	0.687	0.102	0.361	0.276	0.564	0.126	0.745
3rd quintile, 1962 to 1996										
γ	0.83	1.56	1.00	1.28	0.57	1.03	1.96	1.50	1.55	1.14
p-value	0.502	0.016	0.266	0.074	0.903	0.243	0.001	0.023	0.016	0.150
$\gamma\tau(\searrow)$	0.95	0.94	0.66	0.76	0.61	0.82	1.45	1.61	1.17	1.01
p-value	0.326	0.346	0.775	0.613	0.854	0.520	0.031	0.012	0.131	0.258
$\gamma\tau(\nearrow)$	1.05	1.43	0.93	1.14	0.63	0.80	0.93	0.78	0.59	0.86
p-value	0.223	0.033	0.350	0.147	0.826	0.544	0.354	0.578	0.878	0.450
γ Diff.	1.02	1.14	0.45	0.48	0.50	0.89	0.66	0.91	0.72	1.15
p-value	0.246	0.148	0.986	0.974	0.964	0.413	0.774	0.383	0.670	0.143
4th quintile, 1962 to 1996										
γ	0.72	0.61	1.29	0.84	0.61	0.84	1.37	1.37	0.72	0.53
p-value	0.683	0.852	0.071	0.479	0.855	0.480	0.048	0.047	0.682	0.943
$\gamma\tau(\searrow)$	1.01	0.95	0.83	0.96	0.78	0.84	1.34	0.72	0.62	1.01
p-value	0.255	0.330	0.504	0.311	0.585	0.487	0.056	0.680	0.841	0.258
$\gamma\tau(\nearrow)$	0.93	0.66	1.29	0.96	1.16	0.69	0.64	1.16	0.69	0.85
p-value	0.349	0.772	0.072	0.316	0.137	0.731	0.810	0.136	0.720	0.468
γ Diff.	1.10	0.97	0.64	1.16	1.31	0.78	0.64	0.92	0.66	1.10
p-value	0.175	0.301	0.804	0.138	0.065	0.571	0.806	0.363	0.780	0.176
Largest quintile, 1962 to 1996										
γ	1.25	1.16	0.98	0.48	0.50	0.80	0.94	1.76	0.90	1.28
p-value	0.088	0.136	0.287	0.977	0.964	0.544	0.346	0.004	0.395	0.077
$\gamma\tau(\searrow)$	1.12	0.90	0.57	0.78	0.64	1.17	0.91	0.87	0.64	1.20
p-value	0.164	0.386	0.906	0.580	0.806	0.127	0.379	0.442	0.802	0.114
$\gamma\tau(\nearrow)$	0.81	0.93	0.83	0.61	0.69	0.81	0.73	0.87	0.46	0.88
p-value	0.522	0.350	0.495	0.854	0.729	0.532	0.661	0.432	0.982	0.418
γ Diff.	0.71	0.54	0.59	0.64	0.76	1.21	0.85	1.11	0.54	0.79
p-value	0.699	0.934	0.874	0.800	0.607	0.110	0.467	0.170	0.929	0.552

(continued)

Table 2.7 (*continued*)

Statistic	HS	IHS	BTOP	BBOT	TTOP	TBOT	RTOP	RBOT	DTOP	DBOT
All stocks, 1962 to 1966										
γ	1.29	1.67	1.07	0.72	0.75	1.32	1.20	1.53	2.04	1.73
p-value	0.072	0.007	0.202	0.671	0.634	0.062	0.112	0.018	0.001	0.005
$\gamma\tau(\searrow)$	0.83	1.01	1.04	0.80	0.63	1.80	0.66	1.84	1.03	1.54
p-value	0.499	0.260	0.232	0.539	0.826	0.003	0.771	0.002	0.244	0.017
$\gamma\tau(\nearrow)$	1.13	1.13	0.84	0.84	0.58	1.40	1.12	0.83	1.09	1.16
p-value	0.156	0.153	0.480	0.475	0.894	0.040	0.163	0.492	0.183	0.135
γ Diff.	0.65	0.71	0.75	0.76	0.60	1.90	0.68	1.35	0.73	0.83
p-value	0.799	0.691	0.629	0.615	0.863	0.001	0.741	0.052	0.657	0.503
All stocks, 1967 to 1971										
γ	1.10	0.96	0.60	0.65	0.98	0.76	1.29	1.65	0.87	1.22
p-value	0.177	0.317	0.867	0.797	0.292	0.606	0.071	0.009	0.436	0.101
$\gamma\tau(\searrow)$	1.02	0.80	0.53	0.85	0.97	0.77	0.71	1.42	0.97	1.06
p-value	0.248	0.551	0.943	0.464	0.303	0.590	0.700	0.035	0.300	0.214
$\gamma\tau(\nearrow)$	1.08	0.86	0.68	0.91	1.11	0.82	0.79	0.73	0.71	0.96
p-value	0.190	0.454	0.750	0.373	0.169	0.508	0.554	0.660	0.699	0.315
γ Diff.	1.36	0.51	0.53	0.76	0.68	0.71	0.71	0.98	1.06	1.12
p-value	0.049	0.956	0.942	0.616	0.751	0.699	0.701	0.290	0.210	0.163
All stocks, 1972 to 1976										
γ	0.47	0.75	0.87	1.56	1.21	0.75	0.87	0.94	1.64	1.20
p-value	0.980	0.620	0.441	0.015	0.106	0.627	0.441	0.341	0.009	0.113
$\gamma\tau(\searrow)$	0.80	0.40	0.50	1.24	1.21	0.65	1.26	0.63	0.70	1.39
p-value	0.539	0.998	0.966	0.093	0.106	0.794	0.084	0.821	0.718	0.041
$\gamma\tau(\nearrow)$	0.49	0.78	0.94	1.21	1.12	1.03	0.81	0.95	0.84	0.70
p-value	0.970	0.577	0.340	0.108	0.159	0.244	0.521	0.331	0.485	0.719
γ Diff.	0.55	0.56	0.51	0.95	0.81	1.11	1.15	0.62	0.67	1.31
p-value	0.925	0.915	0.960	0.333	0.525	0.170	0.141	0.836	0.767	0.065

All stocks, 1977 to 1981

γ	1.16	0.73	0.76	1.16	0.82	1.14	1.01	0.87	0.86	1.79
p-value	0.138	0.665	0.617	0.136	0.506	0.147	0.263	0.428	0.449	0.003
$\gamma\tau(\searrow)$	1.04	0.73	1.00	1.31	1.10	1.32	0.83	0.80	1.20	1.81
p-value	0.228	0.654	0.274	0.065	0.176	0.062	0.494	0.550	0.113	0.003
$\gamma\tau(\nearrow)$	0.75	0.84	0.88	0.65	0.67	0.76	1.51	1.41	0.86	0.99
p-value	0.623	0.476	0.426	0.799	0.754	0.602	0.020	0.037	0.450	0.280
γ Diff.	0.67	0.94	0.88	0.70	0.65	0.70	1.11	1.29	1.16	0.70
p-value	0.767	0.335	0.423	0.708	0.785	0.716	0.172	0.073	0.137	0.713

All stocks, 1982 to 1986

γ	1.57	0.99	0.59	1.46	1.47	1.04	0.87	0.68	0.76	0.90
p-value	0.015	0.276	0.883	0.029	0.027	0.232	0.431	0.742	0.617	0.387
$\gamma\tau(\searrow)$	1.17	0.68	0.44	1.30	1.53	1.21	1.08	0.93	0.84	0.88
p-value	0.129	0.741	0.991	0.070	0.018	0.106	0.190	0.356	0.478	0.421
$\gamma\tau(\nearrow)$	0.81	1.03	0.74	0.62	0.83	1.23	0.77	0.79	0.63	0.81
p-value	0.533	0.243	0.640	0.831	0.499	0.097	0.597	0.564	0.821	0.528
γ Diff.	0.51	0.79	0.70	0.81	0.74	1.21	0.73	0.75	0.93	0.74
p-value	0.961	0.567	0.717	0.532	0.643	0.107	0.657	0.623	0.352	0.642

All stocks, 1987 to 1991

γ	1.36	1.53	1.05	0.67	0.75	0.86	0.60	1.09	1.20	0.67
p-value	0.048	0.019	0.219	0.756	0.627	0.456	0.862	0.185	0.111	0.764
$\gamma\tau(\searrow)$	0.52	1.16	1.25	0.72	1.03	0.81	0.81	0.61	1.07	0.68
p-value	0.953	0.135	0.087	0.673	0.235	0.522	0.527	0.848	0.201	0.751
$\gamma\tau(\nearrow)$	1.72	1.03	0.64	1.37	0.74	1.10	1.04	1.20	1.02	1.32
p-value	0.006	0.241	0.813	0.046	0.639	0.181	0.232	0.111	0.250	0.062
γ Diff.	1.11	1.29	1.07	1.06	0.67	0.93	0.89	0.74	0.84	1.17
p-value	0.168	0.072	0.201	0.215	0.753	0.357	0.403	0.638	0.483	0.129

(continued)

Table 2.7 *(continued)*

Statistic	HS	IHS	BTOP	BBOT	TTOP	TBOT	RTOP	RBOT	DTOP	DBOT
All stocks, 1992 to 1996										
γ	1.50	1.31	1.05	1.89	1.27	0.94	1.23	0.66	1.72	1.54
p-value	0.022	0.066	0.222	0.002	0.078	0.343	0.095	0.782	0.005	0.018
$\gamma\tau(\searrow)$	0.87	1.05	0.60	0.89	1.11	1.03	0.90	0.65	0.99	1.12
p-value	0.443	0.218	0.858	0.404	0.174	0.242	0.390	0.787	0.283	0.165
$\gamma\tau(\nearrow)$	0.72	0.66	0.75	1.42	1.02	0.58	0.61	0.64	1.36	0.93
p-value	0.670	0.778	0.624	0.036	0.246	0.895	0.854	0.813	0.048	0.357
γ Diff.	0.58	0.88	0.50	0.49	0.43	0.81	0.60	0.46	0.96	0.99
p-value	0.887	0.422	0.966	0.971	0.993	0.528	0.858	0.984	0.314	0.282

Table 2.8 *Kolmogorov–Smirnov test of the equality of conditional and unconditional one-day return distributions for NASDAQ stocks from 1962 to 1996, in five-year subperiods, and in size quintiles. Conditional returns are defined as the daily return three days following the conclusion of an occurrence of one of 10 technical indicators: head-and-shoulders (HS), inverted head-and-shoulders (IHS), broadening top (BTOP), broadening bottom (BBOT), triangle top (TTOP), triangle bottom (TBOT), rectangle top (RTOP), rectangle bottom (RBOT), double top (DTOP), and double bottom (DBOT). All returns have been normalized by subtraction of their means and division by their standard deviations. p-values are with respect to the asymptotic distribution of the Kolmogorov–Smirnov test statistic. The symbols '$\tau(\searrow)$' and '$\tau(\nearrow)$' indicate that the conditional distribution is also conditioned on decreasing and increasing volume trend, respectively*

Statistic	HS	IHS	BTOP	BBOT	TTOP	TBOT	RTOP	RBOT	DTOP	DBOT
All stocks, 1962 to 1996										
γ	2.31	2.68	1.60	1.84	2.81	2.34	2.69	1.90	2.29	2.06
p-value	0.000	0.000	0.012	0.002	0.000	0.000	0.000	0.001	0.000	0.000
$\gamma\tau(\searrow)$	1.86	1.53	1.35	0.99	1.97	1.95	2.16	1.73	1.38	1.94
p-value	0.002	0.019	0.052	0.281	0.001	0.001	0.000	0.005	0.045	0.001
$\gamma\tau(\nearrow)$	1.59	2.10	1.82	1.59	1.89	1.18	1.57	1.22	2.15	1.46
p-value	0.013	0.000	0.003	0.013	0.002	0.126	0.014	0.102	0.000	0.028
γ Diff.	1.08	0.86	1.10	0.80	1.73	0.74	0.91	0.75	0.76	1.52
p-value	0.195	0.450	0.175	0.542	0.005	0.637	0.379	0.621	0.619	0.020
Smallest quintile, 1962 to 1996										
γ	1.51	2.16	1.72	1.68	1.22	1.55	2.13	1.70	1.74	1.98
p-value	0.021	0.000	0.006	0.007	0.101	0.016	0.000	0.006	0.005	0.001
$\gamma\tau(\searrow)$	1.16	1.30	0.85	1.14	1.25	1.62	1.43	1.05	1.08	1.95
p-value	0.139	0.070	0.463	0.150	0.089	0.010	0.033	0.216	0.191	0.001
$\gamma\tau(\nearrow)$	0.85	1.73	1.61	2.00	1.34	0.79	1.58	1.52	1.47	1.20
p-value	0.462	0.005	0.012	0.001	0.055	0.553	0.014	0.019	0.026	0.115
γ Diff.	1.04	0.95	0.83	1.44	1.39	0.78	0.95	0.73	0.94	1.09
p-value	0.227	0.334	0.493	0.031	0.042	0.574	0.326	0.654	0.338	0.184

(continued)

Table 2.8 (*continued*)

Statistic	HS	IHS	BTOP	BBOT	TTOP	TBOT	RTOP	RBOT	DTOP	DBOT
2nd quintile, 1962 to 1996										
γ	1.55	1.46	0.94	1.44	1.24	1.08	1.20	1.10	1.90	1.27
p-value	0.016	0.029	0.341	0.031	0.095	0.192	0.113	0.175	0.001	0.078
$\gamma\tau(\searrow)$	1.11	1.13	1.08	0.92	1.23	0.79	1.34	1.19	1.09	1.61
p-value	0.173	0.157	0.192	0.371	0.097	0.557	0.055	0.117	0.185	0.011
$\gamma\tau(\nearrow)$	1.37	0.87	0.73	0.97	1.38	1.29	1.12	0.91	1.12	0.94
p-value	0.048	0.439	0.665	0.309	0.044	0.073	0.162	0.381	0.165	0.343
γ Diff.	1.23	0.62	0.97	0.69	1.02	1.05	1.09	0.78	0.58	0.51
p-value	0.095	0.835	0.309	0.733	0.248	0.224	0.183	0.579	0.894	0.955
3rd quintile, 1962 to 1996										
γ	1.25	1.72	0.82	1.71	1.41	1.52	1.25	1.84	1.86	1.82
p-value	0.087	0.005	0.510	0.006	0.038	0.020	0.089	0.002	0.002	0.003
$\gamma\tau(\searrow)$	0.93	1.08	0.54	1.23	1.06	1.02	0.79	1.47	1.38	0.88
p-value	0.348	0.194	0.930	0.097	0.213	0.245	0.560	0.026	0.044	0.423
$\gamma\tau(\nearrow)$	0.59	1.14	0.97	1.37	0.75	1.01	1.13	1.34	1.37	1.78
p-value	0.873	0.146	0.309	0.047	0.633	0.262	0.159	0.054	0.047	0.003
γ Diff.	0.61	0.89	0.58	0.46	0.61	0.89	0.52	0.38	0.60	1.09
p-value	0.852	0.405	0.890	0.984	0.844	0.404	0.947	0.999	0.864	0.188
4th quintile, 1962 to 1996										
γ	1.04	0.82	1.20	0.98	1.30	1.25	1.88	0.79	0.94	0.66
p-value	0.233	0.510	0.111	0.298	0.067	0.087	0.002	0.553	0.341	0.779
$\gamma\tau(\searrow)$	0.81	0.54	0.57	1.05	0.92	1.06	1.23	0.72	1.53	0.87
p-value	0.528	0.935	0.897	0.217	0.367	0.215	0.097	0.672	0.019	0.431
$\gamma\tau(\nearrow)$	0.97	1.04	1.29	0.53	2.25	0.71	1.05	0.77	1.20	0.97
p-value	0.306	0.229	0.071	0.938	0.000	0.696	0.219	0.589	0.114	0.309
γ Diff.	1.17	0.89	0.98	0.97	1.86	0.62	0.93	0.73	1.31	0.92
p-value	0.128	0.400	0.292	0.301	0.002	0.843	0.352	0.653	0.065	0.371

Largest quintile, 1962 to 1996

γ	1.08	1.01	1.03	0.66	0.92	0.68	0.85	1.16	1.14	0.67
p-value	0.190	0.255	0.242	0.778	0.360	0.742	0.462	0.137	0.150	0.756
γτ(↘)	1.03	0.54	0.93	0.47	0.77	0.76	0.85	0.62	0.85	1.14
p-value	0.237	0.931	0.356	0.981	0.587	0.612	0.468	0.840	0.465	0.149
γτ(↗)	1.18	1.39	0.50	0.93	0.88	1.25	0.77	1.13	0.98	1.12
p-value	0.123	0.041	0.967	0.358	0.415	0.089	0.597	0.156	0.292	0.160
γ Diff.	0.94	1.25	0.73	0.84	0.76	1.11	0.73	0.86	0.86	0.77
p-value	0.342	0.090	0.668	0.476	0.617	0.169	0.662	0.457	0.454	0.598

All stocks, 1962 to 1966

γ	1.01	0.84	1.08	0.82	0.71	0.70	1.59	0.89	1.12	1.10
p-value	0.261	0.481	0.193	0.508	0.697	0.718	0.013	0.411	0.166	0.175
γτ(↘)	0.95	0.65	0.41	1.05	0.51	1.13	0.79	0.93	0.93	1.21
p-value	0.322	0.798	0.997	0.224	0.956	0.155	0.556	0.350	0.350	0.108
γτ(↗)	0.77	0.96	0.83	0.73	1.35	0.49	1.17	0.62	1.18	1.15
p-value	0.586	0.314	0.489	0.663	0.052	0.972	0.130	0.843	0.121	0.140
γ Diff.	1.10	0.67	0.32	0.69	1.29	0.58	0.80	0.75	0.98	1.06
p-value	0.174	0.761	1.000	0.735	0.071	0.892	0.551	0.620	0.298	0.208

All stocks, 1967 to 1971

γ	0.75	1.10	1.00	0.74	1.27	1.35	1.16	0.74	0.74	1.21
p-value	0.636	0.175	0.273	0.637	0.079	0.052	0.136	0.642	0.638	0.107
γτ(↘)	1.03	0.52	0.70	0.87	1.24	1.33	1.29	0.83	0.72	1.45
p-value	0.241	0.947	0.714	0.438	0.092	0.058	0.072	0.490	0.684	0.031
γτ(↗)	1.05	1.08	1.12	0.64	0.79	0.65	0.55	0.53	0.75	0.69
p-value	0.217	0.192	0.165	0.810	0.566	0.797	0.923	0.941	0.631	0.723
γ Diff.	1.24	0.89	0.66	0.78	1.07	0.88	0.88	0.40	0.91	0.76
p-value	0.093	0.413	0.770	0.585	0.203	0.418	0.423	0.997	0.385	0.602

All Stocks, 1972 to 1976

γ	0.82	1.28	1.84	1.13	1.45	1.53	1.31	0.96	0.85	1.76
p-value	0.509	0.077	0.002	0.156	0.029	0.019	0.064	0.314	0.464	0.004
γτ(↘)	0.59	0.73	-99.00	0.91	1.39	0.73	1.37	0.98	1.22	0.94
p-value	0.875	0.669	0.000	0.376	0.042	0.654	0.046	0.292	0.100	0.344
γτ(↗)	0.65	0.73	-99.00	-99.00	-99.00	-99.00	0.59	0.76	0.78	0.65
p-value	0.800	0.653	0.000	0.000	0.000	0.000	0.878	0.611	0.573	0.798
γ Diff.	0.48	0.57	-99.00	-99.00	-99.00	-99.00	0.63	0.55	0.92	0.37
p-value	0.974	0.902	0.000	0.000	0.000	0.000	0.828	0.925	0.362	0.999

(continued)

Table 2.8 *(continued)*

Statistic	HS	IHS	BTOP	BBOT	TTOP	TBOT	RTOP	RBOT	DTOP	DBOT
All stocks, 1977 to 1981										
γ	1.35	1.40	1.03	1.02	1.55	2.07	0.74	0.62	0.92	1.28
p-value	0.053	0.039	0.236	0.249	0.016	0.000	0.636	0.842	0.369	0.077
$\gamma\tau(\searrow)$	1.19	1.47	−99.00	−99.00	0.96	0.98	0.86	0.79	0.81	0.68
p-value	0.117	0.027	0.000	0.000	0.317	0.290	0.453	0.554	0.522	0.748
$\gamma\tau(\nearrow)$	0.69	0.94	0.80	−99.00	1.46	−99.00	0.56	0.82	1.06	0.94
p-value	0.728	0.341	0.542	0.000	0.028	0.000	0.918	0.514	0.207	0.336
γ Diff.	0.73	0.90	−99.00	−99.00	0.35	−99.00	0.44	0.37	0.80	0.53
p-value	0.665	0.395	0.000	0.000	1.000	0.000	0.991	0.999	0.541	0.944
All stocks, 1982 to 1986										
γ	1.66	1.59	1.17	0.73	1.46	1.69	1.04	1.24	2.44	1.27
p-value	0.008	0.013	0.129	0.654	0.028	0.006	0.232	0.093	0.000	0.078
$\gamma\tau(\searrow)$	1.65	1.10	0.46	0.74	0.95	1.47	0.83	1.18	1.20	0.59
p-value	0.009	0.176	0.984	0.641	0.330	0.027	0.503	0.121	0.112	0.873
$\gamma\tau(\nearrow)$	1.13	1.31	0.86	0.42	1.17	1.04	0.97	1.13	1.68	0.89
p-value	0.153	0.065	0.445	0.995	0.129	0.231	0.302	0.155	0.007	0.405
γ Diff.	0.67	0.39	0.51	0.42	0.85	0.43	0.41	0.67	0.66	0.75
p-value	0.755	0.998	0.957	0.994	0.462	0.993	0.996	0.766	0.782	0.627
All stocks, 1987 to 1991										
γ	1.24	1.29	0.91	0.88	1.28	1.41	2.01	1.49	1.55	1.53
p-value	0.091	0.070	0.384	0.421	0.074	0.039	0.001	0.024	0.017	0.019
$\gamma\tau(\searrow)$	1.05	1.00	1.00	0.78	1.68	0.92	1.67	1.25	0.61	0.86
p-value	0.221	0.266	0.274	0.580	0.007	0.369	0.008	0.087	0.849	0.448
$\gamma\tau(\nearrow)$	1.23	1.26	1.06	1.32	0.65	1.27	1.10	1.26	1.67	1.81
p-value	0.099	0.084	0.208	0.060	0.787	0.078	0.176	0.085	0.007	0.003
γ Diff.	0.80	0.91	1.22	1.28	1.22	0.92	0.87	0.81	1.07	1.05
p-value	0.552	0.375	0.103	0.075	0.102	0.360	0.431	0.520	0.202	0.217

All Stocks, 1992 to 1996

γ	1.21	1.61	0.84	0.90	0.97	0.91	1.60	1.51	1.13	1.00
p-value	0.108	0.011	0.476	0.394	0.299	0.379	0.012	0.021	0.156	0.265
$\gamma\tau(\searrow)$	0.68	1.02	0.81	0.78	0.81	0.93	0.79	1.07	0.94	0.64
p-value	0.752	0.246	0.530	0.578	0.532	0.357	0.558	0.201	0.340	0.814
$\gamma\tau(\nearrow)$	1.56	0.85	0.71	1.00	1.10	1.04	1.43	0.93	0.90	1.44
p-value	0.015	0.470	0.688	0.275	0.180	0.231	0.034	0.352	0.392	0.031
γ Diff.	1.45	0.59	0.94	0.62	1.15	1.14	0.64	0.52	0.59	1.35
p-value	0.030	0.879	0.346	0.840	0.139	0.148	0.814	0.953	0.874	0.052

Kolmogorov–Smirnov test still cannot distinguish between the decreasing and increasing volume-trend conditional distributions, as the last pair of rows of Table 2.8's first panel indicates.

2.5   MONTE CARLO ANALYSIS

Tables 2.9 and 2.10 contain bootstrap percentiles for the Kolmogorov–Smirnov test of the equality of conditional and unconditional one-day return distributions for NYSE/AMEX and Nasdaq stocks, respectively, from 1962 to 1996, for five-year subperiods, and for market-capitalization quintiles, under the null hypothesis of equality. For each of the two sets of market data, two sample sizes, m_1 and m_2, have been chosen to span the range of frequency counts of patterns reported in Tables 2.1 and 2.2. For each sample size m_i, we resample one-day normalized returns (with replacement) to obtain a boot-strap sample of m_i observations, compute the Kolmogorov–Smirnov test statistic (against the entire sample of one-day normalized returns), and repeat this procedure 1000 times. The percentiles of the asymptotic distribution are also reported for comparison under the column labelled 'Δ'.

Tables 2.9 and 2.10 show that for a broad range of sample sizes and across size quintiles, subperiod, and exchanges, the bootstrap distribution of the Kolmogorov–Smirnov statistic is well approximated by its asymptotic distribution, Equation (2.20).

2.6   CONCLUSIONS

In this chapter, we have proposed a new approach to evaluating the efficacy of technical analysis. Based on smoothing techniques such as nonparametric kernel regression, our approach incorporates the essence of technical analysis: to identify regularities in the time series of prices by extracting nonlinear patterns from noisy data. While human judgement is still superior to most computational algorithms in the area of visual pattern recognition, recent advances in statistical learning theory have had successful applications in fingerprint identification, handwriting analysis, and face recognition. Technical analysis may well be the next frontier for such methods.

We find that certain technical patterns, when applied to many stocks over many time periods, do provide incremental information, especially for Nasdaq stocks. While this does not necessarily imply that technical analysis can be used to generate 'excess' trading profits, it does raise the possibility that technical analysis can add value to the investment process.

Moreover, our methods suggest that technical analysis can be improved by using automated algorithms such as ours and that traditional patterns such as

Table 2.9 *Bootstrap percentiles for the Kolmogorov–Smirnov test of the equality of conditional and unconditional one-day return distributions for NYSE/AMEX and Nasdaq stocks from 1962 to 1996, and for size quintiles, under the null hypothesis of equality. For each of the two sets of market data, two sample sizes, m_1 and m_2, have been chosen to span the range of frequency counts of patterns reported in Table 2.1. For each sample size m_i, we resample one-day normalized returns (with replacement) to obtain a bootstrap sample of m_i observations, compute the Kolmogorov–Smirnov test statistic (against the entire sample of one-day normalized returns), and repeat this procedure 1000 times. The percentiles of the asymptotic distribution are also reported for comparison*

	NYSE/AMEX sample					Nasdaq sample				
Percentile	m_1	$\Delta_{m_1,n}$	m_2	$\Delta_{m_2,n}$	Δ	m_1	$\Delta_{m_1,n}$	m_2	$\Delta_{m_2,n}$	Δ
All stocks, 1962 to 1996										
0.01	2076	0.433	725	0.435	0.441	1320	0.430	414	0.438	0.441
0.05	2076	0.515	725	0.535	0.520	1320	0.514	414	0.522	0.520
0.10	2076	0.568	725	0.590	0.571	1320	0.573	414	0.566	0.571
0.50	2076	0.827	725	0.836	0.828	1320	0.840	414	0.826	0.828
0.90	2076	1.219	725	1.237	1.224	1320	1.244	414	1.229	1.224
0.95	2076	1.385	725	1.395	1.358	1320	1.373	414	1.340	1.358
0.99	2076	1.608	725	1.611	1.628	1320	1.645	414	1.600	1.628
Smallest quintile, 1962 to 1996										
0.01	320	0.456	78	0.406	0.441	218	0.459	41	0.436	0.441
0.05	320	0.535	78	0.502	0.520	218	0.533	41	0.498	0.520
0.10	320	0.586	78	0.559	0.571	218	0.590	41	0.543	0.571
0.50	320	0.848	78	0.814	0.828	218	0.847	41	0.801	0.828
0.90	320	1.231	78	1.204	1.224	218	1.229	41	1.216	1.224
0.95	320	1.357	78	1.330	1.358	218	1.381	41	1.332	1.358
0.99	320	1.661	78	1.590	1.628	218	1.708	41	1.571	1.628
2nd quintile, 1962 to 1996										
0.01	420	0.445	146	0.428	0.441	305	0.458	68	0.426	0.441
0.05	420	0.530	146	0.505	0.520	305	0.557	68	0.501	0.520
0.10	420	0.580	146	0.553	0.571	305	0.610	68	0.559	0.571
0.50	420	0.831	146	0.823	0.828	305	0.862	68	0.804	0.828
0.90	420	1.197	146	1.210	1.224	305	1.265	68	1.210	1.224
0.95	420	1.349	146	1.343	1.358	305	1.407	68	1.409	1.358
0.99	420	1.634	146	1.626	1.628	305	1.686	68	1.614	1.628
3rd quintile, 1962 to 1996										
0.01	458	0.442	145	0.458	0.441	279	0.464	105	0.425	0.441
0.05	458	0.516	145	0.508	0.520	279	0.539	105	0.525	0.520
0.10	458	0.559	145	0.557	0.571	279	0.586	105	0.570	0.571
0.50	458	0.838	145	0.835	0.828	279	0.832	105	0.818	0.828
0.90	458	1.216	145	1.251	1.224	279	1.220	105	1.233	1.224
0.95	458	1.406	145	1.397	1.358	279	1.357	105	1.355	1.358
0.99	458	1.660	145	1.661	1.628	279	1.606	105	1.638	1.628

(*continued*)

Table 2.9   (*continued*)

Percentile	NYSE/AMEX sample					Nasdaq sample				
	m_1	$\Delta_{m_1,n}$	m_2	$\Delta_{m_2,n}$	Δ	m_1	$\Delta_{m_1,n}$	m_2	$\Delta_{m_2,n}$	Δ
4th quintile, 1962 to 1996										
0.01	424	0.429	173	0.418	0.441	303	0.454	92	0.446	0.441
0.05	424	0.506	173	0.516	0.520	303	0.526	92	0.506	0.520
0.10	424	0.552	173	0.559	0.571	303	0.563	92	0.554	0.571
0.50	424	0.823	173	0.815	0.828	303	0.840	92	0.818	0.828
0.90	424	1.197	173	1.183	1.224	303	1.217	92	1.178	1.224
0.95	424	1.336	173	1.313	1.358	303	1.350	92	1.327	1.358
0.99	424	1.664	173	1.592	1.628	303	1.659	92	1.606	1.628
Largest quintile, 1962 to 1996										
0.01	561	0.421	167	0.425	0.441	308	0.441	108	0.429	0.441
0.05	561	0.509	167	0.500	0.520	308	0.520	108	0.508	0.520
0.10	561	0.557	167	0.554	0.571	308	0.573	108	0.558	0.571
0.50	561	0.830	167	0.817	0.828	308	0.842	108	0.816	0.828
0.90	561	1.218	167	1.202	1.224	308	1.231	108	1.226	1.224
0.95	561	1.369	167	1.308	1.358	308	1.408	108	1.357	1.358
0.99	561	1.565	167	1.615	1.628	308	1.724	108	1.630	1.628

head-and-shoulders and rectangles, while sometimes effective, need not be optimal. In particular, it may be possible to determine 'optimal patterns' for detecting certain types of phenomena in financial time series, e.g., an optimal shape for detecting stochastic volatility or changes in regime. Moreover, patterns that are optimal for detecting statistical anomalies need not be optimal for trading profits, and vice versa. Such considerations may lead to an entirely new branch of technical analysis, one based on selecting pattern-recognition algorithms to optimize specific objective functions. We hope to explore these issues more fully in future research.

Table 2.10 *Bootstrap percentiles for the Kolmogorov–Smirnov test of the equality of conditional and unconditional one-day return distributions for NYSE/AMEX and Nasdaq stocks from 1962 to 1996, for five-year subperiods, under the null hypothesis of equality. For each of the two sets of market data, two sample sizes, m_1 and m_2, have been chosen to span the range of frequency counts of patterns reported in Table 2.1. For each sample size m_i, we resample one-day normalized returns (with replacement) to obtain a bootstrap sample of m_i observations, compute the Kolmogorov–Smirnov test statistic (against the entire sample of one-day normalized returns), and repeat this procedure 1000 times. The percentiles of the asymptotic distribution are also reported for comparison*

	NYSE/AMEX sample					Nasdaq sample				
Percentile	m_1	$\Delta_{m_1,n}$	m_2	$\Delta_{m_2,n}$	Δ	m_1	$\Delta_{m_1,n}$	m_2	$\Delta_{m_2,n}$	Δ
All stocks, 1962 to 1966										
0.01	356	0.431	85	0.427	0.441	342	0.460	72	0.417	0.441
0.05	356	0.516	85	0.509	0.520	342	0.539	72	0.501	0.520
0.10	356	0.576	85	0.559	0.571	342	0.589	72	0.565	0.571
0.50	356	0.827	85	0.813	0.828	342	0.849	72	0.802	0.828
0.90	356	1.233	85	1.221	1.224	342	1.242	72	1.192	1.224
0.95	356	1.359	85	1.363	1.358	342	1.384	72	1.339	1.358
0.99	356	1.635	85	1.711	1.628	342	1.582	72	1.684	1.628
All stocks, 1967 to 1971										
0.01	258	0.432	112	0.423	0.441	227	0.435	65	0.424	0.441
0.05	258	0.522	112	0.508	0.520	227	0.512	65	0.498	0.520
0.10	258	0.588	112	0.562	0.571	227	0.571	65	0.546	0.571
0.50	258	0.841	112	0.819	0.828	227	0.811	65	0.812	0.828
0.90	258	1.194	112	1.253	1.224	227	1.179	65	1.219	1.224
0.95	258	1.315	112	1.385	1.358	227	1.346	65	1.357	1.358
0.99	258	1.703	112	1.563	1.628	227	1.625	65	1.669	1.628
All stocks, 1972 to 1976										
0.01	223	0.439	82	0.440	0.441	58	0.433	25	0.405	0.441
0.05	223	0.518	82	0.503	0.520	58	0.495	25	0.479	0.520
0.10	223	0.588	82	0.554	0.571	58	0.542	25	0.526	0.571
0.50	223	0.854	82	0.798	0.828	58	0.793	25	0.783	0.828
0.90	223	1.249	82	1.208	1.224	58	1.168	25	1.203	1.224
0.95	223	1.406	82	1.364	1.358	58	1.272	25	1.345	1.358
0.99	223	1.685	82	1.635	1.628	58	1.618	25	1.616	1.628
All stocks, 1977 to 1981										
0.01	290	0.426	110	0.435	0.441	96	0.430	36	0.417	0.441
0.05	290	0.519	110	0.504	0.520	96	0.504	36	0.485	0.520
0.10	290	0.573	110	0.555	0.571	96	0.570	36	0.542	0.571
0.50	290	0.841	110	0.793	0.828	96	0.821	36	0.810	0.828
0.90	290	1.262	110	1.184	1.224	96	1.197	36	1.201	1.224
0.95	290	1.383	110	1.342	1.358	96	1.352	36	1.371	1.358
0.99	290	1.598	110	1.645	1.628	96	1.540	36	1.545	1.628

(continued)

Table 2.10   (*continued*)

Percentile	NYSE/AMEX sample					Nasdaq sample				
	m_1	$\Delta_{m_1,n}$	m_2	$\Delta_{m_2,n}$	Δ	m_1	$\Delta_{m_1,n}$	m_2	$\Delta_{m_2,n}$	Δ
All stocks, 1982 to 1986										
0.01	313	0.462	106	0.437	0.441	120	0.448	44	0.417	0.441
0.05	313	0.542	106	0.506	0.520	120	0.514	44	0.499	0.520
0.10	313	0.585	106	0.559	0.571	120	0.579	44	0.555	0.571
0.50	313	0.844	106	0.819	0.828	120	0.825	44	0.802	0.828
0.90	313	1.266	106	1.220	1.224	120	1.253	44	1.197	1.224
0.95	313	1.397	106	1.369	1.358	120	1.366	44	1.337	1.358
0.99	313	1.727	106	1.615	1.628	120	1.692	44	1.631	1.628
All Stocks, 1987 to 1991										
0.01	287	0.443	98	0.449	0.441	312	0.455	50	0.432	0.441
0.05	287	0.513	98	0.522	0.520	312	0.542	50	0.517	0.520
0.10	287	0.565	98	0.566	0.571	312	0.610	50	0.563	0.571
0.50	287	0.837	98	0.813	0.828	312	0.878	50	0.814	0.828
0.90	287	1.200	98	1.217	1.224	312	1.319	50	1.216	1.224
0.95	287	1.336	98	1.348	1.358	312	1.457	50	1.323	1.358
0.99	287	1.626	98	1.563	1.628	312	1.701	50	1.648	1.628
All Stocks, 1992 to 1996										
0.01	389	0.438	102	0.432	0.441	361	0.447	87	0.428	0.441
0.05	389	0.522	102	0.506	0.520	361	0.518	87	0.492	0.520
0.10	389	0.567	102	0.558	0.571	361	0.559	87	0.550	0.571
0.50	389	0.824	102	0.818	0.828	361	0.817	87	0.799	0.828
0.90	389	1.220	102	1.213	1.224	361	1.226	87	1.216	1.224
0.95	389	1.321	102	1.310	1.358	361	1.353	87	1.341	1.358
0.99	389	1.580	102	1.616	1.628	361	1.617	87	1.572	1.628

REFERENCES

Allen, F. and Karjalainen, R. (1999) Using genetic algorithms to find technical trading rules, *Journal of Financial Economics*, **51**, 245–271.

Beymer, D. and Poggio, T. (1996) Image representation for visual learning, *Science*, **272**, 1905–1909.

Blume, L., Easley, D. and O'Hara, M. (1994) Market statistics and technical analysis: The role of volume, *Journal of Finance*, **49**, 153–181.

Brock, W., Lakonishok, J. and LeBaron, B. (1992) Simple technical trading rules and the stochastic properties of stock returns, *Journal of Finance*, **47**, 1731–1764.

Brown, D. and Jennings, R. (1989) On technical analysis, *Review of Financial Studies*, **2**, 527–551.

Campbell, J., Lo, A. W. and MacKinlay, C. A. (1997) *The Econometrics of Financial Markets*, Princeton University Press, Princeton, NJ.

Chan, L., Jegadeesh, N. and Lakonishok, J. (1996) Momentum strategies, *Journal of Finance*, **51**, 1681–1713.

Chang, K. and Osler, C. (1994) Evaluating chart-based technical analysis: The head-and-shoulders pattern in foreign exchange markets, Working paper, Federal Reserve Bank of New York.

Csáki, E. (1984) Empirical distribution function, in *Handbook of Statistics*, Volume 4 (eds P. Krishnaiah and P. Sen), Elsevier Science Publishers, Amsterdam.

DeGroot, M. (1986) *Probability and Statistics*, Addison-Wesley, Reading, MA.

Edwards, R. and Magee, J. (1966) *Technical Analysis of Stock Trends*, 5th ed, John Magee, Boston, MA.

Grundy, B. and Martin, S. (1998) Understanding the nature of the risks and the source of the rewards to momentum investing, Working paper, Wharton School, University of Pennsylvania.

Härdle, W. (1990) *Applied Nonparametric Regression*, Cambridge University Press, Cambridge.

Hollander, M. and Wolfe, D. (1973) *Nonparametric Statistical Methods*, John Wiley, New York.

Jegadeesh, N. and Titman, S. (1993) Returns to buying winners and selling losers: Implications for stock market efficiency, *Journal of Finance*, **48**, 65–91.

Lo, A.W. and Craig MacKinlay, A. (1988) Stock market prices do not follow random walks: Evidence from a simple specification test, *Review of Financial Studies*, **1**, 41–66.

Lo, A.W. and Craig MacKinlay, A. (1997) Maximizing predictability in the stock and bond markets, *Macroeconomic Dynamics*, **1**, 102–134.

Lo, A.W. and Craig MacKinlay, A. (1999) *A Non-Random Walk Down Wall Street*, Princeton University Press, Princeton, NJ.

Malkiel, B. (1996) *A Random Walk Down Wall Street: Including a Life-Cycle Guide to Personal Investing*, W.W. Norton, New York.

Neely, C., Weller, P. and Dittmar, R. (1997) Is technical analysis in the foreign exchange market profitable? A genetic programming approach, *Journal of Financial and Quantitative Analysis*, **32**, 405–426.

Neely, C. and Weller, P. (1998) Technical trading rules in the European monetary system, Working paper, Federal Bank of St. Louis.

Neftci, S. (1991) Naive trading rules in financial markets and Wiener–Kolmogorov prediction theory: A study of technical analysis, *Journal of Business*, **64**, 549–571.

Neftci, S. and Policano, A. (1984) Can chartists outperform the market? Market efficiency tests for 'technical analyst', *Journal of Future Markets*, **4**, 465–478.

Osler, C. and Chang, K. (1995) Head-and-shoulders: Not just a flaky pattern, Staff Report No. 4, Federal Reserve Bank of New York.

Poggio, T. and Beymer, D. (1996) Regularization networks for visual learning, in *Early Visual Learning* (eds S. Nayar and T. Poggio), Oxford University Press, Oxford.

Press, W., Flannery, B., Teukolsky, S. and Vetterling, W. (1986) *Numerical Recipes: The Art of Scientific Computing* Cambridge University Press, Cambridge.

Pruitt, S. and White, R. (1988) The CRISMA trading system: Who says technical analysis can't beat the market?, *Journal of Portfolio Management*, **14**, 55–58.

Riesenhuber, M. and Poggio, T. (1997) Common computational strategies in machine and biological vision, in *Proceedings of International Symposium on System Life*, Tokyo, Japan, 67–75.

Rouwenhorst, G. (1998) International momentum strategies, *Journal of Finance*, **53**, 267–284.

Simonoff, J. (1996) *Smoothing Methods in Statistics*, Springer-Verlag, New York.

Smirnov, N. (1939a) Sur les écarts de la courbe de distribution empirique, *Rec. Math. (Mat. Sborn.)*, **6**, 3–26.

Smirnov, N. (1939b) On the estimation of the discrepancy between empirical curves of distribution for two independent samples, *Bulletin. Math. Univ. Moscow*, **2**, 3–14.

Tabell, A. and Tabell, E. (1964) The case for technical analysis, *Financial Analyst Journal*, **20**, 67–76.

Treynor, J. and Ferguson, R. (1985) In defense of technical analysis, *Journal of Finance*, **40**, 757–773.

NOTES

1. A similar approach has been proposed by Chang and Osler (1994) and Osler and Chang (1995) for the case of foreign-currency trading rules based on a head-and-shoulders pattern. They develop an algorithm for automatically detecting geometric patterns in price or exchange data by looking at properly defined local extrema.

2. See, for example, Beymer and Poggio (1996), Poggio and Beymer (1996), and Riesenhuber and Poggio (1997).

3. Despite the fact that $K(x)$ is a probability density function, it plays no probabilistic role in the subsequent analysis – it is merely a convenient method for computing a weighted average, and does *not* imply, for example, that X is distributed according to $K(x)$ (which would be a parametric assumption).

4. However, there are other bandwidth-selection methods that yield the same asymptotic optimality properties but which have different implications for the finite-sample properties of kernel estimators. See Härdle (1990) for further discussion.

5. Specifically, we produced fitted curves for various bandwidths and compared their extrema to the original price series visually to see if we were fitting more 'noise' than 'signal', and asked several professional technical analysts to do the same. Through this informal process, we settled on the bandwidth of $0.3 \times h^*$ and used it for the remainder of our analysis. This procedure was followed before we performed the statistical analysis of section 2.4, and we made no revision to the choice of bandwidth afterward.

6. See Simonoff (1996) for a discussion of the problems with kernel estimators and alternatives such as local polynomial regression.

7. After all, for two consecutive maxima to be local maxima, there must be a local minimum in between, and vice versa for two consecutive minima.

8. If we are willing to place additional restrictions on $m(\cdot)$, e.g., linearity, we can obtain considerably more accurate inferences even for partially completed patterns in any fixed window.

9. For example, Chang and Osler (1994) and Osler and Chang (1995) propose an algorithm for automatically detecting head-and-shoulders patterns in foreign exchange data by looking at properly defined local extrema. To assess the efficacy of a head-and-shoulders trading rule, they take a stand on a class of trading strategies and compute the profitability of these across a sample of exchange

rates against the US dollar. The null return distribution is computed by a bootstrap that samples returns randomly from the original data so as to induce temporal independence in the bootstrapped time series. By comparing the actual returns from trading strategies to the bootstrapped distribution, the authors find that for two of the six currencies in their sample (the yen and the Deutsche mark), trading strategies based on a head-and-shoulders pattern can lead to statistically significant profits. See also Neftci and Policano (1984), Pruitt and White (1988), and Brock *et al.* (1992).

10. If the first price observation of a stock is missing, we set it equal to the first non-missing price in the series. If the *t*th price observation is missing, we set it equal to the first non-missing price prior to *t*.

11. In particular, let the price process satisfy

$$dP(t) = \mu P(t)\,dt + \sigma P(t)\,dW(t)$$

where $W(t)$ is a standard Brownian motion. To generate simulated prices for a single security in a given period, we estimate the security's drift and diffusion coefficients by maximum likelihood and then simulate prices using the estimated parameter values. An independent price series is simulated for each of the 350 securities in both the NYSE/AMEX and the Nasdaq samples. Finally, we use our pattern-recognition algorithm to detect the occurrence of each of the ten patterns in the simulated price series.

ACKNOWLEDGMENTS

This research was partially supported by the MIT Laboratory for Financial Engineering, Merrill Lynch, and the National Science Foundation (Grant SBR–9709976). We thank Ralph Acampora, Franklin Allen, Susan Berger, Mike Epstein, Narasimhan Jegadeesh, Ed Kao, Doug Sanzone, Jeff Simonoff, Tom Stoker, and seminar participants at the Federal Reserve Bank of New York, NYU, and conference participants at the Columbia-JAFEE conference, the 1999 Joint Statistical Meetings, RISK 99, the 1999 Annual Meeting of the Society for Computational Economics, and the 2000 Annual Meeting of the American Finance Association for valuable comments and discussion.

Chapter 3

Mean-variance analysis, trading rules and emerging markets

DAAN MATHEUSSEN AND STEPHEN SATCHELL

3.1 INTRODUCTION

It has only been in the last few years that serious study on the statistical properties of emerging markets returns has commenced. Papers in this new literature include, inter alia, Frankel (1995), Behaert and Harvey (1995), Erb, Harvey and Viskanter (1995). The purpose of this chapter is to examine the possibility of using trading rules based on mean-variance analysis on emerging markets. The question, among many others, has been discussed in an important study by Harvey (1995). He finds on the basis of extensive testing that standard global asset pricing models fail to explain expected returns in emerging markets due to large idiosyncratic (country-specific) informational effects. However, Effekhari and Satchell (1995) examine the validity of the capital asset pricing model (CAPM) using monthly emerging markets data and find that, although the data is highly non-normal, they cannot conclude that the mean-variance CAPM gives different betas than the mean semi-variance CAPM. This result is compatible with the data coming from an elliptical distribution and such a result implies the validity of mean-dispersion analysis where dispersion is a measure proportional to variance, thus the analysis is equivalent to mean-variance analysis. Considering twenty emerging market indices, we find skewness present in ten cases whilst kurtosis is present in fifteen. Kurtosis is compatible with elliptical distributions, whereas skewness is not.

This discussion suggests that it would be an interesting, and possibly valid, exercise to construct one-period mean-variance optimized portfolios and base trading rules on them. We do this as part of a broader aim which is to investigate the empirical performance of various dynamic trading rules and strategies to our emerging market database. These new markets are characterized by high costs and optimized strategies may not perform as well as simple rules such as rebalancing every six months, say, which will reduce 'churning' the portfolios and keep costs down. There is a long history of empirical work on strategies and trading rules in finance and we make no attempt to survey this vast literature. Some references on the empirical performance measurement of strategies include Johnston and Shannon (1975) and Bloomfield, Left and Long (1977) to name but two. We present a set of trading rules in section 3.2, our results in section 3.3 and our conclusions in section 3.4.

3.2 DATA AND PORTFOLIO CONSTRUCTION

The data we use is the International Finance Corporation (IFC) monthly one country returns. Diagnostics of this data are presented in Harvey (1995) and Effekhari and Satchell (1995). Essentially, it is highly non-normal, but often elliptical, possesses some but not excessive autocorrelation and in some but not all cases has time-varying heteroskedasticity.

The strategy of our investment is myopic, that is we choose our portfolio across countries based on next period's return distribution. In certain cases this can be shown to be optimal for N periods expected utility maximizations, see Stapleton and Subrahmanyan (1978), for example. The advantage of the myopic strategy is that it only considers one-period returns and, as referred to in section 3.1, we have some evidence that the returns are approximately elliptical. It is perfectly possible for a series that is elliptical through time rather than cross-sectionally to exhibit GARCH behaviour, see Satchell (1995) for results on this phenomenon. All our data is converted to US dollars so that our analysis is from the perspective of a US investor, our returns are arithmetic.

The first portfolio we consider was suggested to us by Kleinwort Benson Investment Management (KBIM). This is the averaged portfolio. We note that this assigns weights equal to $1/N$ where N is the number of countries at the time of investment. This procedure is independent of any predictions of moments. There is an issue of timing; we consider two versions of the equal weight (EW) portfolio, one in which we hold $1/(N+1)$ from the month a new market emerges. We call this EWII. The other we hold $1/(N+1)$ 10 months after the new market emerges. We call this EWI. The reason for this distinction is to keep EWI compatible with the other portfolios, as described later in the text. Another simple strategy used by KBIM, but not included, is a two-tier weight system rather than the equally weighted examples considered in this study.

The next portfolio to consider is the global minimum variance portfolio. To simplify this we assume that the cross-correlations are zero; this seems reasonable for most of the period and agrees with the low empirical cross-correlation in the data. Under this assumption it is a simple exercise to show that the optimal weights $W_{i,t}$ are given by:

$$W_{i,t} = \frac{\dfrac{1}{\sigma_{i,t}^2}}{\displaystyle\sum_{i=1}^{N} \dfrac{1}{\sigma_{i,t}^2}}$$

with $i = 1, \ldots, N$ and $\sigma_{i,t}^2$ is the variance of returns of asset i at time t. We note that the weights are independent of the means, they depend only on the variances, the larger the variance the less of the asset we hold.

The third portfolio is the so-called Markowitz optimal portfolio. In this case, the weights $W_{i,t}$ are given by:

$$W_{i,t} = \frac{M_{i,t}}{\displaystyle\sum_{i=1}^{N} M_{i,t}}$$

with $i = 1, \ldots, N$

$$M_{i,t} = \frac{\mu_{i,t} - r_t}{\sigma_{i,t}^2}$$

and $\mu_{i,t}$ is the expected return of Index i at time t, r_t is the US dollar monthly mid-rate.

In this case the Markowitz portfolio depends on both means and variances. Correlations are assumed to be zero as before. This portfolio corresponds to the tangency portfolio of the familiar mean-variance diagram. It reflects the optimal portfolio of an investor whose net position in bonds is zero and whose total investment in the risky assets is held in proportion to the market. Because it is likely that short positions are not feasible, or, at least, very expensive, in emerging markets, we adjust our weights in the following way. If $M_{i,t} < 0$, then $M_{i,t} = 0$, i.e. all short positions are set to zero and our weights are rescaled to add up to one.

The portfolio returns are presented in Table 3.2 for the cases where we have used the past ten, twenty or all past observations for parameter estimation. We wait ten months before including new assets in our portfolio. The likelihood that the process governing returns are non-stationary through time means that we need to consider rolling windows of data for estimating $M_{i,t}$ and $\sigma_{i,t}^2$. We also present some results on rebalancing. This popular and simple technique consists of fixing a set of portfolio weights at some level and rebalancing the portfolio back to these benchmark weights after some fixed time period. We consider the time periods monthly, three monthly, six monthly and annually. Our procedure is complicated by the introduction of new markets. Here we consider an equally weighted portfolio where we wait ten periods until we invest in a market, i.e. we start the funds in period eleven. However, if a market emerges after period eleven and we rebalance before (or after) ten months subsequent to the period of emergence, we invest in that market.

We consider a snapshot of our portfolios. Thus, for June 1992, when volatility seemed rather high, we compute the weights of the two non-EW portfolios which we report in Table 3.1. This is simply to give an example of the sort of weight patterns that might emerge and to familiarize the reader with the data and models.

3.3   RESULTS

We first discuss our snapshot values. In Table 3.1 we list the Markowitz optimal (MO) weights, second column, the minimum variance weights in the

Table 3.1   *Weights of MO and MV in June 1992*

	Log return in June 1992	MO weights (%)	MV weights (%)	MO return	MV return
Argentina	−0.256 069	1.58	20.4	−0.004 051	−0.052 25
Brazil	−0.036 66	0.11	13.35	−0.000 411	−0.048 96
Chile	0.020 253	20.36	1.69	0.004 123	0.000 343
Columbia	0.139 919	11.98	2.03	0.016 764	0.002 841
Mexico	−0.152 879	4.95	6.74	−0.007 56	−0.010 30
Peru	Not indexed				
Venezuela	−0.007 495	3.56	5.46	−0.000 267	−0.000 41
China	Not indexed				
Korea	−0.004 517	5.63	1.98	−0.000 254	-8.95^{-5}
Philippines	0.137 373	10.04	3.22	0.013 792	0.004 422
Taiwan	0.0045	2.85	6.64	0.000 128	0.000 299
India	0.028 765	4.99	2.69	0.001 434	0.000 775
Indonesia	0.031 279	0.00	2.90	0	0.000 908
Malaysia	0.015 868	1.82	1.78	0.000 289	0.000 282
Pakistan	0.059 784	11.89	0.95	0.007 11	0.000 567
Sri Lanka	Not indexed				
Thailand	0.093 757	7.05	2.16	0.006 61	0.002 024
Greece	0.106 283	3.13	4.48	0.003 33	0.004 758
Hungary	Not indexed				
Jordan	0.023 234 3	0.00	0.72	0	0.000 167
Nigeria	0.055 112	0.00	4.52	0	0.002 492
Poland	Not indexed				
Portugal	−0.000 145	4.21	5.10	-6.10^{-6}	-7.41^{-6}
Turkey	0.245 49	0.56	11.02	0.001 37	0.0270
Zimbabwe	−0.118 589	5.3	2.16	−0.006 28	−0.0026
Total		100.0	100.0	0.0361	−0.0677

Table 3.2 *Sharpe ratio of the considered strategies over entire period taken with respect to averages*

	Return (net cum) (%)	Mean	Standard deviation	Sharpe ratio
All observations				
MO	874	0.023 779	0.055 605	0.333 973
EWI	865	0.022 139	0.043 683	0.387 66
EWII	920	0.022 753	0.045 752	0.383 545
MV	797	0.024 077	0.088 297	0.213 703
20 Observations				
MO	645	0.021 873	0.048 941	0.337 098
EWI	628	0.021 657	0.043 591	0.373 514
MV	631	0.024 556	0.094 221	0.203 575
10 Observations				
MO	1648	0.028 482	0.056 769	0.407 028
EWI	868	0.022 244	0.043 494	0.387 851
MV	660	0.024 491	0.108 757	0.175 766

third column. Note that, although we do not record it, the weights for the equal weight (EW) portfolio would be 5 per cent. The date chosen, 30 June, 1992, was purely for the purpose of providing a snapshot and has no special significance other than showing large differences in monthly returns between the two portfolios.

We concentrate on the differences. The mean-variance portfolio is long in Argentina, Brazil and Turkey, whereas the MO portfolio is long in Chile, Columbia, The Philippines and Pakistan. In the fourth and fifth columns we report the portfolio weights multiplied by the asset return for that month. We see that the MO portfolio gained 4.1 per cent in the month whereas the mean-variance portfolio lost 7 per cent in the month. Overall, these portfolios appear to select quite different assets, no clear picture emerges, the mean-variance portfolio has made substantial profits in Turkey and large losses in Brazil and Argentina.

We also compute the time-series means and variances of the different portfolios. These are presented in Table 3.2.

We first report results for the long period. Using all data MV has the highest return but also the highest risk. On a risk-adjusted basis the KBIMI fund out-performs. Using 20 observations MV has the highest expected return. Again the KBIMI fund out-performs. Using 10 observations the MV fund out-performs for both risk-adjusted and actual returns.

Table 3.3 *Sharpe ratio of the considered strategies over short period taken with respect to averages*

	Return (net cum) (%)	Mean	Standard deviation	Sharpe ratio
All observations				
MO	46.22	0.015 231	0.046 271	0.267 23
EWI	44	0.012 99	0.045 194	0.224 01
EWII	38	0.011 498	0.047 772	0.180 70
MV	32	0.013 645	0.059 122	0.182 33
20 Observations				
MO	31	0.011 372	0.046 618	0.181 47
EWI	44	0.012 99	0.045 194	0.222 99
MV	39	0.014 416	0.052 549	0.218 91
10 Observations				
MO	49	0.015 594	0.044 359	0.285 9
EWI	44	0.012 99	0.045 194	0.222 99
MV	46	0.016 299	0.055 647	0.240 56

Turning to the short period we see that for all data MO has the best risk-adjusted and return characteristic; for 20 observations MV has the highest return whilst KBIM has the best risk-adjusted return, and for 10 observations, MV has the best return whilst MO has the best risk-adjusted performance.

Summarizing, MV performs well but typically has large volatility, MO performs well based on a short window and has the best expected return (in the long period). The KBIMI fund performs well and is in no sense dominated by the others.

We repeated the exercise assuming transaction costs of 2 per cent for a one-way transaction. The results, see Table 3.4, are qualitatively the same as our previous results, this was done using all previous data in our estimations. We omit results for transaction costs for ten and twenty due to lack of space.

Finally, we discuss our rebalancing results, see Table 3.5. Although the Sharpe ratios are lower than those of the MO portfolio, the results are interesting in terms of the optimal rebalancing time. It seems clear that for one-way costs of 2 per cent, a 6-monthly rebalance outperforms other rebalancing periods. If costs are higher, and it may be reasonable to think that they are, then a longer period is likely to be optimal. Such a procedure is a low-cost activity that lies somewhere between active and passive quantitive management, it is easy to understand and seems to produce good results.

Table 3.4   *Transaction costs and their effect on the Sharpe ratio over the entire period*

	MO	EWI	MV
0.0% Commission			
Mean	0.023 779	0.022 139	0.024 077
Standard deviation	0.055 605	0.043 683	0.088 297
Sharpe	0.333 973	0.387 66	0.213 703
0.5% Commission			
Mean	0.023 332	0.022 11	0.023 903
Standard deviation	0.055 54	0.043 688	0.088 354
Sharpe	0.326 33	0.386 822	0.211 592
1% Commission			
Mean	0.022 886	0.022 07	0.023 729
Standard deviation	0.055 479	0.043 694	0.088 413
Sharpe	0.318 641	0.385 979	0.209 481
1.5% Commission			
Mean	0.022 439	0.022 036	0.023 555
Standard deviation	0.055 422	0.043 701	0.088 473
Sharpe	0.310 915	0.385 132	0.207 37
2% Commission			
Mean	0.021 993	0.022 001	0.023 38
Standard deviation	0.055 368	0.043 708	0.088 533
Sharpe	0.303 152	0.384 281	0.205 261

3.4 CONCLUSIONS

In conclusion, simple one-period models that are based on mean-variance analysis perform adequately in emerging markets confirming a possible implication of Effekhari and Satchell (1995). The results are robust to transaction costs and suggest that these simple strategies could be profitable. The difficulty is the extent to which the increased participation by worldwide investors has changed the stochastic structure of these markets and eliminated the investment opportunity present in the historical data.

To expand on the previous remark, it seems to be the case that the portfolio risk structure has changed. Although we do not report the results, we found that the average correlation between emerging markets has increased in recent years suggesting that common factors matter more than previously. The

Table 3.5   *Sharpe ratio for rebalancing over entire period with different levels of transaction costs*

	Monthly	3 Monthly	6 Monthly	Annually	Not rebalanced
0.0% Commission					
Cumulative return	865.26	875.19	966.49	1038.53	881.08
Mean	0.022 139	0.022 279	0.023 213	0.024 056	0.022 723
Standard deviation	0.043 683	0.044 582	0.046 535	0.051 165	0.052 741
Sharpe	0.387 207	0.382 529	0.386 548	0.368 047	0.331 782
0.5% Commission					
Cumulative return	800.95	840.4	957.08	1020.54	868
Mean	0.021 484	0.021 935	0.023 128	0.023 911	0.022 601
Standard deviation	0.043 574	0.044 575	0.046 505	0.051 277	0.052 819
Sharpe	0.373 132	0.374 879	0.384 965	0.364 419	0.328 985
1% Commission					
Cumulative return	740.87	806.81	947.73	1002.8	855.94
Mean	0.020 829	0.021 591	0.023 043	0.023 767	0.022 480
Standard deviation	0.043 469	0.044 574	0.046 482	0.051 396	0.052 902
Sharpe	0.358 959	0.367 172	0.383 329	0.360 756	0.326 157
1.5% Commission					
Cumulative return	684.76	774.38	938.45	985.29	842.25
Mean	0.020 173	0.021 248	0.022 958	0.023 622	0.022 358
Standard deviation	0.043 367	0.044 58	0.046 466	0.051 523	0.052 993
Sharpe	0.344 691	0.359 41	0.381 642	0.357 059	0.323 30
2% Commission					
Cumulative return	632.34	743.08	929.24	968.02	829.58
Mean	0.019 518	0.020 904	0.022 874	0.023 477	0.022 236
Standard deviation	0.043 268	0.044 594	0.046 456	0.051 658	0.053 089
Sharpe	0.330 329	0.351 597	0.379 905	0.353 331	0.320 417

double impact of international investment and financial integration has led to joint market features that represent, perhaps, a less interesting investment environment. New constituent emerging markets may not have the same statistical characteristics as the original ones did at the same stage of their development. Poland, Hungary and China may not be statistically equivalent to Taiwan, Thailand and Columbia at the point at which they join the investment opportunity set.

Why should trading rules based on our optimized portfolios lead to good risk-adjusted returns? One reason is that the MO portfolio is constructed to have the maximum Sharpe ratio in a mean-variance world. Although our returns may appear highly non-normal, conditions for the validity of mean-variance analysis are known to be more general than just multivariate normality. As proved in Chamberlain (1983), a necessary and sufficient condition for the validity of MV analysis is that the random returns are a linear transformation of a spherically distributed random vector, see Dempster (1969) for a definition of a spherical distribution. Furthermore, in the absence of a riskless asset, mean-variance analysis is valid for a vector of N returns if and only the last $(N-1)$ components are spherically distributed conditional on the first, which can have an arbitrary distribution. Thus, it is plausible that our rule of holding the MO portfolio actually maximizes the historical Sharpe ratio; it certainly should on a period by period basis.

However, whilst we have found that the empirical Sharpe ratio of the rule that maximizes the cross-sectional Sharpe ratio is indeed maximal, the rule that minimizes the cross-sectional variance appears to have a huge time-series variance. Further research is needed to understand what sort of stochastic process might give us such a result.

Our results are not in conflict with those of Harvey (1995). Harvey finds that asset pricing models based on unconditional moments are inadequate for emerging markets data. We have found outperformance from trading rules based on conditional, one-period ahead, moments.

We describe our strategies as trading rules. They are trading rules in the sense that they reflect certain features of optimization, but fall short of full optimization. If we regard a trading rule as a compromise between an optimizing strategy and a rule of thumb based on considerations of cost and computability, then our strategies are certainly trading rules. They optimize only in a narrow sense and fall short of the optimal strategy for maximizing expected intertemporal utility. They also seem to work and so are clearly examples of profitable trading rules.

REFERENCES

Behaert, C. and Harvey, C.R. (1995) Time-varying world market integration, *Journal of Finance*, **2**, June, Vol. 50, 403–444.

Bloomfield, T., Left, R. and Long, J.B. (1977) Portfolio strategies and performance, *Journal of Financial Economics*, **5**, 201–18.

Chamberlain, G. (1983) A characterisation of the distributions that imply mean-variance utility functions, *Journal of Economic Theory*, **29**, 185–201.

Dempster, A.P. (1969) *Elements of Continuous Multi-variate Analysis*, Addison-Wesley, Reading, MA.

Effekhari, B. and Satchell, S.E. (1995) *Non-normality of Returns in Emerging Markets*, Mimeo, Economics Department, University of Cambridge.

Effekhari, B. and Satchell, S.E. (1996) A comparison of mean-variance versus mean-lower partial moment asset pricing models. In *International Business and Finance*, Supp. 1 (eds Doukas, J. and Lang, L.H.P.), JAI Press.

Erb, C.B., Harvey, C.R., Viskanta, J.E. (1995) Country risk and global equity selection, *Journal of Portfolio Management*, 74–83.

Frankel, J.A. (1995) The Internationalisation of Equity Markets, NBER working paper No. 4590.

Harvey, C.R. (1995) Predictable risk and returns in emerging markets, *Review of Financial Studies*, **8**, 3, 773–816.

Johnston, K.H. and Shannon, D.S. (1975) Portfolio maintenance strategies revisited, *Atlantic Economic Journal*, **3**, 25–35.

Satchell, S.E. (1995) *Elliptical Distributions and Garch Models of Volatility*, Mimeo, Economics Department, University of Cambridge.

Stapleton, R. and Subrahmanyam, M. (1978) A multiperiod equilibrium asset pricing model, *Econometrica*, **46**, 1077–93.

Chapter 4

Expected returns of directional forecasters

EMMANUEL ACAR

4.1 INTRODUCTION

An important area not yet covered in the literature is an assessment of the profitability of directional forecasters. Can non-zero profit be expected in financial markets from such methods, and if so, what are the parameters of the underlying price process which make the rule profitable? The aim of this paper is to specify the theoretical relationship between rule returns and standard statistical measures of serial dependency. Such a specification, although not pursued in previous research, is useful because rule returns provide a measure of economic significance for serial dependencies in financial returns that otherwise might not be readily interpretable. Gauging the economic significance of observed daily asset return autocorrelations is difficult, because the relationship between the magnitude of observed serial correlation coefficients and profits is not clear. This chapter attempts to resolve this issue by examining how trading rule returns are related to the statistical characteristics of the underlying series. The goal is to show that using stochastic modelling, it is possible to establish the parameters of the underlying price process which generate any non-zero expected return from trading rules.

Many previous studies have used historical returns to explore the profitability of financial forecasting (Bird, 1985; Sweeney, 1986; Dunis, 1989; Surujaras and Sweeney, 1992; Levich and Thomas, 1993; LeBaron, 1991, 1992; Brock, Lakonishok and LeBaron, 1992; Taylor, 1986, 1990a, 1990b, 1992, 1994; Silber, 1994). These studies play an important role in suggesting the historical behaviour of forecasting strategies. However, they may not constitute an appropriate guide because their results are highly dependent on the asset and time period covered by the research. To get a broader view, we will turn to theoretical or stochastic modelling. Very little is known in the literature about the expected returns of dynamic strategies. Theoretical results exist only under the assumption of a random walk with drift for the filter rule

(Praetz, 1976; Bird, 1985; Sweeney, 1986), the option strategy (Cox and Rubinstein, 1985), the stop-loss and constant proportion insurance strategies (Black and Perold, 1992). However, no other results exist for stochastic processes which exhibit dependencies. We believe the random walk to be an unreasonably narrow view of reality and will subsequently establish the expected return of directional forecasts for any Gaussian stochastic process. Two reasons can be given for restricting the study to such processes. First, Gaussian processes describe numerous classes of models and, therefore, monitor a wide range of possible market conditions. So a Gaussian process may be the preliminary step to more complex models. Second, it is questionable whether complicated nonlinear models will bring much additional support to our arguments.

In order to model rule returns, restrictions must also be placed on the nature of the rule used. This is why the set of trading rules investigated in this chapter will be restricted to autoregressive models and linear technical rules which are well defined in the Neftci (1991) sense. This constitutes a considerable improvement on past studies since it covers a wider range of possible market conditions and trading rules. Particular emphasis is given to the expected return and variance of trading rules by providing exact analytical formulae.

Section 4.2 defines the trading rule process. Section 4.3 defines autoregressive forecasts and rule returns, and establishes their expected values under Gaussian processes assumptions. The forecasts which maximize profits are explicited. Section 4.4 shows that many technical indicators can be reformulated as autoregressive models. Section 4.5 measures the effect of conditional heteroskedasticity on linear rule returns. Finally, section 4.6 summarizes our results and conclusions.

4.2   TRADING RULES

4.2.1   Rule signals

Suppose that at each day t, a decision rule is applied with the intention of achieving profitable trades. It is the price trend which is based on market expectations that determines whether the asset is bought or sold. When the asset is bought, the position initiated in the market is said to be 'long'. When the asset is sold, the position initiated in the market is said to be 'short'. A forecasting technique is assessed as useful if, in dealer terms, it can 'make money'. For achieving this purpose, market participants use price-based forecasts. Therefore, the predictor F_t is completely characterized by a function f of past prices:

$$F_t = f\{P_t, P_{t-1}, P_{t-2}, \ldots, P_0\}$$

The only crucial feature which is required from the forecasting technique is its ability to accurately predict the direction of the trend in order to generate profitable buy and sell signals. Trading signals, buy ($+1$) and sell (-1), can then be formalized by the binary stochastic process B_t:

$$\text{sell: } B_t = -1 \quad \text{iff} \quad F_t = f\{P_t, P_{t-1}, P_{t-2}, \ldots, P_0\} < 0$$

Note that the signal of a trading rule is completely defined by one of the inequalities giving a sell or buy order, because if the position is not short, it is long. Only in the trivial case of a buy and hold (sell and hold) strategy, the signal B_t is deterministic and is $+1$ (-1) irrespective of the underlying process. Otherwise, trading signals B_t are stochastic variables. They are time series of binary data generated by an underlying time series of continuous data. The family of discretization mechanisms is broad since it is the one of trading rules. However, in all cases, discretizations arise by a truncation of a continuous-valued process which is a special case of Keenan (1982). By nature, the signal is a highly nonlinear function of the observed price series P_t (Neftci and Policano, 1984; Neftci, 1991) and, therefore, it can be highly dependent through time. B_t remains constant for a certain random period, then jumps to a new level as P_t behaves in a certain way. Trading in the asset occurs throughout the investment horizon at times that depend on a fixed set of rules and future price changes.

4.2.2   Rule returns

The study of the binary process of signals is of limited interest for trading purposes. The focus should be the economic consequence, i.e. the returns process implied by the decision rule, rather than on the generating process of the signal. Let us recall the investment strategy. Assume a position is taken in the market for a given period $[t - 1; t]$ and that no dividends are paid during the period. The logarithmic return during this time is $X_t = \text{Ln}(P_t/P_{t-1})$. The nature of the position (long or short) is given by the signal triggered at time $t - 1$, B_{t-1} following a given technical rule. Returns at time t made by applying such a decision rule are called 'rule returns' and denoted R_t. Their value can be expressed as:

$$R_t = B_{t-1}X_t \quad \Leftrightarrow \quad \begin{cases} R_t = -X_t & \text{if } B_{t-1} = -1 \\ R_t = +X_t & \text{if } B_{t-1} = +1 \end{cases} \tag{4.1}$$

The following two important remarks should be made.

(1) Rule returns are the product of a binary stochastic signal and a continuous-returns random variable. Except in the trivial case of a buy and hold strategy, the signal B_t is a stochastic variable and so rule returns are conditional on the position taken in the market (long $B_t = +1$ or short $B_t = -1$). This is the main feature of rule returns. Up to this point, little attention has been paid to the rule returns process. Earlier studies have mainly focused on the price-change process or underlying returns. The fact is that when evaluating forecasting ability the mean squared error criterion has been used to evaluate their performance rather than any economic evaluation. So their measures have been unconditional to the position taken in the market.

(2) Our rule return definition clearly corresponds to an unrealized return. By unrealized, we mean that rule returns are recorded every day even if the position is neither closed nor reversed, but is simply left open.

4.3 AUTOREGRESSIVE MODELS

4.3.1 Definition

A linear forecast is used to predict the one-step ahead return X_{t+1}, given by:

$$F_t = \delta + \sum_{j=0}^{t} d_j X_{t-j} \qquad (4.2)$$

with δ and the d_j being constants.

We will denote by μ_F the expected value of F_t and by σ_F^2 the variance of F_t.

This type of forecasting technique is referred to as an autoregressive predictor. The predictor is normally defined such that it minimizes the mean squared error between the forecast value and the one-step ahead return to be estimated. If the true process of returns is linear, autoregressive forecasts must yield the best forecasts of a stochastic process in the mean squared error sense. Autoregressive models do not generate explicit trading signals. However, if we assume zero transactions costs, the intuitive decision rule derived from autoregressive models is to go short if the 'one-ahead' forecast is negative and go long if it is positive. That is the forecasting technique implicitly triggers a daily signal B_t specifying a long $(+1)$ or short (-1) position following the decision rule:

$$\text{sell: } B_t = -1 \quad \text{iff} \quad F_t = \delta + \sum_{j=0}^{\infty} d_j X_{t-j} < 0 \qquad (4.3)$$

4.3.2 Rule returns process

(Unrealized) rule returns are the product of a binary stochastic signal B_{t-1}

and a continuous return random variable X_t. Equation (4.1) represents the trading rule return equation assuming discrete trading in markets where the underlying asset is lognormally distributed.

If we assume that the underlying process X_t is Gaussian, and the rule linear, the forecast F_t is Gaussian. It can be seen from Equations (4.1) and (4.3) that in this case, the rule return function is a mixture of marginal density functions of a truncated bivariate normal density. Such a distribution has been studied by Cartinhour (1990). He derived it in a form that can be evaluated using a computer algorithm developed by Schervish (1984). He showed that the marginal density function is a truncated normal density function multiplied by a 'skew function'. In general, the greater the degree of truncation, the more severe the skewing effect will be.

A truncated distribution is a common feature of portfolio insurance strategies. As shown in Trippi and Harriff (1991), the terminal return distribution of dynamic asset allocation rules is highly asymmetric being either left-truncated or positively skewed. Bookstaber and Clarke (1987) showed that the put option strategy truncates the lower tail and maintains the upside potential. Zhu and Kavee (1988) showed, using Monte Carlo simulations, that two strategies, namely the synthetic put approach and the constant proportion strategy, have the ability to reshape the return distribution so as to reduce downward risk and retain a certain part of upward gains.

There is, however, a key difference between option and technical rule returns. On the one hand, when using a put option, the left truncation is fixed at a deterministic level, the exercise price for an option. On the other hand, when applying a mechanical system downside risk reduction still occurs,[1] but the left or right truncation is a random one, due to the signal effect. By nature, a trading rule generates random infrequent trading. The signal of a rule remains constant for a certain random period, then jumps to a new level as the price behaves in a certain way.

This point highlights that rule returns are in fact closely related to the literature of infrequent trading and in particular with the Lo and MacKinlay (1990) approach. The stochastic model of nonsynchronous asset prices they developed is based on sampling with random censoring. They give explicit calculation of the effects of infrequent trading on the time series properties of asset returns. Contrary to Lo and MacKinlay (1990), we will have to consider explicitly two situations they only mentioned. First, our nontrading process is by its nature dependent, trading tomorrow (reversal of signal) depends on the signal of today. Second, we will relax their assumptions of independent and identically distributed underlying returns.

The expected value of rule returns can be established analytically, assuming that underlying returns follow a Gaussian process, although the exact distribution cannot. This is the most important statistic for trading purposes. In addition, the one-period variance can be deduced from the expected value using the relation:

$$\text{Var}(R_t) = E(R_t^2) - (E(R_t))^2 = E(B_{t-1}^2 X_t^2) - (E(R_t))^2$$

We know that by definition:

$$B_{t-1}^2 = 1$$

and

$$E(X_t^2) = \sigma^2 + \mu^2$$

where μ is the expected value or drift of X_t, and σ^2 is the variance of X_t. Therefore:

$$\text{Var}(R_t) = E(X_t^2) - (E(R_t))^2 = \sigma^2 + \mu^2 - (E(R_t))^2 \qquad (4.4)$$

An important observation is that the variance of rule returns is a negative function of its squared expected value. Then for given underlying market parameters, the more profitable the trading rule, the less risky this will be if risk is measured by the volatility of the asset. Consequently, maximizing returns will also maximize returns per unit of risk. This implies that attention need only be focused on the expected rule return.

4.3.3   Expected rule returns

Proposition 1

If the underlying process of returns $\{X_t\}$ follows a linear Gaussian process with drift, the expected value of linear rule returns R_t is given by:

$$E(R_t) = \sqrt{\frac{2}{\pi}} \sigma \, \text{Corr}(X_t, F_{t-1}) \exp(-\mu_F^2/2\sigma_F^2) + \mu(1 - 2\Phi[-\mu_F/\sigma_F]) \quad (4.5)$$

where Φ is the cumulative function of a normal distribution $N(0,1)$, μ and σ^2 are the mean and variance of the underlying series $\{X_t\}$, μ_F and σ_F^2 the mean and variance of $\{F_{t-1}\}$ and $\text{Corr}(X_t, F_{t-1})$ the linear correlation coefficient between the future underlying return $\{X_t\}$ and the forecaster $\{F_{t-1}\}$.

Proofs

$$E(R_t) = E(B_{t-1}X_t) = E(B_{t-1}(\sigma X_t^* + \mu)) = \sigma E(B_{t-1}X_t^*) + \mu E(B_{t-1})$$

where X_t^* designs a unit normal variate, $\mu = E(X_t)$ and $\sigma^2 = \text{Var}(X_t)$.

$$E(B_{t-1}) = \Pr(F_{t-1} > 0) - \Pr(F_{t-1} < 0) = 1 - 2\Pr(F_{t-1} < 0)$$
$$= 1 - 2\Phi(-\mu_F/\sigma_F)$$

$$E(B_{t-1}X_t^*) = \int\limits_{X_t^*} \int\limits_{F_{t-1}^* > -\mu_F/\sigma_F} X_t^* - \int\limits_{X_t^*} \int\limits_{F_{t-1}^* < -\mu_F/\sigma_F} X_t^*$$

where F_{t-1}^* designs a unit normal variate, $\mu_F = E(F_{t-1})$ and $\sigma_F^2 = \text{Var}(F_{t-1})$. Then, using the truncated bivariate moments given by Johnston and Kotz (1972, p. 116), it follows that:

$$E(B_{t-1}X_t^*) = \sqrt{\frac{2}{\pi}}\,\rho\exp\left(-\mu_F^2/2\sigma_F^2\right)$$

with

$$\rho = \text{Corr}(X_t, F_{t-1})$$

Therefore, Equation (4.5) results from the weighted summation of the two previous terms:

$$E(R_t) = \sigma E(B_{t-1}X_t^*) + \mu E(B_{t-1})$$

$$= \sigma\sqrt{\frac{2}{\pi}}\,\rho\exp(-\mu_F^2/2\sigma_F^2) + \mu(1 - 2\Phi[-\mu_F/\sigma_F]) \qquad (4.5)$$

The expected value of rule returns is composed of two components. One comes from the general Gaussian process without drift and the other from the drift component. Equation (4.5) generalizes and refines results from previous researches. The only theoretical formulae to which Equation (4.5) can be compared to are given by Praetz (1976) under the assumption of a random walk with drift. Having noted f, the frequency of short positions, Praetz (1976) has established that:

$$E(R_t) = \mu(1 - 2f)$$
$$\text{Var}(R_t) = \sigma^2$$

Under the random walk with drift assumption, there is no correlation between the forecast and the one-ahead return, then $\rho = \text{Corr}(X_t, F_{t-1}) = 0$. Therefore, Equation (4.5) can be rewritten as:

$$E(R_t) = \mu(1 - 2\Phi[-\mu_F/\sigma_F])$$

Then using the relationships between variance and expected value given by Equation (4.4), it follows that:

$$\text{Var}(R_t) = \sigma^2 + \mu^2 - \{\mu(1 - 2\Phi[-\mu_F/\sigma_F])\}^2$$

$$= \sigma^2 + 4\mu^2\Phi[-\mu_F/\sigma_F](1 - \Phi[-\mu_F/\sigma_F])$$

Equation (4.5) uses the probability of being short given by $\Phi(-\mu_F/\sigma_F)$ rather than the ex-post frequency of short positions, f, derived by Praetz (1976) and used by Bird (1985), Sweeney (1986) and Surujuras and Sweeney (1992).

Another dissimilarity with Praetz (1976) is that directional trading must increase the variance of returns. In fact, the latter result shares one property with nonsynchronous trading (Lo and MacKinlay, 1990). Namely, infrequent trading increases the variance of individual security returns with a non-zero mean. To the best of the author's knowledge, the expected value of rule returns for a general Gaussian process has not been derived before. It is not surprising that an exact analytical formulae for the expected value of linear rule returns can be established for any Gaussian process, since linear rules are well defined (Neftci, 1991). A first comment is that a biased forecast might be suboptimal.[2] This can be simply noted by considering a Gaussian process without drift ($\mu = 0$). Assuming that $\mu_F \neq 0$ gives an expected return equal to:

$$E(R_t) = \sqrt{\frac{2}{\pi}} \, \sigma \, \mathrm{Corr}(X_t, F_{t-1}) \exp(-\mu_F^2/2\sigma_F^2)$$

This is of course below the expected return of a similar but unbiased forecaster having $\mu_F = 0$.

4.3.4   Maximizing returns

Proposition 2
If the underlying process of logarithmic returns X_t is Gaussian, a forecaster F_{t-1} maximizes expected returns if and only if:

(1) it maximizes: $\rho = \mathrm{Corr}(F_{t-1}, X_t)$
(2) $\mu_F/\sigma_F = \mu/(\sigma\rho)$.

Proofs
Expected returns given by Equation (4.5) are functions of the following two variables: $x = \mu_F/\sigma_F$, the ratio mean/standard deviation of the forecast. $\rho = \mathrm{Corr}(F_{t-1}, X_t)$, the correlation between forecast and one-ahead return. Consequently, Equation (4.5) can be rewritten as:

$$E(R_t) = \sqrt{\frac{2}{\pi}} \, \sigma\rho \exp(-x^2/2) + \mu(1 - 2\Phi[-x]) \tag{4.6}$$

The two variables ρ and x are independent. So the forecast which maximizes expected returns must first maximize ρ. Then for a given ρ, the forecast which maximizes profits is obtained by deriving formula (4.6) as a function of x. It follows that the second condition is given by:

$$dE(R_t)/dx = 0 \quad \Leftrightarrow \quad \sqrt{\frac{2}{\pi}}\sigma\rho(-x)\exp(-x/2) + \mu\sqrt{\frac{2}{\pi}}\exp(-x^2/2) = 0$$

$$\Leftrightarrow \quad \sigma\rho x = \mu \quad \Leftrightarrow \quad x = \mu/(\sigma\rho)$$

$$\Leftrightarrow \quad \mu_F/\sigma_F = \mu/(\sigma\rho)$$

A first remark is that the optimal forecast in terms of mean squared error, F_{MSE} satisfies criteria (1) and (2). So if the X_t process is Gaussian, no linear trading rule obtained from a finite history of X_t can generate expected returns over and above vector autoregressions. A similar finding is attributable to Neftci (1991). It has been proven here that minimizing the mean squared error is a sufficient but not necessary condition to maximize returns. The forecast which maximizes profits need not be the forecast which minimizes the mean squared error. For instance, any forecast proportional to F_{MSE}, $a \cdot F_{MSE}$ (with $a > 0$) still maximizes profits. Therefore, there are cases for which a forecast can be highly profitable, although not accurate. When the true model is known, choosing the forecast which minimizes the mean squared error will maximise returns. However, when the true model is unknown, decreasing the mean squared error may be an inappropriate procedure to increase returns. Acar (1993) shows that the relationship between mis-specifications in terms of mean squared error and returns is highly nonlinear. There are cases for which a forecast can be badly mis-specified in terms of mean squared error but almost optimal in terms of returns and vice versa. The striking fact is that one cannot deduce from an increase in mean squared error a decrease in returns and vice versa.

4.4   TECHNICAL INDICATORS

The majority of traders forecast price changes using technical analysis, even though autoregressive techniques should yield better forecasts if the underlying process is linear (Neftci, 1991). Financial market players often prefer technical rules to autoregressive models, mainly because they are not looking for the forecast which minimizes the mean squared error but that which maximizes profits. Technical analysts have claimed that contrary to autoregressive models, technical indicators are able to capture the complex nonlinearity observed in financial prices.

Although technical analysis and autoregressive models might have different objectives, they both use the same information, that is, historical prices. Technical analysis covers a broad category of forecasting rules. However, certain of these are highly subjective and ill-defined. To be objective, buy and sell signals should be based on data available up to the current time t and should be independent of future information. Using the theory of Markov times, Neftci (1991) shows that rules based on mathematical formulae using past prices $\{P_t, \ldots, P_{t-m}, \ldots\}$ are well defined and objective in the sense that their performances can be assessed. It must be emphasized however, that there does not exist any theory or 'research algorithm' to design technical rules. A current practice among traders is to measure the profits and losses generated by an arbitrary set of trading rules and to select the rule which maximizes profits.

4.4.1   Technical indicators as autoregressive models

Technical indicator signals are usually expressed by an inequality in terms of past prices ('price' signal). An equivalent formulation in terms of (logarithmic) returns should be sought whenever possible ('return' signal). There are two reasons for this.

(1)   Ability to model rule returns. It has been shown in the previous section that when the signal is expressed by a linear combination of returns, the expected value of rule returns can be easily found for any underlying Gaussian process.

(2)   Purpose of comparison with autoregressive models. Autoregressive models are expressed in terms of returns. So if technical indicators signals were to stay a function of price, direct comparison with autoregressive models would be difficult.

4.4.2   Technical linear rules

Definition
A rule is said to be 'linear' if it can be expressed in the form of Equation (4.2).

Proposition 3
Any mechanical system triggering a sell signal from a finite linear combination of past prices of the form:

$$\text{sell } B_t = -1 \quad \Leftrightarrow \quad \sum_{j=0}^{m-1} a_j P_{t-j} < 0$$

where m being an integer larger than one and a_j constants admits an (almost) equivalent linear return formulation of the form:

$$\text{sell } \tilde{B}_t = -1 \quad \Leftrightarrow \quad \delta + \sum_{j=0}^{m-2} d_j X_{t-j} < 0 \tag{4.7}$$

where $X_t = \text{Ln}(P_t / P_{t-1})$

$$\delta = \sum_{j=0}^{m-1} a_j, \qquad d_j = -\sum_{i=j}^{m-2} a_i$$

The only required assumption is that rates of returns can be approximated by their logarithmic versions. That is:

$$1 - P_{t-j}/P_t \sim \mathrm{Ln}(P_t/P_{t-j})$$

for $j = 1, m - 1$

Proofs

$$\text{sell } B_t = -1 \quad \Leftrightarrow \quad \sum_{j=0}^{m-1} a_j P_{t-j} < 0$$

$$\Leftrightarrow \quad P_t - \sum_{j=0}^{m-1} b_j P_{t-j} < 0$$

with $b_0 = 1 - a_0$ and $b_j = -a_j$ for $j = 1, m - 1$

$$\Leftrightarrow \quad P_t - \sum_{j=0}^{m-1} b_j P_{t-j} + \sum_{j=0}^{m-1} b_j P_t - \sum_{j=0}^{m-1} b_j P_t < 0$$

$$\Leftrightarrow \quad \sum_{j=1}^{m-1} b_j (P_t - P_{t-j}) + \left(1 - \sum_{j=0}^{m-1} b_j\right) P_t < 0$$

$$\Leftrightarrow \quad \sum_{j=1}^{m-1} b_j (1 - P_{t-j}/P_t) + 1 - \sum_{j=0}^{m-1} b_j < 0$$

Let us assume that

$$1 - P_{t-j}/P_t \sim \mathrm{Ln}(P_t/P_{t-j}) = \sum_{i=0}^{j-1} X_{t-i} \qquad (4.8)$$

for $j = 1, m - 1$. It follows that

$$\sum_{j=1}^{m-1} b_j \sum_{i=0}^{j-1} X_{t-i} + 1 - \sum_{j=0}^{m-1} b_j < 0$$

$$\Leftrightarrow \quad \left(1 - \sum_{j=0}^{m-1} b_j\right) + \sum_{j=0}^{m-2} \left(\sum_{i=0}^{m-2-j} b_{m-1-i}\right) X_{t-j} < 0$$

$$\Leftrightarrow \quad \delta + \sum_{j=0}^{m-2} d_j X_{t-j} < 0$$

with

$$\delta = 1 - \sum_{j=0}^{m-1} b_j = \sum_{j=0}^{m-1} a_j$$

and

$$d_j = \sum_{i=0}^{m-2-j} b_{m-1-i} = -\sum_{i=0}^{m-2-j} a_{m-1-i} = -\sum_{i=j+1}^{m-1} a_i$$

Consequently, many popular technical systems are implicitly linear rules. This is especially the case for moving-average type and momentum indicators. Let us recall their definition through the necessary and sufficient conditions which trigger a short position (when the position is not short, it is long).

(1) Simple moving average of order $m > 1$

$$\text{sell if } P_t < SM_t(m) = \frac{P_t + P_{t-1} + \cdots + P_{t-m+1}}{m}$$

where $SM_t(m)$ denotes the simple moving average over m prices up to P_t.

(2) Weighted moving average of order $m > 1$

$$\text{sell if } P_t < \frac{(m-1)P_t + (m-2)P_{t-1} + \cdots + 1P_{t-m+1}}{m(m-1)/2}$$

(3) Exponential moving average of coefficient $1 > a > 0$

$$\text{sell if } P_t < a(P_t + (1-a)P_{t-1} + \cdots + (1-a)^{m-1}P_{t-m+1})$$

(4) Momentum of order $m > 1$ [3]

$$\text{sell if } P_t < P_{t-m+1}$$

(5) Double moving average of orders $r, m, 0 < r < m$

$$\text{sell if } SM_t(r) < SM_t(m)$$

It must be noted that the simple moving average is a particular case of the double moving average when the short moving average is the price ($r = 1$).

Explicit coefficients d_j in Equation (4.2) for all the technical indicators mentioned above can be found by applying the results of Proposition 3 and are given in Table 4.1.

Validity of logarithmic approximations
The validity of the return signal was checked using Monte Carlo simulations. One hundred samples of 2500 observations have been generated from various simulated normal random walks with steps distributed as $N(\mu, \sigma^2)$. The equivalence between price signals B_t and return signals $\tilde{B}_t$ has been tested

Table 4.1   *Return/price signals equivalence*

Rule	Parameter(s)	Price sell signals	Return sell signals
Simple order		$P_t < \sum_{j=0}^{m-1} a_j P_{t-j}$	$\sum_{j=0}^{m-2} d_j X_{t-j} < 0$
Simple MA	$m \geq 2$	$a_j = \dfrac{1}{m}$	$d_j = (m - j - 1)$
Weighted MA	$m \geq 2$	$a_j = \dfrac{m-j}{[m(m-1)]/2}$	$d_j = \dfrac{(m-j)(m-j-1)}{2}$
Exponential MA	$1 > a > 0, m \geq 2$	$a_j = a(1-a)^j$	see generalization
Momentum	$m \geq 2$	$a_j = 1$ for $j = m - 1$, $a_j = 0$ for $j \neq m - 1$	$d_j = 1$
Double orders		$\sum_{j=0}^{r-1} b_j P_{t-j} < \sum_{j=0}^{m-1} a_j P_{t-j}$	$\sum_{j=0}^{m-2} d_j X_{t-j} < 0$
Double MA	$m > r \geq 1$	$b_j = \dfrac{1}{r}, \quad a_j = \dfrac{1}{m}$	$d_j = (m-r)(j+1)$ $\quad$ for $0 \leq j \leq r - 1$ $d_j = r(m-j-1)$ $\quad$ for $r \leq j \leq m - 1$
Generalization		$\sum_{j=0}^{m-1} a_j P_{t-j} < 0$	$\delta + \sum_{j=0}^{m-2} d_j X_{t-j} < 0$, with: $d_j = -\sum_{i=j+1}^{m-1} a_i$ and $\delta = \sum_{j=0}^{m-1} a_j$

for the simple and weighted moving average rule.[4] As can be seen from Tables 4.2 and 4.3, signals are different in less than 3 per cent of all cases for simulated series. The largest deviation comes from $\mu = 0.001$ and $\sigma = 0.03$, for $m = 200$. Even then, returns signals are identical to price signals in at least 97 per cent of all cases. This case represents an upper bound in terms of both volatility and average returns over ten years for financial series (Taylor, 1986: Tables 3 and 4, pp. 33 and 34). On the basis of the empirical results presented in Tables 4.2 and 4.3, one can safely conclude that return signals lead to essentially the same investment strategies as price signals for values of m as large as 200.

The nice feature of the linear rules, expressed by a linear combination of returns, is that it includes in a unified framework autoregressive predictors (by construction) and technical systems (by reformulation). Finally, it must be emphasized that, although rather general, linear rules do not cover all technical rules used by practitioners.

Table 4.2 *Equivalence between price $\{B_t\}$ and return $\{\tilde{B}_t\}$ signals for the simple moving average rule*

Simulated random walk $N(\mu, \sigma^2)$, 100 replica

		Average (maximum) percentage of days having $B_t \neq \tilde{B}_t$			
Order m	No. obs	$\mu = 0, \sigma = 0.01$	$\mu = 0.001, \sigma = 0.01$	$\mu = 0, \sigma = 0.03$	$\mu = 0.001, \sigma = 0.03$
25	2500	0.18 (0.44)	0.15 (0.48)	0.50 (1.2)	0.50 (0.96)
50	2500	0.22 (0.56)	0.22 (0.44)	0.72 (1.40)	0.19 (1.08)
100	2500	0.37 (0.68)	0.26 (0.60)	1.08 (1.96)	1.05 (1.84)
200	2500	0.48 (0.84)	0.30 (0.68)	1.46 (2.44)	1.46 (2.60)

Table 4.3 *Equivalence between price $\{B_t\}$ and return $\{\tilde{B}_t\}$ signals for the weighted moving average rule*

Price signal B_t/return signal $\tilde{B}_t$: case of the weighted moving average rule

Simulated random walk $N(\mu, \sigma^2)$, 100 replica

		Average (maximum) percentage of days having $B_t \neq \tilde{B}_t$	
Order m	No. obs	$\mu = 0, \sigma = 0.03$	$\mu = 0.001, \sigma = 0.03$
200	2500	1.57 (2.52)	1.55 (2.92)

It is doubtful that signals from certain rules will ever accept an (almost) equivalent formulation of the type given by Equation (4.7). Rules which might be nonlinear are in particular rules based on intraday high and low data or on the maximum and minimum of certain values. An example of such a rule is the channel rule studied by Lukac, Brorsen and Irwin (1988), Taylor (1990a, 1994), Brock, Lakonishok and LeBaron (1992) and Curcio and Goodhart (1992). These rules have not been included in this research because they are not easily modelled.

4.4.3 Expected rule returns

Our purpose is to quantify the profitability of popular trading rules under plausible market conditions. More precisely, we consider the simple moving averages, weighted moving averages and momentum rules in their autoregressive versions given by Table 4.1. Therefore, the exact expected value of rule returns can be established using Equation (4.5) under Gaussian processes assumptions. We will assume that a year includes 250 days and that the daily process which drives underlying logarithmic returns is successively:

(1) a random walk with drift
(2) an autoregressive process of order one without drift, AR(1)
(3) a price-trend model without drift, ARMA(1,1)
(4) a fractional Gaussian process without drift.

Random walk with drift
The underlying model is

$$X_t = \mu + \varepsilon_t$$

where μ is a constant and ε_t is iid $N(0, \sigma^2)$. Figure 4.1 exhibits returns from a buy and hold strategy and from a simple moving average rule of orders 5, 20, 100 as a function of the drift. Overall, the following three remarks can be made.

(1) Expected return will be a fixed percentage of the drift. It will under-perform a buy and hold strategy if the drift is positive and outperform it if the drift is negative. The expected return of the simple moving average rule is a positive function of the absolute value of the drift $|\mu|$ and a negative function of the volatility σ. It is a positive function of the order m of the simple moving average, which can be explained by the fact that the most profitable strategy is buy and hold if the drift is positive. Indeed, it must be stressed that in this case technical trading would be useless and Figure 4.1 is really measuring how much trading rules underperform the optimal buy and hold strategy.
(2) The drift increases the instantaneous variance of return.
(3) Only in the absence of any drift in the data are rule returns uncorre-lated.

Figure 4.2 illustrates that in decreasing order of profitability, we have:

(1) momentum
(2) simple moving average
(3) weighted moving average.

It means that ex ante, certain technical rules will systematically capture the drift better than others.

AR(1)
The process of underlying returns is supposed to be an autoregressive model of order one without drift, defined by:

$$X_t = \alpha X_{t-1} + \varepsilon_t$$

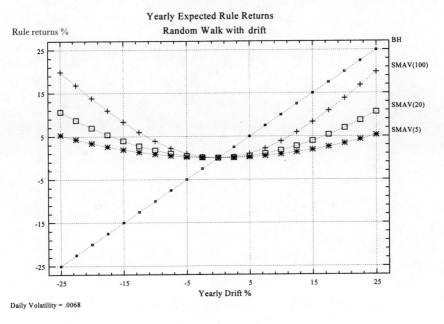

Yearly Expected Rule Returns
Random Walk with drift

Figure 4.1 *Technical returns as a function of the drift*

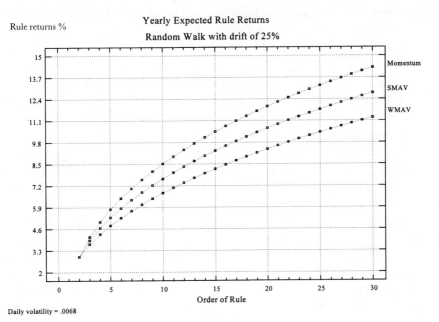

Yearly Expected Rule Returns
Random Walk with drift of 25%

Figure 4.2 *Technical returns as a function of the order of the rule, under the random walk with drift assumption*

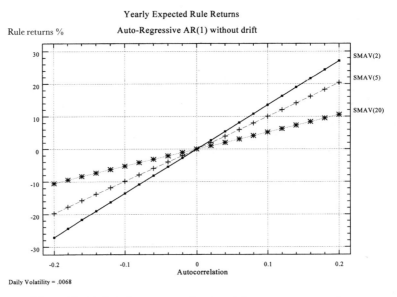

Figure 4.3   *Technical returns as a function of the autoregressive coefficient*

where α is the autoregressive coefficient and the ε_t are iid $N(0, (1 - \alpha^2)\sigma^2)$. Figure 4.3 exhibits that for a given system (moving average type) positive autocorrelation is required to make the investment profitable. The relationship between expected rule returns and first order autocorrelation is almost linear for an AR(1) model without drift and small α (see Equation (4.5)).

Trend-following models require positive autocorrelations to be profitable. However it is perfectly possible to create rules designed to take advantage of negative autocorrelations (e.g. opposite strategies). It is even possible to build rules which display positive expected return whatever the sign of the first-order autocorrelation.[5] Figure 4.4 shows that for a given order of rule, certain strategies perform better than others. The quicker the rule responds to a new price, the more profitable it is. For example, a short-order system captures better the autocorrelation of order one than a long-order system. In addition, the more weight given to the most recent prices, the more profitable it is. For instance, a weighted moving average systematically reflects a new price value better than a simple moving average, which in turn outperforms a momentum. Proposition 2 explains among other things why going from the random walk with drift process to the AR(1) process, the ranking of trading rules highlighted by respectively Figures 4.2 and 4.4 is inverted. Indeed, this shows on the one hand that under the AR(1) process assumption, a trading rule which maximizes profits is the short-term AR(1) forecast which is nothing else than the simple moving average of order 2. On the other hand, under the

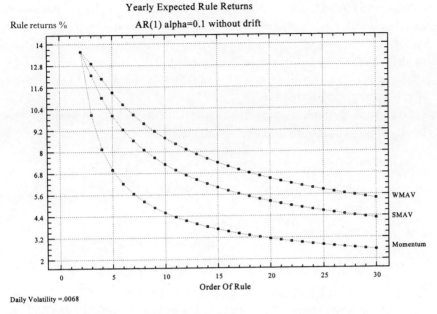

Figure 4.4 *Technical returns as a function of the order of the rule, under the AR(1) assumption*

random walk with drift model, a rule which maximizes profits is the long-term buy and hold strategy.

Finally, it can be noted that these results are consistent with the findings of LeBaron (1992) who performed Monte Carlo simulations to estimate the expected returns following simple moving averages of orders twenty, thirty and fifty under the assumption of AR(1) models.

ARMA(1,1), price-trend model

Taylor (1980) proposes an original approach to model trends in financial prices. The fundamental trend idea is that several returns are influenced in the same way, either towards a positive conditional mean or towards a negative conditional mean (Taylor, 1986). Thus, trends will cause positive autocorrelations. The impact of that current information which is not fully reflected in the current price, on future returns, should diminish as time goes on. Thus, the autocorrelations should decrease as the lag increases. The simplest parametric autocorrelation functions consistent with the observations was first investigated in Taylor (1980), and is defined by:

$$H_1 : \rho_h = Ap^h \qquad A, p, h > 0$$

There are two parameters in H_1. Parameter A measures the proportion of information not reflected by prices within one day. Parameter p measures the speed at which imperfectly reflected information is incorporated into prices. As $A \to 0$ or $p \to 0$, information is used perfectly. Credible price-trend models have typical parameter values $A = 0.03$ and $p = 0.95$ (Taylor, 1986). Low values for A are inevitable whilst values for p near to one indicate trends lasting for a long time.

One simple example assumes the return X_t is the sum of an autoregressive trend component μ_t and an unpredictable residual e_t.

$$X_t = \mu_t + e_t$$

$$\mu_t - \mu = p(\mu_{t-1} - \mu) + \zeta_t \qquad \zeta_t \text{ are iid } N(0, A\sigma^2(1 - p^2))$$
$$A = \text{Var}(\mu_t)/\text{Var}(X_t)$$

The returns then have autocorrelations:

$$\rho_h = Ap^h$$

The processes $\{\mu_t\}$ and $\{e_t\}$ are supposed to be stochastically independent and of a Gaussian nature (hence linear). Prices tend to move in one direction (the trend) for a period of time and these trends themselves change in a random and unpredictable fashion. The mean duration of such trends is denoted m_d and shown to be:

$$m_d = 1/(1 - p)$$

The price-trend model is in fact nothing else than a state representation of an ARMA(1,1) defined by:

$$X_t - \mu - p(X_{t-1} - \mu) = \varepsilon_t - q\varepsilon_{t-1}$$

where the variance reduction A is linked to p and q via:

$$A = (p - q)(1 - pq)/\{p(1 - 2pq + q^2)\}$$

Consequently, this particular price-trend model is a Gaussian process. Therefore, expected rule returns can again be deduced from Equation (4.5). They are as follows, assuming a price-trend model without drift.

(1) An increasing function of A for p and σ fixed – the larger the proportion of the variance of the returns that can be explained by the variance of the trends, the more profitable the trading rules are.
(2) An increasing function of p for A and σ fixed – the more the trend component is autocorrelated, the more profitable the trading rules are.
(3) A proportional (and positive, if trend-following, rule and positive autocorrelations) function of the volatility for A and p fixed.

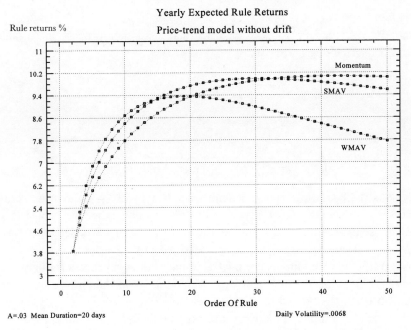

Figure 4.5 *Technical returns as a function of the order of the rule, under the price-trend model assumption*

Figure 4.5 gives an example of some rule returns of orders 2 to 50 for $\{\sigma = 0.0068,\ A = 0.03,\ m_d = 20$ days$\}$. The most profitable simple moving average corresponds to the order $r = 29$ days. It seems logical that given a mean duration of trends, a technical rule finds its optimal parameter around this value. In the case of the moving average, it is slightly bigger (order twenty-nine for a mean duration of twenty days). Ranking between systems is more complex and should be in favour of exponential moving average since Taylor (1986) has remarked that such representations can be very close to the optimal forecast. Rules are no longer uniformly ranked – that is, either systematically in favour of short (AR[1]) or long (see random walk with drift) strategies – but instead depend on the mean duration of the trend.

Such properties of linear trading rules might hold for nonlinear strategies such as the channel rule. Taylor (1994) finds in particular that channel rule returns are a positive function of A for p fixed (property a) and a positive function of p for A fixed (property b). The distribution shape of channel rule returns (Taylor, 1994) is extremely similar to the one of weighted moving average returns (Figure 4.3). The best order of channel rule, as is also the case for the weighted moving average, finds its optimal parameter close to the true mean duration of the trend.

Fractional ARIMA (0, d, 0)

An ARIMA $(0, d, 0)$ process or fractional Gaussian process is formally defined by Hosking (1981) as:

$$\nabla^d(X_t - \mu) = e_t$$

where

$$\nabla^d = (1 - B)^d = \sum_{k=0}^{\infty} \binom{d}{k}(-B)^k$$

$$= 1 - dB - \tfrac{1}{2}d(1 - d)B^2 - \tfrac{1}{6}d(1 - d)(2 - d)B^3 - \cdots$$

and B is the backward operator defined by $B(X_t) = X_{t-1}$, μ the mean return and $\{e_t\}$ the white noise process. In this chapter, the $\{e_t\}$ consists of independent identically distributed (normal) random variables with mean zero and variance σ_e^2.

As in the financial literature, the fractional Gaussian process is interpreted here as a function of the Hurst exponent rather than the parameter d. It is recalled that H is related to d by the relation $H = d + 0.5$.

Financial fractional Gaussian processes usually fall in the range $\tfrac{1}{2} < H < 1$ (Walter, 1991; Peters, 1991). They are characterized by a tendency to have trends and cycles, as in the price-trend model. In contrast, however, the fractional Gaussian process exhibits abrupt discontinuous changes because of an infinite or undefined variance. Cycles are no longer regular but erratic and aperiodic.

Expected rule returns assuming a fractional Gaussian process can also be established using Equation (4.5). Figures 4.6 and 4.7 exhibit that when there is no drift, expected rule returns are very similar to the ones corresponding to an autoregressive process of order one (Figures 4.3 and 4.4). This is because technical indicators do not exploit the main feature of a fractional Gaussian process, namely the long-term dependence (for $H > 0.5$). They only extract the short-term dependence, which is very much that of an AR(1) process.[6] Nevertheless, there does exist a major difference with more usual Gaussian processes: the maximum possible gain is infinite. Indeed, it appears that the optimal forecast defined by Hosking (1981) displays both infinite expected return and variance because the autocorrelations are not summable. Therefore, technical predictors might produce returns very far from the maximum achievable gain. However, it has been claimed (Mandelbrot, 1966) that the best linear forecast is useless for predicting the time series since it relies on parameter estimation.

Consequently, the fractional Gaussian process might constitute a case where technical trading rules might be preferred to the best linear forecast and would contradict Mandelbrot's (1963) opinion that expected gains from

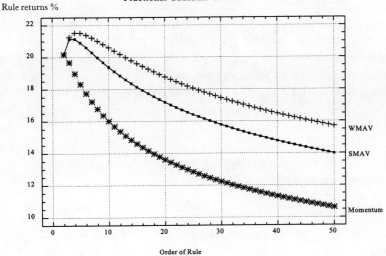

Figure 4.6 *Technical returns as a function of the order of the rule, under the fractional Gaussian process assumption*

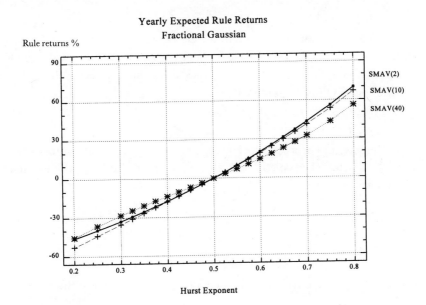

Figure 4.7 *Technical returns as a function of the fractional parameter*

the 'filter method' depend entirely on the assumption that price is continuous. Mandelbrot (1966, p. 242) stated: 'It is also possible to conceive of models where successive price changes are dependent so that prices do not follow a pure random walk, but where the nature of the dependence is such that it cannot be used to increase expected profits'. This does not apply to the fractional Gaussian process. Indeed, in the latter case, technical rules are quite profitable and do not rely on parameter estimation.

4.5   CONDITIONAL HETEROSKEDASTICITY AND LINEAR RULE RETURNS

4.5.1   ARCH(p) model

It has been recognized that models for returns should have either nonstationary variance or, conditional upon past observations, a variance dependent on such observations and additional variables. The pioneering work of Engle (1982) defines a μ-mean, autoregressive conditional heteroskedasticity ARCH(p) process, X_t, by:

$$X_t = \mu + \left\{ \sqrt{\alpha_0 + \sum_{i=1}^{p} \alpha_i (X_{t-i} - \mu)^2} \right\} \varepsilon_t$$

there being $p + 1$ non-negative parameters α_i with $\alpha_0 > 0$ and ε_t Gaussian white noise, with $\varepsilon_t \sim N(0, 1)$. This model has a very complicated unconditional distribution and it is difficult to establish conditions for stationarity or to subsequently find the moments.

Proposition 4
If the underlying process of returns $\{X_t\}$ is a zero-mean autoregressive conditional heteroskedasticity ARCH(p) process, the expected value of linear rule returns R_t is zero.

Proofs

$$E(R_t) = E\{E^{\{X_{t-1}\}}(B_{t-1} X_t)\}$$

where $E^{\{X_{t-1}\}}$ means the expected value of X_{t-1} conditional to the knowledge of

$$\{X_{t-1}\} = \{X_{t-1}, X_{t-2}, \ldots, X_{t-m}, \ldots\}$$

$$E(R_t) = E\left(B_{t-1}\sqrt{\alpha_0 + \sum_{i=1}^{p} \alpha_i X_{t-i}^2 \varepsilon_t}\right)$$

$$= E\left(B_{t-1}\sqrt{\alpha_0 + \sum_{i=1}^{p} \alpha_i X_{t-i}^2 E^{\{X_{t-1}\}}(\varepsilon_t)}\right)$$

Since the stochastic process ε_t is independent of $\{X_{t-1}\}$, it follows that

$$E^{\{X_{t-1}\}}(\epsilon_t) = 0$$

Then

$$E(R_t) = E\left(B_{t-1}\sqrt{\alpha_0 + \sum_{i=1}^{p} \alpha_i X_{t-i}^2 0}\right) = 0$$

Proposition 4 has just established the expected value of rule returns for one of these alternatives, namely the ARCH(p) model, still assuming process without drift. As long as the X_t are uncorrelated, no non-zero rule returns can be expected. So mean nonlinearities might be necessary to generate non-zero profits as in the case of the fractional Gaussian process.

4.5.2 Price-trend model with conditional heteroskedasticity

The ARCH process is constructed from strict white noise and, therefore, will always be uncorrelated. Extensions have been proposed to introduce small autocorrelations (Taylor, 1986). An example of this is given by the price-trend model with conditional heteroskedasticity:

$$X_t = \mu_t + e_t$$

where

$$\mu_t = p\mu_{t-1} + \nu_t, \quad \mathrm{Corr}(X_t, X_{t+\tau}) = Ap^\tau \quad \text{and} \quad A = \mathrm{Var}(\mu_t)/\mathrm{Var}(X_t)$$

The conditional heteroskedasticity is added through:

$$e_t = V_t \varepsilon_t$$

where

$$\mathrm{Ln}(V_t) - \alpha = \phi[\mathrm{Ln}(V_{t-1}) - \alpha] + \eta_t$$

with ε_t iid $N(0, 1 - A)$ and η_t iid $N(0, \beta^2(1 - \phi^2))$. It is not possible to derive analytical expected rule returns for such models. However, expected returns can be established using Monte Carlo simulations. We generated 500 samples of 1500 rates following a price-trend model with conditional heteroskedasticity. The parameters considered are typical of exchange rates models

Table 4.4   *Conditional heteroskedasticity and annualized returns from linear rules*

Price-trend model with conditional heteroskedasticity	S(5)	S(10)	S(20)	S(40)
Simulated return	7.33	9.38	10.78	10.63
Expected linear return	7.61	9.69	11.00	10.85
AR(2)-GARCH(1,1) model	**S(5)**	**S(10)**	**S(20)**	**S(40)**
Simulated return	24.06	17.90	12.77	9.39
Expected linear return	24.56	18.66	13.57	9.72

(Taylor, 1994). They are $A = 0.03$, $p = 0.95$, $\alpha = -5.15$, $\beta = 0.422$, $\phi = 0.973$.

Average returns were measured for the simple moving average of orders five, ten, twenty and forty (Table 4.4). Conditional heteroskedasticity makes the rule marginally more profitable than without conditional heteroskedasticity. The expected rule return resulting from the simulations is slightly higher than the expected return assuming a pure linear models given by Equation (4.5). However, the differences are rather small and the ranking between strategies remains unchanged.

4.5.3   AR(2)-GARCH(1,1) model

Another popular model including both conditional heteroskedasticity and serial dependencies is the AR(2)-GARCH(1,1) model (LeBaron, 1991) defined by:

$$X_t = a + b_1 X_{t-1} + b_2 X_{t-2} + \varepsilon_t$$

with

$$\varepsilon_t = \sqrt{h_t} z_t, \quad h_t = \alpha_0 + \alpha_1 \varepsilon_{t-1}^2 + \beta h_{t-1} \quad \text{and} \quad z_t \text{ iid } N(0,1)$$

As for the price-trend model with conditional heteroskedasticity, it is not possible to derive analytical expected rule returns for the AR(2)-GARCH(1,1) model. However, expected returns can be established using Monte Carlo simulations. Five hundred samples of 1500 rates following an AR(2)-GARCH(1,1) model were generated. The parameters considered are typical of exchange rates models (LeBaron, 1991). They are:

$$a = 0, \quad b_1 = 0.0832, \quad b_2 = 0.0324, \quad \alpha_0 = 2.294E - 5,$$
$$\beta = 0.77287, \quad \alpha_1 = 0.1680$$

As before, average returns were measured for the simple moving average of orders five, ten, twenty and forty (Table 4.4). This time, conditional heteroskedasticity makes the rule marginally less profitable than without conditional heteroskedasticity. The expected rule return resulting from the simulations is slightly lower than the expected return assuming a pure linear models given by Equation (4.5). The differences are again rather small and the ranking between strategies also continues unchanged.

To conclude, we do not believe that the presence of conditional heteroskedasticity will drastically affect returns generated by linear rules. That is, the presence of conditional heteroskedasticity, if unrelated to serial dependencies, may be neither a source of profits nor losses for linear rules.

4.6 CONCLUSIONS

Under the assumption that underlying asset returns follow a Gaussian process, the linear rule returns distribution is a mixture of marginal density functions of a truncated bivariate density function. Exact expected values can be obtained and are of importance because for given underlying market parameters, maximizing returns will also minimize risk.

The expected return following a linear trading rule is zero if the underlying process is a random walk without drift. This is non-zero if the underlying process exhibits a drift and/or autocorrelations. If the underlying process is a random walk with drift, the expected return of a trend-following trading rule is a positive function of the drift and a negative function of the volatility. If the underlying process exhibits positive (negative) autocorrelations but no drift, the expected return of a trend-following (contrarian) strategy is a positive function of the volatility.

Under the assumptions of an underlying Gaussian process and a linear forecast, minimizing the mean squared error is a sufficient but not necessary condition to maximize expected returns. Consequently, maximizing returns over and above autoregressive models is not possible. However, when the true price model is unknown, a non-optimal forecast has to be used. In these situations, the degree of mis-specification can be quite different in terms of mean squared error and returns.

Many popular technical trading rules can be expressed as autoregressive forecasts. Such re-formulations permit the application of both technical and statistical predictors in a unified framework called 'linear rules'.

To conclude, the purpose of this research has not been to test market efficiency, in itself a difficult task, rather to provide an understanding of the performances of some forecasting strategies relative to plausible models of financial prices.

4.7   APPENDIX

This appendix writes down Equation (4.5) for the different stochastic processes and trading rules investigated in this paper.

Proposition 1 has shown that if the underlying process of returns $\{X_t\}$ follows a linear Gaussian process with drift μ and volatility σ, the expected value of linear rule returns R_t is given by:

$$E(R_t) = \sqrt{\frac{2}{\pi}}\, \sigma \operatorname{Corr}(X_t, F_{t-1}) \exp(-\mu_F^2/2\sigma_F^2) + \mu(1 - 2\Phi[-\mu_F/\sigma_F])$$

$$(4.5)$$

where

$$F_t = \delta + \sum_{j=0}^{t} d_j X_{t-j}$$

with δ and the d_j being constants, μ_F the expected value of F_t and σ_F^2 the variance of F_t. Then it follows that:

$$\mu_F = \delta + \mu \sum_{j=0}^{t} d_j$$

and

$$\sigma_F = \sigma \sqrt{\sum_{j=0}^{t} d_j^2 + 2 \sum_{j=0}^{t} \sum_{i=j+1}^{t-1} d_i d_j \rho_{i-j}}$$

where

$$\rho_{i-j} = \operatorname{Corr}(X_{t-j}, X_{t-i})$$

$$\operatorname{Corr}(X_t, F_{t-1}) = \frac{\displaystyle\sum_{j=0}^{t} d_j \rho_{j+1}}{\sqrt{\displaystyle\sum_{j=0}^{t} d_j^2 + 2 \sum_{j=0}^{t} \sum_{i=j+1}^{t-1} d_i d_j \rho_{i-j}}}$$

Figures 4.1 to 4.7 illustrate expected rule returns for varied underlying processes and trading forecasts, namely the simple moving averages, weighted moving averages and momentum rules in their autoregressive versions given by Table 4.1.

REFERENCES

Acar, E. (1993) *Economic Evaluation of Financial Forecasting*, PhD Thesis, City University, London.

Bird, P.J.W.N. (1985) The weak form efficiency of the London Metal Exchange, *Applied Economics*, **17**, 571–87.

Black, F. and Perold, A.F. (1992) Theory of constant proportion portfolio insurance, *Journal of Economic Dynamics and Control*, **16**, 403–26.

Bookstaber, R. and Clarke, R. (1987) Options can alter portfolio returns, *Journal of Portfolio Management*, Spring, 63–70.

Brock, W., Lakonishok, J. and LeBaron, B. (1992) Simple technical rules and the stochastic properties of stock returns, *Journal of Finance*, **47**, 1731–64.

Cartinhour, J. (1990) One-dimensional marginal density functions of a truncated multivariate normal density function, *Commun. Statist.-Theory Meth*, **19**(1), 197–203.

Cox, J.C. and Rubinstein, M. (1985) *Options Markets*, Prentice Hall, Englewood Cliffs, New Jersey.

Curcio, R. and Goodhart, C.A.E. (1992) When support/resistance levels are broken, can profits be made? Evidence from the foreign exchange market, LSE Financial markets group discussion paper series, L142, July.

Davies, R. and Harte, D. (1987) Tests for Hurst effect, *Biometrika*, **74**, 95–101.

Dunis, C. (1989) Computerised technical systems and exchange rate movements. In *Exchange Rates Forecasting* (eds C. Dunis and M. Feeny), Woodhead-Faulkner, pp. 165–205.

Engle, R.F. (1982) Autoregressive conditional heteroskedasticity with estimates of the variance, *Econometrica*, **50**, September, 987–1007.

Hosking, J.R.M. (1981) Fractional differencing, *Biometrika*, **68**, 165–76.

Johnson, N.L. and Kotz, S. (1972) *Distributions in Statistics: Continuous Multivariate Distributions*, New York: Wiley.

Kaufman, P.J. (1987) *The New Commodity Trading Systems and Methods*, John Wiley & Sons.

Keenan, D.M. (1982) A time-series analysis of binary data, *Journal of the American Statistical Association*, **77**, 816–21.

LeBaron, B. (1991) Technical Trading Rules and Regime Shifts in Foreign Exchange, University of Wisconsin, Social Systems Research Institute, Working Paper 9118.

LeBaron, B. (1992) Do Moving Average Trading Rule Results Imply Nonlinearities in Foreign Exchange Markets?, University of Wisconsin, Social Systems Research Institute, Working Paper 9222.

Levich, R.M. and Thomas, L.R. (1993) The significance of technical trading-rule profits in the foreign exchange market: a bootstrap approach, *Journal of International Money and Finance*, **12**, 451–74.

Lo, A.W. and MacKinlay, A.C. (1990) An econometric analysis of nonsynchronous trading, *Journal of Econometrics*, **45**, 181–211.

Lukac, L.P., Brorsen, B.W. and Irwin, S.H. (1988) A test of futures market disequilibrium using twelve different technical trading systems, *Applied Economics*, **20**, 623–39.

Mandelbrot, B. (1963) The variation of certain speculative prices, *Journal of Business*, **36**, 394–419, reprinted in *The Random Character of Stock Market Prices* (ed. P. Cootner), MIT Press, Cambridge, MA, pp. 297–337.

Mandelbrot, B. (1966) Forecasts of future prices, unbiased markets, and 'Martingale' Models, *Journal of Business*, **39**, 242 55.

Neftci, S.N. (1991) Naive trading rules in financial markets and Wiener-Kolmogorov prediction theory: a study of technical analysis, *Journal of Business*, **64**, 549–71.

Neftci, S.N. and Policano, A.J. (1984) Can chartists outperform the market? Market efficiency tests for technical analysis, *Journal of Futures Markets*, **4**(4), 465–78.

Peters, E.E. (1991) *Chaos and Order in the Capital Markets*, John Wiley & Sons.

Praetz, P.D. (1976) Rates of return on filter tests, *Journal of Finance*, **31**, 71–5.

Schervish, M.J. (1984) Algorithm AS 195: Multivariate normal probabilities with error bound, *Applied Statistics*, **33**, 81–94.

Silber, W. (1994) Technical trading: when it works and when it doesn't, *The Journal of Derivatives*, Spring, 39-44.

Surujaras, P. and Sweeney R.J. (1992) *Profit-making Speculation in Foreign Exchange Markets. The Political Economy of Global Interdependence*, Westview Press.

Sweeney, R.J. (1986) Beating the foreign exchange market, *Journal of Finance*, **41**, 163–82.

Taylor, S.J. (1980) Conjectured models for trends in financial prices, tests and forecasts, *Journal of the Royal Statistical Society*, **143**A, 338–62.

Taylor, S.J. (1986) *Modelling Financial Time Series*, Chichester, England, John Wiley & Sons.

Taylor, S.J. (1990a) Reward available to currency futures speculators: Compensation for risk or evidence of inefficient pricing? *Economic Record (supplement)*, **68**, 105–116.

Taylor, S.J. (1990b) Profitable currency futures trading: a comparison of technical and time-series trading rules. In *The Currency Hedging Debate* (ed. L.R. Thomas), IFR Publishing Ltd., London, pp. 203–39.

Taylor, S.J. (1992) Efficiency of the Yen futures market at the Chicago Mercantile Exchange. In *Rational Expectations and Efficient in Future Markets* (ed. B.A. Goss), pp. 109–28.

Taylor, S.J. (1994) Trading futures using the channel rule: a study of the predictive power of technical analysis with currency examples, *Journal of Futures Markets*, **14**(2), 215–35.

Trippi, R.R. and Harriff, R.B. (1991) Dynamic asset allocation rules: survey and synthesis, *Journal of Portfolio Management*, Summer, 19–26.

Walter, C. (1991) L'utilisation des lois levy-stables en finance: une solution possible au problème posé par les discontinuités des trajectoires boursières (dernière partie), *Bulletin de l'Institut des Actuaires Français*, January, 350, 3–23.

Zhu, Y. and Kavee, R.C. (1988) Performance of portfolio insurance strategies, *Journal of Portfolio Management*, Spring, 48–54.

NOTES

1. The distribution of realized rule returns is highly skewed (Acar, 1993; Chapter 3, pp. 83–5).
2. An in-depth discussion on mis-specified forecasts can be found in Acar (1993; Chapter 4).
3. $m - 1$ in Kaufmann (1987).
4. Return and price signals are strictly identical for the momentum rule. The reason is that:

$$P_t < P_{t-m+1} \quad \Leftrightarrow \quad \mathrm{Ln}(P_t/P_{t-m+1}) < 0 \quad \Leftrightarrow \quad \sum_{j=0}^{m-2} X_{t-j} < 0$$

5. An example of such a strategy is:

$$\begin{cases} B_t = -1 & \Leftrightarrow & X_{t-1} < 0 \\ B_t = +1 & \Leftrightarrow & X_{t-1} > 0 \end{cases}$$

6. Distinguishing a fractional Gaussian process from an AR(1) model is recognized in the literature as a difficult task (Davies and Harte, 1987)

ACKNOWLEDGMENTS

I wish to acknowledge Banque Nationale de Paris plc who provided the opportunity for me to undertake this research. A special debt of gratitude must be paid to my ex-colleague at the 'technical desk', Pierre Lequeux. I am indebted to Dr Elias Dinenis who gave me encouragement and advice throughout the course of this research.

Chapter 5

Some exact results for moving-average trading rules with applications to UK indices

GEORGE W. KUO

5.1 INTRODUCTION

Technical analysis is commonly used by traders in financial markets to detect main turning points of the market at an early stage. The assumption underlying technical analysis is that investors respond to similar market events in very consistent ways. Such consistency implies future re-occurrences of historical price patterns, and, therefore, makes developing trading rules to identify certain price patterns a rewarding business. Numerous trading rules have been designed to provide investors and traders with trading suggestions based on the buying and selling signals they generate. However, the signals from most trading rules are always not decisive and have to be interpreted by users heuristically and subjectively. This makes systematic studies of all trading rules very difficult. Thus, the studies are usually confined to a subset of trading rules which can be mathematically well defined.

According to Neftci (1991), for a trading rule to be mathematically well defined it has to be able to issue signals that are Markov times.[1] Note that Markov times cannot depend on future information. Neftci (1991) shows that the moving-average rule can generate Markov times such that it is mathematically well defined. Because of this characteristic, the moving-average rule is of most interest to academics and practitioners because it generates trading signals mechanically without depending on traders' subjective judgements which always implicitly incorporate future information.

Recently, the feasibility of the moving-average rule in various financial markets has been studied. The common null hypothesis of these studies is that the moving-average rule can produce average returns that are statistically significant. Applying bootstrap methodology, Levich and Thomas (1993) find that a subclass of the moving-average rule does produce statistically significant average returns for futures contracts on the British pound, the Canadian dollar, the German mark, the Japanese yen and the Swiss franc. LeBaron (1991) also finds significant weekly average returns from certain moving-average rules in the quoted exchange rates for the British pound, the German mark and the Japanese yen. Furthermore, in order to identify the possible generating processes of these major foreign exchange rates, he simulates the returns from these moving-average rules based on several models with regime shifts and persistent trends[2] and compares them with the realized returns. He finds that these models cannot capture certain aspects of the realized returns. In addition, Brock, Lakonishok and LeBaron (1992) report that the moving-average rule produces statistically significant returns in the US stock market. Using bootstrap technique, they simulate returns from moving-average rules, etc., based on the random walk model, the AR(1) model, the GARCH-M model, and the exponential GARCH model, and compare these simulated returns with those realized returns. As LeBaron (1991), they conclude that these four models still cannot fully capture the characteristics of the realized returns.

Although LeBaron (1991) and Brock, Lakonishok and LeBaron (1992) have examined the probability distribution of realized returns from the moving-average rule empirically, it has not been investigated theoretically yet. Adopting Acar's (1993) general framework for studying trading rules, Acar and Satchell (1997) derive the probability distribution of realized returns from a simple moving-average rule given that asset returns are Markovian. In this chapter, we first derive some exact results for a special case of Acar and Satchell's Markovian framework and then extend these results to another moving-average rule in a different context. Finally, we apply the results for the first rule to UK FT100 index and futures.

As Acar (1993) suggests, in order to investigate the probability distribution of realized returns from a trading rule, we have to explicitly specify the nature of the trading rule, the underlying stochastic process for asset returns, and the particular return concept involved. The trading rule we study here is the moving-average rule. The return concept involved is the realized return from a sequential trading strategy based on the moving-average rule. The most important part in this framework is the assumption about the stochastic process that generates asset returns. This process should be able to account for the empirical characteristics already found in financial time series: asymmetry and fat tails.

In the literature, many processes have been proposed to explain these two empirical properties of financial time series. Tucker (1992) categorizes these processes into two types:

(1) the time-independent process

(2) the time-dependent process.

Many time-independent processes have been applied to account for the asymmetry and fat tails, e.g., the stable Paretian process (Mandelbrot, 1963; Fama, 1965), the symmetric Student process (Blattberg and Gonedes, 1974), the mixed diffusion-jump process (Merton, 1976), the lognormal-normal subordinated process (Clark, 1973), the mixed normal process (Kon, 1984) and the asymmetric stable Paretian process (Tucker, 1992). There also are some examples of the same application of the time-dependent processes. Akgiray (1989) uses ARCH-type processes to fit the returns in the US stock market, based on the fact that the independence and linearity of stock returns are not required to achieve market efficiency. In addition, recognizing the important implications of the asymmetry of stock returns in searching for an appropriate measure of risk in financial economics, Knight, Satchell and Tran (1995) propose a mixed scale gamma process to capture such asymmetry. They assume that whether the stock return will stay above or below its long-term mean depends on the realization of a positive or negative shock in the present period. Both shocks come from scale gamma processes with different parameters and their conditional switching probabilities are controlled by a Markov process. Strictly speaking, Knight, Satchell and Tran's process is a time-dependent one. The dependence comes from the Markov process, which describes the evolution of the conditional probabilities for the stock return to stay above and below its long-term mean.

Although Knight, Satchell and Tran assume in their empirical study that the asset return has a mixed gamma distribution, they actually propose a more general process for the asset return. Specifically, they assume the asset return to have a mixed distribution of two non-negative random variables, whose distributions satisfy certain moment conditions. This general Knight–Satchell–Tran process is the one we use for the generating process of asset returns.

The first moving-average rule we analyse is a naive geometric one which uses only the information about whether the asset return in the present period is positive or not to issue trading signals. We show that for investors following a sequential trading strategy based on this rule to make profits, either one of the following two conditions is sufficient provided that the stochastic process generating asset returns is the general Knight–Satchell–Tran process. The first condition is that the expected value of the positive shocks to the asset return is much greater than the expected value of the negative shocks. The second condition is that the positive shocks have to be very persistent themselves and much more persistent than the negative shocks. If we further assume that the asset return is independently identically distributed, we prove that either one of these conditions is still sufficient for investors to make profits. However, if conditioning the expected realized return on the event that investors already hold the target asset when they decide for the first time to adopt the sequential trading strategy, we show that the same first condition is still sufficient whereas the second one changes to be that the unexpected positive shocks must be highly persistent no matter how persistent the negative ones are.

The second case we study is a geometric moving-average rule which produces trading signals based on the whole past history of asset prices. We show that the corresponding sequential trading strategy always delivers negative realized returns to investors given that the general Knight–Satchell–Tran process generates asset prices. What is more interesting is that the negative average realized return can be minimized if the asset price actually follows a random walk.

Apart from deriving theoretical results, we also provide an example by using the empirically estimated numbers from Knight, Satchell and Tran (1995) to illustrate the implications of our results for the first moving-average rule. Interestingly, the example shows that on average investors can make profits by following the first moving-average rule in both UK FT100 index and FT100 futures markets if the asset return is not independently identically distributed. These profits are around 0.3 per cent and 6.0 per cent per month on average in the stock and futures markets respectively.

The rest of the chapter is organized as follows. Section 5.2 describes the moving-average rule. Section 5.3 presents the general Knight–Satchell–Tran process and the trading strategy based on a naive geometric moving-average rule and also derives the probability distribution as well as the expected value of the realized return. Section 5.4 extends the results in section 5.3 to a geometric moving-average rule utilizing the past history of asset prices to issue trading signals. Section 5.5 applies the theoretical results in section 5.3 to UK stock and futures markets. Finally, section 5.6 concludes the results.

5.2 THE MOVING-AVERAGE TRADING RULE

The moving-average rule is one of the trend-determining techniques in technical analysis. The feasibility of these techniques hinges on the assumption that crowd psychology makes the asset price move in discernible trends. However, the trends can be very volatile, almost haphazard at times. A moving average serves to smooth down the fluctuations of asset prices so that distortions can be reduced to a minimum.

In practice, a moving-average rule usually consists of two moving averages with different lengths. It delivers a buying or selling signal depending on whether a valid penetration exists. A valid penetration happens when the moving average with a shorter length penetrates the one with a longer length either from the below or from the above respectively. To be precise, we denote a moving-average rule, which consists of two moving averages with n and m lags respectively $(n > m)$, as moving-average (n, m). Mathematically, a moving-average (n, m) rule can be defined as:

$$B_t = \left(1/m \sum_{j=0}^{m-1} P_{t-j}\right) - \left(1/n \sum_{j=0}^{n-1} P_{t-j}\right) \tag{5.1}$$

where $\{P_t\}$ is a sequence of asset prices. Note that $B_t \geq 0$ implies a valid penetration from the below of the m-lag moving average into its n-lag counterpart and that $B_t < 0$ implies the opposite. In other words, a moving-average (n, m) rule will generate a buying signal for the next period when $B_t \geq 0$ and a selling signal for the next period when $B_t < 0$.

The validity of a moving-average (n, m) rule depends mainly on its time lags, m and n. These time lags should be determined according to the length of the market cycle to be detected. Since market cycles have been found to be nonperiodic, there does not exist a universal principle for choosing the time lags. This makes deciding optimal time lags for a moving-average (n, m) rule much more a science of art. Thus, many experiments are needed to search for optimal moving-average rules in different financial markets.

Academics and financial practitioners have devoted much effort in searching for optimal moving-average (n, m) rules. Among the optimal rules found so far, the moving-average $(n, 1)$-type rules, such as MA(150, 1) and MA(200, 1), are the simplest and most popular. Although these rules have passed standard empirical tests and passed them well, their feasibility has not yet been theoretically justified.

In general, there are two classes of moving-average rules: the arithmetic moving-average rule and the geometric moving-average rule. The moving-average (n, m) rule that can be described by Equation (5.1) belongs to the former. Specifically, an arithmetic moving-average $(n, 1)$ rule, denoted as AMA$(n, 1)$, can be defined as:

$$B_t \geq 0, \text{ iff } P_t \geq \left(1/n \sum_{j=0}^{n-1} P_{t-j}\right); \quad B_t < 0, \text{ otherwise} \tag{5.2}$$

whereas a geometric moving-average $(n, 1)$ rule, denoted by GMA$(n, 1)$ can be defined as:

$$B_t \geq 0, \text{ iff } P_t \geq \left(\prod_{j=0}^{n-1} P_{t-j}\right)^{1/n}; \quad B_t < 0, \text{ otherwise} \tag{5.3}$$

Taking the natural logarithm of the inequality in Equation (5.3) and rearranging, we have:

$$R_t \geq -\sum_{j=1}^{n-2} \frac{[n-(j+1)]}{n-1} R_{t-j} \tag{5.4}$$

where $\{R_t\}$ is a sequence of asset returns. Equation (5.4) shows that as long as the asset return at present time t is greater than or equal to the negative of the weighted average of the asset returns in the past $(n-2)$ periods, a geometric moving-average $(n,1)$ rule will suggest investors to hold the asset for the next period. Otherwise, it will issue a selling signal suggesting investors to close their positions at the beginning of the next period. Under a specific assumption,[3] we can also simplify the arithmetic moving-average $(n,1)$ rule in Equation (5.2) as the weighted average of the past asset returns expressed as Equation (5.4). The primary results derived in the next two sections are mainly based upon the geometric moving-average $(n,1)$ rules.

5.3 THE STOCHASTIC PROCESS FOR ASSET RETURNS

Knight, Satchell and Tran (1995) assume daily asset returns to follow the stochastic process:

$$R_t = \mu_l + Z_t \varepsilon_t - (1 - Z_t)\delta_t \tag{5.5}$$

where μ_l is the long-term mean of daily asset returns; ε_t and δ_t are two non-negative independently identically distributed random variables, e.g., two different scale gamma processes with probability density functions:

$$pdf_\varepsilon(x) = \begin{cases} \dfrac{\lambda_1^{\alpha_1} x^{\alpha_1 - 1}}{\Gamma(\alpha_1)} \exp(-\lambda_1 x) & \text{if } x \geq 0 \\ 0 & \text{otherwise} \end{cases} \tag{5.6}$$

$$pdf_\delta(x) = \begin{cases} \dfrac{\lambda_2^{\alpha_2} x^{\alpha_2 - 1}}{\Gamma(\alpha_2)} \exp(-\lambda_2 x) & \text{if } x \geq 0 \\ 0 & \text{otherwise} \end{cases} \tag{5.7}$$

where $\Gamma(\cdot)$ is a gamma function; the random variable Z_t is a stationary two-state Markov process with the transition probabilities:

$$\begin{aligned} &\Pr[Z_t = 1 \mid Z_{t-1} = 1] = p \\ &\Pr[Z_t = 0 \mid Z_{t-1} = 1] = 1 - p \\ &\Pr[Z_t = 1 \mid Z_{t-1} = 0] = 1 - q \\ &\Pr[Z_t = 0 \mid Z_{t-1} = 0] = q \end{aligned} \tag{5.8}$$

where $0 \leq p, q \leq 1$.

As Z_t is stationary, we can compute the stationary probability of state one, Π, by:

$$\Pi = \frac{1-q}{2-p-q}$$

Therefore, in the stationary state, the asset return will stay above its own long-term mean with probability Π and below its long-term mean with probability $1 - \Pi$, namely:

$$\begin{cases} R_t = \mu_l + \varepsilon_t \geq \mu_l & \text{with probability } \Pi \\ R_t = \mu_l - \delta_t < \mu_l & \text{with probability } 1 - \Pi \end{cases}$$

We also assume that ε_t, δ_t and Z_t are independent to one another for $\forall t$. Note that although, in their empirical study, Knight, Satchell and Tran (1995) use scale gamma distributions for the unexpected shocks – ε_t, δ_t – they actually propose a more general process for the asset return. We call it the general Knight–Satchell–Tran process. This process, as described by Equation (5.5), just requires the unexpected shocks be two non-negative independently identically distributed random variables with characteristic functions $\Phi_\varepsilon(s)$ and $\Phi_\delta(s)$[4] and to satisfy certain moment conditions.[5] In addition, we presume the long-term mean of asset return to be zero.[6]

After assigning the general Knight–Satchell–Tran process as the generating stochastic process of the asset return, we still need to clarify the concept of the realized return from the geometric moving-average $(n, 1)$ rule whose probabilistic properties we want to examine. We assume that an investor follows a sequential trading strategy according to the trading signals generated by the geometric moving-average $(n, 1)$ rule. Suppose that an investor decides to hold an asset A for whatever reason at the very beginning of period one according to a buying signal he receives at the end of period zero, that is, $B_0 \geq 0$. Since then, he has to decide sequentially at the beginning of every subsequent period whether he is going to keep holding asset A or sell it based on the signal generated by the geometric moving-average $(n, 1)$ rule at the end of the previous period. Note that the only information he has when he makes the decision is either a buying or a selling signal he receives at the end of the previous period. He has no prior information other than the knowledge of the return generating process about what will happen during the period after he takes his action. Thus, according to the nature of this sequential trading strategy, if an investor decides to keep holding asset A until the end of period T, it means that he or she observes buying signals from Equation (5.3) in the first $T - 1$ periods, i.e.

$$B_t \geq 0, 1 \leq t \leq T - 1$$

and receives a selling signal at the end of period T[7], namely, $B_T < 0$. Note that T here is actually a random variable. Now we can define the realized return for T periods as:

$$RR_T = \sum_{t=1}^{T} R_t \times I_{\{B_{t-1} \geq 0\}} \tag{5.9}$$

where $I_{\{B_t \geq 0\}}$ is an indicator function whose value equals one when $B_t \geq 0$ and zero when otherwise. We next present a proposition, Proposition 1, which gives a particular form for the characteristic function of realized returns. Our proof mainly follows Acar and Satchell (1997). We specialize our results to the case where the asset return is generated by Equation (5.5).

Proposition 1
Assume that the general Knight–Satchell–Tran process is the underlying stochastic process of asset returns. The probability distribution of the realized return in Equation (5.9) resulting from the geometric moving-average $(2, 1)$ rule can be described by the following characteristic function.

$$\Phi_{RR_T}(s) = (1 - \Pi)\Phi_\delta(-s) + \Pi(1 - p)\frac{\Phi_\delta(-s)}{1 - p\Phi_\varepsilon(s)} \tag{5.10}$$

Proof
From Equation (5.4) we see that the geometric moving-average $(2, 1)$ rule can be expressed as:

$B_t \geq 0$, iff $R_t \geq 0$; $B_t < 0$, otherwise

Moreover, we can also see from Equation (5.5) that:

$R_t \geq 0$, iff $Z_t = 1$; $R_t < 0$, iff $Z_t = 0$

Therefore, the information contained in the sequence of trading signals, $\{B_0, \ldots, B_t\}$, is identical to that contained in the sequence of Markovian random variables, $\{Z_0, \ldots, Z_t\}$.

To derive the distribution of the realized return, we have to compute the probability for an investor to hold the target asset until the end of period T conditional on the event that a buying signal is generated by the geometric moving-average $(2, 1)$ rule at the end of period zero.

$$\begin{aligned}
\Pr(N = T) &= \Pr(B_T < 0, B_{T-1} \geq 0, \ldots, B_1 \geq 0, B_0 \geq 0) \\
&= \Pr(Z_T = 0, Z_{T-1} = 1, \ldots, Z_1 = 1, Z_0 = 1) \\
&= \Pr(Z_T = 0, Z_{T-1} = 1, \ldots, Z_1 = 1 \mid Z_0 = 1) \Pr(Z_0 = 1) \\
&= \begin{cases} \Pi p^{T-1}(1-p) & \text{if } T \geq 1 \\ 1 - \Pi & \text{if } T = 0 \end{cases}
\end{aligned}$$

where Π is the stationary distribution of state one of the Markov process in Equation (5.8).

Now we can derive the conditional characteristic function of the realized return for T periods, RR_T, from the sequential trading strategy based on the geometric moving-average $(2, 1)$ rule as follows.

$$\begin{aligned}
\Phi_{RR_T|N=T}(s) &= E[e^{\{i[\sum_{t=1}^{N}(R_t \times I_{\{B_{t-1} \geq 0\}})]s\}} \mid N = T] \\
&= E[e^{\{i[\sum_{t=1}^{T}(R_t \times I_{\{B_{t-1} \geq 0\}})]s\}} \mid B_0 \geq 0, \ldots, B_T < 0] \\
&= E[e^{\{i(\sum_{t=1}^{T} R_t)s\}} \mid Z_0 = 1, \ldots, Z_T = 0] \\
&= E[e^{i(\varepsilon_1 + \cdots + \varepsilon_{T-1} - \delta_T)s}] \\
&= \begin{cases} \Phi_\varepsilon^{T-1}(s)\Phi_\delta(-s) & \text{if } T \geq 1 \\ \Phi_\delta(-s) & \text{if } T = 0 \end{cases}
\end{aligned}$$

Because T is a random variable, we have to compute the unconditional characteristic function of the realized return as follows.

$$\begin{aligned}
\Phi_{RR_T}(s) &= \sum_{T=0}^{\infty} E[e^{\{i[\sum_{t=1}^{N}(R_t \times I_{\{B_{t-1} \geq 0\}})]s\}} \mid N = T] \Pr(N = T) \\
&= \sum_{T=1}^{\infty} [\Phi_\varepsilon^{T-1}(s)\Phi_\delta(-s)\Pi p^{T-1}(1-p)] + (1-\Pi)\Phi_\delta(-s) \\
&= (1-\Pi)\Phi_\delta(-s) + \Pi(1-p)\frac{\Phi_\delta(-s)}{1 - p\Phi_\varepsilon(s)}
\end{aligned}$$

Note that the function form of $\Phi_{RR_T}(s)$ is a special case of Proposition 1 of Acar and Satchell (1995).

Proposition 2

If we condition the result in Equation (5.10) on the event $\{R_0 \geq 0\}$, we have

$$\Phi_{RR_T}(s) = \frac{(1-p)\Phi_\delta(-s)}{1 - p\Phi_\varepsilon(s)} \tag{5.11}$$

Proof

Substitute $\Pi = 1$ into Equation (5.10) and the result follows.

Proposition 3

If the asset return, R_t, is independently identically distributed, we have

$$\Phi_{RR_T}(s) = \frac{q\Phi_\delta(-s)[1+p-p\Phi_\varepsilon(s)]}{1-p\Phi_\varepsilon(s)} \qquad (5.12)$$

Proof

The assumption that the asset return is independently identically distributed implies that p and q in Equation (5.8) satisfy the condition $p + q = 1$, which in turn implies

$$\Pi = \frac{1-q}{2-p-q} = 1-q = p$$

Substitute this condition into Equation (5.10), rearrange it and the result follows.

Proposition 4

For the realized return from the geometric moving-average $(2, 1)$ rule, we can compute the expected realized return, $E(RR_T)$, as

$$E(RR_T) = \frac{1}{1-p}\{\Pi p\mu_\varepsilon - (1-p)\mu_\delta\} \qquad (5.13)$$

where μ_ε and μ_δ are the means of the unexpected shocks, ε_t and δ_t, respectively.

Proof

To derive the expected realized return, we first have to differentiate the characteristic function of the realized return.

$$\Phi'_{RR_T}(s) = -(1-\Pi)\Phi'_\delta(-s) + \Pi(1-p)\left\{ \frac{p\Phi_\delta(-s)\Phi'_\varepsilon(s)}{[1-p\Phi_\varepsilon(s)]^2} - \frac{\Phi'_\delta(-s)}{1-p\Phi_\varepsilon(s)} \right\}$$

Since

$$E(RR_T) = -i\Phi'_{RR_T}(0)$$

we have

$$E(RR_T) = i(1 - \Pi)\Phi_\delta'(0) - i\Pi(1 - p)\left\{ \frac{p\Phi_\delta(0)\Phi_\varepsilon'(0)}{[1 - p\Phi_\varepsilon(0)]^2} - \frac{\Phi_\delta'(0)}{1 - p\Phi_\varepsilon(0)} \right\}$$

$$= -(1 - \Pi)\mu_\delta + \Pi(1 - p)\left\{ \frac{p\mu_\varepsilon}{(1 - p)^2} - \frac{\mu_\delta}{1 - p} \right\}$$

$$= \frac{1}{1 - p}[\Pi p\mu_\varepsilon - (1 - p)\mu_\delta]$$

From Equation (5.13), we know that for the expected realized return to be positive, the inequality

$$\mu_\varepsilon \geq \frac{1 - p}{\Pi p}\mu_\delta$$

must be satisfied. One sufficient condition for that inequality to be satisfied is that:

$$\mu_\varepsilon \geqslant \mu_\delta$$

This condition basically states that if the unexpected positive shocks in the market generally have much more impact on the asset return than the unexpected negative shocks, the sequential trading strategy based on the signals from the geometric moving-average $(2, 1)$ rule will on average create positive realized returns. Furthermore, the inequality can be satisfied too as long as:

$$\Pi p \geqslant (1 - p) \text{ if } \mu_\varepsilon \approx \mu_\delta$$

This second sufficient condition implies that the unexpected positive shocks are highly persistent and much more persistent than the unexpected negative ones even when their means are not much different from each other. To see this, we substitute:

$$\Pi = \frac{1 - q}{2 - p - q}$$

into the coefficient of the RHS of the inequality and rearrange it as:

$$\frac{1}{1 - p}\left(1 + \frac{1 - p}{1 - q}\right)$$

Obviously, we know from this coefficient that in order to have a positive expected realized return, state one in which the asset return is positive must be very persistent, say, $p \geq 0.90$, and much more persistent than state zero in which the asset return is negative, i.e., $p \geqslant q$. For example, suppose that p is equal to 0.90, and that q is equal to 0.99, which means that state zero is even more persistent than state one. Then, in order to have positive expected realized return, the inequality

$$\mu_\varepsilon \geq 1.22\mu_\delta$$

should be satisfied. In this case, it will be easily violated if the mean of negative shocks is more or less equal to that of positive shocks. However, if state zero is much less persistent than state one, e.g., $q = 0.5$, the inequality becomes:

$$\mu_\varepsilon \geq 0.13\mu_\delta$$

and can be more easily satisfied than the previous one.

Proposition 5

If we condition the result in Equation (5.13) on the event $\{R_0 \geq 0\}$, we have:

$$E(RR_T) = \frac{1}{1-p}[p\mu_\varepsilon - (1-p)\mu_\delta] \tag{5.14}$$

Proof

Substitute $\Pi = 1$ into Equation (5.13) and the result follows.

Proposition 6

Assume that the asset return, R_t is independently identically distributed, the expected realized return in Equation (5.13) becomes:

$$E(RR_T) = \frac{1}{q}\{p^2\mu_\varepsilon - q\mu_\delta\} \tag{5.15}$$

Proof

Substitute $p + q = 1$ and $\Pi = p = 1 - q$ into Equation (5.13) and the result follows.

Basically, Equations (5.14) and (5.15) present similar results. Both equations have the same first sufficient condition for getting a positive expected realized return as Equation (5.13). However, the second condition of Equation (5.14) says that as long as state one is highly persistent, an investor, who already owns the target asset when he or she decides to adopt the sequential trading strategy, can make profits on average. In this case, whether state zero is persistent or not is irrelevant. In contrast to Equation (5.14), Equation (5.15) even has the same second condition as Equation (5.13), but the degree of persistence of state one relative to state zero required by the former is much higher than the latter. For example, we also assume that $p = 0.9$ and $q = 0.5$.

The inequality:

$$\mu_\varepsilon \geq \frac{q}{p^2}\mu_\delta$$

becomes

$$\mu_\varepsilon \geq 0.31\mu_\delta$$

This inequality is apparently much more restricted than:

$$\mu_\varepsilon \geq 0.13\mu_\delta$$

5.4 THE MOVING-AVERAGE $(\infty, 1)$ RULE

For the moving-average $(\infty, 1)$ rule, Equation (5.4) becomes:

$$R_t \geq -\lim_{n \to \infty}\left(\sum_{j=1}^{n-2}\frac{[n-(j+1)]}{n-1}R_{t-j}\right) \tag{5.16}$$

In order to make the moving-average $(\infty, 1)$ rule work, the RHS of Equation (5.16) has to converge to a random process or a scalar. This requires the sequence of coefficients:

$$\left\{\frac{n-(j+1)}{n-1}\right\}$$

to be absolutely summable. Obviously, it is not because the summation equals:

$$\frac{(n-2)}{2}$$

In other words, the RHS of Equation (5.16) does not converge in probability to a random process or a scalar even though the asset return is assumed to follow a stationary process. Therefore, we cannot extend the results of the geometric moving-average $(2, 1)$ rule to the geometric moving-average $(\infty, 1)$ rule based on Equation (5.16). However, if we take the natural logarithm on both sides of Equation (5.3), we can have:

$$\ln P_t \geq \sum_{j=0}^{n-1}\ln(P_{t-1})/n \tag{5.17}$$

Assuming the natural logarithm of asset price, $\ln P_t$, to follow a stationary process, we can assert that the RHS of Equation (5.17), according to the Law of Large Numbers, will converge in probability to its long-term mean level, denoted by μ_1. Hence, Equation (5.17) becomes:

$$\ln P_t \geq \mu_1 \tag{5.18}$$

Similarly, provided that the asset price follows a stationary stochastic process, the arithmetic moving-average rules described by Equation (5.2) can be simplified to be:

$$P_t \geq \mu_2 \qquad\qquad\qquad (5.19)$$

where μ_2 is the long-term mean of P_t.

As usual, our purpose is to derive the distribution of the realized return from the sequential trading strategy based on the moving-average $(\infty, 1)$ rule. In order to work on asset returns, we choose to focus on the case of the natural logarithm of asset prices as described by Equation (5.18). However, the following derivation can be easily duplicated for the case of asset price levels. Accordingly, the geometric moving-average $(\infty, 1)$ rule will generate a buying signal when the natural logarithm of the asset price is greater than or equal to its long-term mean and a selling signal when the opposite happens. Based on this characteristic, we assume that the natural logarithm of the asset price is generated by the general Knight–Satchell–Tran process:

$$\ln P_t = \mu_1 + Z_t \varepsilon_t - (1 - Z_t)\delta_t \qquad\qquad\qquad (5.20)$$

where the random variables ε_t, δ_t and Z_t have the same specifications as described in Section 5.3 and are independent to one another for $\forall t$.

Equation (5.20) states that the natural logarithm of the asset price fluctuates around its long-term mean and whether it is greater than the long-term mean or not depends on the outcome of the Markovian random variable Z_t. It can be easily shown that $\ln P_t$ is stationary. Moreover, we can present the asset return, denoted by:

$$R_t = \ln P_t - \ln P_{t-1}$$

as

$$R_t = Z_t \varepsilon_t - Z_{t-1}\varepsilon_{t-1} - (1 - Z_t)\delta_t + (1 - Z_{t-1})\delta_{t-1} \qquad\qquad\qquad (5.21)$$

It can be shown that the asset return is a first-order moving-average process which satisfies:

$$E(R_t) = 0$$

$$\mathrm{Var}(R_t) = 2[\Pi(\sigma_\varepsilon^2 + \mu_\varepsilon^2) + (1 - \Pi)(\sigma_\delta^2 + \mu_\delta^2)]$$

$$E(R_{t-i}R_{t-j}) = \begin{cases} -[\Pi(\sigma_\varepsilon^2 + \mu_\varepsilon^2) + (1 - \Pi)(\sigma_\delta^2 + \mu_\delta^2)] & \text{if } |i - j| = 1 \\ 0 & \text{if } |i - j| > 1 \end{cases}$$

Proposition 7

Assume that the asset return is generated by the first-order moving-average process as described by Equation (5.21). The probability distribution of the realized return resulting from the geometric moving-average $(\infty, 1)$ rule can be described by the characteristic function:

$$\Phi_{RR_T}(s) = (1 - \Pi)q[\Phi_\delta(s) + \Phi_\delta(-s)] + [1 - p(1 - \Pi)][\Phi_\varepsilon(-s) + \Phi_\delta(-s)]$$

$$(5.22)$$

Proof

From Equation (5.18) we see that the geometric moving-average $(\infty, 1)$ rule can be expressed as:

$$B_t \geq 0, \text{ iff } \ln P_t \geq \mu_1; \quad B_t < 0, \text{ otherwise}$$

Moreover, we can also see from Equation (5.20) that:

$$\ln P_t \geq 0, \text{ iff } Z_t = 1; \quad \ln P_t < 0, \text{ iff } Z_t = 0$$

Therefore, the information contained in the sequence of trading signals, $\{B_0, \ldots, B_t\}$, is identical to that contained in the sequence of Markovian random variables, $\{Z_0, \ldots, Z_t\}$.

To derive the distribution of the realized return, we have to compute the probability for an investor to hold the target asset until the end of period T conditional on the event that a buying signal is generated by the geometric moving-average $(\infty, 1)$ rule at the end of period zero.

$$\begin{aligned}
\Pr(N = T) &= \Pr(B_T < 0, B_{T-1} \geq 0, \ldots, B_1 \geq 0, B_0 \geq 0) \\
&= \Pr(Z_T = 0, Z_{T-1} = 1, \ldots, Z_1 = 1, Z_0 = 1) \\
&= \Pr(Z_T = 0, Z_{T-1} = 1, \ldots, Z_1 = 1 \mid Z_0 = 1) \Pr(Z_0 = 1) \\
&= \begin{cases} \Pi p^{T-1}(1-p) & \text{if } T \geq 1 \\ 1 - \Pi & \text{if } T = 0 \end{cases}
\end{aligned}$$

where Π is the stationary distribution of state one of the Markov process in Equation (5.8).

Now we can derive the conditional characteristic function of the realized return for T periods from the sequential trading strategy based on the geometric moving-average $(\infty, 1)$ rule as follows:

$$\begin{aligned}
\Phi_{RR_T|N=T}(s) &= E[e^{\{i[\sum_{t=1}^{N}(R_t \times I_{\{B_{t-1} \geq 0\}})]s\}} \mid N = T] \\
&= E[e^{\{i[\sum_{t=1}^{T}(R_t \times I_{\{B_{t-1} \geq 0\}})]s\}} \mid B_0 \geq 0, \ldots, B_T < 0] \\
&= E[e^{\{i[\sum_{t=1}^{T}(R_t)]s\}} \mid Z_0 = 1, \ldots, Z_T = 0] \\
&= E[e^{i[(\varepsilon_1 - \varepsilon_0) + (\varepsilon_2 - \varepsilon_1) + \cdots + (\varepsilon_{T-1} - \varepsilon_{T-2}) + (-\delta_t - \varepsilon_{T-1})]s}] \\
&= \begin{cases} \Phi_\varepsilon(-s) + \Phi_\delta(-s) & \text{if } T \geq 1 \\ q[\Phi_\delta(s) + \Phi_\delta(-s)] + (1-p)[\Phi_\varepsilon(-s) + \Phi_\delta(-s)] & \text{if } T = 0 \end{cases}
\end{aligned}$$

Finally, the unconditional characteristic function becomes:

$$\Phi_{RR_T}(s) = \sum_{T=0}^{\infty} E[e^{\{i[\sum_{t=1}^{N}(R_t \times I_{\{B_{t-1} \geq 0\}})]s\}} \mid N = T] \Pr(N = T)$$

$$= \Pi(1-p)[\Phi_\varepsilon(-s) + \Phi_\delta(-s)] \sum_{T=1}^{\infty} p^{T-1}$$

$$+ (1-\Pi)\{q[\Phi_\delta(s) + \Phi_\delta(-s)]$$

$$+ (1-p)[\Phi_\varepsilon(-s) + \Phi_\delta(-s)]\}$$

$$= (1-\Pi)q[\Phi_\delta(s) + \Phi_\delta(-s)]$$

$$+ [1 - p(1-\Pi)][\Phi_\varepsilon(-s) + \Phi_\delta(-s)]$$

Proposition 8
If we condition the result in Equation (5.22) on the event:

$$\{\ln P_0 \geq \mu_1\}$$

we have:

$$\Phi_{RR_T}(s) = \Phi_\varepsilon(-s) + \Phi_\delta(-s) \tag{5.23}$$

Proof
Substitute $\Pi = 1$ into Equation (5.22) and the result follows.

Proposition 9
If the natural logarithm of asset price, $\ln P_t$, is independently identically distributed, we have:

$$\Phi_{RR_T}(s) = q^2[\Phi_\delta(s) + \Phi_\delta(-s)] + (1-pq)[\Phi_\varepsilon(-s) + \Phi_\delta(-s)] \tag{5.24}$$

Proof
The assumption that the natural logarithm of asset price is independently identically distributed implies that p and q in Equation (5.8) satisfy the condition $p + q = 1$, which in turn implies:

$$\Pi = \frac{1-q}{2-p-q} = 1 - q = p$$

Substitute this condition into Equation (5.22), rearrange it and the result follows.

Proposition 10
For the realized return from the geometric moving-average $(\infty, 1)$ rule as in Equation (5.22), we can compute the expected realized return, $E(RR_T)$,

as follows:

$$E(RR_T) = -[1 - p(1 - \Pi)][\mu_\varepsilon + \mu_\delta] \qquad (5.25)$$

where μ_ε and μ_δ are the means of the unexpected shocks, ε_t and δ_t, respectively.

Proof

To derive the expected realized return, we have to first differentiate the characteristic function of the realized return.

$$\Phi'_{RR_T}(s) = (1 - \Pi)q[\Phi'_\delta(s) - \Phi'_\delta(-s)] - [1 - p(1 - \Pi)][\Phi'_\varepsilon(-s) + \Phi'_\delta(-s)]$$

Since:

$$E(RR_T) = -i\Phi'_{RR_T}(0)$$

we have:

$$E(RR_T) = -i(1 - \Pi)q[\Phi'_\delta(0) - \Phi'_\delta(0)] + i[1 - p(1 - \Pi)][\Phi'_\varepsilon(0) + \Phi'_\delta(0)]$$
$$= -[1 - p(1 - \Pi)][\mu_\varepsilon + \mu_\delta]$$

Proposition 11

If we condition the result in Equation (5.25) on the event:

$$\{\ln P_0 \geq \mu_1\}$$

we have:

$$E(RR_T) = -[\mu_\varepsilon + \mu_\delta] \qquad (5.26)$$

Proof

Substitute $\Pi = 1$ into Equation (5.25) and the result follows.

Proposition 12

Assume that the natural logarithm of asset price, $\ln P_t$, is independently identically distributed, the expected realized return in Equation (5.25) becomes:

$$E(RR_T) = -[1 - pq][\mu_\varepsilon + \mu_\delta] \qquad (5.27)$$

Proof

Substitute $p + q = 1$ and $\Pi = p = 1 - q$ into Equation (5.25) and the result follows.

Equation (5.25), Equation (5.26) and Equation (5.27) all suggest that as long as the asset price follows the general Knight–Satchell–Tran process, investors will lose money on average by taking the sequential trading strategy that exploits the information contained in the whole past history of asset prices. In addition, if an investor already owns the target asset when he begins to follow the strategy, he has to take the risk of losing more money than he has to if he does not own it in the first place. This is because $p(1 - \Pi)$ is always positive. Interestingly, if the natural logarithm of the asset price is actually independently identically distributed and $p + q \geq 1$, the sequential trading strategy based on the geometric moving-average $(\infty, 1)$ rule does the least damage to investors' terminal wealth. Furthermore, if it actually follows a random walk,[8] the possible loss from the trading strategy can be reduced to a minimum.

5.5 APPLICATIONS TO UK STOCK AND FUTURES MARKETS

In order to illustrate the implications of the theoretical results in Section 5.3, we use the empirical results of Knight, Satchell and Tran to actually calculate the expected realized returns of UK FT100 index and futures from the sequential trading strategy based on the geometric moving-average $(2, 1)$ rule. Knight, Satchell and Tran assume that the unexpected shocks, ε_t and δ_t, follow two different scale gamma distributions with parameters (α_1, λ_1) and (α_2, λ_2), as described by Equation (5.6) and Equation (5.7) respectively. Table 5.1 presents the maximum likelihood estimates of the parameters. These ML estimates suggest that in both markets neither state one nor state zero is very persistent. On the contrary, they are quite transitory. In other words, once the asset return enters one of the two states today, it has about 50 per cent chance to switch to the other state tomorrow. Besides, state zero is relatively persistent to state one in both markets. The fact that the sum of the estimates of p and q is very close to one, i.e., $\hat{p} + \hat{q} \approx 1$, implies that asset return is almost independently identically distributed in both markets.

Before we calculate the expected realized return, $E(RR_T)$, we first have to calculate the expected values of ε_t and δ_t. We know that the characteristic

Table 5.1 *Parameter estimates of FT100 futures and FT100 index*

	Futures	Index
$\hat{\alpha}_1$	1.3835	1.3640
$\hat{\lambda}_1$	171.38	204.40
$\hat{\alpha}_2$	0.7497	0.7499
$\hat{\lambda}_2$	98.750	214.04
$\hat{p}$	0.4805	0.4816
$\hat{q}$	0.4859	0.5080

function of a scale gamma distribution with parameters (α, λ) is:

$$\left(\frac{\lambda}{\lambda - is}\right)^{\alpha}$$

Hence, from the characteristic functions of ε_t and δ_t, we can calculate their expected values by:

$$\mu_{\varepsilon} = \frac{\alpha_1}{\lambda_1}$$

and

$$\mu_{\delta} = \frac{\alpha_2}{\lambda_2}$$

respectively. According to the ML estimates of parameters for the FT100 futures, we can compute $\mu_{\varepsilon} = 0.0081$ and $\mu_{\delta} = 0.0076$. Note that there is not much difference between μ_{ε} and μ_{δ}. Therefore, we can expect that the geometric moving-average $(2, 1)$ rule cannot create much profit for investors in FT100 futures market. We calculate the expected realized return in Equation (5.13) and Equation (5.15) as follows:

$$E(RR_T) = \frac{1.0}{0.5195}[(1.0336)(0.4805)(0.0081) - (0.5195)(0.0076)] = 0.014\%$$

$$E(RR_T) = \frac{1.0}{0.4859}[(0.4805)^2(0.0081) - (0.4859)(0.0076)] = -0.38\%$$

As we expect, the geometric moving-average $(2, 1)$ rule does not work very well in FT100 futures market. On average, it produces only 0.014 per cent per day. On the other hand, if futures return is very close to independently identically distributed, it will make investors in this market lose 0.38 per cent per day on average.

In the case of FT100 index, we can calculate $\mu_{\varepsilon} = 0.0067$ and $\mu_{\delta} = 0.0035$. Note that the expected value of positive shocks in UK stock market is much greater than the expected value of negative shocks. In fact, the former is almost a double of the latter. This leads us to expect that the geometric moving-average $(2, 1)$ rule would work well in the stock market or at least much better than it does in FT100 futures market. We compute the expected realized return in Equation (5.13) and Equation (5.15) for FT100 index as follows:

$$E(RR_T) = \frac{1.0}{0.5184}[(1.0104)(0.4816)(0.0067) - (0.5184)(0.0035)] = 0.28\%$$

$$E(RR_T) = \frac{1.0}{0.5080}[(0.4816)^2(0.0067) - (0.5080)(0.0035)] = -0.04\%$$

Interestingly, although the geometric moving-average $(2, 1)$ rule still cannot bring investors in the stock market profit if the stock return is independently identically distributed, it does confer investors positive average return up to around 0.3 per cent per day.

5.6 CONCLUSIONS

We have analysed theoretically the probability characteristics of the realized returns from two naive moving-average trading rules. Our results say that even a naive geometric moving-average $(2, 1)$ rule, which generates trading signals according to the information contained in the asset return at present time, can bring investors profits as long as the positive shocks to Markovian asset returns in financial markets have on average much more influence than the negative shocks. The other sufficient condition to make such a moving-average rule profitable is that the positive shocks must be very persistent themselves and much more persistent than the negative ones. For the geometric moving-average $(\infty, 1)$ rule, we prove that it always delivers negative realized returns to investors provided that the asset price follows the general Knight–Satchell–Tran process. However, this negative return can be reduced to a minimum if the asset price is in fact a random walk.

Although we apply the results for the geometric moving-average $(2, 1)$ rule to UK FT100 index and futures markets by using the empirical results of Knight, Satchell and Tran and find that it can let investors make profits in both markets up to on average 0.3 per cent and 6.0 per cent per month respectively if asset returns are not independently identically distributed, we do not statistically test whether these numbers are significant or not. Therefore, the empirical test of the theoretical results in this article will be the topic of our future research.

REFERENCES

Acar, E. (1993) Economic evaluation of financial forecasting, PhD Thesis, City University, London.

Acar, E. and Satchell, S.E. (1997) A theoretical analysis of trading rules: an application to the moving average case with Markovian returns, *Applied Mathematical Finance*, **4**, 1–16.

Akgiray, V. (1989) Conditional heteroscedasticity in time series of stock returns: Evidence and forecasts, *Journal of Business*, **62**, 55–80.

Blattberg, R.C. and Gonedes, R.C. (1974) A comparison of the stable and student distributions as statistical models for stock prices, *Journal of Business*, **47**, 244–80.

Brock, W., Lakonishok, J. and LeBaron, B. (1992) Simple technical rules and the stochastic properties of stock returns, *Journal of Finance*, **47**, 1731–64.

Clark, P.K. (1973) A subordinated stochastic process model with finite variance for speculative prices, *Econometrica*, **41**, 135–55.

Fama, E. (1965) The behaviour of stock prices, *Journal of Business*, **47**, 244–80.

Knight, J.L., Satchell, S.E. and Tran, K.C. (1995) Statistical modelling of asymmetric risk in asset returns, *Applied Mathematical Finance*, **2**, 155–72.

Kon, S.J. (1984) Models of stock returns: a comparison, *Journal of Finance*, **39**, 147–65.

LeBaron, B. (1991) Technical trading rules and regime shifts in foreign exchange, Working Paper, Department of Economics, University of Wisconsin-Madison.

Levich, R.M. and Thomas, L.R. (1993) The significance of technical trading-rule profits in the foreign exchange market: a bootstrap approach, *Journal of International Money and Finance*, **12**, 451–74.

Mandelbrot, B. (1963) The variations of certain speculative prices, *Journal of Business*, **36**, 394–419.

Merton, R. (1976) Option pricing when underlying stock returns are discontinuous, *Journal of Financial Economics*, **3**, 125–44.

Neftci, S.N. (1991) Naive trading rules in financial markets and Wiener-Kolmogorov prediction theory: a study of 'technical analysis', *Journal of Business*, **64**, 549–71.

Tucker, A.L. (1992) A re-examination of finite- and infinite-variance distributions as models of daily stock returns, *Journal of Business and Economic Statistics*, **10**, 73–81.

NOTES

1. A random variable B is a Markov time if the event

$$A_t = \{B < t\}$$

   is Ω_t-measurable – that is, whether B is less than t or not can be decided given the information available at time t, Ω_t. See Neftci (1991) for an example that describes the difference between Markov times and non-Markov times.

2. The models he uses are the GARCH$(1,1)$ and the Markov switching model developed by Hamilton (1989).

3. As is standard in this literature, we assume the following approximation

$$1 - \frac{P_{t-j}}{P_t} \approx \ln\left(\frac{P_t}{P_{t-j}}\right) = \ln\left(\frac{P_t}{P_{t-1}} \cdots \frac{P_{t-(j-1)}}{P_{t-j}}\right) = \sum_{i=0}^{j-1} R_{t-i}$$

4. For example, the unexpected shocks may come from the exponential distribution and the chi-square distribution.

5. We assume that

$$E|\varepsilon_t^4| < \infty$$

   and

$$E|\delta_t^4| < \infty$$

   such that the 4th-order differentiations of $\Phi_\varepsilon(s)$ and $\Phi_\delta(s)$ exist and equal $E(\varepsilon_t^4)$ and $E(\delta_t^4)$ respectively, namely, $\Phi_\varepsilon^{(4)}(0) = E(\varepsilon_t^4)$ and $\Phi_\delta^{(4)}(0) = E(\delta_t^4)$.

6. This presumption should not affect our results because we can expect the long-term mean of daily returns for financial assets to be reasonably close to zero. In fact, Knight, Satchell and Tran (1995) fit their model described by Equations (5.5) to (5.8) to daily returns of UK FT100 index and futures and estimate their long-term means to be 0.00042 and 0.0000 respectively. Their results support our presumption about the long-term mean here.

7. We assume that an investor will take his or her action immediately at the beginning of each period right after he or she observes a signal at the end of the previous period. We also assume that there is no price change between the end of the previous period and the beginning of the present period.

8. The natural logarithm of the asset price will follow a random walk only when the condition $p = q = \frac{1}{2}$ is satisfied.

ACKNOWLEDGMENTS

The author thanks his supervisor, Dr Stephen Satchell, for his helpful guidance and comments.

Chapter 6

The portfolio distribution of directional strategies

EMMANUEL ACAR AND STEPHEN SATCHELL

6.1 INTRODUCTION

This chapter is concerned with the rates of returns distribution generated by a set of dynamic strategies. In order to calculate the risk of a portfolio, a passive investor applying buy-and-hold strategies needs to know how related are the two underlying markets. This information is necessary for an active investor but not sufficient alone. The active investor also needs to know how the two forecasting strategies he or she follows can differ. Very little is known about the exact distribution of portfolio of active strategies. Active strategies differ from passive ones in that they include an in-built timing. Market timing affects not only the returns from a given asset, but also its volatility and correlation with other assets.

In recent years, and particularly for banking institutions involved with unstable financial markets, the need for worthwhile forecasts has been generally recognized by treasurers and academics alike. The choice of which dynamic strategy to follow depends on the expectations one has about the stochastic process which drives prices. Many forecasting strategies can be used to predict future price moves from fundamental to technical indicators without ignoring more advanced techniques such as neural networks and genetic algorithms. Unfortunately, the study of financial forecasts used for trading is relatively new.

There are three reasons for investigating the distribution of portfolio of trading rules. First, rules distributions would provide a measure of similarity between trading systems. With the exception of Lukac, Brorsen and Irwin (1988), rules have been merely listed rather than classified on the basis of their properties. Many forecasting systems have been proposed and are often considered to be different when they are extremely similar if not identical. Second, rules distributions would permit the construction of an efficient portfolio of rules. Until now such portfolios have been built empirically for given financial time series (Brorsen and Lukac, 1990), but have never been established theoretically for given stochastic processes. Indeed, establishing theoretical correlations between trading rules has been considered an extremely difficult task (Brock, Lakonishok and LeBaron, 1992). Third, and perhaps more important, it will allow the joint profitability of a set of trading rules to be tested. Brock, Lakonishok and LeBaron (1992), Surujaras and Sweeney (1992) and Prado (1992) have emphasized that such a test might have power, especially against nonlinear alternatives. The resulting tests of non-zero profitability could then be more powerful than any single test.

The primary purpose of this chapter is to establish the distribution of returns generated by a portfolio including two active strategies for given stochastic processes. Section 6.2 defines our forecasting strategies. The timing is triggered by linear forecasts for the sake of tractability. Section 6.3 establishes the exact distribution of a portfolio of trading rules. Section 6.4 generalizes previous results assuming elliptical processes. The extension is of some interest as future and foreign exchange markets are often characterized by return distributions that are symmetric about the mean due to the ability of investors taking long and short positions at equal costs. However, the same returns are typically kurtotic and exhibit fatter tails than normal distributions. The elliptical family have this property of being asymmetric and kurtotic. The most important finding of our analysis is that conventional portfolio theory might not apply to active directional strategies even when the underlying assets follow a multivariate normal distribution.

6.2 PORTFOLIO RETURNS OF DIRECTIONAL STRATEGIES

6.2.1 Directional strategies

Let us first define the trading process. A forecast F_t is used to predict the one-step ahead return X_{t+1}. If we assume zero transactions costs, the intuitive decision rule is to go short if the [one-ahead] forecast is negative and go long if it is positive. That is the forecasting technique implicitly triggers a daily signal B_t specifying a long $(+1)$ or short (-1) position following the decision rule:

sell $B_t = -1$ iff $F_t < 0$

sell $B_t = +1$ iff $F_t > 0$

Returns at time t made by applying such a decision rule are called 'rule returns' and denoted R_t. Their value can be expressed as:

$$R_t = B_{t-1}X_t \quad \Leftrightarrow \quad \left\{ \begin{array}{l} R_t = -X_t \text{ if } B_{t-1} = -1 \\ R_t = +X_t \text{ if } B_{t-1} = +1 \end{array} \right\}$$

6.2.2   Portfolio returns

Now, two trading rules are applied separately and simultaneously to two different underlying assets. Both trading rules generate returns $R_{1,t} = B_{1,t-1}X_{1,t}$ and $R_{2,t} = B_{2,t-1}X_{2,t}$ where $X_{i,t}$ is the underlying return of asset i. Then the investor decides to allocate a weight ω to the first active strategy applied to asset one and $(1 - \omega)$ to the second active strategy applied to asset two. The corresponding portfolio returns is given by:

$$R_t = \omega B_{1,t-1}X_{1,t} + (1 - \omega)B_{2,t-1}X_{2,t} \tag{6.1}$$

6.3   EXACT DISTRIBUTION UNDER THE NORMAL RANDOM WALK ASSUMPTION

We now make the following assumptions.

(1) Two financial series, with underlying returns $X_{1,t}$ and $X_{2,t}$, follow a zero mean bivariate normal law with variances σ_1^2 and σ_2^2 and correlation coefficient ρ_x.

(2) Two trading rules (similar or different) $F_{1,t}$ and $F_{2,t}$ are respectively applied to the two processes $\{X_{1,t}\}$ and $\{X_{2,t}\}$ to predict one-step ahead returns. Both forecasts are zero-mean and follow a bivariate normal law. The correlation coefficient between the two trading rules is denoted by ρ_F.

(3) Forecasts and one-ahead returns are independent.

Assumption (3) may seem very limiting since it implies that the forecasts used in the trading process have no value. However, the purpose of this section is not to test the usefulness of active strategies but to derive their stochastic properties under the random walk assumption. By doing so, new tests of the random walk hypothesis will be permitted.

Proposition 1
The portfolio returns R_t specified by Equation (6.1) exhibit a characteristic function given by:

$$E(\exp(izR_t)) = \left[\frac{1}{2} + \frac{1}{\pi} \arcsin(\rho_F)\right]$$

$$\times \exp\left[-\frac{z^2}{2}(\omega^2\sigma_1^2 + (1-\omega)^2\sigma_2^2 + 2\omega(1-\omega)\rho_x\sigma_1\sigma_2)\right]$$

$$+ \left[\frac{1}{2} - \frac{1}{\pi}\arcsin(\rho_F)\right]$$

$$\times \exp\left[-\frac{z^2}{2}(\omega^2\sigma_1^2 + (1-\omega)^2\sigma_2^2 - 2\omega(1-\omega)\rho_x\sigma_1\sigma_2)\right]$$

$$(6.2)$$

Then from the characteristic function, we can deduce the density function. This is given by:

If:

$$(\omega^2\sigma_1^2 + (1-\omega)^2\sigma_2^2 - 2\omega(1-\omega)\rho_x\sigma_1\sigma_2) \neq 0$$

$$g(x) = \left[\frac{1}{2} + \frac{1}{\pi}\arcsin(\rho_F)\right]\frac{1}{\sqrt{2\pi(\omega^2\sigma_1^2 + (1-\omega)^2\sigma_2^2 + 2\omega(1-\omega)\rho_x\sigma_1\sigma_2)}}$$

$$\times \exp\left[-\frac{x^2}{2(\omega^2\sigma_1^2 + (1-\omega)^2\sigma_2^2 + 2\omega(1-\omega)\rho_x\sigma_1\sigma_2)}\right]$$

$$+ \left[\frac{1}{2} - \frac{1}{\pi}\arcsin(\rho_F)\right]\frac{1}{\sqrt{2\pi(\omega^2\sigma_1^2 + (1-\omega)^2\sigma_2^2 + 2\omega(1-\omega)\rho_x\sigma_1\sigma_2)}}$$

$$\times \exp\left[-\frac{x^2}{2(\omega^2\sigma_1^2 + (1-\omega)^2\sigma_2^2 + 2\omega(1-\omega)\rho_x\sigma_1\sigma_2)}\right]$$

If:

$$(\omega^2\sigma_1^2 + (1-\omega)^2\sigma_2^2 + 2\omega(1-\omega)\rho_x\sigma_1\sigma_2) = 0$$

that is $\rho_x = 1$ and $\omega\sigma_1 = (1-\omega)\sigma_2$

$$g(x) = \left[\frac{1}{2} + \frac{1}{\pi}\arcsin(\rho_F)\right]\frac{1}{\sqrt{\pi 8\omega\sigma_1}}\exp\left[-\frac{x^2}{8\omega^2\sigma_1^2}\right] + \left[\frac{1}{2} - \frac{1}{\pi}\arcsin(\rho_F)\right]$$

Proofs

$$E(\exp(izR_t)) = \Pr[B_{1,t-1} = 1, B_{2,t-1} = 1]E(\exp(iz[\omega X_{1,t} + (1-\omega)X_{2,t}]))$$

$$+ \Pr[B_{1,t-1} = 1, B_{2,t-1} = -1]E(\exp(iz[\omega X_{1,t} - (1-\omega)X_{2,t}]))$$

$$+ \Pr[B_{1,t-1} = -1, B_{2,t-1} = +1]E(\exp(iz[-\omega X_{1,t} + (1-\omega)X_{2,t}]))$$

$$+ \Pr[B_{1,t-1} = -1, B_{2,t-1} = -1]E(\exp(-iz[\omega X_{1,t} + (1-\omega)X_{2,t}]))$$

The probability of the truncated bivariate normal $[0,0]$ is given in Johnson and Kotz (1972). This is equal to:

$$\Pr[B_{1,t-1}=1, B_{2,t-1}=1] = \Pr[F_{1,t-1}>0, F_{2,t-1}>0] = \frac{1}{4}+\frac{1}{2\pi}\arcsin(\rho_F)$$

Similarly,

$$\Pr[B_{1,t-1}=1, B_{2,t-1}=-1] = \Pr[F_{1,t-1}<0, F_{2,t-1}<0] = \frac{1}{4}+\frac{1}{2\pi}\arcsin(\rho_F)$$

$$\Pr[B_{1,t-1}=1, B_{2,t-1}=1] = \Pr[F_{1,t-1}<0, F_{2,t-1}>0] = \frac{1}{4}-\frac{1}{2\pi}\arcsin(\rho_F)$$

$$\Pr[B_{1,t-1}=1, B_{2,t-1}=-1] = \Pr[F_{1,t-1}>0, F_{2,t-1}<0] = \frac{1}{4}-\frac{1}{2\pi}\arcsin(\rho_F)$$

Then by substitution, we obtain:

$$E(\exp(izR_t)) = \left[\frac{1}{2}+\frac{1}{2\pi}\arcsin(\rho_F)\right]$$

$$\times \exp\left[-\frac{z^2}{2}(\omega^2\sigma_1^2 + (1-\omega)^2\sigma_2^2 + 2\omega(1-\omega)\rho_x\sigma_1\sigma_2)\right]$$

$$+\left[\frac{1}{2}-\frac{1}{\pi}\arcsin(\rho_F)\right]$$

$$\times \exp\left[-\frac{z^2}{2}(\omega^2\sigma_1^2 + (1-\omega)^2\sigma_2^2 - 2\omega(1-\omega)\rho_x\sigma_1\sigma_2)\right]$$

Active portfolio returns exhibit different variance than passive strategies. The variance of the portfolio of trading rules is given by:

$$\mathrm{Var}(R_t) = \omega^2\sigma_1^2 + (1-\omega)^2\sigma_2^2 + 2\omega(1-\omega)\sigma_1\sigma_2\rho_x\left(\frac{2}{\pi}\arcsin(\rho_F)\right)$$

This obviously differs from the variance of a passive portfolio which would be equal to:

$$\mathrm{Var}(R_t) = \omega^2\sigma_1^2 + (1-\omega)^2\sigma_2^2 + 2\omega(1-\omega)\sigma_1\sigma_2\rho_x$$

The portfolio of active strategies will exhibit lower variance than passive ones if and only if $0 < \rho_x$.

Portfolio of active strategies do not exhibit any skewness under the normal random walk assumption. They do, however, display kurtosis. To illustrate this point, we have chosen the case where two active strategies are applied to the same asset ($\sigma_1 = \sigma_2 = \sigma$ and $\rho_x = 1$) and given equal weight ($\omega = 0.5$). The amount of kurtosis can be derived from the characteristic function in

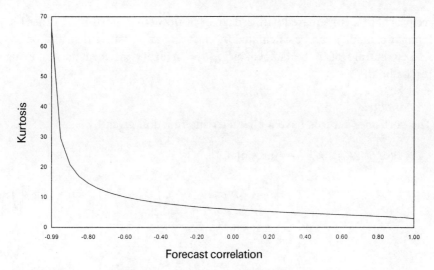

Figure 6.1   *Kurtosis = F (forecast correlation)*

Equation (6.2). This is equal to:

$$K = \frac{3}{0.5 + \dfrac{1}{\pi}\arcsin(\rho_F)} \tag{6.3}$$

Kurtosis of active portfolio returns is a negative function of the correlation coefficient between forecasts ρ_F. The more negatively correlated the forecasts, the higher the amount of kurtosis (see Figure 6.1) In principle, one could calculate K for an arbitrary portfolio using Equation (6.2), the result is long and cumbersome and we therefore omit it.

6.4   GENERALIZATION

We now generalize proposition 1 to consider examples of processes where:

$$\begin{pmatrix} X_{1,t} \\ X_{2,t} \end{pmatrix} \Big/ s_t \sim N(0, s_t^2 \Sigma) \quad \text{where } \Sigma = \begin{pmatrix} \sigma_1^2 & \rho_x \sigma_1 \sigma_2 \\ \rho_x \sigma_1 \sigma_2 & \sigma_2^2 \end{pmatrix}$$

and likewise the forecasts are:

$$\begin{pmatrix} F_{1,t} \\ F_{2,t} \end{pmatrix} \Big/ q_t \sim N(0, q_t^2 \Sigma_F) \quad \text{where } \Sigma_F = \begin{pmatrix} \sigma_{1,F}^2 & \rho_F \sigma_{1,F} \sigma_{2,F} \\ \rho_F \sigma_{1,F} \sigma_{2,F} & \sigma_{2,F}^2 \end{pmatrix}$$

and s_t and q_t are independent. This characterization consists of a large family of possible processes, indeed these are a subclass of the elliptical class. Different choices for s_t (or q_t) lead to a mixture of normals if δ_t is Bernoulli or a multivariate t with ν degrees of freedom, if δ_t is distributed as the reciprocal of a chi-squared with ν degrees of freedom divided by ν, other less familiar examples can be calculated by choosing any positive distribution for s_t. Let the mgf of s_t^2 be defined by $\phi_s(\theta) = E(\exp(s^2\theta))$ then the following results hold.

Proposition 2

The portfolios returns have a characteristic function given by:

$$E(\exp(izR_t)) = \left[\frac{1}{2} + \frac{1}{\pi}\arcsin(\rho_F)\right]$$

$$\times \left(\phi_s\left[-\frac{z^2}{2}(\omega^2\sigma_1^2 + (1-\omega)^2\sigma_2^2 + 2\omega(1-\omega)\rho_x\sigma_1\sigma_2)\right]\right)$$

$$+ \left[\frac{1}{2} - \frac{1}{\pi}\arcsin(\rho_F)\right]$$

$$\times \left(\phi_s\left[-\frac{z^2}{2}(\omega^2\sigma_1^2 + (1-\omega)^2\sigma_2^2 - 2\omega(1-\omega)\rho_x\sigma_1\sigma_2)\right]\right)$$

$$(6.4)$$

Proof

The steps are exactly the same as in proposition 1 except that in Equation (6.4) we would have:

$$E[\exp(izR_t)/s] = \left(\frac{1}{2} + \frac{1}{\pi}\arcsin(\rho_F)\right)$$

$$\times \exp\left(-\frac{s^2z^2}{2}(\omega^2\sigma_1^2 + (1-\omega)^2\sigma_2^2 + 2\omega(1-\omega)\rho_x\sigma_1\sigma_2)\right)$$

$$+ \left(\frac{1}{2} - \frac{1}{\pi}\arcsin(\rho_F)\right)$$

$$\times \exp\left(-\frac{s^2z^2}{2}(\omega^2\sigma_1^2 + (1-\omega)^2\sigma_2^2 - 2\omega(1-\omega)\rho_x\sigma_1\sigma_2)\right)$$

The general form of this expression is for constants C_1, C_2, C_3, C_4

$$E[\exp(izR_t)/s] = C_1 \exp(s^2C_2) + C_3 \exp(s^2C_4)$$

Using the relationship

$$E[\exp(izR_t)/s] = E_s[E(\exp(izR_t)/s]$$

and noting that $\phi_s(C_j) = E_s(\exp(s^2C_j))_{j=2,4}$ gives us the result. Q.E.D.

It is not possible to advance this argument further without specifying the pdf of s_t^2. For the case of a Bernoulli where $s_t^2 = \lambda_1^2$ with probability p and $s_t^2 = \lambda_2^2$ with probability $1 - p$, we see that

$$\phi_s(\theta) = E[\exp(s_t^2\theta)] = p \exp(\lambda_1^2\theta) + (1-p)\exp(\lambda_2^2\theta)$$

and thus replacing t by

$$-\frac{z^2}{2}(\omega^2\sigma_1^2 + (1-\omega)^2\sigma_2^2 + 2\rho_x\sigma_1\sigma_2)$$

will give us the mgf of a mixture of normals. It is apparent that the returns will have a pdf which is the mixture of four normals with the following probability weights and variances.

Weights	Variances
$\left(\frac{1}{2} + \frac{1}{\pi}\arcsin(\rho_F)\right)p$	$\lambda_1^2(\omega^2\sigma_1^2 + (1-\omega)^2\sigma_2^2 + 2\rho_x\sigma_1\sigma_2)$
$\left(\frac{1}{2} + \frac{1}{\pi}\arcsin(\rho_F)\right)(1-p)$	$\lambda_2^2(\omega^2\sigma_1^2 + (1-\omega)^2\sigma_2^2 + 2\rho_x\sigma_1\sigma_2)$
$\left(\frac{1}{2} - \frac{1}{\pi}\arcsin(\rho_F)\right)p$	$\lambda_1^2(\omega^2\sigma_1^2 + (1-\omega)^2\sigma_2^2 - 2\rho_x\sigma_1\sigma_2)$
$\left(\frac{1}{2} - \frac{1}{\pi}\arcsin(\rho_F)\right)(1-p)$	$\lambda_2^2(\omega^2\sigma_1^2 + (1-\omega)^2\sigma_2^2 - 2\rho_x\sigma_1\sigma_2)$

6.5   CONCLUSIONS

Under the normal random walk assumption, both buy and hold and active strategies exhibit zero returns. However, when more than one directional strategy is used, the distribution is no longer normal. When two forecasts are used to time the markets, the distribution is a mixture of two normal laws. The mixture coefficient depends on the correlation coefficient between the two forecasts. A portfolio of directional strategies introduces a substantial amount of kurtosis which is a decreasing function of the correlation coefficient between forecasting strategies. The more negatively correlated the forecasts, the higher is the kurtosis. This is due to the fact that most often there will be no position taken in the market. One forecast will trigger a long position whereas the other will trigger a short position. Consequently, the return distribution will have many zero values with sparse non-zero observations. This, in turn, explains the positive kurtosis. Results have been generalized for a subclass of the elliptical family of distributions. The knowledge of theoretical active portfolio returns has many potential applications. First, this might help to build an efficient portfolio. Second, it might allow the building of new tests of a random walk from the joint profitability of active strategies.

Finally, our results could be extended to consider multiple assets and rules although expressions for the probabilities as defined in section 6.3 may require numerical solutions.

REFERENCES

Brock, W., Lakonishok, J. and LeBaron, B. (1992) Simple technical rules and the stochastic properties of stock returns, *Journal of Finance*, **47**, 1731–64.

Brorsen, B.W. and Lukac, L.P. (1990) Optimal portfolios for commodity futures funds, *Journal of Futures Markets*, **10(3)**, 247–58.

Lukac, L.P., Brorsen, B.W. and Irwin, S.H. (1988) Similarity of computer guided technical trading systems, *Journal of Futures Markets*, **8(1)**, 1–13.

Prado, R. (1992) *Design, Testing and Optimization of Trading Systems*, John Wiley & Sons.

Surujaras, P. and Sweeney, R.J. (1992) Profit-making speculation in foreign exchange markets, *The Political Economy of Global Interdependence*, Westview Press.

Chapter 7

The profits to technical analysis in foreign exchange markets have not disappeared

JOHN OKUNEV AND DEREK WHITE

7.1 INTRODUCTION

The relative efficacy of foreign exchange trading rules has been examined intensively during the previous two decades. Most would argue that in the absence of a risk-based explanation the profitability for simple trading rules should have disappeared during this time if foreign exchange markets are efficient. However, numerous papers have shown many trading strategies for individual currencies would have generated significant returns (Sweeney, 1986; Schulmeister, 1988; Levich and Thomas, 1993; Taylor, 1994; Kho, 1996; Neely, Weller, and Dittmar, 1997; LeBaron, 1999; Marsh, 2000). While these studies, among many others, have clearly documented the profitability to technical trading rules in the foreign exchange market, we must be careful to ensure that the results are not due to an ex post selection of the successful methods (Brock, Lakonishok, and LeBaron, 1992; Sullivan, Timmerman, and White, 1999). Some studies justify the analysis of only a few strategies by claiming to examine the trading rules that 'are most commonly used in the market'. Unfortunately, this defence is invalid as the trading rules that are used in the market are those that have performed well ex post. While some would counter that the exact specification of the trading rule does not matter, many studies are further hamstrung in that they only consider the performance relative to one base currency of reference. This is perhaps a more insidious form of data-snooping and ex post selection bias. It is not at all clear that a profitable trading rule using the US dollar as a base currency would also earn excess returns from a Japanese yen perspective. The stability of trading rules needs to be examined not only over time, but also across as many base currencies as possible. Anything less may leave the study subject to ex post selection critiques.

In this chapter, we wish to analyse the performance of several *classes* of foreign exchange trading rules. That is, instead of analysing individual trading rules, we examine multiple specifications of a given trading rule and then average the returns across those specifications to determine the return for that *class* of trading techniques. For example, one individual moving-average specification may involve a short-run moving-average length of four months and a long-run moving-average of 36 months. The moving-average rule *class* returns are calculated by averaging the returns of many individual short-run, long-run moving-average combinations.

Okunev and White (2002) examined the class of short-run, long-run moving-average rules that identify a most attractive and least attractive currency and then initiate the appropriate long–short positions in those currencies. Specifically, 354 individual moving-average rules were examined across eight base currencies of reference for the period January 1980 to June 2000. Okunev and White (2002) found the long–short strategies across currencies generate returns of about 7 per cent per year on average and that the results are robust to the exact specification of the moving-average rule and the base currency of reference. Moreover, neither a static nor a time-varying risk premium could explain the results.

In this chapter, we wish to extend the analysis to include multiple classes of trading rules. Broadly speaking, we will examine trading rules that maintain either long or short positions in all individual non-domestic currencies with those that allocate exposures to a subset of the non-domestic currencies (e.g. a long exposure to one currency and a short exposure to another currency). We will identify two *divisions* of trading rules: those that trade in all individual non-domestic currencies every month as *Long–Short Within* and those that trade in only a subset of the non-domestic currencies as *Long–Short Across*. *Long–Short Within* trading rules will not consider other non-domestic currencies when setting a long or short position in an individual currency. *Long–Short Across* trading rules will evaluate whether to trade in a given non-domestic currency and the type of position (long or short) by comparing technical performance across other non-domestic currencies. Within each *division*, we will examine the following classes of trading rules: momentum, buying/selling based upon relative interest rates, and multiple parameterizations for moving-average rules.

In earlier work, Surajaras and Sweeney (1992) examine the *Long–Short Across* trading strategies using moving-average rules based upon daily foreign exchange movements. In addition, they also conduct portfolio type tests similar to that used in this chapter. A number of differences between their methodology and ours may be identified. First, the parameters for technical trading rules were optimized for each currency in their paper. We take a more conservative approach by averaging the performance of individual parameterizations rather than by attempting to find the best specification. Second, their tests focused on moving averages using daily returns and assumed trading in spot rather than futures markets. Our approach is to use monthly returns and to assume futures trading (realised returns are interest adjusted). Third, their tests used only the US dollar as the base currency of reference. We conduct our tests across eight base currencies. This is especially important when attempting to benchmark performance. In addition, their tests examined a much earlier time period (1978–1986). Finally, they find performance to be particularly weak during the mid 1980s. We find our results to be particularly strong during this time period. If technical trading rules can be arbitraged away, they should have long since disappeared.

In general, we find that *Long–Short Across* foreign exchange trading rules outperform the *Long–Short Within* division.[1] The moving-average class in both divisions tends to outperform the momentum and interest rate based strategies, however, significant benefits may accrue through the combination of these strategies. Moreover, on a risk-adjusted basis, the moving-average strategy in the *Long–Short Within* class compares very favourably with the moving-average rule in the *Long–Short Across* class. All tests are conducted using eight base currencies of reference: the Australian dollar, the British pound, the Canadian dollar, the French franc, the German mark, the Japanese yen, the Swiss franc, and the United States dollar. We show our results are robust to the base currency of reference and we analyse the results for the period January 1980 to June 2000.

The results of our chapter are especially relevant for a corporation with multiple foreign currency exposures or an international funds institution. These entities have a natural foreign exchange exposure that they can hedge completely, leave unhedged, or tilt towards currencies they expect to appreciate while their exposure persists. Hedging and tilting currency exposures can be easily accomplished through the use of futures positions. For an international funds institution an extra 1 per cent gained through astute foreign currency management may mean the difference between operating at the median or the upper quartile of performance. For a corporation with multiple currency exposures, shrewd foreign currency risk management may produce a significant positive revenue impact.

The methods we advocate are very simple, involving minimal trading and transactions cost. We examine monthly returns and our holding period is at least one month. Perhaps a shorter time horizon would increase the profitability of the methods we analyse – but that is outside the scope of this chapter. Prior studies have advocated simple strategies over more complex ones and have shown them to perform just as well (Taylor, 1992; Ntungo and Boyd, 1998). While the chapter does focus on classes of foreign exchange trading strategies, the positions need not be executed this way in practice.

Many of the individual foreign exchange trading strategies within a given class will outperform other specifications within that same class. By focusing on classes of trading rules instead of individual trading rules, we are presenting the results in a conservative manner – and as free from ex post selection bias as possible. In effect, we are mixing the weak with the strong in each class and reporting on those results.[2]

The chapter is organized as follows. Section 7.2 describes the data and methodology. Section 7.3 details the divisions and classes of foreign exchange trading rules analysed in the chapter. Section 7.4 outlines the results. Section 7.5 concludes with the findings of the chapter.

7.2   DATA AND METHODOLOGY

The dataset consists of three-month government yields and spot exchange rates taken from the Global Financial Database.[3] We obtained end-of-month data for Australia, Canada, France, Germany, Japan, Switzerland, the United Kingdom, and the United States for a period spanning January 1975 to June 2000. In addition, we obtained MSCI capitalization weights for the same period from Morgan Stanley. We computed currency returns using each country as the domestic currency. That is, we computed all combinations of currency returns for the eight countries. We will define this return series as *base currency returns*. The base currency return from month $t - 1$ to t is computed as follows:

$$R_{B,t} = \frac{S_t}{S_{t-1}} - 1 \tag{7.1}$$

where the base currency return is $R_{B,t}$, the spot exchange rate at month t is S_t and the spot exchange rate at month $t - 1$ is S_{t-1}. All exchange rates are expressed as the ratio of units of domestic currency per unit of foreign currency.

In addition, we computed a similar series of currency returns adjusted for interest rate differentials. An investor who uses futures to invest in currencies or borrows in one country to invest in another would actually experience these returns.[4] The futures price at month, $t - 1$, is denoted as F_{t-1}. The *interest-adjusted currency return* from month $t - 1$ to t is computed as follows:

$$R_{I,t} = \frac{S_t}{F_{t-1}} - 1 \tag{7.2}$$

where

$$F_{t-1} = S_{t-1} \exp[(r - r_f) * (1/12)]$$

$R_{l,t}$ is the interest-adjusted currency return, r is the domestic interest rate and r_f is the foreign interest rate. Note that:

$$R_{l,t} \approx (r_f - r) * (1/12) + \frac{S_t}{S_{t-1}} - 1 \tag{7.3}$$

Note that we can subdivide the actual returns from investing in currency into two components: the return due to interest differentials between the non-domestic and domestic currency and the return due to pure currency appreciation. Direct examination of Equation (7.3) reveals the return due to interest differentials to be:

$$(r_f - r) * (1/12) \tag{7.4}$$

and the return due to pure currency appreciation is:

$$\frac{S_t}{S_{t-1}} - 1 \tag{7.5}$$

We can see from Equations (7.4) and (7.5) that the return to investing in a relatively strong currency may be mitigated by the relative interest rate differential between the non-domestic and the domestic countries. In section 7.4 we will examine the component of trading rule returns due to the interest rate differential.

Table 7.1 lists summary statistics for the monthly base currency returns of each country with each base currency in the far-left column and the reference currencies in the subsequent columns. For example, using the Australian dollar as the domestic currency the average monthly appreciation of Canadian dollars is 0.192 per cent. The MSCI column gives the return to a basket of currencies with the individual country allocation determined by its MSCI weight. The allocations are determined by excluding the MSCI weight of the domestic currency. That is, if we have four currencies, each with an MSCI weight of 25 per cent, we would give each of the other three currencies a weight of 33 per cent when we determined the MSCI return for each base currency. The Equal benchmark equally weights the seven non-domestic currencies for computing a return relative to a base currency.

We can easily observe from Table 7.1 that the Australian dollar has experienced the greatest depreciation during the previous twenty years. The Japanese yen has had the greatest appreciation. Because of the relatively large standard deviation in monthly foreign exchange returns, most of the base currency mean returns are insignificantly different from zero. The Ljung–Box–Pierce (LBP) statistics are presented in the next to last row for each base currency and test the joint significance of the first ten autocorrelations. The p-values for the LBP statistics are given in parentheses in the last row for each base currency. In nearly all cases, the p-values are insignificant with the most

Table 7.1 *Descriptive statistics: base currency returns*

	[Australia]	Canada	[France]	Germany	[Japan]	[Swiss]	[UK]	[US]	[MSCI]	[Equal]
Australia Mean Ret (%)	n.a.	0.192	0.112	0.268	0.675*	0.336	0.165	0.292	0.392*	0.291
Median Ret (%)	n.a.	−0.031	−0.230	0.107	0.005	−0.007	0.066	0.113	0.021	−0.088
Std Dev (%)	n.a.	2.790	4.044	4.229	4.344	4.428	3.824	2.913	3.086	3.290
t-stat	n.a.	1.081	0.434	0.993	2.436	1.192	0.679	1.570	1.991	1.390
Skewness	n.a.	0.852	0.728	0.781	1.086	0.885	0.519	1.097	1.391	1.180
Kurtosis	n.a.	3.197	1.386	1.786	2.298	2.163	1.399	4.201	4.599	3.178
Autocorrelations										
1	n.a.	0.001	0.059	0.065	0.009	0.089	0.115	0.048	0.031	0.067
2	n.a.	−0.013	0.037	0.041	0.064	0.026	−0.023	0.032	0.036	0.019
3	n.a.	−0.022	0.010	−0.013	−0.089	−0.011	−0.084	−0.003	−0.073	−0.052
4	n.a.	−0.133*	−0.037	−0.062	−0.002	−0.064	−0.062	−0.159*	−0.119	−0.097
5	n.a.	−0.054	0.028	0.022	−0.046	0.009	−0.008	−0.072	−0.046	−0.014
6	n.a.	0.046	−0.033	−0.027	−0.075	−0.060	−0.093	0.054	−0.003	−0.024
7	n.a.	0.011	0.079	0.077	0.060	0.041	0.034	−0.010	0.053	0.054
8	n.a.	0.109	0.024	0.020	0.025	0.010	−0.010	0.122	0.030	0.037
9	n.a.	−0.010	0.070	0.064	0.096	0.097	0.085	0.082	0.117	0.089
10	n.a.	−0.093	0.052	0.048	0.031	0.003	−0.069	−0.040	−0.022	0.002
LBP (10)	n.a.	10.829	5.525	5.862	8.366	6.730	11.307	14.640	10.193	7.307
p-value	n.a.	(0.629)	(0.146)	(0.173)	(0.407)	(0.249)	(0.666)	(0.854)	(0.576)	(0.304)

Canada	Mean Ret (%)	-0.116	n.a.	-0.067	0.084	0.500*	0.155	-0.010	0.105	0.210	0.093
	Median Ret (%)	0.031	n.a.	-0.220	-0.189	-0.091	-0.163	-0.341	0.059	0.096	-0.149
	Std Dev (%)	2.731	n.a.	3.309	3.406	3.796	3.698	3.193	1.325	1.853	2.331
	t-stat	-0.666	n.a.	-0.319	0.388	2.064	0.656	-0.048	1.239	1.778	0.625
	Skewness	-0.500	n.a.	0.062	0.064	0.769	0.247	0.149	0.356	0.068	0.097
	Kurtosis	2.401	n.a.	-0.023	0.039	1.996	0.120	1.875	1.130	0.562	0.350
Autocorrelations											
	1	-0.005	n.a.	0.038	0.035	-0.015	0.059	0.026	-0.072	-0.056	-0.002
	2	-0.022	n.a.	0.108	0.083	0.076	0.047	-0.004	-0.007	0.025	0.060
	3	-0.019	n.a.	0.058	0.033	-0.014	0.021	-0.005	-0.021	-0.006	0.022
	4	-0.139*	n.a.	0.029	0.002	0.024	0.018	0.099	-0.015	0.023	0.021
	5	-0.056	n.a.	0.055	0.040	-0.014	0.008	0.007	-0.028	0.016	0.022
	6	0.059	n.a.	-0.061	-0.057	-0.098	-0.087	-0.103	-0.073	-0.081	-0.062
	7	0.005	n.a.	0.064	0.058	-0.015	0.048	0.021	0.093	0.029	0.024
	8	0.111	n.a.	-0.030	-0.029	0.023	-0.036	-0.080	0.083	-0.044	-0.041
	9	-0.002	n.a.	0.053	0.028	0.084	0.047	-0.036	0.126	0.063	0.019
	10	-0.091	n.a.	0.034	0.024	-0.005	-0.023	-0.128	0.085	-0.018	-0.051
	LBP (10)	11.590	n.a.	8.034	4.751	5.975	4.966	11.225	12.460	4.446	3.410
	p-value	(0.687)	n.a.	(0.375)	(0.093)	(0.183)	(0.107)	(0.660)	(0.745)	(0.075)	(0.030)

(continued)

Table 7.1 (*continued*)

		[Australia]	Canada	[France]	Germany	[Japan]	[Swiss]	[UK]	[US]	[MSCI]	[Equal]
France	Mean Ret (%)	0.047	0.177	n.a.	0.152**	0.605**	0.222*	0.095	0.272	0.346*	0.224
	Median Ret (%)	0.230	0.220	n.a.	0.012	0.321	0.109	0.206	0.100	0.256	0.095
	Std Dev (%)	3.952	3.321	n.a.	0.894	3.288	1.603	2.595	3.275	2.411	1.882
	t-stat	0.188	0.837	n.a.	2.676	2.885	2.170	0.576	1.301	2.250	1.870
	Skewness	-0.411	0.137	n.a.	3.447	0.790	0.958	-0.054	0.299	0.407	0.404
	Kurtosis	0.689	0.068	n.a.	19.742	1.805	4.472	1.275	0.513	0.914	0.562
	Autocorrelations										
	1	0.048	0.035	n.a.	-0.028	-0.013	0.109	0.078	0.046	0.026	0.035
	2	0.041	0.106	n.a.	0.057	0.129*	-0.071	-0.012	0.083	0.125	0.102
	3	0.017	0.059	n.a.	0.033	0.000	0.001	0.074	0.073	0.091	0.092
	4	-0.040	0.028	n.a.	0.040	0.139*	0.125	-0.013	0.007	0.059	0.061
	5	0.019	0.052	n.a.	0.049	0.037	-0.068	-0.062	0.062	0.089	0.071
	6	-0.034	-0.067	n.a.	0.075	-0.064	-0.095	-0.135*	-0.081	-0.055	-0.058
	7	0.080	0.063	n.a.	0.028	0.018	0.030	0.117	0.079	0.108	0.112
	8	0.023	-0.031	n.a.	0.255**	0.076	0.113	-0.017	0.007	0.009	0.026
	9	0.068	0.049	n.a.	0.193*	0.054	0.089	-0.036	0.070	0.048	0.055
	10	0.056	0.033	n.a.	0.043	0.033	0.026	0.093	0.029	0.072	0.116
	LBP (10)	5.405	7.806	n.a.	29.465**	12.557	16.651	14.127	8.933	14.131	15.115
	p-value	(0.137)	(0.352)	n.a.	(0.999)	(0.751)	(0.918)	(0.833)	(0.462)	(0.833)	(0.872)

Germany										
Mean Ret (%)	−0.094	0.032	−0.145**	n.a.	0.457*	0.069	−0.051	0.125	0.196	0.056
Median Ret (%)	−0.107	0.190	−0.012	n.a.	−0.003	−0.033	0.097	0.114	0.143	0.097
Std Dev (%)	4.111	3.409	0.866	n.a.	3.326	1.328	2.667	3.349	2.500	1.979
t-stat	−0.359	0.146	−2.619	n.a.	2.154	0.818	−0.301	0.588	1.231	0.445
Skewness	−0.418	0.147	−3.196	n.a.	0.861	0.090	−0.154	0.200	0.215	0.161
Kurtosis	0.919	0.162	17.780	n.a.	1.967	0.691	0.889	0.378	0.689	0.183
Autocorrelations										
1	0.053	0.030	−0.028	n.a.	−0.035	0.137*	0.052	0.043	0.011	0.019
2	0.048	0.079	0.058	n.a.	0.098	−0.107	0.010	0.066	0.087	0.075
3	−0.009	0.033	0.031	n.a.	−0.009	−0.025	0.099	0.039	0.050	0.043
4	−0.065	0.001	0.041	n.a.	0.119	0.036	0.009	−0.031	0.014	−0.006
5	0.015	0.036	0.051	n.a.	0.034	−0.142*	−0.053	0.053	0.080	0.051
6	−0.026	−0.060	0.077	n.a.	−0.066	−0.098	−0.059	−0.067	−0.032	−0.022
7	0.080	0.055	0.028	n.a.	0.009	−0.029	0.111	0.081	0.103	0.097
8	0.023	−0.027	0.249**	n.a.	0.072	0.015	−0.014	0.005	−0.001	0.012
9	0.065	0.021	0.185*	n.a.	0.047	−0.038	−0.068	0.042	0.020	0.001
10	0.055	0.023	0.046	n.a.	0.002	−0.063	0.099	0.025	0.052	0.085
LBP (10)	5.963	4.346	28.156**	n.a.	9.233	16.531	11.253	6.051	7.685	6.787
p-value	(0.182)	(0.070)	(0.998)	n.a.	(0.490)	(0.915)	(0.662)	(0.189)	(0.340)	(0.255)

(continued)

Table 7.1 (continued)

		[Australia]	Canada	[France]	Germany	[Japan]	[Swiss]	[UK]	[US]	[MSCI]	[Equal]
Japan	Mean Ret (%)	-0.492	-0.358	-0.497*	-0.348	n.a.	-0.288	-0.425	-0.267	-0.286	-0.382*
	Median Ret (%)	-0.005	0.091	-0.320	0.003	n.a.	-0.111	0.040	0.066	0.101	-0.019
	Std Dev (%)	4.136	3.682	3.185	3.224	n.a.	3.227	3.493	3.566	3.155	2.886
	t-stat	-1.867	-1.526	-2.448	-1.694	n.a.	-1.401	-1.908	-1.174	-1.422	-2.077
	Skewness	-0.707	-0.416	-0.509	-0.572	n.a.	-0.301	-0.864	-0.504	-0.747	-0.769
	Kurtosis	1.457	1.214	0.970	1.096	n.a.	0.964	2.445	0.867	1.715	1.822
	Autocorrelations										
	1	0.008	-0.009	-0.004	-0.027	n.a.	0.001	0.059	0.046	0.035	-0.012
	2	0.072	0.068	0.132*	0.096	n.a.	0.072	0.045	0.038	0.054	0.092
	3	-0.086	-0.006	0.008	-0.004	n.a.	0.036	-0.031	0.018	0.002	-0.030
	4	-0.004	0.026	0.140*	0.120	n.a.	0.128*	0.107	0.018	0.059	0.110
	5	-0.052	-0.008	0.041	0.035	n.a.	-0.002	-0.044	-0.043	-0.035	-0.025
	6	-0.073	-0.098	-0.062	-0.066	n.a.	-0.090	-0.102	-0.124	-0.111	-0.101
	7	0.072	-0.007	0.020	0.010	n.a.	0.020	-0.038	-0.017	-0.027	-0.010
	8	0.031	0.025	0.083	0.078	n.a.	0.048	0.067	0.089	0.098	0.083
	9	0.100	0.076	0.046	0.041	n.a.	0.022	0.121	0.060	0.074	0.086
	10	0.029	-0.006	0.029	-0.005	n.a.	-0.001	-0.005	-0.016	-0.010	0.007
	LBP (10)	9.191	5.301	12.832	9.210	n.a.	8.302	12.407	8.210	9.094	11.395
	p-value	(0.486)	(0.130)	(0.767)	(0.488)	n.a.	(0.401)	(0.741)	(0.392)	(0.477)	(0.672)

Switzerland										
Mean Ret (%)	-0.147	-0.019	-0.196	-0.052	0.396	n.a.	-0.106	0.074	0.138	-0.007
Median Ret (%)	0.007	0.163	-0.109	0.033	0.111	n.a.	0.095	0.115	0.147	0.077
Std Dev (%)	4.279	3.674	1.576	1.326	3.297	n.a.	2.851	3.586	2.666	2.275
t-stat	-0.539	-0.081	-1.952	-0.611	1.882	n.a.	-0.584	0.322	0.811	-0.050
Skewness	-0.487	-0.017	-0.713	0.018	0.592	n.a.	-0.481	-0.048	-0.111	-0.228
Kurtosis	1.099	0.139	3.384	0.780	1.508	n.a.	1.180	0.187	0.444	0.243
Autocorrelations										
1	0.074	0.054	0.104	0.136*	-0.012	n.a.	0.077	0.090	0.079	0.089
2	0.036	0.045	-0.075	-0.107	0.074	n.a.	0.034	0.050	0.061	0.030
3	-0.007	0.025	0.001	-0.029	0.029	n.a.	0.077	0.015	0.034	0.033
4	-0.065	0.017	0.118	0.034	0.132*	n.a.	0.003	-0.026	0.016	0.010
5	0.004	0.008	-0.075	-0.143*	-0.001	n.a.	-0.016	0.014	0.032	-0.003
6	-0.064	-0.091	-0.097	-0.099	-0.090	n.a.	-0.048	-0.114	-0.098	-0.096
7	0.048	0.044	0.027	-0.030	0.021	n.a.	0.033	0.054	0.053	0.039
8	0.021	-0.026	0.106	0.016	0.049	n.a.	-0.071	-0.008	-0.041	-0.021
9	0.098	0.041	0.088	-0.037	0.024	n.a.	-0.029	0.068	0.040	0.049
10	0.007	-0.027	0.030	-0.059	0.002	n.a.	0.074	-0.025	-0.007	-0.001
LBP (10)	6.741	4.680	16.096	16.549	8.589	n.a.	6.865	8.017	6.813	5.706
p-value	(0.250)	(0.088)	(0.903)	(0.915)	(0.428)	n.a.	(0.262)	(0.373)	(0.257)	(0.161)

(continued)

Table 7.1 (continued)

	[Australia]	Canada	[France]	Germany	[Japan]	[Swiss]	[UK]	[US]	[MSCI]	[Equal]
UK										
Mean Ret (%)	-0.022	0.112	-0.028	0.123	0.555*	0.189	n.a.	0.209	0.304	0.163
Median Ret (%)	-0.066	0.342	-0.206	-0.097	-0.040	-0.095	n.a.	0.152	0.180	0.100
Std Dev (%)	3.767	3.200	2.604	2.691	3.664	2.909	n.a.	3.233	2.643	2.354
t-stat	-0.090	0.547	-0.167	0.717	2.376	1.020	n.a.	1.012	1.805	1.083
Skewness	-0.177	0.225	0.313	0.387	1.280	0.744	n.a.	0.245	0.432	0.607
Kurtosis	1.005	2.140	1.549	1.140	3.863	1.775	n.a.	2.171	3.426	2.789
Autocorrelations										
1	0.110	0.031	0.081	0.059	0.056	0.082	n.a.	0.084	0.092	0.106
2	-0.023	-0.004	-0.013	0.008	0.048	0.030	n.a.	-0.002	0.003	-0.035
3	-0.083	0.003	0.072	0.100	-0.035	0.078	n.a.	0.008	-0.012	0.005
4	-0.061	0.092	-0.012	0.011	0.099	0.003	n.a.	0.030	0.091	0.047
5	-0.010	0.008	-0.062	-0.052	-0.044	-0.019	n.a.	-0.017	-0.016	-0.048
6	-0.099	-0.108	-0.132*	-0.058	-0.100	-0.048	n.a.	-0.135*	-0.121	-0.127
7	0.038	0.021	0.118	0.117	-0.039	0.034	n.a.	0.029	0.020	0.029
8	-0.010	-0.079	-0.021	-0.016	0.062	-0.076	n.a.	0.026	0.010	-0.043
9	0.086	-0.037	-0.042	-0.072	0.122	-0.038	n.a.	0.005	0.025	-0.015
10	-0.072	-0.134	0.086	0.097	-0.001	0.072	n.a.	-0.074	-0.064	-0.042
LBP (10)	11.435	11.640	13.922	11.804	11.872	7.274	n.a.	8.182	8.958	9.182
p-value	(0.675)	(0.69)	(0.823)	(0.702)	(0.706)	(0.301)	n.a.	(0.389)	(0.464)	(0.485)

USA										
Mean Ret (%)	−0.209	−0.087	−0.165	−0.014	0.399	0.055	−0.105	n.a.	0.152	−0.018
Median Ret (%)	−0.113	−0.059	−0.100	−0.114	−0.066	−0.115	−0.152	n.a.	0.001	−0.141
Std Dev (%)	2.826	1.317	3.241	3.334	3.675	3.607	3.218	n.a.	2.678	2.272
t-stat	−1.159	−1.038	−0.799	−0.066	1.702	0.241	−0.510	n.a.	0.888	−0.124
Skewness	−0.698	−0.238	−0.070	0.028	0.802	0.282	0.148	n.a.	0.262	0.105
Kurtosis	2.929	1.024	0.310	0.248	1.618	0.280	2.177	n.a.	0.021	0.352
Autocorrelations										
1	0.049	−0.075	0.048	0.046	0.045	0.094	0.073	n.a.	0.074	0.072
2	0.020	−0.007	0.090	0.075	0.041	0.055	−0.005	n.a.	0.024	0.047
3	0.003	−0.020	0.070	0.038	0.010	0.010	0.002	n.a.	0.032	0.041
4	−0.163*	−0.015	0.011	−0.025	0.013	−0.020	0.042	n.a.	−0.029	−0.043
5	−0.073	−0.026	0.065	0.056	−0.048	0.013	−0.023	n.a.	−0.005	0.003
6	0.069	−0.075	−0.076	−0.064	−0.123	−0.111	−0.132*	n.a.	−0.130*	−0.094
7	−0.012	0.095	0.084	0.086	−0.025	0.058	0.031	n.a.	0.017	0.038
8	0.130	0.085	0.007	0.004	0.083	−0.019	0.024	n.a.	0.057	0.057
9	0.088	0.122	0.073	0.050	0.065	0.075	0.004	n.a.	0.060	0.068
10	−0.041	0.085	0.025	0.021	−0.013	−0.025	−0.072	n.a.	−0.028	−0.033
LBP (10)	16.136	12.553	9.358	6.708	8.168	8.503	7.773	n.a.	7.973	7.355
p-value	(0.904)	(0.750)	(0.502)	(0.247)	(0.388)	(0.42)	(0.349)	n.a.	(0.369)	(0.308)

The dataset consists of monthly returns for individual currencies from January 1980 to June 2000. The period consists of 246 months. The base currency is denoted on the far left and the columns to the right give the return statistics of the seven other currencies with respect to the base currency. MSCI and Equal returns are calculated relative to the base currency. The MSCI column is calculated using the MSCI weights excluding the base currency. The Equal column calculates the currency return assuming an equal proportion allocated to the seven currencies. The Ljung and Box Q-statistic is denoted as LBP(10) and tests whether the 10 autocorrelations are jointly significant. The p-value for the Q-statistic is given in the last row for each base currency. ** and * indicate significance at the 1 and 5 per cent levels.

Table 7.2 *Descriptive statistics: interest-adjusted currency returns*

	[Australia]	Canada	[France]	Germany	[Japan]	[Swiss]	[UK]	[US]	[MSCI]	[Equal]
Australia Mean Ret (%)	n.a.	0.076	−0.007	−0.104	0.145	−0.145	0.105	0.021	0.084	0.013
Median Ret (%)	n.a.	−0.162	−0.290	−0.363	−0.618	−0.671	−0.081	−0.183	−0.242	−0.366
Std Dev (%)	n.a.	2.800	4.017	4.193	4.334	4.414	3.837	2.931	3.085	3.274
t-stat	n.a.	0.426	−0.029	−0.388	0.525	−0.517	0.430	0.111	0.426	0.062
Skewness	n.a.	0.722	0.695	0.738	1.044	0.862	0.509	0.957	1.264	1.113
Kurtosis	n.a.	2.837	1.280	1.621	2.206	1.999	1.334	3.675	4.161	2.939
Autocorrelations										
1	n.a.	0.007	0.049	0.056	0.014	0.090	0.118	0.063	0.035	0.062
2	n.a.	−0.010	0.026	0.031	0.070	0.023	−0.024	0.046	0.038	0.012
3	n.a.	−0.023	−0.002	−0.024	−0.086	−0.019	−0.085	0.008	−0.073	−0.062
4	n.a.	−0.133*	−0.050	−0.075	−0.001	−0.071	−0.064	−0.145*	−0.119*	−0.108
5	n.a.	−0.055	0.016	0.012	−0.045	0.001	−0.011	−0.058	−0.044	−0.023
6	n.a.	0.043	−0.046	−0.039	−0.074	−0.069	−0.096	0.063	−0.003	−0.034
7	n.a.	0.008	0.067	0.067	0.060	0.032	0.029	0.001	0.054	0.045
8	n.a.	0.101	0.013	0.008	0.024	0.002	−0.015	0.128	0.029	0.028
9	n.a.	−0.018	0.060	0.053	0.096	0.090	0.079	0.086	0.114	0.080
10	n.a.	−0.100	0.041	0.038	0.031	−0.004	−0.077	−0.034	−0.024	−0.007
LBP (10)	n.a.	10.722	4.377	5.017	8.345	6.789	11.755	14.546	10.145	7.353
p-value	n.a.	(0.620)	(0.071)	(0.110)	(0.405)	(0.255)	(0.698)	(0.851)	(0.572)	(0.308)

Canada										
Mean Ret (%)	0.001	n.a.	−0.069	−0.169	0.088	−0.209	0.048	−0.050	0.018	−0.051
Median Ret (%)	0.162	n.a.	−0.225	−0.362	−0.415	−0.482	−0.290	−0.095	−0.057	−0.295
Std Dev (%)	2.756	n.a.	3.325	3.419	3.814	3.724	3.244	1.359	1.876	2.357
t-stat	0.006	n.a.	−0.325	−0.775	0.361	−0.880	0.231	−0.572	0.148	−0.342
Skewness	−0.380	n.a.	0.072	0.060	0.744	0.238	0.167	0.341	0.047	0.107
Kurtosis	2.176	n.a.	−0.044	−0.010	1.873	−0.043	1.724	0.926	0.486	0.229
Autocorrelations										
1	0.003	n.a.	0.046	0.045	0.003	0.075	0.051	−0.028	−0.032	0.019
2	−0.016	n.a.	0.115	0.091	0.091	0.062	0.018	0.019	0.041	0.078
3	−0.018	n.a.	0.063	0.042	0.002	0.033	0.014	−0.004	0.009	0.039
4	−0.137*	n.a.	0.034	0.010	0.037	0.029	0.112	−0.001	0.034	0.035
5	−0.055	n.a.	0.059	0.047	−0.001	0.018	0.019	−0.014	0.029	0.036
6	0.057	n.a.	−0.057	−0.050	−0.085	−0.075	−0.092	−0.054	−0.067	−0.047
7	0.004	n.a.	0.067	0.064	−0.006	0.057	0.027	0.112	0.042	0.035
8	0.105	n.a.	−0.027	−0.023	0.031	−0.025	−0.077	0.101	−0.028	−0.030
9	−0.008	n.a.	0.055	0.032	0.091	0.057	−0.034	0.146*	0.075	0.028
10	−0.095	n.a.	0.038	0.031	0.004	−0.012	−0.123	0.105	−0.002	−0.037
LBP (10)	11.236	n.a.	8.925	5.684	6.373	5.983	11.572	14.708	4.266	4.131
p-value	(0.661)	n.a.	(0.461)	(0.159)	(0.217)	(0.183)	(0.685)	(0.857)	(0.065)	(0.059)

(continued)

Table 7.2 (continued)

		[Australia]	Canada	[France]	Germany	[Japan]	[Swiss]	[UK]	[US]	[MSCI]	[Equal]
France	Mean Ret (%)	0.165	0.180	n.a.	-0.100	0.193	-0.141	0.154	0.119	0.157	0.082
	Median Ret (%)	0.291	0.225	n.a.	-0.135	-0.114	-0.207	0.219	-0.132	-0.005	-0.023
	Std Dev (%)	3.940	3.336	n.a.	0.876	3.272	1.588	2.624	3.287	2.410	1.867
	t-stat	0.659	0.845	n.a.	-1.784	0.927	-1.397	0.921	0.569	1.019	0.685
	Skewness	-0.383	0.125	n.a.	3.030	0.796	0.716	-0.081	0.273	0.386	0.378
	Kurtosis	0.647	0.030	n.a.	16.213	1.922	3.690	1.231	0.417	0.850	0.487
	Autocorrelations										
	1	0.038	0.043	n.a.	-0.068	-0.016	0.096	0.093	0.060	0.032	0.023
	2	0.031	0.113	n.a.	0.016	0.126*	-0.095	0.001	0.095	0.129*	0.091
	3	0.005	0.064	n.a.	-0.020	-0.003	-0.030	0.082	0.082	0.092	0.079
	4	-0.053	0.033	n.a.	-0.011	0.134*	0.098	-0.004	0.017	0.059	0.047
	5	0.010	0.055	n.a.	0.003	0.030	-0.094	-0.052	0.068	0.087	0.058
	6	-0.046	-0.064	n.a.	0.035	-0.073	-0.123*	-0.124	-0.078	-0.062	-0.075
	7	0.070	0.065	n.a.	-0.024	0.007	-0.002	0.122	0.079	0.101	0.096
	8	0.012	-0.029	n.a.	0.209**	0.066	0.080	-0.011	0.009	0.003	0.010
	9	0.059	0.050	n.a.	0.139	0.042	0.062	-0.033	0.071	0.041	0.039
	10	0.046	0.038	n.a.	-0.006	0.019	-0.005	0.096	0.032	0.066	0.104
	LBP (10)	4.419	8.695	n.a.	17.241	11.387	15.248	14.365	10.359	13.830	11.718
	p-value	(0.074)	(0.439)	n.a.	(0.931)	(0.672)	(0.877)	(0.843)	(0.590)	(0.819)	(0.696)

Germany										
Mean Ret (%)	0.276	0.287	0.107*	n.a.	0.299	−0.042	0.260	0.226	0.268	0.202
Median Ret (%)	0.364	0.363	0.135	n.a.	−0.152	−0.134	0.391	0.116	0.259	0.239
Std Dev (%)	4.114	3.439	0.856	n.a.	3.329	1.338	2.704	3.376	2.515	1.981
t-stat	1.053	1.308	1.965	n.a.	1.407	−0.489	1.507	1.049	1.669	1.598
Skewness	−0.384	0.147	−2.805	n.a.	0.836	0.033	−0.104	0.210	0.255	0.198
Kurtosis	0.857	0.099	14.565	n.a.	1.890	0.752	0.982	0.280	0.701	0.257
Autocorrelations										
1	0.044	0.039	−0.067	n.a.	−0.030	0.142*	0.063	0.058	0.021	0.014
2	0.040	0.088	0.017	n.a.	0.101	−0.106	0.018	0.080	0.096	0.071
3	−0.020	0.042	−0.023	n.a.	−0.006	−0.032	0.103	0.051	0.057	0.038
4	−0.076	0.009	−0.010	n.a.	0.121	0.032	0.014	−0.019	0.020	−0.012
5	0.008	0.043	0.004	n.a.	0.036	−0.145*	−0.050	0.063	0.086	0.047
6	−0.036	−0.053	0.037	n.a.	−0.066	−0.102	−0.056	−0.058	−0.027	−0.027
7	0.071	0.061	−0.023	n.a.	0.006	−0.037	0.114	0.085	0.104	0.092
8	0.012	−0.023	0.201**	n.a.	0.067	0.006	−0.012	0.010	−0.001	0.004
9	0.055	0.024	0.132	n.a.	0.040	−0.047	−0.067	0.045	0.018	−0.009
10	0.046	0.031	−0.003	n.a.	−0.005	−0.075	0.099	0.029	0.052	0.079
LBP (10)	5.212	5.255	16.075	n.a.	9.106	17.874	11.765	7.339	8.556	6.027
p-value	(0.123)	(0.127)	(0.903)	n.a.	(0.478)	(0.943)	(0.699)	(0.307)	(0.425)	(0.187)

(continued)

Table 7.2 (continued)

		[Australia]	Canada	[France]	Germany	[Japan]	[Swiss]	[UK]	[US]	[MSCI]	[Equal]
Japan	Mean Ret (%)	0.035	0.054	−0.089	−0.190	n.a.	−0.241	0.043	−0.009	0.012	−0.057
	Median Ret (%)	0.621	0.416	0.114	0.152	n.a.	−0.143	0.492	0.271	0.388	0.284
	Std Dev (%)	4.176	3.733	3.195	3.239	n.a.	3.260	3.535	3.612	3.191	2.914
	t-stat	0.133	0.228	−0.436	−0.922	n.a.	−1.158	0.190	−0.039	0.061	−0.305
	Skewness	−0.664	−0.396	−0.507	−0.550	n.a.	−0.272	−0.837	−0.464	−0.702	−0.740
	Kurtosis	1.410	1.123	1.055	1.040	n.a.	0.927	2.389	0.753	1.598	1.744
	Autocorrelations										
	1	0.014	0.009	−0.008	−0.022	n.a.	0.017	0.070	0.068	0.054	0.000
	2	0.079	0.085	0.129*	0.099	n.a.	0.086	0.055	0.059	0.072	0.103
	3	−0.081	0.011	0.005	0.000	n.a.	0.045	−0.020	0.038	0.019	−0.019
	4	−0.002	0.039	0.134*	0.122	n.a.	0.137*	0.114	0.037	0.074	0.118
	5	−0.046	0.006	0.034	0.037	n.a.	0.004	−0.037	−0.026	−0.021	−0.016
	6	−0.071	−0.084	−0.072	−0.066	n.a.	−0.085	−0.095	−0.108	−0.098	−0.094
	7	0.075	0.003	0.009	0.008	n.a.	0.022	−0.032	−0.004	−0.017	−0.006
	8	0.031	0.034	0.072	0.074	n.a.	0.048	0.069	0.098	0.104	0.084
	9	0.101	0.083	0.033	0.034	n.a.	0.023	0.122	0.068	0.079	0.087
	10	0.031	0.003	0.015	−0.011	n.a.	−0.005	−0.003	−0.004	−0.002	0.008
	LBP (10)	9.268	5.874	11.536	9.162	n.a.	9.435	12.840	9.112	10.105	11.879
	p-value	(0.493)	(0.174)	(0.683)	(0.483)	n.a.	(0.509)	(0.767)	(0.479)	(0.569)	(0.707)

Switzerland										
Mean Ret (%)	0.336	0.348	0.167	0.060	0.350	n.a.	0.316	0.286	0.323	0.266
Median Ret (%)	0.676	0.484	0.208	0.134	0.143	n.a.	0.517	0.348	0.329	0.302
Std Dev (%)	4.310	3.726	1.578	1.340	3.324	n.a.	2.901	3.639	2.709	2.306
t-stat	1.221	1.465	1.657	0.698	1.650	n.a.	1.711	1.233	1.869	1.810
Skewness	−0.474	−0.024	−0.487	0.079	0.562	n.a.	−0.421	−0.039	−0.072	−0.209
Kurtosis	1.027	−0.027	2.855	0.884	1.444	n.a.	1.175	0.005	0.262	0.108
Autocorrelations										
1	0.074	0.070	0.092	0.141*	0.002	n.a	0.094	0.113	0.102	0.102
2	0.036	0.061	−0.097	−0.106	0.088	n.a.	0.048	0.074	0.086	0.043
3	−0.013	0.036	−0.029	−0.035	0.038	n.a.	0.082	0.032	0.048	0.037
4	−0.072	0.029	0.093	0.030	0.140*	n.a.	0.011	−0.008	0.032	0.016
5	0.000	0.018	−0.099	−0.145*	0.005	n.a.	−0.011	0.029	0.045	0.001
6	−0.071	−0.079	−0.123	−0.102	−0.085	n.a.	−0.042	−0.098	−0.084	−0.092
7	0.040	0.053	−0.003	−0.038	0.023	n.a.	0.037	0.064	0.061	0.039
8	0.013	−0.017	0.075	0.007	0.048	n.a.	−0.065	0.003	−0.031	−0.018
9	0.093	0.049	0.064	−0.046	0.025	n.a.	−0.020	0.077	0.050	0.054
10	0.001	−0.016	0.001	−0.071	−0.002	n.a.	0.078	−0.013	0.001	0.002
LBP (10)	6.695	5.616	15.012	17.744	9.553	n.a.	7.755	9.717	9.035	6.560
p-value	(0.246)	(0.154)	(0.868)	(0.941)	(0.519)	n.a.	(0.347)	(0.534)	(0.471)	(0.234)

(continued)

Table 7.2 (continued)

		[Australia]	Canada	[France]	Germany	[Japan]	[Swiss]	[UK]	[US]	[MSCI]	[Equal]
UK	Mean Ret (%)	0.040	0.057	-0.085	-0.186	0.087	-0.231	n.a.	-0.001	0.035	-0.046
	Median Ret (%)	0.081	0.291	-0.218	-0.390	-0.490	-0.514	n.a.	-0.024	-0.116	-0.105
	Std Dev (%)	3.785	3.245	2.632	2.708	3.671	2.932	n.a.	3.268	2.674	2.382
	t-stat	0.164	0.277	-0.506	-1.078	0.370	-1.234	n.a.	-0.003	0.208	-0.300
	Skewness	-0.172	0.195	0.341	0.348	1.253	0.692	n.a.	0.173	0.382	0.574
	Kurtosis	0.926	1.907	1.560	1.235	3.749	1.778	n.a.	1.938	3.186	2.687
	Autocorrelations										
	1	0.113	0.056	0.097	0.070	0.067	0.098	n.a.	0.106	0.113	0.124
	2	-0.023	0.019	0.001	0.015	0.057	0.043	n.a.	0.018	0.023	-0.019
	3	-0.084	0.023	0.081	0.104	-0.025	0.082	n.a.	0.024	0.004	0.018
	4	-0.063	0.105	-0.003	0.015	0.106	0.010	n.a.	0.044	0.103	0.057
	5	-0.012	0.021	-0.052	-0.050	-0.037	-0.014	n.a.	-0.006	-0.005	-0.039
	6	-0.102	-0.096	-0.122	-0.055	-0.093	-0.043	n.a.	-0.123	-0.109	-0.117
	7	0.034	0.025	0.125	0.119	-0.033	0.037	n.a.	0.036	0.028	0.035
	8	-0.014	-0.077	-0.014	-0.014	0.065	-0.070	n.a.	0.028	0.012	-0.040
	9	0.081	-0.036	-0.038	-0.071	0.124	-0.030	n.a.	0.008	0.027	-0.012
	10	-0.079	-0.129	0.089	0.097	0.002	0.075	n.a.	-0.069	-0.060	-0.041
	LBP (10)	11.916	12.101	14.357	12.349	12.288	8.032	n.a.	8.783	9.948	9.498
	p-value	(0.709)	(0.722)	(0.843)	(0.738)	(0.734)	(0.374)	n.a.	(0.447)	(0.555)	(0.514)

USA										
Mean Ret (%)	0.063	0.068	-0.012	-0.112	0.142	-0.153	0.107	n.a.	0.079	0.015
Median Ret (%)	0.183	0.095	0.132	-0.115	-0.270	-0.347	0.024	n.a.	-0.124	-0.030
Std Dev (%)	2.869	1.356	3.266	3.354	3.698	3.643	3.274	n.a.	2.706	2.307
t-stat	0.346	0.787	-0.057	-0.526	0.604	-0.660	0.515	n.a.	0.461	0.101
Skewness	-0.572	-0.228	-0.049	0.009	0.756	0.257	0.208	n.a.	0.254	0.114
Kurtosis	2.571	0.828	0.250	0.151	1.457	0.079	2.054	n.a.	-0.065	0.217
Autocorrelations										
1	0.067	-0.031	0.063	0.062	0.066	0.117	0.096	n.a.	0.098	0.104
2	0.037	0.020	0.102	0.089	0.061	0.078	0.017	n.a.	0.048	0.077
3	0.015	-0.004	0.080	0.050	0.029	0.027	0.018	n.a.	0.053	0.066
4	-0.147*	0.000	0.021	-0.014	0.030	-0.002	0.056	n.a.	-0.008	-0.016
5	-0.057	-0.012	0.070	0.065	-0.033	0.027	-0.012	n.a.	0.012	0.023
6	0.081	-0.057	-0.073	-0.055	-0.108	-0.096	-0.119	n.a.	-0.112	-0.072
7	0.002	0.114	0.085	0.090	-0.014	0.068	0.039	n.a.	0.029	0.054
8	0.138*	0.104	0.010	0.009	0.090	-0.006	0.028	n.a	0.067	0.072
9	0.094	0.142*	0.076	0.053	0.072	0.086	0.008	n.a.	0.068	0.082
10	-0.032	0.105	0.028	0.025	-0.002	-0.014	-0.067	n.a.	-0.016	-0.016
LBP (10)	16.224	14.692	10.984	8.127	8.796	10.387	8.310	n.a.	9.196	10.193
p-value	(0.907)	(0.856)	(0.641)	(0.384)	(0.448)	(0.593)	(0.401)	n.a.	(0.486)	(0.576)

The dataset consists of interest-adjusted monthly returns for individual currencies from January 1980 to June 2000. The period consists of 246 months. The base currency is denoted on the far left and the columns to the right give the return statistics of the seven other currencies with respect to the base currency. MSCI and Equal returns are calculated relative to the base currency. The MSCI column is calculated using the MSCI weights excluding the base currency. The Equal column calculates the currency return assuming an equal proportion allocated to the seven currencies. The Ljung and Box Q-statistic is denoted as LBP(10) and tests whether the 10 autocorrelations are jointly significant. The p-value for the Q-statistic is given in the last row for each base currency. ** and * indicate significance at the 1 and 5 per cent levels.

notable exception of the eighth and ninth autocorrelations of the French and German currencies with respect to each other.

Table 7.2 provides similar summary statistics for the monthly interest-adjusted currency returns. These are the actual returns that an investor would face when trading in the currency markets. Of particular note, the interest-adjusted currency returns are much smaller in magnitude than the base currency returns. Any trading strategy relying on these returns would have a much greater hurdle to overcome to exceed a benchmark of simply holding the MSCI or Equal benchmark basket of currencies. Note that on an interest-adjusted basis the rankings of performance differ markedly from Table 7.1. The Swiss franc is now the worst-performing currency even though it was one of the strongest for base currency returns. The Australian dollar's interest-adjusted performance is no longer quite so poor, and the Japanese yen has an interest-adjusted return very close to zero in magnitude. These results can be easily explained by the very low historical interest rates in Japan and Switzerland and the high historical interest rate in Australia relative to the other countries. While those who invested in Japan and Switzerland would have benefited from currency appreciation, the returns due to interest yields in these countries have been relatively modest.

7.3 TRADING STRATEGIES

We analyse the trading strategies in this chapter from the following eight base currencies of reference: the Australian dollar, the British pound, the Canadian dollar, the French franc, the German mark, the Japanese yen, the Swiss franc, and the United States dollar. From the perspective of a given base currency a foreign exchange trader can initiate either long or short positions in up to seven non-domestic currencies during any given month. A foreign exchange trader might take a position in a subset or all seven non-domestic currencies. We will analyse two divisions of foreign exchange trading techniques. One technique is for the foreign exchange trader to take positions (either long or short) in all seven non-domestic currencies every month. We will classify this division of trading as *Long–Short Within*. For example, from a US dollar base currency of reference, a foreign exchange trader may initiate a long or short position in Australian dollars, British pounds, and Japanese yen while shorting Canadian dollars, French francs, German marks, and Swiss francs. The second technique is for a foreign exchange trader to take positions in only a subset of the seven non-domestic currencies during any given month. We will classify this second division of trading rule as *Long–Short Across*. *Long–Short Within* trading rules will not consider other non-domestic currencies when setting a long or short position in an individual currency. *Long–Short Across* trading rules will evaluate whether to trade in a given non-domestic currency and the type of position (long or short) by comparing technical performance across non-domestic currencies. Within each division we will analyse three classes of foreign exchange trading rules: momentum, interest rate-based strategies, and moving-average rules.

Within the *Long–Short Within* division, all non-domestic currencies will either be bought or sold every month depending upon the class of trading rules followed. For momentum strategies, a non-domestic currency will be bought/sold if the prior *n-month* base return of the currency is positive/ negative. The interest rate strategies will dictate that a non-domestic currency be bought/sold if the non-domestic interest rate is greater than/less than the local interest rate. The motivation for following the interest rate strategy can be easily seen by examining Equation (7.4). By buying/selling high/low interest rate currencies, the foreign exchange trader is guaranteed of locking in a return equal to the interest rate differential between the non-domestic and domestic currency. If a foreign exchange trader believes that any remaining return is random noise, then following this strategy should yield positive excess returns. The final class of trading rules is to use moving-average strategies. A moving-average rule requires that a currency be bought/sold if the short-run moving average is greater than less than the long-run moving average of prior base currency returns.

We now need to define the moving average rules. At time t the short-run moving average and the long-run moving average are computed as:

$$SR_{j,t} = \frac{R_{B,t} + (j-1)SR_{j,t-1}}{j} \tag{7.6}$$

$$LR_{k,t} = \frac{R_{B,t} + (k-1)LR_{k,t-1}}{k} \tag{7.7}$$

where $SR_{j,t}$ is the short-run moving average at month t using the prior j months of returns and $LR_{k,t}$ is the long-run moving average at month t using the prior k months of returns.[5] A given short-run/long-run moving-average rule, $(MA(j,k))$, would require a currency be bought at time t if $SR_{j,t} > LR_{k,t}$ or sold at time t if $SR_{j,t} < LR_{k,t}$.

Within the momentum class, we examined trading rules based upon prior one-month, three-month, six-month, nine-month, and one-year base currency returns. By construction, only one trading rule exists for the interest rate trading rule class. For the moving-average rules, the short-run moving average values from one to twelve months and the long-run moving average values from two to thirty-six months. For all combinations of short-run, long-run moving-average rules, the number of months used to compute the short-run moving average must be less than the number of months used to compute the long-run moving average. For example, using a short-run moving average of one month, we determine the currency positions using: $SR_{1,t} - LR_{2,t}, SR_{1,t} - LR_{3,t}, \ldots, SR_{1,t} - LR_{36,t}$. Using a short-run moving average of two months, we determine the currency positions using: $SR_{2,t} - LR_{3,t}, SR_{2,t} - LR_{4,t}, \ldots, SR_{2,t} - LR_{36,t}$. In total, we evaluate 354 moving-average combinations. In effect, the moving-average class is giving a weighted allocation to the seven non-domestic currencies as different moving-average rules will provide different buy/sell signals for individual currencies. The returns to the moving-average class in the *Long–Short Within* division will be determined by averaging the returns of all combinations of moving-average rules for each non-domestic currency each month and then averaging the returns across the seven non-domestic currencies each month. In this way, we will construct the monthly returns to the moving-average class of trading rules in the *Long–Short Within* division.

Within the *Long–Short Across* division, the momentum trading rule will buy the non-domestic currency with the highest prior *n-month* base currency returns and short the non-domestic currency with the lowest prior *n-month* base currency returns. Unlike the momentum rule in the *Long–Short Within* division, only two non-domestic currencies will be traded in any given month. The interest rate strategy will buy the non-domestic currency with the highest interest rate and short the non-domestic currency with the lowest interest rate.[6] For the *Long–Short Across* division, we will evaluate two classes of moving-average rules. One class of moving-average rules will determine $SR_{j,t} - LR_{k,t}$ and then buy/sell the currency with the greatest/smallest difference. We will refer to this first class of moving-average rules as $MA(1 - 7)$. The second class of moving-average rules will buy the three currencies (equally weighted) with the greatest difference $SR_{j,t} - LR_{k,t}$ and short the currency with the smallest value of $SR_{j,t} - LR_{k,t}$.[7] We will refer to this second class of moving-average rules as $MA(1, 2, 3 - 7)$. With both classes of moving-average rules we will once again average across the returns for multiple parameterizations each month to calculate the monthly return.

As we have been careful to state, we do not wish to evaluate individual specifications of trading rules. Instead, we wish to consider broad classes of trading rules. To do this, we average across the return series for all the individual specifications of trading rules within one class to determine the overall performance for a given class of trading rules. Okunev and White (2002) found that the moving-average class within the *Long–Short Across* division has performed quite well throughout the 1980s and the 1990s. We therefore view this class as the benchmark by which to compare the other strategies.

We generally found the momentum trading rules in both divisions to perform very poorly compared with the interest rate rules and the moving-average rules. In fact, we found the best performing momentum rule to underperform both the interest rate and the moving-average rules. In order to present the momentum trading rules in the most favourable manner with respect to our benchmark, we will show only the results for the three-month momentum.[8] We did, however, in separate tests evaluate the one-month, six-month, nine-month, and one-year momentum trading rules.

For the moving-average rules, we will present only the results for the short-run moving average ranging from four to six months and the long-run moving average ranging from five to thirty-six months. Okunev and White (2002) found the performance for this particular range of parameterizations to be stable across time and base currencies of reference. This subset will comprise 93 combinations of moving-average rules and we will average across the returns of the individual specifications when calculating the monthly returns to the moving-average class. The complete results and analysis for the 354 moving-average rules as a class are given in Okunev and White (2002).[9]

In the end, for the *Long–Short Within* division we will present the results for the three-month momentum rule, the interest rate rule, and the moving-average class comprising rules $MA(4,5) - MA(6,36)$. In the *Long–Short Across* division we will present the results for the three-month momentum rule, the interest rate rule, and two moving-average classes comprising rules $MA(4,5) - MA(6,36)$. One moving-average class will go long in one currency and short in another currency based upon the difference between the short- and long-run moving average. The second moving-average class will go long in the top three currencies and short in the lowest currency as measured by the difference between the short- and long-run moving average.

For both the momentum and the moving-average rules we will use *base currency returns* to determine the buy/sell signals. The actual realized returns, however, will depend upon *interest-adjusted currency returns*. As Table 7.2 shows, the interest-adjusted returns are markedly lower in magnitude than the base currency returns. This will make earning excess returns in foreign exchange markets through any trading rule much more difficult. The tests are repeated using each currency as the base currency.

7.4 RESULTS

In the presentation of the results we will examine several summary performance measures for the classes of trading rules. Most will be self-evident, but a few will require explanation. One measure we will examine closely is the *interest differential* performance for each of the strategies. The formula to calculate the interest differential is given by Equation (7.4) and is simply the component of total realized return due to locking in the difference in interest rates between the non-domestic and the domestic currency. We are assuming for the purposes of this study that all transactions are conducted through the use of futures contracts and that the initial contract price is set by the futures price. The futures price, as detailed by Equation (7.2), incorporates the interest differential and must hold strongly in the absence of arbitrage. In short, buying/selling a non-domestic currency with a higher/lower interest rate than the interest rate with the domestic currency will result in a positive return before consideration of movements in the underlying exchange rate.

Another measure we will examine is the monthly performance of the trading strategies with respect to three different benchmarks. No consensus exists regarding the appropriate benchmark for risk-adjusting the strategies. If currency returns are unpredictable, one might argue the appropriate benchmark is a zero expected return. On the other hand, an appropriate benchmark might be to maintain a currency exposure with the same composition as a broad international index such as the MSCI. However, using the MSCI currency index may likewise be an inappropriate benchmark to use to evaluate currency performance. The MSCI has, at times, given excessive weight to one individual currency – most recently, the US dollar. As a basis of comparison, a benchmark that equally weights currency exposure should also be relevant. These benchmarks are computed using the base currency returns presented in Table 7.1.[10] We will also attempt to risk-adjust performance by presenting the information ratio (mean return divided by standard deviation) for each of the trading rule strategies.[11]

Table 7.3 presents summary results of the monthly returns for the trading rule classes as well as the MSCI and Equal currency benchmarks over the entire sample period. We can see that all the trading rule classes examined in this chapter have positive mean monthly returns for all the base currencies of reference.[12] In general, the trading rules in the *Long–Short Across* division had much higher mean returns than the trading rules in the *Long–Short Within* division. In all cases, both moving-average classes in the *Long–Short Across* division had mean returns significantly different from zero with the strategies performing the best in Australia and the worst in Switzerland. For all base currencies, the moving-average classes in the *Long–Short Across* division would have generated annual returns of at least 6 per cent. With the possible exception of Australia and Germany, the momentum rules have been the worst performing among the trading strategies.

If performance is measured by the information ratio, the moving-average class in the *Long–Short Within* division also has performed markedly well over the sample period. In many cases, while the mean monthly return is relatively low, the information ratio for this class of trading rule is actually greater than the information ratio for the moving-average class in the *Long–Short Across* division. That the risk for the moving-average rule in the *Long–Short Within* division is lower should not be surprising. All classes of trading rules in the *Long–Short Within* division maintain a position in the seven non-domestic currencies every month, providing greater diversification benefits than that for the *Long–Short Across* strategies.

The *Long–Short Across* interest rate rule also has performed quite well over the sample period with the caveat that the risk level to this strategy is quite high and the resulting information ratio in many cases relatively low. In fact, for four of the base currencies the mean return to the interest rate rule was the greatest among all the trading strategies. We can note that the performance attributable to the interest rate differential with the interest rate rule is often greater than the mean performance of the interest rate rule itself. For example, in the case of Canada the *Long–Short Across* interest rate rule had a mean return of 0.484 per cent each month while the average return due to investing in higher interest rate, non-domestic markets was 0.686 per cent on average each month. Therefore, while the interest rate rule did experience a positive mean overall return, the return due to currency appreciation of the strategy was actually negative. In fact, in seven out of eight cases the interest rate rule performance suffered due to currency depreciation. It is interesting to note that the return due to interest differential for the moving-average and the momentum rules is very nearly zero. That is, unlike the interest rate rules, the moving-average and momentum strategies experience positive returns primarily from pure currency movements.

Another undesirable characteristic for the interest rate rules is that in all eight cases for the *Long–Short Across* and the *Long–Short Within* division, the interest rate strategy returns were negatively skewed. This is in marked contrast to the positive skewness of $MA(1, 2, 3 - 7)$ for seven of the eight base currencies.

Analysis of the autocorrelation structure of returns reveals very little other than that both *Long–Short Across* moving-average rules are slightly negatively autocorrelated for all base currencies. Of particular note, the fourth autocorrelation for $MA(1 - 7)$ is significantly different from zero in seven out of eight cases.

The paired *t*-tests presented in Table 7.3 measure the statistical significance of excess monthly returns for the short-run, long-run moving-average strategies against the MSCI and Equal benchmarks.[13] The Wilcoxon test is a nonparametric test of the statistical significance of the excess returns. Related to an examination of excess returns, Table 7.3 also provides the

Table 7.3 *Performance of selected strategies: January 1980–June 2000*

		Long-Short Within			Long-Short Across				Currency benchmarks	
		[Momentum] 3-month	Interest [rate]	[MA 4 – 6]	[Momentum] 3-month	Interest [rate]	[MA 4 – 6] (1 – 7)	[MA 4 – 6] (1, 2, 3 – 7)	[MSCI]	[Equal]
Australia	Mean Ret (%)	0.112	0.080	0.244	0.624**	0.795**	0.685***	0.693***	0.392*	0.291
	Median Ret (%)	−0.084	0.273	0.224	0.843	0.942	0.907	0.858	0.021	−0.088
	Std Dev (%)	2.710	2.841	2.665	3.570	3.424	3.303	2.952	3.086	3.290
	t-stat	0.648	0.444	1.434	2.739	3.639	3.254	3.680	1.991	1.390
	Information Ratio	0.041	0.028	0.091	0.175	0.232	0.207	0.235	0.127	0.089
	Interest Differential (%)	−0.016	0.334	0.017	0.009	0.610	0.097	0.109	−0.308	−0.278
	Skewness	0.653	−1.560	0.371	−0.347	−1.084	−0.437	−0.501	1.391	1.180
	Kurtosis	5.726	6.437	6.865	0.350	3.873	0.615	1.233	4.599	3.178
	Autocorrelations									
	1	−0.011	0.057	−0.045	−0.203**	0.091	−0.165***	−0.130*	0.031	0.067
	2	−0.033	0.060	−0.053	0.110	0.094	0.049	0.041	0.036	0.019
	3	−0.100	−0.097	−0.058	0.025	0.066	−0.011	−0.014	−0.073	−0.052
	4	−0.139*	−0.104	−0.171**	−0.137*	0.038	−0.153*	−0.105	−0.119	−0.097
	5	0.095	0.054	0.077	0.073	−0.062	0.115	0.183**	−0.046	−0.014
	6	0.017	−0.048	0.038	−0.070	−0.079	−0.105	−0.061	−0.003	−0.024
	7	−0.053	0.024	−0.097	0.142*	0.028	0.105	0.078	0.053	0.054
	8	0.172**	0.042	0.099	0.031	0.086	−0.059	−0.090	0.030	0.037
	9	−0.004	0.082	−0.109	−0.034	0.055	−0.038	−0.031	0.117	0.089
	10	−0.069	−0.013	−0.009	0.061	0.025	0.070	0.035	−0.022	0.002
	LBP (10)	18.763*	10.081	18.443*	26.335**	10.926	23.851**	20.229*	10.193	7.307
	(p-value)	(0.957)	(0.567)	(0.952)	(0.997)	(0.637)	(0.992)	(0.973)	(0.576)	(0.304)
	Prob >0 (%)	47.561	56.098	56.098	58.130	67.073	61.789	65.041		
	Prob >MSCI (%)	44.309	51.220	49.187	55.691	60.163	57.317	57.317		
	paired t-test	−1.199	−0.865	−0.591	0.805	1.302	1.026	1.101		
	Wilcoxon test	−1.702	0.308	−0.309	1.385	2.413*	2.282*	2.144*		
	Prob >Equal (%)	41.057	54.065	46.341	55.285	58.537	55.285	57.317		
	paired t-test	−0.728	−0.567	−0.183	1.094	1.588	1.312	1.397		
	Wilcoxon test	−3.628**	1.444	−2.096*	0.909	1.305	0.833	1.705		
	Proportion >0 (%)	n.a.	n.a.	100.000	n.a.	n.a.	100.000	100.000		
	Proportion >MSCI (%)	n.a.	n.a.	0.000	n.a.	n.a.	100.000	100.000		
	Proportion >Equal (%)	n.a.	n.a.	0.000	n.a.	n.a.	100.000	100.000		

Canada										
Mean Ret (%)	0.251*	0.304**	0.331**	0.307	0.484	0.597**	0.589**	0.210	0.093
Median Ret (%)	0.200	0.324	0.331	0.368	0.776	0.532	0.590	0.096	-0.149
Std Dev (%)	1.938	1.647	1.850	3.833	4.245	3.606	3.103	1.853	2.331
t-stat	2.032	2.894	2.807	1.256	1.786	2.598	2.977	1.778	0.625
Information Ratio	0.130	0.185	0.179	0.080	0.114	0.166	0.190	0.113	0.040
Interest Differential (%)	0.019	0.249	0.051	-0.015	0.686	0.094	0.078	-0.193	-0.145
Skewness	-0.032	-0.398	-0.396	0.081	-0.983	-0.039	0.344	0.068	0.097
Kurtosis	0.529	1.724	1.038	1.763	2.703	2.925	3.725	0.562	0.350
Autocorrelations									
1	-0.043	0.048	-0.149*	-0.019	0.028	-0.087	-0.058	-0.056	-0.002
2	0.110	0.057	0.113	0.058	0.109	-0.008	-0.031	0.025	0.060
3	0.007	-0.015	-0.021	-0.058	-0.042	0.009	0.051	-0.006	0.022
4	-0.157*	-0.015	-0.187**	-0.095	-0.048	-0.110	-0.066	0.023	0.021
5	-0.028	0.010	0.052	0.050	0.009	0.091	0.115	0.016	0.022
6	-0.030	-0.014	-0.058	-0.017	-0.062	-0.013	-0.001	-0.081	-0.062
7	0.063	0.029	0.069	0.101	0.072	-0.012	-0.019	0.029	0.024
8	0.065	-0.013	-0.040	0.093	0.124	0.070	0.048	-0.044	-0.041
9	0.056	0.100	0.054	0.026	0.056	-0.091	-0.019	0.063	0.019
10	-0.017	-0.055	-0.050	-0.004	-0.007	0.018	0.035	-0.018	-0.051
LBP (10)	12.580	4.980	21.364*	9.380	10.861	10.166	7.009	4.446	3.410
(p-value)	(0.752)	(0.108)	(0.981)	(0.504)	(0.632)	(0.574)	(0.275)	(0.075)	(0.030)
Prob >0 (%)	54.472	61.382	59.756	54.878	63.415	60.976	61.382		
Prob >MSCI (%)	55.691	54.878	54.878	53.659	58.130	55.691	58.943		
paired t-test	0.256	0.482	0.712	0.361	0.833	1.456	1.612		
Wilcoxon test	1.943	1.828	1.408	1.290	2.447*	0.939	2.563*		
Prob >Equal (%)	48.780	55.285	52.439	55.691	59.350	59.756	61.382		
paired t-test	0.835	0.957	1.209	0.731	1.152	1.760	1.933		
Wilcoxon test	-1.851	1.631	-0.264	2.051*	2.761**	2.771**	3.344**		
Proportion >0 (%)	n.a.	n.a.	100.000	n.a.	n.a.	100.000	100.000		
Proportion >MSCI (%)	n.a.	n.a.	95.699	n.a.	n.a.	100.000	100.000		
Proportion >Equal (%)	n.a.	n.a.	100.000	n.a.	n.a.	100.000	100.000		

(continued)

Table 7.3 (*continued*)

	Long–Short Within			Long–Short Across				Currency benchmarks	
	[Momentum] 3-month	Interest [rate]	[MA 4 – 6]	[Momentum] 3-month	Interest [rate]	[MA 4 – 6] (1 – 7)	[MA 4 – 6] (1, 2, 3 – 7)	[MSCI]	[Equal]
France									
Mean Ret (%)	0.146	0.172	0.264**	0.467	0.639*	0.631**	0.608***	0.346*	0.224
Median Ret (%)	0.138	0.246	0.251	0.682	0.989	0.679	0.750	0.256	0.095
Std Dev (%)	1.603	1.437	1.546	3.920	4.303	3.603	3.136	2.411	1.882
t-stat	1.426	1.880	2.672	1.870	2.330	2.745	3.042	2.250	1.870
Information Ratio	0.091	0.120	0.170	0.119	0.149	0.175	0.194	0.144	0.119
Interest Differential (%)	-0.031	0.262	0.023	0.022	0.669	0.089	0.089	-0.189	-0.143
Skewness	0.117	-0.786	-0.111	0.110	-0.946	-0.031	0.159	0.407	0.404
Kurtosis	0.608	3.337	0.968	1.508	2.402	2.467	3.107	0.914	0.562
Autocorrelations									
1	-0.061	0.007	-0.045	-0.041	0.034	-0.124	-0.110	0.026	0.035
2	0.069	0.026	0.054	0.063	0.096	0.000	-0.008	0.125	0.102
3	0.018	-0.027	0.020	-0.046	-0.018	-0.019	0.005	0.091	0.092
4	-0.157*	0.025	-0.150*	-0.090	-0.030	-0.143*	-0.101	0.059	0.061
5	0.053	-0.033	0.089	0.069	0.016	0.084	0.096	0.089	0.071
6	-0.002	-0.099	-0.039	-0.034	-0.063	-0.001	-0.004	-0.055	-0.058
7	0.065	0.028	0.045	0.058	0.039	-0.022	0.019	0.108	0.112
8	0.044	0.066	-0.010	0.078	0.121	0.072	0.027	0.009	0.026
9	-0.031	-0.044	0.006	0.021	0.081	-0.086	-0.037	0.048	0.055
10	-0.082	0.006	-0.049	0.063	0.007	0.017	0.058	0.072	0.116
LBP (10)	12.225	4.893	10.159	8.669	9.426	13.726	9.102	14.131	15.115
(p-value)	(0.730)	(0.102)	(0.573)	(0.436)	(0.508)	(0.814)	(0.478)	(0.833)	(0.872)
Prob >0 (%)	54.472	63.008	60.163	56.098	63.821	60.976	60.976		
Prob >MSCI (%)	43.902	52.846	48.780	51.220	56.911	55.285	52.439		
paired t-test	-1.177	-0.860	-0.470	0.445	0.986	1.070	1.095		
Wilcoxon test	-1.634	1.626	-0.185	0.279	1.242	1.594	0.149		
Prob >Equal (%)	44.715	53.252	49.187	55.691	60.163	56.098	58.537		
paired t-test	-0.538	-0.309	0.262	0.917	1.491	1.613	1.703		
Wilcoxon test	-1.844	1.024	-0.838	2.062*	2.491*	1.365	2.575**		
Proportion >0 (%)	n.a.	n.a.	100.000	n.a.	n.a.	100.000	100.000		
Proportion >MSCI (%)	n.a.	n.a.	0.000	n.a.	n.a	100.000	100.000		
Proportion >Equal (%)	n.a.	n.a.	84.946	n.a.	n.a.	100.000	100.000		

Germany	Mean Ret (%)	0.193	0.228*	0.322**	0.512*	0.610*	0.601**	0.601**	0.196	0.056
	Median Ret (%)	0.194	0.306	0.330	0.691	0.947	0.623	0.653	0.143	0.097
	Std Dev (%)	1.705	1.635	1.619	3.818	4.282	3.593	3.076	2.500	1.979
	t-stat	1.775	2.184	3.117	2.104	2.234	2.625	3.064	1.231	0.445
	Information Ratio	0.113	0.139	0.199	0.134	0.142	0.167	0.195	0.078	0.028
	Interest Differential	-0.005	0.251	0.031	-0.002	0.696	0.096	0.101	0.071	0.145
	Skewness	0.029	-0.132	-0.157	0.043	-1.018	-0.027	0.086	0.215	0.161
	Kurtosis	1.469	0.785	1.548	1.498	2.800	2.533	2.779	0.689	0.183
	Autocorrelations									
	1	-0.089	-0.008	-0.073	-0.033	0.025	-0.120	-0.101	0.011	0.019
	2	0.090	0.070	0.031	0.025	0.118	-0.010	-0.008	0.087	0.075
	3	0.019	-0.035	-0.049	-0.007	-0.030	-0.002	0.016	0.050	0.043
	4	-0.166**	-0.014	-0.145*	-0.060	-0.019	-0.157*	-0.090	0.014	-0.006
	5	0.046	-0.013	0.078	0.024	0.021	0.098	0.113	0.080	0.051
	6	-0.003	-0.046	-0.036	-0.007	-0.080	-0.001	-0.001	-0.032	-0.022
	7	0.048	0.066	0.008	0.012	0.080	-0.024	0.019	0.103	0.097
	8	-0.003	-0.002	-0.025	0.097	0.109	0.070	0.032	-0.001	0.012
	9	-0.012	0.031	-0.021	0.031	0.076	-0.081	-0.030	0.020	0.001
	10	-0.001	0.010	0.058	0.011	-0.006	0.013	0.036	0.052	0.085
	LBP (10)	11.669	3.429	10.079	4.051	11.353	14.794	8.512	7.685	6.787
	(p-value)	(0.692)	(0.031)	(0.566)	(0.055)	(0.669)	(0.860)	(0.421)	(0.340)	(0.255)
	Prob >0 (%)	54.472	60.976	60.976	57.317	64.634	60.569	62.195		
	Prob >MSCI (%)	49.593	56.504	52.439	52.033	60.163	54.878	53.659		
	paired t-test	-0.017	0.220	0.717	1.159	1.391	1.486	1.659		
	Wilcoxon test	0.038	2.652**	0.565	-0.017	2.827**	0.932	0.068		
	Prob >Equal (%)	58.943	66.260	59.350	55.691	63.008	57.724	60.976		
	paired t-test	0.863	1.499	1.769	1.711	2.019*	2.114*	2.377*		
	Wilcoxon test	3.401**	5.595**	2.511*	1.238	3.629**	1.626	2.884**		
	Proportion >0 (%)	n.a.	n.a.	100.000	n.a.	n.a.	100.000	100.000		
	Proportion >MSCI (%)	n.a.	n.a.	100.000	n.a.	n.a.	100.000	100.000		
	Proportion >Equal (%)	n.a.	n.a.	100.000	n.a.	n.a.	100.000	100.000		

(continued)

Table 7.3 (continued)

	Long-Short Within			Long-Short Across				Currency benchmarks	
	[Momentum] 3-month	Interest [rate]	[MA 4 – 6]	[Momentum] 3-month	Interest [rate]	[MA 4 – 6] (1 – 7)	[MA 4 – 6] (1, 2, 3 – 7)	[MSCI]	[Equal]
Japan									
Mean Ret (%)	0.272	0.110	0.296*	0.422	0.513*	0.505*	0.602**	-0.286	-0.382*
Median Ret (%)	0.187	0.315	0.427	0.502	0.591	0.581	0.640	0.101	-0.019
Std Dev (%)	2.333	2.630	2.121	3.621	3.895	3.534	3.096	3.155	2.886
t-stat	1.830	0.654	2.185	1.826	2.066	2.242	3.047	-1.422	-2.077
Information Ratio	0.117	0.042	0.139	0.116	0.132	0.143	0.194	-0.091	-0.132
Interest Differential (%)	-0.009	0.343	0.041	-0.005	0.641	0.085	0.058	0.298	0.325
Skewness	0.081	-0.802	0.059	0.095	-0.711	0.109	0.211	-0.747	-0.769
Kurtosis	1.291	3.058	2.018	1.739	1.736	2.619	1.927	1.715	1.822
Autocorrelations									
1	-0.051	0.032	-0.075	-0.032	0.024	-0.044	-0.022	0.035	-0.012
2	-0.010	0.128*	0.007	0.012	0.043	0.006	-0.003	0.054	0.092
3	-0.012	-0.035	-0.007	0.046	-0.032	0.012	0.009	0.002	-0.030
4	-0.069	0.090	-0.009	-0.111	-0.055	-0.171**	-0.142*	0.059	0.110
5	0.018	-0.030	0.056	0.107	0.053	0.060	0.047	-0.035	-0.025
6	-0.005	-0.103	-0.092	-0.073	-0.097	0.007	-0.006	-0.111	-0.101
7	0.096	0.019	0.055	-0.004	0.043	-0.077	-0.047	-0.027	-0.010
8	-0.004	0.122	0.002	0.136*	0.039	0.119	0.098	0.098	0.083
9	-0.104	0.082	-0.140*	0.000	0.067	-0.049	0.038	0.074	0.086
10	0.060	0.042	0.090	0.061	-0.046	0.017	0.047	-0.010	0.007
LBP (10)	7.713	15.100	11.794	13.333	6.959	14.112	9.400	9.094	11.395
(p-value)	(0.343)	(0.872)	(0.701)	(0.794)	(0.271)	(0.832)	(0.505)	(0.477)	(0.672)
Prob >0 (%)	54.878	57.317	60.163	56.098	63.821	58.943	63.415		
Prob >MSCI (%)	54.065	60.569	54.065	56.504	55.285	54.065	54.878		
paired t-test	2.243*	4.887**	2.543*	2.348*	2.905**	2.684**	3.178**		
Wilcoxon test	0.454	1.056	0.307	1.254	0.147	-0.075	0.004		
Prob >Equal (%)	63.415	88.211	65.447	54.878	57.317	56.098	59.350		
paired t-test	2.701**	9.361**	3.100**	2.697**	3.234**	3.066**	3.599**		
Wilcoxon test	4.581**	10.420**	4.978**	0.084	0.823	0.624	1.887		
Proportion >0 (%)	n.a.	n.a.	100.000	n.a.	n.a	100.000	100.000		
Proportion >MSCI (%)	n.a.	n.a.	100.000	n.a.	n.a	100.000	100.000		
Proportion >Equal (%)	n.a.	n.a.	100.000	n.a.	n.a.	100.000	100.000		

Switzerland Mean Ret (%)	0.313*	0.358**	0.408**	0.265	0.329	0.527*	0.516**	0.138	-0.007
Median Ret (%)	0.351	0.365	0.470	0.339	0.587	0.388	0.547	0.147	0.077
Std Dev (%)	1.922	1.966	1.783	3.685	4.234	3.554	3.054	2.666	2.275
t-stat	2.551	2.852	3.591	1.128	1.219	2.324	2.650	0.811	-0.050
Information Ratio	0.163	0.182	0.229	0.072	0.078	0.148	0.169	0.052	-0.003
Interest Differential (%)	0.026	0.317	0.064	-0.018	0.659	0.081	0.086	0.183	0.272
Skewness	-0.097	-0.391	-0.098	0.051	-0.778	0.016	0.135	-0.111	-0.228
Kurtosis	1.006	0.927	1.338	1.205	2.160	2.047	2.092	0.444	0.243
Autocorrelations									
1	-0.051	0.053	-0.078	-0.058	-0.020	-0.112	-0.081	0.079	0.089
2	0.034	0.109	0.023	0.067	0.119	-0.035	-0.026	0.061	0.030
3	0.004	0.001	-0.037	-0.035	-0.071	-0.004	-0.002	0.034	0.033
4	-0.128*	-0.001	-0.115	-0.100	-0.040	-0.139*	-0.087	0.016	0.010
5	0.031	0.028	0.069	0.059	-0.018	0.068	0.092	0.032	-0.003
6	0.005	-0.085	-0.046	0.051	-0.072	0.037	0.038	-0.098	-0.096
7	-0.032	0.050	0.046	0.110	0.062	-0.023	0.007	0.053	0.039
8	0.042	-0.052	0.012	0.121	0.137*	0.074	0.029	-0.041	-0.021
9	-0.011	0.048	-0.027	0.050	0.108	-0.092	-0.043	0.040	0.049
10	0.054	-0.011	0.118	-0.010	0.002	-0.020	0.034	-0.007	-0.001
LBP (10)	6.544	7.335	10.846	13.279	14.957	13.067	6.922	6.813	5.706
(p-value)	(0.232)	(0.307)	(0.630)	(0.791)	(0.866)	(0.780)	(0.267)	(0.257)	(0.161)
Prob >0 (%)	59.350	63.821	65.447	54.065	61.382	59.350	60.569		
Prob >MSCI (%)	50.000	60.163	52.033	51.220	55.691	56.504	51.626		
paired t-test	0.856	1.726	1.396	0.456	0.625	1.395	1.489		
Wilcoxon test	-0.575	2.474*	-0.217	0.297	1.469	2.003*	-0.650		
Prob >Equal (%)	62.195	77.642	65.447	54.472	56.911	58.130	54.878		
paired t-test	1.687	3.578**	2.353*	0.988	1.211	2.002*	2.160*		
Wilcoxon test	4.030**	8.062**	4.603**	1.390	1.577	2.133*	0.179		
Proportion >0 (%)	n.a.	n.a.	100.000	n.a.	n.a.	100.000	100.000		
Proportion >MSCI (%)	n.a.	n.a.	100.000	n.a.	n.a.	100.000	100.000		
Proportion >Equal (%)	n.a.	n.a.	100.000	n.a.	n.a.	100.000	100.000		

(continued)

Table 7.3 (continued)

	Long-Short Within			Long-Short Across				Currency benchmarks	
	[Momentum] 3-month	Interest [rate]	[MA 4 − 6] 3-month	[Momentum] 3-month	Interest [rate]	[MA 4 − 6] (1 − 7)	[MA 4 − 6] [(1, 2, 3 − 7)]	[MSCI]	[Equal]
UK									
Mean Ret (%)	0.142	0.270*	0.293**	0.353	0.628*	0.536*	0.536*	0.304	0.163
Median Ret (%)	0.155	0.278	0.282	0.407	0.975	0.645	0.700	0.180	0.100
Std Dev (%)	1.839	1.798	1.691	3.953	4.268	3.774	3.326	2.643	2.354
t-stat	1.209	2.357	2.716	1.400	2.306	2.227	2.529	1.805	1.083
Information Ratio	0.077	0.150	0.173	0.089	0.147	0.142	0.161	0.115	0.069
Interest Differential (%)	0.019	0.280	0.053	−0.024	0.669	0.086	0.079	−0.270	−0.209
Skewness	0.270	−0.682	0.089	0.136	−0.993	−0.126	0.144	0.432	0.607
Kurtosis	1.430	2.331	1.696	1.837	2.798	2.720	3.076	3.426	2.789
Autocorrelations									
1	−0.042	0.073	−0.073	−0.079	−0.027	−0.106	−0.063	0.092	0.106
2	−0.017	−0.025	−0.033	0.032	0.127*	−0.040	−0.021	0.003	−0.035
3	0.043	0.040	−0.046	−0.053	−0.087	−0.049	−0.026	−0.012	0.005
4	−0.006	0.031	0.007	−0.128*	−0.034	−0.139*	−0.135*	0.091	0.047
5	0.004	0.016	0.036	0.078	0.019	0.102	0.134*	−0.016	−0.048
6	0.045	0.000	0.030	0.011	−0.081	−0.015	−0.012	−0.121	−0.127
7	0.002	0.006	0.043	0.023	0.032	−0.038	0.014	0.020	0.029
8	0.168**	0.076	0.075	0.039	0.087	0.029	−0.010	0.010	−0.043
9	−0.066	0.054	−0.079	−0.006	0.085	−0.058	−0.002	0.025	−0.015
10	−0.092	−0.028	−0.017	−0.012	−0.007	0.036	0.021	−0.064	−0.042
LBP (10)	11.595	4.462	6.041	8.415	11.736	12.646	10.236	8.958	9.182
(p-value)	(0.687)	(0.076)	(0.188)	(0.412)	(0.697)	(0.756)	(0.580)	(0.464)	(0.485)
Prob >0 (%)	54.065	58.537	61.382	54.472	63.008	59.350	60.569		
Prob > MSCI (%)	48.374	50.813	51.220	52.033	56.911	56.098	56.098		
paired t-test	−0.859	−0.128	−0.059	0.161	0.978	0.789	0.863		
Wilcoxon test	−0.007	0.077	0.561	0.568	1.331	1.680	1.737		
Prob >Equal (%)	45.122	55.691	47.967	53.252	58.537	58.130	59.350		
paired t-test	−0.115	0.429	0.731	0.631	1.462	1.295	1.419		
Wilcoxon test	−2.440*	2.121*	−1.723	0.625	1.733	2.144*	2.750**		
Proportion >0 (%)	n.a.	n.a.	n.a.	n.a.	100.000	100.000	100.000		
Proportion >MSCI (%)	n.a.	n.a.	n.a.	n.a.	100.000	100.000	100.000		
Proportion >Equal (%)	n.a.	n.a.	n.a.	n.a.	100.000	100.000	100.000		

Median Ret (%)	0.319	0.353	0.350	0.344	0.941		0.606	0.132	−0.018
Std Dev (%)	1.916	1.480	1.825	3.885	4.163	3.628	3.155	2.678	2.272
t-stat	2.878	3.595	3.329	1.377	1.785	2.563	2.767	0.888	−0.124
Information Ratio	0.183	0.229	0.212	0.088	0.114	0.163	0.176	0.057	−0.008
Interest Differential (%)	0.042	0.245	0.043	−0.034	0.685	0.105	0.086	−0.073	0.032
Skewness	−0.071	−0.838	−0.210	0.065	−0.986	−0.029	0.329	0.262	0.105
Kurtosis	0.790	3.138	1.014	1.829	2.813	2.984	3.587	0.021	0.352
Autocorrelations									
1	−0.116	0.134*	−0.141*	−0.047	0.013	−0.090	−0.061	0.074	0.072
2	0.000	0.037	0.064	0.057	0.150*	−0.021	−0.031	0.024	0.047
3	0.019	0.066	−0.007	−0.021	−0.038	−0.012	0.024	0.032	0.041
4	−0.089	−0.129*	−0.151*	−0.103	0.012	−0.153*	−0.101	−0.029	−0.043
5	0.086	−0.084	0.103	0.068	0.052	0.084	0.115	−0.005	0.003
6	−0.075	−0.170**	−0.104	0.029	−0.054	0.033	0.027	−0.130*	−0.094
7	0.068	−0.039	0.072	0.047	0.067	−0.024	−0.009	0.017	0.038
8	0.018	0.146*	−0.017	0.091	0.090	0.069	0.034	0.057	0.057
9	0.022	0.019	0.038	0.048	0.108	−0.086	−0.020	0.060	0.068
10	−0.065	0.053	−0.056	0.053	−0.019	0.029	0.044	−0.028	−0.033
LBP (10)	10.779	24.893**	18.961*	9.147	13.278	13.132	7.983	7.973	7.355
(p-value)	(0.625)	(0.994)	(0.959)	(0.482)	(0.791)	(0.784)	(0.369)	(0.369)	(0.308)
Prob >0 (%)	60.163	65.447	61.382	54.065	62.602	59.756	61.382	61.382	
Prob >MSCI (%)	55.285	56.504	54.878	54.878	56.504	56.911	56.911	56.911	
paired t-test	0.948	0.892	1.095	0.630	0.855	1.492	1.520		
Wilcoxon test	1.509	1.988*	1.061	1.349	1.492	1.451	1.473		
Prob >Equal (%)	58.943	63.821	58.130	54.472	60.163	58.130	60.163		
paired t-test	1.894	1.974*	2.049*	1.221	1.451	2.173*	2.289*		
Wilcoxon test	2.517*	4.767**	1.891	0.855	2.795**	1.659	2.619**		
Proportion >0 (%)	n.a.	n.a.	100.000	n.a.	n.a.	100.000	100.000		
Proportion >MSCI (%)	n.a.	n.a.	100.000	n.a.	n.a.	100.000	100.000		
Proportion >Equal (%)	n.a.	n.a.	100.000	n.a.	n.a.	100.000	100.000		

This table shows performance measures and statistics for selected foreign exchange trading strategies. The base currency is denoted on the far left. The MSCI and Equal columns are reproduced from Table 7.1. The first t-stat is used to test the significance of the mean return relative to a null hypothesis of zero. The [Interest Differential] rows give the mean monthly return due to the interest differential of the non-domestic relative to the domestic currency. The Ljung and Box Q-statistic is denoted as LBP(10) and tests whether the 10 autocorrelations are jointly significant. The p-value for the Q-statistic is given below the LBP(10) row. The [Prob >] rows give the percentage of the total months that the given strategy has exceeded zero, the MSCI benchmark, and the Equal benchmark. The paired t-test is used to test the significance of the excess returns of each of the ranks and the long–short strategies relative to the MSCI benchmark and the Equal benchmark. The Wilcoxon is a nonparametric test of the excess returns. The [Proportion >] rows give the percentage of the 93 MA combinations that exceed zero, the MSCI benchmark average return, and the Equal benchmark average return. ** and * indicate significance at the 1 and 5 per cent levels.

percentage of months the strategies had a positive return, a return greater than the MSCI currency benchmark, and a return greater than the Equal currency benchmark.

For all base currencies, the moving-average and interest rate strategies in the *Long–Short Across* division had a positive return in about 60 per cent of the months. The probabilities that the returns were greater than the MSCI and Equal benchmarks were also greater than 50 per cent for all base currencies, and for most currencies were above 55 per cent. For most base currencies, either the paired *t*-test or the Wilcoxon test also showed the strategies to yield statistically significant excess returns. However, the statistical significance of the moving-average and interest rate returns was not, in general, as great with the MSCI and Equal benchmark as they were with the zero benchmark. As was documented in Okunev and White (2002), nearly all moving-average specifications have an average performance greater than zero, the MSCI currency benchmark, and the Equal currency benchmark.

Tables 7.4 to 7.7 summarize the subperiod performance of the strategies. Clearly, the period 1980–1984 was the golden era for market inefficiency in the foreign exchange market. By examining Table 7.4 we can see that during this time, the *Long–Short Across* interest rate strategy generated annual returns of over 12 per cent on average. In fact, all strategies in the *Long–Short Across* division performed markedly well. Even in the *Long–Short Within* division, all the trading rules generated substantial returns during this time.

At first sight, one interesting result for the period 1980–1984 is that the *Long–Short Within* interest rate rule outperforms the Equal benchmark during 90 per cent of the months for Japan and 95 per cent of the months for Switzerland. This result, however, is not as impressive as it first appears. During this time both Japan and Switzerland had very low interest rates compared to the other base currencies. Consequently, for both the Japanese yen and the Swiss franc as base currencies, the *Long–Short Within* interest rate rule specified long positions in nearly all non-domestic currencies most of the time. Because the interest rate rule gave equal weight to all non-domestic currencies, the positions in both Japan and Switzerland for the interest rate rule were very close in construction to the Equal currency benchmark. The Equal currency benchmark returns is determined using *base currency returns*, whereas the performance of the trading rules is determined using *interest-adjusted currency returns*. Since the domestic interest rates in both Japan and Switzerland were low relative to the non-domestic rates, the interest-adjusted currency returns were generally greater than the base currency returns. Because of this, any strategy (earning interest-adjusted currency returns) that gave equal, positive weight to all non-domestic currencies would be expected to outperform the Equal currency benchmark (earning base currency returns). This can be easily seen by direct comparison of Equation (7.1) with Equation (7.3).

Table 7.5 shows that during the 1985–1989 period the moving-average classes in both the *Long–Short Within* and the *Long–Short Across* divisions experienced substantial returns. The momentum and the interest rate rules did not fare nearly as well during this time period. During this time, German, Japanese and Swiss interest rates were much lower than the other countries considered in the study. Because of this, the *Long–Short Within* interest rate rule had returns greater than the Equal benchmark in most of the months during this time period for the mark, the yen, and the Swiss franc.

Table 7.6 shows the 1990–1994 period to be entirely different from the other subperiods in the analysis. While the two classes of moving-average rules in the *Long–Short Across* division continued to generate positive mean returns, the performance is not nearly as strong as in the other subperiods considered. All the strategies in the *Long–Short Within* division performed rather poorly. It is not surprising that some might have thought technical analysis to be dead during the mid-1990s. The notable exception is that the three-month momentum rule in the *Long–Short Across* division performed quite well during this time period. We should, however, remain somewhat sceptical concerning the potential of the momentum rule class. In separate tests, the one-month momentum rule also had very strong returns, however, the six-month, nine-month, and one-year momentum rules did not perform particularly well during this time. It is not at all clear that this particular result for the three-month momentum rule is not entirely due to chance.

Table 7.7 shows the *Long–Short Across* moving-average rules to perform markedly well once again for all base currencies during the 1995–2000 period. In addition, the *Long–Short Across* interest rate rule has also generated substantial returns during this time period. Because Japan's domestic interest rate was then extremely low, the *Long–Short Within* interest rate rule outperformed the Equal benchmark in all of the months during this time period with the yen as the base currency.

In general, the *Long–Short Across* MA(1, 2, 3 − 7) class outperforms all other classes for all base currencies over the period of the study. In general, this class has a higher mean return and information ratio than the other strategies considered by this study. The *Long–Short Across* interest rate rule is intriguing and it is perhaps possible that combining it with the MA(1, 2, 3 − 7) class could benefit currency exposures. While the *Long–Short Within* moving-average class does not perform as well on average, its relatively low risk level and high information ratio may cause it to add some

Table 7.4 *Performance of selected strategies: sub-period analysis: 1980–1984*

		Long-Short Within			Long-Short Across				Currency benchmarks	
		[Momentum] 3-month	Interest [rate]	[MA 4 – 6]	[Momentum] 3-month	Interest [rate]	[MA 4 – 6] (1 – 7)	[MA 4 – 6] [(1, 2, 3 – 7)]	[MSCI]	[Equal]
Australia	Mean Ret (%)	0.362	0.205	0.342	1.020*	1.318**	0.699	0.530	0.313	-0.142
	Median Ret (%)	0.153	0.283	0.258	1.503	1.414	1.331	0.985	-0.032	-0.271
	Std Dev (%)	1.503	1.551	1.509	3.883	2.916	3.526	3.247	1.869	2.029
	t-stat	1.864	1.025	1.754	2.035	3.501	1.536	1.265	1.297	-0.542
	Information Ratio	0.241	0.132	0.226	0.263	0.452	0.198	0.163	0.167	-0.070
	Interest Differential (%)	0.010	0.329	0.023	0.002	0.877	0.156	0.186	-0.188	-0.210
	Skewness	-0.083	-3.414	0.124	-1.019	-0.912	-1.273	-1.389	3.064	1.913
	Kurtosis	0.146	20.912	0.428	1.350	3.008	2.074	3.402	15.967	8.111
	Prob >0 (%)	55.000	61.667	58.333	66.667	75.000	68.333	68.333		
	Prob >MSCI (%)	50.000	56.667	50.000	60.000	70.000	60.000	56.667		
	paired t-test	0.162	-0.260	0.100	1.306	2.150*	0.780	0.461		
	Wilcoxon test	0.015	0.905	0.059	1.053	2.275*	1.347	0.508		
	Prob >Equal (%)	53.333	65.000	56.667	61.667	68.333	63.333	63.333		
	paired t-test	1.401	0.786	1.381	1.898	2.869**	1.484	1.230		
	Wilcoxon test	-0.317	2.017*	0.442	0.883	1.178	1.664	1.561		
Canada	Mean Ret (%)	0.489*	0.684**	0.422*	0.818	0.878*	0.624	0.392	0.023	-0.460
	Median Ret (%)	0.574	0.573	0.306	1.219	0.973	0.898	0.619	0.000	-0.478
	Std Dev (%)	1.703	1.489	1.545	3.514	3.174	3.251	2.929	1.209	1.857
	t-stat	2.222	3.561	2.116	1.802	2.142	1.487	1.037	0.144	-1.918
	Information Ratio	0.287	0.460	0.273	0.233	0.276	0.192	0.134	0.019	-0.248
	Interest Differential (%)	0.105	0.358	0.155	-0.023	0.854	0.140	0.121	-0.271	-0.295
	Skewness	-0.734	-0.049	-0.856	-1.010	-0.879	-1.272	-1.268	0.231	0.807
	Kurtosis	1.160	0.607	1.840	2.134	2.614	2.945	3.769	0.412	1.127
	Prob >0 (%)	61.667	71.667	63.333	66.667	71.667	63.333	66.667		
	Prob >MSCI (%)	61.667	63.333	56.667	63.333	65.000	58.333	60.000		
	paired t-test	1.502	2.052*	1.308	1.529	1.843	1.225	0.812		
	Wilcoxon test	1.038	1.524	0.221	1.141	1.384	0.169	0.876		
	Prob >Equal (%)	65.000	70.000	65.000	68.333	68.333	68.333	65.000		
	paired t-test	2.311*	2.770**	2.180*	2.083*	2.587**	1.867	1.542		
	Wilcoxon test	0.847	2.326*	1.170	1.921	1.701	2.105*	1.251		

France	Mean Ret (%)	0.291	−0.070	0.196	0.930*	1.612**	0.759	0.722	1.337**	0.980**
	Median Ret (%)	0.283	0.108	0.186	1.374	2.277	1.021	0.803	1.212	0.866
	Std Dev (%)	1.771	1.739	1.596	3.616	3.160	3.292	3.111	2.650	1.988
	t-stat	1.272	−0.313	0.951	1.993	3.951	1.786	1.798	3.907	3.819
	Information Ratio	0.164	−0.040	0.123	0.257	0.510	0.231	0.232	0.504	0.493
	Interest Differential (%)	−0.137	0.382	0.006	0.088	0.845	0.178	0.193	−0.297	−0.334
	Skewness	0.000	−0.911	0.130	−0.870	−1.101	−1.177	−1.292	0.069	0.294
	Kurtosis	1.595	4.835	1.866	1.723	3.078	2.581	3.734	2.198	2.070
	Prob >0 (%)	63.333	55.000	60.000	66.667	75.000	63.333	65.000		
	Prob >MSCI (%)	20.000	35.000	28.333	48.333	56.667	48.333	41.667		
	paired t-test	−3.937**	−2.810**	−3.667**	−0.988	0.690	−1.456	−1.726		
	Wilcoxon test	−3.394**	−0.928	−1.848	0.250	0.206	0.766	−0.883		
	Prob >Equal (%)	30.000	33.333	26.667	61.667	65.000	53.333	56.667		
	paired t-test	−3.117**	−2.431*	−3.069**	−0.122	1.620	−0.568	−0.720		
	Wilcoxon test	−1.642	−1.855	−3.165**	2.503*	1.399	1.009	1.826		
Germany	Mean Ret (%)	0.512*	0.464*	0.416	0.866	1.247**	0.656	0.662	0.885*	0.457
	Median Ret (%)	0.344	0.471	0.324	1.198	1.583	1.065	0.767	0.784	0.210
	Std Dev (%)	1.873	1.445	1.720	3.575	3.105	3.150	2.996	2.691	2.025
	t-stat	2.118	2.489	1.873	1.877	3.111	1.614	1.711	2.547	1.747
	Information Ratio	0.273	0.321	0.242	0.242	0.402	0.208	0.221	0.329	0.226
	Interest Differential (%)	0.022	0.336	0.084	−0.042	0.894	0.147	0.178	0.195	0.215
	Skewness	0.264	−0.410	−0.023	−0.882	−0.956	−1.284	−1.454	−0.140	0.021
	Kurtosis	2.042	0.475	2.006	1.685	2.670	3.357	5.232	1.735	0.857
	Prob >0 (%)	61.667	71.667	63.333	65.000	73.333	63.333	65.000		
	Prob >MSCI (%)	38.333	43.333	40.000	50.000	56.667	48.333	48.333		
	paired t-test	−1.432	−1.963*	−1.851	−0.047	0.848	−0.551	−0.616		
	Wilcoxon test	−1.480	0.206	−0.942	0.066	0.714	0.000	−0.236		
	Prob >Equal (%)	66.667	56.667	68.333	58.333	65.000	55.000	65.000		
	paired t-test	0.256	0.050	−0.202	0.998	2.038*	0.500	0.577		
	Wilcoxon test	3.158**	1.575	3.850**	0.979	1.627	0.294	2.459*		

(continued)

Table 7.4 (continued)

	Long–Short Within			Long–Short Across				Currency benchmarks	
	[Momentum] 3-month	[Interest] [rate]	[MA 4 – 6]	[Momentum] 3-month	[Interest] [rate]	[MA 4 – 6] [1 – 7]	[MA 4 – 6] [1, 2, 3 – 7]	[MSCI]	[Equal]
Japan									
Mean Ret (%)	0.320	0.157	0.046	0.973*	0.848*	0.828*	0.841*	-0.099	-0.590
Median Ret (%)	0.561	0.347	0.386	1.301	0.940	1.146	0.742	0.610	-0.183
Std Dev (%)	2.166	2.215	2.109	3.036	3.311	2.895	2.714	3.047	2.662
t-stat	1.146	0.549	0.168	2.482	1.984	2.217	2.402	-0.252	-1.717
Information Ratio	0.148	0.071	0.022	0.320	0.256	0.286	0.310	-0.033	-0.222
Interest Differential (%)	-0.026	0.442	0.029	0.017	0.852	0.208	0.190	0.440	0.406
Skewness	-0.840	-0.673	-1.232	-0.716	-0.993	-0.688	-0.633	-1.005	-0.829
Kurtosis	4.340	0.739	3.903	1.765	2.170	1.948	2.606	1.141	0.767
Prob >0 (%)	60.000	60.000	60.000	66.667	68.333	66.667	71.667		
Prob >MSCI (%)	50.000	46.667	41.667	60.000	58.333	53.333	56.667		
paired t-test	0.954	1.527	0.376	2.216*	1.681	1.973*	2.076*		
Wilcoxon test	-0.398	-1.921	-1.899	0.721	0.670	-0.663	0.250		
Prob >Equal (%)	66.667	90.000	68.333	65.000	61.667	65.000	63.333		
paired t-test	2.064*	7.678**	1.683	3.015**	2.520*	2.842**	2.926**		
Wilcoxon test	2.393**	4.792**	2.893**	1.178	0.501	1.274	0.663		
Switzerland Mean Ret (%)	0.662**	0.840**	0.593*	0.766	0.167	0.423	0.476	0.680	0.244
Median Ret (%)	0.674	0.594	0.401	1.208	0.587	0.646	0.628	0.937	0.160
Std Dev (%)	1.969	2.120	1.875	3.451	3.277	3.293	3.099	2.846	2.302
t-stat	2.606	3.070	2.449	1.720	0.394	0.994	1.189	1.851	0.822
Information Ratio	0.336	0.396	0.316	0.222	0.051	0.128	0.153	0.239	0.106
Interest Differential (%)	0.104	0.511	0.191	-0.038	0.772	0.087	0.109	0.446	0.499
Skewness	-0.047	-0.430	-0.043	-0.824	-0.590	-0.798	-0.913	-0.825	-0.934
Kurtosis	2.487	1.320	2.410	1.574	0.582	1.543	2.896	2.320	2.340
Prob >0 (%)	71.667	75.000	70.000	65.000	60.000	60.000	61.667		
Prob >MSCI (%)	33.333	51.667	38.333	51.667	41.667	50.000	48.333		
paired t-test	-0.055	1.127	-0.290	0.200	-0.918	-0.564	-0.482		
Wilcoxon test	-2.834**	-0.353	-1.693	0.191	-1.458	0.655	-0.147		
Prob >Equal (%)	60.000	95.000	70.000	61.667	53.333	55.000	56.667		
paired t-test	1.401	8.840**	1.288	1.201	-0.155	0.401	0.559		
Wilcoxon test	1.090	6.088**	3.033**	1.516	0.707	0.685	0.714		

UK									
Mean Ret (%)	0.466	0.354*	0.318	0.660	1.078**	0.420	0.384	1.017**	0.563
Median Ret (%)	0.495	0.296	0.453	1.028	1.234	0.516	0.699	0.974	0.323
Std Dev (%)	1.967	1.391	1.910	3.714	3.145	3.451	3.120	2.610	2.504
t-stat	1.836	1.970	1.288	1.378	2.655	0.942	0.953	3.018	1.742
Information Ratio	0.237	0.254	0.166	0.178	0.343	0.122	0.123	0.390	0.225
Interest Differential (%)	0.048	0.324	0.067	−0.042	0.859	0.168	0.188	−0.176	−0.182
Skewness	−0.646	0.357	−0.807	−0.861	−0.731	−1.037	−1.114	−0.059	0.381
Kurtosis	0.575	0.860	1.358	1.871	2.841	2.321	2.267	0.364	0.882
Prob >0 (%)	68.333	58.333	66.667	60.000	66.667	58.333	61.667		
Prob >MSCI (%)	41.667	38.333	41.667	51.667	53.333	50.000	43.333		
paired t-test	−1.444	−1.463	−1.820	−0.601	0.119	−1.073	−1.274		
Wilcoxon test	−0.729	−1.413	−0.442	0.736	0.618	0.714	−0.633		
Prob >Equal (%)	43.333	53.333	45.000	55.000	58.333	56.667	56.667		
paired t-test	−0.245	−0.455	−0.619	0.150	0.969	−0.236	−0.320		
Wilcoxon test	−1.597	1.340	−0.942	0.736	1.090	1.502	1.546		
USA									
Mean Ret (%)	0.507*	0.390*	0.431	0.875*	1.240**	0.672	0.406	−0.441	−0.687*
Median Ret (%)	0.806	0.308	0.497	1.243	1.619	0.913	0.606	−1.114	−1.231
Std Dev (%)	1.867	1.391	1.739	3.447	2.828	3.152	2.879	2.398	2.205
t-stat	2.103	2.169	1.920	1.965	3.397	1.651	1.093	−1.426	−2.415
Information Ratio	0.271	0.280	0.248	0.254	0.439	0.213	0.141	−0.184	−0.312
Interest Differential (%)	0.079	0.293	0.097	0.001	0.892	0.184	0.152	−0.203	−0.100
Skewness	−0.447	−0.421	−0.530	−1.220	−0.718	−1.426	−1.329	0.758	0.554
Kurtosis	0.219	3.837	0.673	2.970	1.753	3.865	4.424	0.025	0.127
Prob >0 (%)	61.667	61.667	63.333	66.667	73.333	66.667	65.000		
Prob >MSCI (%)	65.000	63.333	60.000	75.000	70.000	73.333	70.000		
paired t-test	1.987*	1.882	1.791	2.061*	3.137**	1.868	1.469		
Wilcoxon test	1.759	1.288	0.567	3.688***	1.943	3.246**	2.459*		
Prob >Equal (%)	70.000	68.333	71.667	73.333	76.667	73.333	71.667		
paired t-test	2.545*	2.533*	2.360*	2.474*	3.757**	2.322*	1.931		
Wilcoxon test	2.503*	2.105*	3.173**	2.989**	3.254**	2.996**	2.643**		

This table shows performance measures and statistics for selected foreign exchange trading strategies. The base currency is denoted on the far left. The MSCI and Equal columns are reproduced from Table 7.1. The first t-stat is used to test the significance of the mean return relative to a null hypothesis of zero. The [Interest Differential] rows give the mean monthly return due to the interest differential of the non-domestic relative to the domestic currency. The [Prob >] rows give the percentage of the total months that the given strategy has exceeded zero, the MSCI benchmark, and the Equal benchmark. The paired t-test is used to test the significance of the excess returns of each of the ranks and the long–short strategies relative to the MSCI benchmark and the Equal benchmark. The Wilcoxon is a nonparametric test of the excess returns. The [Proportion >] rows give the percentage of the 93 MA combinations that exceed zero, the MSCI benchmark average return, and the Equal benchmark average return. ** and * indicate significance at the 1 and 5 per cent levels.

Table 7.5 *Performance of selected strategies: sub-period analysis: 1985–1989*

		Long–Short Within			Long–Short Across				Currency benchmarks	
		[Momentum] 3-month	[Interest rate]	[MA 4–6]	[Momentum] 3-month	[Interest rate]	[MA 4–6] (1–7)	[MA 4–6] (1,2,3–7)	[MSCI]	[Equal]
Australia	Mean Ret (%)	0.048	−0.214	0.307	0.165	0.755*	1.017*	1.019*	0.605	0.838
	Median Ret (%)	−0.370	0.590	0.359	0.641	0.745	1.519	1.506	−0.484	−0.115
	Std Dev (%)	3.888	4.637	4.080	3.882	2.617	3.687	3.179	4.526	4.632
	t-stat	0.095	−0.357	0.582	0.329	2.234	2.135	2.483	1.035	1.402
	Information Ratio	0.012	−0.046	0.075	0.043	0.288	0.276	0.321	0.134	0.181
	Interest Differential (%)	−0.095	0.623	0.016	−0.036	0.601	0.185	0.123	−0.684	−0.623
	Skewness	0.763	−1.176	0.306	−0.236	−0.590	−0.531	−0.524	1.370	1.157
	Kurtosis	4.523	1.692	3.890	0.218	1.188	0.498	0.494	2.338	1.655
	Prob >0 (%)	46.667	55.000	60.000	58.333	65.000	68.333	71.667		
	Prob >MSCI (%)	40.000	56.667	53.333	56.667	56.667	65.000	61.667		
	paired t-test	−0.823	−0.696	−0.380	−0.570	0.195	0.510	0.539		
	Wilcoxon test	−1.943	−1.406	0.368	1.789	0.493	2.930**	1.929		
	Prob >Equal (%)	36.667	55.000	45.000	50.000	55.000	56.667	58.333		
	paired t-test	−1.160	−0.879	−0.674	−0.874	−0.105	0.221	0.237		
	Wilcoxon test	−1.877	1.237	−0.861	0.383	0.648	0.942	1.215		
Canada	Mean Ret (%)	0.134	0.146	0.515	−0.322	0.194	0.830	0.880	0.241	0.443
	Median Ret (%)	0.230	0.104	0.616	0.003	0.897	0.899	0.756	−0.023	0.119
	Std Dev (%)	2.358	1.849	2.417	4.498	5.431	4.555	3.697	2.210	2.672
	t-stat	0.441	0.613	1.652	−0.555	0.277	1.412	1.845	0.846	1.283
	Information Ratio	0.057	0.079	0.213	−0.072	0.036	0.182	0.238	0.109	0.166
	Interest Differential (%)	−0.015	0.313	0.063	−0.108	0.895	0.184	0.072	−0.277	−0.160
	Skewness	−0.307	−0.098	−0.652	0.745	−0.766	0.247	1.112	−0.105	0.001
	Kurtosis	−0.306	0.620	0.405	3.889	0.803	3.674	5.257	0.051	−0.001
	Prob >0 (%)	56.667	55.000	68.333	50.000	58.333	68.333	60.000		
	Prob >MSCI (%)	55.000	51.667	63.333	41.667	51.667	56.667	61.667		
	paired t-test	−0.290	−0.192	0.628	−0.940	−0.052	0.885	1.216		
	Wilcoxon test	0.640	0.640	2.069*	−0.972	0.147	0.663	1.826		
	Prob >Equal (%)	41.667	48.333	51.667	40.000	50.000	53.333	58.333		
	paired t-test	−0.775	−0.548	0.157	−1.220	−0.268	0.568	0.818		
	Wilcoxon test	−1.656	0.228	−0.147	−0.935	0.066	0.361	1.347		

France									
Mean Ret (%)	0.127	0.264	0.433*	−0.294	0.316	0.800	0.821	−0.414	−0.302
Median Ret (%)	0.046	0.374	0.537	0.238	0.883	0.948	0.867	−0.417	−0.470
Std Dev (%)	1.553	1.106	1.651	4.563	5.382	4.545	3.695	2.244	1.754
t-stat	0.634	1.847	2.032	−0.498	0.455	1.364	1.721	−1.427	−1.335
Information Ratio	0.082	0.238	0.262	−0.064	0.059	0.176	0.222	−0.184	−0.172
Interest Differential (%)	−0.013	0.290	0.067	−0.065	0.895	0.146	0.062	−0.197	−0.074
Skewness	−0.110	−1.022	−0.694	0.599	−0.649	0.231	0.954	0.461	0.576
Kurtosis	−0.194	2.937	1.363	2.996	0.688	3.092	4.449	1.310	0.608
Prob >0 (%)	51.667	71.667	61.667	51.667	58.333	70.000	61.667		
Prob >MSCI (%)	56.667	66.667	66.667	53.333	61.667	66.667	63.333		
paired t-test	1.367	2.178*	2.112*	0.178	1.177	1.805	2.061*		
Wilcoxon test	0.530	1.723	1.671	0.582	1.207	2.238*	1.156		
Prob >Equal (%)	51.667	66.667	68.333	51.667	65.000	65.000	61.667		
paired t-test	1.288	2.649**	2.173*	0.013	1.096	1.737	2.012*		
Wilcoxon test	−0.758	1.553	1.988**	0.456	2.385*	1.862	0.861		
Germany									
Mean Ret (%)	0.060	−0.029	0.401	−0.082	0.320	0.847	0.882	−0.609	−0.505
Median Ret (%)	0.359	−0.138	0.491	0.306	1.036	1.043	0.964	−0.490	−0.726
Std Dev (%)	1.824	2.045	1.797	4.421	5.519	4.543	3.600	2.590	2.133
t-stat	0.254	−0.108	1.729	−0.144	0.449	1.445	1.898	−1.821	−1.835
Information Ratio	0.033	−0.014	0.223	−0.019	0.058	0.187	0.245	−0.235	−0.237
Interest Differential (%)	−0.046	0.352	0.024	−0.049	0.893	0.208	0.116	0.171	0.334
Skewness	−0.529	0.400	−0.557	0.585	−0.840	0.238	0.729	0.384	0.431
Kurtosis	1.467	0.370	1.950	3.170	1.019	2.802	3.278	0.656	0.187
Prob >0 (%)	53.333	46.667	63.333	51.667	60.000	65.000	65.000		
Prob >MSCI (%)	61.667	76.667	68.333	56.667	65.000	65.000	65.000		
paired t-test	1.400	3.506**	2.215*	0.787	1.531	2.097*	2.401*		
Wilcoxon test	1.480	3.526**	1.885	1.104	1.796	1.590	1.362		
Prob >Equal (%)	65.000	93.333	75.000	53.333	68.333	66.667	66.667		
paired t-test	1.340	8.064**	2.303*	0.649	1.523	2.067*	2.388*		
Wilcoxon test	2.098*	5.845**	3.335**	0.294	2.797**	2.024*	1.649		

(continued)

Table 7.5 (continued)

		Long–Short Within			Long–Short Across				Currency benchmarks	
		[Momentum] 3-month	[Interest rate]	[MA 4 – 6]	[Momentum] 3-month	[Interest rate]	[MA 4 – 6] (1 – 7)	[MA 4 – 6] (1, 2, 3 – 7)	[MSCI]	[Equal]
Japan	Mean Ret (%)	0.157	0.121	0.431	-0.171	-0.012	0.673	0.818	-0.648	-0.371
	Median Ret (%)	0.040	0.238	0.703	0.276	0.324	1.177	0.755	-0.238	-0.066
	Std Dev (%)	1.925	2.101	1.798	4.603	5.311	4.778	3.775	3.097	2.629
	t-stat	0.632	0.446	1.858	-0.288	-0.018	1.091	1.678	-1.621	-1.093
	Information Ratio	0.082	0.058	0.240	-0.037	-0.002	0.141	0.217	-0.209	-0.141
	Interest Differential (%)	-0.059	0.357	0.095	-0.063	0.874	0.115	0.019	0.260	0.332
	Skewness	0.121	-0.338	-0.113	0.441	-0.523	0.099	0.371	-0.311	-0.607
	Kurtosis	0.081	-0.142	0.480	2.481	0.597	2.343	2.381	-0.094	0.104
	Prob >0 (%)	50.000	56.667	65.000	55.000	55.000	66.667	63.333		
	Prob >MSCI (%)	58.333	65.000	66.667	61.667	55.000	63.333	58.333		
	paired t-test	1.529	3.889**	2.428*	0.623	1.058	1.804	2.222*		
	Wilcoxon test	0.994	0.582	2.451*	2.289*	0.272	1.597	0.037		
	Prob >Equal (%)	56.667	78.333	68.333	43.333	53.333	55.000	58.333		
	paired t-test	1.081	3.047**	2.038*	0.278	0.571	1.507	1.973*		
	Wilcoxon test	0.905	4.078**	2.635**	-1.605	0.184	0.037	0.530		
Switzerland	Mean Ret (%)	0.207	0.143	0.491*	-0.634	0.230	0.777	0.827	-0.417	-0.308
	Median Ret (%)	0.244	0.215	0.582	-0.244	0.815	0.769	0.864	-0.546	-0.371
	Std Dev (%)	2.002	2.342	1.886	4.119	5.337	4.514	3.526	2.769	2.468
	t-stat	0.799	0.473	2.015	-1.192	0.334	1.334	1.817	-1.168	-0.968
	Information Ratio	0.103	0.061	0.260	-0.154	0.043	0.172	0.235	-0.151	-0.125
	Interest Differential (%)	-0.022	0.375	0.047	-0.111	0.865	0.178	0.109	0.193	0.363
	Skewness	0.136	-0.218	0.100	0.553	-0.604	0.176	0.597	-0.084	-0.066
	Kurtosis	0.920	-0.174	1.030	3.026	0.659	2.474	2.403	0.174	-0.091
	Prob >0 (%)	53.333	56.667	66.667	48.333	60.000	68.333	60.000		
	Prob >MSCI (%)	58.333	78.333	68.333	53.333	66.667	65.000	61.667		
	paired t-test	1.302	3.990**	2.033*	-0.304	1.085	1.671	1.933		
	Wilcoxon test	0.788	3.556**	2.422*	1.340	2.532*	2.179*	1.104		
	Prob >Equal (%)	61.667	95.000	73.333	50.000	63.333	65.000	60.000		
	paired t-test	1.160	8.012**	1.975*	-0.467	1.059	1.586	1.846		
	Wilcoxon test	1.597	5.875**	3.335**	0.648	1.870	2.253*	0.714		

UK

Statistic									
Mean Ret (%)	-0.164	0.292	0.339	0.013	0.290	0.993	0.931	-0.097	0.062
Median Ret (%)	-0.039	0.263	0.583	0.263	0.897	0.674	0.677	0.081	-0.198
Std Dev (%)	1.859	1.851	1.720	4.743	5.426	4.824	4.025	2.704	2.362
t-stat	-0.683	1.221	1.527	0.021	0.414	1.594	1.792	-0.278	0.205
Information Ratio	-0.088	0.158	0.197	0.003	0.053	0.206	0.231	-0.036	0.026
Interest Differential (%)	-0.048	0.367	0.048	-0.076	0.895	0.173	0.065	-0.407	-0.278
Skewness	-0.245	-0.577	-0.219	0.786	-0.722	0.189	0.825	-1.198	-0.559
Kurtosis	-0.010	2.360	0.124	3.194	0.901	2.574	3.682	3.780	1.815
Prob >0 (%)	46.667	60.000	65.000	51.667	58.333	65.000	56.667		
Prob >MSCI (%)	43.333	51.667	56.667	50.000	56.667	63.333	66.667		
paired t-test	-0.159	0.705	1.049	0.159	0.536	1.648	1.753		
Wilcoxon test	-1.266	-0.140	0.832	-0.265	0.434	1.487	2.547*		
Prob >Equal (%)	38.333	56.667	48.333	48.333	58.333	63.333	63.333		
paired t-test	-0.619	0.451	0.790	-0.074	0.331	1.470	1.577		
Wilcoxon test	-2.128*	1.207	-0.950	-0.339	1.185	1.782	1.870		

USA

Statistic									
Mean Ret (%)	0.426	0.588	0.612	-0.493	0.205	0.713	0.840	0.863*	0.698
Median Ret (%)	0.588	0.240	0.680	-0.547	0.891	0.773	0.744	0.532	0.669
Std Dev (%)	2.469	1.101	2.494	4.541	5.450	4.690	3.851	3.373	2.780
t-stat	1.335	0.869	1.900	-0.842	0.292	1.178	1.689	1.982	1.945
Information Ratio	0.172	0.112	0.245	-0.109	0.038	0.152	0.218	0.256	0.251
Interest Differential (%)	0.019	0.284	0.057	-0.129	0.895	0.183	0.078	-0.054	0.106
Skewness	-0.370	-1.164	-0.529	0.889	-0.759	0.242	0.903	-0.116	-0.038
Kurtosis	0.193	2.456	0.256	3.817	0.787	3.150	4.388	-0.769	-0.244
Prob >0 (%)	61.667	66.667	68.333	41.667	58.333	61.667	60.000		
Prob >MSCI (%)	50.000	46.667	50.000	40.000	46.667	53.333	48.333		
paired t-test	-0.889	-1.436	-0.467	-1.998*	-0.649	-0.197	-0.039		
Wilcoxon test	0.420	0.375	0.287	-0.626	-0.471	1.009	-0.449		
Prob >Equal (%)	50.000	45.000	55.000	38.333	46.667	50.000	50.000		
paired t-test	-0.622	-1.381	-0.181	-1.816	-0.537	0.021	0.254		
Wilcoxon test	0.758	-0.029	1.384	-1.009	-0.559	0.140	-0.022		

This table shows performance measures and statistics for selected foreign exchange trading strategies. The base currency is denoted on the far left. The MSCI and Equal columns are reproduced from Table 7.1. The first t-stat is used to test the significance of the mean return relative to a null hypothesis of zero. The [Interest Differential] rows give the mean monthly return due to the interest differential of the non-domestic relative to the domestic currency. The [Prob >] rows give the percentage of the total months that the given strategy has exceeded zero, the MSCI benchmark, and the Equal benchmark. The paired t-test is used to test the significance of the excess returns of each of the ranks and the long–short strategies relative to the MSCI benchmark and the Equal benchmark. The Wilcoxon is a nonparametric test of the excess returns. The [Proportion >] rows give the percentage of the 93 MA combinations that exceed zero, the MSCI benchmark average return, and the Equal benchmark average return. ** and * indicate significance at the 1 and 5 per cent levels.

Table 7.6 Performance of selected strategies sub-period analysis: 1990–1994

		Long–Short Within			Long–Short Across				Currency benchmarks	
		[Momentum] 3-month	[Interest rate]	[MA 4 – 6]	[Momentum] 3-month	[Interest rate]	[MA 4 – 6] (1 – 7)	[MA 4 – 6] (1, 2, 3 – 7)	[MSCI]	[Equal]
Australia	Mean Ret (%)	0.001	0.109	-0.041	0.796*	0.533	0.564	0.572	0.295	0.211
	Median Ret (%)	-0.333	0.213	-0.126	0.673	0.430	0.494	0.632	-0.074	-0.077
	Std Dev (%)	2.470	1.918	2.208	3.104	3.331	3.055	2.903	2.620	3.039
	t-stat	0.004	0.439	-0.142	1.986	1.239	1.430	1.527	0.872	0.539
	Information Ratio	0.001	0.057	-0.018	0.256	0.160	0.185	0.197	0.113	0.070
	Interest Differential (%)	-0.021	0.199	-0.015	0.002	0.492	-0.029	0.012	-0.224	-0.109
	Skewness	0.970	-0.009	0.812	0.197	-0.617	0.198	0.249	0.834	0.489
	Kurtosis	1.853	1.744	1.692	-0.200	0.711	-0.687	-0.382	1.285	0.203
	Prob >0 (%)	38.333	58.333	46.667	60.000	60.000	60.000	61.667		
	Prob >MSCI (%)	45.000	48.333	48.333	55.000	55.000	53.333	56.667		
	paired t-test	-0.776	-0.410	-0.790	1.278	0.553	0.629	0.651		
	Wilcoxon test	-0.648	-0.096	0.309	-0.015	0.228	0.479	1.274		
	Prob >Equal (%)	46.667	46.667	43.333	56.667	55.000	45.000	51.667		
	paired t-test	-0.516	-0.214	-0.568	1.338	0.876	0.754	0.775		
	Wilcoxon test	-0.375	-0.589	-1.067	0.405	0.265	-1.620	-0.184		
Canada	Mean Ret (%)	0.290	0.124	0.221	0.622	0.439	0.455	0.471	0.576*	0.522
	Median Ret (%)	0.200	0.201	0.265	0.302	0.355	0.407	0.376	0.546	0.227
	Std Dev (%)	1.978	1.439	1.796	3.438	3.285	3.284	3.069	1.959	2.396
	t-stat	1.137	0.668	0.953	1.402	1.034	1.072	1.188	2.278	1.688
	Information Ratio	0.147	0.086	0.123	0.181	0.133	0.138	0.153	0.294	0.218
	Interest Differential (%)	-0.020	0.175	-0.040	0.019	0.503	-0.004	0.033	-0.173	-0.050
	Skewness	0.563	-0.967	0.196	0.288	-0.441	0.111	0.497	-0.158	-0.580
	Kurtosis	0.305	3.359	1.073	0.159	0.530	0.551	0.638	-0.386	0.587
	Prob >0 (%)	53.333	60.000	58.333	55.000	56.667	60.000	60.000		
	Prob >MSCI (%)	48.333	45.000	50.000	51.667	51.667	51.667	51.667		
	paired t-test	-0.896	-1.547	-1.243	0.093	-0.319	-0.246	-0.216		
	Wilcoxon test	0.383	0.125	1.259	0.501	0.729	0.456	0.721		
	Prob >Equal (%)	40.000	43.333	45.000	51.667	56.667	53.333	55.000		
	paired t-test	-0.638	-1.311	-0.917	0.189	-0.223	-0.131	-0.100		
	Wilcoxon test	-1.620	-0.331	-0.272	0.537	2.002*	0.920	1.494		

France	Mean Ret (%)	0.109	0.217	0.186	0.861	0.132	0.423	0.310	0.124	0.000
	Median Ret (%)	0.162	0.236	0.172	0.501	0.190	0.430	0.475	−0.291	−0.256
	Std Dev (%)	1.679	1.512	1.608	3.443	3.597	3.172	3.007	2.377	1.848
	t-stat	0.505	1.110	0.896	1.937	0.285	1.032	0.799	0.405	0.001
	Information Ratio	0.065	0.143	0.116	0.250	0.037	0.133	0.103	0.052	0.000
	Interest Differential (%)	0.001	0.236	−0.008	0.004	0.442	−0.021	0.012	−0.285	−0.170
	Skewness	0.394	−0.368	0.289	0.419	−0.825	0.027	0.311	0.853	0.644
	Kurtosis	0.661	1.199	0.802	0.075	0.905	0.211	0.288	0.595	0.393
	Prob >0 (%)	51.667	60.000	55.000	56.667	55.000	56.667	56.667		
	Prob >MSCI (%)	51.667	61.667	53.333	53.333	51.667	56.667	55.000		
	paired t-test	−0.038	0.191	0.161	1.320	0.011	0.536	0.349		
	Wilcoxon test	−0.044	2.289*	0.331	−0.228	−0.184	0.964	0.744		
	Prob >Equal (%)	48.333	60.000	51.667	58.333	51.667	56.667	61.667		
	paired t-test	0.315	0.517	0.566	1.617	0.207	0.819	0.629		
	Wilcoxon test	−1.001	1.583	−0.346	0.810	−0.243	0.839	2.319*		
Germany	Mean Ret (%)	0.064	0.206	0.158	0.960*	0.321	0.413	0.307	0.107	−0.017
	Median Ret (%)	0.049	0.290	0.061	0.809	0.347	0.453	0.327	−0.111	−0.070
	Std Dev (%)	1.740	1.449	1.634	3.406	3.417	3.196	3.017	2.451	1.936
	t-stat	0.287	1.100	0.748	2.183	0.728	1.000	0.787	0.339	−0.068
	Information Ratio	0.037	0.142	0.097	0.282	0.094	0.129	0.102	0.044	−0.009
	Interest Differential (%)	−0.013	0.172	−0.014	0.025	0.505	−0.014	0.022	−0.131	−0.002
	Skewness	0.312	−0.352	0.250	0.373	−0.672	0.090	0.397	0.774	0.497
	Kurtosis	0.831	2.130	1.346	0.125	0.845	0.196	0.130	0.923	0.808
	Prob >0 (%)	50.000	63.333	53.333	63.333	56.667	58.333	56.667		
	Prob >MSCI (%)	51.667	56.667	55.000	58.333	60.000	58.333	53.333		
	paired t-test	−0.103	0.212	0.132	1.511	0.303	0.547	0.372		
	Wilcoxon test	0.088	1.148	0.780	0.626	1.737	1.355	0.221		
	Prob >Equal (%)	51.667	58.333	48.333	63.333	60.000	58.333	58.333		
	paired t-test	0.224	0.554	0.531	1.812	0.532	0.828	0.650		
	Wilcoxon test	0.243	1.303	−1.347	1.796	1.575	1.259	1.355		

(continued)

Table 7.6 (continued)

		Long–Short Within					Long–Short Across		Currency benchmarks	
		[Momentum] 3-month	Interest [rate]	[MA 4 – 6]	[Momentum] 3-month	Interest [rate]	[MA 4 – 6] (1 – 7)	[MA 4 – 6] [(1,2,3 – 7)]	[MSCI]	[Equal]
Japan	Mean Ret (%)	0.311	-0.125	0.330	0.411	0.458	0.105	0.237	-0.542	-0.538
	Median Ret (%)	0.065	0.002	0.326	0.045	0.439	0.026	0.153	-0.268	-0.234
	Std Dev (%)	2.253	2.173	1.983	3.366	3.255	3.145	3.028	2.382	2.429
	t-stat	1.068	-0.445	1.289	0.945	1.090	0.260	0.607	-1.762	-1.717
	Information Ratio	0.138	-0.057	0.166	0.122	0.141	0.034	0.078	-0.228	-0.222
	Interest Differential (%)	-0.005	0.245	0.009	-0.034	0.467	-0.049	-0.035	0.117	0.232
	Skewness	0.585	0.279	0.508	0.297	-0.466	0.490	0.546	-0.058	0.015
	Kurtosis	0.141	0.492	0.808	0.350	1.573	0.990	0.990	0.026	0.069
	Prob >0 (%)	51.667	50.000	61.667	50.000	68.333	50.000	56.667		
	Prob >MSCI (%)	63.333	73.333	65.000	55.000	56.667	51.667	53.333		
	paired t-test	1.956	2.508*	2.227*	1.683	1.848	1.217	1.478		
	Wilcoxon test	1.782	3.143**	2.010*	-0.265	-0.103	-0.368	-0.125		
	Prob >Equal (%)	66.667	83.333	66.667	56.667	58.333	48.333	56.667		
	paired t-test	1.905	4.305**	2.170*	1.694	2.058*	1.245	1.498		
	Wilcoxon test	2.687**	4.446**	2.451*	0.184	0.383	-1.207	0.751		
Switzerland	Mean Ret (%)	0.139	0.133	0.220	0.626	0.327	0.454	0.247	-0.018	-0.157
	Median Ret (%)	0.360	0.194	0.470	0.368	0.345	0.363	0.286	-0.421	-0.444
	Std Dev (%)	1.939	1.346	1.784	3.438	3.414	3.256	3.054	2.596	2.169
	t-stat	0.556	0.767	0.956	1.411	0.742	1.080	0.627	-0.052	-0.561
	Information Ratio	0.072	0.099	0.123	0.182	0.096	0.139	0.081	-0.007	-0.072
	Interest Differential (%)	-0.010	0.159	-0.015	0.015	0.505	0.004	0.027	-0.095	0.036
	Skewness	-0.606	-0.840	-0.703	0.756	-0.652	0.196	0.551	0.789	0.586
	Kurtosis	0.746	4.015	1.466	0.459	0.813	-0.061	0.519	0.336	-0.101
	Prob >0 (%)	58.333	63.333	63.333	53.333	56.667	56.667	58.333		
	Prob >MSCI (%)	56.667	60.000	55.000	53.333	58.333	58.333	55.000		
	paired t-test	0.325	0.341	0.509	1.148	0.496	0.821	0.495		
	Wilcoxon test	0.788	1.524	0.169	0.118	1.038	1.067	0.493		
	Prob >Equal (%)	65.000	61.667	63.333	55.000	55.000	55.000	56.667		
	paired t-test	0.670	0.766	0.890	1.433	0.772	1.127	0.805		
	Wilcoxon test	2.415*	1.531	1.369	0.324	-0.015	0.007	0.677		

									MSCI	Equal
UK										
Mean Ret (%)	0.049	0.032	0.259	0.756	0.459	0.282	0.246	0.350	0.214
Median Ret (%)	−0.252	0.145	0.032	0.650	0.447	0.680	0.693	−0.307	0.112
Std Dev (%)	2.048	2.025	1.824	3.611	3.099	3.495	3.268	3.185	2.621
t-stat	0.184	0.124	1.099	1.622	1.147	0.625	0.583	0.850	0.632
Information Ratio	0.024	0.016	0.142	0.209	0.148	0.081	0.075	0.110	0.082
Interest Differential (%)	0.022	0.211	0.048	−0.026	0.492	−0.042	−0.010	−0.310	−0.171
Skewness	1.264	−1.330	1.178	0.214	−0.456	−0.595	−0.123	1.648	1.677
Kurtosis	3.187	3.216	3.118	0.355	0.746	2.030	1.778	3.911	5.170
Prob >0 (%)	45.000	56.667	53.333	58.333	58.333	61.667	61.667		
Prob >MSCI (%)	48.333	60.000	51.667	51.667	53.333	55.000	51.667		
paired t-test	−0.774	−0.485	−0.222	0.618	0.162	−0.101	−0.165		
Wilcoxon test	0.221	2.039*	0.412	−0.567	0.029	0.832	0.140		
Prob >Equal (%)	43.333	53.333	46.667	55.000	53.333	55.000	55.000		
paired t-test	−0.479	−0.311	0.127	0.897	0.423	0.113	0.057		
Wilcoxon test	−1.281	0.324	−0.942	0.103	−0.155	0.596	0.810		
USA										
Mean Ret (%)	0.254	0.345	0.255	0.881	−0.055	0.491	0.375	0.379	0.151
Median Ret (%)	0.129	0.563	0.189	0.333	−0.066	0.227	0.252	0.445	0.283
Std Dev (%)	1.776	1.905	1.594	3.731	3.157	3.308	3.047	2.366	2.055
t-stat	1.106	1.404	1.240	1.829	−0.136	1.149	0.953	1.241	0.571
Information Ratio	0.143	0.181	0.160	0.236	−0.018	0.148	0.123	0.160	0.074
Interest Differential (%)	0.024	0.249	−0.026	−0.032	0.459	0.004	0.035	0.138	0.234
Skewness	0.608	−1.222	0.374	0.142	−0.315	0.381	0.641	−0.425	−1.002
Kurtosis	0.874	3.016	0.442	0.592	−0.546	0.685	0.921	0.580	1.910
Prob >0 (%)	55.000	63.333	58.333	56.667	50.000	55.000	58.333		
Prob >MSCI (%)	45.000	51.667	50.000	51.667	48.333	46.667	51.667		
paired t-test	−0.366	−0.184	−0.368	0.992	−0.837	0.229	−0.008		
Wilcoxon test	−0.449	0.758	0.346	−0.317	0.309	−0.994	0.501		
Prob >Equal (%)	60.000	80.000	53.333	51.667	50.000	48.333	56.667		
paired t-test	0.327	2.300*	0.339	1.424	−0.490	0.719	0.496		
Wilcoxon test	2.208*	5.124**	0.589	−0.589	0.324	−0.935	1.355		

This table shows performance measures and statistics for selected foreign exchange trading strategies. The base currency is denoted on the far left. The MSCI and Equal columns are reproduced from Table 7.1. The first t-stat is used to test the significance of the mean return relative to a null hypothesis of zero. The [Interest Differential] rows give the mean monthly return due to the interest differential of the non-domestic relative to the domestic currency. The [Prob >] rows give the percentage of the total months that the given strategy has exceeded zero, the MSCI benchmark, and the Equal benchmark. The paired t-test is used to test the significance of the excess returns of each of the ranks and the long-short strategies relative to the MSCI benchmark and the Equal benchmark. The Wilcoxon is a nonparametric test of the excess returns. The [Proportion >] rows give the percentage of the 93 MA combinations that exceed zero, the MSCI benchmark average return, and the Equal benchmark average return. ** and * indicate significance at the 1 and 5 per cent levels.

Table 7.7 *Performance of selected strategies: sub-period analysis: 1995–2000*

	Long-Short Within			Long-Short Across				Currency benchmarks	
	[Momentum] 3-month	Interest [rate]	[MA 4 − 6]	[Momentum] 3-month	Interest [rate]	[MA 4 − 6] (1 − 7)	[MA 4 − 6] (1,2,3 − 7)	[MSCI]	[Equal]
Australia									
Mean Ret (%)	0.044	0.209	0.356	0.523	0.593	0.482	0.653*	0.358	0.261
Median Ret (%)	0.116	0.081	0.522	−0.068	0.952	0.032	0.695	0.732	0.673
Std Dev (%)	2.443	2.211	2.177	3.312	4.395	2.893	2.431	2.722	2.873
t-stat	0.147	0.767	1.327	1.282	1.096	1.354	2.181	1.068	0.739
Information Ratio	0.018	0.094	0.163	0.158	0.135	0.167	0.268	0.132	0.091
Interest Differential (%)	0.036	0.200	0.040	0.064	0.483	0.077	0.113	−0.151	−0.180
Skewness	−0.006	−0.276	−0.176	0.076	−1.248	0.216	0.214	−0.032	0.133
Kurtosis	0.077	0.567	0.851	−0.361	3.934	−0.093	−0.483	−0.317	−0.343
Prob >0 (%)	50.000	50.000	59.091	48.485	68.182	51.515	59.091		
Prob >MSCI (%)	42.424	43.939	45.455	51.515	59.091	51.515	54.545		
paired t-test	−0.736	−0.256	−0.006	0.312	0.333	0.251	0.636		
Wilcoxon test	−0.885	−1.498	−1.108	0.042	1.575	0.022	0.648		
Prob >Equal (%)	28.788	50.000	40.909	53.030	56.061	56.061	56.061		
paired t-test	−0.479	−0.086	0.231	0.480	0.458	0.431	0.807		
Wilcoxon test	−4.481**	−0.003	−2.482*	0.214	0.553	1.070	0.814		
Canada									
Mean Ret (%)	0.106	0.265	0.181	0.128	0.429	0.490	0.611	0.019	−0.113
Median Ret (%)	−0.024	0.327	0.133	−0.276	0.874	0.123	0.864	0.033	−0.136
Std Dev (%)	1.631	1.708	1.506	3.697	4.601	3.179	2.642	1.830	2.193
t-stat	0.526	1.259	0.975	0.281	0.758	1.253	1.877	0.085	−0.418
Information Ratio	0.065	0.155	0.120	0.035	0.093	0.154	0.231	0.010	−0.051
Interest Differential (%)	0.008	0.157	0.027	0.047	0.510	0.059	0.084	−0.062	−0.080
Skewness	0.631	−0.586	−0.260	0.001	−1.196	0.039	0.005	0.281	0.166
Kurtosis	2.352	2.840	0.504	−0.491	3.958	−0.248	1.000	1.663	1.113
Prob >0 (%)	46.970	59.091	50.000	48.485	66.667	53.030	59.091		
Prob >MSCI (%)	57.576	59.091	50.000	57.576	63.636	56.061	62.121		
paired t-test	0.313	0.616	0.526	0.212	0.587	1.028	1.448		
Wilcoxon test	1.741	1.332	−0.425	1.856*	2.386*	0.444	1.504		
Prob >Equal (%)	48.485	59.091	48.485	62.121	62.121	63.636	66.667		
paired t-test	0.675	0.856	0.824	0.444	0.747	1.219	1.611		
Wilcoxon test	−0.987	1.204	−1.140	2.635**	1.734	2.188*	2.578**		

		1	2	3	4	5	6	7	8	9
France	Mean Ret (%)	0.064	0.269	0.241	0.381	0.509	0.549	0.582	0.337	0.220
	Median Ret (%)	0.037	0.418	0.282	-0.070	0.899	0.167	0.499	0.655	0.205
	Std Dev (%)	1.395	1.297	1.316	3.849	4.542	3.243	2.662	2.026	1.700
	t-stat	0.371	1.686	1.488	0.803	0.911	1.374	1.777	1.351	1.052
	Information Ratio	0.046	0.208	0.183	0.099	0.112	0.169	0.219	0.166	0.129
	Interest Differential (%)	0.021	0.151	0.028	0.059	0.510	0.056	0.088	0.004	-0.007
	Skewness	0.050	-0.512	-0.187	0.241	-1.098	0.204	-0.030	-0.031	-0.057
	Kurtosis	-0.597	-0.365	-0.282	0.424	4.011	-0.079	0.963	-0.924	-0.963
	Prob >0 (%)	51.515	65.152	63.636	50.000	66.667	54.545	60.606		
	Prob >MSCI (%)	46.970	48.485	46.970	50.000	57.576	50.000	50.000		
	paired t-test	-1.063	-0.290	-0.377	0.086	0.287	0.471	0.661		
	Wilcoxon test	0.227	-0.208	-0.252	0.010	1.255	-0.291	-0.380		
	Prob >Equal (%)	48.485	53.030	50.000	51.515	59.091	50.000	54.545		
	paired t-test	-0.658	0.248	0.090	0.323	0.491	0.751	1.011		
	Wilcoxon test	0.195	0.316	0.118	0.157	1.223	-0.744	0.252		
Germany	Mean Ret (%)	0.141	0.265	0.313*	0.324	0.557	0.499	0.558	0.383	0.269
	Median Ret (%)	0.071	0.507	0.319	-0.060	0.948	0.160	0.521	0.578	0.418
	Std Dev (%)	1.322	1.497	1.298	3.708	4.556	3.310	2.626	2.020	1.686
	t-stat	0.866	1.440	1.960	0.710	0.993	1.226	1.726	1.540	1.296
	Information Ratio	0.107	0.177	0.241	0.087	0.122	0.151	0.212	0.190	0.160
	Interest Differential (%)	0.017	0.155	0.030	0.053	0.510	0.049	0.092	0.050	0.044
	Skewness	-0.070	-0.511	-0.320	-0.004	-1.106	0.052	0.051	-0.083	-0.196
	Kurtosis	-0.626	0.642	-0.464	-0.047	4.008	0.672	1.009	-0.811	-0.876
	Prob >0 (%)	53.030	62.121	63.636	50.000	68.182	56.061	62.121		
	Prob >MSCI (%)	46.970	50.000	46.970	43.939	59.091	48.485	48.485		
	paired t-test	-0.997	-0.606	-0.277	-0.115	0.291	0.253	0.471		
	Wilcoxon test	0.291	0.310	-0.112	-1.555	1.568	-0.508	-0.731		
	Prob >Equal (%)	53.030	57.576	46.970	48.485	59.091	51.515	54.545		
	paired t-test	-0.571	-0.025	0.191	0.110	0.493	0.511	0.806		
	Wilcoxon test	1.543	1.370	-0.470	-0.655	1.242	-0.188	0.380		

(continued)

Table 7.7 (continued)

		Long-Short Within			Long-Short Across				Currency benchmarks	
		[Momentum] 3-month	Interest [rate]	[MA 4 – 6] 3-month	[Momentum] 3-month	Interest [rate]	[MA 4 – 6] (1 – 7)	[MA 4 – 6] [1, 2, 3 – 7]	[MSCI]	[Equal]
Japan	Mean Ret (%)	0.298	0.270	0.368	0.469	0.736	0.423	0.518	0.106	-0.062
	Median Ret (%)	0.226	0.982	0.321	0.256	0.867	0.425	0.606	0.452	0.679
	Std Dev (%)	2.834	3.597	2.477	3.216	3.302	2.986	2.743	3.796	3.578
	t-stat	0.855	0.610	1.207	1.185	1.811	1.150	1.535	0.226	-0.141
	Information Ratio	0.105	0.075	0.149	0.146	0.223	0.142	0.189	0.028	-0.017
	Interest Differential (%)	0.046	0.331	0.033	0.055	0.394	0.070	0.057	0.367	0.331
	Skewness	0.183	-1.127	0.643	0.169	-0.432	0.185	0.051	-1.142	-1.141
	Kurtosis	0.585	2.682	1.414	-0.792	0.430	-0.320	0.229	2.923	2.705
	Prob >0 (%)	57.576	62.121	54.545	53.030	63.636	53.030	62.121		
	Prob >MSCI (%)	45.455	57.576	43.939	50.000	51.515	48.485	51.515		
	paired t-test	0.346	1.669	0.475	0.649	1.270	0.544	0.733		
	Wilcoxon test	-1.051	0.412	-1.524	-0.329	-0.399	-0.712	0.010		
	Prob >Equal (%)	63.636	100.000	59.091	54.545	56.061	56.061	59.091		
	paired t-test	0.669	56.547**	0.807	0.951	1.544	0.839	1.038		
	Wilcoxon test	3.153**	7.062**	2.035*	0.501	0.431	1.000	1.581		
Switzerland	Mean Ret (%)	0.249	0.318	0.337	0.298	0.568	0.460	0.514	0.291	0.174
	Median Ret (%)	0.165	0.538	0.361	-0.061	0.955	0.157	0.398	0.238	0.457
	Std Dev (%)	1.743	1.842	1.567	3.540	4.525	2.999	2.469	2.330	2.110
	t-stat	1.161	1.401	1.746	0.683	1.020	1.246	1.691	1.014	0.670
	Information Ratio	0.143	0.172	0.215	0.084	0.126	0.153	0.208	0.125	0.082
	Interest Differential (%)	0.032	0.231	0.035	0.053	0.510	0.055	0.098	0.189	0.198
	Skewness	0.097	-0.714	0.190	-0.208	-1.084	0.025	-0.096	-0.129	-0.366
	Kurtosis	-0.249	0.718	-0.141	-0.172	3.920	-0.109	1.214	-0.972	-0.510
	Prob >0 (%)	54.545	60.606	62.121	50.000	68.182	53.030	62.121		
	Prob >MSCI (%)	51.515	51.515	46.970	46.970	56.061	53.030	42.424		
	paired t-test	-0.126	0.161	0.150	0.014	0.477	0.380	0.571		
	Wilcoxon test	0.744	0.246	-0.604	-0.987	0.910	0.604	-2.239*		
	Prob >Equal (%)	62.121	60.606	57.576	51.515	56.061	57.576	46.970		
	paired t-test	0.237	1.083	0.556	0.252	0.693	0.658	0.891		
	Wilcoxon test	2.948**	1.306	1.683	0.112	0.591	1.587	-1.536		

UK									
Mean Ret (%)	0.210	0.391	0.260	0.016	0.678	0.457	0.580	−0.020	−0.157
Median Ret (%)	0.136	0.342	0.210	−0.278	1.175	0.123	0.843	0.030	−0.042
Std Dev (%)	1.390	1.838	1.276	3.599	4.804	3.117	2.774	1.808	1.838
t-stat	1.225	1.728	1.653	0.036	1.147	1.191	1.698	−0.091	−0.694
Information Ratio	0.151	0.213	0.203	0.004	0.141	0.147	0.209	−0.011	−0.085
Interest Differential (%)	0.051	0.222	0.049	0.041	0.454	0.048	0.074	−0.193	−0.205
Skewness	0.942	−0.283	0.529	−0.107	−1.254	0.064	−0.006	0.130	0.122
Kurtosis	1.949	0.516	1.266	−0.240	3.398	−0.084	0.759	0.110	0.593
Prob >0 (%)	56.061	59.091	60.606	48.485	68.182	53.030	62.121		
Prob >MSCI (%)	59.091	53.030	54.545	54.545	63.636	56.061	62.121		
paired t-test	0.724	0.953	0.898	0.076	0.995	1.105	1.467		
Wilcoxon test	1.575	−0.112	0.310	1.032	1.920	0.501	1.805		
Prob >Equal (%)	54.545	59.091	51.515	54.545	63.636	57.576	62.121		
paired t-test	1.105	1.229	1.298	0.352	1.180	1.370	1.727		
Wilcoxon test	0.125	1.402	−0.597	0.642	1.555	0.521	1.530		
USA									
Mean Ret (%)	0.232	0.485**	0.264	0.124	0.502	0.504	0.601	−0.163	−0.214
Median Ret (%)	0.198	0.503	0.248	0.129	0.935	0.243	1.036	−0.200	−0.118
Std Dev (%)	1.435	1.395	1.272	3.584	4.519	3.171	2.743	2.268	1.737
t-stat	1.316	2.822	1.683	0.281	0.903	1.292	1.780	−0.582	−1.002
Information Ratio	0.162	0.347	0.207	0.035	0.111	0.159	0.219	−0.072	−0.123
Interest Differential (%)	0.047	0.161	0.044	0.020	0.510	0.054	0.080	−0.165	−0.101
Skewness	0.527	−0.251	0.505	−0.094	−1.265	−0.115	0.007	0.593	0.251
Kurtosis	2.118	−0.085	1.415	−0.257	4.371	0.073	0.981	2.119	0.558
Prob >0 (%)	62.121	69.697	56.061	51.515	68.182	56.061	62.121		
Prob >MSCI (%)	60.606	63.636	59.091	53.030	60.606	54.545	57.576		
paired t-test	1.154	1.502	1.323	0.546	0.848	1.380	1.659		
Wilcoxon test	1.722	1.958	1.217	−0.010	1.096	−0.227	0.399		
Prob >Equal (%)	56.061	62.121	53.030	54.545	66.667	60.606	62.121		
paired t-test	1.476	1.898	1.702	0.686	1.029	1.570	1.936		
Wilcoxon test	0.169	1.306	−0.731	0.374	2.629**	1.319	1.389		

This table shows performance measures and statistics for selected foreign exchange trading strategies. The base currency is denoted on the far left. The MSCI and Equal columns are reproduced from Table 7.1. The first t-stat is used to test the significance of the mean return relative to a null hypothesis of zero. The [Interest Differential] rows give the mean monthly return due to the interest differential of the non-domestic relative to the domestic currency. The [Prob >] rows give the percentage of the total months that the given strategy has exceeded zero, the MSCI benchmark, and the Equal benchmark. The paired t-test is used to test the significance of the excess returns of each of the ranks and the long–short strategies relative to the MSCI benchmark and the Equal benchmark. The Wilcoxon is a nonparametric test of the excess returns. The [Proportion >] rows give the percentage of the 93 MA combinations that exceed zero, the MSCI benchmark average return, and the Equal benchmark average return. ** and * indicate significance at the 1 and 5 per cent levels.

Table 7.8 *Mean returns across countries for selected strategies*

		[1980–1984]	[1985–1989]	[1990–1994]	[1995–2000]	$\begin{bmatrix}\text{Average}\\\text{Overall}\end{bmatrix}$	$\begin{bmatrix}\text{Average}\\\text{1985–2000}\end{bmatrix}$
Long–Short Within	Momentum	0.451	0.124	0.152	0.168	0.224	0.148
		(8)	(7)	(8)	(8)		
	Interest rate	0.378	0.106	0.130	0.309	0.231	0.182
		(7)	(6)	(7)	(8)		
	MA 4–6	0.346	0.441	0.199	0.290	0.319	0.310
		(8)	(8)	(7)	(8)		
Long–Short Across	Momentum	0.863	−0.227	0.739	0.283	0.415	0.265
		(8)	(2)	(8)	(8)		
	Interest rate	1.049	0.287	0.327	0.572	0.559	0.395
		(8)	(7)	(7)	(8)		
	MA 4–6 [1–7]	0.635	0.831	0.398	0.483	0.587	0.571
		(8)	(8)	(8)	(8)		
	MA 4–6 (1, 2, 3–7)	0.552	0.877	0.346	0.577	0.588	0.600
		(8)	(8)	(8)	(8)		
Average	L–S Within	0.392	0.224	0.160	0.256	0.258	0.213
	L–S Across	0.775	0.442	0.453	0.479	0.537	0.458
	All	0.611	0.348	0.327	0.383	0.417	0.353

This table shows the mean monthly returns to the foreign exchange strategies averaged across countries. The numbers in parentheses give the count of countries in each time period that had a positive mean return for a given trading strategy.

value to foreign exchange performance. We will examine these possibilities later in the chapter.

Table 7.8 gives the average monthly return across base currencies for each class of trading rules. As detailed earlier, the *Long–Short Within* strategies had their greatest performance during the 1980–1984 period. In addition, the *Long–Short Across* interest rate rule also did extremely well during the 1980–1984 period. What is clear from an examination of Table 7.8 is that the *Long–Short Within* strategies have not performed as well during the 1990s as during the 1980s. This is especially true for the *Long–Short Within* moving-average rules. While it is certainly possible to identify select specifications in select base currencies ex post to show that moving-average rules still work, we should view such results with a fair degree of scepticism. At least on a monthly basis, such trading rules do not appear to earn significant returns.

On the other hand, we can see that the performance of the *Long–Short Across* moving-average class has been remarkably stable during the previous 20 years. In fact, the performance during the 1995–2000 period has been very strong. In general, with the exception of the momentum rules, the *Long–Short Across* strategies identified in this chapter still appear to work quite well.

In Table 7.9 we show the correlations of the individual trading strategies for each base currency. From the Table we can see that the *Long–Short Across* interest rate rule has nearly a zero correlation with the *Long–Short Across* moving-average rules. In spite of the much higher standard deviation to the *Long–Short Across* interest rate rule, it does appear that substantial diversification benefits would accrue to a combination of the two. Moreover, it also appears that for many base currencies the *Long–Short Within* moving-average rules may be combined with the *Long–Short Across* rules to gain even greater benefits. Clearly, one need not choose one trading strategy to the exclusion of the others.

As an additional layer of diversification, one may wish to initiate exposures across multiple base currencies for selected strategies. Table 7.10 gives the correlations across base currencies for individual strategies. While the correlations between the same strategies across multiple base currencies are greater than the correlations between different strategies in the same base currency, there are also potential diversification benefits by initiating multiple positions across different base currencies. In particular, base currencies can be identified that offer the greatest potential diversification benefits (e.g. using Australia or Japan with any other base currency).

7.5 CONCLUSIONS

The simple strategies we analyse in this chapter may be easily implemented. We find that following the *Long–Short Across* moving-average rules will

Table 7.9 *Correlations across strategies*

		Long-Short Within			Long-Short Across				Currency benchmarks	
		[Momentum]	Interest [rate]	[MA 4 – 6]	[Momentum]	Interest [rate]	[MA 4 – 6] (1 – 7)	[MA 4 – 6] (1, 2, 3 – 7)	[MSCI]	[Equal]
Australia										
Long–Short Within	Momentum		−0.122	0.848	0.331	0.138	0.334	0.345	0.209	0.181
	Int Rate			0.009	−0.002	0.331	0.062	0.079	−0.813	−0.812
	MA 4 – 6				0.303	0.142	0.346	0.364	0.074	0.061
Long–Short Across	Momentum					0.008	0.849	0.815	0.085	0.040
	Int Rate						0.072	0.105	−0.109	−0.095
	MA 4 – 6 (1 – 7)							0.926	0.013	−0.019
	MA 4 – 6 (1, 2, 3 – 7)								−0.008	−0.038
Currency benchmarks	MSCI									0.951
	Equal									
Canada										
Long–Short Within	Momentum		0.072	0.812	0.581	−0.059	0.563	0.563	0.121	0.041
	Int Rate			0.236	0.085	0.675	0.178	0.103	−0.521	−0.496
	MA 4 – 6				0.550	0.102	0.643	0.614	−0.036	−0.080
Long–Short Across	Momentum					−0.034	0.836	0.793	0.030	−0.052
	Int Rate						0.117	0.055	−0.320	−0.244
	MA 4 – 6 (1 – 7)							0.906	−0.073	−0.105
	MA 4 – 6 (1, 2, 3 – 7)								−0.047	−0.079
Currency benchmarks	MSCI									0.888
	Equal									

France

Long–Short Within									
	Momentum	0.072	0.875	0.652	0.085	0.636	0.658	0.164	0.141
	Int Rate		0.147	−0.012	0.501	0.065	0.045	−0.311	−0.260
	MA 4 – 6			0.617	0.102	0.707	0.703	0.088	0.079
Long–Short Across	Momentum				0.020	0.850	0.817	0.147	0.111
	Int Rate					0.150	0.106	0.124	0.187
	MA 4 – 6 (1 – 7)						0.910	0.079	0.068
	MA 4 – 6 (1, 2, 3 – 7)							0.101	0.074
Currency benchmarks	MSCI								0.948
	Equal								

Germany

Long–Short Within									
	Momentum	0.102	0.890	0.642	0.050	0.642	0.656	0.131	0.096
	Int Rate		0.132	0.115	0.695	0.122	0.153	0.473	0.521
	MA 4 – 6			0.608	0.093	0.730	0.730	0.164	0.155
Long–Short Across	Momentum				−0.034	0.819	0.795	0.133	0.067
	Int Rate					0.103	0.083	0.133	0.222
	MA 4 – 6 (1 – 7)						0.910	0.048	0.033
	MA 4 – 6 (1, 2, 3 – 7)							0.070	0.038
Currency benchmarks	MSCI								0.947
	Equal								

(continued)

Table 7.9 (continued)

		Long-Short Within		Long-Short Across			Currency benchmarks	
		Interest [Momentum] [rate]	[MA 4 – 6] [Momentum]	Interest [rate]	[MA 4 – 6] [(1 – 7)]	[MA 4 – 6] [(1, 2, 3 – 7)]	[MSCI]	[Equal]
Japan								
Long-Short Within	Momentum	0.010	0.315	-0.035	0.343	0.349	0.010	-0.050
	Int Rate	0.126	-0.019	0.315	0.031	-0.017	0.919	0.960
	MA 4 – 6		0.257	0.036	0.366	0.347	0.118	0.087
Long-Short Across	Momentum			-0.019	0.855	0.839	0.032	-0.020
	Int Rate				0.142	0.046	0.265	0.207
	MA 4 – 6 (1 – 7)					0.935	0.047	0.010
	MA 4 – 6 (1, 2, 3 – 7)						0.018	-0.026
Currency benchmarks	MSCI							0.934
	Equal							
Switzerland								
Long-Short Within	Momentum	0.165	0.593	0.015	0.570	0.602	0.052	0.002
	Int Rate	0.231	0.053	0.563	0.114	0.087	0.666	0.725
	MA 4 – 6		0.573	0.033	0.631	0.636	0.110	0.084
Long-Short Across	Momentum			-0.080	0.816	0.778	0.077	0.005
	Int Rate				0.100	0.061	0.089	0.214
	MA 4 – 6 (1 – 7)					0.915	0.033	0.018
	MA 4 – 6 (1, 2, 3 – 7)						0.034	0.004
Currency benchmarks	MSCI							0.951
	Equal							

UK

Long–Short Within	Momentum	0.014	0.833	0.347	0.021	0.298	0.343	0.160	0.107
	Int Rate		0.092	0.032	0.407	0.042	0.039	-0.737	-0.791
	MA 4 – 6			0.386	0.092	0.408	0.439	0.091	0.074
Long–Short Across	Momentum				0.031	0.862	0.837	0.003	-0.066
	Int Rate					0.114	0.099	-0.074	-0.057
	MA 4 – 6 (1 – 7)						0.932	0.002	-0.037
	MA 4 – 6 (1, 2, 3 – 7)							0.014	-0.030
Currency benchmarks	MSCI								0.921
	Equal								

USA

Long–Short Within	Momentum	0.178	0.873	0.573	-0.020	0.516	0.518	-0.009	-0.061
	Int Rate		0.176	0.087	0.604	0.177	0.160	-0.193	-0.104
	MA 4 – 6			0.577	0.032	0.614	0.596	-0.092	-0.136
Long–Short Across	Momentum				-0.082	0.825	0.785	0.000	-0.056
	Int Rate					0.081	0.031	-0.468	-0.304
	MA 4 – 6 (1 – 7)						0.914	-0.061	-0.067
	MA 4 – 6 (1, 2, 3 – 7)							-0.020	-0.026
Currency benchmarks	MSCI								0.925
	Equal								

Table 7.10 *Correlations across countries for individual strategies*

Long–Short Within Momentum 3-Month

	Australia	Canada	France	Germany	Japan	Switzerland	UK	USA
Australia		0.427	0.539	0.556	0.398	0.570	0.350	0.429
Canada			0.759	0.728	0.435	0.710	0.512	0.830
France				0.926	0.487	0.797	0.524	0.680
Germany					0.459	0.825	0.500	0.672
Japan						0.462	0.406	0.477
Switzerland							0.439	0.684
UK								0.498
USA								

Long–Short Within Interest rate

	Australia	Canada	France	Germany	Japan	Switzerland	UK	USA
Australia		0.680	0.542	0.660	0.392	0.618	0.387	0.513
Canada			0.565	0.819	0.508	0.745	0.509	0.655
France				0.502	0.410	0.458	0.449	0.590
Germany					0.468	0.841	0.542	0.677
Japan						0.418	0.366	0.474
Switzerland							0.452	0.636
UK								0.640
USA								

Long–Short Within MA 4 – 6

	Australia	Canada	France	Germany	Japan	Switzerland	UK	USA
Australia		0.497	0.556	0.585	0.354	0.589	0.372	0.463
Canada			0.745	0.753	0.492	0.714	0.532	0.863
France				0.937	0.471	0.777	0.549	0.700
Germany					0.489	0.821	0.565	0.713
Japan						0.425	0.451	0.448
Switzerland							0.475	0.694
UK								0.524
USA								

Long–Short Across Momentum 3-month

	Australia	Canada	France	Germany	Japan	Switzerland	UK	USA
Australia		0.762	0.782	0.763	0.615	0.765	0.714	0.772
Canada			0.945	0.938	0.782	0.927	0.891	0.945
France				0.953	0.793	0.946	0.905	0.951
Germany					0.787	0.932	0.894	0.938
Japan						0.762	0.739	0.787
Switzerland							0.863	0.932
UK								0.896
USA								

Long–Short Across Interest rate

	Australia	Canada	France	Germany	Japan	Switzerland	UK	USA
Australia		0.770	0.746	0.786	0.543	0.719	0.723	0.743
Canada			0.941	0.982	0.792	0.910	0.928	0.953
France				0.957	0.784	0.877	0.899	0.936
Germany					0.823	0.923	0.938	0.968
Japan						0.743	0.754	0.785
Switzerland							0.869	0.898
UK								0.920
USA								

Long–Short Within MA 4 – 6 (1 – 7)

	Australia	Canada	France	Germany	Japan	Switzerland	UK	USA
Australia		0.781	0.808	0.801	0.642	0.787	0.741	0.784
Canada			0.975	0.977	0.843	0.956	0.911	0.968
France				0.985	0.845	0.960	0.928	0.972
Germany					0.850	0.962	0.928	0.978
Japan						0.817	0.793	0.839
Switzerland							0.892	0.955
UK								0.912
USA								

Long–Short Within MA 4 – 6 (1, 2, 3 – 7)

	Australia	Canada	France	Germany	Japan	Switzerland	UK	USA
Australia		0.778	0.810	0.809	0.695	0.790	0.768	0.788
Canada			0.960	0.958	0.858	0.935	0.905	0.973
France				0.987	0.870	0.961	0.923	0.964
Germany					0.865	0.965	0.922	0.964
Japan						0.839	0.839	0.858
Switzerland							0.897	0.945
UK								0.922
USA								

outperform other trend-chasing technical approaches. These results have been stable over the previous twenty years across all base currencies and have been particularly strong during the 1995–2000 period. Potential diversification benefits may also be obtained through combining the *Long–Short Across* interest rate rule and moving-average rules. These strategies have outperformed the MSCI and Equal currency benchmarks for all the base currencies as well. In Okunev and White (2002) we found no evidence for the presence of time-varying risk explanations for the *Long–Short Across* moving-average rules. In additional tests not shown in this chapter we also found little evidence for a time-varying risk premium for the *Long–Short Across* interest rate strategy. In short, we do not believe that risk can fully explain the results of this chapter.

In general, following *Long–Short Across* approaches will outperform strategies that trade within individual currencies in isolation. That is, the potential for excess returns is much greater when we consider the technical performance of all currencies with respect to each other when we set our positions. While individual specifications of select trading rules within a given currency may have historically performed quite well, we cannot ascertain whether the result is driven by chance. This is especially true if only one base currency is considered when a trading rule is evaluated.

We do not yet know why, but pure momentum as a strategy for currencies does not appear to be a viable trading approach. This is in stark contrast to what has been found for equities (Jegadeesh and Titman, 1993, 2001). It is not clear what fundamental difference exists between momentum and moving-average approaches, and one potential avenue for future research would be to determine the conditions explaining why one approach might succeed and the other not. Perhaps a deeper process is at work differentiating equity and currency markets.

If this chapter makes any further contribution, we hope it will motivate others to consider as broad a range of assets as possible when testing sets of technical trading rules. In addition, by averaging across many specifications for a given class of strategies, the studies will be as free as possible from ex post selection bias criticisms. Even though we have found that the results in this chapter are remarkably stable across base currencies, we recommend that tests be substantiated using multiple base currencies.

We should emphasize that we do not necessarily advocate our approach as a speculative tool. The returns the moving-average strategies generate average only 7 per cent per year and they are not risk-free. Instead we expect our findings to be of use to those who have natural positions in a foreign currency and who would like to tilt their exposure to select currencies to enhance performance. Any foreign exchange manager can calculate a moving average of returns for multiple currencies and look up interest rate differentials. We simply advocate using these as tools when considering an institution's overall currency exposure.

REFERENCES

Arnott, R.D. and Pham, T.K. (1993) Tactical currency allocation, *Financial Analysts Journal*, **49**, 47–52.

Banerjee, A.V. (1992) A simple model of herd behavior, *Quarterly Journal of Economics*, **107**, 797–817.

Black, F. (1989) Equilibrium exchange rate hedging, *Journal of Finance*, **43**, 899–908.

Brock, W., Lakonishok, J. and LeBaron, B. (1992) Simple technical trading rules and the stochastic properties of stock returns, *Journal of Finance*, **47**, 1731–64.

Clarida, R.H. and Taylor, M.P. (1997) The term structure of forward exchange premiums and the forecastability of spot exchange rates: correcting the errors, *Review of Economic and Statistics*, **79**, 353–61.

Fama, E.F. (1965) The behavior of stock market prices, *Journal of Political Economy*, **38**, 34–105.

Fama, E.F. (1984) Forward and spot exchange rates, *Journal of Monetary Economics*, **36**, 697–703.

Frankel, J.A. and Froot, K.A. (1990) Chartists, fundamentalists, and trading in the foreign exchange market, *American Economic Review*, **80**, 181–85.

Frenkel, M. and Stadtmann, G. (2000) Trading rule profitability and interventions in the dollar–deutschmark market, Working paper.

Froot, K.A. (1993) Currency hedging over long horizons, Bureau of Economic Research Working Paper 4355.

Gastinaeu, G.L. (1995) The currency hedging decision: a search for synthesis in asset allocation, *Financial Analysts Journal*, **51**, 8–17.

Jegadeesh, N. and Titman, S. (1993) Returns to buying winners and selling losers: implications for stock market efficiency, *Journal of Finance*, **48**, 65–91.

Jegadeesh, N. and Titman, S. (2001) Profitability of momentum strategies: an evaluation of alternative explanations, *Journal of Finance*, **56**, 699–720.

Kho, B. (1996) Time varying risk premia, volatility, and technical reading profits: evidence from foreign currency futures markets, *Journal of Financial Economics*, **41**, 249–90.

Kritzman, M. (1989) Serial dependence in currency returns: investment implications, *Journal of Portfolio Management*, **16**, 96–102.

LeBaron, B. (1999) Technical trading rule profitability and foreign exchange intervention, *Journal of International Economics*, **49**, 125–43.

LeBaron, B. (2000) The stability of moving average technical trading rules on the Dow Jones Index, *Derivative Use, Trading & Regulation*, **5**, 324–38.

Levich, R.M. (1985) Empirical studies of exchange rates: price behaviour, rate determination and market efficiency, in *Handbook of International Economics* (eds R.W Jones and P.B. Kenen), **2**, 980–1036.

Levich, R.M. (Fall, 1989) Is the foreign exchange market efficient? *Oxford Review of Economic Policy*, **5**, 40–60.

Levich, R.M. (1989) Forward rates as the optimal future spot rate forecast, in *Exchange Rate Forecasting* (eds C. Dunis and W. Feeny), Woodhead-Faulkner, Cambridge, pp. 75–98.

Levich, R.M and Thomas, L.R. (1993) The significance of technical trading-rule profits in the foreign exchange market: a bootstrap approach, *Journal of International Money and Finance*, **12**, 451–74.

Marsh, I.W. (2000) High-frequency Markov switching models in the foreign exchange market, *Journal of Forecasting*, **19**, 123–34.

Neely, C.J. (1998) Technical analysis and the profitability of U.S. foreign exchange intervention. *Federal Reserve Bank of St Louis Review*, July/August, 3–17.

Neely, C.J. (2000) The temporal pattern of trading rule returns and central bank intervention: intervention does not generate technical trading rule profits, Working Paper, St Louis Federal Reserve Bank.

Neely, C.J. and Weller, P. (2001) Intraday technical trading in the foreign exchange market, Working Paper, St Louis Federal Reserve Bank.

Neely, C.J. and Weller, P. (2001) Technical analysis and central bank intervention, *Journal of International Money and Finance*, **20**, 949–70.

Neely, C.J., Weller, P. and Dittmar, R. (1997) Is technical analysis profitable in foreign exchange markets? A genetic programming approach, *Journal of Financial and Quantitative Analysis*, **32**, 405–26.

Neftci, S.N. (1991) Naive trading rules in financial markets and Weiner–Kolmogorov prediction theory: a study of technical analysis, *Journal of Business*, **64**, 549–71.

Ntungo, C. and Boyd, M. (1998) Commodity futures trading performance using neural network models versus ARIMA models, *Journal of Futures Markets*, **18**, 965–83.

Okunev, J. and White, D. (2002) Do momentum-based strategies still work in foreign currency markets? *Journal of Financial and Quantitative Analysis*, forthcoming.

Perold, A. and Schulman, E. (1988) The free lunch in currency hedging: implications for investment policies and performance standards, *Financial Analysts Journal*, **44**, May/June, 45–50.

Raj, M. (2000) Transaction data tests of efficiency in the Singapore futures markets, *Journal of Futures Markets*, **20**, 687–704.

Schulmeister, S. (1988) Currency speculation and dollar fluctuations, *Quarterly Review*, Banca Nationale del Lavoro, **167**, 343–65.

Shleifer, A. and Summers, L.H. (1990) The noise trader approach to finance, *Journal of Economic Perspectives*, **4**, 19–33.

Sullivan, R., Timmermann, A. and White, H. (1999) Data-Snooping, Technical Trading Rule Performance, and the Bootstrap, *Journal of Finance*, **54**, 1647–91.

Surajaras, P. and Sweeney, R.J. (1992) *Profit-Making Speculation in Foreign Exchange Markets*, Westview Press, Boulder, CO.

Sweeney, R.J. (1986) Beating the foreign exchange market, *Journal of Finance*, **41**, 163–82.

Sweeney, R.J. (1988) Some new filter rule tests: methods and results, *Journal of Financial and Quantitative Analysis*, **23**, 285–300.

Sweeney, R.J. (1997) Do central banks lose on foreign exchange intervention? A review article, *Journal of Banking and Finance*, **21**, 1667–84.

Szakmary, A.C. and Mathur, I. (1997) Central bank intervention and trading rule profits in foreign exchange markets, *Journal of International Money and Finance*, **16**, 513–35.

Taylor, S.J. (1992) Efficiency in the yen futures market at the Chicago Mercantile Exchange, in *Rational Expectations and Efficiency in Futures Markets*, Routledge, London, pp. 109–28.

Taylor, S.J. (1994) Trading futures using a channel rule: a study of predictive power of technical analysis with currency examples, *Journal of Futures Markets*, **14**, 215–35.

Taylor, M.P. and Allen, H. (1992) The use of technical analysis in the foreign exchange market, *Journal of International Money and Finance*, **11**, 304–14.

NOTES

1. Surajaras and Sweeney (1992) find that optimized *Long–Short Across* trading strategies underperform optimized *Long–Short Within* methods. Our approach does not attempt to identify the optimal specification for a given trading rule. Instead, we evaluate the performance of selected *classes* of trading rules by averaging returns across multiple parameterizations.

2. In fact, we show that the very best strategy from the momentum class underperforms the moving-average class as a whole.

3. Because we employ one-month trading strategies, we should ideally use one-month yields in our dataset. However, we did not have access to this data for all the currencies for the time period of the analysis. In Okunev and White (2002) we showed through bootstrapping tests that using this proxy for the cash rate does not explain the returns earned by the moving-average strategy. In general, very little difference exists between the one-month rate and the three-month rate expressed on a one-month basis.

4. While the *Long–Short Across* strategies could, in theory, be considered zero-cost and the resulting returns infinite, we choose to frame the returns in terms of an unlevered position in currency futures where full margin is given for both long and short positions. The *Long–Short Within* strategies are not zero cost as it is possible to go long or short in all seven non-domestic currencies during any given month.

5. Return-based momentum strategies are preferred as the price momentum strategy would tend to favour currencies with greater price adjustments such as the yen. The largest change in price may not reflect the largest change in percentage terms.

6. Note that if a given base currency has the lowest interest rate among all eight base currencies, it will still go short a currency with a higher interest rate since

the rule compares only the non-domestic interest rates with each other. Conversely, if a given base currency has the highest interest rate, it will still go long a currency with a lower interest rate.

7. The sum of the weights for the long positions will be equal to the weight of the short position.

8. As will be quite evident in section 7.4, we face a difficult space constraint in the presentation of the results. Because of this, we will have to discuss some of the results of the chapter without giving supporting tables. In general, our objective is to test the moving-average rules against the very best specification possible for the momentum rules. The interest rate strategy, by construction, has only one specification.

9. Using all 354 moving-average strategies as a class would lower the returns by five to ten basis points each month for the base currencies considered.

10. An additional benchmark not tested might be a policy of completely hedging currency exposure through the use of futures contracts. In this case, the benchmark expected return would be the interest rate differential between the two countries. The average interest rate differential may be calculated by subtracting the mean return to the MSCI-weighted and Equal-weighted currency benchmarks of Table 7.1 from Table 7.2. Because these differences are typically lower in magnitude than the base currency returns identified in Table 7.1, any test that shows statistical significance relative to the base currency returns would likely have even greater significance using interest rate differentials.

11. We chose to use the information ratio instead of the Sharpe ratio as no consensus exists regarding the appropriate risk-free rate for a zero-cost, zero expected return strategy in international currency markets.

12. We did not include a transactions cost in the analysis. Most studies use a ten basis point round-trip transactions cost for trading in currency futures markets.

13. This test is identical to the standard t-test for statistical significance on excess returns.

Chapter 8

The economic value of leading edge techniques for exchange rate prediction

CHRISTIAN L. DUNIS

8.1 INTRODUCTION

During the past decade, empirical evidence has emerged that pockets of predictability do exist in financial markets. Academics have developed new mathematical and statistical tools to help predict future price movements. These new techniques, which rely heavily on the analysis of nonlinearities, are now used by some major trading institutions and fund managers and there is an ever increasing interest from large corporates too.

Today's financial markets are characterized by a large number of participants, with their different appetites for risk, their different time horizon and their different motivations and reactions to unexpected news. In the circumstances, it would come as a surprise if all these complex interactions were to average out in a linear fashion. Furthermore, the introduction of nonlinearities in the modelling approach should allow one to explain some price moves that seemed random previously without resorting to stochastic mechanisms.

The development in nonlinear modelling spans a wide range of approaches, from formalizing chartist techniques to artificial neural networks (ANNs), from ARCH/GARCH processes to chaotic dynamics.

Combined with extensive data banks and the greater availability of powerful computers, these new techniques now make it possible to devise systems that can help take and manage risk positions in different asset markets.

This chapter investigates the application of ANNs to high frequency forecasting of the following exchange rates: the GBP/DEM, the DEM/FRF, the DEM/ITL, the USD/DEM, the USD/CHF and the DEM/JPY.

For benchmarking purposes, our models' results are compared to those of two naive linear models. They are evaluated not only on the basis of their respective forecasting accuracy, but also on the basis of their economic significance, i.e. the models are also tested by means of a trading strategy.

Such tests are necessitated by the fact that the expected returns from high frequency forecasts can easily be wiped out by the associated transaction costs and the time lags between when the price is recorded, when the model is run and, finally, when the order is executed.

In section 8.2, we briefly describe the principles of ANNs, the data preprocessing they require and the modelling procedure that we have adopted. In section 8.3, we present some of our first results and some further experiments that we conducted.

8.2   BASIC CONCEPTS, DATA PROCESSING AND MODELLING PROCEDURE

The reason why we have chosen the ANN technology for high frequency foreign exchange forecasting is fairly simple: having used linear models and nonlinear parametric filters for several years, we wished to further enlarge our toolbox of forecasting techniques by adding models where no specific functional form was a priori assumed.[1] It can be shown, as in Refenes, Bentz and Burgess (1994) for instance, that ANNs are equivalent to nonlinear nonparametric models. Furthermore, following Cybenko (1989) and Hornik, Stinchcombe and White (1989), it can be demonstrated that specific ANNs, if they are sufficiently large, can approximate any continuous function.[2]

The general specification of the intraday foreign exchange models presented in this chapter therefore uses ANN methodology. The network architecture that we have used in practice is reasonably straightforward. If there are many different types of ANN models, we chose probably the most commonly used, i.e. the backpropagation multi-layer perceptron (MLP) which feeds its inputs along a series of weighted connections and applies a nonlinear transformation in its processing elements (see Figure 8.1).

ANNs are a tool for determining the relative importance of an input (or a combination of inputs) for predicting a given outcome. They are a class of models made up of layers of elementary processing units, called neurons or nodes, which elaborate information by means of a nonlinear transfer function. Most of the computing takes place in these processing units (for more details, see Simpson, 1990). The input signals come from an input vector $A = (a_1, a_2, \ldots, a_n)$ where a_i is the activity level of the ith input. A series of weight vectors $W_j = (w_{1j}, w_{2j}, \ldots, w_{nj})$ is associated with the input vector so that the weight w_{ij} represents the strength of the connection between the input a_i and the processing unit b_j. Each node may additionally have also a bias input θ_j modulated with the weight w_{0j} associated with the inputs. The total

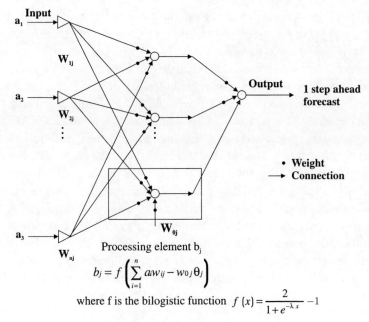

$$b_j = f\left(\sum_{i=1}^{n} a_i w_{ij} - w_{0j}\theta_j\right)$$

where f is the bilogistic function $f(x) = \dfrac{2}{1+e^{-\lambda x}} - 1$

Figure 8.1 *ANN architecture*

input of the node b_j is formally the dot product between the input vector A and the weight vector W_j, minus the weighted input bias. It is then passed through a nonlinear transfer function to produce the output value of the processing unit b_j:

$$b_j = f\left(\sum_{i=1}^{n} a_i w_{ij} - w_{0j}\theta_j\right) = f(X_i)$$

In our case, we used a bilogistic sigmoid:[3]

$$f(X_i) = \frac{2}{1+e^{-\lambda X_i}} - 1$$

At the beginning, the modelling process is initialized with random values for the weights. The output value of the processing unit b_j is then passed on to the single output node of the output layer. The ANN error, i.e. the difference between the ANN forecast and the actual value, is analysed through the root mean squared error. The latter is systematically minimized by adjusting the weights according to the level of its derivative with respect to these weights. The adjustment obviously takes place in the direction that reduces the error. As can be expected, ANNs with two hidden layers are more complicated. In general, they are better suited for discontinuous functions. They tend to have better generalization capabilities, but are also much harder to train. In summary, ANNs depend crucially on the choice of the number of hidden layers, the number of nodes and the type of nonlinear transfer function (in our case, a bisymmetric sigmoid).

A good predictive model should be capable of forecasting with a reasonable degree of accuracy not only in-sample, but also out-of-sample, i.e. it should be able to generalize to previously unseen data. Preventing overfitting of the model is crucial. This is achieved by using, on top of the in- and out-of-sample data sets (respectively the 'training' and the 'test' data sets in ANN jargon), a third data set called the 'validation' set. We show an example of such a partition of the total data set for the DEM/FRF (Figure 8.2). Periodically, during the training period, the error of the ANN is measured on the validation set.[4] Thus, overfitting is avoided by training the ANN on the in-sample period until the forecasting error on the validation set goes up significantly. Indeed, the final ANN chosen for the USD/CHF is the one with the lowest error on the validation set (see Figure 8.3). Note also the necessity of having powerful computers as ANN training finished after 15 000 epochs (each ANN model took in the order of 8 hours to train on a SunSparc 20).

Input selection, data scaling and preprocessing are of crucial importance to the successful development of ANN models (Klimasauskas, 1994; Deboeck and Cader, 1994).

Potential inputs were selected using traditional statistical analysis: these included the raw exchange rate series and lags thereof, descriptive statistics and data transformations. Input selection relied mostly on correlation analysis to detect valuable input variables and cross-correlations were used to avoid multicolinearity as this may cause certain inputs to seem less important than they really are. Correlations were calculated for the entire data set and independently for the three subsets to check for their relative stability over time. Inputs showing an unstable correlation (or, even worse, a reversal in the sign of the correlation) with the output were discarded, as the exchange rate series was then clearly non-stationary with respect to them.

Data scaling is necessary as ANN models cannot cope with the entire range of a time series: this data transformation was basically handled such as to allow for new highs and lows in the test data set.

Data preprocessing was conducted with a view to removing underlying trends. Furthermore, the relevant lag structure of potential inputs was analysed using traditional statistical analysis, mostly the partial autocorrelation function (PACF) and the Akaike information criterion (AIC). We looked to determine the maximum lag for which the PACF coefficient was statistically significant and the lag giving the minimum AIC. Although these

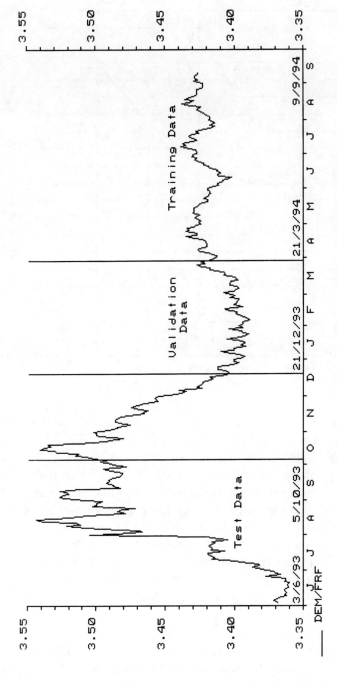

Figure 8.2 *DEM/FRF – training, validation and test data*

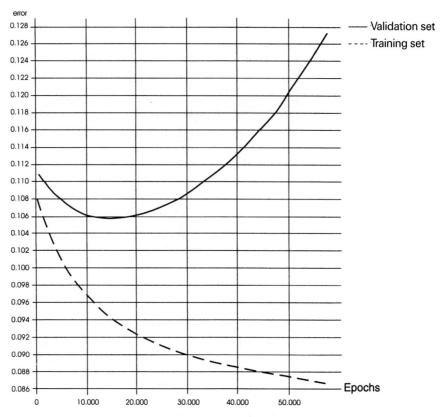

Figure 8.3   *USD/CHF error*

are, in reality, linear techniques, they were deemed to provide a useful tool for the determination of the input lag structure.

As the ANN models output was the forecast price one hour ahead, forecasting accuracy was analysed via the root mean squared error, the mean absolute error, the largest absolute error and the percentage of correct directional forecasts of the network. Still, as forecasting accuracy does not necessarily demonstrate economic significance, we devised a simple trading strategy that we superimposed on the ANN models forecast (see Nabney et al., 1996). To this effect, we decided to band the price predictions into five classes (see Figure 8.4): 'large up', 'small up', 'no change', 'small down' and 'large down'. The 'change threshold' defining the boundary between small and large movements was determined according to the bid-ask spread of each market. The resulting trading model is documented in the lower part of the figure where the boxes denote the 'current position' and the arrows show the transitions carried out when the model makes the prediction given by the attached label.

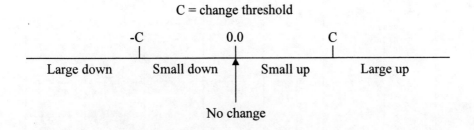

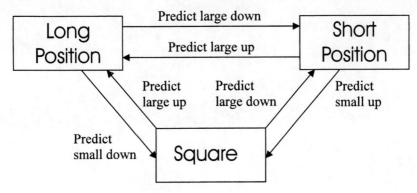

Figure 8.4 *The neuro trade model*

8.3 EMPIRICAL RESULTS AND FURTHER DEVELOPMENTS

The results of ANN models trained from various days in March to 9 September, 1994, and tested over the period 3 June to 5 October, 1993, are shown for the following six exchange rates: the GBP/DEM, the DEM/FRF, the DEM/ITL, the USD/DEM, the USD/CHF and the DEM/JPY (see Table 8.1). Note the shifting of the training, evaluation and test data sets in order to minimize the impact of structural change in the marketplace.

The main performance statistics reported for our ANN-based trading models are the percentage annualized cumulative Gain (ACG) and the Sharpe ratio (SR), a measure of profitability weighted by the volatility of the series of gains and losses commonly used by fund managers. We also report the number of days for the training, the validation and the test period, the number of predictions during each period, the average holding period of each position, the percentage of correct directional forecasts by the models, the percentage of winning trades and the gain-to-loss ratio (i.e. the ratio of the average gain weighted by the percentage of winning trades over the average loss weighted by the percentage of losing trades).

Although satisfactory at first sight, these results show that the same ANN model can see its forecasting accuracy improve at the same time as the trading

Table 8.1 *Neural network trading models – summary results*

	Period start	Period end	Number of days	Number of predictions	Number of positions	Mean hours in position	% of correct direction	% Gain positions	ACG	Sharpe ratio (SR)	Gain/loss ratio
GBP/DEM											
Training	07 03 94:2115	09 09 94:2115	129	1032	38	5.97	53.83	86.84	17.28	2.76	9.15
Validation	07 12 93:2115	07 03 94:2015	64	512	12	16.42	51.67	83.30	8.90	1.75	4.47
Test	03 06 93:1115	27 09 93:2115	81	654	31	5.16	52.37	70.97	15.61	2.16	3.33
DEM/FRF											
Training	21 03 94:1115	09 09 94:2115	119	958	7	5.57	50.89	85.71	0.93	0.60	18.94
Validation	21 12 93:1115	21 03 94:1015	64	512	8	5.50	54.79	100.00	3.93	2.23	0.00
Test	03 06 93:1115	05 10 93:1815	87	702	31	11.16	53.35	80.65	27.66	4.44	14.33
DEM/ITL											
Training	22 12 93:1615	09 09 94:1615	182	1457	40	3.35	59.55	80.00	13.30	1.84	10.46
Validation	07 10 93:1515	22 12 93:1515	54	433	13	4.15	55.09	69.23	10.97	1.22	2.49
Test	08 06 93:0915	07 10 93:1415	86	694	11	34.18	49.21	81.82	18.19	2.43	191.17
USD/DEM											
Training	21 03 94:1615	09 09 94:2115	120	960	47	6.91	56.93	80.85	48.05	5.84	14.56
Validation	21 12 93:0715	21 03 94:0615	64	512	17	16.82	53.03	88.24	31.03	4.29	25.71
Test	03 06 93:1115	05 10 93:1615	87	702	42	6.64	53.21	88.10	44.07	4.37	5.98
USD/CHF											
Training	21 03 94:1115	09 09 94:2115	119	958	47	6.55	55.80	74.47	34.46	3.26	7.96
Validation	21 12 93:1115	21 03 94:1015	64	512	25	7.76	54.60	72.00	33.25	3.76	6.78
Test	03 06 93:1115	05 10 93:1815	87	702	24	14.79	54.92	87.50	23.04	2.16	4.61
DEM/JPY											
Training	21 03 94:1215	09 09 94:2115	119	957	34	5.91	54.29	82.35	32.15	3.82	26.88
Validation	12 12 93:1215	21 03 94:1115	64	512	27	4.81	54.60	88.89	48.46	4.68	28.27
Test	03 06 93:1115	05 10 93:1915	87	702	47	6.83	52.35	85.11	95.08	6.64	16.02

Table 8.2   *Naive forecasting models – training set results*

	Model #1 % correct direction	Model #1 ACG (%)	Model #2 % correct direction	Model #2 ACG (%)
USD/CHF	49.16	−43.81	46.76	−97.53
DEM/FRF	61.67	−12.15	41.32	−2.79

Model #1 generates a forecast $P_{t+1} = 2P_t - P_{t-1}$.
Model #2 generates a forecast $P_{t+1} = P_{t-1}$.

performance deteriorates. This is, for example, the case of the USD/CHF model when one compares the validation period with the training period: the percentage of correct direction of the ANN predictions increases from 54.6 per cent to 55.8 per cent, but, at the same time, the Sharpe ratio drops from 3.76 to 3.26.

For benchmarking purposes, we compared the performance of our trading models to that of two naive linear models and we show these results for both the USD/CHF and the DEM/FRF (see Table 8.2).

The first naive model assumes that the price one step ahead is equal to twice the current price minus the price one step back, i.e. $P_{t+1} = 2P_t - P_{t-1}$. The second naive model simply assumes that the price one step ahead equals the price one step back, i.e. $P_{t+1} = P_{t-1}$. As can be seen, the results of these models are very negative. Note that using an AR(1) forecast where the parameter would equal one, so that $P_{t+1} = P_t$, was not possible, as, from the point of view of a trading model, predicting the price one step ahead equal to the current price would result in no position being taken at all. On the whole, improvements to the forecasting accuracy of our ANN models need to be made. For example, in the case of the USD/CHF, the errors on the training data set are approximately symmetrically distributed about a near zero mean, whereas the errors on the test data set are clearly biased with a non-zero mean (see Figure 8.5). Moreover, it seems that the USD/CHF prediction network may be overtrained as its trading performance consistently deteriorates over time in the test set (see Figure 8.6).

This certainly implies, as advocated by Klimasauskas (1994), integrating financial criteria rather than statistical ones in the very selection process of the 'best' network model. True, our ANN trading models are set up to minimize the prediction error, i.e. forecast minus actual, when in reality we wish to maximize trading profits for a given level of risk. These two objectives are not absolutely identical even though intuitively it seems reasonable to assume that a lower prediction error should result in higher profitability. However, backpropagation can only minimize a differentiable function, such as squared

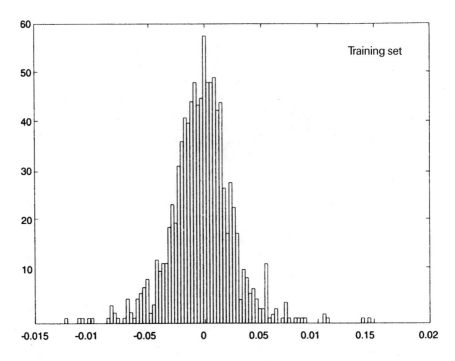

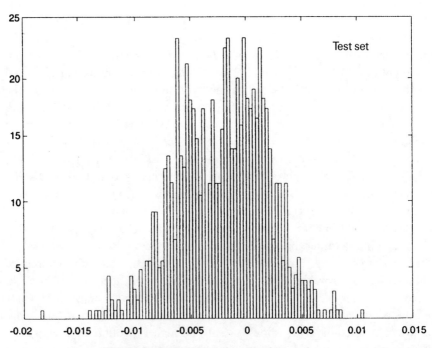

Figure 8.5   *USD/CHF model – distribution of errors*

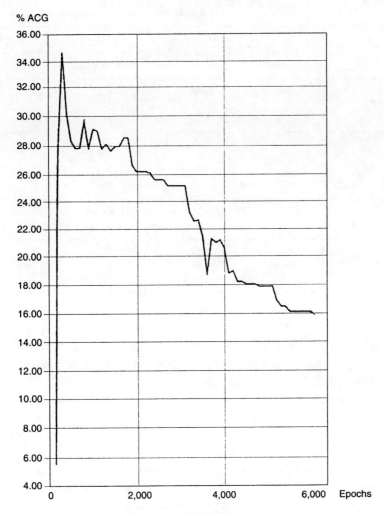

Figure 8.6 *USD/CHF – test set*

error; it cannot minimize a function based on loss or, conversely, it cannot maximize a function based on profitability.[5]

Within the framework of MLP-based ANN models, a potential improvement could be the introduction of a direct connection between the inputs and the output: this implies the existence of some linear relationship between the explanatory variables and the output. We show the results of some experiments we conducted in this respect for the USD/CHF, the USD/DEM and the GBP/DEM (see Table 8.3). The evidence is mixed: if direct connections definitely improve the forecasting accuracy, albeit marginally, and the trading

Table 8.3   *Neural networks with direct connections – training set results*

	ACG (no direct connections)	ACG (direct connections)	% correct dir. (no direct connections)	% correct dir. (direct connections)
USD/CHF	26.54	22.80	53.38	54.72
USD/DEM	31.84	35.69	56.45	55.87
GBP/DEM	5.50	11.78	53.60	53.95

Table 8.4   *Neural networks with intercept correction – training set results*

	ACG (no correction)	ACG (correction on)	% correct dir. (no correction)	% correct dir. (correction on)
USD/CHF	26.54	15.27	53.38	55.77
USD/DEM	31.84	19.55	56.45	58.26
GBP/DEM	5.50	1.31	53.60	55.28

performance in the case of the GBP/DEM, the improvement lies either with the trading model for the USD/DEM or with the forecasting model in the case of the USD/CHF.

We experimented with modifications to our basic ANN architecture. Initial results from using recurrent networks (i.e. dynamic ANNs with a feedback block in the hidden layer) were disappointing but in line with findings reported elsewhere (see Barucci and Landi, 1993). Along the same lines, we experimented with the introduction of an intercept correction (i.e. in our case, the average of the price prediction error over the last five hours), an idea which has since been used by Burgess and Refenes (1996). Here again, the results of the trading models proved disappointing, even if the forecasting accuracy of the original ANNs was notably improved (see Table 8.4).

Finally, we also varied the number of nodes of the ANN forecasting models and the change threshold of the trading model. As can be seen with the case of the USD/CHF, the best level of the Sharpe ratio is reached for a combination of 15 hidden nodes and a 0.001 threshold during the training set (with 20 hidden nodes and a 0.003 threshold a close competitor), but a combination of 25 hidden nodes and a 0.001 threshold during the validation set (see Table 8.5).

In general, more parsimonious models seemed to produce better results for a given threshold level (e.g. the validation set results for the USD/CHF with threshold levels of 0.003, 0.004 and 0.005), but there were clear exceptions

Table 8.5 *USD/CHF model sensitivity to threshold and number of nodes*

USD/CHF validation set Sharpe ratio

| Hidden nodes | Change threshold | | | | |
	0.001	0.002	0.003	0.004	0.005
10	3.304	2.993	2.103	1.742	1.871
15	2.216	2.913	2.033	1.525	1.742
20	3.489	2.600	1.848	1.541	1.670
25	3.584	3.049	1.848	1.541	1.670
30	3.480	2.622	1.957	1.582	1.711

USD/CHF training set Sharpe ratio

| Hidden nodes | Change threshold | | | | |
	0.001	0.002	0.003	0.004	0.005
10	2.277	2.529	2.643	2.621	2.445
15	3.105	2.778	2.920	2.694	2.602
20	2.793	2.780	3.102	2.782	2.734
25	2.628	2.612	2.933	2.584	2.537
30	2.265	2.315	2.658	2.461	2.437

also (with the 0.001 and, to a lesser extent, the 0.002 thresholds for the same data set). Adding a second hidden layer did not improve our trading models performance either, a result similar to that reported by Tan (1995) for daily USD/DEM data.

8.4 CONCLUSIONS

In conclusion, the results we have obtained using ANN technology for high frequency foreign exchange modelling are interesting, but much improvement is still needed.

Perhaps on-line learning will help resolve the key problem of non-stationarity of the data: this is certainly an appealing approach, but a practical validation scheme will need to be developed to make it operational, as in this case no out-of-sample data set is really available.

As we have seen, integrating financial and not only statistical criteria into the modelling procedure is certainly a promising avenue for future research. Clearly, forecasting accuracy and trading performance are two different concepts.

In any case, it would seem that ANN modelling is pretty much an n-parameter modelling exercise, some would even argue ANN models are $(n+1)$-parameter models. As such, with the fine tuning of so many parameters so critical to the final outcome, their successful use for financial modelling is probably as much an art as it is a science.

REFERENCES

Barucci, E. and Landi, L. (1993) A neural network model for short-term interest rate forecasting: the 12-month BOT Italian auction rate, *Neural Network World*, **3**, 625–56.

Burgess, A.N. and Refenes, A.N. (1996) The use of error feedback terms in neural network modelling of financial time series. In *Forecasting Financial Markets* (ed. C. Dunis). op. cit.

Cybenko, G. (1989) Approximation by superposition of a sigmoidal function, *Mathematical Control, Signals and Systems*, **2**, 303–14.

Deboeck, G.J. (1994) (ed.) *Trading on the Edge – Neural, Genetic and Fuzzy Systems for Chaotic Financial Markets*, John Wiley & Sons, New York.

Deboeck, G.J. and Cader, M. (1994) Pre- and post-processing of financial data. In *Trading on the Edge* (ed. G.J. Deboeck), pp. 27–44.

Dunis, C. (1996) (ed.) *Forecasting Financial Markets*, John Wiley & Sons, Chichester.

Hornik, K., Stinchcombe, M. and White, H. (1989) Multilayer feedforward networks are universal approximators, *Neural Networks*, **2**, 359–66.

Klimasauskas, C.C. (1993) Applying neural networks. In *Neural Networks in Finance and Investing* (eds R.R. Trippi and E. Turban), Irwin Professional, London.

Klimasauskas, C.C. (1994) Neural network techniques. In *Trading on the Edge* (ed. G.J. Deboeck), pp. 3–26.

Nabney, I., Dunis, C., Dallaway, R., Leong, S. and Redshaw, W. (1996) Leading edge forecasting techniques for exchange rate prediction. In *Forecasting Financial Markets* (ed. C. Dunis).

Refenes, A.N., Bentz, Y. and Burgess, N. (1994) Neural networks in investment management, *Gestion Collective*, Avril, 95–101.

Simpson, P.K. (1990) *Artificial Neural Systems – Foundations, Paradigms, Applications and Implementations*, Pergamon Press, New York.

Tan, P.Y. (1995) Using neural networks to model chaotic properties in currency exchange markets, Working Papers in Financial Economics, Chemical Bank, **3**, 8–15.

Trippi, R.R. and Turban, E. (1993) *Neural Networks in Finance and Investing*, Probus Publishing Company, Chicago.

NOTES

1. Strictly speaking, the use of an ANN model implies assuming a functional form, namely that of the 'transfer function'. However, if it contains enough elements in its hidden layer, it will be able to accurately approximate any given function (Cybenko, 1989; Hornik, Stinchcombe and White, 1989).

2. This very feature also explains why it is so difficult to use ANN models, as one may in fact end up fitting the noise in the data rather than the underlying statistical process.

3. This function is similar to the 'hyperbolic tangent' and, likewise, it varies in the interval $[-1, +1]$. In fact, it can be shown that we have:

$$f(X_j) = \tanh\left(\frac{\lambda X_j}{2}\right)$$

4. It is known that the training process of an ANN model can be sensitive to the relative size of the validation versus the training set, particularly given a small number of data points. This is not our case here. Conforming with standard heuristics, we partition the total data set into three subsets, using roughly 50 per cent of the data for training, 25 per cent for validation and the remaining 25 per cent for testing. Furthermore, the very size of our training set more than satisfies the heuristic rule that one should have at least five examples per connection (Klimasauskas, 1993).

5. Genetic algorithms can in fact maximize a profit function. As they require writing the evaluation function explicitly, one can introduce into them financial criteria such as profit and risk. The genetic algorithm then optimizes the trading model with respect to this function.

Chapter 9

Is more always better? Head-and-shoulders and filter rules in foreign exchange markets

P.H. KEVIN CHANG AND CAROL L. OSLER

9.1 INTRODUCTION

The profitability of technical trading strategies such as filter rules and moving averages has been extensively documented in a number of empirical studies. Excess returns based on technical trading rules are documented in the stock market by Brock, Lakonishok, and LeBaron (1992) and in the foreign exchange market by Logue, Sweeney, and Willett (1978), Dooley and Shafer (1984), Sweeney (1986), LeBaron (1991), Levich and Thomas (1993) and LeBaron (1994).

In practice, however, technical traders often take positions in the market based on more complex trading strategies. Typically, these more complex trading rules are based on visual patterns in the data. Indeed, the names of many of these patterns – 'head-and-shoulders', 'roundings tops and bottoms', 'triangles', 'diamonds', 'wedges', 'flags and pennants', 'scallops and saucers' – refer directly to the corresponding geometrical image in a chart of prices over time.

Despite the importance of these more complex image-based chart patterns, little research has been conducted concerning their profitability. For example, Brock, Lakonishok and LeBaron (1992: 1758) emphasize that although their 'analysis focuses on the simplest trading rules, other more elaborate rules may generate even larger differences between conditional returns'. The lack of empirical testing of these more elaborate rules may stem from the apparent 'subjectivity' involved in identifying such patterns, making them difficult to evaluate in any rigorous objective way. If these visual chart patterns could be systematically identified, they could potentially improve upon the already profitable simpler rules.

This chapter investigates the **incremental** profitability of one such visually based chart pattern: the 'head-and-shoulders' pattern, considered to be one of the best-known and most reliable patterns. Technical analysts claim that this pattern, identified when the second of a series of three peaks is higher than the first and the third, indicates an imminent trend reversal. Relative to rules known to be profitable, such as filter rules, we wish to answer a number of questions regarding the 'head-and-shoulders' pattern: Does a more elaborate rule such as head-and-shoulders generate a greater profit than filter rules? What overlap might exist between head-and-shoulders and the simpler filter rules? Can head-and-shoulders be used in conjunction with filter rules to increase returns still further?

To test whether the head-and-shoulders rule can enhance filter rules' profitability, we use daily spot rates for six currencies versus the dollar: the yen, the mark, the Canadian dollar, the Swiss franc, the French franc and the UK pound. Our data cover most of the floating rate period (19 March, 1973, to 13 June, 1994), a 21-year span that provided over 5500 daily observations. Currency markets seem especially appropriate for testing technical signals, as they are characterized by very high liquidity, low bid-ask spreads, and round-the-clock decentralized trading. Furthermore, because of their size, these markets are relatively immune to insider trading.

To complete this study, we first design an objective algorithm for identifying long and short positions based on filter rules and the head-and-shoulders pattern. This search mechanism is programmable into a computer, and is replicable in real time, permitting simulated trading to take place based on the technical signals we identify. We then evaluate the strategies of both filter rules and head-and-shoulders on a stand-alone basis and whether head-and-shoulders can increase the profitability of filter rules beyond current levels.

9.2 DEFINING FILTER RULES AND HEAD-AND-SHOULDERS PATTERNS

In this section, we first define the two technical trading strategies studied in this chapter – filter rules and head-and-shoulders patterns. Then, we describe specifically how we identify such patterns in the data.

9.2.1 Implementing filter rules

As will become clear from our discussion of each, filter rules are far simpler to implement than the head-and-shoulders rule. The filter rule requires taking a long position whenever the spot rate has risen by x per cent (the filter size) above the previous low and a short position whenever the spot rate has fallen by x per cent from the previous high. According to the filter rule, as soon as a trader enters a long position, he or she begins to keep track of the maximum price attained since entry, updating as necessary. As soon as the price has dropped x per cent from that maximum, the long position is closed and a short position entered. At that point, the trader keeps track of the minimum price attained since entering the short position, and again reverses his/her position as soon as the price has risen x per cent above that minimum.

Basic filter rules always involve either a long or short position in the underlying commodity. Filter rules fall into a category sometimes referred to as 'naive' trading rules, either because they are relatively easy to implement, or because they have no feedback mechanism, i.e. rules for future periods are not updated as a function of the profitability of past periods. Moving-average rules also fall into this category.

9.2.2 Defining the head-and-shoulders pattern

Technical analysis manuals[1] concur in the definition of a head-and-shoulders pattern: a sequence of three peaks with the highest in the middle, as shown in Figure 9.1. The left and right peaks are referred to as 'shoulders', the center peak as the 'head'. The straight line connecting the troughs between the head and each shoulder is referred to as the 'neckline'. The head-and-shoulders pattern is 'confirmed' when the price crosses the neckline after forming the right shoulder, indicating that one should enter a short position.

According to the manuals, after the price crosses the neckline, it sometimes rises back towards the neckline briefly before continuing on its downward trend. Whether or not this temporary 'pull-back' to the neckline occurs,

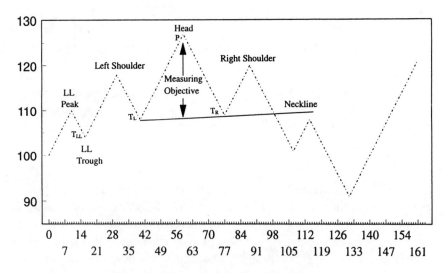

Figure 9.1 *Hypothetical head-and-shoulders pattern*

manuals indicate that the price should ultimately fall to a specific minimum level referred to as a 'price objective' or 'measuring objective'. This objective is reached when the price has fallen by a vertical distance equal to the height of the head, i.e. the vertical distance between the neckline and the middle peak.

Head-and-shoulders can occur both at peaks (where they are 'tops') and at troughs (where they are 'bottoms'). All the price factors that apply to head-and-shoulders tops apply equally, with a sign change, to head-and-shoulders bottoms. Our sources concur that the head-and-shoulders is specifically a reversal pattern: a head-and-shoulders top indicates that an earlier upward trend is about to be followed by a price decline, while a head-and-shoulders bottom indicates that an earlier downward trend is about to be followed by a price rise.

9.2.3 An algorithm to identify head-and-shoulders

To identify head-and-shoulders tops or bottoms, we begin by tracing out a zigzag pattern in the data. A zigzag pattern is essentially a modified version of the original data in which the maxima and minima of the original data are preserved, but in which all variation between these maxima and minima are smoothed. Thus, a zigzag consists of peaks and troughs connected with upward and downward diagonal trend lines. We define a peak as a local maximum at least χ per cent higher than the preceding trough, and a trough as a local minimum at least χ per cent lower than the preceding peak, where χ is referred to as the 'cutoff'. The number of peaks and troughs in a given data sample is inversely related to the value of the cutoff. An increase or a decrease in the cutoff generates a different series of peaks and troughs, which will result in a different set of head-and-shoulders patterns.[2]

To capture most of the head-and-shoulders patterns occurring for these currencies we scan the data ten times, each time with a different value of cutoff. The ten different levels of cutoff are chosen with reference to each currency's volatility.[3] Specifically, we set one standard deviation of daily exchange rate changes as a lower bound for cutoff, to distinguish local peaks and troughs from a single day's upward or downward movement, and consider the following higher multiples of that standard deviation: 1.25, 1.50, 1.75, 2.00, 2.50, 3.00, 3.50, 4.00 and 4.50.[4] Each time we scan the data at a new cutoff, we eliminate duplicate patterns.[5] Using these ten indices typically leads us to take positions in each currency one to two times a year on average, a frequency consistent with anecdotal descriptions in the practitioners' literature.

For each cutoff, the computer searches for a head-and-shoulders top following each peak, and a head-and-shoulders bottom following each trough. To qualify as a head-and-shoulders top, a given set of four consecutive peaks (see Figure 9.1) – the last three of which represent the left shoulder, head and right shoulder – is required to satisfy a number of descriptive criteria identified only qualitatively in technical manuals. Thus, we formalize those criteria as follows.

(1) The height of the head must exceed that of the left and right shoulders.
(2) Since the pattern should **presage a trend reversal**, it must occur following an uptrend. Thus,
     (a) the left shoulder must exceed the previous peak (point P)
     (b) the first trough within the head-and-shoulders (point T_L) must exceed the previous trough (point T_{LL}).
(3) To avoid extreme **vertical asymmetries**, the pattern must be only moderately sloped. The right shoulder must exceed, and the right trough must not exceed, the midpoint between the left shoulder and left trough (T_L). Likewise, the left shoulder must exceed, and the left trough must not exceed, the midpoint between the right shoulder and right trough (T_R).
(4) To avoid extreme **horizontal asymmetries**, the time between the left shoulder and the head must be no greater than 2.5 times the time between the head and the right shoulder; likewise, the time between the head and the right shoulder should be no greater than 2.5 times the time between the left shoulder and the head.
(5) Since the head-and-shoulders pattern in principle indicates an **imminent** trend reversal, the time required for the price to cross the neckline must be no longer than the time interval between right and left shoulders.

These criteria apply with reverse sign for head-and-shoulders bottoms.

A useless technical trading rule could by pure chance prove profitable for a particular price series and time period. This rule might then attract the market's attention as a potentially valuable trading tool. If one evaluated the rule using a similar price series and time period, one would be likely to find profits very similar to those that attracted the market's attention in the first place. However, if one tested the same rule on a completely unrelated time series during a completely unrelated time period, it would be extremely unlikely to find profits. It is important, therefore, to test any trading rule on a time series or for a time period that is not correlated with the data in which the rule was originally found to be profitable.

The rules used by chartists to enter speculative positions were originally determined to be important in pre-1948 equity data for head-and-shoulders (Edwards and Magee, 1966; pp. 50–72) and pre-1961 equity data for filters (Alexander 1961, 1964). Since we test the significance of this set of signals on post-1972 exchange rate data (that is, data from a later time period on a different set of financial prices) our test data are independent from the data that originally suggested the pattern's significance. For this reason, our tests are analogous to 'out of sample' tests of other predictive rules.

9.3 MEASURING PROFITS FROM TECHNICAL SIGNALS

We now evaluate the profits that a market participant would earn if he or she entered and exited the market as prescribed by the technical analysis manuals.

9.3.1 Filter rules

Like the identification algorithm, the computation of profits is far simpler for filter rules than for the head-and-shoulders rule. Under filter rules, the trader is in the market holding either a long or short position at virtually all times. In contrast, under a head-and-shoulders trading rule, which is much stricter, the trader is out of the market much of the time, waiting for a new pattern to emerge before entering.

Under filter rules, the trader begins out of the market, and assumes a long or short position depending on the evolution of prices. In particular, the trader begins with no position at all, and keeps track of both the maximum and a minimum price observed over time. (On day one, the maximum and minimum are both set to that day's price.) As soon as the price is either at least x per cent above the minimum or at least x per cent below the maximum, the trader enters a long or short position respectively. From that point forward, the trader is always holding either a long or short position. As a long position is closed, a short position is opened, and vice versa.

One can measure profits over an extended period of time by computing the daily return from the trader's long or short position, then averaging this daily return over the period. Each day's return is treated as a separate position and expressed as a percentage of the price at entry. Thus, the daily return from day t to day $t + 1$ will be simply $(P_{t+1}/P_t) - 1$, where P_t denotes the price at time t. This approach to measuring profits treats profits earned early in the time period the same way as those earned later. Since the 'daily average return' measure does not incorporate interest, we do not give a relatively larger weight to early gains or losses.

9.3.2 The head-and-shoulders pattern

To compute profits from head-and-shoulders positions, we need to define entry and exit criteria, including two caveats for exiting.

Entry

According to the technical manuals, one enters a position only after the price line has crossed the neckline.[6,7] We use as our entry price the recorded price on the day of the neckline's penetration. In our analysis, the reported daily price was used rather than the price at which the head-and-shoulders pattern actually crossed the neckline.[8] Since peaks and troughs are identified only after they occur, the pattern could conceivably cross the neckline before the price has declined by the cutoff per cent required to identify the right shoulder ex post as a peak. When this occurs, we enter only when the cutoff has been reached, thereby guaranteeing that positions do not benefit from future information.[9]

Exit

Although very clear about when to enter a position, technical analysis manuals are ambiguous about when to exit. We calculate profits by choosing an exit point, as might an actual market participant, when prices appear to have 'conclusively' stopped moving in the predicted direction. Like the technical analysis manuals themselves, the term 'conclusively' is subjective. To be consistent and objective, we determine that a price has conclusively stopped moving when a new peak or trough, as defined earlier, occurs. Thus, for a head-and-shoulders top, investors exit their short positions as soon as a new trough has been identified, i.e. when the price has risen cutoff per cent above that local minimum. Naturally, the holding period depends on the evolution of prices after one enters a position.

There are two important exceptions to this exit rule.

Exception 1: Stop-loss

We impose a 'stop-loss' to limit losses when the theory proves wrong. Specifically, we close our position when the exchange rate moves by stop-loss per cent in the direction opposite to that predicted. In our analysis, we set stop-loss at 1 per cent of the original price at entry. Note that the actual loss could exceed this because we exit at the day's recorded price.

Exception 2: Bounce

As mentioned earlier, prices may exhibit a temporary movement back toward the neckline following a confirmed head-and-shoulders pattern. To exit one's position at this point would, according to the manuals, be premature, because the reversal would not have completed its course and reached its true minimum or maximum. To reflect this aspect of the paradigmatic head-and-shoulders pattern, we allow for a possible 'bounce' or brief interruption in the reversal pattern. Specifically, if a downward trend turns upward before falling by at least 25 per cent of its 'measuring objective', then investors maintain their short positions unchanged until one of the following two conditions is met.

(1) If the price rises to at least 1 per cent above the entry price, triggering the stop-loss discussed earlier.
(2) A second trough (of any size) is reached in the zigzag.

We chose the 25 per cent bounce parameter after discussions with practising technical analysts.[10] These rules are applied with reverse sign for long positions following confirmed head-and-shoulders bottoms.

9.4 EMPIRICAL PROFITABILITY OF THE TECHNICAL TRADING RULES IN FX DATA

9.4.1 Data description

To determine empirical profits, we apply the technical trading algorithms to daily exchange rates on the dollar versus the yen, the mark, the Canadian dollar, the Swiss franc, the French franc and the UK pound from 19 March, 1973, to 13 June, 1994.[11] We use the average of daily bid and ask quotes recorded by the BIS. Data are expressed according to the market convention of foreign currency units per dollar, except for the UK pound and the Canadian dollar, which are expressed in dollars per unit of foreign currency.

9.4.2 Profitability of filter and head-and-shoulders rules[12]

Table 9.1 reports the average daily return on filter rules where the filter has been set to 0.5 per cent, 1 per cent or 2 per cent. The column marked 'Unconditional' reports the average daily return over the full sample. Columns A, B and C indicate returns as a function of the contemporaneous head-and-shoulders trading signal, and will be discussed later. Unconditional daily average returns from filter rules for these six currencies are positive for all six currencies, and significantly above head-and-shoulders returns. For the mark, the yen and the French franc, the three filter rules generate daily returns in the range of 11.3–37.9 basis points, with an average of 24 basis points.

Table 9.2 summarizes the results from applying our head-and-shoulders trading algorithm to the data. For each currency, we take on average one to two positions per year, lasting on average a few weeks, leaving us with open positions (either short or long) about 10 per cent of the time.

For each position, we compute 'per cent profits' as a percentage of the price at entry. For each currency, we sum the per cent profits over all positions in

Table 9.1   *Filter rule returns as function of head-and-shoulders and filter rules' overlap*

Curr.	Filter (%)	Average daily return on filter rules				Number of days		
		Unconditional (%)	A (%)	B (%)	C (%)	A	B	C
DEM	0.5	0.379	0.354	0.481	0.377*	275	160	5097
	1	0.265	0.210	0.494	0.264	334	101	5096
	2	0.146	0.083	0.443	0.149	405	30	5065
JPY	0.5	0.296	0.213	0.366	0.300	331	105	5105
	1	0.193	0.131	0.431	0.196	381	45	5105
	2	0.113	0.096	0.534	0.113	420	16	5030
CAD	0.5	0.079	0.103	0.115	0.076	223	251	5044
	1	0.040	0.061	0.072	0.037	211	263	4961
	2	0.018	0.036	0.049	0.015	200	274	4856
CHF	0.5	0.454	0.278	0.495	0.459	177	104	5255
	1	0.320	0.163	0.507	0.324	209	72	5250
	2	0.180	0.047	0.662	0.185	259	22	5220
FRF	0.5	0.357	0.253	0.410	0.362	335	161	5040
	1	0.253	0.155	0.491	0.257	406	90	5035
	2	0.135	0.061	0.140	0.141*	440	56	5004
GBP	0.5	0.347	0.109	0.400	0.365	404	112	5023
	1	0.237	0.061	0.225	0.251*	404	112	5009
	2	0.125	0.014	0.519	0.135	501	15	4986

A ≡ days on which H&S and filter rules have same non-zero position.
B ≡ days on which H&S and filter rules have opposite non-zero position.
C ≡ days on which H&S has zero position, filter rules positive or negative.

Table 9.2   *Profitability of positions following head-and-shoulders patterns, 1973–1994*

	JPY	DEM	CAD	CHF	FRF	GBP
Average % profit	1.5158	0.7784	−0.0377	0.0959	0.5653	−0.0699
Average daily % profit	0.683	0.469	−0.0018	0.0083	0.0349	−0.0035
Average holding period	22.2	16.6	18.7	11.5	16.2	20.0
Number of positions	20	32	29	27	33	27

*Head-and-shoulders identification and profit-taking algorithms applied to actual exchange rate data, assuming exit takes place when trough (or peak) has been identified following entry.

the sample period, and divide by the number of positions to reach an 'average per cent profit', which is reported in Table 9.1. Average per cent profits are positive for four of our six currencies, and in the range of 0.5–1.5 per cent for the yen, the mark and the French franc for positions held on average 3–4 weeks. Average per cent profits are considerably less for the Swiss franc, and negative for the UK pound and the Canadian dollar.

Average per cent profit is divided by average holding period (in days) per position to determine the 'average daily per cent profit' (also reported in Table 9.2) from the head-and-shoulders trading. Average daily per cent profit figures from head-and-shoulders can be compared with filter rules.

A comparison of average per cent profit obtained by each of the two rules indicates that profitability from filter rules is several times that of the head-and-shoulders rules. Moreover, the filter rules generate these average returns over the entire sample, whereas head-and-shoulders rules are out of the market nearly 90 per cent of the time. Thus, filter rules appear to dominate the head-and-shoulders pattern in terms of consistency (across currencies) of positive profits, the magnitude of positive profits, and the constancy (over time) with which the profits are earned.

9.5 THE INCREMENTAL PROFITABILITY OF THE HEAD-AND-SHOULDERS PATTERN

Although resulting in far lower profits on a stand-alone basis, head-and-shoulders signals could nonetheless prove to be incrementally valuable by reinforcing or contradicting signals from filter rules. At the margin, head-and-shoulders rules would add value if, for example, days in which filter and head-and-shoulders rules coincided proved more profitable than days in which they did not. Since the profitability of filter rules is already well known, we focus on the incremental rather than absolute value of head-and-shoulders rules.

To test the incremental value of head-and-shoulders rules, we compare daily positions from head-and-shoulders and filter rules, classifying them into one of three categories:

(A) head-and-shoulders and filter rules have the same non-zero position
(B) head-and-shoulders and filter rules have the opposite non-zero position
(C) head-and-shoulders has a zero position and the filter rule has a positive or negative position.

We then compare the average daily returns for days of type (A), (B) and (C). If head-and-shoulders rules do provide useful information incrementally, then average daily returns on the filter rule should be ranked:

$$A_{\text{daily return}} > C_{\text{daily return}} > B_{\text{daily return}}$$

An empirical comparison leads to the opposite conclusion: head-and-shoulders technical signals do not add value to filter rules. Table 9.1 lists the filter rules' average daily returns as well as the number of days of type (A) – same sign, (B) – opposite sign and (C) – no head-and-shoulders position, for all six currencies and filters of size 0.5 per cent, 1 per cent and 2 per cent. The average daily return on type (A) days (when head-and-shoulders and filter rules have the same sign) is never higher than on type (B) days (when head-and-shoulders and filter rules have the opposite sign). Furthermore, average daily returns are higher on type (C) days (when there is no head-and-shoulders signal and only the filter rule indicates a non-zero position) than type (B) days in only three out of eighteen cases, indicated by * in Table 9.1. Both these results indicate that the head-and-shoulders rule does not contribute information to an existing filter rule.[13,14]

Nonetheless, the overall profitability of the head-and-shoulders rule can be explained through its positive correlation with filter rules, whose average daily return is positive on days of types (A), (B) and (C). As Table 9.1 indicates, type (A) days consistently outnumber type (B) days by a substantial margin, except for the Canadian dollar, for which the head-and-shoulders rule is in any case not profitable.

Table 9.3 summarizes more rigorous measures of correlation between head-and-shoulders positions and the filter rules. We represent a long position by +1, a short position by −1, and no position by 0. We can, thus, compute a 'position correlation' between head-and-shoulders positions and those based on filter rules. As Table 9.3 indicates, head-and-shoulders positions are positively correlated with those from all three filter rules. We also compute a 'return correlation' using returns from head-and-shoulders positions and those based on filter rules. This would differ significantly from 'position correlation' if head-and-shoulders systematically differed from filter rules when returns were abnormally high or low (although such a phenomenon is not suggested by Table 9.1). A casual comparison of these two conditions does not suggest a systematic difference of this type, echoing the returns rankings reported in Table 9.1.

Since it generates smaller profits, one can think of the head-and-shoulders trading rule as a noisy but, nonetheless, positively correlated version of filter rules, adding no incremental value of its own. Overall, a comparison with filter rules indicates that head-and-shoulders rules are both more difficult to implement and less reliable than either filter rules or moving averages. Moreover, a technical analyst already relying on filter rules would not gain

Table 9.3   *Correlation between head-and-shoulders rules and filter rules*

Position correlation

Filter size	DEM	JPY	CAD	CHF	FRF	GBP
0.5% Filter	0.240	0.264	0.134	0.189	0.143	0.285
1% Filter	0.079	0.143	0.126	0.064	0.225	0.167
2% Filter	0.157	0.225	0.167	0.114	0.264	0.166

Return correlation

Filter size	DEM	JPY	CAD	CHF	FRF	GBP
0.5% Filter	0.057	0.147	0.126	0.016	0.147	0.039
1% Filter	0.092	0.191	0.167	0.041	0.192	0.069
2% Filter	0.199	0.228	0.134	0.127	0.228	0.153

Position correlation: correlation of daily positions of two different trading strategies, with long
positions represented by $+1$, short by -1, and neutral positions by 0.
Return correlation: correlation between daily returns of two different strategies.

incrementally (and may even lose) by combining filter rules with head-and-
shoulders signals. The profitability of head-and-shoulders-based rules can be
understood through the positive correlation of head-and-shoulders-based
positions with those based on filter rules.

9.6   CONCLUSIONS

This chapter assesses the incremental value of the head-and-shoulders
pattern, consistently cited by technical analysts as particularly frequent and
reliable, relative to filter rules, which have already been proven profitable in
earlier studies. Previously, non-linear visual chart patterns such as the head-
and-shoulders, though strongly recommended by technical analysis manuals,
remained largely untested empirically. To evaluate the pattern's incremental
contribution to profitability, we first define a head-and-shoulders pattern,
then describe algorithms to recognize such patterns and to measure profits
derived from following these trading rules in daily foreign exchange data.

On a stand-alone basis, filter rules clearly dominate the head-and-shoulders
pattern as a technical trading signal. Head-and-shoulders rules generate
positive profits for four out of six currencies, but the average daily return is
several times greater using filter rules. Furthermore, filter rules generate these
average profits over the entire sample period. In contrast, head-and-
shoulders-based trading takes a market position only about 10 per cent of
the time for a given currency, remaining completely out of the market

otherwise. In sum, profit from filter rules is more consistent, much higher and sustainable for longer holding periods than profits from head-and-shoulders.

On an incremental basis, we show that the head-and-shoulders trading rules add noise but no value. Days on which filter rules and head-and-shoulders indicate the same long/short position are no more profitable, and sometimes less so, than days on which the two rules indicate opposite positions or days on which head-and-shoulders rules are out of the market. Thus, a trader would do no better, and possibly worse, by following both head-and-shoulders and filter rules instead of filter rules only. However, one can successfully explain head-and-shoulders-based profits in terms of positive correlation with filter rules, which are simpler and more reliable. In sum, our analysis strongly favours relying only on filter rules and ignoring the head-and-shoulders pattern.

The economic justification for profits from any of these technical rules remains unclear. Such profits may indicate the presence of market inefficiencies or, as suggested by LeBaron (1994) and Silber (1994), the presence of non-profit-maximizing agents such as central banks. Much more research is needed before we will understand the underlying economic forces behind profits from any technical trading rules – the simpler algorithms such as filter rules, or more complex, visually based rules such as head-and-shoulders.

REFERENCES

Alexander, S.S. (1961) Price movements in speculative markets: trends or random walks, *Industrial Management Review*, **II**, May, 7–26.

Alexander, S.S. (1964) Price movements in speculative markets: trends or random walks, No. 2, *Industrial Management Review*, Spring, 25–46.

Arnold, C. and Rahfeldt, D. (1986) *Timing the Market: How to Profit in Bull and Bear Markets with Technical Analysis*, Chicago: Probus Publishing.

Brock, W., Lakonishok, J. and LeBaron, B. (1992) Simple technical trading rules and the stochastic properties of stock returns, *Journal of Finance*, **48**, **5**, December, 1731–64.

Chang, P.H.K. and Osler, C.L. (1996) Head and shoulders: just a flaky pattern?, Federal Reserve Bank of New York Working Paper.

Dooley, M.P. and Shafer, J.H. (1984) Analysis of short-run exchange rate behaviour: March 1973 to November 1981. In *Floating Exchange Rates and the State of World Trade and Payments* (eds Bigman and Taya), Ballinger Publishing Company, Cambridge, MA, pp. 43–70.

Edwards, D. and Magee, J. (1966) *Technical Analysis of Stock Trends*, Fifth edition, Boston: John Magee Inc.

Hardy, C. Colburn (1978) *The Investor's Guide to Technical Analysis*, New York: McGraw-Hill.

Kaufman, P. (1978) *Commodity Trading Systems and Methods*, New York: Ronald Press.

LeBaron, B. (1991) Technical Trading Rules and Regime Shifts in Foreign Exchange, Mimeo, University of Wisconsin.

LeBaron, B. (1994) Technical Trading Rule Profitability and Foreign Exchange Intervention, Mimeo, University of Wisconsin.

Levich, R. and Thomas, L. (1993) The significance of technical trading-rule profits in the foreign exchange market: a bootstrap approach, *Journal of International Money and Finance*, **12**, 5, 451–74.

Logue, D., Sweeney, R. and Willett, T. (1978) The speculative behaviour of foreign exchange rates during the current float, *Journal of Business Research*, **6**, May, 159–74.

Murphy, J.J. (1986) *Technical Analysis of the Futures Market: A Comprehensive Guide to Trading Methods and Applications*, Prentice Hall, New York.

Neftci, S. (1991) Naive trading rules in financial markets and Wiener-Kolmogorov prediction theory: a study of 'technical analysis', *Journal of Business*, **64**, 4, 549–71.

Pring, M. (1985) *Technical Analysis Explained: The Successful Investor's Guide to Spotting Investment Trends and Turning Points*, Third Edition, New York, McGraw-Hill.

Silber, William L. (1994) Technical trading: when it works and when it doesn't, *The Journal of Derivatives*, Spring, 39–44.

Sklarew, A. (1980) *Techniques of a Professional Commodity Chart Analyst*, New York, Commodity Research Bureau.

Sweeney, R.J. (1986) Beating the foreign exchange market, *Journal of Finance*, **41**, 1, 163–82.

NOTES

1. Those manuals are Arnold and Rahfeldt (1986), Edwards and Magee (1966), Hardy (1978), Kaufmann (1978), Murphy (1986), Pring (1985) and Sklarew (1980).
2. In our analysis, we exclude duplicates when examining the aggregate of **all** head-and-shoulders positions found for a range of cutoffs.
3. In this sample, standard deviations of daily per cent changes were as follows: DEM 0.697 per cent, JPY 0.615 per cent, CAD 0.274 per cent, CHF 0.794 per cent, GBP 0.657 per cent and FRF 0.698 per cent.
4. Increasing the cutoff beyond 4.50 times the standard deviation of daily exchange rate changes resulted in very few additional positions taken.
5. If a head-and-shoulders pattern using one cutoff suggested entering a position within two days of a previously identified entry date, we do not

include the new position in our analysis. Our results are unaffected by whether we identify such positions with successively higher cutoffs or successively lower cutoffs.

6. Entry always entails going long or short one unit in the priced currency, i.e. the denominator in a conventional quote, with profits measured in terms of the numeraire currency, i.e. the numerator in the quote. Thus, for all currencies but the UK pound, positions involve a long or a short position in one dollar. For the UK pound, positions involve one UK pound. This had no effect, however, on the interpretation of our results, which are always expressed in terms of 'per cent return'.

7. In practice, we find that 25–40 per cent of all head-and-shoulders patterns are confirmed by penetration of the neckline, depending on the currency.

8. Manuals giving detailed instructions on this point stress that the penetration must be 'decisive' and, furthermore, we do not observe prices intraday.

9. Neftci (1991) asserts that acting on the head-and-shoulders pattern necessarily requires future information. This assertion could be correct only in the context of his particular representation of the head-and-shoulders pattern, which does not correspond to representations in the technical analysis manuals we studied. The assertion also relies on the requirement that the right and left trough be very nearly identical, which is not required in the manuals and which we do not require in our algorithm.

10. In practice, we find that for most currencies the bounce possibility was invoked about 15 per cent of the time.

11. Japanese data were sampled as the 'Tokyo market closing middle rate'. Mark data were taken at the official fixing, 1:00 pm Frankfurt time. The UK pound and Swiss franc rates represent 'current market rates at 2:15 pm Swiss time'. French franc rates are 'indicate rates at 2:15 pm'. Canadian dollar rates represent 'London market middle rates at around noon Swiss time'. (Source: BIS Data Bank, Courtesy of the Federal Reserve Bank of New York.)

12. In this chapter, we report returns from technical trading rules without discussing their statistical significance. For a discussion of the statistical significance or riskiness of these rules' profits, see Chang and Osler (1996), which is more technical and more detailed.

13. In fact, for the majority of cases, it appears that head-and-shoulders signals reduce the profitability of the filter rules. We have not computed the statistical significance of this asymmetry. In any case, the evidence does not support the hypothesis that head-and-shoulders rules add value to filter rules.

14. Of course, it is still possible that the head-and-shoulders rule adds value to some other technical rule.

Chapter 10

Informative spillovers in the currency markets: a practical approach through exogenous trading rules

PIERRE LEQUEUX

10.1 INTRODUCTION

The concept of a global currency market, well established in the dealing community, is generally accepted by all schools of thought – be they those that describe themselves as favouring an approach according to fundamentals, technical analysis or quantitative analysis. A market move will trigger a chain of events that will in time affect other markets by creating temporal imbalances in the equilibrium relationship that rules these markets. Described mathematically, there is a strong belief in cross-correlation of an order different from zero at various time lags.

The very few that might contest this concept usually come back to their senses when a financial crisis occurs. Market participants, indeed, become painfully aware of these dependencies between markets in times of extreme volatility. A recent example occurred in September 1992 when financial shockwaves destabilized the ERM. During this well-documented crisis (Sease, 1992) huge losses and profits were made overnight from derivatives and cash trading books. The level of correlation between the assets that were at the basis of their diversification changed drastically, resulting in large unwanted equity swings.

Because of the inter-market relationships, there is a common quest amongst traders to try to find which market will trigger another. The link between currencies and interest rates is a well-known feature of the foreign exchange market. On 30 June, 1996, the currency section of the *Financial Times* reported: 'The dollar fell sharply on the foreign exchanges on Friday, due partly to resurgent expectations of higher German interest rates as euromark futures were sold off. Traders this week will be looking for further clues as to the likely timing and direction of future German and US interest rate changes.' There is indeed a strong belief that the interest rates markets lead the currency market as money flows from one country to another. Johnson (1994: 44–46) reported: 'International long and short term bonds, notes and deposit rates abound with untapped insights into the future values of currencies.'

For a systematic trader, such a line of thinking is quite attractive, since if such cross-correlation does exist it might enable him or her to devise efficient trading strategies. On the one hand, the correlation might generate more accurate buy or sell signals by using information with less noise. On the other hand, if the cross-correlation is of order higher than zero, it will provide a new source of predictive information. Then an exogenous model might prove more effective than an endogenous one.

In section 10.2 of this chapter we look at the statistical properties of interest rates and spot currency prices. We go on looking at some empirical facts on the relationship between spot currency price and interest rate series. In section 10.3, we explain the design of our endogenous and exogenous trading rules and why we chose more particularly some time horizon than other. We discuss issues about transactions cost and performance evaluation. Finally, we look at the results for the endogenous[1] and exogenous[2] trading rules and draw some conclusions.

10.2   THE SERIES AND THEIR STATISTICAL PROPERTIES

10.2.1   The data

The relatively tranquil nature of the forward premiums series fails to mirror the volatile behaviour of spot price currency exchange rates and, as a result, the forward premium is considered a poor forecaster (Levich, 1989). Accordingly, we have chosen instead to use the implied interest rates derived from the three months' interest rates contracts traded on the Liffe futures market. Our opinion is that these instruments are more receptive to the bias induced by the expectation of the markets' participants. We calculated the interest rates differential time series associated with various currency pairs. The logarithmic forward premium (discount) of a currency can be defined as $\mathrm{Ln}[(1+i)/(1+i')]$ (Bilson, 1993) where i is the interest rate of the base currency and i' the interest rate of the quoted currency. Because there is a time lag of six hours between the series of interest rates and spot rates, this will induce some spurious correlation. This is worth bearing in mind as it will most certainly affect unfavourably the signals generated by the trading rules studied here. From the data in Table 10.1, we have built three types of time

Table 10.1   *Characteristics of the daily data*

Instrument	Source	Period	Settlement
Spot GBP-USD	Reuters FXFX page	07/02/91–20/12/95	22:00 GMT
Spot USD-DEM	Reuters FXFX page	07/02/91–20/12/95	22:00 GMT
Spot USD-CHF	Reuters FXFX page	07/02/91–20/12/95	22:00 GMT
Futures 3 months Euro dollar	Liffe (1st available contract)	07/02/91–20/12/95	16:00 GMT
Futures 3 months Euro Sterling	Liffe (1st available contract)	07/02/91–20/12/95	16:05 GMT
Futures 3 months Euro Deutschemark	Liffe (1st available contract)	07/02/91–20/12/95	16:10 GMT
Futures 3 months Euro Swiss franc	Liffe (1st available contract)	07/02/91–20/12/95	16:05 GMT

price series as defined in Equations (10.1), (10.2) and (10.3). Daily spot rates return series:

$$X_t = \mathrm{Ln}(S_t/S_{t-1})$$
$$S_t = \text{spot price of the currency pair on day } t \qquad (10.1)$$

Daily interest rates return series:

I_t = interest rates variation on day t

$$I_t = \mathrm{Ln}\left(\frac{1+(100-F_t)/100}{1+(100-F_{t-1})/100}\right) \qquad (10.2)$$

F_t = price of the interest rate future on day t

Daily interest rates differential return series:

Id_t = interest rates differential variation on day t

$$Id_t = \mathrm{Ln}\left(\frac{1+(100-FB_t)/100}{1+(100-FQ_t)/100}\right) - \mathrm{Ln}\left(\frac{1+(100-FB_{t-1})/100}{1+(100-FQ_{t-1})/100}\right) \qquad (10.3)$$

FB_t = price of the base currency interest rate future on day t

FQ_t = price of the quoted currency interest rate future on day t

The series of cumulated daily returns for the differential of interest and the spot price of the associated currency pair do not seem to exhibit any obvious relationships, except in some periods such as 1991–1992, when both curves head in the same direction (Figures 10.1 to 10.3). The chartist 'eyeball' method would not be very helpful in generating profitable forecast in this case. This is in contradiction with the interest rate 'parity theorem', which suggests that the forward rate is an unbiased predictor of the future spot rate.

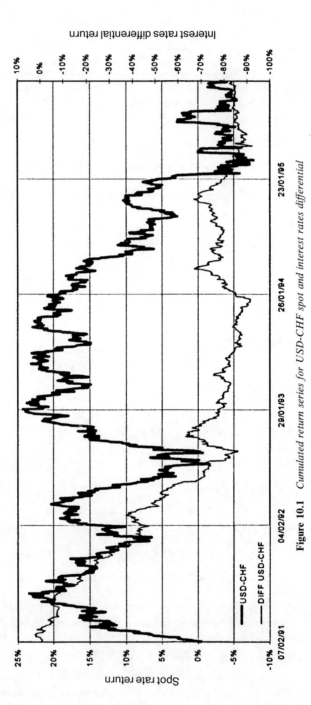

Figure 10.1 Cumulated return series for USD-CHF spot and interest rates differential

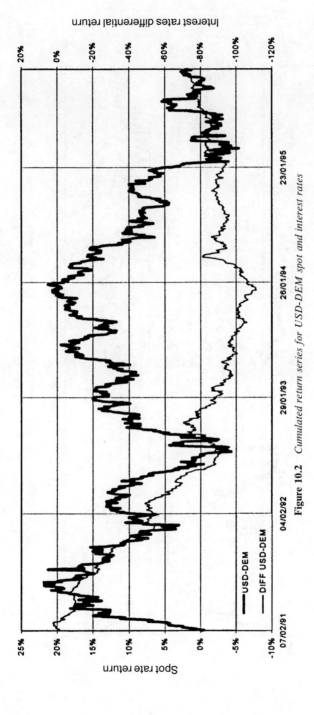

Figure 10.2 *Cumulated return series for USD-DEM spot and interest rates*

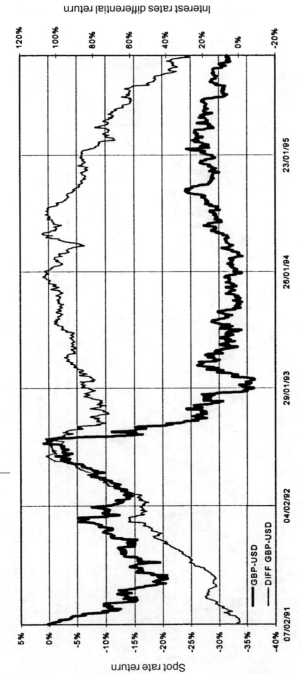

Figure 10.3 *Cumulated return series for GBP-USD spot and interest rates*

10.2.2 Summary statistics

The variety of hypotheses about the distributions of price changes and their generating process is great, but most practitioners and academics agree that daily changes are leptokurtic[3] and that there is substantial deviation from a Gaussian model (Olsen, 1995). The summary statistics of kurtosis and skew for our daily returns series (Tables 10.2 to 10.4) support this view. Various explanations for the distribution instability have been proposed, the most popular among them being the process of reaction to cluster of information through time that are not taken into account by market participants.

The skewness statistics are used to assess the degree of asymmetry of a distribution around its mean. Positive skewness indicates a distribution with an asymmetric tail extending towards more positive values. Negative skewness indicates a distribution with an asymmetric tail extending towards more negative values. In our case, most of the distributions analysed are symmetric,

Table 10.2 *Daily spot rates return series*

	USD-DEM	GBP-USD	USD-CHF
Mean	0.000 02	−0.000 26	−0.000 03
Median	0.000 00	−0.000 12	0.000 00
Standard deviation	0.007 73	0.007 26	0.008 43
Kurtosis	1.96	3.21	1.90
Standardized kurtosis	13.96	22.79	13.52
Skewness	0.04	−0.23	−0.10
Standardized skewness	0.5889	−3.2363	−1.4415
Minimum	−0.032 51	−0.043 90	−0.035 51
Maximum	0.034 90	0.032 99	0.038 37
Count	1212	1212	1212

Table 10.3 *Daily interest rates return series*

	Euro USD	Euro GBP	Euro DEM	Euro CHF
Mean	−0.000 69	−0.000 32	−0.000 10	−0.000 44
Median	0.000 00	0.000 00	0.000 00	0.000 00
Standard deviation	0.008 89	0.011 48	0.006 31	0.010 31
Kurtosis	6.85	159.29	10.17	3.21
Standardized kurtosis	48.70	1131.94	72.27	22.81
Skewness	−0.53	−7.85	−1.16	−0.22
Standardized skewness	−7.52	−111.52	−16.44	−3.16
Minimum	−0.058 71	−0.239 47	−0.055 92	−0.058 59
Maximum	0.045 99	0.051 07	0.024 10	0.048 34
Count	1212	1212	1212	1212

Table 10.4   *Daily interest rates differential return series*

	Diff. USD-DEM	Diff. GBP-USD	Diff. USD-CHF
Mean	−0.000 60	0.000 25	−0.000 69
Median	−0.000 29	0.000 11	−0.000 04
Standard deviation	0.009 91	0.012 53	0.008 91
Kurtosis	4.52	2.85	6.87
Standardized kurtosis	32.10	20.28	48.83
Skewness	0.14	−0.22	−0.52
Standardized skewness	1.95	−3.18	−7.44
Minimum	−0.052 44	−0.073 33	−0.058 81
Maximum	0.058 61	0.063 11	0.046 28
Count	1212	1212	1212

except for the GBP (and to a lesser extent DEM) interest rates series. This might be explained by a stronger and sustained monetary policy of the respective central bank over the period studied than, say, for the Swiss franc.

Kurtosis characterizes the relative peakedness or flatness of a distribution compared to the normal distribution. Positive kurtosis indicates a relatively peaked distribution and negative kurtosis indicates a relatively flat distribution. In our case, not surprisingly, we have high coefficients of kurtosis because our sample exhibits many outliers, a situation we would not expect to find in a normal distribution. This phenomenon is even more pronounced in the interest rates series. This is the reflection of the structural behaviour of money market rates, which usually exhibit small daily returns, but which are subject to large adjustments whenever central banks change the level of their base rates. The behaviour of interest rates has been extensively studied and ample references can be found in the financial literature (Murphy, 1990).

The standardized values for both kurtosis and skew outside the range of ±2 indicate that the observed data depart significantly from a normal distribution. This is the case for all the observed series. The very high value of kurtosis and skew shown for GBP series comes from the 1992 crisis when the UK puzzled the market by withdrawing from the European Rate Mechanism (ERM). This was due to increasing speculative pressures on the GBP, notably from hedge funds such as the one headed by George Soros. The Bank of England reacted by raising its interest rates in a very aggressive way at first and then brought them to previously unseen low levels as it exited the ERM, to the dismay of other European countries. Overall, the rates implied by the futures market went sharply from highs of near 13 per cent to lows of 5 per cent over the period studied (Figure 10.4).

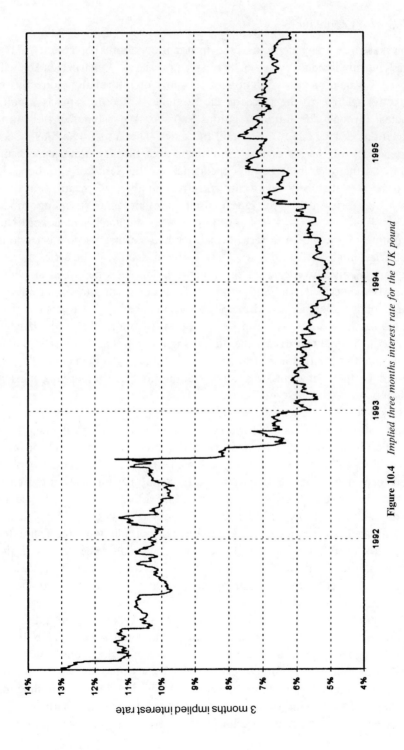

Figure 10.4 *Implied three months interest rate for the UK pound*

10.2.3   Autocorrelations

A market order may contain some information about perception of the underlying fundamental value of the asset price level. A market maker will adjust his valuation as a function of the flow of information (directly or indirectly) relative to the price of the asset he is trading. This is usually reflected through the autocorrelations statistic. We estimated the auto-correlations of lags one to ten for all the series. The autocorrelations reflect the tendency of the series to repeat themselves through time, expressing as they do the magnitude of the dependencies in the series of variations. If we have a statistically significant positive number, it means that our underlying series tends to repeat itself through time (trending mode $+++++-----++++++----$). If the coefficient is negative, we are in the presence of a series which tends to reverse its past behaviour (contrarian mode $+-+-+-+-+-+$) and, finally, if the series do not show any significant coefficient of autocorrelations it is described as white noise, often described as a 'random walk'. These coefficients are important for a directional trader because they reflect the predictability of a given series. The higher the absolute value of the coefficient the more likely it is that the trader will be able to forecast the underlying market. The systematic trader will be able to use either a contrarian or trend-following system depending on the sign of the coefficient of autocorrelations to trade underlying market profitably.

Market efficiency depends upon rational, profit motivated investors (Arnott and Pham, 1993). However, the two largest participants in the foreign exchange markets have no direct profit motive. International corpora-tions will try to hedge their currency risk while the task of the central bank is to dampen fluctuations in its currency rate. Serial dependencies in currency markets have been observed (Kritzman, 1989; Silber, 1994) and linked to central bank activity as well. The central banks tend to try to dampen the volatility in their currency because stability assists trade flows and facilitates the control of inflation level. A central bank might intervene directly in the currency market in times of high volatility, such as the ERM crisis in 1992, or act as a discreet price smoothing agent by manipulating their domestic interest rate levels.

The spot series (Table 10.5) do not seem to exhibit significant auto-correlations in comparison with the price differential series (Table 10.6). This infers a tendency to trend which is more evident in the interest rates time price series than in the foreign exchange market (more smoothing in the interest rates market than in the currency one). This is a significant finding for us, since in the following we will use moving averages to generate directional forecasts on spot currency exchange rates. Moving averages are trend-

Table 10.5 *Autocorrelations for the currencies series*

Lag	USD-DEM	USD-CHF	GBP-USD
1	0.013 26	−0.000 74	−0.009 87
2	−0.030 76	−0.021 15	0.0247
3	−0.020 73	−0.012 48	0.009 03
4	0.045 71	0.016 59	0.038 23
5	−0.000 57	0.002 58	0.034 18
6	−0.080 59*	−0.070 06*	−0.092 78*
7	0.031 49	0.043 42	0.013 95
8	0.0189	0.038 79	0.042 54
9	0.044 38	0.0295	0.003 14
10	−0.019 76	−0.010 19	0.015 18
$\sum$	0.001 33	0.016 26	0.0783

*Significant at the level of 5%.

following trading rules and perform best in markets that exhibit positive serial dependencies.

10.2.4   Inter-market correlations

When looking at two related variables, correlation analysis is frequently the first calculation done. The statistic should be looked at with caution as series can be linearly uncorrelated and nonlinearly dependent when in the presence of non-normal series (DeRosa, 1996). Here we look at both parametric and non-parametric methods. The Pearson product-moment correlation assumes that the data is normally distributed. The results given by such an analysis (Table 10.7) will tend to exaggerate the impact of high variations and it will be particularly sensitive to highly leptokurtic distributions.

When the assumption of a normal distribution is not justifiable, the correlation can be calculated by the non-parametric Kendall method which is then more robust. This measures the relative degree of agreement or disagreement between the two variables. The calculation proceeds by first ordering one variable from smallest to largest, then reordering the second variable according to the ranks of the first and, finally, calculating how well the ranks of the second variable agree with the ranks of the first variable.

The Kendall measure of correlation tends to be smaller because of the lesser impact of the leptokurtic form of the distribution (Table 10.8). This in turn indicates the non-normality of the series studied. Over the whole period the correlation between the interest series and the currency series was minimal. Nevertheless, when one looks at the relationship on the basis of a 'rolling 12 months', the picture is quite different. Indeed the ratio of

Table 10.6 *Autocorrelations for the interest rates series*

Lag	Euro USD	Euro GBP	Euro DEM	Euro CHF	Diff. USD-CHF	Diff. USD-DEM	Diff. GBP-USD
1	0.007 52	0.020 26	−0.026 53	0.057 49*	0.008 65	0.020 78	0.077 85*
2	0.019 37	−0.073 78*	0.044 58	−0.028 66	0.019 53	0.057 35*	0.011 63
3	0.049 63*	0.101 94*	−0.028 69	−0.040 08	0.049 69*	0.022 69	0.018 96
4	−0.028 08	0.022 2	0.015 53	−0.021 74	−0.027 48	0.003 76	−0.013 2
5	0.052 72*	0.009 1	−0.000 19	0.045 48	0.052 3*	0.059 49*	0.073 56*
6	0.007 56	−0.033 99	0.013 81	0.027 45	0.007 1	−0.001 43	0.017 16
7	−0.063 56*	−0.038 56	−0.026 03	−0.017 85	−0.063 31*	−0.031 53	−0.003 89
8	0.041 29	−0.029 13	0.012 22	−0.020 52	0.041 26	0.019 17	−0.019 72
9	0.023 49	−0.018 11	0.023 99	−0.014 36	0.023 53	0.029 28	0.017 54
10	0.045 5	0.040 38	0.054 45*	0.012 53	0.045 67	0.053 28*	0.015 75
$\sum$	0.155 44	0.000 31	0.083 14	−0.000 26	0.156 94	0.232 84	0.195 64

*Significant at the level of 5%.

Table 10.7 *Pearson correlation coefficients between spot and interest rates series*

Interest rates/spot S_t	USD-DEM	GBP-USD	USD-CHF
Dollar I_t	0.138	−0.161	0.143
Non-dollar I_t	−0.113	0.103	0.037
Differential Id_t	0.196	0.135	0.155

Table 10.8 *Kendall rank correlation between spot and interest rates series*

Interest rates/spot S_t	USD-DEM	GBP-USD	USD-CHF
Dollar I_t	0.057	−0.066	0.060
Non-dollar I_t	−0.055	0.081	−0.001
Differential Id_t	0.097	0.047	0.08

correlation has been changing drastically over time shown to be unstable. This might be due to central banks adjusting their monetary policy and being more or less aggressive in their market interventions, depending on the prevailing economic factors.

As illustrated in Figure 10.5, the correlation between the series of daily variations for the interest rates differential and the currency spot prices have been as high as 40 per cent in the past but have steadily decreased over the past few years. Indeed, recently the correlation has been negative. Meanwhile the interest rate differential (Figure 10.6) varied from levels of −8 per cent to +4 per cent. This narrowing in the interest rates differential might confuse the market in terms of which direction to trade the currency exchange rate and they probably use other sources of information in order to decide at what level the exchange rate of the currency they trade should be. The question is: do interest rate differentials affect currency variations and if so how? To try to answer this question we investigate the relationship between the yearly average interest rate differential and yearly currency volatility and correlation between variation in the spot price and the differential of interest rates.

Figure 10.7 clearly shows the relationship between interest rates spread and the level of correlation between the daily variation of interest rates differential and spot currency exchange rates. Respective R^2 of 0.945 for USD-DEM, 0.841 for GBP-USD and 0.856 for USD-CHF were obtained when fitting each series by a simple linear regression.

We plotted the 250 days average differential of interest rates versus the 1-year volatility of the spot return (Figure 10.8). A linear regression was used

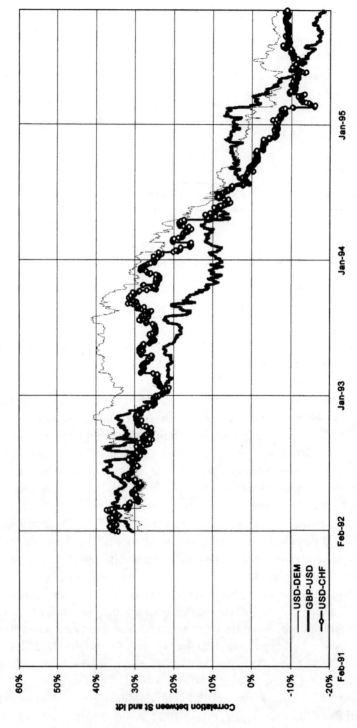

Figure 10.5 *Rolling 12-month correlation between spot currency and corresponding interest rates series*

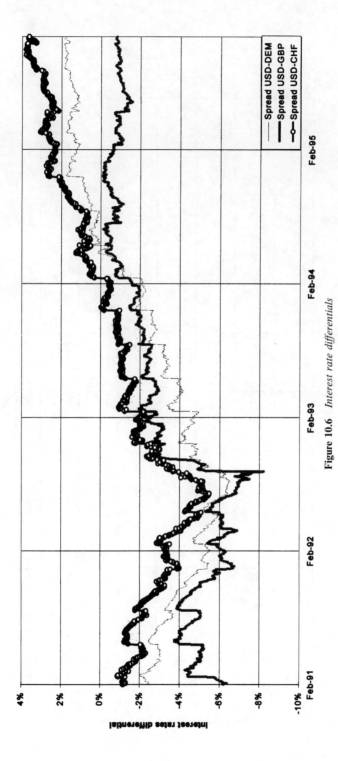

Figure 10.6 Interest rate differentials

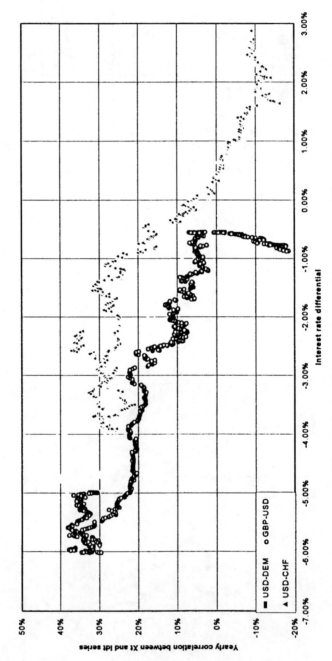

Figure 10.7 *Correlation as a function of the interest rate differential*

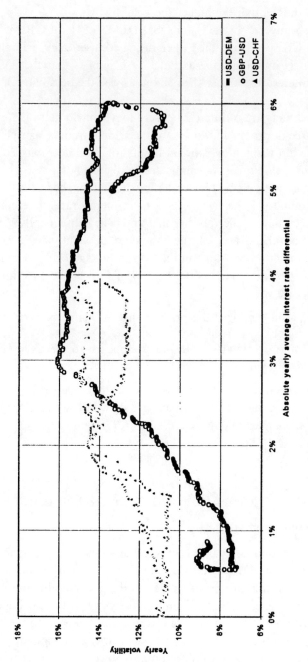

Figure 10.8 *Volatility as a function of the interest rate differential*

to model the scatter of data. The slope of the fit reflects the relationship between the interest rates differential and the volatility of the currency pair. The higher the differential, the higher the volatility.

This time respective R^2 of 0.371 for USD-DEM, 0.541 for GBP-USD and 0.612 for USD-CHF were obtained when fitting each series by a simple linear regression. This is important for a trader as it implies that the higher the differential of interest, the higher the risk but as well the possibility of greater reward.

These stylized facts are of interest because they contribute to the explanation of the source of profits and losses for directional traders, as well as how such traders obtain their informational inputs for their decision process for when to buy or sell. For a systematic trader these finding are even more important because not only do they underline the fact that currency directions are partly determined by the variations in their interest rates differential, but also that the accuracy of the forecast that could be subsequently generated will depend upon the extent of the difference in yield of the currency. Considerable work has been done in the field of linkage between geographically separate but related markets (Olsen, 1995). Two of the most important findings in our case are:

(1) when volatility is high, the price change in major markets tends to become highly correlated
(2) correlation in volatility and prices appears to be asymmetric in causality between the USA and other countries.

The US movement may affect other markets, but not vice versa.

From the previously noted stylized facts, we show how some of the features of the interest rates market could be used to forecast direction of exchange rates in the currency market.

10.3   THE ENDOGENOUS AND EXOGENOUS TRADING RULES

10.3.1   The timing method

Until recently, economists regarded technical analysis as unprofessional and lacking in credibility, despite its widespread use by market practitioners. However, the increasing number of studies on the predictability of time price series suggest that the dismissal of technical analysis as a forecasting method might have been premature. In this context, it is also relevant to mention the huge volume of assets managed in a systematic way by commodity trading advisors. Technical analysis covers a broad category of forecasting rules, amongst which the moving average would seem to be the most widely used by practitioners (Kaufman, 1987; Schwager, 1984) or academics (LeBaron, 1992; Taylor, 1986) alike. Trading rules have the advantage of enabling the trader to take decisions in the financial markets without having to rely on an analysis of the fundamentals (Dunis, 1989), the hypothesis being that all available information and economic market data flows, are already fully taken into account in the rate.

The rule is used in the following way: when the rate of the instrument traded penetrates from below (above) a moving average of a given length, a buy (sell) signal is generated. A formal way to describe this decision rule is given by:

$$
\left.
\begin{aligned}
\text{sell} &\Leftrightarrow P_t < \frac{P_t + P_{t-1} + \cdots + P_{t-m+1}}{m} \\[2ex]
\text{buy} &\Leftrightarrow P_t > \frac{P_t + P_{t-1} + \cdots + P_{t-m+1}}{m}
\end{aligned}
\right\}
\tag{10.4}
$$

where P_t is the price of the asset recorded once on each trading day t, always at the same time of day, and $m[>1]$ is the length (or order) of the moving average. Rules based on mathematical formulas using past prices $\{P_t, \ldots, P_{t-m}, \ldots\}$ are well defined and objective in the sense that their performances can be assessed. The selection of the adequate order for the moving average is generally based on both the technical consideration of the predictive quality and the need to determine price trends over a specific time horizon for commercial use. This is usually done through the optimization of the risk–return ratio. Figure 10.9 provides an illustration of the use of the moving-average method.

The moving-average rule is considered as a trend-following system because of its innate design. In a rising price environment the price will always be higher than the moving average, thus requiring a long position. Similarly, a short position is called for in a falling price environment. In this way, the trader will always follow the trend represented by the mean price. The trading rule, although simple, is not optimal, as the signal will always 'lag' the price structure. The rule will never sell near the high or buy near the low, so the trader using it will always miss the first part of the move and possibly surrender a significant proportion of the unrealised profits before reversing a position from long to short or vice versa. Nevertheless, the existence of central bank price-smoothing action in the short-term interest rates and currencies markets, as described in the statistical analysis in this chapter, suggests that the abnormal profit from trend-following methods will persist over time and, as such, justifies the use of simple trading rules to exploit market inefficiencies (Silber, 1994).

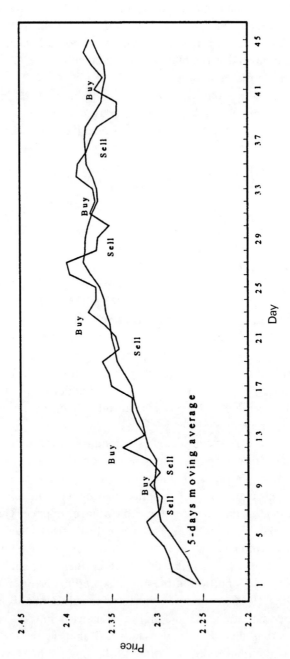

Figure 10.9 *Moving-average trading rule*

To examine the properties of exogenous trading models versus endogenous ones, we use the moving-average rules as previously described. We generate the signals for the endogenous trading model by applying the moving-average trading rule on the past daily spot rates to forecast the spot series (system A). Similarly, the signals for the exogenous trading models will be generated by applying the moving-average trading rule on the interest rates series to forecast the spot series (system B).

In the design of our endogenous trading rules, we use the Equation (10.5) as defined in Acar and Lequeux (1995):

$$F_t = \sum_{j=1}^{m-1}(m-j)X_{t-j+1} \cong F_t = P_t - \sum_{j=0}^{m-1}\frac{P_{t-j}}{m} \tag{10.5}$$

In the description of system A (endogenous) we define the moving average of order m by the function:

$$\left.\begin{array}{l} F_t = \sum_{j=1}^{m-1}(m-j)X_{t-j+1} \\[2mm] X_t = \mathrm{Ln}(S_t/S_{t-1}) \\[2mm] S_t = \text{spot price of the currency pair} \end{array}\right\} \tag{10.6}$$

In the description of system B (exogenous) the exogenous trading rules are similar to the moving-average endogenous trading rule but for the source of the signal:

$$F_t = \sum_{j=1}^{m-1}(m-j)Y_{t-j+1} \tag{10.7}$$

With $Y_t = I_t$ for the exogenous trading rules using only one of the two interest rate series to generate their signal and $Y_t = Id_t$ for the ones using the interest rates differential. I_t and Id_t are defined respectively in Equations (10.2) and (10.3). The return R_t generated by the trading rules at time t is called 'rule return' and its value expressed as in Equation (10.8).

$$\left\{\begin{array}{l} R_t = -X_t \quad \text{if } F_{t-1} < 0 \\ R_t = +X_t \quad \text{if } F_{t-1} > 0 \end{array}\right\} \tag{10.8}$$

where X_t is the price change during a given period $[t-1,t]$.

10.3.2 The time horizon of the trading rules

To chose the various order of the trading rules that we would test, we first need to recognize that not all investors work their strategies over the same time horizons. For example, a day trader can trade anonymously with a

Table 10.9   *Trading rules correlation*

ρ	$S(2)$	$S(3)$	$S(5)$	$S(9)$	$S(17)$	$S(32)$	$S(61)$	$S(117)$
$S(2)$	1	0.705	0.521	0.378	0.272	0.196	0.142	0.102
$S(3)$		1	0.71	0.512	0.366	0.264	0.19	0.137
$S(5)$			1	0.705	0.501	0.361	0.26	0.187
$S(9)$				1	0.699	0.501	0.359	0.258
$S(17)$					1	0.707	0.504	0.361
$S(32)$						1	0.705	0.502
$S(61)$							1	0.704
$S(117)$								1

pension fund; the former trades frequently for short-terms gains, the latter trades infrequently for long-term financial security. Each participates simultaneously and each diversifies the other. To adequately represent all time horizons in our study, we use the statistical properties of technical indicators (Acar and Lequeux, 1996). Assuming that an underlying time series, X_t follows a centred normal law, the returns $R_{1,t}$ and $R_{2,t}$ generated by moving averages of order m_1 and m_2 exhibit linear correlation coefficient ρ_R given by:

$$\rho_R(m_1, m_2) = \frac{2}{\pi} \text{Arcsin} \left(\frac{\sum_{i=0}^{\text{Min}(m_1,m_2)-2} (m_1 - i - 1)(m_2 - i - 1)}{\sqrt{\sum_{i=0}^{m_1-2} (m_1 - i - 1)^2} \sqrt{\sum_{i=0}^{m_2-2} (m_2 - i - 1)^2}} \right) \quad (10.9)$$

For example it is possible to evaluate the level of correlation between the cash flows generated by two moving averages of respective order five and nine by using Equation (10.9), $\rho[S(5), S(9)]$ would be 0.705 independently of the underlying series. Table 10.9 shows the coefficient of correlation between the rule returns triggered by two different moving averages applied to the same underlying market.

The orders of the rules have been chosen such that they are almost equicorrelated (around 0.70) under the normal random walk assumption. As such, we can demonstrate that the simple moving averages of order {2, 3, 5, 9, 17, 32, 61, 117} are representative of holding periods from 2 to 120 days. It is possible to demonstrate that the reduction in risk of such an equally distributed portfolio is very close to that which would be obtained by using quadratic minimization on the whole universe of moving averages of order 2–120. Therefore, it can be said that our elementary basket of trading rules achieves satisfactory diversification when compared to an optimal portfolio of moving averages. In addition, from a practitioner point of view, an equally weighted portfolio of trading rules is much easier to implement than a minimum variance portfolio involving heavily unbalanced and non-tradable weights.

10.3.3   Transaction costs

Because we wanted to look at the performance of the forecaster and not the overall return of a trading strategy, the results expressed in the following tables do not take into account the cost of transactions that would be generated by using such trading rules. This cost can be easily evaluated by using the statistical properties of technical indicators (Acar and Lequeux, 1995). The expected number of round turns generated by a moving-average method of order m supposing that a position is opened at the beginning of the period and that the last position is closed at the end day of the period, is:

$$E(N) = 1 + (T - 2)\left[\frac{1}{2} - \frac{1}{\pi}\arcsin(\rho_F)\right] \tag{10.10}$$

where

$$\rho_F = \sum_{i=0}^{m-2}(m - i - 1)(m - i - 2) \bigg/ \sum_{i=0}^{m-2}(m - i - 1)^2$$

if $m \geq 2$. Then the expected value of a transaction costs is given by:

$$E(TC) = -cE(N) \quad \text{where } c \text{ is the trading cost per round turn} \quad (10.11)$$

Table 10.10 indicates the expected number of round turns in a year of 250 days under the random walk assumption. The last column gives the resulting yearly cost in percentage terms for a cost equal to $c = 0.03$ per cent per round turn.

10.3.4   Performance evaluation

To evaluate the robustness of our results, we use the Student t-statistic which is generally accepted by academics and practitioners to test the hypothesis that the returns generated by technical analysis are zero. Its popularity is due in part to its simplicity as well as its intuitive appeal. It can be defined as:

$$T = \sqrt{N}\frac{\bar{R}}{\sigma_R} \tag{10.12}$$

Table 10.10   *Expected number of round turns and cost under the random walk assumption*

Moving average	$E(N) =$ Expected number of round turns	Expected yearly cost $\%c = 0.03\%$
$S(2)$	125.00	−3.75
$S(3)$	92.52	−2.77
$S(5)$	67.40	−2.02
$S(9)$	48.62	−1.46
$S(17)$	34.92	−1.05
$S(32)$	25.46	−0.76
$S(61)$	18.62	−0.56
$S(117)$	13.68	−0.41

Assumes a year of 250 trading days.

with N number of (daily) observations, $\bar{R}$ the average (daily) rule returns and σ_R the standard deviation of (daily) rule returns.

If T is above 1.645, the returns are said to be significantly positive at the critical threshold of 5 per cent. If T is above 0.841, the returns are said to be significantly positive at the critical threshold of 20 per cent (that is, 5 per cent and 20 per cent probability, respectively, that this conclusion is incorrect).

It is interesting to note that the t-statistic is similar to a ratio widely used by the managed funds industry, the Sharpe ratio – Equation (10.13). It is general practice to report performance in absolute terms as well as in a risk adjusted form (De Rosa, 1996; Murphy, 1990). It has been shown that since investors are, generally speaking, risk averse, a good measure of performance would be the ratio of reward per unit of risk taken (Murphy, 1986). Sharpe defined the difference between the return on a risky asset and the risk-free return on another secure asset as a good measure of the reward and the variance of the return on the asset as being an appropriate measure of risk. The formula of the Sharpe ratio is:

$$\text{Sharpe ratio} = \frac{\bar{R} - R_f}{\sigma_R} \tag{10.13}$$

with $\bar{R}$ the annualized return of the trading rule, R_f, the annualized risk free returns of the asset under management, and σ_R annualized standard deviation of (daily) rule returns.

One of the drawbacks of the Sharpe ratio compared with the t-statistic is that it is not weighted by the number of observations. Hence, it does not properly reflect the impact of time and does not reward long-term performance. The Sharpe ratio will mechanically decrease over time. Neither ratio can distinguish between intermittent and consecutive losses. This is because the measure of risk (standard deviation) that they both use is independent on the order of the data. Various attempts have been made to design a modified measure to overcome this shortcoming, but as to date such proposals have been unable to retain the simplicity of the *t*-statistic and the Sharpe ratio, which has impeded their acceptance and implementation.

10.3.5 Performance of the trading rules

For each currency we look at the gross returns generated by the exogenous trading rule from the point of view of each interest rate, as well as from their differential we discussed previously in the data section (Tables 10.11, 10.13 and 10.15). The period where the absolute differential between the interest rates of the currencies involved is below 2 per cent has been highlighted in grey on the Figures 10.10 to 10.12. We also show the correlation between the endogenous and exogenous trading rules of same order (Tables 10.12, 10.14 and 10.16).

Overall, it would seem that the exogenous trading rules performed better than the endogenous ones over the period studied. We note that there were many more positive and significant *t*-statistics for the exogenous trading rules than for the endogenous ones. The USD interest rate would seem to explain most of the profitability of the endogenous systems for the USD-DEM and USD-GBP parities. Nevertheless, the best results are obtained when using the interest rate differential. The volatility of the cash flows is similar for endogenous and exogenous trading strategies. One of the most interesting features for a system trader is the level of correlation between endogenous and exogenous trading rules, which would provide a high level of expected diversification. The performance outside the 2 per cent interest rates differential bands appears to be superior, but further study should be made to verify this point. Most of the short-term rules would be eliminated because of the high level of transactions and hence costs that they generate.

10.4 CONCLUSIONS

The use of interest rates in the design of exogenous trading rules can represent a simple and efficient tool for systems traders. Not only can it provide a new source of information for forecasting, but also provide an improved level of diversification within a multisystem[4] environment. The study of the relationship between markets affords new areas of research for a technical trader, whether the focus is on the issues of forecasting, diversification, asset allocation or risk management.

Table 10.11 *Results of the trading rules for USD-CHF*

Endogenous rule	S(2)	S(3)	S(5)	S(9)	S(17)	S(32)	S(61)	S(117)	Average
Yearly return	−2.55%	−5.88%	−9.00%	−9.30%	−5.28%	3.23%	1.77%	1.29%	−3.21%
Yearly volatility	13.13%	13.13%	13.12%	13.12%	13.13%	13.13%	13.13%	13.13%	9.08%
T-statistic	−0.41	−0.94	−1.44	−1.48	−0.84	0.52	0.28	0.20	−0.74
Euro USD rule	S(2)	S(3)	S(5)	S(9)	S(17)	S(32)	S(61)	S(117)	Average
Yearly return	4.49%	8.15%	5.97%	9.98%	15.84%	12.89%	6.62%	3.86%	8.47%
Yearly volatility	13.13%	13.12%	13.13%	13.12%	13.09%	13.11%	13.13%	13.13%	9.80%
T-statistic	0.71	1.30	0.95	1.59	2.53	2.06	1.05	0.62	1.81
Euro CHF rule	S(2)	S(3)	S(5)	S(9)	S(17)	S(32)	S(61)	S(117)	Average
Yearly return	4.15%	1.95%	2.68%	10.71%	7.39%	11.28%	16.92%	11.81%	8.36%
Yearly volatility	13.13%	13.13%	13.13%	13.12%	13.12%	13.11%	13.09%	13.11%	10.07%
T-statistic	0.66	0.31	0.43	1.71	1.18	1.80	2.70	1.88	1.74
Diff. rule	S(2)	S(3)	S(5)	S(9)	S(17)	S(32)	S(61)	S(117)	Average
Yearly return	1.96%	8.30%	6.86%	11.74%	15.29%	12.29%	6.56%	2.66%	8.21%
Yearly volatility	13.13%	13.12%	13.13%	13.11%	13.10%	13.11%	13.13%	13.13%	9.70%
T-statistic	0.31	1.32	1.09	1.87	2.44	1.96	1.05	0.42	1.77

Table 10.12 *Correlation of endogenous versus exogenous trading rules, USD-CHF*

Correlation	S(2)	S(3)	S(5)	S(9)	S(17)	S(32)	S(61)	S(117)	Average
Euro USD	0.03	0.06	0.10	0.11	0.10	0.10	0.15	0.11	0.09
Euro CHF	0.05	0.01	0.00	0.03	0.06	0.09	0.14	0.25	0.06
Diff.	0.14	0.10	0.10	0.13	0.11	0.10	0.15	0.12	0.10

Table 10.13 Results of the trading rules for USD-DEM

Endogenous rule	S(2)	S(3)	S(5)	S(9)	S(17)	S(32)	S(61)	S(117)	Average
Yearly return	−4.32%	−7.93%	−5.03%	−5.23%	−3.68%	3.71%	−1.21%	1.27%	−2.80%
Yearly volatility	11.91%	11.90%	11.91%	11.91%	11.91%	11.91%	11.91%	11.91%	8.22%
T-statistic	−0.76	−1.39	−0.88	−0.92	−0.65	0.65	−0.21	0.22	−0.71
Euro USD rule	S(2)	S(3)	S(5)	S(9)	S(17)	S(32)	S(61)	S(117)	Average
Yearly return	4.52%	6.11%	6.19%	9.88%	13.93%	9.94%	5.49%	0.85%	7.12%
Yearly volatility	11.91%	11.90%	11.90%	11.89%	11.88%	11.89%	11.91%	11.91%	9.02%
T-statistic	0.79	1.07	1.09	1.74	2.45	1.75	0.97	0.15	1.65
Euro DEM rule	S(2)	S(3)	S(5)	S(9)	S(17)	S(32)	S(61)	S(117)	Average
Yearly return	1.10%	4.41%	1.46%	5.02%	0.63%	1.92%	−1.63%	0.87%	1.72%
Yearly volatility	11.91%	11.91%	11.91%	11.91%	11.91%	11.91%	11.91%	11.91%	8.28%
T-statistic	0.19	0.77	0.26	0.88	0.11	0.34	−0.29	0.15	0.44
Diff. rule	S(2)	S(3)	S(5)	S(9)	S(17)	S(32)	S(61)	S(117)	Average
Yearly return	4.94%	8.75%	1.50%	8.03%	3.60%	0.53%	2.80%	5.87%	4.50%
Yearly volatility	11.91%	11.90%	11.91%	11.90%	11.91%	11.91%	11.91%	11.90%	8.58%
T-statistic	0.87	1.54	0.26	1.41	0.63	0.09	0.49	1.03	1.10

Table 10.14 Correlation of endogenous versus exogenous trading rules, USD-DEM

Correlation	S(2)	S(3)	S(5)	S(9)	S(17)	S(32)	S(61)	S(117)	Average
Euro USD	0.03	0.03	0.11	0.08	0.16	0.20	0.32	0.32	0.19
Euro DEM	0.10	0.08	0.10	0.13	0.11	0.10	0.05	−0.10	0.08
Diff.	0.16	0.24	0.17	0.11	0.12	0.12	0.20	0.05	0.19

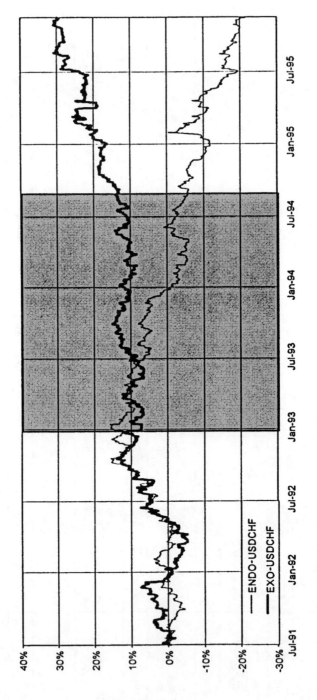

Figure 10.10 *Performance of the basket of moving averages on USD-CHF (exogenous and endogenous)*

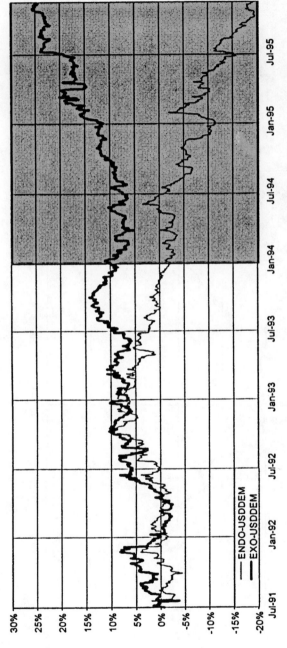

Figure 10.11 *Performance of the basket of moving averages on USD-DEM (exogenous and endogenous)*

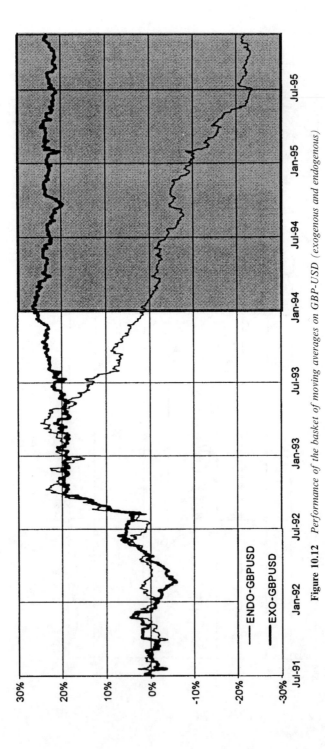

Figure 10.12 *Performance of the basket of moving averages on GBP-USD (exogenous and endogenous)*

Table 10.15 Results of the trading rules for GBP-USD

Endogenous rule	S(2)	S(3)	S(5)	S(9)	S(17)	S(32)	S(61)	S(117)	Average
Yearly return	-0.85%	-2.23%	-3.65%	-4.25%	-4.65%	-2.58%	-2.80%	-5.25%	-3.28%
Yearly volatility	11.18%	11.18%	11.18%	11.18%	11.18%	11.18%	11.18%	11.18%	8.02%
T-statistic	-0.16	-0.42	-0.68	-0.79	-0.87	-0.48	-0.52	-0.98	-0.86
Euro USD rule	S(2)	S(3)	S(5)	S(9)	S(17)	S(32)	S(61)	S(117)	Average
Yearly return	1.64%	1.43%	-2.09%	0.40%	5.67%	1.40%	0.08%	-4.98%	0.44%
Yearly volatility	11.18%	11.18%	11.18%	11.18%	11.17%	11.18%	11.18%	11.18%	8.45%
T-statistic	0.31	0.27	-0.39	0.08	1.06	0.26	0.01	-0.93	0.11
Euro GBP rule	S(2)	S(3)	S(5)	S(9)	S(17)	S(32)	S(61)	S(117)	Average
Yearly return	-4.18%	-5.92%	-4.25%	2.27%	-0.36%	4.88%	0.82%	0.54%	-0.78%
Yearly volatility	11.18%	11.17%	11.18%	11.18%	11.18%	11.18%	11.18%	11.18%	7.93%
T-statistic	-0.78	-1.11	-0.80	0.42	-0.07	0.91	0.15	0.10	-0.20
Diff. rule	S(2)	S(3)	S(5)	S(9)	S(17)	S(32)	S(61)	S(117)	Average
Yearly return	3.35%	7.59%	4.03%	8.24%	6.64%	9.40%	8.72%	6.07%	6.76%
Yearly volatility	11.18%	11.17%	11.18%	11.17%	11.17%	11.16%	11.17%	11.17%	7.70%
T-statistic	0.63	1.42	0.75	1.54	1.24	1.76	1.63	1.14	1.83

Table 10.16 Correlation of endogenous versus exogenous trading rules GBP-USD

Correlation	S(2)	S(3)	S(5)	S(9)	S(17)	S(32)	S(61)	S(117)	Average
Euro USD	0.09	-0.01	0.04	0.08	0.05	0.04	0.05	0.04	-0.02
Euro GBP	0.14	0.21	0.11	0.12	0.26	0.20	0.18	0.27	0.21
Diff.	0.10	0.09	0.13	0.20	0.21	0.19	0.37	0.20	0.21

REFERENCES

Acar, E. and Lequeux, P. (1995) Trading rules profits and the underlying time series properties, First International Conference on High Frequency Data in Finance, Zurich, Switzerland.

Acar, E. and Lequeux, P. (1996) Dynamic strategies: a correlation study. In *Forecasting Financial Markets* (ed. C. Dunis), Wiley, pp. 93–123.

Arnott, R.D. and Pham, T.K. (1993) Tactical currency allocation, *Financial Analysts Journal*, September, 47–52.

Bilson, O. (1993) Value, yield and trend: A composite forecasting approach to foreign exchange trading. In *Strategic Currency Investing* (ed. A. Gitlin), Probus, Chicago, pp. 366–403.

DeRosa, D.F. (1996) *Managing Foreign Exchange Risk*, Irwin, Chicago.

Dunis, C. (1989) Computerized technical systems and exchange rate movements. In *Exchange Rates Forecasting* (eds C. Dunis and M. Feeny), Woodhead-Faulkner, Cambridge, pp. 165–205.

Johnson, T. (1994) Interest rate comparison reveal currency trends, *Futures Magazine*, February, pp. 44–6.

Kaufman, P.J. (1987) *The New Commodity Trading Systems and Methods*, John Wiley & Sons, New York.

Kritzman, M. (1989) Serial dependence in currency returns: investment implications, *Journal of Portfolio Management*, Fall, 96–102.

LeBaron, B. (1992) Persistence of the Dow Jones index on rising volume, Working Paper 9201, University of Wisconsin, Social Science Research.

Levich, R.M. (1989) Forward rates as the optimal future spot rate forecast. In *Exchange Rates Forecasting* (eds C. Dunis and M. Feeny), Woodhead-Faulkner, Cambridge, pp. 75–98.

Murphy, J.A. (1986) Futures fund performance: a test of the effectiveness of technical analysis, *Journal of Futures Markets*, **6**, 2, 175–85.

Murphy, J.E. (1990) *The Random Character of Interest Rates*, McGraw-Hill, London.

Olsen, A. (1995) High Frequency Data in Financial Markets: Issues and Applications, First International Conference on High Frequency Data in Finance, Zurich, Switzerland.

Schwager, J. (1984) *A Complete Guide to the Futures Markets*, John Wiley & Sons, New York.

Sease, D.R. (1992) Pound crisis shakes world currency markets, *Wall Street Journal*, 28 September 1992.

Silber, L.W. (1994) Technical trading: when it works and when it doesn't, *The Journal of Derivatives*, Spring, 39–44.

Taylor, S.J. (1986) *Modelling Financial Time Series*, John Wiley & Sons, Chichester, England.

NOTES

1. Endogenous trading rule: trading rule that uses the price of one market to forecast this same market (e.g. forecasting USD-DEM with USD-DEM).

2. Exogenous trading rule: trading rule that uses the price of one market to forecast another market (e.g. forecasting USD-DEM with USD and DEM interest rates).
3. Leptokurtic: characteristic of a distribution exhibiting an abnormally high number of unexpected events under the assumption of a normal distribution. The well-known bell-shaped curve of the distribution will then have fatter tails and a higher peak due to the number of 'abnormal' events.
4. Multisystem: trading strategy that involves more than one trading rule applied to the same underlying (e.g. trading USD-DEM with a moving average of order twenty and a moving average of order five).

Chapter 11

Stop-loss rules as a monitoring device: theory and evidence from the bond futures market

BERNARD BENSAID AND OLIVIER DE BANDT

11.1 INTRODUCTION

Since Schiller's (1981) seminal paper, the economic profession has faced a long-standing debate about market volatility, opposing two conflicting views on the functioning of financial markets. On the one hand, advocates of the rational expectation hypothesis have stressed the forward-looking properties of financial markets regarding changes in business conditions. On the other hand, models have been developed highlighting various 'anomalies' in financial markets, like the existence of bubbles or 'fad' effects, among others. Actually the opposition between these two views is not as irreducible as it might seem at first glance and large movements of prices can be explained by the optimizing behaviour of rational agents. We argue in the chapter that it is the case, in particular, of stop-loss strategies which can trigger dramatic price changes in equity, exchange rates and/or future markets. Those trading strategies leading investors to liquidate massively portfolios exhibiting heavy losses seem to have played a major role during the 1929 and 1987 crashes (Schiller, 1989), as well as during other periods of speculative attacks in foreign exchange rate markets (see Krugman and Miller, 1993).

Obviously, given the mean-reverting property of financial prices, such strategies cannot be justified by classical arguments. As indicated by Friedman (1953), speculators tend to buy when prices are low and to sell when prices are high, otherwise they lose money. In addition, information theory in the line of Grossman and Stiglitz (1978), Kyle (1985), Grossman (1988) and Genotte and Leland (1991) does not provide satisfactory explanations of stop-loss strategies. According to these studies, in a context of asymmetric information, uninformed traders infer from falling prices that informed traders have received bad news about the future return of the stock. As a consequence, uninformed investors, independently of their past performance, adjust their expectations downward as prices fall.

Stop-loss orders have to be distinguished from other strategies that may also entail selling off a risky asset when its price falls, but in less dramatic proportions: for example, in the case of portfolio insurance, it is used to replicate a put option designed to limit potential losses. Hence, positions are adjusted quasi-continuously. Similarly, with 'drawdown' rules (gradual sell-offs), traders are forced to pull out of risky assets, as the net worth of their assigned portfolio declines.

Regarding the motives of stop-loss strategies, there is no shortage of explanations. First of all, one can mention psychological motives. A stop-loss order allows investors to calm down after heavy losses and to make a fresh start. Carrying over and over a losing position may prevent traders from taking the right decisions. In the line of Kahneman and Tversky (1979) 'prospect theory', traders may also be psychologically more reluctant to realize losses than gains (see also Shefrin and Statman, 1985), so that it is suggested to impose stop-loss orders on them.

In this chapter, we focus on motives related to the internal organization of the investment firm. In such organizations, relationships between employees and the firm are usually plagued with adverse selection and/or moral hazard problems. With adverse selection, the firm, searching for a trader in a pool of traders of unknown quality, uses the whole series of observations on the trader's past performance to revise its beliefs on the trader's actual quality. Following bad performances the firm decides to fire the trader and to liquidate its position. However, this explanation of stop-loss strategies is only relevant for young traders and cannot explain the bulk of stop-loss strategies.

To get a more convincing explanation of stop-loss orders, the chapter suggests a model with moral hazard. The model is based on a conflict of interest between an investment firm and its traders. The investment firm relies on the technical expertise of traders who do not naturally maximize the firm's profits. In this context, we show that the optimal behaviour of the firm is to enforce a stop-loss rule, i.e. to constrain the trader to liquidate the asset when his or her performance is poor. There are many possible causes of divergence between the investment firm and the traders. First of all a trader may derive prestige from trading and will prefer a high to a low level of activity, hence a suboptimal point on the mean-variance frontier. A trader may also be concerned by his or her own value on the job market and try to accumulate human capital at the expenses of the firm, by investing in exotic assets or new products, or by keeping, at the individual level, minimal turnover in some segments of the market that would not be justified at the level of the investment firm. Finally, traders may not be able to resist the temptation to buy and sell shares on the firm's behalf to generate commissions paid to their private account (bribery). As in the principal–agent model, the trader can choose among a set of financial strategies, i.e. among different distribution functions of the return on the asset. If the trader derives more utility from selecting another strategy than the one which is the most preferred by the firm, a variable wage is designed to make the choice of the latter strategy incentive compatible. Under reasonable conditions on the distribution of returns, the wage schedule is monotonic. When the trader has limited liability, we show that the firm may actually increase its profit by committing to liquidate the asset when the return is too low.

Section 11.2 of this chapter develops a theoretical model which gives a rationale for stop-loss rules. Section 11.3 presents the methodology we use in order to find out empirical evidence of stop-loss strategies in the French Treasury bond future market. Section 11.4 gives the results of the tests.

11.2 THE MODEL

In this section, we consider a situation in which a fund provider hires a fund manager in order to enhance his capital returns in financial markets. The fund manager is hired because of his or her skills and expertise in highly leveraged, volatile and sophisticated markets or in exotic markets. Accordingly, his or her performance determines his or her appointments. The fund provider can be any financial institution with market oriented activities in which case, the fund manager is said to be a proprietary trader. Like in the literature of corporate governance, we assume some conflict of interests between the fund provider and the fund manager. The fund manager does not naturally maximize the provider's gains because he can derive prestige and/or bribe from his position by following suboptimal strategies. Because the financial strategies carried out by the trader are dynamic and complex, they are not observable or they are observable at a very high cost. No complete contracts based on such financial strategies can be written. Moral hazard problem will therefore spoil the relationships between the fund provider and the fund manager.

We use the principal–agent framework to model this conflict of interest. In the standard principal–agent model, the principal (the fund provider) observes perfectly the realized gains of the agent (the fund manager) and pays him or her a bonus. Here, we make the principal–agent model more realistic by constraining the bonus to be lower bounded.[1] Moreover, we assume that the principal can enforce some kind of stop-loss rules when the agent's results are strongly deficient. Ex post, this rule is always inefficient, since it denies the trader expertise. The aim of this section is to show that, because of the incentive compatibility conditions, the commitment to follow such a rule can however become optimal under certain conditions.

The assumptions and notations of the model are the following. The realized gains are denoted x and the bonus $w(x)$. The fund provider is risk-neutral and the trader's von Neumann–Morgenstern utility function is $u(\cdot)$. He or she can choose a financial strategy a in a finite set A and his or her preferences over the different financial strategies are represented by a desutility function $c(\cdot)$. Given the bonus scheme w and the strategy a, his or her utility is separable and writes $u(w) - c(a)$.

The usual assumptions are made concerning $u(\cdot)$ and $c(\cdot)$. Function u is increasing and concave and function c is increasing and convex. Despite the trader's expertise, the gains of the fund provider are unknown. These gains depend on the financial strategy carried out; the trader can only control the distribution of the gains. We denote $f(x|a)$ the density function of these gains ($f(x|a) > 0$), and $F(x|a)$ the associated distribution function. These functions reflect the financial expertise of the trader. Then, the standard principal's problem, denoted by $\mathscr{P}$ is to:

$$\text{maximize}_{a \in A, w(\cdot)} \int (x - w(x)) f(x|a)\, dx$$

subject to the incentive compatibility condition:

$$a \in \arg\ \max_{a' \in A} \int u(w(x)) f(x|a')\, dx - c(a')$$

and to the agent's individual rationality condition:

$$\int u(w(x)) f(x|a)\, dx - c(a) \geq \underline{U}$$

Under perfect observability and verifiability of the strategy a (no moral hazard problem), the optimal contract is characterized by full insurance of the trader (the funds provider is risk-neutral while the trader is risk-adverse) i.e. by a fixed wage w^* (no bonus). The fixed wage w^* is defined by:

$$u(w^*) = \underline{U} + c(a^*)$$

and the first best strategy a^* maximizes:

$$\int x f(x|a)\, dx - u^{-1}(\underline{U} + c(a))$$

In general, the first best contract (a^*, w^*) is different from the solution $(a^{**}, w^{**}(x))$ of $\mathscr{P}$ because of the incentive compatibility condition. The usual principal agent model is commonly solved under the Mirlees's conditions (Mirlees and Milgrom, 1975). These conditions are that the density function with the agent's strategy as parameter has a monotone likelihood ratio (MLRC) and, in addition, that the distribution function of gains is convex for each level of gain (CDFC). Formally:

$$\text{if } c(a) > c(a'), \; x \mapsto \frac{f(x|a')}{f(x|a)} \text{ is decreasing in } x \qquad \text{(MLRC)}$$

and,

$$\text{if } 0 \leq \alpha \leq 1, \text{ for all } x, \qquad \text{(CDFC)}$$
$$F(x|\alpha a + (1 - \alpha)a') \leq \alpha F(x|a) + (1 - \alpha)F(x|a')$$

MLRC has the natural interpretation that a less preferred strategy for the trader implies higher gains for the principal. This condition also ensures that the incentive scheme is increasing with the realized gains. CDFC has the more controversial interpretation (see Jewitt, 1988) that the trader's financial expertise exhibits decreasing returns with respect to less preferred strategy.

In this chapter, we depart from the standard principal–agent model as just described. First, we require the incentive scheme w to be lower bounded, i.e.:

$$w(x) \geq \underline{w} \qquad \text{(LL)}$$

This very natural constraint can be interpreted as the trader's limited liability. It could also be some institutional constraint imposed on the incentive scheme, for example a minimal wage requirement.[2]

In addition to the standard principal–agent framework, we also assume that the principal can enforce a more or less stringent liquidation rule. More precisely, the principal can commit to liquidate the portfolio into a risk-free asset according to the observed trader's results, whether results are potential or realized. The enforcement of the rule is assumed to be costly to both the principal and the agent. The cost for the principal can be interpreted as the cost associated with the abrupt liquidation of the strategy. The portfolio is sold in very bad conditions of liquidity and fundamentals. This cost can also be interpreted as the fund provider's opportunity cost of a risk-free portfolio. The cost for the trader can be interpreted as the cost due to the loss of prestige and the bribe option implicit to the trader's activity.[3] Actually, all these costs depend both on the trader's performance and on the intensity of the liquidation rule.

We denote by $s(x) \in [0, 1]$ the liquidation rule chosen by the fund provider. Given the stylized approach of the modelling, there is no loss of generality to assume that the liquidation cost incurred by the fund provider can be simply written $b(x)s(x)$. Similarly, we write $d(x)s(x)$ the liquidation cost incurred by the trader with $b(x), d(x) \geq 0$. Then, the fund provider's utility becomes $x - w - b(x)s(x)$ and the trader's utility writes $u(w) - c(a) - d(x)s(x)$.

Under these two extensions, the principal's problem becomes:

$$\text{maximize}_{a \in A, w(\cdot), s(\cdot)} \; U_P(a, w, s) = \int (x - w(x) - b(x)s(x)) f(x|a) \, dx$$

subject to the incentive compatibility conditions:

$$\text{for all } a' \neq a, \; U_A(a, w, s) = \int (u(w(x)) - d(x)s(x)) f(x|a) \, dx - c(a)$$

$$\geq U_A(a', w, s), \qquad \qquad (\text{IC}_a^{a'})$$

the trader's individual rationality condition:

$$\int (u(w(x)) - d(x)s(x)) f(x|a) \, dx - c(a) \geq \underline{U} \qquad \qquad (\text{IR})$$

and the trader's limited liability condition:

$$w(x) \geq \underline{w} \qquad \qquad (\text{LL})$$

We denote $\hat{\mathcal{P}}(\underline{w})$ this problem and $(\hat{a}, \hat{w}(\cdot), \hat{s}(\cdot))$ a solution.[4] In a model of perfect information, there is no rationale for the fund provider to enforce ex post an inefficient rule. No stop-loss rule ($s = 0$) should be observed. But if there is some imperfect observability of the trader's strategy, the principal can be induced to enforce $s \neq 0$ in order to soften the incentive compatibility condition. This intuition is developed in the following.

We first prove that the optimal liquidation rule is necessarily binary: either $s = 0$ (no liquidation) or $s = 1$ (full liquidation of the portfolio).

Lemma 1

If $(\hat{a}, \hat{w}(\cdot), \hat{s}(\cdot))$ is a solution of program $\hat{\mathcal{P}}(\underline{w})$, then $\hat{s}(x)$ can take only two values: 0 or 1. When $\hat{w}(x) > \underline{w}$, one has $\hat{s}(x) = 0$. Moreover, if $\underline{w} = -\infty$ $(a^{**}, w^{**}(x), 0)$ is a solution of program $\hat{\mathcal{P}}$.

Proof (see Appendix)

This lemma says that without the limited liability condition, committing to take an ex post inefficient decision does not actually enlarge the set of admissible incentive compatible contracts. Conversely, committing to ex post inefficiencies can be valuable only if the limited liability condition holds. Thus, a stop-loss rule can only be optimal when the fund provider faces some kind of limited liability of the fund manager.

We need an additional assumption to insure stop-loss to be triggered only in bad performance states. This assumption is called decreasing inefficiency (DI).

Assumption DI

Functions $d(x)$ and $d(x)/b(x)$ are non-increasing.

The fact that function $d(x)$ is decreasing is quite natural. It says that inefficiency of the stop-loss rule is decreasing with a higher performance of the portfolio. Liquidating a portfolio which generates positive profits is simply realizing gains and should not generate costs for the fund manager. The second part of assumption DI must be interpreted as the fact that the cost of abrupt liquidation of the portfolio decreases more for the manager than for the provider when the performance improves. Note that assumption DI is satisfied when functions b and d are constants.

Result

Under assumptions MLRC, CDFC and DI, a solution $(\hat{a}, \hat{w}(\cdot), \hat{s}(\cdot))$ of program $\hat{\mathcal{P}}$ necessarily satisfies that:

   (1) $\hat{w}(\cdot)$ is non-decreasing with respect to x
   (2) $\hat{s}(\cdot)$ is non-increasing with respect to x.

Proof

See Appendix.

   Result 1 is depicted in Figure 11.1. This result has a straightforward interpretation in terms of stop-loss strategies. It concludes that the fund provider, by committing to ex post inefficiencies,[5] under the form of stop-loss rules, will be able to increase his profit when the limited liability constraint of the fund manager is binding. This rule ensures that stop-loss orders will occur in the lower range of the support of returns. As a consequence, the provider will only use stop-loss orders when the trader's results are poor. Another interpretation of the model is that the fund provider follows a 'stick and carrot' policy. To save on the carrot (the bonus), the fund provider can use sticks of different sizes and shapes. One big stick would be to fire the trader. However, this is very costly for both the trader and the fund provider since the trader's human capital and knowledge are lost and, after the firing, the position cannot remain unchanged. Liquidation of the position in extreme situations, without firing the trader is therefore less costly and still allows him or her to save on the bonus.

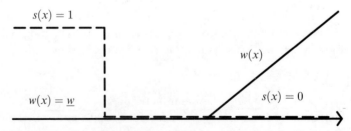

Figure 11.1   *The optimal liquidation rule $s(x)$ and the optimal reward $w(x)$*

11.3 A TEST OF THE EXISTENCE OF STOP-LOSS STRATEGIES

We now provide empirical evidence in favour of the existence of stop-loss strategies, using data on the French Treasury bond futures market, one of the most active contracts in the world. At this point, the focus is on stop-loss strategies at the individual level of investment firms; the effect of stop-loss strategies on the aggregate market equilibrium is reserved for future work. The empirical strategy has to face an identification problem. It is necessary to define a test of the existence of stop-loss strategies, as opposed to other trading strategies that may have similar effects. In our view, a useful distinction is between strategies exclusively determined by prices, and those which also depend on other factors. Hedging, portfolio rebalancing and positive-feedback strategies[6] fall into the first category. This is also the case, as will be stressed later, of the 'neo-classical' model of demand for risky assets. On the contrary, the second category includes stop-loss strategies, where realized losses become a crucial determinant of the demand for assets.

However, it seems difficult to distinguish between the different explanations of stop-loss strategies. In particular, as mentioned above, psychological motives, highlighted by 'prospect theory', imply traders' reluctance to realize losses so that principals are also induced to use stop-loss orders to avoid carrying over losing positions. The following subsections include:

(1) a definition of stop-loss strategies
(2) the description of the dataset used in the analysis, namely the end-of-day positions of all direct participants in the French Treasury bond future market
(3) summary statistics on the accounts available in the dataset
(4) the derivation of the two tests suggested to measure stop-loss orders.

11.3.1 Definition

Loosely speaking, a stop-loss order means the liquidation of the investor's portfolio following heavy losses. A stop-loss rule is associated with a threshold of losses under which stop-loss orders are triggered. In the following, we define formally a stop-loss rule. First, we denote by PO_t^j the position of firm $j = 1, \ldots, J$ at date $t = 1, \ldots, T$. (This is the number of contracts the trader has bought or sold.) ΔP_t is the first difference in the price of the contract, and $R_{\theta t}^j$ is the corresponding profit of firm j between dates $t - \theta$ and t. The latter variable is simply defined as:

$$R_{\theta t}^j = \sum_{k=0}^{\theta-1} PO_{t-k-1}^j \Delta P_{t-k} \tag{11.1}$$

Then, a stop-loss rule is described by the commitment:

$$R^j_{\theta t} \leq \bar{R}^j (< 0) \quad \Rightarrow \quad PO^j_t = 0 \tag{11.2}$$

which can be interpreted as saying that, below a given threshold, bad performances trigger liquidation of the portfolio. It is important to note that the standard neo-classical model of demand for risky assets is unable to account for stop-loss rules. In this model, investors have different horizons and different expectations. They determine their portfolios according to the current price as given by:

$$PO^j_t = \Omega^j E^j_t (P_{t+n} - P_t) \tag{11.3}$$

where Ω^j is the ratio of their absolute risk aversion and the conditional variance of the price. Without revision of expectations, since P_t enters negatively in Equation (11.3), the main implications of the neo-classical model are:

(1) the negative response of the position to an increase in prices, akin to a 'profit-taking' behaviour
(2) the positive response to a decrease in prices, akin to a 'cost-averaging' behaviour.

11.3.2   Data sources

The data used are end-of-day positions of all direct participants (seat owners) in the French Treasury bond future market (future contracts). They are accounting data compiled by MATIF SA, the market's clearinghouse. For each of the 140 seat owners, we have information on their 'customer' account (132 accounts) as well as on their 'own' account (94 accounts, including the account of 9 market makers for the corresponding option contract).[7] Each seat owner may have customers which are indirect participants to the future market. The 'customer' account of a seat owner is an aggregate account of the end-of-day positions of all its customers. It is also important to note that the 'own account' of a direct participant may also be an aggregation of different private accounts, including his or her error account, if any. All accounts are anonymous, only identified by a code number and by the statute of the owner of the seat (bank, broker, 'local', Globex-associated dealer, interbank market dealer). For each account, daily positions (short/long) in number of lots on all contracts are available from 1 May, 1993, to 31 March, 1995 (565 trading days). Actually contracts on four different maturities are available at each point in time (e.g. March, June, September, December), so that PO^j_t is computed as the combined position on the different contracts, namely:

$$PO^j_t = \sum_{m=1}^{4} PO^j_{t,m} \tag{11.4}$$

Similarly, the profit is computed using $P_{t,m}$, the price of the contract of maturity m and Equation (11.1) becomes:

$$R^j_{\theta t} = \sum_{k=0}^{\theta-1} \sum_{m=1}^{4} PO^j_{t-k-1,m} \Delta P_{t-k,m} \tag{11.5}$$

Such a comprehensive view of investors (for all maturities) offers a better measurement of investors' effective exposure to price movements in the bond future market, and takes into account the common strategy of buying the different maturities of the contract if one anticipates non-parallel shifts in the term structure of interest rates (in that case the notional position for each maturity has little meaning). Since positions are given in terms of future contracts, the total net aggregate position is necessarily null: the equalities $\sum_j PO^j_t = 0$ and $\sum_j R^j_{\theta t} = 0$ hold at each date t.[8]

11.3.3 Summary statistics

Several remarks can be made concerning the relative size of the different accounts and their time-series properties.

First, the market is highly concentrated. On the one hand, among non-zero accounts at each date (i.e. for which $PO^j_t \neq 0$ at date t), the top quartile of firms ranked by $|PO^j_t|$ hold about 80 per cent of the daily open interest.[9] On the other hand, when the average position is computed from the first to the last day where a firm is active (i.e. $PO^j_t \neq 0$), 7.2 per cent of the accounts, holding more than 6000 lots in average (0.6 billion dollars), share about 50 per cent of the daily open interest, with a high variability (the minimum is 40 per cent and the maximum is 70 per cent). Concerning the nature of the position, the smallest accounts at each date are slightly more likely to have a short than a long position. When accounts are ranked by $|PO^j_t|$, the accounts below the median are short with a probability of 40–45 per cent. However, according to the Student t-test, the proportion is not significantly different from 50 per cent ($t = 1.49$).

Second, an important feature of the data is that a significant number of accounts are either inactive for most of the time or active during a fraction of the sample period only (this includes the opening of new accounts, but also the closure of accounts, at the beginning/end of the calendar year).[10] As indicated in Table 11.1, 122 out of 226 accounts (53.9 per cent) are in that case. This includes 27 accounts present in the market less than 30 days, as well as 95 accounts which, from the first to the last day of presence have a position different from zero less than 95 per cent of the time. Among the latter 95 accounts, some share a very similar pattern in the sense that they exhibit a zero position most of the time and a few extremely short-lived peaks and

Table 11.1   *Results from Dickey–Fuller unit root tests*

Accounts	$I(1)$	$I(0)$ trend	$I(0)$ +intercept	$I(0)$	Present < 30 days	30 days ≤ active <95% (error accounts)	Total
Customer accounts	19	10	6	30	17	50 (38)	132
Own accounts							
– Market makers	1	1	–	4	1	2 (1)	9
– Non-market makers	11	4	6	12	9	45 (36)	85
Total	31	15	12	46	27	95 (75)	226

troughs. Two explanations of this behaviour are possible. Either they correspond to the positions of firms with a very short horizon (one day or less), but in that case stop-loss strategies cannot be tested; or they are effectively what is known as 'error accounts'. Seventy-five accounts appear under this heading in Table 11.1. Inspection of their graph reveals a systematic behaviour: those operators have a target position equal to zero, but may miss their target and adjust their position back to zero the following day. Therefore, they use the following rule: $PO^j_{t-1} = 0$ with probability p, and $PO^j_{t-1} = \varepsilon_t$ with probability $1 - p$. These accounts are not very well approximated by a white noise process, since the realization $PO^j_t = 0$ should not obtain with such a high frequency. Among them, most of the customer accounts are locals or Globex-associated dealers, whose horizon is extremely short.

This justifies why in the following only the 104 remaining accounts will be investigated. Using Dickey–Fuller unit root tests on individual positions, it turns out that 31 accounts are non-stationary, whereas 73 are $I(0)$ as indicated in Table 11.1.[11]

11.3.4   Tests of stop-loss strategies

The formal definition of a stop-loss rule provided earlier is of little help in uncovering stop-loss strategies when data are observed at an aggregated level. In most cases, it seems difficult to disentangle the different strategies (hedging, arbitrage, speculation) followed by investment firms on their own account. In other cases, data can be only observed with aggregation of different investment firms on the same customer account. For these reasons, we provide tests which can only validate less restrictive definitions of stop-loss rules. Loosely speaking, our intent is to prove that poor past performances are significant determinants of current positions. Two tests are presented. The first one looks for evidence of holding reversion behaviours associated with very negative profits. The second is based on causality tests of low performance indicators in the contract holding equation.

Holding reversion behaviour

The first method measures the effect of large losses on the likelihood of closing down a position. Since investors are allowed to choose between a long or a short position, closing down a position means reverting to the zero position, so that the movement is in opposite direction for long and short positions. Hence, the relevant indicator is $\Delta PO_t^j / PO_{t-1}^j$. However, PO_{t-1}^j may be very close to zero during some periods. In addition, due to heterogeneity of investors, one faces aggregation problems with the indicator $\text{sgn}(PO_{t-1}^j)\Delta PO_t^j$ when data are pooled across time and investors. We find it, therefore, more convenient to concentrate on another statistic, namely:

$$z_t^j = \text{sgn}(PO_{t-1}^j \Delta PO_t^j) \tag{11.6}$$

which can take the values: $-1, 0, 1$. Only the value -1 can be assimilated to a reversion to the zero position. We also define

$$z_t^j = z_t^j \mathbf{1}_{\{|\Delta PO_t^j| > \frac{\sigma^j}{s}\}} \tag{11.7}$$

where σ^j is the standard deviation of ΔPO_t^j, s is a constant that we choose arbitrarily, and $\mathbf{1}_{\{|\Delta PO_t^j| > \frac{\sigma^j}{s}\}}$ is a dummy variable equal to 1 when $|\Delta PO_t^j| > \frac{\sigma^j}{s}$ and 0 otherwise. This indicator focuses on significant changes in positions.

In accordance with our previous remarks, under the neo-classical model $\Pr\{z_t^j < 0\}$ and $\Pr\{z_t^j > 0\}$ only depend on changes in prices. However, given the correlation between changes in prices and realized one-period profits, an additional implication of the neo-classical model is the negative correlation between z_t^j and realized one-period profits. Therefore, according to this model, z_t^j should be positive (respectively negative) more frequently when one-period profits are negative (respectively positive). Conversely, if stop-loss rules are followed by investment firms, $\Pr\{z_t^j < 0\}$ should be higher when profits are negative. Based, on the preceding remark, our test computes the distribution of $\Pr\{z_t^j\}$ conditional on different classes of realized profits, using pooled data. If stop-loss strategies are effectively used, the conditional distribution should give more weight to the event $z_t^j < 0$ for the lowest classes of profits. The firm's investment horizon may well exceed one day, so that this property is expected to remain true when profits over several periods are considered.

To confirm the preceding analysis, we use logistic regressions measuring the effect of profit dummy variables X_t^j on the probability of reversing a position. The dependent variable, z_t^j or $\tilde{z}_t^j$ is still defined as a discrete indicator, taking the value -1, 0 or 1. In the case of a binary response model, we assume that z_t^j takes the value -1 whenever a latent variable z_t^{j*} is such that $z_t^{j*} > r_1$. Otherwise, z_t^j is equal to 1. z_t^{j*} depends linearly on realized profits: $z_t^{j*} = X_t^j b + u_t^j$, where u_t^j is a measurement error on z_t^j. u_t^j is assumed to be identically logistically distributed. Finally:

$$\Pr\{z_t^j = -1|X_t^j\} = \Pr\{u_t^j > r_1 - X_t^j b\} = 1 - F(r_1 - X_t^j b)$$

Causality of poor performance

To test the effect of profits on positions, we now use a non-structural approach. We allow current holdings to be partially determined by past holdings, but we do not take a stand on whether positions should be stationary or not. We, therefore, fit an autoregressive model on positions, adding price changes in the equation, as advocated by the neo-classical theory. We also introduce a profit indicator and test whether current performance, when poor, helps to explain current positions. Our empirical strategy does not restrict the value of the coefficient on PO_{t-1}^j so that we define tests compatible with stationary as well as non-stationary positions.

When PO_t^j is stationary, we run for each firm the regression:

$$PO_t^j = \alpha_0 + \sum_{k=1}^{5} \alpha_k^i PO_{t-k}^j + \beta^i \Delta P_t + \gamma^j PO_{t-1}^j \mathbf{1}_{\{R_{\theta t}^j < c\%\}} + \eta_t^j \qquad (11.8)$$

where $\mathbf{1}_{\{R_{\theta t}^j < c\%\}}$ is a dummy variable equal to 1 if $R_{\theta t}^j$ is lower than the bottom $c\%$ of firm j's realized profits and 0 otherwise. The null hypothesis of no stop-loss is $H_0 : \gamma^j = 0$. The alternative hypothesis of stop-loss is $H_1 : \gamma^j < 0$. Under H_1, the position at t is smaller when realized profits are very negative. In that case, the coefficient on PO_{t-1}^j is reduced by β_1. When the process of PO_t^j contains a unit-root, Equation (11.8) is run in first difference:

$$\Delta PO_t^j = \alpha_0 + \alpha_1^j \Delta PO_{t-1}^j + \beta^j \Delta P_t + \gamma^j PO_{t-1}^j \mathbf{1}_{\{R_{\theta t}^j < c\%\}} + \eta_t^j \qquad (11.9)$$

11.4   EMPIRICAL RESULTS

As justified before, the two types of tests defined in the preceding section are not run on the whole data set, but only on the sample of the accounts active more than 95 per cent of the time (104 accounts). In particular, this sample does not include the error accounts. In this sample, each account will be treated as a trading unit.

11.4.1 Conditional distribution of z_t^j on pooled data

The first test is implemented by computing, for each account, the distribution of profits and losses on the whole sample period. We define classes of profits and measure the probability of getting the different occurrences of z_t^j and $\tilde{z}_t^j$. Stop-loss orders are likely to occur, as shown in section 11.2, for extremely low values of profits. Hence, we condition z_t^j by different classes of realized profits. To avoid drawing conclusions from a very small subsample of conditioned observations for each trading unit, we pool data across all accounts. We compute p_{ki}, the proportion of realizations $k = -1, 0, 1$ of z_t^j in each profit class i.[12] For each trading unit, 7 classes are defined: the 1 per cent lowest profits, the fractions 1–10 per cent, 10–25 per cent, 25–75 per cent, 75–90 per cent, 90–99 per cent and the top 1 per cent profits. For a given trading unit and for each class of profit, the number of realizations of the different occurrences of z_t^j and $\tilde{z}_t^j$ are computed. Then, aggregating those results across all 104 trading units, class by class, one gets the conditional distribution of the proportion of the different occurrences of z_t^j and $\tilde{z}_t^j$ for the whole population.

Note however, that in order to run the test, we remove from the sample all observations corresponding to $PO_t^j = PO_{t-1}^j$ as well as the observations where $PO_{t-1}^j = 0$. The aim of these exclusions is to avoid taking into account hedging positions, in the first case, as well as zero profits, in the second case. As a consequence, z_t^j has two occurrences instead of three and

$$\Pr\{z_t^j > 0\} = 1 - \Pr\{z_t^j < 0\}$$

The results for the conditional distribution of z_t^j are exhibited in Figure 11.2 and Table 11.2 for profits measured over one period. The bottom part of the graph is $\Pr\{z_t^j < 0\}$. The dashed line is the unconditional proportion and the solid line is the conditional distribution. Only the relevant window is displayed. The graph reveals general characteristics of trading as well as evidence in favour of stop-loss strategies.

Concerning the general characteristics of trading, the first remark that can be made is that the unconditional distribution is slightly biased in favour of $z_t^j < 0$ (54 per cent versus 46 per cent). Therefore, positions in our data set exhibit mean-reversion. One possible explanation is that firms active in the Treasury bond future market have to meet daily deposit requirements by the clearinghouse. Most firms have a target position, so that, when the target is missed, the constraint of deposit requirement entails a liquidation of the position, independently of the level of realized profits. On the other hand, due to aggregation problems positions may still be affected by noises and include some components of 'error accounts' – for which the correlation between ΔPO_t^j and PO_{t-1}^j is negative with probability $1 - p$, while $\Delta PO_t^j = PO_t^j = 0$

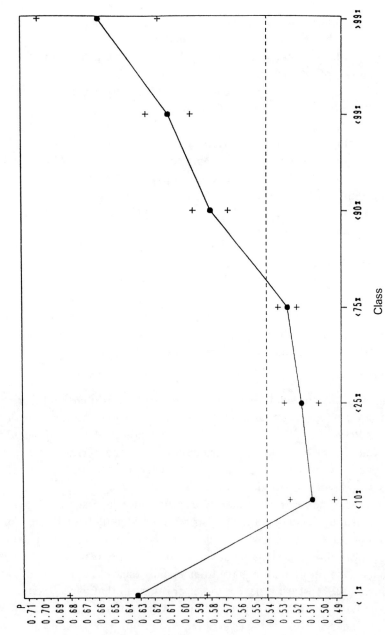

Figure 11.2 *Indicator of selloffs – accounts active more than 95 per cent of the sample period without constant positions conditioned by profits (over 1 day)*

Table 11.2 *Conditional distribution of z_t^j*

$$\Pr\{z_t^j < 0 \mid R_{1t}^j \in c_i\}$$

c_i are classes of one-period realized profits
t_u: Student t of difference of proportion with uncond. proportion
t_c: Student t of difference of proportion with 25–75% class
t_1: Student t of difference of proportion with 1% class
t_{99}: Student t of difference of proportion with 99% class

104 accounts
$T \times J = 43\,176$ observations

c_i	p	σ_p	t_u	t_c	t_1	t_{99}
Unconditional proportion	54.06	0.002	–	–	–	–
$R_t^j < 1\%$	63.24	0.024	3.63	4.18	–	–
$1\% \le R_t^j < 10\%$	50.76	0.008	−4.12	−2.05	−4.70	–
$10\% \le R_t^j < 25\%$	51.52	0.006	−4.09	−1.45	−4.49	–
$25\% \le R_t^j < 75\%$	52.55	0.003	−4.44	–	–	–
$75\% \le R_t^j < 90\%$	58.00	0.006	6.36	7.71	–	−3.44
$90\% \le R_t^j < 99\%$	60.97	0.008	8.63	9.68	–	−2.13
$R_t^j \ge 99\%$	65.92	0.021	5.28	5.88	–	–

with probability p – which induces a bias in the distribution of z_t^j in favour of $z_t^j = 0$ or $z_t^j < 0$. As a consequence, our task is to prove that the global mean reversion behaviour of market participants is more pronounced for bad realizations of profits.

Figures 11.2 to 11.4 show that the conditional distribution of the occurrence $z_t^j < 0$ is consistent with the existence of stop-loss strategies: the proportion of mean reverting changes in position is much higher in the bottom 1 per cent profit class (60.9 per cent) than in the unconditional proportion (54 per cent), or the central 25–75 per cent profit class (52.6 per cent) (the two-standard deviation band is drawn around the point estimates). It is also higher than in the adjacent classes (the Student t-statistic of difference of proportion is highly significant, see Table 11.2).

On the other hand the conditional distribution exhibits some of the basic features of the standard neo-classical model of trading: except for the first (bottom) class, the likelihood of the occurrence $z_t^j < 0$ is increasing with higher classes of realized profits. When profits are very positive, investment firms reduce their position in 66.1 per cent of the cases and realize their profits.

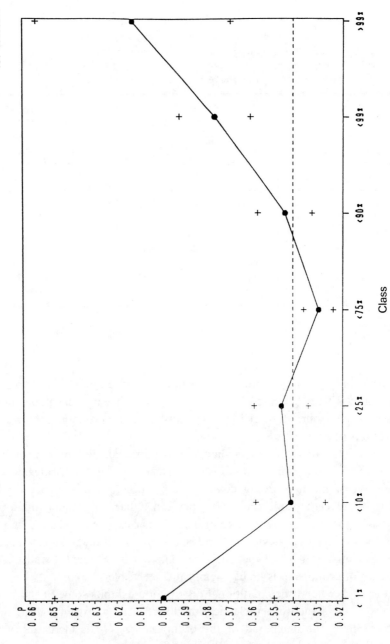

104 accounts

Figure 11.3 *Indicator of selloffs – accounts active more than 95 per cent of the sample period without constant positions conditioned by profits (over 5 days)*

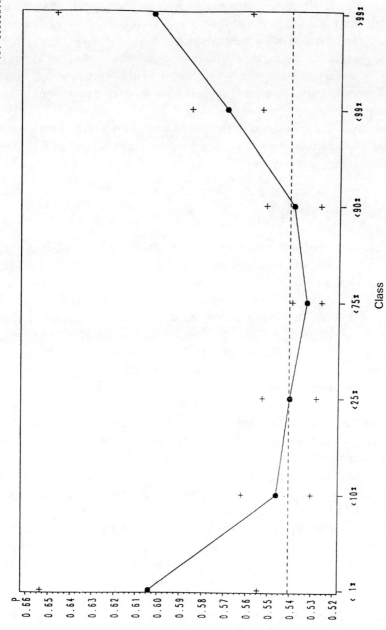

Figure 11.4 *Indicator of selloffs – accounts active more than 95 per cent of the sample period without constant positions conditioned by profits (over 15 days)*

As shown in Figures 11.3 and 11.4, when profits are computed on a longer period ($\theta = 5$ and 15), stop-loss effects remain apparent, albeit in a weaker fashion. This result suggests that our findings are independent of continuous hedging strategies, which would mainly appear at intradaily frequencies and would be inexistent at other frequencies.

Also notice the asymmetry between profits and losses, with position reversion concentrated in the lower bound of the distribution of profits. Stop-loss orders are, therefore, triggered after significant deviations in terms of profits.

To confirm the robustness of the results and to avoid taking into account infinitesimal changes of positions that may blur the picture, the same test is run for the indicator

$$\tilde{z}_t^j = z_t^j \mathbf{1}_{\{|\Delta PO_t^j| > \frac{\sigma^j}{4}\}}$$

This indicator excludes a high proportion of observations with very small changes (38 per cent of the changes in positions are smaller than $\sigma^j/4$). In Figures 11.5, 11.6 and 11.7, the two dashed lines are the unconditional proportion of $\tilde{z}_t^j < 0$ (lower line) and $1 - \Pr\{\tilde{z}_t^j > 0\}$ (upper line). The three solid lines correspond to the conditional distribution of the three occurrences $\tilde{z}_t^j < 0$, $\tilde{z}_t^j = 0$ and $\tilde{z}_t^j > 0$. The occurrence $\tilde{z}_t^j = 0$ corresponds to small changes in positions, either positive or negative.

As in the case of z_t^j, the conditional distribution of $\tilde{z}_t^j < 0$ is V-shaped; it offers evidence in favour of profit-taking and stop-loss behaviours: in the bottom class of realized profits, the proportion of $\tilde{z}_t^j < 0$ is 52 per cent versus 34.6 per cent for the unconditional distribution and 31.2 per cent in the central class (see Table 11.3). The comparison of Figures 11.2 and 11.5 reveals that, when profits are very negative, the bulk of mean reverting position changes ($z_t^j < 0$) is largely supported by large position changes.

The results of logistic regression models are exhibited in the appendix (Tables A.11.1 and A.11.2). For details see 'Holding reversion behaviour' earlier. The profit dummy variables have a strong effect on $z_t^j = -1$ for the bottom 1 per cent profits and the top 25 per cent (i.e. above the 75th centile) in the binary response model. In the ordered response model they are the only significant variables, with the largest effect for the first and last classes.

To conclude this section, we interpret the results presented so far as evidence in favour of stop-loss strategies. Although one may argue that the tests are simply tests of mean reversion, there is, to our knowledge, no alternative convincing explanation of the strong correlation between low profits over different horizons and reversion of positions.

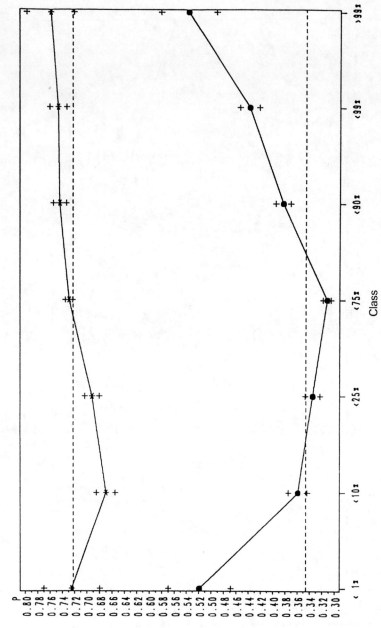

Figure 11.5 *Indicator of selloffs – accounts active more than 95 per cent of the sample period without constant positions conditioned by profits (over one day); — middle proportion is ±0.25 std of position changes*

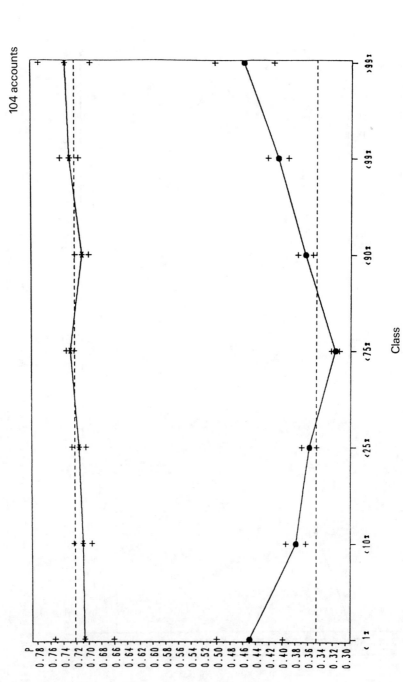

Figure 11.6 *Indicator of selloffs – accounts active more than 95 per cent of the sample period without constant positions conditioned by profits (over five days); middle proportion is ±0.25 std of position changes*

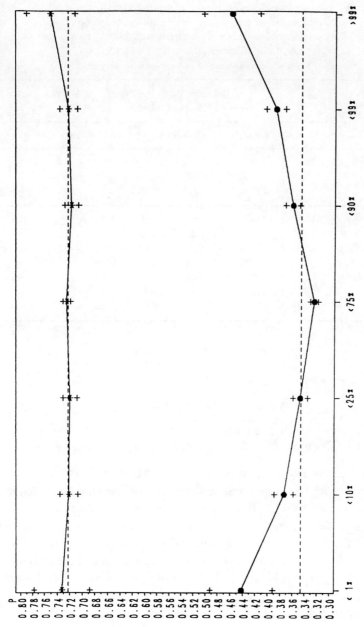

Figure 11.7 *Indicator of selloffs – accounts active more than 95 per cent of the sample period without constant positions conditioned by profits (over 15 days); middle proportion is ±0.25 std of position changes*

Table 11.3   *Conditional distribution of $\tilde{z}_t^j$*

$$\Pr\{\tilde{z}_t^j < 0 \mid R_{1t}^j \in c_i\}$$

c_i are classes of one-period realized profits
t_u: Student t of difference of proportion with uncond. proportion
t_c: Student t of difference of proportion with 25–75% class
t_1: Student t of difference of proportion with 1% class
t_{99}: Student t of difference of proportion with 99% class

104 accounts
$T \times J = 43\,176$ observations

c_i	p	σ_p	t_u	t_c	t_1	t_{99}
Unconditional proportion:						
$\tilde{z}_t^j = -1$	34.61	0.002	–	–	–	–
$\tilde{z}_t^j = 1$	27.80	0.002	–	–	–	–
$R_t^j < 1\%$	51.93	0.025	7.18	8.71	–	–
$1\% \le R_t^j < 10\%$	35.93	0.008	1.72	5.80	−6.21	–
$10\% \le R_t^j < 25\%$	33.53	0.006	−1.82	3.52	−7.41	–
$25\% \le R_t^j < 75\%$	31.21	0.003	−10.51	–	–	–
$75\% \le R_t^j < 90\%$	38.29	0.006	6.22	10.64	–	−6.68
$90\% \le R_t^j < 99\%$	43.74	0.008	11.95	15.28	–	−4.12
$R_t^j \ge 99\%$	53.55	0.022	8.84	10.54	–	–

11.4.2   Causality tests on individual data

We now go more deeply into our assessment of stop-loss strategies by:

(1)   controlling for price changes
(2)   providing estimates of the effect of losses on individual accounts.

Using the framework of Equations (11.8) and (11.9), we carry out a t test separately on each individual unit to determine whether the introduction of realized losses improves the forecasting power of the regression.[13]

We present the results for the sample of accounts active more than 95 per cent of the time, distinguishing $I(0)$ and $I(1)$ accounts. In Table 11.4, we tally the results on each account to measure how widespread the causality is. We then discuss the robustness of the results, by introducing alternative specifications.

The RHS variables in the Equations (11.8) and (11.9) are the price changes, the lagged endogenous variable and the realized profit dummy variables. Price changes are computed by selecting the price of the most active contract at each date and removing the step that appears when the contact is changed

Table 11.4 *OLS estimates on individual accounts: equations (11.8) and (11.9)*

'Tally' of accounts where realized profits are significant
Student t test significantly different from 0 at 10% level

$I(0)$ accounts – total number: 73

	Number of accounts			
	$\gamma^j > 0$		$\gamma^j < 0$	
Def. of RHS (c%)	nb accounts	%	nb accounts	%
$R_t^j < 1\%$	5	6.8	16	21.9
$R_t^j < 5\%$	8	11	15	20.5
$5\% \le R_t^j < 10\%$	8	11	8	11
$10\% \le R_t^j < 15\%$	7	9.6	3	4.1
$85\% \le R_t^j < 90\%$	3	4.1	6	8.2
$90\% \le R_t^j < 95\%$	3	4.1	6	8.2
$R_t^j \ge 95\%$	7	9.6	16	21.9
$R_t^j \ge 99\%$	9	12.2	14	19.2

$I(1)$ accounts – total number: 31

	Number of accounts			
	$\gamma^j > 0$		$\gamma^j < 0$	
Def. of RHS (c%)	nb accounts	%	nb accounts	%
$R_t^j < 1\%$	2	6.4	8	25.8
$R_t^j < 5\%$	1	3.2	8	25.8
$5\% \le R_t^j < 10\%$	2	6.4	2	6.4
$10\% \le R_t^j < 15\%$	2	6.4	2	6.4
$85\% \le R_t^j < 90\%$	0	–	5	16.1
$90\% \le R_t^j < 95\%$	0	–	3	9.7
$R_t^j \ge 95\%$	0	–	10	32.2
$R_t^j \ge 99\%$	0	–	3	9.7

(for details, see Bensaid and Boutillier, 1995). We use Akaike criterion to determine the optimal number of lags in the AR part, with a maximal lag length of five. Concerning the dummy variables, different indicators of realized profits are introduced as shown in Table 11.4.

For $I(0)$ accounts, the top panel of Table 11.4 shows that, out of 73 accounts, there is a significant effect of profits for 28.7 per cent of the accounts. Among them, 16 (21.9 per cent) exhibit a significant negative effect of low realized profits (bottom 1 per cent and bottom 5 per cent). The effect of losses is statistically less significant for upper classes of realized returns: only 3 accounts react negatively to profits in the 10–15 per cent class. This confirms the idea that stop-loss occurs only for extremely low profits. Evidence contradicting such a strategy is scarce: very negative profits have a positive effect on positions for only 5 accounts (6.8 per cent). As predicted by the neo-classical theory, the highest realizations of returns also have a negative effect on positions: it is the case for 14 accounts (19.2 per cent).

In the case of I(1) accounts, 8 out of 31 accounts (25.8 per cent) exhibit a restrictive effect of negative profits on position changes. Evidence in favour of stop-loss strategies is therefore stronger in the sample of $I(1)$ accounts than for $I(0)$ accounts. On the contrary, the impact of very positive profits on selloffs is somewhat weaker than in the $I(0)$ case: the indicator of profits in the top 99 per cent class is significant in 3 cases only (10 in the top 5 per cent class).

To check the robustness of the results, we investigate more thoroughly the impact of changes in prices, which are expected to be significant according to the standard neo-classical theory. First, the variable $\Delta P_t / P_{t-1}$ is substituted to variable ΔP_t, since P_t fluctuates in a narrow range, with very similar result. Second, we proceed to test how significant the coefficient of the profit indicator is. We use the subsample of accounts for which the neo-classical theory is not strongly rejected (i.e. where the coefficient β on prices is not positive). Table A.11.3 in the Appendix shows that on 60 $I(0)$ and 24 $I(1)$ accounts (columns $t_\beta < 0$ or n.s.), the profit indicator has a negative sign ($t_\gamma < 0$) in one out of four cases.

11.5   CONCLUSIONS

Although we only investigate one (large) market, the French Treasury bond futures market, the paper provides evidence in favour of stop-loss strategies, that we interpret as optimal responses to agency conflicts inside the investment firms. Both types of tests presented here are consistent with mean-reversion of positions when performance is poor. Since selloffs are associated with very negative profits, it appears that at least some firms use stop-loss strategies. Empirical evidence shows that around 20 per cent of the firms follow that kind of strategy. Given the level of the threshold of profits triggering stop-loss orders, the evidence favours the explanation of stop-loss orders by moral hazard rather than adverse selection. In the latter case, selection of traders is likely to induce smaller loss limits than the one we have uncovered. Unfortunately, we cannot distinguish between the implications of the optimal level of liquidation under moral hazard and psychological motives.

Such findings may have systemic consequences, since selloffs induced by stop-loss orders in a few firms may rapidly spread to a significant proportion of other firms, triggering large adjustments in the market. However, other studies have shown that the market was efficient during the period under review (Bensaid–Boutillier, 1995). We can, therefore, conclude that the market was resilient enough to absorb the potentially destabilizing effect of stop-loss strategies.

11.6 STATISTICAL APPENDIX

Table A.11.1 *Logistic regression: binary response model*

$$z^j_t = \text{sgn}(\Delta PO^j_t PO^j_{t-1}) = -1, 1$$
$$\text{logit}(\Pr\{y^j_t = -1\}) = X^j_t \beta$$
where $X^j_t = (X_1, \ldots, X_6)$ are profit dummy variables

Number of observations: 43 176
$\chi^2(6) = 497.310$ (*p*-value $= 0.0001$)

Variable	Estimate	Wald statistic	*p*-value
X_1: $R^j_{1t} \leq 1\%$	0.5425	26.61	0.0001
X_2: $1\% \leq R^j_{1t} \leq 25\%$	0.0495	6.33	0.0118
X_3: $25\% \leq R^j_{1t} \leq 75\%$	0.1030	57.07	0.0001
X_4: $75\% \leq R^j_{1t} \leq 90\%$	0.3236	164.75	0.0001
X_5: $90\% \leq R^j_{1t} \leq 99\%$	0.4460	183.82	0.0001
X_6: $R^j_{1t} \geq 99\%$	0.6599	48.22	0.0001

Table A.11.2 *Logistic regression: ordered response model*

$$\tilde{z}^j_t = \text{sgn}(\Delta PO^j_t PO^j_{t-1}) 1_{|\Delta PO^j_t| \geq \sigma^j/4} = -1, 0, 1$$
$$\text{logit}(\Pr\{\tilde{z}^j_t = -1\}) = X^j_t \beta$$
where $X^j_t = (X_1, \ldots, X_4)$ are profit dummy variables

Number of observations: 43 176
$\chi^2(4) = 254.32$ (*p*-value $= 0.0001$)

Variable	Estimate	Wald statistic	*p*-Value
First intercept	−0.7140	2836.15	0.0001
Second intercept	0.8856	5599.51	0.0001
X_1: $R^j_{1t} \leq 1\%$	0.5650	34.85	0.0001
X_2: $75\% \leq R^j_{1t} \leq 90\%$	0.2144	72.38	0.0001
X_3: $90\% \leq R^j_{1t} \leq 99\%$	0.3667	135.07	0.0001
X_4: $R^j_{1t} \geq 99\%$	0.6860	63.79	0.0001

Table A.11.3   *OLS estimates on individual accounts: prices and profits variables*

Comparison of significance of β^j and γ^j

t_β: Student t for ΔP_t

t_γ: Student t for $1_{\{R^j_{1,t}<c\%\}}$

$I(0)$ accounts

	$t_\beta < 0$		t_β n.s.		$t_\beta > 0$		Total	
	nb	% column	nb	% column	nb	% column	nb	% column
$t_\gamma > 0$	1	4.1	4	11.1	0	–	5	6.8
$t_\gamma < 0$	3	12.5	12	33.3	1	7.6	16	21.9
Total (% line)	24	100 (32.8)	36	100 (49.3)	13	100 (17.8)	73	100 (100)

$I(1)$ accounts

	$t_\beta < 0$		t_β n.s.		$t_\beta > 0$		Total	
	nb	% column	nb	% column	nb	% column	nb	% column
$t_\gamma > 0$	1	7.1	1	10.0	0	–	2	6.4
$t_\gamma < 0$	3	21.4	3	30.0	2	28.5	8	25.0
Total (% line)	14	100 (19.1)	10	100 (32.2)	7	100 (22.5)	31	100 (100)

Table A.11.4   *Whiteness of the residuals in equations (11.8)–(11.9)*

$$I(0) : PO^j_t = \alpha^j_0 + \sum_{k=1}^{5} \alpha^j_{1,k} PO^j_{t-k} + \beta^j \Delta P_t + \gamma^j PO^j_{t-1} 1_{R^j_{1t}<1\%} + \varepsilon^j_t$$

$$I(1) : \Delta PO^j_t = \alpha^j_0 + \sum_{k=1}^{5} \alpha^j_{1,k} \Delta PO^j_{t-k} + \gamma^j PO^j_{t-1} 1_{R^j_{1t}<1\%} + \varepsilon^j_t$$

Test of whiteness of ε^j_t

% of accounts where p-value is greater than 1% or 5%

	Final unit root diagnostic:			
	$I(0)$		$I(1)$	
Degrees of freedom	$p > 1\%$	$p > 5\%$	$p > 1\%$	$p > 5\%$
6	94%	83%	100%	90%
12	96%	93%	96%	86%
18	94%	93%	93%	93%
24	92%	92%	93%	93%
30	92%	90%	93%	93%

Table A.11.5 *Whiteness of the residuals in Dickey–Fuller unit root tests*

Eq.: $\Delta PO_t^j = \alpha^j + \beta^j t + \delta PO_{t-1}^j + \sum_{k=1}^{4} \gamma_k^j \Delta PO_{t-k}^j + \varepsilon_t^j$

Test of whiteness of ε_t^j

% of accounts where p-value greater than 1% or 5%

Final unit root diagnostic:

Degrees of freedom	I(0) with trend and intercept		I(0) with intercept		I(0) without intercept		I(1) without trend, or intercept	
	$p > 1\%$	$p > 5\%$	$p > 1\%$	$p > 5\%$	$p > 1\%$	$p > 5\%$	$p > 1\%$	$p > 5\%$
6	100%	100%	100%	100%	100%	100%	100%	100%
12	100%	93%	100%	100%	98%	98%	97%	97%
18	93%	93%	92%	92%	96%	93%	97%	93%
24	93%	80%	100%	92%	96%	76%	93%	93%
30	87%	87%	92%	92%	96%	74%	97%	93%

11.7   MATHEMATICAL APPENDIX

Proof of Lemma 1

Let us denote $\lambda(a')$ the multiplier associated with the incentive compatibility condition $(IC_a^{a'})$, μ the multiplier associated with the trader's individual rationality constraint (IR) and $\nu(x)f(x|a)$ the multiplier associated with the trader limited liability condition (LL). Then the Lagrangian of program $\hat{\mathscr{P}}(\underline{w})$ is given by:

$$\mathscr{L} = \int (x - w(x) - b(x))f(x|a)\,dx$$

$$+ \sum_{a' \neq a} \lambda(a') \int (u(w(x)) - d(x)s(x))(f(x|a) - f(x|a'))\,dx$$

$$- \sum_{a' \neq a} \lambda(a')(c(a) - c(a')) + \mu \int (u(w(x)) - d(x)s(x))f(x|a)\,dx - \mu c(a)$$

$$+ \int \nu(x)(w(x) - \underline{w})f(x|a)\,dx$$

A necessary condition for $(a, w(x), s(x))$ to solve the principal agent problem is that:

$$\frac{\partial \mathscr{L}}{\partial w(x)} = 0 \quad \text{and} \quad \frac{\partial \mathscr{L}}{\partial s(x)} = 0 \text{ if } 0 < s(x) < 1,$$

$$\geq 0 \text{ if } s(x) = 1,$$

$$\leq 0 \text{ if } s(x) = 0$$

Let us compute $\dfrac{\partial \mathscr{L}}{\partial w(x)}$ and $\dfrac{\partial \mathscr{L}}{\partial s(x)}$. One has:

$$\frac{\partial \mathscr{L}}{\partial w(x)} = -f(x|a) + \sum_{a' \neq a} \lambda(a')u'(w(x)$$

$$\times (f(x|a) - f(x|a')) + \mu u'(w(x))f(x|a) + \nu(x)f(x|a)$$

and

$$\frac{\partial \mathscr{L}}{\partial s(x)} = -\frac{d(x)}{u'(w(x))}\frac{\partial \mathscr{L}}{\partial w(x)} - f(x|a)\left(b(x) + (1 - \nu(x))\frac{d(x)}{u'(w(x))}\right)$$

Thus, if $w(x) > \underline{w}$, the exclusion condition gives $\nu(x) = 0$ and $\dfrac{\partial \mathscr{L}}{\partial s(x)}$ is then equal to:

$$-f(x|a)\left(b(x) + \frac{d(x)}{u'(w(x))}\right) < 0$$

which in turn implies that $s(x) = 0$. Moreover, when $s(x) = 1$, one has necessarily $\nu(x) > 0$ and thus $w(x) = \underline{w}$. Finally, since $w(x)$ is determined by the necessary condition $\dfrac{\partial \mathscr{L}}{\partial w(x)} = 0$, $\dfrac{\partial \mathscr{L}}{\partial s(x)}$ is either strictly positive or strictly negative and, therefore, $s(x)$ can only take the values 0 or 1. Q.E.D.

Proof of result 1

Let us consider program $\tilde{\mathscr{P}}$ defined by:

$$\text{maximize}_{a \in A, w(\cdot), s(\cdot)} \int (x - w(x) - b(x)s(x)) f(x|a) \, dx$$

subject to (IR), (LL) and $(IC_a^{a'})$ for all $a, a' \in A$ such that $a' < a$. We consider the function:

$$\Lambda(x, a) = \mu + \sum_{a' < a} \lambda(a') \left(1 - \frac{f(x|a')}{f(x|a)} \right)$$

Since $\lambda(a') \geq 0$ and $a' < a$, MLRC implies that function $\Lambda(x, a)$ is increasing in x for all $a \in A$. A necessary condition for $(\tilde{a}, \tilde{w}, \tilde{s})$ to solve $\tilde{\mathscr{P}}$ is that:

$$\text{if } \tilde{w}(x) \neq \underline{w}, \frac{1}{u'(\tilde{w}(x))} = \Lambda(x, a) \text{ and } \nu(x) = 0,$$

$$\text{if } \tilde{w}(x) = \underline{w}, \frac{1 - \nu(x)}{u'(\underline{w})} = \Lambda(x, a)$$

This condition and the concavity of $u(\cdot)$ implies that $\tilde{w}(x)$ is non-decreasing with x.

Let us show now that $\tilde{s}(\cdot)$ is non-increasing with respect to x. Lemma 1 tells us that it is the case when $\tilde{w}(x) \neq \underline{w}$ ($\tilde{s}$ is constantly equal to 0). When $\tilde{w}(x) = \underline{w}$, one has:

$$\frac{\partial \mathscr{L}}{\partial s(x)} = -f(x|a) d(x) \left(\frac{b(x)}{d(x)} + \Lambda(x, a) \right)$$

Since $b(x)/d(x) + \Lambda(x, a)$ is increasing with x, the sign of the derivative of the Lagrangian with respect to s can change at most once. This is sufficient to prove that $\hat{s}(\cdot)$ is non-increasing with respect to x.

To finish the proof, we have to show that a solution of program $\tilde{\mathscr{P}}$ is also a solution of program $\hat{\mathscr{P}}$. Since programs $\tilde{\mathscr{P}}$ and $\hat{\mathscr{P}}$ differ only by the number of constraints ($\hat{\mathscr{P}}$ is more constrained than $\tilde{\mathscr{P}}$), it is sufficient to show that $(\tilde{a}, \tilde{w}, \tilde{s})$ is admissible for $\hat{\mathscr{P}}$ which is equivalent to show that for all $a' > \tilde{a}$, condition $(IC_{\tilde{a}}^{a})$ holds. Denoting $U_A(a', \tilde{w}, \tilde{s})$ the utility function of the agent, we have to show that

$$\forall a' > \tilde{a}, \quad U_A(\tilde{a}, \tilde{w}, \tilde{s}) > U_A(a', \tilde{w}, \tilde{s})$$

Let us consider a strategy $a'' < \tilde{a}$ such that $U_A(a'', \tilde{w}, \tilde{s}) = U_A(\tilde{a}, \tilde{w}, \tilde{s})$ and a parameter α $(0 < \alpha < 1)$ defined by $\tilde{a} = \alpha a'' + (1 - \alpha) a'$. Since the function

$u(\tilde{w}(x)) - d(x)\tilde{s}(x)$ is increasing in x (function $d(x)$ is non-increasing), the condition (CDFC) and the convexity of function $c(\cdot)$ imply that

$$U_A(\tilde{a}, \tilde{w}, \tilde{s}) \geq \alpha U_A(a'', \tilde{w}, \tilde{s}) + (1 - \alpha)U_A(a', \tilde{w}, \tilde{s})$$

which is equivalent to

$$U_A(\tilde{a}, \tilde{w}, \tilde{s}) \geq U_A(a', \tilde{w}, \tilde{s})$$

(Recall that (CDFC) implies first order stochastic dominance.) Q.E.D.

REFERENCES

Bensaid, B. and Boutillier, M. (1995) Le contrat notionnel: efficience et causalité, Bank of France, Notes d'Etudes et de Recherche, 44.

Friedman, M. (1953) *Essays in Positive Economics*, Chicago University Press, 1953

Gennotte, G. and Leland, H. (1991) Market liquidity, hedging and crashes, *American Economic Review*, December, **80**, 999–1021.

Grossman, S. (1988) An analysis of the implications for stock and futures price volatility of program trading and dynamic hedging strategies, *Journal of Business*, **61**, 3, 275–98.

Grossman, S. and Stiglitz, J. (1978) On the impossibility of informationally efficient markets, *American Economic Review*, June, **22**, 477–98.

Jewitt, I. (1988) Justifying the first-order approach to principal-agent problems, *Econometrica*, **56**, 1177–90.

Kahneman, D. and Tversky, A. (1979) Prospect theory: an analysis of decision under risk, *Econometrica*, **47**, 2, 263–91.

Krugman, P. and Miller, M. (1993) Why have a target zone, *Carnegie-Rochester Conference Series on Public Policy*, **38**, 279–314.

Kyle, A.S. (1985) Continuous auctions and insider trading, *Econometrica*, November, **53**, 1, 315–35.

Mirlees, J.A. and Milgrom, P. (1975) The theory of moral hazard and unobservable behaviour, Nuffield College, Oxford.

Schiller, R. (1981) Do stocks prices move too much to be justified by subsequent changes in dividends?, *American Economic Review*, June, **71**, 3, 421–35.

Shefrin, H and Statman, M. (1985) The disposition to sell winners too early and ride losers too long: theory and evidence, *The Journal of Finance*, 777–92.

NOTES

1. In any case, the trader cannot be responsible on his own wealth.
2. It is only very recently that the financial industry has overcome this constraint by delaying over time distribution of bonuses, then allowing negative bonuses. For example, in 1994 Salomon Brothers Corporation

introduced intertemporal tie-ins to its pay system: a portion of the annual bonus is withheld in case the firm's subsequent performance is poor (*The Economist*, April 15, 1995).

3. It may also be the cost associated with early closure of the wage contract, although it need not be the case.
4. $1 \geq s(x) \geq 0$ holds necessarily.
5. When the investment firm faces a large pool of traders, such a commitment is credible from a reputational point of view.
6. A positive-feedback strategy is characterized by an increase of long holdings when prices rise.
7. As a given firm may have more than one seat, there is a discrepancy between the numbers of 'own' and 'customer' accounts.
8. Although we rely in equation (11.5) on one type of discretization of continuous profits, the following results are not sensitive to the definition of this indicator. Except for 'error accounts' (defined in section 11.3.3 and eventually excluded from the analysis), the cumulative values of $PO_{t-1}\Delta P_t$ and $PO_t\Delta P_t$ are very similar.
9. The open interest is defined as $(1/2)\sum_j |PO_t^j|$.
10. It was the case, in particular, for a few large accounts.
11. Tests of whiteness of the residuals in the ADF equations are provided in Table 11.9 of the Appendix.
12. The standard error of this proportion is simply

$$\sqrt{\frac{pk_i(1 - pk_i)}{n_{ki}}},$$

where n_{ki} is the number of observations in class i, pooled across accounts. When comparing the proportion in class l and m, we compute

$$t_{klm} = \frac{p_{kl} - p_{km}}{\sigma_{klm}}$$

with

$$\sigma_{klm} = \sqrt{p_{klm}(1 - p_{klm})\left(\frac{1}{n_{kl}} + \frac{1}{n_{km}}\right)}$$

and

$$p_{klm} = \frac{p_{kl}n_{kl} + p_{km}n_{km}}{n_{kl} + n_{km}}.$$

We concentrate on the case where $k = -1$.
13. We use simple OLS regressions. Table A.11.5 in the Appendix provides information about the whiteness of residuals of regression equations (11.8) and (11.9). In most cases, there is no evidence of autocorrelation in the error term.

ACKNOWLEDGMENTS

Research assistance from Valerie Golitin is gratefully acknowledged. The paper does not necessarily reflect the views of the Bank of France.

Chapter 12

Evolving technical trading rules for S&P 500 futures

RISTO KARJALAINEN

12.1 INTRODUCTION

In recent years, various machine learning techniques such as genetic algorithms and neural networks have made their debut in financial markets. With earning your living as a trader being as hard as it is, any approach where you set up a computer to learn trading rules for you instead of applying your limited time and resources to the same task has an obvious appeal. Machine learning algorithms have indeed attracted attention in recent years (*The Economist*, 1993) and are likely to inspire an increasing amount of research on the technical aspects of the new trading techniques (Deboeck, 1994).

Since a machine learning paradigm is relatively new in finance, it is understandable that much of the research has so far concentrated on developing the methodology and describing the results obtained in various applications. At some point, however, we need a theory of why these learning algorithms work (if they do; if they don't, the theory of efficient markets provides us with an explanation). An apparently successful application may simply have targeted a market or a time period where conditions favoured the researcher's approach. If the approach had not been successful (or had been too successful), the results would never have been published.

In this chapter, we take an initial step in trying to find out why there appear to be price patterns that are captured by a genetic algorithm. In the course of this work, we set up the algorithm to learn trading rules for the Standard & Poor's 500 futures markets in a careful way, separating the data into training, validation, and out-of-sample test periods. It is found that the rules found by the algorithm perform better than a simple buy-and-hold strategy in the out-of-sample period adjusted for risk. We look at what kinds of price patterns trigger the trading rule signals, and then analyse trading activity in a related options market. It turns out that the rules are activated by particular price patterns and are essentially making profits by betting against short-term overreaction by the market. The price patterns coincide with systematic changes in option volume and open interest, even though these data were not used as inputs to the genetic algorithm. The patterns in the option data are stable across the training and test periods. These findings indicate that in the S&P 500 futures market, the genetic algorithm is able to find rules that generalize out-of-sample because the underlying regularities in the market behaviour have remained relatively constant throughout the years.

This chapter is organized as follows. Section 12.2 presents a brief summary of genetic algorithms and their applications to finance. Section 12.3 describes how a genetic algorithm was applied to find trading rules for S&P 500 futures. The rules are tested in section 12.4, and the trading rule signals are analysed in more detail in section 12.5. Implications of the findings are discussed in section 12.6.

12.2   GENETIC ALGORITHMS

This section describes the basic features of genetic algorithms. Only the general principles are reviewed here. For a more thorough introduction, there are a number of accessible books and papers on genetic algorithms, including Goldberg (1989), Beasley, Bull and Martin (1993), Colin (1994) and Davis (1994).

A genetic algorithm refers to a search, adaptation and optimization technique based on the principles of natural evolution. Genetic algorithms were developed by Holland (1962, 1975) and have been developed further and applied to many different problems since the late 1960s by many others (for a summary, see Goldberg, 1989). A genetic algorithm is one example of so-called evolutionary algorithms, all of which are based broadly on the same principles. Other evolutionary algorithms include evolution strategies (Rechenberg, 1973; Schwefel, 1981), evolutionary programming (Fogel, Owens and Walsh, 1966), classifier systems (Holland, 1976, 1980) and genetic programming (Koza, 1992).

Genetic algorithms implement a stylized version of the Darwinian paradigm of the 'survival of the fittest'. A genetic algorithm starts with a population of randomly generated solution candidates to the problem of interest. Each of the solution candidates is then evaluated according to a problem-specific fitness function, which is simply a measure of the quality of a solution. To create a new generation, relatively fit members of the current population are recombined to create new solutions. These new individuals are used to replace the less fit members of the population. Over successive generations, the average fitness of the population typically increases in a more or less steady manner. The evolution is allowed to continue until a predetermined termination criterion is satisfied, which usually occurs either when the best members of the population are acceptable solutions to the problem or when the genetic algorithm makes no further progress.

Different evolutionary algorithms share the basic paradigm, although the representation of the candidate solutions and the details of the generation cycle vary widely. In a basic genetic algorithm, the candidate solutions (which we will call 'genomes') are represented by fixed-length bit strings (e.g. 00111001), which are mapped to the original solution space. These bit strings are recombined through a 'crossover' operator, where each of the two parent genomes is broken apart at a randomly chosen location, and one part from each parent is put together to create an 'offspring' (e.g. parents 00000000 and 11111111 could be recombined to 00011111). In earlier days, it was popular to create a new generation by copying a fraction of the old generation over intact, and filling in the rest through a recombination operator. Currently, so-called 'continuous reproduction' is often used, where a small number of the relatively poor genomes are replaced by new offspring, so that successive generations overlap (Syswerda, 1989; Whitley, 1989). In each case, the parents for recombination are chosen at random while favouring the fit individuals. This has the effect of increasing the average fitness of the population over time, while still occasionally exploring different regions of the search space. The in-built randomness reduces the likelihood of the algorithm becoming trapped in a local optimum.

Genetic algorithms are popular because they offer a number of advantages over traditional optimization methods. They can be applied to problems where the objective function is non-differentiable or discontinuous. They are also useful in optimization problems with several local optima, which often pose difficulties for hill-climbing or gradient-based methods. In some situations, the search space is simply too large for other approaches. While genetic algorithms may not find the global optimum in such problems, they often converge to acceptable solutions relatively quickly. However, evolutionary algorithms offer no panacea. In well-understood problems, they are unlikely to perform better than special-purpose algorithms. Genetic algorithms also suffer from the lack of a rigorous theoretical foundation. While they have been found to be quite useful in practice, there is no general result that guarantees convergence to a global optimum. Hence, one should view evolutionary algorithms as a complement rather than a replacement for traditional optimization methods.

Evolutionary algorithms have been applied to a large number of problems in the past three decades (see Goldberg, 1989; Nissen, 1993). In economics, genetic algorithms have been applied to time-series forecasting by Packard

(1990) and Meyer and Packard (1992) and to econometric estimation by Dorsey and Mayer (1995), to give just a few examples (for more references, see Karjalainen, 1994). In finance, Allen and Karjalainen (1993) used a genetic algorithm to find technical trading rules for the S&P 500 stock index. Bauer (1994) applied a genetic algorithm to finding market-timing strategies based on fundamental data for stock and bond markets. Colin (1994) and Davis (1994) describe other practical applications to finance. Arthur et al. (1996) have used classifier systems to model traders in an artificial stock market at the Santa Fe Institute.

12.2.1 Genetic programming

In this research, we used a variant of the basic genetic algorithm called genetic programming. It was developed by Koza (1992), although Antonisse (1991) and Colin (1994) have independently come up with similar algorithms. In a basic genetic algorithm, the solution candidates are represented as bit strings of fixed length. While this representation is quite adequate for many problems, it is restrictive in situations where the size or the form of the solution is not known beforehand. In genetic programming, solution candidates are represented as hierarchical compositions of functions. In these tree-like genomes, the successors of each node provide the arguments for the function identified with the node. The terminal nodes (i.e. the nodes without successors) correspond to the input data. The structure of the tree does not need to be specified beforehand. Instead, one defines a problem-dependent set of functions and terminal nodes, and allows the genetic algorithm to recombine the tree structures to create new solution candidates. The genetic programming package used to implement this process was developed on a Unix workstation and written in C (for details, see Karjalainen, 1994).

In genetic programming, the evolution starts with a population of randomly generated tree structures. The root node of each tree is chosen at random among the available functions. Each argument of that function is then selected among the available functions, taking care that only functions of the appropriate type are considered. This process continues in a recursive manner, extending the tree until each branch terminates at a function with no arguments.

The crossover operator recombines two genomes by replacing a randomly selected subtree in the first parent by a subtree from the second parent. To maintain the syntactic validity of the trees, the subtree in the second parent is chosen among those whose root node is of the same type as the chosen subtree in the first parent (this procedure preserves a so-called 'closure' property).

When evolving new generations, continuous reproduction is used. This process involves choosing two parents at random, while biased towards choosing the relatively fit genomes. The two parents are then recombined into one offspring. This offspring replaces a randomly chosen member of the population, this time biased towards the less fit individuals. Each generation consists of N repetitions of the crossover operation, where N is the population size.

12.3 EVOLVING TECHNICAL TRADING RULES

This section describes how a genetic algorithm was set up to find technical trading rules for the S&P 500 futures. Because the rules make trading decisions based on past prices only on one of the most efficient markets in the world, we should not expect the rules to lead to dramatic profits. However, evolving and testing purely technical rules provides us with a base case and the methodology can be easily extended to handle other inputs beyond prices. Moreover, there are some previous studies which suggest that even purely price-based technical trading rules can be useful. These include a paper by Brock, Lakonishok and LeBaron (1992) on the Dow Jones index, Sweeney (1988) on individual stocks, and Lukac and Brorsen (1990) on several commodity futures markets.

12.3.1 The futures data

We used daily closing prices for 47 contracts of the S&P 500 futures, starting on 21 April, 1982, and ending on 15 September, 1993, with a total of 2885 trading days (ignoring the overlap between the contracts). In a preliminary data analysis, sample autocorrelation function of the daily log returns was found to be significantly negative for the first lag, with a coefficient of -0.10. At higher-order lags, there was no evidence of significant autocorrelation. There was evidence, however, of nonlinearity. If the returns are generated by a linear process (such as a random walk), the absolute and squared returns should show no evidence of autocorrelation, after linear dependence has been controlled for (Taylor, 1986). It turns out, however, that there is significant serial dependence in the absolute residuals from an AR(5) model fitted to the daily returns (Karjalainen, 1994). This analysis does not explain where the nonlinearity comes from; it may simply be evidence of conditional hetero-skedasticity in the data. Nevertheless, technical trading rules may be useful for S&P 500 futures if they manage to exploit the nonlinearity of the returns.

Because the trading volume was very small in the beginning, the first three contracts were dropped, so that the first contract used by the genetic algorithm was March 1983. For each contract, daily closing prices in the delivery month and in the preceding four months were retained, so that the different contracts partly overlap. The data were normalized by dividing each closing price by the first price of the contract and multiplying the results by 100.

12.3.2   Evolving trading rules

The trading rules were set up so that they returned a boolean value of either 'true' or 'false' at the close of each trading day, corresponding to a 'buy' or a 'sell' signal, respectively. The rules were represented by tree structures, as explained earlier on the section on genetic programming. The tree structures were hierarchical compositions of various logical and real-valued functions and constants. The logical functions included an 'if-then-else' function, operators 'and', 'or', and 'not', as well as comparisons of two real numbers ('<' and '>'). The real-valued functions included division, addition, subtraction, multiplication of two real numbers, a 'norm' function (absolute difference of two real numbers), a moving average, a maximum and a minimum of past prices (with the time window specified by a real-valued argument), today's closing price, as well as a 'lag' function which causes all the functions in the subtree to be applied to prices lagged by a specified number of days. There were also logical constants ('true' and 'false') and real-valued constants (drawn from a uniform distribution between 0 and 100, and truncated to integer values when appropriate). Figure 12.1 shows two simple trading rules that can be created using these functions and an offspring created by recombining the two parents. To interpret any of the rules in the figure, start at the root of the tree and follow the arguments down to the leaves. Parent 1 in Figure 12.1, for instance, returns a 'buy' signal if today's price is greater than a fifty-day moving average and a maximum of the past thirty days' prices is below today's price. To evaluate a trading rule, it was applied to each trading day. If the rule returned a 'buy' signal, a long position was taken (or maintained, if the rule was already long) for the following day. If the rule returned a 'sell' signal, a short position was taken (or maintained) for the day after. Whenever a trade extended beyond the first day of the delivery month, the position was covered at the first switch to a new position, and the processing shifted over to the next contract. If the rule returned the same signal for each day in the delivery month, the position was covered on the expiry. Depending on the exact rollover day, the rules had access to 4–6 weeks of past prices on the first day in a new contract.

The fitness of a rule was defined as the excess cash flow above a buy-and-hold strategy, marking the position to market each day. For S&P 500 futures, the daily cash flow is equal to 500 times the size of the position (one contract)

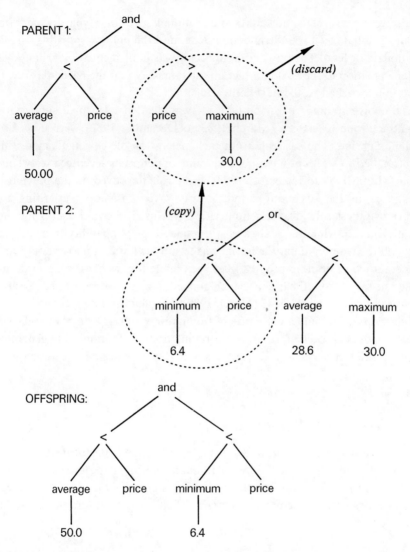

Figure 12.1 *Illustration of two simple trading rules and the crossover operator. The crossover creates a new trading rule by recombining the two parent rules. A randomly chosen subtree (designated by the dotted line) in the first parent is discarded. The discarded subtree is replaced by a subtree of the same type, chosen from the second parent. The offspring is shown in the bottom of the figure*

times the price change from the previous day's close. To compute the fitness, the cash flow for each day in a long position was added to the cumulative balance for the rule. The cash flow for each day in the short position was subtracted from the balance. Every time the position was changed, a commission of 100 dollars was subtracted from the cash balance (this is a conservative estimate; nowadays, institutional investors typically pay less than 15 dollars as a roundtrip commission, and the bid-ask spread is usually 50 dollars or less). The buy-and-hold policy was implemented by rolling over a long position to the next contract on the same day that the particular rule in question switched to the next contract.

To evolve trading rules, the data set was divided into three subperiods. Contracts one to sixteen (March 1983 to December 1986) were used as a training period. The best rule from each generation of the genetic algorithm was applied to a selection period, consisting of contracts seventeen to twenty-four (March 1987 to December 1988). If the rule improved on the previously best rule in the selection period, it was saved instead, overwriting the previously best rule. The selection period was used to avoid overfitting, i.e. stop evolution while the best rules still retained their capability to generalize beyond the training data. Each trial was terminated after a maximum of fifty generations, or until no progress had been made for twenty-five generations. The rule saved from the trial was then applied to an out-of-sample test period, consisting of contracts 25–43 (March 1989 to September 1993), covering 1211 trading days. To build a collection of trading rules to test, a total of 100 trials were conducted, each starting with a population of 500 randomly generated trading rules. The test results for the saved 100 rules are described below.

12.4   TESTING THE TRADING RULES

This section describes the out-of-sample test results for the trading rules evolved for the S&P 500 futures. Although one might be interested in the absolute profits for the rules, the results for a simple buy-and-hold strategy are also presented for comparison. The riskiness of the trading rules is also analysed.

12.4.1   Trading rule results

The average buy-and-hold cash flow for holding a long position of one contract during the test period in 1989–1993 was 3546 dollars per 3-month contract, accruing a 100 dollars commission for each rollover. The average cash flow for the 100 trading rules was 4306 dollars, using the same 100 dollars roundtrip commissions. The average trading rule cash flow ranges from −2320 dollars to 9043 dollars. The average daily cash flow for long positions was 106.94 dollars; the average for short positions was −31.27 dollars.

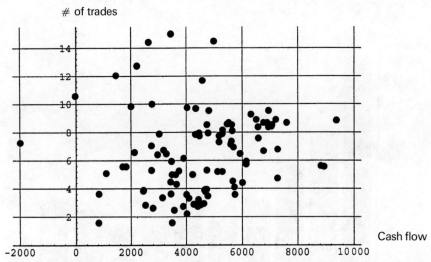

Figure 12.2 *The average cash flow and the average number of trades per contract for the 100 trading rules for the S&P 500 futures. The rules were evolved using price data for contracts from March 1983 to December 1988, and tested on contracts from March 1989 to September 1993*

Figure 12.2 shows the average cash flow versus trading frequency. Across the rules, there was an average of 6.53 trades per contract or one trade every 10 days. The frequency ranges from less than two days per contract (a trade every thirty to forty days) to a high of fifteen trades per contract (a trade every four days), indicating that there is a fair range of diversity in the trading strategies.

To get a different view of the trading rule performance, consider Figures 12.3 and 12.4. They show the distribution of the daily profit (ignoring commissions) for trades of different duration for long (Figure 12.3) and short (Figure 12.4) positions. The graphs are truncated at ten days, because there are relatively few observations for the long-term trades. It can be noted that the average cash flows are positive for long positions and negative for short, regardless of the duration of the trade. The largest profits are made on short-term trades of one to three days.

Figure 12.5 shows the cumulative cash flow for a 'portfolio' of trading rules. The portfolio corresponds to a trading strategy where the daily position is equal to the net position (between −1 and +1) across the rules. Figure 12.5 indicates that the trading rules did miss the big market upswings, but made up the gap achieving relatively small but steady gains. The cash balance for the buy-and-hold strategy in the end of test period on 31 August, 1993 was 73 150 dollars, starting from zero on 30 November, 1988. The ending cash balance for the trading rule portfolio was 84 013 dollars.

Cash flow

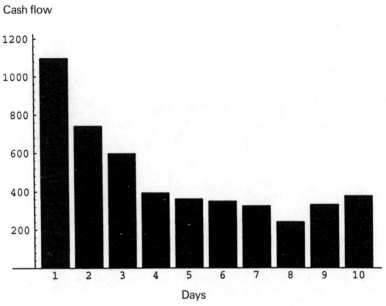

Figure 12.3   *The distribution of the average daily profit for trades in long positions for the S&P 500 futures, using trading rules found by a genetic algorithm. The results are averaged over the 100 trading rules over the test period from December 1988 to August 1993*

Cash flow

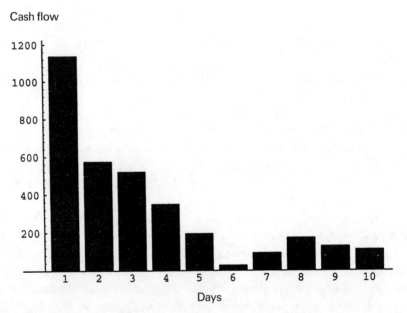

Figure 12.4   *The distribution of the average daily profit for trades in short positions for the S&P 500 futures, using trading rules found by a genetic algorithm. The results are averaged over the 100 trading rules over the test period of December 1988 to August 1993*

Cash flow

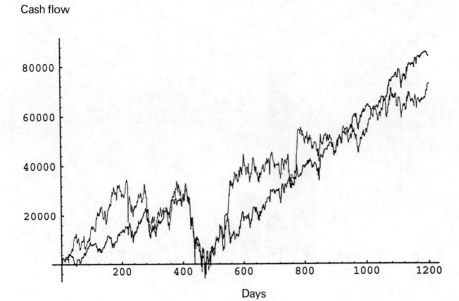

Figure 12.5 *The cumulative cash balance for a portfolio of 100 trading rules for S&P 500 futures during the test period from December 1988 to August 1993. The horizontal axis corresponds to the trading days and the vertical axis to the cumulative cash balance. The thick line corresponds to the portfolio of trading rules and the thin line to the buy-and-hold strategy*

12.4.2 Trading rule risk

Measuring the trading rule risk is obviously important. So far, the results indicate that the trading rules led to slightly higher profits in the out-of-sample period than a simple buy-and-hold strategy. The difference is not great, however, and there have been periods of up to two years when the rules' performance lagged the passive holding policy. Even the small increase in the profits might, of course, be due to bearing increased risk. On the other hand, even matching the market would be a good result if the rules reduced risk. The trading rule risk is measured below by the Sharpe ratio and by the maximum drawdown of the cash balance. The results are compared to the buy-and-hold strategy. The risk measures are also computed for a portfolio of trading rules, with the signals aggregated into a daily net position.

The Sharpe ratios were computed for the average cash flow in successive twenty-day periods, corresponding roughly to monthly cash flows (the results were similar for different periods). The annualized Sharpe ratio for the buy-and-hold strategy in the test period was 0.63. The average Sharpe ratio for the 100 trading rules was 0.79. Had the rules been used as portfolio, the Sharpe ratio would have increased to 1.15. Based on these results, the trading rules do not appear to be particularly risky.

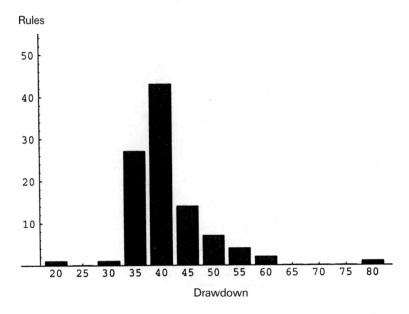

Figure 12.6 *The distribution of the maximum drawdown for the 100 trading rules for S&P 500 futures during the test period from December 1988 to August 1993. The drawdown is defined as the greatest decline in the cumulative cash position before a new high balance is reached*

Another measure of risk often used in practice is the drawdown of equity. Here, the maximum drawdown was defined as the greatest decline of the cash position before a new high balance was reached. For the buy-and-hold strategy, the maximum drawdown of 40 675 dollars occurred between 9 October, 1989 and 10 October, 1990. The average drawdown for the trading rules was 41 343 dollars (the median was 39 187 dollars). The drawdown ranges from 22 215–81 300 dollars. As Figure 12.6 shows, the distribution is skewed. The drawdown was bigger than for the passive strategy for only 39 rules out of the 100. Again, diversification across the rules is advantageous, as the maximum drawdown for the portfolio was 33 703 dollars (between 19 July, 1990, and 11 October, 1990), smaller than for an average trading rule.

Using the risk measures considered earlier, it appears that the trading rules are not more risky than a buy-and-hold strategy. Moreover, a significant reduction of risk (30 per cent lower volatility) can be achieved by combining the rules into a portfolio, where the daily net position is aggregated across the rules. Despite the relatively low volatility, however, the trading rules do carry a risk of underperforming the market for long periods of time. There is also the possibility that the trading rules make money by assuming a risk of being on the wrong side of the market on rare occasions, and the risks were simply not realized during the relatively short test period.

12.5 ANALYSING TRADING RULE SIGNALS

So far, we have found that the trading rules found by the genetic algorithm led to profits comparable to a buy-and-hold strategy but with somewhat subdued volatility. The next question we address is how did the trading rules achieve their performance, i.e. what kinds of price patterns did they rely on? We start by looking at the daily cash flow in 'event time', i.e. time relative to the trading rule signals. This is done by labelling each day relative to the signal, and averaging the cash flows across the rules and across the event days. As shown below, a surprisingly clear pattern emerges when we look at prices in this way. Of course, the pattern is only evident because the averaging process cancels out much of the noise in the market; any individual trading rule signal is unlikely to be preceded by an equally smooth return sequence. This section only looks at the average behaviour of the 100 rules that were saved. While this helps to smooth out the noise in the data, it also masks individual differences. A more detailed analysis for different groups of rules is presented by Karjalainen (1994).

12.5.1 Price patterns

Figure 12.7 shows the cash flow in event time for transitions from long to short positions, averaged across the 100 rules for each day. For instance, cash flow for day −1 is the average cash flow on the last day in a long position, day −2 the cash flow on day next to last, etc. Similarly, day 0 is the first day in a short position, day 1 the second day, etc. Figure 12.7 indicates that the rules tend to switch from a long position to a short one after a sequence of positive returns, triggered finally by an exceptionally large price increase. Figure 12.8 shows the transitions from short to long positions, with days labelled in a similar manner. It appears that the rules switch from a short position to a long one after a day or two of negative returns, triggered by a large price decline. Although figures are omitted to save space, very similar patterns were also evident in the training period.

The observed price patterns suggest that the trading rules at least partly rely on the reversal of returns on a short horizon. These findings are consistent with evidence from stock markets. For instance, Bremer and Sweeney (1991) found that daily stock returns smaller than −10 per cent are partially reversed during the following two days. Brown, Van Harlow and Tinic (1988) reported that returns smaller than −2.5 per cent rebounded by a cumulative 0.53 per cent by the 60th day after the event. For a summary of related evidence, see De Bondt and Thaler (1989).

One possible interpretation of these findings is an overreaction by investors either to news or to recent price changes themselves (there is evidence that

Cash flow

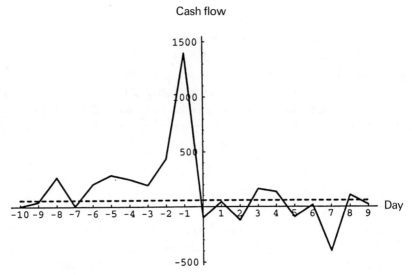

Figure 12.7   *The average daily cash flow in event time for transitions from long to short positions for the 100 trading rules for S&P 500 futures during the test period from December 1988 to August 1993. The horizontal axis corresponds to the event time, relative to the signal on day −1. The vertical axis corresponds to the average cash flow for each event day (500 times the price change). The dashed horizontal line indicates the average daily cash flow for the 100 rules*

Cash flow

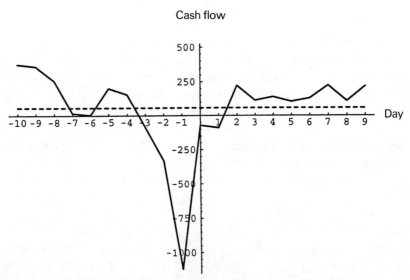

Figure 12.8   *The average daily cash flow in event time for transitions from short to long positions for the 100 trading rules for S&P 500 futures during the test period from December 1988 to August 1993. The horizontal axis corresponds to the event time, relative to the signal on day −1. The vertical axis corresponds to the average cash flow for each event day (500 times the price change). The dashed horizontal line indicates the average daily cash flow for the 100 rules*

investors find recent price movements salient information that they take into account when making decisions; see Schachter et al., 1987). As new information comes in, returns are partially reversed as investors realize that the initial reaction was disproportionate. Put another way, sometimes the prices are moved by 'noise', and the price movements without a fundamental reason are then corrected over the next couple of days. However, one should keep in mind the fact that the time period considered here is relatively short. As alluded to above in the section on trading rule risk, it is possible that large returns that the rules bet against do sometimes lead to even larger returns which justify the initial reaction of the markets. The rules may have simply made money because they assumed the risk of rare events that just did not materialize during the training or test periods.

12.5.2   Option trading activity

If the price patterns observed earlier reflect overreaction by the markets, assessment of investor sentiment becomes important. Option data are particularly interesting in this respect, since option markets offer a more detailed picture of market behaviour that can be achieved by looking at the underlying market alone. In this section, we study volume and open interest data for options to see where there are any regularities corresponding to the observed price patterns and the timing of the trading rule signals.

In the past, researchers have usually looked at a so-called 'put-call ratio', i.e. the ratio of put option volume to call volume, sometimes smoothed by taking a moving average. The reasoning behind the ratio is that when trading is concentrated on the put options (i.e. the put-call ratio is high), investor sentiment is bearish. From a contrarian viewpoint, this is considered to be a buy signal. Similarly, a low put-call ratio is thought to be an indicator or bullish sentiment, which is taken as a signal to sell. Billingsley and Chance (1988) tested two such indicators using data from the S&P 100 options, but found no evidence of abnormal stock market returns after transaction costs. Chance (1990) showed that the correlation between the S&P 500 return and the put-call ratio was largely contemporaneous. However, he also found that some of the trading strategies he tested were at least marginally profitable, especially in futures where transaction costs are low.

There are several active markets for options related to S&P 500 futures, including options for the S&P 100 index (OEX), options for the S&P 500 index (SPX), as well as options for the futures themselves. Of these three markets, the S&P 100 options are the most liquid, being in fact the most actively traded option market in the world. There is also evidence that OEX options are actually priced off the S&P 500 futures (Figlewski, 1988). Because trading volume and open interest data for all the tree markets are highly correlated with one another, OEX data was used in the following tests.

Using a methodology similar to looking at cash flows in event time, we analysed the option data relative to the trading rule signals during the test period from December 1988 to August 1993. Put-call ratios were formed for both the trading volume (as in the previous research) and for open interest. In the trading volume put-call ratio, there was indeed a pattern where put-call ratio declines to its trough on the precise day that the rules switch over from a long position to a short one, and bounces back during the next few days. Similarly, the put-call ratio achieved its peak on the day when the rules send a buy signal.

While the volume data were suggestive, the open interest data turned out to be even more revealing. Figure 12.9 shows the open interest put-call ratio (PCO) in event time. For transitions from long to short positions, the put-call ratio steadily increases before the trading rule signal, and keeps growing for another three to four days afterwards. Figure 12.10 shows that the pattern for buy signals is essentially a mirror image from the sell signals. Were the two figures pasted together, we would see a pattern very much resembling a sinewave, with the put-call ratio fluctuating from peak to trough, with the

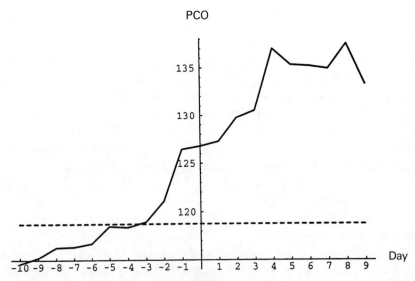

Figure 12.9   *The open interest put-call ratio (PCO) in event time for transitions from long to short positions for the 100 trading rules for S&P 500 futures during the test period from December 1988 to August 1993. The horizontal axis corresponds to the event time, relative to the signal on day −1. The vertical axis corresponds to the average put-call ratio for each event day. The dashed horizontal line indicates the average put-call ratio for the 100 rules*

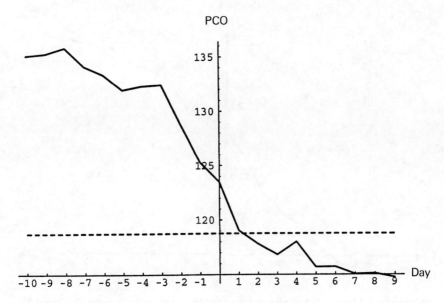

Figure 12.10 *The open interest put-call ratio (PCO) in event time for transitions from short to long positions for the 100 trading rules for S&P 500 futures during the test period from December 1988 to August 1993. The horizontal axis corresponds to the event time, relative to the signal on day −1. The vertical axis corresponds to the average put-call ratio for each event day. The dashed horizontal line indicates the average put-call ratio for the 100 rules*

curve punctuated by the trading rule signals at the midpoint between the extremes.

Figures 12.11 and 12.12 show the open interest put-call ratio during the combined training and selection period. The option data exhibit patterns very similar to the test period. This suggests that the trading rules worked out-of-sample because the market behaved similarly across the different periods. There is some evidence, however, of a fastened pace in the markets. The peaks and troughs tend to follow each other with a higher frequency in the test period, compared with the more tranquil training years. The trading volume data are also largely similar to the test period, except that the put-call ratio achieves its extrema one to three days after the signal.

To summarize the analysis of the trading rule signals, it was found that the rules made bets against the market, stepping in and buying when prices fell and selling after large price increases. In the time period studied here, the strategy was profitable because large returns were partially reversed after a few days. A study of option data on a related market showed that the rules held long positions when the open interest and volume was concentrated on call options, and were short when the option trading activity was focused on puts. The results are consistent with a contrarian view of the markets where

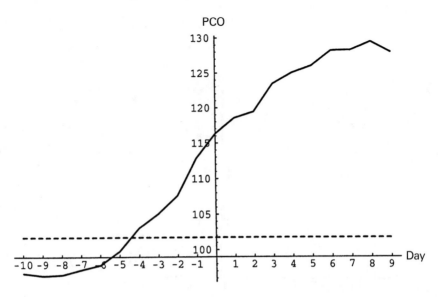

Figure 12.11   *The open interest put-call ratio (PCO) in event time for transitions from long to short positions for the 100 trading rules for S&P 500 futures during the training and selection periods from June 1983 to November 1988. The horizontal axis corresponds to the event time, relative to the signal on day −1. The vertical axis corresponds to the average put-call ratio for each event day. The dashed horizontal line indicates the average put-call ratio for the 100 rules*

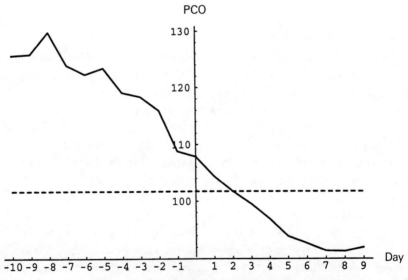

Figure 12.12   *The open interest put-call ratio (PCO) in event time for transitions from short to long positions for the 100 trading rules for S&P 500 futures during the training and selection periods from June 1983 to November 1988. The horizontal axis corresponds to the event time, relative to the signal on day −1. The vertical axis corresponds to the average put-call ratio for each event day. The dashed horizontal line indicates the average put-call ratio for the 100 rules*

bullish sentiment precedes price declines and bearish sentiment peaks before price increases. While the observed patterns may be due to rational hedging activity, the fact remains that the patterns are there, even though the option data were not used as inputs to the genetic algorithm. The patterns were stable throughout the years, allowing the algorithm to find rules in the training period that generalized to an out-of-sample test period.

12.6 CONCLUSIONS

In this chapter, a variant of genetic algorithms called genetic programming was used to find technical trading rules for S&P 500 futures, using daily prices as inputs. The rules were found using a training period from March 1983 to December 1986, and one rule from each of the 100 trials was saved as long as it also worked in a selection period from March 1987 to December 1988. The rules were tested out-of-sample from March 1989 to September 1993. It was found that the rules led to profits slightly higher than the buy-and-hold strategy in the test period, with smaller realized risk. The rules were typically contrarian, betting against large price movements. There were also identifiable patterns in the put-call ratios for related S&P 100 index (OEX) options. In particular, the volume and open interest were systematically higher in call options than in put options before the rules switched from long to short positions, and vice versa.

The results indicate that the trading rules found by a genetic algorithm led to higher risk-adjusted profits than a passive holding policy in the out-of-sample test period in one of the most efficient financial markets. However, it would be premature to claim that such rules could be expected to consistently 'beat the market'; perhaps they simply made profits by assuming a risk of rare events that did not materialize during the time period we studied. Even if that were not the case, the rules still had to bear the risk of underperforming the market for periods of up to two years. For investors with the S&P 500 index as the benchmark, such rules might not be very attractive. Nevertheless, the results certainly encourage further applications of genetic algorithms in finance. In developing practical trading rules one would probably not want to limit oneself to using past prices only in the information set.

From a theoretical viewpoint, the findings about the option put-call ratios suggest that there is a link between changes in investor sentiment and trading rule signals. The results are consistent with overreaction of investors either to news or to price changes themselves. However, without a more detailed study of the motivation and actual decisions of investors in these markets we cannot actually show that the price patterns we found are caused by irrational changes in investor sentiment; it is possible that patterns reflect rational hedging activity. Still, the fact that the patterns in option data exist and are consistent across training and test periods implies that the trading rule results are not (even inadvertently) caused by data snooping or overfitting. In other words, there are genuine patterns in market behaviour based on past prices only, and genetic algorithms offer one way of finding these patterns. We are not claiming that there is a deterministic mechanism that drives the market, as a simplistic application of chaos theory would imply. Rather, it seems that investors' reactions to either exogenous information (news) or endogenous information (recent price changes) follow patterns that are systematic enough to detect when one looks at a sufficiently large number of events that trigger trading rule signals.

REFERENCES

Allen, F. and Karjalainen, R. (1993) Using genetic algorithms to find technical trading rules, Rodney L. White Center, The Wharton School, University of Pennsylvania, Working paper, 20–93.

Antonisse, H.J. (1991) A grammar-based genetic algorithm. In *Foundations of Genetic Algorithms* (ed. G.J. Rawlins), Morgan Kaufmann, San Mateo, California, pp. 193–204.

Arthur, W.B., Holland, H.J., LeBaron, B., Palmer, R. and Taylor, P. (1996) Asset pricing under endogenous expectations in an artificial stock market, Santa Fe Institute, Santa Fe, New Mexico, Working paper 96–12–093.

Bauer, R.J. Jr. (1994) *Genetic Algorithms and Investment Strategies*, Wiley, New York.

Beasley, D., Bull, D.R. and Martin, R.R. (1993) An overview of genetic algorithms: part I, fundamentals, *University Computing*, **15**, 2, 58–69.

Billingsley, R.S. and Chance, D.M. (1988) Put-call ratios and market timing effectiveness, *Journal of Portfolio Management*, Fall, 25–8.

Bremer, M. and Sweeney, R.J. (1991) The reversal of large stock-price decreases, *Journal of Finance*, **46**, 2, 747–54.

Brock, W., Lakonishok, J. and LeBaron, B. (1992) Simple technical trading rule and the stochastic properties of stock returns, *Journal of Finance*, **47**, 5, 1731–64.

Brown, K.C., Van Harlow, W. and Tinic, S.M. (1988) Risk aversion, uncertainty information and market efficiency, *Journal of Financial Economics*, **22**, 355–85.

Chance, D.M. (1990) Option volume and stock market performance, *Journal of Portfolio Management*, Summer, 42–51.

Colin, A.M. (1994) Genetic algorithms for financial modeling. In *Trading on the Edge* (ed. G.J. Deboeck), Wiley, New York, pp. 148–73.

Davis, L. (1994) Genetic algorithms and financial applications. In *Trading on the Edge* (ed. G.J. Deboeck), Wiley, New York, pp. 133–47.

Deboeck, G.J. (ed.) (1994) *Trading on the Edge*, Wiley, New York.

De Bondt, W.F.M. and Thaler, R.H. (1989) A mean-reverting walk down Wall Street, *Journal of Economic Perspectives*, **3**, 1, 189–202.

Dorsey, R.E. and Mayer, W.J. (1995) Genetic algorithms for estimation problems with multiple optima, nondifferentiability, and other irregular features, *Journal of Business & Economic Statistics*, **13**, 53–66.

The Economist (1993) Frontiers of finance, **328** (7832), 9 October, a survey.

Figlewski, S. (1988) Arbitrage-based pricing of stock index options, *Review of Futures Markets*, **7**, 2, 250–70.

Fogel, L.J., Owens, A.J. and Walsh, M.J. (1966) *Artificial Intelligence through Simulated Evolution*, Wiley, New York.

Goldberg, D.E. (1989) *Genetic Algorithms in Search, Optimization and Machine Learning*, Addison-Wesley, Reading, Massachusetts.

Holland, J.H. (1962) Outline for a logical theory for adaptive systems, *Journal of the Association for Computing Machinery*, **3**, 197–217.

Holland, J.H. (1975) *Adaptation in Natural and Artificial Systems*, University of Michigan Press, Ann Arbor, MI.

Holland, J.H. (1976) Adaptation. In *Progress in Theoretical Biology* (eds R. Rosen and F.M. Snell), Vol. 4, Academic Press, New York, pp. 263–93.

Holland, J.H. (1980) Adaptive algorithms for discovering and using general patterns in growing knowledge-bases, *International Journal of Policy Analysis and Information Systems*, **4**, 3, 217–40.

Karjalainen, R. (1994) *Using genetic algorithms to find technical trading rules in financial markets*, PhD dissertation, University of Pennsylvania.

Koza, J.R. (1992) *Genetic Programming: On the Programming of Computers by Means of Natural Selection*, MIT Press, Cambridge, MA.

Lukac, L.P. and Brorsen, B.W. (1990) A comprehensive test of futures market disequilibrium, *Financial Review*, **25**, 4, 593–622.

Meyer, T.P. and Packard, N.H. (1992) Local forecasting of high-dimensional chaotic dynamics. In *Nonlinear Modelling and Forecasting* (eds M. Casdagli and S. Eubank), Santa Fe Institute Studies in the Sciences of Complexity, Proc. Vol. XII, 249–263, Addison-Wesley, Reading, MA.

Nissen, V. (1993) Evolutionary algorithms in management science, Interdisziplinaeres Graduiertenkolleg, Universitaet Goettingen, Papers on Economics and Evolution, 9303.

Packard, N.H. (1990) A genetic learning algorithm for the analysis of complex data, *Complex Systems*, **4**, 543–72.

Rechenberg, I. (1973) *Evolutionsstrategie: Optimierung technischer Systeme nach Prinzipien der Biologischen Evolution*, Frommann-Holzboog Verlag, Stuttgart.

Schachter, S., Ouellette, R., Whittle, B. and Gerin, W. (1987) Effects of trend and of profit or loss on tendency to sell stock, *Basic and Applied Social Psychology*, **8**, 4, 259–71.

Schwefel, H.-P. (1981) *Numerical Optimization of Computer Models*, Wiley, Chichester.

Sweeney, R.J. (1988) Some new filter rule tests: methods and results, *Journal of Financial and Quantitative Analysis*, **23**, 3, 285–300.

Syswerda, G. (1989) Uniform crossover in genetic algorithms. In *Proceedings of the Third International Conference on Genetic Algorithms* (ed. D.J. Schaffer), Morgan Kaufmann, San Mateo, CA, 2–9.

Taylor, S. (1986) *Modeling Financial Time Series*, Wiley, New York

Whitley, D. (1989) The GENITOR algorithm and selection pressure: Why rank-based allocation of reproductive trials is best. In *Proceedings of the Third International Conference on Genetic Algorithms* (ed. D.J. Schaffer), Morgan Kaufmann, San Mateo, CA, 116–21.

ACKNOWLEDGMENTS

This article is based on my dissertation at the Wharton School in the University of Pennsylvania. I would like to thank my dissertation advisors Paul Kleindorfer and Franklin Allen for their encouragement, support, and advice. Helpful comments and suggestions were also made by Blake LeBaron, Colin Camerer, Larry Fisher, Steve Kimbrough, Michele Kreisler, Howard Kunreuther, Jim Laing, George Mailath, John Miller, and by the editors. Financial support by the Academy of Finland is gratefully acknowledged. Correspondence should be addressed to Risto Karjalainen, Flat 4, 1 Greenaway Gardens, London NW3 7DJ. Email: risto.karjalainen@dial.pipex.com.

Chapter 13

Commodity trading advisors and their role in managed futures

DEREK EDMONDS

13.1 INTRODUCTION

The primary purpose of this chapter is to examine the merits of using managed futures as a diversifying vehicle for traditional investments, to analyse the variables that are considered in the evaluation, selection and monitoring processes of building a portfolio of traders, and ultimately to probe into the characteristics of the traders that comprise a multi-advisor portfolio.

Section 13.2 discusses the major advantages for investing in this asset class, including powerful arguments for diversification, ability to potentially profit from all types of market conditions, access to global markets and limited liability. In order to achieve the desired results, a sound system of analysing potential traders needs to be employed. As a leader in the futures industry, Refco has developed a comprehensive quantitative and qualitative evaluation system that is used in the evaluation, selection and monitoring processes. These vital criteria are described in greater detail in section 13.3.

Section 13.4 goes on to examine the Nobel-prize winning argument for incorporating a multiple group of non-correlated diversified return streams into a single portfolio that results in an improved risk-return profile. Using this premise of a multi-advisor platform, section 13.5 details the step-by-step process of customizing a program designed to suit an investor's needs as well as a system for monitoring the ongoing performance of the portfolio.

Finally, sections 13.6 and 13.7 delve into an in-depth examination of the performance characteristics of the two most popular schools of thought concerning trading. The relative performance for each style of trading is studied in each of the various market sectors, yielding some surprising results. Conclusions drawn from this type of analysis may well provide invaluable insights into arriving at an effective mix of traders in a multi-advisor portfolio.

13.2   BENEFITS OF INVESTING IN MANAGED FUTURES

The typically managed futures portfolio incorporates the services and trading strategies from one to several dozen individual commodity trading advisors (CTAs). The CTAs are professional money managers who are registered with the Commodity Futures and Trading Commission (CFTC), the governmental body in the USA that is responsible for overseeing the activities in the US futures markets. The major advantages for an investment in a multi-advisor managed futures product are as follows.

(1) **Diversification**. Managed futures provide investment diversification because of their low correlation with global stocks, bonds, real estate and venture capital. A multi-advisor fund offers further diversification because the assets of the fund are allocated to multiple CTAs who trade diversified markets using proprietary strategies.

(2) **Profitability in 'up' and 'down' markets**. Because the CTAs can trade futures on both the long and short sides of a market, profits can be generated irrespective of the direction of any particular market.

(3) **Professional trading management**. Investment decisions will be made by proven professionals who are actively engaged in futures trading.

(4) **Risk monitoring**. Refco has developed a set of risk management systems which will enable it to closely monitor the futures positions of each advisor on a daily basis.

(5) **Global investment**. Managed futures funds will allow investors to participate in the growth of the global markets.

(6) **Daily net asset value (NAV)**. The net asset value will be calculated on a daily basis based on the closing value of all positions.

(7) **Limited liability**. The careful selection of managers, the conservative use of leverage, and the employment of daily risk management systems are designed to limit the risk of managed futures funds and thereby protect the investor.

(8) **Cost**. Refco's managed futures funds have been designed with an institutional fee structure which will provide investors with a highly competitive cost structure.

13.3   MEASURES OF INVESTMENT AND RETURN

The measurement of performance of a CTA trading futures and options is an area that has received limited attention from the academic and practitioner. Refco has developed a comprehensive performance measurement system, which provides diagnostic analysis in addition to more traditional return review. The system has been developed to measure risk–return relationships and provides input to support the selection, monitoring and allocation decisions. The performance measurement tools outlined next are presented to demonstrate the quantitative and qualitative inputs recommended for a meaningful review of a CTA. The most difficult step in the model-building cycle is identification of significant information. This is because, although a number of general principles can be laid down, there exists no sure fire deterministic approach to the data analysis problem. Rather, it is necessary to exert a degree of judgement, the facility for which is greatly improved by experience.

13.3.1 Quantitative measures

Refco employs a variety of quantitative statistical measures of CTA performance as presented in the Refco Derivative Advisor Database. The various categories that are analysed include return statistics, recent returns, worst drawdowns, linear and scatter correlations and horizon analysis.

Return statistics
A primary variable is the monthly rate of return for a CTA. The time series of returns, $r_{i,t}$ for each CTA i, for month t, provides the source of data to compute the following.

Average rate of return for CTA i, $A_{[ri]}$. The average rate of return, also called the historical rate of return, is found for different intervals of time, one month, three months, six months, twelve months, two years, three years and five years. The analysis is done by linking together previous returns for all the consecutive holding periods. For example, with thirty-six months of return data we would generate thirty-four quarterly return numbers and twenty-five annual returns.

Standard deviation of returns for CTA i, $SD_{[ri]}$. The standard deviation is calculated on the linked returns for rolling periods of time corresponding to the calculation for the expected rate of return. As a statistical measure of volatility, the standard deviation of a CTA's returns provides a good tool to measure risk.

Sharpe ratio for CTA i, $SM_{[ri]}$. The Sharpe ratio provides a tool to measure the efficiency of a CTA. It is calculated by taking a CTA's actual return minus the risk-free T-Bill return and dividing the result by the standard deviation of the CTA's returns. The Sharpe ratio attempts to evaluate a CTA's performance by considering risk as well as returns and allows more level comparisons between CTAs with vastly different returns and/or risk profiles. A value of 1.0 on an annual basis is considered very good.

Gain statistics for CTA i {average, max, min, SD}. The gain statistics are also useful in addressing the risk of a CTA. Upside volatility is weighted lower than downside volatility such that a CTA will not be penalized for 'making too much money'. This distinction is especially important in light of the fact that the standard deviation measure makes no distinction between upside and downside volatility and, thus, unfairly penalizes traders who perform exceedingly well. The distribution of the period of times the CTA gains money also serves as a meaningful tool to define rebalance decisions.

Loss statistics for CTA i {average, max, min, SD}. The loss statistics are useful in addressing the risk of a CTA. Downside volatility is especially important in the evaluation of the risk of a CTA and is a vital supplement to the standard deviation measure. The distribution of the period of times a CTA loses money is also a meaningful tool to define rebalance decisions.

Distribution percentage of up/down periods. The percentage of one-month, three-month, six-month or twelve-month periods in which a CTA is up or down is also a good measure for the consistency of a CTA over time.

Recent returns

The recent returns is an important tool both in the analysis of the quality of a CTA as well as being invaluable in defining rebalancing decisions. The longer-term returns over the past twelve-month, eighteen-month, twenty-four-month, and thirty-six-month periods can be useful in identifying different types of CTAs that are more likely to generate above average returns in the future. The shorter-term returns over the past one-month, three-month, six-month and twelve-month periods are used primarily in the rebalancing decisions.

Improving CTAs. The CTAs that have improved their returns without increasing their risk or have maintained their returns while lowering volatility would be looked upon more favourably. This would be especially true if the CTA employs a computerized technical system, as this would suggest that the recent improvements in performance will more likely be an ongoing phenomenon.

Cyclical/seasonal CTAs. The CTAs that have demonstrated a pattern in their past track record to be either cyclical or seasonal may, at a given point in time, provide a greater probability to produce above-average returns. An example of this type of situation would be identifying a grain specialist that produced exceptional results due to a severe drought some five years ago followed by mediocre performance over the next few years. Due to the cyclical nature of weather patterns, the CTA may offer better risk–reward statistics in the short term than his average returns, standard deviation and Sharpe ratio may suggest.

Impact of growth and/or extraordinary circumstances. The CTAs recent returns may be reflective of internal changes that might be worth considering in the allocation process. For example, poor recent returns in contrast to a good previous track record may indicate that the CTA may be taking on too much money and the burden of the new administrative work may be affecting his trading. Likewise, the CTA may be undergoing some difficult times in his personal life, such as a divorce or death in the family, that may be affecting his trading. CTAs who are running small operations consisting of only one or two employees may also be affected if the principal is frequently travelling in an attempt to raise new capital.

Worst drawdowns

Drawdowns are measured as the percentage decline from the peak to the valley with the duration measured by the time from the initial decline to the establishment of a new high. Analysis of a CTA's worst drawdowns is an extremely useful tool in the evaluation of a CTA's risk and can also be helpful in rebalancing decisions.

Magnitude of drawdowns. The magnitude of drawdowns is the most commonly used criteria in assessing the downside risk of a CTA. Refco routinely analyses the four largest drawdown periods for each CTA in an effort to assess what the worst case scenario for each CTA would be and whether the fund–client will be able to tolerate such a scenario.

Duration of worst drawdowns. The duration of drawdown periods, in conjunction with the magnitude of the decline, is very helpful in determining the suitability of a CTA given the goals and constraints of a fund.

Length of recovery time. The length of time a CTA takes to emerge from drawdown periods is also an important criteria in determining client suitability. A consistently short recovery period from drawdowns will be preferable to CTAs who languish incessantly after difficult trading periods.

Disparity between largest drawdowns. CTAs whose largest drawdowns vary significantly from one another generally hold less predictive power than CTAs with consistent drawdowns. Technical traders with historical drawdowns in similar ranges tend to have the most predictable downside risk. On the other hand, discretionary CTAs, especially ones with large disparities between historical drawdowns, are generally less defined with regards to downside risk. Caution must be exercised with some of these CTAs in that the single largest drawdown may have been caused by the CTA being over-leveraged during a drawdown in a futile attempt to make up the previous losses.

Proven history of drawdown recoveries. CTAs with long track records complete with numerous drawdowns and subsequent recoveries may be especially useful in the reallocation decision process. The risk–reward ratios for such CTAs are typically more favourable while they are in the midst of a drawdown and are likewise less attractive after a prolonged period of superior performance. Decisions with regards to rebalancing should properly address the timing for such CTAs.

Linear and scatter correlation

Linear correlation coefficient. The calculation of correlation of the CTAs' returns with other CTAs and benchmarks provide insight to diversification of returns and subsequently the reduction of risk. The linear correlation coefficient measures the degree of relationship between two series of returns, with the results being any value between −1 and 1. The closer the value is to 1, the more related the two series of returns, and the more predictive one series is to the other. Similarly, the closer the value is to −1, the more the two series are diametrically opposite and would also be predictive of each other. A value around 0 means that the two series are unrelated and the returns of one series hold no predictive value in the returns of the other. In accordance with modern portfolio theory, significant reductions in volatility can be achieved by combining negatively correlated CTAs in a fund, significant reductions in volatility can be achieved.

While linear correlation coefficients are extremely useful in portfolio allocation and combining CTAs with the goal of minimizing volatility, there are some limitations to using them in evaluating CTAs. The main problem with the linear correlation coefficient is that in the search for negatively correlated investments, the important fact that negative correlation is not necessarily good and positive correlation is not necessarily bad was lost. For example, if the client has already invested with CTA A and is searching for a second CTA (CTA B), then a linear measurement does not differentiate between desirable negative correlation (e.g. CTA B is up when CTA A is down) and undesirable negative correlation (e.g. CTA B is down when CTA A is up). Furthermore, although the linear measurement does properly penalize undesirable positive correlation (e.g. CTA B is down when CTA A is down), it also wrongly penalizes desirable positive correlation (e.g. CTA B is up when CTA A is up).

Scatter correlation graphs. Scatter correlation graphs provide a terrific supplement to simple linear correlation coefficient values. Assuming that the client already has exposure to a benchmark index or is invested in a CTA (CTA A), and is looking to add a CTA B, the scatter correlation graph provides invaluable information. By graphing the distribution of returns for CTA A against those of CTA B, a clear picture of CTA B's suitability with CTA A develops. It is desirable if CTA B's returns are positive when CTA A is down (negative correlation) as it is if CTA B's returns are positive when CTA A is up (positive correlation). Overall, a desirable scatter correlation graph would be in the general shape of an upward sloping parabola consisting of negative correlation on the left half of the graph and positive correlation on the right half of the graph.

Horizon analysis

Interval returns analysis. Horizon analysis reviews returns over intervals of various length, (one month, three months, six months, twelve months, etc.) to assess the momentum of a CTA. The rebalance decisions are aided by this tool. However, caution must be taken in assessing the relative impact of the most recent month's effect on the average versus the back month that is being dropped. Often a large drop in the average horizon is the result of dropping a spectacular month rather than the addition of an extremely poor month, and interpretations that a CTA may be losing momentum may be premature. Rather, this reallocation tool is most useful when viewed from a number of different intervals to arrive at a more precise consensus of which direction a CTA has a greater probability of heading towards in the future.

13.3.2 Qualitative measures

While the use of quantitative statistical analysis is important in the CTA selection process, Refco also arranges numerous personal meetings with the CTAs themselves in their offices, at Refco's offices or during industry conferences. Refco believes that the qualitative due diligence trips are tremendously important in determining whether the CTAs being considered are likely to be able to duplicate past results in the future. Refco considers factors such as trading style, key personnel, depth and quality of organization, research, execution, cost and credibility to be relevant factors in the evaluation of a CTA.

Trading style. Perhaps the most significant qualitative distinction is that of trading style. It is important that there is diversification by trading style as well as having mathematically non-correlated CTAs. The categories which are generally considered include technical versus fundamental, systematic versus discretionary, diversified versus specialized, and short- versus intermediate- and long-term.

(1) Technical versus fundamental. These classifications relate to how a CTA makes trading decisions, i.e. what things are important to the CTA's decisions. Technical analysis is based on the study of the markets themselves in order to provide a means of anticipating future prices. Technical analysis of markets often includes a study of the actual daily, weekly and monthly price volume and open interest data

and price pattern data. Charts and/or computers are often used for the analysis of these items. Sentiment indicators, such as call-to-put ratios and relative strength, are also technical analysis instruments. Fundamental analysis is based on the study of the commodity itself. Fundamental analysis looks at the external factors that affect the supply and demand of a particular commodity in order to predict future prices. Items such as government actions, the release of information concerning weather conditions or the release of statistical information which result in probable or actual significant price movements are considered. Many CTAs use a combination of technical and fundamental analysis. These CTAs usually use fundamental analysis to determine the general direction of a given commodity and then use technical analysis for entry and exit.

(2) Systematic versus discretionary. These classifications relate to how a CTA executes trading decisions. If the CTA executes a trade based on a system signal (usually a computer system) we categorize the CTA as a systems trader. To a certain degree, the CTA has eliminated discretion from trading decisions. A discretionary CTA makes trading decisions with the use of human input and emotions. Personal experiences are used to make and execute trading decision but some sort of computer system may be employed as well. The key in this case is that the CTA may or may not, with almost equal probability, follow the signals being generated by the 'system'. A CTA who primarily relies on a system but very infrequently overrides the system's signals is systematic/discretionary.

(3) Diversified versus specialized. This classification relates to which markets a CTA will trade. Diversified indicates that the CTA may trade a wide variety of futures contracts. For the most part, this type of CTA will purposely diversify a portfolio of futures contracts and options to reduce non-systematic risk. In most cases, a CTA who trades a diversified portfolio relies primarily on technical analysis. Specialized indicates that the CTA will trade a narrow group of futures contracts. CTAs in this category are most often arbitrage or tactical managers. The futures management programs often involve some sort of arbitrage technique.

(4) Short- versus intermediate- and long-term. This classification refers to the typical duration of a CTA's trades. The average duration for a short-term trader ranges from one day to perhaps one week. CTAs with a short-term horizon tend to be much more active. While the risk exposure of the client's capital tends to be minimized due to the short-term exposure to possible market fluctuations, transaction costs become more significant to the CTA. The average duration for an intermediate-term trader ranges from one to two weeks to three to six months. Additional market risks are usually present for such CTAs, however the impact of transaction costs tend not to be as great as for

short-term CTAs. The average duration for a long-term trader ranges from over a month to up to several years. Because of the longer time horizon, these CTAs are exposed to the greatest market risks but the additional risk is somewhat offset by the generally lower transaction costs.

(5) Key personnel. An important consideration with the selection process is the experience and education of the key personnel of the organization. Much information can be gathered through interviews with the head trader or the system designer and a good idea of how the trader/system would handle various potential market situations can be obtained. Additional care must be taken in selecting CTAs that place a heavy reliance on one or two key principals, especially if trading decisions are discretionary rather than systematic.

(6) Organization. The depth and quality of a CTA's organization is also important in assessing reliability. The importance of having a good support staff capable of handling the administration, marketing and other non-trading aspects of a business cannot be overstated. Again, caution must be taken in selecting CTAs who must perform all the operational functions in addition to trading, especially if trading decisions are discretionary rather than systematic. Furthermore, special attention needs to be paid to emerging CTAs who have taken on significant amounts of new funds, as the sudden increase in administrative work often leads to a deterioration in performance.

(7) Research. While CTAs with proven track records convey a greater sense of security and are more attractive to investors, those CTAs who show a genuine interest in making improvements to their trading models or markets should be particularly noted. Because markets are in a state of constant change, methods that proved to be successful in the past may not be applicable in trading environments in the future. CTAs who recognize and emphasize the need for additional research should have a higher probability for success in the future.

(8) Execution. The quality of a CTA's execution broker and order flow system can be a factor, especially during turbulent markets when poor execution could potentially lead to large losses.

(9) Cost. The CTA's fees for managing client funds is also a consideration in that excessively high fees reduce the client's chances for profitability. Similarly, excessively high commissions and/or a high number of transactions by the CTA can severely detract from the returns for the client.

(10) Credibility. The most subjective of all the qualitative measures, the question of the CTA's credibility and trustworthiness can be taken into account as a final screen before the final allocations. Previous negative experiences with the CTA and/or information gathered from reliable sources that may suggest a high probability of impropriety by the CTA could be a factor in the final allocation decision.

13.4   MODERN PORTFOLIO THEORY

Modern portfolio theory was introduced in 1952 and tells how to maximize returns while minimizing risk. The foundation for this theory rests on the conviction that investors be concerned *only* with expected returns and risks of portfolios, *not* with individual investments, with the underlying assumption that all investors are risk-averse. The theory emphasizes the formation of portfolios that are sufficiently diversified so that no other portfolio has:

(1)   the same expected return with lower expected risk
(2)   the same expected risk with higher expected return.

Historical data is used in screening potential investments to be included in the portfolio building process, hereafter called 'optimization'. By combining investments with low or negative correlation coefficients, substantial reductions in expected risk levels are attainable. The initial choice of investments may consider many factors other than historical returns. This may include, but is not limited to, qualitative factors such as key personnel, organization, research, execution and cost. While these covert factors are frequently overlooked and are not considered in the basic model, Refco employs them as qualitative inputs to its model.

Keeping the foregoing factors in mind, one may proceed to the first step; construction of the efficient frontier. The efficient frontier is constructed through a mathematical algorithm utilizing:

(1)   the weights of individual assets
(2)   the expected returns of individual assets
(3)   the variance of assets
(4)   the covariance between assets.

Points of expected risk return levels are the result and represent all possible combinations of the assets in the portfolio that are of maximum efficiency. An expected risk versus expected return graph may be plotted to accompany this resulting set of data. The frontier provides the investor with the ability to select any point along the frontier that is equal to, or greater than the minimum variance portfolio.

Selection of the appropriate point (a mix of assets) is the second step and is based on the personal risk preferences that satisfy the investor – where expected risk is lowest and expected return is highest. The final allocations will be based on the investor's decisions with regards to returns expectations and/or risk tolerances.

13.4.1   Diversification

Integrating multiple CTAs. The typical institutionally managed futures fund is structured to combine multiple CTAs. It has been determined that the benefits of the multiple-advisor fund exceed the greater expenses of the structure. The single-advisor account will usually have lower costs for two reasons:

(1) CTAs will charge less for larger accounts
(2) the operating costs such as accounting and custodial expenses are for only one account.

The multiple-advisor structure is significantly more attractive for the following three reasons:

(1) Specialization. A multiple-advisor fund allows the inclusion of CTAs that specialize in market segments such as currencies, agriculturals, financials or metals.
(2) Diversification of styles. Also called 'process diversification', the diversification of the investment decision tools is highly recommended. Since each CTA's approach is susceptible to being incorrect in its assessment of the markets, a commitment to a single CTA increases the concerns regarding the results of the total fund should the CTA perform poorly. To reduce this exposure, it is advantageous to diversify among several conceptually appealing but different approaches. Typical classifications of CTAs by process would be whether the CTAs are systematic/discretionary or employ fundamental/technical inputs.
(3) Diversification of markets. The multi-advisor format allows more CTAs to participate in more markets using different approaches. A major benefit of multiple CTAs trading multiple markets rests with the fact that most CTAs tend to carry larger positions in the same direction during trending markets and smaller positions in different directions during choppy markets. Hence, profits tend to be maximized and losses minimized when the multi-advisor approach trading in different markets is adopted.

13.5 OVERVIEW OF CREATING A MANAGED FUTURES PROGRAM

13.5.1 Selection and allocation process

The objective of the selection and allocation process is to determine the most efficient allocation of the fund's assets among the multiple CTAs who will achieve the risk/return parameters set for the fund. This process determines the appropriate percentage of the fund's assets to allocate to each CTA, in order to produce the lowest overall volatility for a given rate of return. In addition to historical data, the procedure makes use of the data generated by the performance measurement tools as applied to the monitoring of specific CTAs and qualitative factors such as key personnel, organization, research, execution, cost and credibility. The design for a group of CTAs should follow the following algorithm.

Target return. Select a target return level or range for the fund.

Minimum criteria. Select minimum screening criteria for all CTAs: dollars under management, years of experience, registration, depth of organization, institutional clients, minimum return, largest acceptable drawdown, Sharpe ratio, etc.

Diversification requirements. Select diversification requirements for the fund (minimum and maximum exposure by market segment, contract, CTA or trading style).

Database search. Screen the database for CTAs who fulfill the minimum criteria.

Qualitative inputs. Considerations of qualitative factors are used to either screen out certain CTAs or add other CTAs who may not have qualified under a certain screen that extenuating circumstances may deem the CTA to be a viable choice.

Correlation study. Calculate coefficients of correlation on both a monthly and quarterly basis to identify a diversified and non-correlated group of CTAs.

Optimization. The EnCORR/analyser and optimizer completes the process by determining the optimal allocation for the chosen group of CTAs.

13.5.2   Monitoring and management process

The process of selecting CTAs and allocating assets among them is crucial to the design of the fund, but there are two further tasks that are equally as important:

(1) monitoring the fund
(2) actively managing each CTA.

Before being included in the fund, each CTA is assigned certain parameters based upon his or her historical returns. These parameters are generated from the distribution of the monthly losses and the distribution of monthly gains. It is based upon these parameters that Refco will first monitor the CTAs and then, when required, actively manage each CTA's role in the fund.

The monitoring process involves the collection of data as generated by the daily performance measurement system reports. If any material changes occur in the CTA's system which exceed the defined parameters, the management process immediately ensues. The managing process will include the following.

Drawdown/stop loss. Reduce/eliminate a CTA's allocation if the CTA's NAV declines to a pre-defined stop-loss point.

Exceptional performance. Reduce a CTA's allocation if the performance rises beyond a pre-defined strike point (account momentum is unsustainable).

Changes in group correlation. Increase/decrease a CTA's allocation based on significant changes in the correlation between group correlation.

Maintenance of desired risk–reward ratio. Add CTAs when necessary to maintain the desired risk–reward ratio. This will require an on-going process of identifying and analysing new CTAs both in the US as well as overseas CTAs. Currently, the Refco derivative advisor database monitors over 550 programs.

13.6   COMMODITY TRADING ADVISORS

Although there are over 2500 registered CTAs currently, perhaps only around 1000 are active. As a means of tracking the universe of CTAs who can be considered for possible allocations in a portfolio, the Refco derivative advisor database maintains and updates the performance histories of approximately 550 individual CTA programs. Despite the relative diversity amongst the CTA universe with regards to the combination of different trading styles and strategies as well as the markets being traded, two major broad classifications can be made on the group as a whole.

Trading styles. There are two major schools of thought as to how CTAs should approach their decision-making process – systematic versus discretionary. The premise behind the systematic approach is that the key to successful trading lies not only in having good trading rules and strategies, but, more importantly, in being able to eliminate the human emotions that often lead to many traders' downfalls. Most systematic traders tend also to be highly computerized and utilize mostly technical indicators, which are much better suited for inputs that can be analysed by computers. On the other hand, discretionary traders believe that successful results are generated from trading skills and that the ability to make decisions that make common sense more than offset the possible disadvantages of human emotion. Discretionary traders tend to be more varied in their decision-making inputs in that while most rely predominantly on their fundamental views of the markets, they also tend to employ a variety of technical indicators for timing entry and exit points.

Markets traded. In classifying the universe of CTAs, the second major distinction that can be made is in the markets that are being traded. Refco's classification scheme generally breaks down the CTAs into groups that include diversified, agricultural, energy, equity, financial, foreign exchange, interest rate, metal, softs and stock index. Generally, CTAs are considered to be diversified if they are trading markets from both the commodity (agricultural, energy, metal and softs) as well as the financial (foreign exchange, interest rate and stock index) sectors. Financial traders are, thus, CTAs who trade in two or all three areas of the financial sector.

13.7   SYSTEMATIC VERSUS DISCRETIONARY TRADERS

The debate over the relative merits of the two contrasting methodologies produces an array of management preferences for asset allocators. Based on the latest data from the Refco derivative advisor database using data from the past five years ending in March 1996, systematic traders account for approximately 71 per cent of all the trading programs while discretionary programs make up only 26 per cent of the total, with the remaining 3 per cent considering their programs a 50/50 mix of the two approaches. Furthermore, over 80 per cent of the total assets are invested with the systematic programs, whereas only 19 per cent are placed with discretionary traders. The reasons behind the seemingly higher popularity of the systematic programs can be explained by three major factors.

Absence of large discretionary traders. While systematic traders are typically managing more assets than their discretionary counterparts, the few successful discretionary 'stars' such as Paul Tudor Jones and Louis Bacon, accumulate tremendous assets and become closed to new investments. As a result, these large traders stop providing information to databases and are not represented in the overall statistics.

Longevity of systematic traders. Because the systematic traders are able to encode their methodologies into computers, they enjoy a tremendous advantage over their discretionary counterparts in longevity. Since the systematic approach is much more conducive to a company's continued existence, the vast majority of programs that have existed for more than one or two decades are systematic, even though the original developers of the systems may or may not still be active in the company. While discretionary traders can maintain excellence over time periods of as long as several years, it is very unusual to find consistently successful discretionary traders over longer periods of ten or twenty years. Often, the continuing high demands placed on the discretionary traders wears them down over time, leading to either poorer performance and/or the retirement from the business. Thus, in the absence of effective means of transferring their skills, the business lifespans of discretionary traders tend to be far shorter than those of their systematic counterparts.

Preferences of large asset allocators. Due to their more substantial assets under management, the longer track records, as well as their more readily quantifiable approaches, larger asset allocators tend to favour systematic traders. As a result, systematic programs receive more assets under management, which makes them more attractive candidates for further allocations, and the overall group thus grows even larger versus their discretionary traders.

Performance comparisons. The performance summaries in Tables 13.1 to 13.11 illustrate the differences between systematic and discretionary traders in each of the respective market sectors, where a number of fascinating truisms seem to surface.

Total of all traders. Perhaps the single most surprising result of the comparison between systematic and discretionary programs is highlighted by the statistics from Table 13.1. While the systematic traders have produced a very respectable average annual return of 13.43 per cent with an average annual standard deviation of 12.79 per cent, the discretionary programs have been able to achieve similar returns at 13.94 per cent but with much lower volatility at 6.06 per cent average annual standard deviation. Consequently, the Sharpe ratio for the discretionary traders is more than twice that for the systematic programs (1.62 versus 0.73). The historical worst drawdown statistic is even more impressive, with the discretionary traders enjoying over a 3:1 edge over the systematic group (3.73 per cent versus 11.70 per cent). The shocking aspect is that despite poorer performance from both an absolute and especially volatility adjusted basis, systematic traders have been able to maintain a dominant position in the overall industry in terms of both number of traders as well as assets under management.

Diversified traders. Keeping in mind the vastly superior results displayed by the discretionary traders when compared to the systematic group in the overall results, the data from Table 13.2 may appear to be inconsistent. In stark contrast to the total results, an evaluation of diversified programs shows

Table 13.1 *Systematic versus discretionary programs*

TOTAL	Systematic	50/50 Sys/disc	Discretionary
Number	384	14	143
Assets (millions)	13 067	123	2977
Average 12M ROR	13.43	9.20	13.94
Average 12M STD	12.79	9.72	6.06
12M Sharpe ratio	0.73	0.52	1.62
Worst drawdown	(11.70)	(19.19)	(3.73)

Table 13.2   *Diversified sector*

DIVERSIFIED	Systematic	50/50 Sys/disc	Discretionary
Number	181	7	44
Assets (millions)	3918	82	487
Average 12M ROR	16.14	6.11	9.59
Average 12M STD	9.26	16.00	10.11
12M Sharpe ratio	1.30	0.13	0.54
Worst drawdown	(16.54)	(28.04)	(14.59)

that the systematic traders have fared far better than their discretionary counterparts. Due to the much higher average annual return of 16.14 per cent versus 9.59 per cent with similar average annual standard deviation of 9.26 per cent versus 10.11 per cent, the systematic group's Sharpe ratio is a much higher 1.30 versus 0.54 for the discretionary traders. While this result may seem surprising at first glance, a closer examination of the possible reasons behind this discrepancy unveils a solid explanation. Since diversified traders tend to be involved with so many different markets, a computerized systematic approach may well be the most effective trading style. On the other hand, it is extremely difficult for discretionary traders to keep track of and be profitable in trading a diversified portfolio, whereas they experience much more success when their focus is narrowed to trading specific sectors.

Agricultural traders (see Table 13.3). Discretionary traders dominate this sector, the most traditional of all the commodity markets. While most of the diversified programs also trade the agricultural markets systematically, a pure systems-based program trading only in agriculture is very rare and usually not terribly successful. Since these markets often react to fundamental factors such as weather conditions and crop reports, discretionary traders that tend

Table 13.3   *Agricultural sector*

AGRICULTURAL	Systematic	50/50 Sys/disc	Discretionary
Number	1		18
Assets (millions)	0		201
Average 12M ROR	9.23		9.14
Average 12M STD	23.76		6.33
12M Sharpe ratio	0.21		0.79
Worst drawdown	(39.62)		(14.29)

Table 13.4 *Energy sector*

ENERGY	Systematic	50/50 Sys/disc	Discretionary
Number	2		2
Assets (millions)	12		15
Average 12M ROR	17.13		7.70
Average 12M STD	20.43		13.82
12M Sharpe ratio	0.63		0.26
Worst drawdown	(20.86)		(19.62)

to employ mainly fundamental information in making their trading decisions are typically the most successful.

Energy traders. One may expect that markets in the energy sector may be more amenable to discretionary traders due to the nature of oil prices being influenced by fundamental factors such as weather patterns, OPEC policies, and political and military developments in the Middle East. While this may not seem to be the case in light of the scarcity of energy specialists in Table 13.4, there are some prominent traders such as Willem Kookyer from Blenheim whose roots can be traced back to the energy sector. However, there are very few pure energy specialists remaining currently and this small sample size makes the statistics from Table 13.4 not very meaningful.

Equity traders (see Table 13.5). As equity managers are not a major portion of the universe that Refco tracks, the statistical significance of this huge sector is low due to the small sample size. Furthermore, the data is further skewed by the fact that a number of the large systematic traders that are tracked by Refco employ non-directional long/short equity programs, which tend to be much less volatile than the directional equity portfolios.

Financial traders (see Table 13.6). Due to the tendencies for financial markets to be influenced by significantly more variables than the commodity

Table 13.5 *Equity sector*

EQUITY	Systematic	50/50 Sys/disc	Discretionary
Number	11	2	24
Assets (millions)	959	24	891
Average 12M ROR	9.20	19.20	18.11
Average 12M STD	5.37	8.29	14.50
12M Sharpe ratio	0.95	1.80	0.97
Worst drawdown	(2.31)	(4.35)	(20.02)

Table 13.6   *Financial sector*

FINANCIAL	Systematic	50/50 Sys/disc	Discretionary
Number	77	4	20
Assets (millions)	3220	9	523
Average 12M ROR	13.17	11.11	9.40
Average 12M STD	14.37	13.87	5.45
12M Sharpe ratio	0.63	0.51	0.97
Worst drawdown	(15.77)	(16.41)	(4.57)

markets, the use of technical inputs tends to be more popular than fundamental analysis. Consequently, over 75 per cent of the traders in this sector employ a systematic approach, managing over 85 per cent of the assets. However, in sharp contrast to the diversified sector (where systematic traders handily outperformed their discretionary peers), the differences in the financial sector are much more subtle. While systematic programs did manage a higher return (13.17 per cent versus 9.40 per cent), this did come at a cost of much higher volatility (14.37 per cent versus 5.45 per cent), resulting in a poorer risk-adjusted return as measured by the Sharpe ratio (0.63 versus 0.97). The worst drawdown was also considerably higher at 15.77 per cent versus an impressive 4.57 per cent for the discretionary group. One of the main reasons for this relatively unimpressive performance by the systematic group can be attributed to the very difficult trading conditions in the foreign exchange sector over the past four years.

Foreign exchange traders (see Table 13.7). Another sector that has been dominated historically by systematic traders, the past few years have been very trying times in the new low volatility environment. The volatility for the systematic programs has been equivalent to that of the discretionary traders (21.69 per cent versus 23.99 per cent) and the worst drawdowns have been

Table 13.7   *Foreign exchange sector*

FOREIGN EXCHANGE	Systematic	50/50 Sys/disc	Discretionary
Number	52		21
Assets (millions)	3958		655
Average 12M ROR	11.59		29.53
Average 12M STD	21.69		23.99
12M Sharpe ratio	0.35		1.06
Worst drawdown	(21.59)		(21.13)

Table 13.8 *Interest rate sector*

INTEREST RATE	Systematic	50/50 Sys/disc	Discretionary
Number	22		5
Assets (millions)	779		173
Average 12M ROR	13.14		10.36
Average 12M STD	2.57		7.15
12M Sharpe ratio	3.52		0.87
Worst drawdown	(0.39)		(12.72)

very similar as well (21.59 per cent versus 21.13 per cent). However, the big difference between the two groups lies in the raw returns that have been generated, with the discretionary group faring far better with an average annual return of 29.53 per cent as compared to the systematic group's 11.59 per cent, resulting in a much higher Sharpe ratio of 1.06 versus 0.35. Since the mid-1980s into the early 1990s, the favourable trending conditions in the FX markets generated significant profits for a large number of the systematic traders, spawning dozens of new currency programs. Given the performance results over the past five years and if the current environment persists, it appears that discretionary methods may well be better suited to currency trading.

Interest rate traders (see Table 13.8). On the surface, it appears that systematic traders have achieved incredibly good returns (13.14 per cent) with very little volatility (2.57 per cent), resulting in a stratospheric Sharpe ratio of 3.52 and a practically non-existent worst drawdown of 0.39 per cent. However, this result is very skewed in that around 90 per cent of the assets in the systematic interest rate sector is managed by three very low-risk, yield enhancement firms. Hence, even though it appears that the results appear to be reasonably sound statistically with twenty-two traders in this category, the fact is that the dollar-weighting method unfortunately reduces this group to little more than an index for the three yield enhancement firms.

Metal traders. As can be seen clearly from Table 13.9, not very many traders are focused exclusively on the metal sector. Hence, any comparison between the systematic and discretionary programs in this sector will not be very meaningful.

Softs traders (see Table 13.10). Similar to the energy and metal sectors, the softs group does not contain sufficient members in order to provide a meaningful analysis between the systematic and discretionary programs.

Stock index traders (see Table 13.11). Unlike the equity sector in which there are more than twice as many discretionary as systematic traders, the stock index group is predominantly systems based by a ratio of nearly 6:1.

Table 13.9   *Metal sector*

METAL	Systematic	50/50 Sys/disc	Discretionary
Number	2		1
Assets (millions)	7		0
Average 12M ROR	11.64		45.73
Average 12M STD	8.82		16.39
12M Sharpe ratio	0.85		2.44
Worst drawdown	(9.60)		(17.92)

Table 13.10   *Softs sector*

SOFTS	Systematic	50/50 Sys/disc	Discretionary
Number	1		2
Assets (millions)	11		2
Average 12M ROR	28.35		21.05
Average 12M STD	26.60		29.78
12M Sharpe ratio	0.91		0.56
Worst drawdown	(26.99)		(15.01)

Table 13.11   *Stock index sector*

STOCK INDEX	Systematic	50/50 Sys/disc	Discretionary
Number	35		6
Assets (millions)	204		29
Average 12M ROR	12.20		3.69
Average 12M STD	8.72		22.60
12M Sharpe ratio	0.93		(0.02)
Worst drawdown	(11.88)		(43.94)

Judging from the vastly superior results over the data period, it is quite easy to understand why such a discrepancy in popularity exists. Though the sample size is rather small with only six programs, the most likely explanation for the discretionary group's dismal results can be attributed to the relentless rise in the US stock market and the very tempting discretionary tendency to want to short the market.

13.8   CONCLUSIONS

Drawing from the observations made in the aforementioned study between systematic and discretionary traders, some generalizations can be reached that could prove to be extremely valuable in the construction of a diversified portfolio of CTAs. Even though the managed futures industry appears to be dominated by systematic traders, a strong case can certainly be made for the inclusion of a number of discretionary advisors in a diversified portfolio, especially in the agricultural, currency and financial sectors. Of course, systematic traders will still play a very prominent role in the allocation mix, not only as core CTAs in the diversified category but also at some sectors such as stock index, interest rate or even in financial or foreign exchange.

The type of information generated from this type of analysis is only one of the many variables that enables asset allocators to make better decisions. As expressed in the previous sections, numerous quantitative and qualitative factors still need to be carefully examined prior to the actual hiring of the advisors. Nevertheless, the statistics on the performance differences between systematic versus discretionary CTAs are tremendously useful when used in conjunction with the other more traditional measurements of advisor results.

Chapter 14

BAREP futures funds

DAVID OBERT AND EDOUARD PETITDIDIER*

14.1 INTRODUCTION

BAREP (Banque de Réescompte et de Placement), a French bank and a fully owned subsidiary of SOCIETE GENERALE, has an asset management structure, which creates, markets and manages a full range of products and services provided to clients.

This structure has developed a futures funds' asset management based on two leading concepts:

(1) Technical systematic asset management, with investment strategies based on models of historical behaviour in futures markets.
(2) Concentration of the decision-making process within the BAREP management team acting as its own commodity trading advisor (CTA).

Section 14.2 of the chapter is an introduction of BAREP's specific approach, with a presentation of its organization and its advantages.

Section 14.3 seeks to explain precisely BAREP's management and techniques used to trade futures: the systematic, the technical analyses and the trading horizon.

Section 14.4 speaks about money management with asset allocation and leverage policies.

Finally, sections 14.5 and 14.6 describe BAREP's funds performance over the last two years.

14.2 BAREP'S ORGANIZATION

BAREP decided to concentrate all the necessary competencies and skills inside the bank, in terms of research, development, management, presence on the markets and back office. Today, this strategy is clearly justified, although

---

* This chapter was written while the authors were at BAREP Asset Management.

it requires the use of significant technical and intellectual resources. Finally, this method presents a lot of advantages in terms of security and coherence.

14.2.1 The organization

BAREP implements important human means in order to dispose of a total management independence (Figure 14.1). This team consists of three principal poles, each concerned with different competence fields.

The research and fund management team is in charge of operational finance research and the daily life of the funds, that is:

(1) database maintenance with the quotation on all markets
(2) execution of the orders on all markets
(3) creation of new trading models (conception, data processing)
(4) implementation of tests to measure the efficiency of models in the past from a risk-reward point of view
(5) measurement of the robustness and quantification of the models' stability in the long run
(6) following up on the different strategies
(7) setting up and following up on the asset allocation strategy.

Because markets are always changing, the team always tries to improve existing strategies and procedures as well as find totally new ways to make money.

The data-processing team is in charge of data-processing developments during all stages of the project, which are the creation, the setting up and the following up, without any subcontracting.

The main executions are:

(1) reliable tool to test all trading strategies
(2) an operational instrument allowing the managers to deal in excellent and secure conditions on more than 600 strategies and 30 markets
(3) real time screen to follow up each fund value, results by markets and by strategy
(4) home-made computerized system for the back office positions enabling us to value all the instruments of the funds (futures, cash, exchange swap).

The back office team is in charge of all administrative operations concerning the funds, especially

(1) control of the orders on futures markets
(2) management of credit transfers (margin calls)
(3) administration of all monetary instruments used by the funds
(4) control and follow up of the net asset values calculated by an external company.

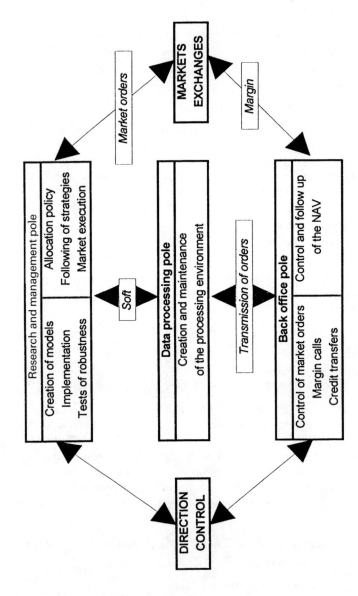

Figure 14.1 *BAREP's organization*

The interconnection between the three teams is very important because the setting up of the whole structure has been conceived from a very coherent point of view. This organization allows us to develop swiftly but harmoniously at the same time.

14.2.2 Advantages

Position taking and asset allocation are integrated and assure us of a permanent control of all management aspects. The risk-return ratio is managed on a whole portfolio scale, that allows us to reduce eventual hedge costs and to optimise yield.

An integrated approach to management allows us to apply the principle of transparency: the investor is able to take his or her investment decision with very objective parameters regarding the risk/return ratio.

Principles of management are defined and tested since the beginning; their pertinence is regularly checked to allow steadiness of performance.

All the characteristics of the decision process, in terms of model selection or asset allocation, are rational. Human factors regarding the specific state of mind of each manager are not taken into account in the management method chosen by BAREP. The quality of methods has been tested and is independent from all modification of our managers' states of mind.

The performance of management is improved by the absence of intermediaries. In-house asset management provides investors with an attractive performance which is not eroded by profit sharing with external partners.

The liability of all administrative operations is secured by the action of fimat, broker of the SOCIETE GENERALE Group, and the first world's leading broker on futures markets.

This type of investment has to be considered with a medium-term point of view. This length of time period enables investors to benefit from the exceptional yield of these markets.

14.3 TRADING CONCEPTS

BAREP follows three principle trading concepts. First, our trading is systematic with decisions made on a computer system and no use of human inputs and emotions. Then, we make our decisions with technical trading strategies and we computerize them in order to test their robustness and to study their risk-return ratio. Finally, we try to have short-term horizons as well as long-term horizons.

14.3.1   Systematic

This type of management is based on the setting up of a formal trading organization. The managers create models that allow them to take a position with a precise timing and at a defined buy–sell level. The managers are not free to interpret the signals before executing the orders in the market; their action is concentrated on the follow-up of performance and the improvement of models.

Systematic management requires a significant study and development period in order to set up the trading models. The structure of the organization and the rigour of the decision-taking process assure the managers of the permanence of the methods used. The trading strategies contribute to efficient daily management and allow the manager to extract him or herself from the day-to-day administration.

Futures markets have been studied very precisely by the asset managers, in terms of evolution, liquidity and volume, in order to understand their characteristics and choose the most efficient and liquid ones.

We intervene simultaneously on the main principal futures markets in Europe, the USA and Asia, and on more than 45 different markets:

(1) long interest rates: Notionnal, Bund, Gilt, BTP, Bonos, JGB, Tbond, Tnote5y, TNote10y, CGB
(2) short interest rates: Pibor, Euro DM, Short £, Euro ITL, EuroUSD
(3) currencies: USD/DEM, USD/GBP, USD/CHF, USD/JPY, USD/CAD, USD/AUD, DEM/JPY, GBP/DEM, DEM/ITL
(4) Stock indices : CAC, Dax, Footsie, Nikkei, S&P 500
(5) commodities: crude oil, natural gas, heating oil, NY harbour gasoline, sugar, coffee, cacao, gold, silver, copper, corn, wheat, soybean, soybean oil, soybean meal, live cattle.

Each day, the database is updated with the quotes from all these markets.

14.3.2   Technical analysis

The aim of technical analysis is not prediction; it tries to derive benefits from the repetitive behaviour of markets. The main postulate adopted is that markets are endowed with a memory inscribed in historical records of quotations and that it is possible to extract a behaviour continuity in the market. Managers identify these cyclical components to create adapted trading models. These systems are tested with historical prices in order to evaluate them in terms of yield and risk.

The development of strategies is specific to BAREP's research teams, based on technical, statistical and chartist methods, excluding any discretionary trading.

Strategy

We assume that a financial market memory does exist, which is linked to the operators' one. Thus, some developments in the financial markets do reoccur with constant characteristics.

The objective of the models' research is to create a system of decisions which aim to understand the market's behaviour in the past and enable the managers to design computerised decision-making models, which are still studied and parametered according to market developments.

Therefore, fund managers search for as many trading approaches as possible to catch many different market moves.

The analytic forms of these trading concepts are called strategies. The number of parameters represents the number of rules which affect either the price or the time of entry and exit. Each strategy created is evaluated in order to see its return, its risk and its stability.

Strategies are based on statistical and technical studies, and it uses indicators able to give buying or selling signals to the managers. Of course, stop-loss mechanisms exist guaranteeing the system's safety.

The trading rules of strategies are the same for each asset manager, whatever their anticipations in the evolution of the market.

Selection

The managers select their strategies and assets by the measure of the robustness and the quantification of the models' stability in the long run.

(1) Tests are implemented to measure the efficiency of the models in the past on a risk–reward point of view. The strategies are selected according to the following three fundamental criteria.

  (a) The return, including brokerage and slippage. Slippage represents the risk the market will trade through a protective stop, or getting filled at prices which are worse than expected. The knowledge of each potential market is essential (liquidity, quality of execution, length of life, brokerage) to estimate the eventual slippage.

  (b) The Sharpe ratio is here the average return divided by the return's standard deviation. It represents a measurement of the return's consistency of a trading method.

  (c) The drawdown is the maximum loss ever registered, analysed according to its depth, drop time and recovery time.

(2) The test of parameters' stability aims at measuring and quantifying the models' stability in the long run. The principal tool is the mapping which studies the movements of two parameters in a period of time in a specific market. We want to check the stability of these parameters.

Example

Let's explain our research approach by presenting one of our strategies. It is based on a pattern recognition: support and resistance.

Theory says that subjective analysis is not easily checked using mathematical methods. We want to computerize the research of patterns (channels, triangles, support and resistance points) and use this research to initiate and manage positions on futures markets.

A support is a level on the chart under the market where buying interests are sufficiently strong to overcome selling pressure. As a result, a decline is halted and the price turns back again. Usually a support level is identified beforehand by a previous low.

A resistance is the opposite of support and is identified by a previous peak.

Whenever a support or resistance level is penetrated by a significant amount, they reverse their role and become the opposite. If the resistance point is broken, the level becomes a support point, and vice versa.

The strategy uses these situations to initiate buy orders when a resistance level is broken and sell orders when a support level is penetrated. The problem resides in determining whether a penetration is significant or not.

It has a few parameters, including:

(1) the length of the period of time to search for the best supports and resistance levels
(2) the management of trades: stop-loss and take-profit objectives.

When the strategy is computerized, the test of its potentialities is made on different markets to decide if this strategy will be introduced into our portfolios.

In our example, we study, thanks to mapping, the stability of two parameters of the strategy:

(1) the length of the period of time, in order to search for the best support and resistance levels
(2) the stop-profit objective.

Mapping studies the variations of these two parameters and gives the net return, the Sharpe ratio and the drawdown ratio for each couple of parameters (the drawdown ratio represents the average return divided by the maximum drawdown).

- Market: JGB
- Time: 1 June, 1989, to 3 June, 1996
- First parameter: thirty–ninety days
- Second parameter: one–three market points.

Inside the mapping (Table 14.1), the first number represents the net return, the second the Sharpe ratio and the last one the drawdown ratio.

The first remark is the stability of these two parameters. Whatever their coefficients are, the return stays roughly the same, with a Sharpe ratio above one and a very good drawdown ratio.

The strategy seems interesting on the JGB and a few assets will be chosen in this mapping for the constitution of the JGB portfolio explained as follows.

14.3.3 Trading horizon

BAREP works its trading horizons in terms of types of markets, models and time horizons.

Market

The principal financial markets, in Europe, the USA and Asia can be divided in different classes and trading horizons.

(1) Stock indices:
  (a) frequent and violent accelerations
  (b) very volatile
  (c) short-term trends
  (d) importance of entry and exit points
  (e) profit-taking
(2) Long interest rates:
  (a) technical and chartist
  (b) medium- and long-term trend-following
  (c) volatility
(3) Currencies
  (a) medium- and long-term trend-following
  (b) no profit-taking
(4) Commodities
  (a) violent accelerations
  (b) long-term trends
  (c) profit-taking.

Model

Different kinds of models are used in our portfolios. These models are studied on an open–high–low–close basis.

A 'volatility breakout trading system' is based on the following principles. If the market moves a certain percentage from a previous price level, it breaks out of a trading range and is a buy or sale.

A 'trend-following system' (Figure 14.2) represents techniques which try to catch trends in a market. The systems buy when the market is going up and

Table 14.1 *A mapping*

	ENC 30	ENC 40	ENC 50	ENC 60	ENC 70	ENC 80	ENC 90
ES 1	23.7/1.13/3.67	25.4/1.18/3.93	20.4/0.99/2.68	28.1/1.26/5.44	29.1/1.28/5.14	31.4/1.39/5.55	24.7/1.12/3.98
ES 1.5	33.0/1.33/5.14	33.3/1.29/5.09	27.4/1.08/2.86	35.8/1.33/5.03	36.6/1.34/4.81	36.5/1.38/4.80	30.3/1.17/3.49
ES 2	39.0/1.38/5.81	38.4/1.31/5.64	31.0/1.09/3.14	41.3/1.35/5.59	41.9/1.35/5.32	38.9/1.30/4.93	37.4/1.25/4.17
ES 2.5	39.9/1.30/5.36	45.2/1.39/5.98	37.7/1.19/3.56	47.6/1.41/5.85	49.7/1.44/5.76	47.1/1.41/5.46	45.6/1.36/4.70
ES 3	38.6/1.21/5.18	44.1/1.33/5.84	41.8/1.25/3.94	46.0/1.32/5.65	34.6/1.05/4.00	32.2/1.01/3.72	30.5/0.96/3.14

A trend-following strategy:

– does not try to anticipate market's movements
– allows to win on increasing or decreasing markets
– allows to be always present in big trends
– cannot be a long time against the market.

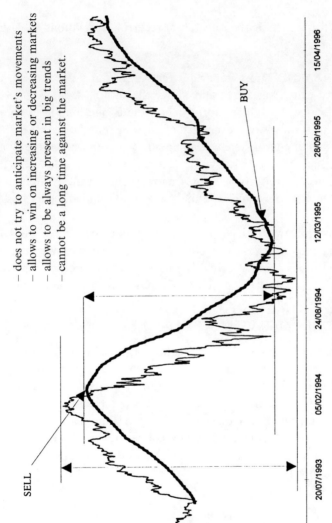

Figure 14.2 *Trend-following strategy*

sell when it is going down. They don't anticipate short-, medium- or long-term trends, they just follow them.

A 'contrarian system' takes position in the opposite way of trend-following systems.

A 'chartist system' is the research of recurring formations or patterns.

Time

Time is one of the most important factors affecting uncertainty, precisely because we can never be certain about the future. A large range of time horizons is used, as well as short-, intermediate- and long-term ones.

Figure 14.3 shows two examples of trading time horizons, a short-term system and a long-term system. On one side, the graph shows the evolution of the Notionnal from 1 January, 1990, to 15 November, 1996. On the other side, it shows the returns of a short-term system on the Notionnal. We use two different returns, which are the realized and unrealized profits, and the realized profit.

A short-term strategy has an average duration from one day to two weeks and is very active. Transaction costs and slippage can be very important. A long-term strategy (see Figure 14.4) lasts between three months to several years and takes only a few positions. Transaction costs and slippage are low.

14.4   MONEY MANAGEMENT

Money management covers the allocation of funds. It includes such areas as portfolio make up, diversification, how much money to invest or risk in any market, the use of stops, reward–risk ratios, what to do after a period of success or adversity, and whether to trade conservatively or aggressively.

We undertake money management by elaborating market portfolios (asset allocations between different strategies), a general portfolio (asset allocation between the different market portfolios) and determining the most efficient use of investment capital.

14.4.1   Diversification

Diversification is a way to achieve higher returns with the same or less amount of risk, and is clearly an important aspect of money management. Different ways to diversify include using different markets, time frames and methods.

Asset-allocation policy is determined for every market and implemented strategy, in order to keep the global level of exposure (leverage) unchanged. It begins by elaborating portfolios of each selected market and then by combining these portfolios. A combination of strategies and markets offering

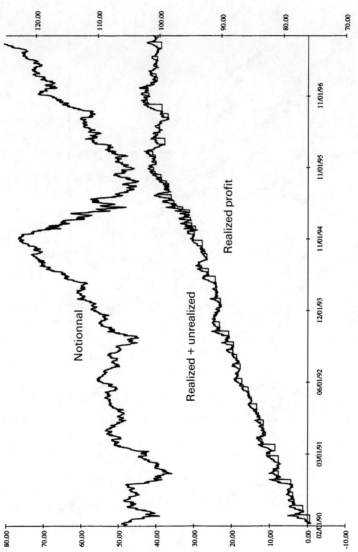

Figure 14.3 *A short-term system*

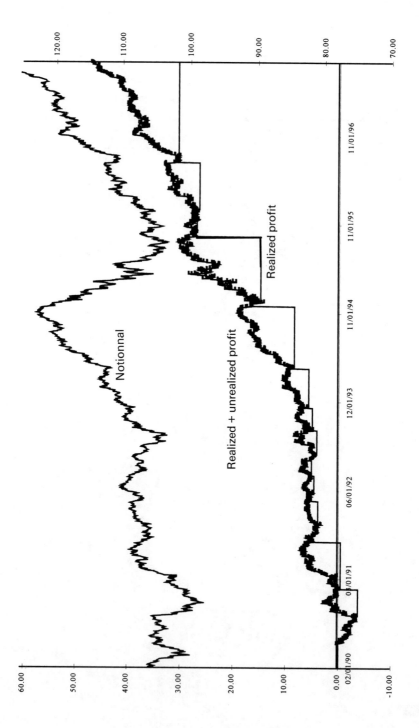

Figure 14.4 *A long-term system*

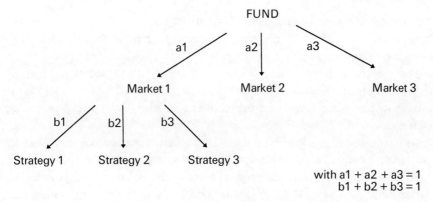

Figure 14.5 *Asset allocation*

low correlation with the others, good Sharpe ratio and low drawdown generates a portfolio which offers a high, regular and also steady performance (Figure 14.5).

The managers benefit from a quick intervention, thanks to the development of computerized valuation instruments in real time. The managers re-study the various strategies integrated in the fund constantly.

A market portfolio

In the portfolio, all strategies are managed independently. Indeed, it is possible to follow, at the same time and on a same market, complementary but different approaches.

Our global exposure on a market depends on each asset evolution and on its relative weighting inside this market.

Using several strategies in a same market is one way to catch different kinds of movements, different trading horizons and timings to enter the markets. Some trading methods perform well in trendy markets (small variations or long movements), others in chartist or contrarian situations.

The choice and the weighting of these assets, in each market, depend on:

(1) a good historical return on investment (the return on investment is the amount made or lost in a certain period of time divided by the amount invested and represents one of the best measures of return)
(2) a decrease in the risk (risk is evaluated by the standard deviation of returns and the maximum drawdown – the largest drawdown during a period of time and, therefore, the worse case scenario)
(3) a large diversification and a low correlation between assets (diversification is a way to achieve return and reduce risk; successful diversification is achieved by choosing models with the lowest correlation possible).

An example of market diversification (Figure 14.6)
It is possible to achieve a diversification with one trend-following strategy using moving averages.

The moving average is one of the most versatile and widely used of all technical indicators. Because of the way it is constructed and the fact that it can be so easily quantified and tested, it is a good basis for trend-following systems.

Its purposes are to identify or signal that a new trend has begun or that an old one has ended or reversed, and so to track the progress of the trend.

With a strategy using moving averages, the selection of couples of parameters gives several assets and at the same time different timing and trading horizons.

● Market: Notionnal
● 40 days moving average
● 150 days moving average.

The portfolio, with this two equi-weighted assets, is long in a bullish trendy market, neutral if a correction happens in a trend, and short in a bearish trendy market.

We can generalize about this diversification with other different assets of this strategy and with other approaches we have created.

The multi-market portfolio
Trading different markets should tend to reduce risk and is probably the most familiar and widely used way of diversifying. Trading markets with low correlation coefficients is a good start in proper diversification.

As we are completely systematic, the number of contracts can be important. The problem lies in the liquidity of each market. Trading markets which are not really liquid can reduce, because of the slippage, any of the benefits of increased diversification. That's why we only trade on liquid markets.

In order to minimize global risk and increase profit opportunities, the logic of each market's diversification is extrapolated to a diversification of markets all together. This study creates the multi-market portfolio.

The choice and the weighting of these different markets depend on:

(1) a good historical return on investment
(2) a decrease of the global risk
(3) a significant diversification and a low correlation between markets.

The end result is a multi-markets and a multi-strategies portfolio, with a multitude of methods, concepts and trading horizons.

We actually trade different assets and strategies on the same market,

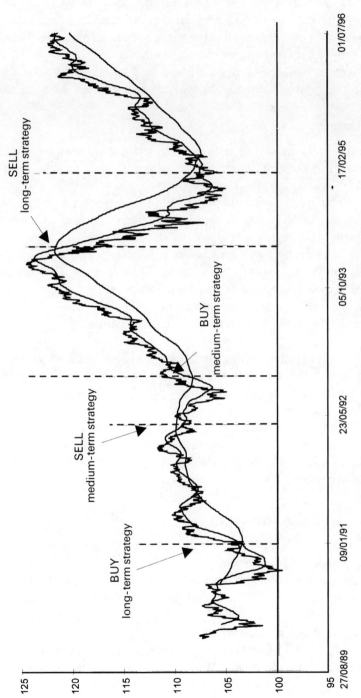

Figure 14.6 *Example of medium-term and long-term diversification*

according to the trading horizons (short-, medium-, long-term). In our funds, more than 300 assets are managed in real time on 25 different markets.

The global purpose of diversification is to generate a regular performance on a medium-term investment maturity, given the fact that at any time during the investment period, the portfolio must contain at least one market with a trend, and the appropriate model to extract a performance from this trend.

14.4.2   Leverage

The leverage is defined as the ratio between the sum of nominal values of every contract in position adjusted by their market price and the net asset amount of the fund.

The portfolio created gives the weighting of each market and each asset. The number of contracts traded depends on the fund's size and on the degree of risk sought. This degree determines the global leverage.

The assets' allocation has determined a trading portfolio which gives indication concerning historical rewards and drawdowns. The maximum drawdown is used to calculate the general leverage of the fund.

Finally, the level of a non-guaranteed fund leverage is defined in order to support eight times the historical maximum drawdown of our simulated portfolio.

BAREP reinvests the trading profits of the fund when profit-making represents half a drawdown. In the same way, we lower the leverage when the losses represent half a drawdown.

In certain situations, we can hedge a part of the portfolio, with the purchase of options. This hedge is done to conserve a part of the portfolio's return after a strong bullish or bearish movement, to cover the risk of a market consolidation. But we never modify the orders given by the strategies on futures markets.

14.5   EPSILON FUTURES FUND

Epsilon futures fund is a FCIMT without any capital guaranteed. A FCIMT (Fonds Communs d'Intervention sur les Marchés à Terme) is a French futures fund registered under French law and accepted by the 'Commission des Opérations de Bourse' (COB), with daily valuation, FFR denominated.

Total invested funds in a FCIMT is limited to 50 per cent of total capital. The balance is placed in Treasury bills.

The trading of our funds began in August, 1994, on three markets (Notionnal, CAC, Bund), about fifteen assets and with one million dollars. After less than two years, we manage 200 million dollars on 28 markets and 600 assets.

Net asset value is actually above 1,200 million francs (200 million dollars) or 18.900 francs per share (Figure 14.7).

14.5.1 Characteristics

- Legal status: futures fund (FCIMT under French law), authorized by COB
- Currency: French franc
- Valuation: daily
- Management fee: 2.5 per cent of the net asset value
- Performance fee: 30 per cent of the profits net of brokerage and management fees gained on the futures markets, on a half-yearly basis
- Front fee: up to FRF 5 000 000: 3.5 per cent
            above FRF 5 000 000: 2.5 per cent
- Redemption fee: 0.5 per cent maximum in case of 7 days prior notice, 10 per cent otherwise
- Investment maturity: open, one year minimum advised
- Tax: depending on the law of the country of residence of the investor
- Document available: investors can obtain each business day in Paris the latest net asset value of the fund, the leverage component, the deposit, and all legal documents.

(Futures funds constitute a volatile type of investment, with the possibility of loss of all the capital invested. It is strongly advised that investors who don't have a sufficient knowledge about the futures markets and the risks involved should not invest in this kind of fund. It is the investor's responsibility to obtain the necessary information on the futures market. BAREP will not be held responsible for any lack of information on these markets.)

14.5.2 Actual markets' allocation (for 20 million dollars)

The futures markets' weights of our multi-markets portfolio allocation is represented in Table 14.2 for an amount of 20 million dollars and a leverage calculated in order to support eight times the historical maximum drawdown.

In our portfolios' allocation long-term bonds represent above 40 per cent of the funds' allocations, short-term bonds 10 per cent, currencies 30 per cent and equities 20 per cent (Figure 14.8).

14.5.3 Performance

Historic volatility of Epsilon, our non-guaranteed fund, has decreased as the net asset value (represented by the shares' number) has risen strongly. This has been possible by an increasingly significant diversification in terms of assets and markets. We did not have problems with the increase in our funds' size (Figure 14.9).

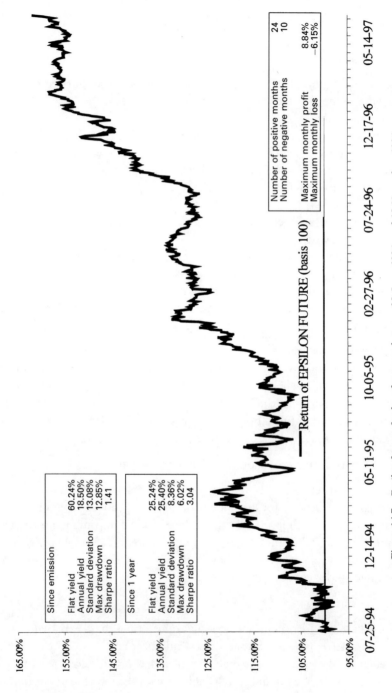

Figure 14.7 *Epsilon futures fund performance between 25 June, 1994, and 15 November, 1996*

The following data appear within the figure:

Since emission

Flat yield	60.24%
Annual yield	18.50%
Standard deviation	13.08%
Max drawdown	12.85%
Sharpe ratio	1.41

Since 1 year

Flat yield	25.24%
Annual yield	25.40%
Standard deviation	8.36%
Max drawdown	6.02%
Sharpe ratio	3.04

Number of positive months	24
Number of negative months	10
Maximum monthly profit	8.84%
Maximum monthly loss	−6.15%

Return of EPSILON FUTURE (basis 100)

Table 14.2 *Futures market's weights*

Contracts	Numbers	Daily volatilities for a contract (in dollars)*
Long-term bonds		
Notionnal	1400	520
Bund	840	825
Gilt	280	565
TNote 10 years	350	619
JGB	105	5778
Bonos	350	598
BTP	490	1040
TNote 5 years	490	423
T-Bond	350	981
Short-term bonds		
Pibor	700	388
Euro-DM	700	173
Short sterling	700	289
Euro-Dollar	700	166
Currencies		
USD/DM	350	684
USD/GBP	350	571
USD/CHF	700	945
USD/JPY	700	1156
USD/AUD	105	520
USD/CAD	105	560
Equities		
CAC	490	1106
Dax	350	1926
Nikkei	420	1857
S&P	140	2080
FTSE	280	1300

*The volatility in dollars is the average amount in dollars of daily movements on a contract.

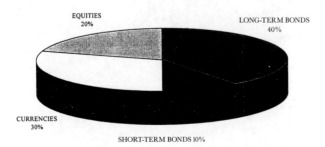

Figure 14.8 *Portfolio allocations*

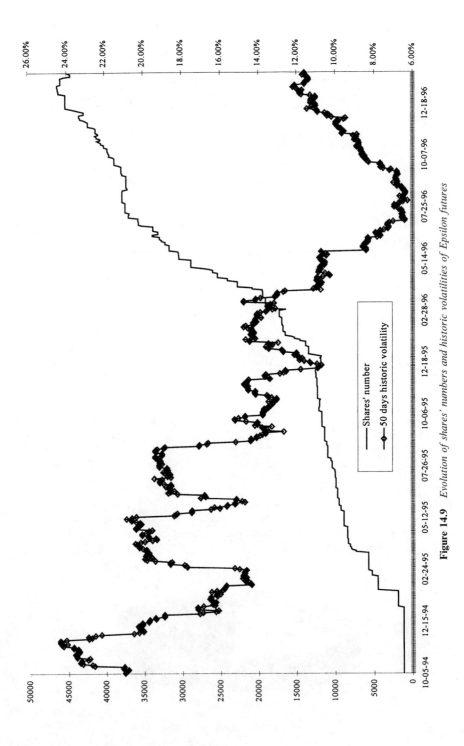

Figure 14.9 *Evolution of shares' numbers and historic volatilities of Epsilon futures*

14.5.4 Comparison

Weekly performance between Epsilon and two benchmarks

The two benchmarks chosen are 'The JP Morgan Global Bond' for bonds' performance and 'The Morgan Stanley Global Equity' for stocks' performance (see Tables 14.3 and 14.4). Epsilon futures performance is taken after the deduction of management and performance fees while stocks and bond indices don't include fees.

Epsilon outperformed by over 60 per cent in three years as in the same time the two benchmarks increase by 24 per cent and 50 per cent. The learning phase at the beginning of Epsilon saw a quite high volatility. Nevertheless, the volatility on the period is decreasing as we saw it (Figure 14.10) and it is actually around 9 per cent.

Table 14.3   *Rewards and risks since the beginning of Epsilon (1 August, 1994 to 5 July, 1997)*

	Epsilon	JP Morgan Global Bond	Morgan Stanley Global Equity	50% Epsilon + 50% Bond JP	50% Epsilon + 50% Equity MS
Flat yield	60.24%	23.74%	50.26%	41.97%	55.27%
Annual yield	18.50%	7.97%	15.79%	13.45%	17.16%
Volatility	13.08%	4.91%	9.46%	7.32%	8.10%
Max drawdown	12.85%	3.98%	6.11%	4.95%	3.99%
Sharpe ratio	1.41	1.62	1.67	1.84	2.12
Number of positive months	24	19	26	25	25
Number of negative months	10	15	8	9	9
Maximum monthly profit	8.84%	5.20%	6.80%	5.30%	6.80%
Maximum monthly loss	−6.15%	−2.15%	−4.61%	−3.29%	−3.06%

*The volatility is calculated with weekly returns.

Table 14.4   *Rewards and risks since one year (16 November, 1995 to 5 July, 1997)*

	Epsilon	JP Morgan Global Bond	Morgan Stanley Global Equity	50% Epsilon + 50% Bond JP	50% Epsilon + 50% Equity MS
Flat yield	25.24%	5.62%	22.55%	15.86%	23.93%
Annual yield	25.40%	5.65%	22.69%	15.95%	24.08%
Volatility	8.36%	4.07%	10.94%	5.14%	7.75%
Max drawdown	6.02%	2.52%	4.83%	3.63%	3.99%
Sharpe ratio	3.04	1.39	2.07	3.10	3.11

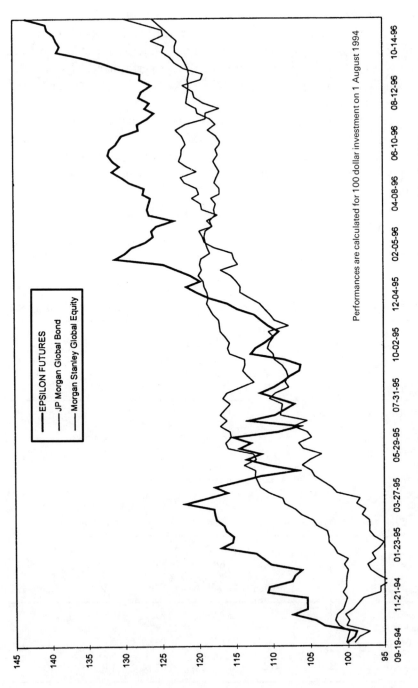

Figure 14.10 *Compared performance between 19 September, 1994 and 3 July, 1997*

Table 14.5 *Correlation between different weekly returns*

	Epsilon	JP Morgan Global Bond	Morgan Stanley Global Equity
Epsilon	100.00%	10.28%	−9.79%
JP Morgan Global Bond	10.28%	100.00%	44.24%
Morgan Stanley Global Equity	−9.79%	44.24%	100.00%

The second year of trading shows a management more secure with a higher diversification in terms of markets and more approaches and strategies.

The global yield kept very high (about 25 per cent flat) while JP Morgan Global Bonds increase only by 22 per cent. The maximum drawdown is weaker and represents only one-quarter of the flat return. Table 14.5 shows a very low correlation between Epsilon and the two benchmarks with 10.28 per cent with the first one and −9.79 per cent with the other one. On the opposite, the correlation between the two benchmarks is quite high with nearly 50 per cent. To conclude, Epsilon outperformed both benchmarks with a higher, but falling, volatility and is a very good instrument of asset diversification.

Figure 14.11 proves that Epsilon is a very good instrument of asset diversification. If you allocate a portfolio with 50 per cent of Epsilon and 50 per cent of Morgan Stanley Global Equity instead of Morgan Stanley Global Equity alone, the yield is higher with a better Sharpe ratio (from 1.67 to 2.12) and a lower maximum drawdown (from 6.11 per cent to 3.99 per cent).

14.5.5 Probability curves

Our management methods being totally systematic, we can simulate a proxi portfolio on market historical prices and check the daily gain. We have studied the empirical distribution of this daily gain and compared it to a Gaussian process. We do obtain the results in Figure 14.12. Several tests of normality (test of χ^2, kurtosis and skewness) show a significant level of confidence to make the assumption that the daily gain of the proxi portfolio follows a Gaussian process which mean and standard deviation are estimated empirically (m, σ).

Daily gain $= m + u_i$

$u_i \to N(0, \sigma_i)$

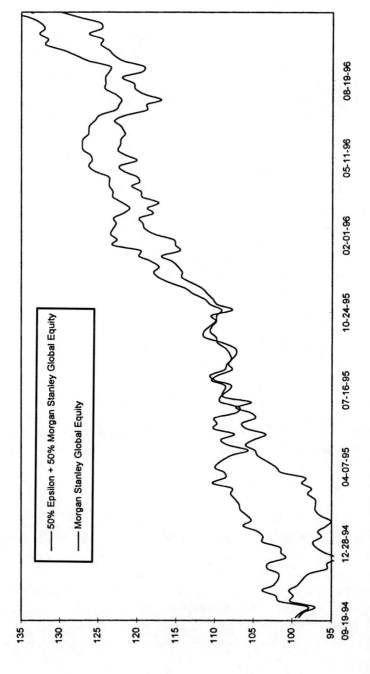

Figure 14.11 *Compared evolutions between 19 September, 1994 and 3 July, 1997*

* Performances are calculated for 100 dollar investment.

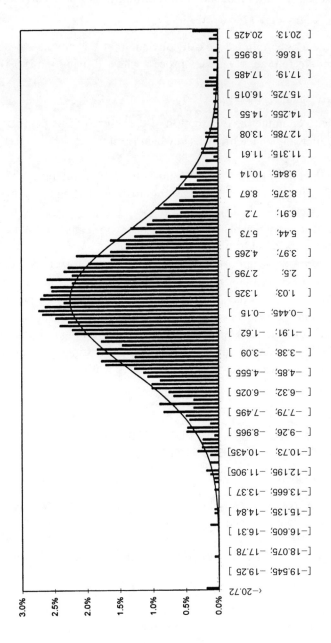

Figure 14.12 *Empirical distribution of the daily gain of a proxi portfolio*

We suppose that the perturbations are homoskedastics: $Vu_i = \sigma \forall i$. The Durbin–Watson test shows that the perturbations are not autocorrelated:

$$\text{cov}(u_i, u_j) = 0 \quad \forall i \neq j$$

Under all these assumptions, we can conclude that the cumulative gain of the proxi portfolio follows a Gaussian process whose distribution is perfectly known.

Cumulative gain $(i) \rightarrow N(im, \sqrt{i}\sigma)$

We are able to compute the distribution of the return of Epsilon fund over any period of time and define brackets in which Epsilon valorization has good probability to evolve.

If we draw the real valorization of Epsilon since the beginning of the fund, we can note that it fits quite well with the anticipations that had been made at the beginning (see Figure 14.13).

The 30 per cent curve means that the fund has a probability of 30 per cent to do less than the level indicated by the curve.

Since the inception, we almost realized our objective (target at 50 per cent) with a realization between 40–50 per cent.

Epsilon futures fund is today an indispensable instrument as its presence in a classic portfolio reduces the average risk while improving global return. Given the market diversification which is used (short- and long-term interest rates, currencies, stocks and commodities) and specific strategies, the FCIMT can be considered as a new autonomous asset class with no correlation with classic investments.

14.6   PERFORMANCE FUTURES FUND AND BAREP COMMODITIES FUTURES FUND

14.6.1   Performance futures fund

Performance futures fund is a FCIMT with a capital guaranteed. Each investor benefits from a principal guarantee at maturity date which is given by BAREP on 100 per cent of the invested principal on the advised investment period, which runs from 17 November, 1994, to 17 November, 1997.

Net asset value is actually above 200 million francs (50 million dollars), or 142.000 francs per share. The trading concepts and the markets traded are the same as for Epsilon futures fund. Only the global leverage of the fund changes, because of the capital guarantee (see Figure 14.14).

The other curb represents the linear-performance of a 3 years rate calculated on 17 November, 1994.

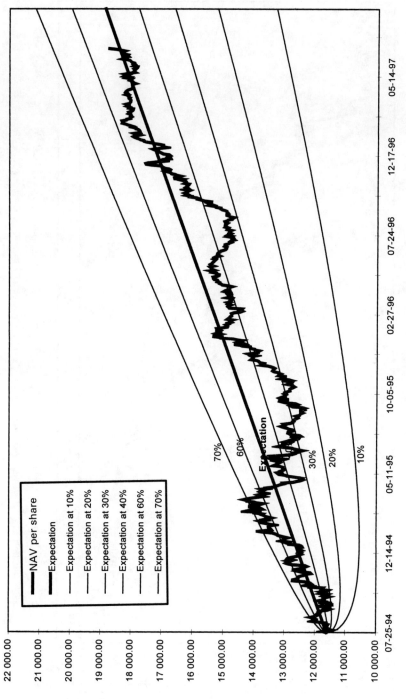

Figure 14.13 *Epsilon futures – anticipation and actual*

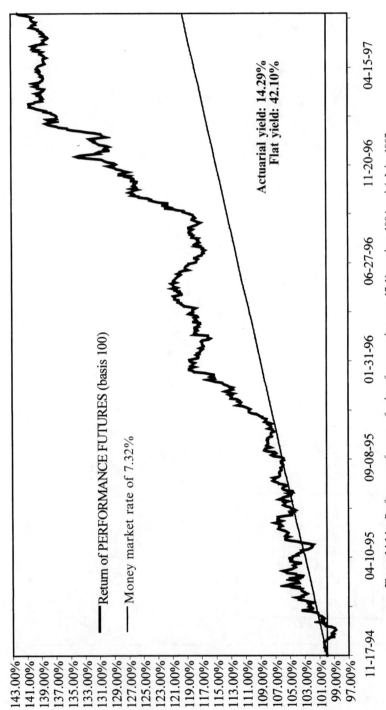

Figure 14.14 *Performance futures – fund performance between 17 November, 1994 and 4 July, 1997*

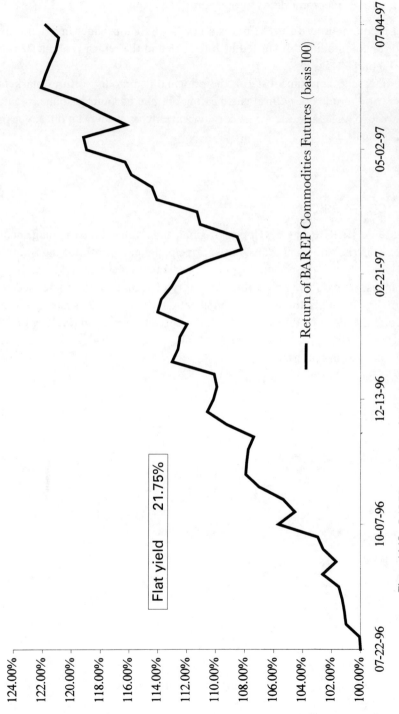

Figure 14.15 *BAREP commodities futures fund performance between 22 July, 1996 and 5 November, 1997*

14.6.2   BAREP commodities futures fund

BAREP commodities futures fund is a new BAREP's product invested only in futures commodities. It started in July 1996 and the return is about 22 per cent (Figure 14.15).

We intervene simultaneously on the principal commodity futures markets in the world: crude oil, natural gas, heating oil, NY harbour gasoline, sugar, coffee, cacao, gold, silver, copper, corn, wheat, soybean, soybean oil, soybean meal, live cattle.

14.7   CONCLUSIONS

Since 1994, BAREP has developed original, high value-added management strategies in the futures markets, based principally on trend-following trading techniques. Since the beginning, we conducted extensive research into techniques for reducing the natural volatility of futures funds, which led to new trading methods and greater diversification of the contracts handled. For example, the Epsilon futures fund is now spread over 28 markets with 20 management strategies per market. All in all, it requires nearly 600 strategies to be followed in real time.

Chapter 15

The need for performance evaluation in technical analysis

FELIX GASSER

15.1 INTRODUCTION

15.1.1 Why I chose this subject

The last ten years I have worked in the field of computer-supported technical analysis, for a large commodity trading advisor (CTA), as a product manager for technical analysis software and as trading system developer in the banking industry, including the 3 years in my current position at Credit Suisse Private Banking. During the course of developing and testing hundreds of trading strategies, my objective in these positions has always been the development of better-performing trading strategies. This has increasingly led me to more involved performance testing and to the development of proprietary performance-evaluation tools. Today, I feel confident that I can make a contribution to the field and dedicate this chapter to the subject.

15.1.2 The importance of performance evaluation

Technical analysis (TA) is defined as the analysis of pure market price movement as time series called charts. Although this is a clear definition, anyone who has read a book on TA knows it's not necessarily straightforward. If we include all the tools and theories labelled technical – from the highly scientific to the rather esoteric – the subject can become controversial and confusing.

The flood of technical instruments has turned TA into an alchemist's melting pot, resulting in scepticism especially among the academic community. On the other hand, the influx from other disciplines, most of all statistics and the computer sciences, has added powerful analytical tools, strengthening the position of TA as a valid discipline in the investment community and increasingly in academia as well.

The question of who can now be the objective judge of what is valid and what is not can only have one answer. Consequently, it must be determined by the resulting investment performance measured in dollars and cents. Valid are those strategies which give us in the long run a financial edge in the market. It is the aim of this chapter to explain and highlight the importance of performance results as an instrument to evaluate indicators, strategies and market behaviour. I will discuss the pros and cons of standard performance figures and add some of the tools I have developed.

15.2   TOOLS AND DEFINITIONS

15.2.1   Trading report performance summary

There is an increasing number of technical analysis tools on the market, such as Trade Station and Metastock, which are two of the high-end packages. Most charting packages – especially those included by data-service providers – are limited to visual display, without the option of a statistical performance evaluation. The main handicap of visual charting is the deception of the naked eye, when it subjectively tries to recognize pattern. On the other hand, a strategy defined as an algorithm in the form of a trading system produces clear-cut buy and sell levels, resulting in a detailed performance report in dollars and cents. Regardless of what is used for analysis, whether a simple spreadsheet or complex proprietary software, one has to be concerned with the same questions regarding performance figures. Accordingly, this chapter is not only aimed at the classical, visual chartist, but also at users of high-end analytical tools, which provide ready-made performance statistics. While the second group especially runs the risk of drawing wrong and overly optimistic conclusions from their ready-made performance reports, the chartist may not know the performance statistics of his or her trading approach at all.

In the remainder of this section I present the reader with definitions of performance statistics and also some technical terms to describe market conditions.

15.2.2   Definitions of performance data

- **Net profit:** The total amount of dollars made or lost by a trading strategy during an observed test period (see details in Section 15.3.1).
- **Max drawdown:** The drawdown is the equity decrease from a previous equity high. The max drawdown is the dollar amount (or better, the percentage) of the largest equity drop. Remember the drawdown in percentage is not symmetric, a 50 per cent drop needs a 100 per cent

recovery to equal the same net equity. The unrealized largest drawdown of a single trade is called the maximum adverse excursion (see details in Section 15.3.2).

- **Runup:** The opposite of the drawdown, the max runup is a strategy's maximum profit gain during the course of trading. The runup during a single trade is the maximum profit potential called the maximum favourable excursion of a trade.

- **Trade efficiency:**

  Long trades = (exit price – entry price)/(highest – lowest price)

  Short trades = (entry price – exit price)/(highest – lowest price)

  Trade efficiency measures the efficiency as a percentage of how close to the top and bottom within a trade the entry and exit was placed. Unrealized runups, for example, are accounted with a loss of efficiency. Unfortunately the price moves before the entry and after the trade exit are not accounted for, which severely limits the value of the efficiency numbers. This excludes opportunity losses before a potential trade and after an actual trade. Stopped-out trades, on the other hand, are considered to exit at the lowest and worst level of a trade and are not credited for avoiding what could have been a possibly ruinous equity drop. This results in consistent lower ratings for the exit-efficiency versus the entry-efficiency and severely limits the use of trade efficiency ratings as a whole.

- **Largest loser:** This is the largest losing trade and can be directly controlled with the stop-loss.

- **Average profit per trade:** The average profit or loss of all winning and losing trades. This figure is especially crucial for short-term and intra-day trading and must be large enough to account for all trading costs (see Section 15.3.3).

- **Per cent profitable:** The percentage of winning trades produced by a trading strategy. Trend-following strategies have a winning percentage of 35–45 per cent. Although they have more losing trades, these strategies are profitable because winners are larger than the more frequent, but smaller, losers. These strategies are much less focused on predicting the next market move, but more on letting their profits run. A percentage under 30 per cent is dangerous and carries a high probability of financial ruin. There are few strategies with over 50 per cent winning trades because they need the rarely successful element of predicting the next market direction after trade entry. Strategies with over 50 per cent should be carefully performance tested. They are usually a result of over-optimization (curve fitting), or too tightly set stop-losses, resulting in many winners, which are critically smaller compared to losers.

- **Average winner to loser:** This is the counterpart performance figure of per cent profitable and measures the ratio of the size of winners to losers. An average winner to loser of 2.5 would mean that winners are, on average, 2.5 times bigger than losing trades. For all strategies with 35–50 per cent winning trades, we look for a ratio over 2. Anything under 1.5 can again be ruinous.

- **Number of trades:** The number of trades is crucial for statistical relevance. In a random environment, we would need at least 30 trades for a sound statistical sample. Since we often carry out testing in a non-random environment (hopefully so) of unknown distribution, we look for as many trades as possible before we draw conclusions regarding the robustness and profitability of a strategy. Since testing of one strategy on one market (one market system) produces insufficient trades, the same strategy has to be tested across many markets for relevance of performance results.

15.2.3   Definitions of market conditions

- **Trends:** One-directional price moves that can last for months, but include moves of small magnitude as well. Statistically, trends are serial-correlated moves, in which a higher price has a higher probability to be followed by another price rise again and vice versa. This leads to a series of correlated climbing or falling prices. Moving averages are a statistical tool to capture such serial correlation. If they (usually two averages) are systematically profitable over time a trending price chart is underlying.
- **Monetary definition of trend:** The point of interest from a trading perspective is how long a directional move has to be to qualify as a trend. As traders, we look for a definition in terms of dollars and cents. A trend has the size of a move long enough to allow us to recognize it as directional and to enter it. On the exit side, we again need the time to recognize the end of the move and to exit it. The trading profit from the trend movements after costs has to be large enough to cover all unprofitable small moves (false breakouts). In a random market, the unprofitable false breakouts will kill off all profits of the longer moves. If strategies like trend-following breakouts or moving-average systems are profitable in the long run, we have a certain degree of trending tendency in the market, which is also called black noise.
- **Black noise:** Market behaviour which is partially random and partially trending. Black noise is what we recognize as trending movement, like most of the interest-rate markets. Even the most favourable trending markets do not trend all the time; they are a mix of randomness and directional correlated moves which result in black noise. Black noise can be profitably traded.

- **White noise:** This is pure randomness. In a purely random market, we will always lose money, at least at the same rate of the occurring trading costs. We will experience financial ruin with mathematical certainty in the long run. Markets have changing and different degrees of randomness. Pure white noise cannot be profitably traded. Modern Portfolio Theory taught at most business schools assumes random markets with a natural distribution. This although most price charts display trends with according fat-tail distributions (similar to a Levy–Pareto distribution).
- **Pink noise:** This is price behaviour in which the direction changes more often than randomly. The fast-reversing price direction is typical for range-driven markets and short-term price action. This reversing-price behaviour can be illustrated and measured with the parameter distribution resulting from an optimization of an inverted-trend-following strategy. Pink noise can be profitably traded within an unknown and limited time frame. The lag in recognizing the beginning and end of the process constitutes the risk and cost of range trading and limits its practical use virtually to zero. I have not yet come across a stable and profitable range trading strategy.

15.3   PRACTICAL USE OF PERFORMANCE TOOLS

All tests in this study are performed with Trade Station and Excel. The concept and ideas do, however, apply to all technical analyses and are not limited to these programs.

15.3.1   Total net profit (NP)

Since the performance of an indicator or a trading strategy cannot be reduced to one number, technical analysts look at several performance figures to assess risk and return. Of these numbers, total net profit is still the most popular single figure to be optimized. This is not necessarily wrong as long as it does not involve curve fitting and is not done at the cost of uneven performance distribution over time. In particular, tests that only show the final summary reports can obscure the fact that a strategy resulted in total losses several times before it showed a profit. Even if we examine additional data like maximum drawdown, average annual return or the Sharpe ratio, we cannot see the entire picture. All performance numbers measured at the end of a trading or test period can hide the fact that we earned all profits within one trend, which could have been years ago. There is a need to visualize net profit in the form of a chart in order to see the performance data over time.

This allows us to observe performance throughout its entire development and evaluate the probability of future profits in changing markets. The display of single equity curves is available in programs like Trade Station. However, it is better for analysts to custom-build equity curves in a spreadsheet for the following reasons.

- To compare the performance and correlations of different strategies
- To display many Profit and Loss (P & L) curves on the same printout
- To display performance as a percentage of invested capital for comparison of markets
- To compare trading strategy results in different currency denominations
- To add equity curves to market or system baskets and to entire portfolios
- To produce all the necessary performance statistics of combined P & L curves
- To produce the raw material for equity-curve trading
- And finally, to produce great marketing material.

The first step in producing equity curves involves sending performance data for each bar of the chart to a file. We can do that in the form of an indicator applied to the chart. For Trade Station, I have written the following indicator that sends all requested performance data to an ASCII file, which can be opened and charted in Excel or Lotus. The input of the indicator allows us to enter the initial margin or starting capital for the market. As soon as the indicator is applied to a chart with a trading system, the accrued, daily percentage return of the initial margin is exported. The resulting graph displays accrued percentage returns over time.

Indicator to send Performance Date to ASCII file

```
Input: InitialMargin(1600);
vars:OpenEqu(0), TotalEquity(0), RPP(0),PP(0);
{- - - - - - - - - - - - - - - - - - - - - - - - - - - - - -}
{This step is only for Trade Station users! It corrects the bug of a wrong open equity function}
OpenEqu = (I_OpenEquity-I_ClosedEquity); TotalEquity = I_OpenEquity;
{- - - - - - - - - - - - - - - - - - - - - - - - - - - - - -}
{Accrued P & L in Percent}              {Daily P & L change in Percent}
RPP = (TotalEquity/InitialMargin*100);   PP = (TotalEquity/TotalEquity[1])/InitialMargin*100;
{- - - - - - - - - - - - - - - - - - - - - - - - - - - - - - - - - - - - - - - - - - - - - - - - - - -}
{Sends the accrued and the daily returns to ASCII file}
Print(file("c:\Performance\T-Note.txt"),FixDate(date),";",RPP:4:0,";", PP:3:2) ;
{- - - - - - - - - - - - - - - - - - - - - - - - - - - - - -}
{Plots indicator to screen}
Plot1(RPP,"RPP"); Plot2(PP,"PP");
```

The following function called FixDate has to be used with the indicator above to send correct dates after 1/1/2000 from Trade Station to Excel.

Correction ELDate function

Inputs: DateSelect(Numeric);   Variables: YearPortion(""), StringMonth(""), StringDay("");
YearPortion = NumToStr(1900 + IntPortion(DateSelect * .0001), 0);
If DateSelect > = 1000000 Then   StringMonth = MidStr(NumToStr(DateSelect, 0), 4, 2)   else
                         StringMonth = MidStr(NumToStr(DateSelect, 0), 3, 2);
StringDay = RightStr(NumToStr(DateSelect, 0), 2); FixDate =YearPortion + StringMonth + StringDay

---

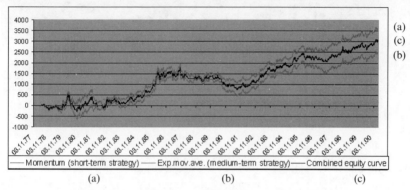

(a)   (b)   (c)

Figure 15.1   *Thirty-year T-bond return in % of margin*

If we look at the equity curves of the two strategies in Figure 15.1, we see the typical performance gap of the US 30-year Treasury bond from 1986–1991. Most strategies on T-bonds had the same performance difficulties during these years. After 1991, we see good results coming from the medium-term exponential moving average. But the short-term momentum strategy never picked up again, which suggests that it is the wrong strategy for T-bonds.

On the US 10-year T-note (Figure 15.2), the two strategies perform in reverse order. The momentum strategy performs better than the exponential

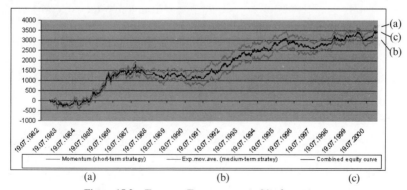

(a)   (b)   (c)

Figure 15.2   *Ten-year T-note return in % of margin*

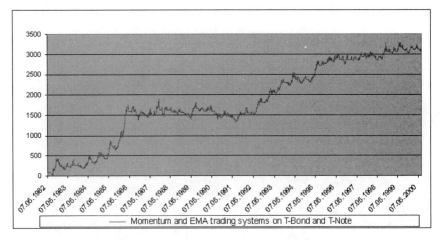

Figure 15.3 *Combined T-bond and T-note equity curve return in % of margin*

moving average from beginning to end. Interestingly, it also performs during the difficult 1986–1991 period. The performance comparison of different strategies during varying market behaviour gives us useful feedback on both trading strategies and markets. As expected, for a trend-following strategy, the performance of the exponential moving average is heavily dependent on a few, strong trends, and it is advisable that it not be used alone. Although the shorter-term momentum clearly performs better on the T-note, we could choose a position that is split between the strategies to produce a combined equity curve seeking lower volatility and a better Sharpe ratio (Figure 15.3).

The good news emanating from the combined equity curve is that drawdowns are minimal. The bad news is that the period from 1986–1991 is still a non-performing flat-line period. Figure 15.3 demonstrates the following points.

- After long periods of non-trending price action, a market can come back to trends
- Most profitable strategies produce similar equity curves in the same market
- Equity curves of trading systems are good indicators of a market's underlying price behaviour.

15.3.2   Drawdown and Max drawdown (DD and MaxDD)

Most trading strategies are in a drawdown state from their last equity high up to 70 per cent of the time. It is important to accept this fact psychologically, and it should encourage efforts to diversify as effectively as possible. Drawdowns are the result of the size and frequency of losing trades. The size of losing trades can be controlled with a stop-loss. But the frequency of losing trades cannot be easily controlled since it results from the interplay of trading strategy logic and the underlying market behaviour, which falls often into randomness. Max drawdown is the largest historical equity dip and has become one of the most widely used measures of risk. In order to compare drawdowns of strategies in different markets, they should be measured as a percentage of capital, referring to the last equity high as 100 per cent. Most software packages calculate DD only in reference to the starting capital, which is dangerous and produces overly optimistic risk expectations, resulting in over-trading and ruin with mathematical certainty as time progresses. Equity swings above the initial starting capital – i.e. from 150 per cent back down to 120 per cent – constitute the same risk as a drop at the beginning of trading. An analyst has to assume that trading can start at any given point in time, including the worst possible moment. This is in fact of some importance, because we are forced to apply reinvestment, regearing or

---

Draw Down Indicator

```
Input: StartEqu(20000), -DDLimit(20);
Vars: MyEquity(0),HighEquity(0), DD(0),MxDD(0),PrcDD(0), MxPrcDD(0), MxCount(0), TextNumber1(0),
TextNumber2(0);
{- - - - - - - - - - - - - - - - - - - - - - - - - - - - - - - - - - - - - - - - - -}
{Calculates Draw Down and Max. Draw Down in percent}
MyEquity = StartEqu  + I_OpenEquity;
if MyEquity > HighEquity then HighEquity = MyEquity;
DD = HighEquity – MyEquity;
If DD > MxDD then MxDD = DD;
If HighEquity < > 0 then PrcDD = DD/(HighEquity/100);
If PrcDD > MxPrcDD then MxPrcDD  =  PrcDD;
{- - - - - - - - - - - - - - - - - - - - - - - - - - - - - - - - - - - - - - - - - -}
{Plots indicator and text to screen}
Plot1(Round(Neg(PrcDD),1),"Current%DD");
Plot2(Round(Neg(MxPrcDD),1),"Mx%DD");
Plot3(Neg(DDLimit)," StopLimitDD");
If Plot2 crosses under Plot3 then begin
Value97 = Text_New(Date, Time, High + (C/80), "Close of account");
If GetBackGroundColor = 1 then

Value98 = Text_SetColor(Value97, Tool_Cyan)
Else beginIf GetBackGroundColor < > 1 then Value99 = Text_SetColor(Value97, Tool_Blue);end;end;
{- - - - - - - - - - - - - - - - - - - - - - - - - - - - - - - - - - - - - - - - - -}
{ Sends draw Down to ASCII file}
Print(file("c:\Performance\IMMCHF.txt"),FixDate(date),";",- PrcDD:3:0,";",- MxPrcDD:3:0,";", DDLimit:3:0) ;
```

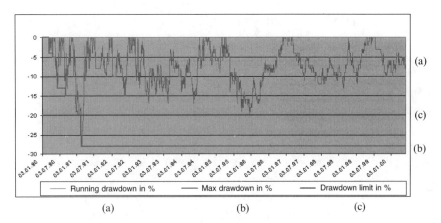

Figure 15.4   *Swiss franc IMM: DD with 1 unit traded*

money management to our trading strategy. *From a risk point of view, each time the position size is increased a new trading start is initiated.*

The above is the formula of an indicator I have written in Trade Station to calculate the percentage MDD and the daily DD for every bar. It allows us to enter initial starting capital and set a DD limit. If this limit is crossed, an alert is shown.

Figure 15.4 is the DD in per cent, of a strategy with one unit traded and no reinvestment or money management. Most tests are performed like this, which gives misleading risk assumptions. The daily DD ((a) in Figure 15.4) reaches its maximum of around −27 per cent in the second year, breaking below the chosen DD alert limit (c). Later, it never drops below −20 per cent and stays above −15 per cent in the last 5 years. Does this mean that the strategy improves over time? Of course not. It is the growing capital base that makes the drawdown of one unit appear smaller and smaller. In real trading, we are, however, forced to increase trading size with capital growth to maintain the same percentage returns. Accordingly, we will also maintain the same DD magnitude due to increased positions as seen in Figure 15.5.

This is the same strategy's DD in per cent if money management or reinvestment is applied. The position size is increased according to capital growth, with the result that the chosen DD limit of 20 per cent is consistently broken. This demonstrates that DDs remain at the same high level and bear the risk of producing a marginally higher MaxDD at any time in the future. This demonstrates what many analysts agree on: that money management (position sizing) is one of the most important aspects of trading. To summarize, the size of drawdown risk is a function of the following underlying factors.

● Market behaviour

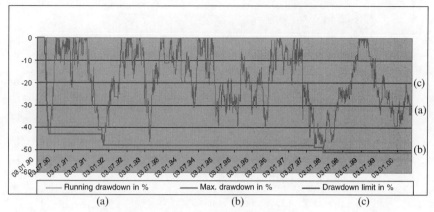

------- Running drawdown in %	—— Max. drawdown in %	—— Drawdown limit in %
(a)	(b)	(c)

Figure 15.5 *Swiss franc IMM: DD with reinvestment*

- Methodology of the trading strategy
- Size of position.

A change in any of these three factors heightens the risk of higher MaxDDs. If the methodology of a trading strategy cannot be improved any further, and the MaxDD in testing is still crossing limit levels, then the trading size has to be decreased until the limit is no longer reached. This tool is not only helpful in determining the DD risk for any strategy, it can also find the optimal investment size and facilitate money management. If we optimize the initial capital as a function of MaxDD, it tells us how much capital for a given trading strategy is needed. Of course, there has to be a safety margin, assuming that marginally larger MaxDDs will occur at some point in the future.

15.3.3 Average profit per trade (AT)

In an increasingly competitive trading environment made up of day traders, scalpers and computer-supported traders, profit margins have decreased to a point where trading costs have become a key factor. The average trade is an indicator of the amount of leeway available for commission, slippage or testing errors, including some degree of unwanted curve fitting resulting from testing. A special warning has to go to the optimization of net profit while neglecting the average trade. The result can be strategies with high trading frequency and a very low profit per trade. As soon as we lose a little of our edge in the market or more slippage occurs, these strategies systematically result in losses.

The following is the code I have written to send the average trade from Trade Station to an ASCII file. In this example, I have added it to a breakout

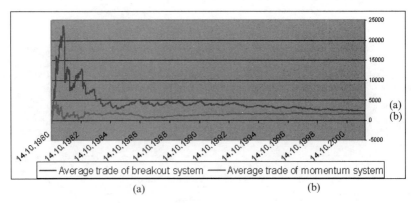

(a)   (b)

Figure 15.6   *Swiss francs (IMM 1980–2000)*

system, but of course it can be added to any other strategy. In Figure 15.6, we can monitor the development of the average trade over its entire history.

Send Average Trade to file

Input: Length(45); vars: TotalEquity(0),Trades(0), AveTr(0);
{- -}
{regular Break-out system}
IF Close > = Highest(c,Length)[1] Then Buy on Close; IF Close < = Lowest(c,Length)[1] Then Sell on Close;
{- -}
{ Calculates and sends "Average Trade" to file}
TotalEquity = NetProfit + OpenPositionProfit; Trades = TotalTrades + 1; AveTr = TotalEquity/Trades;
Print(file("c:\Averagetradefile\sfr.txt"),FixDate(date),";",AveTr:5:0) ;

Looking at the average profit per trade of the Swiss franc from 1980–2000, we see that the trend-following breakout strategy did much better in the beginning of the 1980s. The strong trends back then gave the trend follower such a lead in average profit per trade that the resulting average is still better today, which is misleading (as shown in Figure 15.7).

From 1990–2000, we had a considerably less pronounced trend movement. Looking at the average trade size from 1990–2000, we see that the performance of the two systems is very similar, and that short-term momentum trading has become equally good as the trend follower with regard to average trade size. In fact, it has become the superior strategy because it does not hold trades for as long and has smaller drawdowns. In this example, we can demonstrate how the evaluation of trading strategies documents the long-term change in the markets from long, sustained trends to shorter trends with higher volatility.

The resulting AT chart can also be used for money or risk management, with the aim of decreasing the trading size for strategies that fall under a

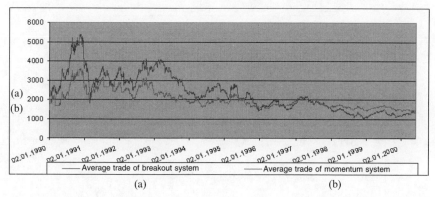

Figure 15.7 *Swiss francs (IMM 1990–2000)*

minimum floor of average profit per trade. The size of this floor must account for trading costs and a margin for white noise (randomness) volatility of a market.

15.4 ROBUSTNESS TESTS

15.4.1 Parameter selection and distribution

At this point we have to talk about the robustness of performance tests. All tests are built on the assumption that future performance will be sufficiently similar to historical performance to allow some degree of generalization. However, in the unstable stationarity (see Glossary at the end of chapter) of market price distributions, we look for additional tests to assess the robustness of our strategies in a changing environment.

The first and easiest test is to apply the same trading rule or indicator to different markets, looking for trading strategies with stable performance across markets. Next we test for different parameter inputs of variables. Variables are all elements which allow for different inputs. For example, a ten-day moving average is a variable with the parameter ten. The more variables or trading rules we apply, the less general and less robust our strategy will be. We are talking about a loss in *degrees of freedom*. Robust strategies use between one to four variables, which can be changed or optimized. It is well known that optimization of historical data tunes parameters and rules to past and often singular price behaviour. The result is curve fitting with unreliable future performance. Nonetheless, optimization is a very powerful tool if used correctly. Optimization should be referred to as visualizing the distribution of parameter performance. We are not interested in the single most profitable setting of the past, but the distribution of profitable parameters across different markets.

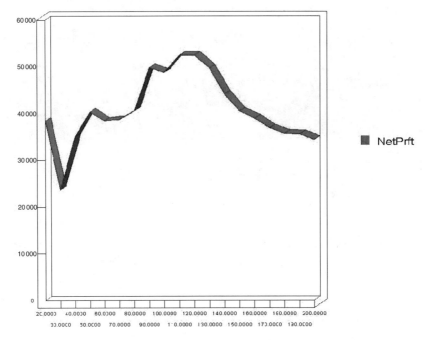

Figure 15.8 *C1Day length*

Figures 15.8–15.10 display the Net Profit (NetPrft) for every parameter length of a system called C1 Day.

Figure 15.8 is a parameter optimization of the number of look-back bars (from 20 to 200) for a breakout strategy on the Euro Bund. We see that all parameters are profitable especially between the wide range from 50 to 150 bars look-back. This reflects a very stable strategy on a tradable black noise market, which suggests that this trading system can be traded in the future with the same parameters between 50 and 150.

Figure 15.9 is the same optimization on the gold price from 1990 to 2000 which produces a much more unstable distribution with losing parameters from 20 up to 100. This result reflects a strategy which is unsuitable for this market, or a market with too much randomness (white noise). From other tests, I see that gold is in fact a difficult market for most strategies, but has in the long run tradable trends and could be included in a trading portfolio as diversification.

Figure 15.10 shows a simple breakout system on the British pound from 1980–1993. Although the performance for different parameters is not very stable, all parameter lengths of the breakout system produced profitable results. This reflects the strong trends (black noise) during that period. After

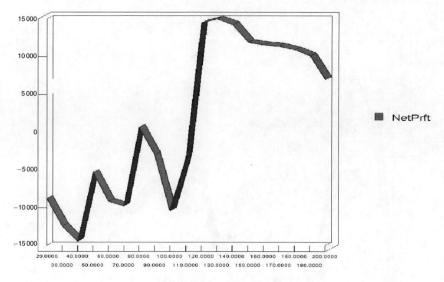

Figure 15.9 *C1Day length*

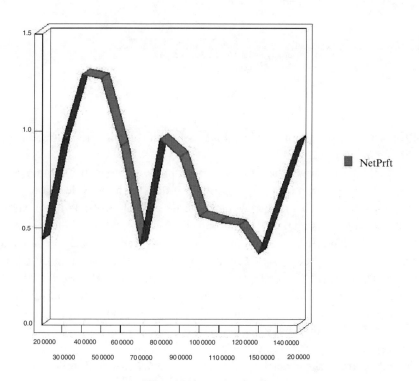

Figure 15.10 *C1Day length*

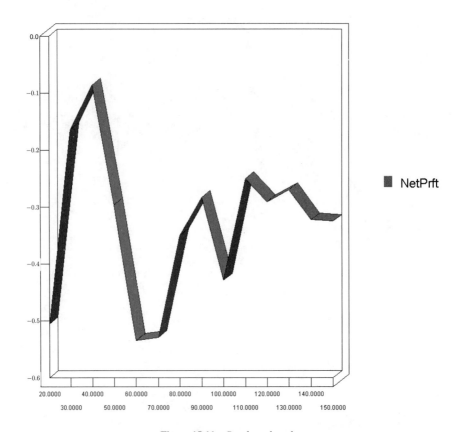

Figure 15.11   *Breakout length*

1993, the British pound changed its behaviour from strong trending to volatile mean reverting.

Figure 15.11 shows the same optimization on the British pound from 1993–2000. All parameters (from 20 to 150 days) produced deeply negative trading results. In this case it would even be possible to trade the breakout system inverted, changing the buy signals to sell signals. The market has changed from a strongly trending to a strongly reversing market. It changes price direction as soon as we are able to measure the beginning of a trend move. This frequent reversing within a range is what we describe as pink noise. This example shows that performance evaluation cannot only produce generalizations about the behaviour of trading strategies, but also about the behaviour of the underlying market. The price behaviour of the British pound is, after the year 2000, again interesting. It has changed with the launch of the Euro, from the reverting range trading back to trend-following price action.

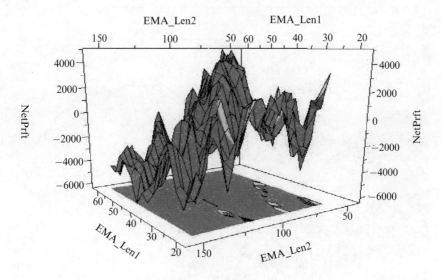

Figure 15.12 *Three-dimensional evaluation*

Figure 15.12 is an example of an optimization of two moving averages on silver, producing a three-dimensional evaluation. We not only have a lot of negative results, but also a very unstable distribution. Silver has a lot of randomness and is accordingly difficult to trade. Most strategies lose money in silver, especially trend followers like moving averages. If the randomness in silver is, as I suspected, mostly white noise, then there is no strategy that can beat this market in the long term.

15.4.2 Parameter diversification

As we see from the results above, there are changing optimal parameters for each trading system. This is even more pronounced across different markets and different years. As a result of this instability of parameter performance, we will never be in a position to continuously trade at an optimum. What we are looking for instead is a spread of robust parameters with a high probability to produce continuously profitable results. Since the optimal peaks are unstable and move around, we are better off using several parameters diversifying our trading signals.

Figure 15.13 is an example of using a combination of moving averages. The buy (up) and sell (down) arrows show how the different parameters are spreading the signals and with it the risk, across the chart. The resulting performance figures in the left corner of the chart are expectedly good and stable.

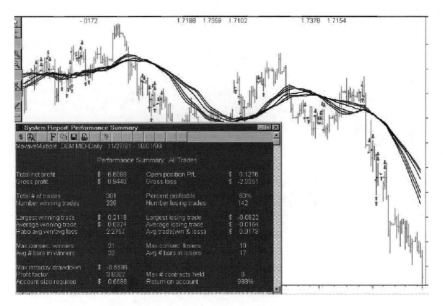

Figure 15.13   *A combination of moving averages*

15.4.3   Optimization of diversified parameters

To observe the stabilizing effect of diversifying across several parameters, we have optimized a system with multi-parameter inputs by moving all parameter inputs parallel at the same time in percentage moves up and down. The following is the formula of a simple breakout strategy with the option of three inputs (50,100,150) moving together from −90 per cent to +90 per cent in any desired increment (use odd numbers to avoid a system failure at zero input).

Multi-parameter optimization

```
Input: Perc(-91);{-99 bis 99}
vars:perc2(0), Len1(0), Len2(0), Len3(0);

If (50/100*perc) < > 0 then begin   If (100/100*perc) < > 0 then begin   If (150/100*perc) < > 0 then begin
Len1 = 50 + (50/100*perc);end;      Len2 = 100 + (100/100*perc);end;     Len3 = 150 + (150/100*perc);end;

IF CurrentBar > 1 and Close > = Highest(c,Len1)[1] Then Buy("Buy1") close;
IF CurrentBar > 1 and Close < = Lowest(c,Len1)[1] Then Sell("Sell1") close;
IF CurrentBar > 1 and Close > = Highest(c,Len2)[1] Then Buy("Buy2") close;
IF CurrentBar > 1 and Close < = Lowest(c,Len2)[1] Then Sell("Sell2") close;
IF CurrentBar > 1 and Close > = Highest(c,Len3)[1] Then Buy ("Buy3") close;
IF CurrentBar > 1 and Close < = Lowest(c,Len3)[1] Then Sell("Sell3") close;
```

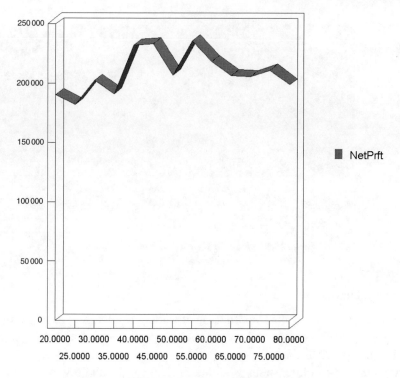

Figure 15.14   *Breakout systems*

Figure 15.14 is the optimization of the above formula on the Euro Bund over the last 10 years. The relative flat and even performance distribution, without performance gaps visualizes the diversification effect across three parameters very well.

The optimization result shows not only a stable return distribution, but in addition we are also exposed to less risk. Indeed, we are, due to the scaling, not continuously engaged with the full amount of contracts. This results in higher returns per total initial margin requirement.

Figure 15.15 is the equity curve resulting from the use of three parameters trading three contracts. Despite a good growth rate, the trading speed diversification (several parameters), cannot avoid the performance stagnation of the last years. This is a sign of changing market behaviour and highlights again the fact that equity curves of trading strategies are the best indicator to analyse market behaviour. This opens an entirely new chapter, which I cannot unfortunately address here. It involves equity curve trading. The use of equity curves as an analytical tool can define parameter and trading system selection as well as money and risk management.

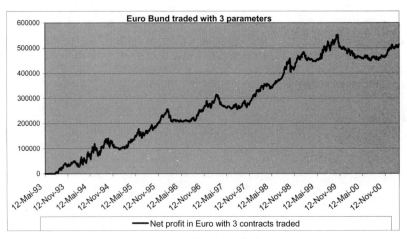

Figure 15.15   *Euro Bund traded with three parameters.*

15.5 CONCLUSIONS

Valuable analysis results from looking at trading results from as many angles as possible. The exclusion of one single aspect can dramatically decrease reliability of performance test results. In a competitive trading environment characterized by diminishing profit margins, in hand with growing computing power, we cannot forfeit the analytic advantage available to anyone with a computer. This is an appeal to test everything you use in technical analysis, the observed market, the trading strategy or indicators and the evaluation tool itself. One should understand not only the indicators and trading systems that are applied, but also the analytical data used for evaluation. The more transparent everything is – from strategies to evaluations – the greater the chance that future performance will be in line with expectations.

Although I have tried to address all the relevant performance measurement figures of trading in this chapter, it cannot be regarded as conclusive to the subject. Performance evaluation is an ongoing process that is changing along with the evolution of markets and the trading tools. Everyone who needs to maintain an edge in the market cannot stop developing and testing on a continuing basis.

GLOSSARY

Algorithm   The naked formula of a strategy. This can be the basis for a trading strategy or an indicator (i.e. a moving average, average(price, length)).

Degrees of freedom   Every rule uses a degree of freedom with the effect that strategies with a lot of variables and rules use up a great deal of freedom and become less general and robust in changing market behaviour.

Indicator   Visual display of an algorithm or trading strategy in the form of lines.

Methodology   Trading method.

Money management   How much money we risk on a trade. MM defines the size of the trade and, with it, the risk we assume with respect to our total trading capital.

Optimization   The search for the best-performing parameter.

Parameter   The number entered as input in indicators or strategies.

Robustness   The reliability of a trading strategy to perform steadily in different market conditions and in the future. We look for robustness or universality in trading strategies.

Slippage   The difference between the actual traded price and the trade signal price calculated by the computer.

Stationarity   A time series is stationary if the underlying rules that generate it do not change over time. Non-stationary distributions change their probability distributions over time. This is the case in trading. An example of a stable probability distribution would be a casino game like roulette.

Trading system   Algorithm or trading strategy that results in trading signals placing orders in the market.

Variables   All elements of an indicator or a strategy that allow different definitions or inputs.

FURTHER READING

Kaufman, J.P. (1998) *Trading Systems and Methods*, John Wiley, Chichester.
Peters, E.E. (1994) *Fractal Market Analysis*, John Wiley, Chichester.
Schwager, D.J. (1998) *Managed Trading*, John Wiley, Chichester.
Sherry, J.C. (1992) *Mathematics of Technical Analysis*, Probus Publishing Company, London.
Vince, R. (1995) *The New Money Management*, John Wiley, Chichester.

Index